Handbook Section	Handbook Changes	Page Number(s)
Section II – Origination through Post-Closing/Endorsement		
II.A.1.b.ii(A)(1)(a) General Borrower Eligibility Requirements – Social Security Number – Standard	Clarified the guidance for individuals exempt from providing Social Security Numbers to address World Bank and foreign embassy employees.	131
II.A.1.b.ii.(A)(3)(a) Borrower Minimum Decision Credit Score – Definition	Updated definition to address application of a median score.	132
II.A.3.a.ii(O)(1) Water Supply Systems – Public Water Supply System	Added clarifying requirement to the Public Water Supply System requirements.	166
II.A.3.a.ii(O)(2) Water Supply Systems – Individual Water Supply Systems (Wells)	Removed language regarding treatment methods for termites.	166
II.A.3.a.ii(O)(2)(a) Individual Water Supply Systems (Wells) – Requirements for Well Water Testing; II.A.3.a.ii(O)(3)(a) Shared Wells – Requirements for Well Water Testing	Added requirements for well water testing.	166-167, 168-169
II.A.3.a.ii(O)(2)(b) Individual Water Supply Systems (Wells) – Required Documentation; II.A.3.a.ii(O)(3)(b) Shared Wells – Required Documentation	Added location where a valid water test can be obtained.	168, 171
II.A.3.a.ii.R Minimum Property Requirements and Minimum Property Standards – Termites	Inserted guidance about soil poisoning as a treatment method for termites. Guidance was moved from the Individual Water Supply Systems (Wells) section.	175
II.A.4.a.i Underwriting with an Automated Underwriting System – Use of TOTAL Mortgage Scorecard	Added language clarifying that Mortgages made to nonprofit/Governmental Entity Borrowers do not need to be scored through TOTAL Mortgage Scorecard.	178

Handbook Section	Handbook Changes	Page Number(s)
II.A.4.b.ii(A) Credit Reports (TOTAL) – Requirements for the Credit Report (TOTAL); II.A.5.a.ii(A)(1) Traditional Credit (Manual) – Requirements for the Credit Report	Added guidance regarding credit report requirements.	183, 253
II.A.4.c.i Income Requirements (TOTAL) – General Income Requirements (TOTAL); II.A.5.b.i Income Requirements (Manual) – General Income Requirements (Manual)	Added clarification on when tax returns must be analyzed and added a link to Appendix 2.0 – Analyzing IRS Forms.	199, 274
II.A.4.c.v(A) Overtime, Bonus or Tip Income (TOTAL) – Definition; II.A.4.c.v(B) Overtime, Bonus or Tip Income (TOTAL) – Standard; II.A.5.b.v(A) Overtime, Bonus or Tip Income (Manual) – Definition; II.A.5.b.v(B) Overtime, Bonus or Tip Income (Manual) – Standard	Added clarifying language to the definition and standard to replace "and" with "or" for context.	202, 277
II.A.4.c.v(C) Overtime, Bonus or Tip Income (TOTAL) – Calculation of Effective Income; II.A.5.b.v(C) Overtime, Bonus or Tip Income (Manual) – Calculation of Effective Income	Updated guidance regarding calculating Effective Income based upon the length of time of receipt and the trend in level of such income.	202, 277
II.A.4.c.ix(C) Commission Income (TOTAL) – Required Documentation; II.A.4.c.ix(D) Commission Income (TOTAL) – Calculation of Effective Income; II.A.5.b.ix(C) Commission Income (Manual) – Required Documentation; II.A.5.b.ix(D) Commission Income (Manual) – Calculation of Effective Income	Updated guidance regarding unreimbursed business expenses to align with IRS tax laws.	204-205, 280

Handbook Section	Handbook Changes	Page Number(s)
II.A.4.c.xii(G)(2) Automobile Allowances (TOTAL) – Required Documentation; II.A.4.c.xii(G)(3) Automobile Allowances (TOTAL) – Calculation of Effective Income; II.A.5.b.xii(G)(2) Automobile Allowances (Manual) – Required Documentation; II.A.5.b.xii(G)(3) Automobile Allowances (Manual) – Calculation of Effective Income	Updated guidance regarding unreimbursed business expenses to align with IRS tax laws.	212, 288
II.A.4.d.i(B)(2)(h) Cash to Close (TOTAL) – Mortgagee Responsibility for Estimating Settlement Requirements – Premium Pricing on FHA-Insured Mortgages; II.A.5.c.i(B)(2)(h) Cash to Close (Manual) – Mortgagee Responsibility for Estimating Settlement Requirements – Premium Pricing on FHA-Insured Mortgages	Added clarifying language to the definition for Premium Pricing to address aggregate credits and clarified the existing guidance when such credits are not included in Interested Party Contributions.	225, 300
II.A.4.d.iii(G)(1) Interested Party Contributions (TOTAL) – Definition; II.A.5.c.iii(G)(1) Interested Party Contributions (Manual) – Definition	Added clarifying language to the definition of Interested Parties to address Mortgagees and Third-Party Originators.	233, 308
II.A.4.d.iii(G)(2) Interested Party Contributions (TOTAL) – Standard; II.A.5.c.iii(G)(2) Interested Party Contributions (Manual) – Standard	Added new subsection for exceptions to Interested Party Contributions to address Premium Pricing.	234, 309
II.A.4.d.iii(G)(3) Interested Party Contributions (TOTAL) – Required Documentation; II.A.5.c.iii(G)(3) Interested Party Contributions (Manual) – Required Documentation	Added clarifying language to the required documentation section about Interested Party Contributions that are documented outside of the sales contract.	234, 309

Handbook Section	Handbook Changes	Page Number(s)
II.A.4.d.iii(H)(3) Inducements to Purchase (TOTAL) – Rent Below Fair Market (TOTAL); II.A.5.c.iii(H)(3) Inducements to Purchase (Manual) – Rent Below Fair Market (Manual)	Updated language to clarify when reduced rent is considered an inducement to purchase and clarified guidance on the calculation of such inducement.	235, 311
II.A.5.d.x(B) Borrower Approval or Denial (Manual) – Documentation of Final Underwriting Review Decision	Removed guidance to align with ML 2016-21 and ML 2017-08, which eliminated Pre-closing submissions for Test Case lenders applying on or after 5/15/17.	332
II.A.6.c.ii Required Documentation for Disbursement of Mortgage Proceeds	Provided guidance on the seller's Closing Disclosure to align with industry standards when such disclosure is received separately from the Borrower's disclosure.	350
II.A.7.b.iii Mortgagee Pre-Endorsement Review Requirements – Note (Including Any Secondary Mortgage)	Removed language to align with FHA's model note requirements.	351
II.A.7.b.v Mortgagee Pre-Endorsement Review Requirements – Closing Disclosure and Settlement Certification	Provided guidance on the seller's Closing Disclosure to align with industry standards when such disclosure is received separately from the Borrower's disclosure.	352
II.A.7.c Inspection and Repair Escrow Requirements for Mortgages Pending Closing or Endorsement in Presidentially-Declared Major Disaster Areas	Updated guidance to clarify damage inspection report requirements for individuals in Presidentially-Declared Major Disaster Areas designed for individual assistance, and provided guidance for the time period when such inspections may be performed.	354
II.A.7.d.ii(B) Assembly of Case Binder – Uniform Case Binder Format	Removed guidance to align with ML 2016-21 and ML 2017-08, which eliminated Pre-closing submissions for Test Case lenders applying on or after 5/15/17.	357

Handbook Section	Handbook Changes	Page Number(s)
II.A.7.d.ii(C) Assembly of Case Binder – Uniform Case Binder Stacking Order	Removed obsolete requirement for 10-Year Warranty; clarified existing requirement to include "all" closing disclosures or similar legal documents with Addenda to address when separate Borrower and seller disclosures are obtained.	358, 359
II.A.7.d.vii Procedures for Endorsement – Mortgagee with Conditional Direct Endorsement Approval (Test Case)	Removed guidance to align with ML 2016-21 and 2017-08, which eliminated Pre-closing submissions for Test Case lenders applying on or after 5/15/17.	363
II.A.8.d.ii(D)(1) Refinances – General Eligibility – General Mortgage Eligibility – Standard	Removed dates associated with the "eminent domain" exclusionary language.	411
II.A.8.d.vi(C)(4)(c)(i) Net Tangible Benefit of Streamline Refinances – Definitions	Clarified the definition for Net Tangible Benefit and added definition for Reduction in Term.	422-423
II.A.8.d.vi(C)(4)(c)(ii) Net Tangible Benefit of Streamline Refinances – Standard for Refinances without a Term Reduction; II.A.8.d.vi(C)(4)(c)(iii) Net Tangible Benefit of Streamline Refinances – Standard for Refinances with a Term Reduction	Updated to align terminology and clarify guidance to distinguish requirements for refinances with or without a term reduction.	423-424
II.A.8.d.vi(C)(5)(b) Streamline Refinance Non-Credit Qualifying – Special Documentation and Procedures for Non-Credit Qualifying Streamline Refinances	Updated title to use consistent terminology.	427
II.A.8.e Refinance of Borrowers in Negative Equity Positions Program (Short Refi) [EXPIRED]	Added "[EXPIRED]" in bracketed text and watermark in this section to reflect the December 31, 2016 expiration of this program.	429
II.A.8.i.i New Construction – Definitions; II.A.8.i.iii New Construction – Required Documentation for Maximum Financing	Updated definition and documentation requirements for Early Start Letter to clarify when one can be issued based upon the property jurisdiction's requirement for building permits.	442; 444

Handbook Section	Handbook Changes	Page Number(s)
II.A.8.i.ii(A)(3) New Construction – Inspections or Warranties for Maximum Financing – Existing for Less than One Year (100 Percent Complete)	Updated guidance to remove the building permit and appraisal requirements.	443
II.A.8.i.vii(A)(6)(a) Individual Water Supply Systems (Wells) – Requirements for Well Water Testing	Added new language to identify parties that may perform water testing and to address handling of test samples.	447
II.A.8.i.vii(A)(6)(b) Individual Water Supply Systems (Wells) – Required Documentation	Added new language regarding required water well testing documentation.	448
II.A.8.j Construction to Permanent	Updated product sheet per ML 2019-08.	449-452
II.A.8.k Building on Own Land	Updated product sheet per ML 2019-08.	453-454
II.D.2 General Appraiser Requirements	Clarified General Appraiser Requirements by consolidating language.	486-487
II.D.3.a Acceptable Appraisal Reporting Forms and Protocols – Additional Required Documentation for Appraisals of New Construction	Removed Appraiser language that has been moved to the general section.	488
II.D.3.c.iii(C)(7) Externalities – Required Analysis and Reporting – Stationary Storage Tanks	Removed unnecessary language from guidance on Stationary Storage Tanks.	496
II.D.3.g Utilities – Mechanical Components	Updated section title and added guidance for inspection while utilities are off.	507
II.D.3.p.iii Utility Services – Public Water Supply Systems	Added Public Water Supply Systems section and renumbered all sections that follow.	515
II.D.3.p.iv Utility Services – Community Water Systems	Moved Community Water Systems section from II.D.3.p.v, updated Required Analysis and Reporting guidance, and renumbered all sections that follow.	515-516, 519-520
II.D.3.p.v(B) Utility Services – Individual Water Supply Systems – Standard	Removed language regarding treating termites.	516

Handbook Section	Handbook Changes	Page Number(s)
II.D.3.p.v(C) Utility Services – Individual Water Supply Systems – Required Analysis and Reporting	Updated Required Analysis and Reporting guidance and removed redundant sub-heading.	516-517
II.D.3.p.vi(B) Utility Services – Shared Wells – Required Analysis and Reporting	Added clarification that water testing may be required.	517
II.D.4.a Valuation and Reporting Protocols – Photograph, Exhibits and Map Requirements	Added clarifying language to support photograph requirements.	519
II.D.4.c.i.(C) Development of the Market Value – Value Required – Required Analysis and Reporting	Added consistent guidance to align with other related policy.	520
II.D.5.l Property Acceptability Criteria for Manufactured Housing for Title II Insured Mortgages – Estimate of Cost New for Manufactured Housing	Removed unnecessary reference to the FHA Single Family Housing Appraisal Report and Data Delivery Guide.	536
II.D.7.d Valuation of Leasehold Interests – Mixed Use One- to Four-Unit Single Family Properties	Moved guidance on Mixed Use One- to Four-Unit Single Family Properties to II.D.13.	538
II.D.12.e.iii(F)(2) Statement of Insurability – Insurable With Repair Escrow; II.D.12.e.iii(F)(3) Statement of Insurability – Uninsurable	Updated repair escrow amounts to comply with current regulations.	551
II.D.13 Mixed Use One- to Four-Unit Single Family Properties	Added guidance on Mixed Use One- to Four-Unit Single Family Properties from II.D.7.d.	554

Section III – Servicing and Loss Mitigation		
III.A.2.k.v(B)(2) FHA-HAMP – Eligibility – Borrower Qualifications	Technical correction to FHA-HAMP Borrower qualification criteria.	626

Section V – Quality Control, Oversight and Compliance		
V.A.2.b.iii(C)(2) Fair Housing and Fair Lending – Fair Housing or Discrimination Violations – Required Documentation	Updated the HUD Form 903 Online Compliant link.	922

Handbook Section	Handbook Changes	Page Number(s)
V.E.3.a.i(A)(5) Test Case Phase Review Status	Revised guidance to align with ML 2016-21 changes, which eliminates the pre-closing submission/Test Case Phase review process.	949
Appendix 2.0 Analyzing IRS Forms	Removed guidance to align with IRS tax law changes.	974
Handbook Section	**Handbook Changes**	**Page Number(s)**
Throughout Document		
	Various technical edits including hyperlinks, punctuation, formatting, grammar, spelling, and capitalization.	13, 62, 108, 143, 174, 208, 256, 257, 284, 333, 334, 337, 346, 349, 363, 375, 379, 441, 445, 463, 486, 488, 489, 490, 532, 551, 572, 581, 589, 591, 593, 604, 608, 610, 615, 625, 629, 635, 637, 638, 650, 660, 667, 669, 670, 676, 677, 678, 679, 680, 683, 684, 685, 687, 691, 694, 704, 708, 716, 719, 724, 726, 727, 745, 748, 749, 832, 834, 839, 861, 862, 864, 873, 876, 883, 900, 919, 942, 944, 987

3. Implementation

Handbook changes identified in Section 2 of this Transmittal incorporated to reflect a Mortgagee Letter are effective as previously announced in the corresponding Mortgagee Letter. Changes identified in Section II.A may be implemented immediately, but must be implemented for mortgages with case numbers assigned on or after September 9, 2019. All other changes may be implemented immediately, but must be implemented no later than September 9, 2019.

4. Public Feedback:

HUD welcomes feedback from interested parties for a period of 30 calendar days from the date of issuance. To provide feedback on this policy document, please send any feedback to the FHA Resource Center at answers@hud.gov. HUD will consider the feedback in determining the need for future updates.

5. Superseded Policy:

Previous versions of Handbook 4000.1 are amended as described in this Transmittal. All previously superseded or canceled Mortgagee Letters, Housing Notices, and/or Handbooks remain canceled or superseded, except for items notated by * below. All superseded or canceled policy documents will continue to be available for informational purposes only on HUD's website. Policy documents that have been superseded in full by the Handbook can always be found on HUD's Client Information Policy Systems (HUDCLIPS) web pages, accessible from the Single Family Housing Superseded Policy Documents page at
http://portal.hud.gov/hudportal/HUD?src=/program_offices/administration/hudclips/sfhsuperseded.

Mortgagee Letter(s) Superseded in Whole	ML Number
2016 Nationwide Forward Mortgage Limits	2015-30
2016 Nationwide Home Equity Conversion Mortgage (HECM) Limits	2015-29
Federal Housing Administration's (FHA) Maximum Loan Limits Effective for Case Numbers Assigned on or after January 1, 2015 through December 31, 2015	2014-25
Federal Housing Administration's (FHA) Maximum Loan Limits Effective for Case Numbers Assigned on or after January 1, 2014 through December 31, 2014	2013-43
Federal Housing Administration's (FHA) Maximum Loan Limits Effective October 1, 2011 through December 31, 2011	2011-29
2010 FHA Maximum Loan Limits	2009-50
2009 FHA Maximum Loan Limits	2008-36
Temporary Loan Limit Increase for FHA	2008-06
2008 FHA Maximum Mortgage Limits	2008-02
2006 FHA Maximum Mortgage Limits	2005-49
2005 FHA Maximum Mortgage Limits	2004-46

Handbook(s) Superseded in Whole	Handbook Number
Central Water and Sewage Systems (Ownership and Organization)	4075.12

6. Paperwork Reduction Act:

The information collection requirements contained in this document have been approved by the Office of Management and Budget (OMB) under the Paperwork Reduction Act of 1995 (44 U.S.C. 3501-3520) and assigned OMB control numbers 2502-0005; 2502-0059; 2502-0117; 2502-0189; 2502-0302; 2502-0306; 2502-0322; 2502-0358; 2502-0404; 2502-0414; 2502-0429; 2502-0494; 2502-0496; 2502-0525; 2502-0527; 2502-0538; 2502-0540; 2502-0556; 2502-0561; 2502-0566; 2502-0569; 2502-0570; 2502-0583; 2502-0584; 2502-0589; 2502-0595 and 2502-0600. In accordance with the Paperwork Reduction Act, HUD may not conduct or sponsor, and a person is not required to respond to, a collection of information unless the collection displays a currently valid OMB control number.

FHA Single Family Housing Policy Handbook
TABLE OF CONTENTS

Handbook 4000.1   vi
Effective Date: 09/14/2015 | Last Revised: 07/10/2019
*Refer to the online version of SF Handbook 4000.1 for specific sections' effective dates

Handbook 4000.1
Effective Date: 09/14/2015 | Last Revised: 07/10/2019
*Refer to the online version of SF Handbook 4000.1 for specific sections' effective dates

vii

Handbook 4000.1   viii
Effective Date: 09/14/2015 | Last Revised: 07/10/2019
*Refer to the online version of SF Handbook 4000.1 for specific sections' effective dates

I. DOING BUSINESS WITH FHA

A. FHA LENDERS AND MORTGAGEES

The Doing Business with FHA section in this *FHA Single Family Housing Policy Handbook (SF Handbook)* covers Federal Housing Administration (FHA) approval and eligibility requirements for both Title I lenders and Title II Mortgagees, as well as other FHA program participants. The term "Mortgagee" is used throughout for all types of FHA approval (both Title II Mortgagees and Title I lenders) and the term "Mortgage" is used for all products (both Title II Mortgages and Title I loans), unless otherwise specified.

A Mortgagee must fully comply with all of the following approval and eligibility requirements in order to be approved by FHA to participate in the origination, underwriting, closing, endorsement, servicing, purchasing, holding, or selling of FHA-insured Title I or Title II Mortgages.

The requirements outlined below in subsections 1 through 9 apply to both Single Family (one-to four-units) and Multifamily Mortgagees. If there are any exceptions or program-specific requirements that differ from those set forth below, the exceptions or alternative program requirements are explicitly stated or hyperlinked to the appropriate guidance. Terms and acronyms used in this *SF Handbook* have their meanings defined in the Glossary and Acronyms and in the specific section of the *SF Handbook* in which the definitions are located.

Handbook 4000.1
Effective Date: 09/14/2015 | Last Revised: 07/10/2019
*Refer to the online version of SF Handbook 4000.1 for specific sections' effective dates

1

1. Types of Program Approvals

FHA approves Mortgagees separately for participation in the Title I and Title II programs. FHA approval is conveyed to a specific legal Entity and cannot be shared with or extended to other Entities, such as a parent or subsidiary, or any Affiliates of the Mortgagee.

a. Title I

i. Definition

A Title I Mortgagee is a Mortgagee that (a) holds a valid Title I contract of insurance and is approved by FHA, or (b) held a Title I contract that has been terminated or suspended but remains responsible for servicing or selling the Title I Mortgages that it holds and is authorized to file insurance claims on these Mortgages.

ii. Standard

A Title I Mortgagee may be approved to originate, underwrite, close, endorse, service, purchase, hold, or sell loans under the Property Improvement program and/or the Manufactured Housing program. Unless otherwise specified, Title I Mortgagees must meet the same approval requirements and follow the same procedures as Title II Mortgagees.

b. Title II

i. Definition

A Title II Mortgagee is a Mortgagee that has been approved to participate in Title II and/or Title XI programs under the National Housing Act (12 U.S.C. § 1707 et seq. and 12 U.S.C. § 1749aaa et seq.).

ii. Standard

A Title II Mortgagee may be approved to originate, underwrite, close, endorse, service, purchase, hold, or sell FHA Single Family insured Mortgages or multifamily Mortgages.

2. Types of Approved Mortgagees

FHA approves Mortgagees as one of the following four types: Supervised, Nonsupervised, Government, or Investing.

a.   Supervised Mortgagee

i.   Definitions

(A) Supervised Mortgagee

A Supervised Mortgagee is a financial institution that is a member of the Federal Reserve System (FRS) or whose accounts are insured by the Federal Deposit Insurance Corporation (FDIC) or the National Credit Union Administration (NCUA) (collectively, "Federal Banking Agencies").

(B) Large Supervised Mortgagee

A Large Supervised Mortgagee is a Supervised Mortgagee that has consolidated assets greater than or equal to the threshold for audited financial reporting established by the Federal Banking Agency with oversight of the Mortgagee. Thresholds are codified at 12 CFR §§ 363.1(a), 562.4(b)(2) and 715.4(c), and are subject to change.

(C) Small Supervised Mortgagee

A Small Supervised Mortgagee is a Supervised Mortgagee that has consolidated assets below the threshold for audited financial reporting established by the Federal Banking Agency with oversight of the Mortgagee. Thresholds are codified at 12 CFR §§ 363.1(a), 562.4(b)(2), and 715.4(c), and are subject to change.

ii.   Standard

A Supervised Mortgagee must meet the general approval requirements set forth below.

iii.   Activities Authorized

A Supervised Mortgagee may originate, underwrite, close, endorse, service, purchase, hold, or sell FHA-insured Mortgages.

b.   Nonsupervised Mortgagee

i.   Definition

A Nonsupervised Mortgagee is a lending institution that has as its principal activity the lending or investing of funds in real estate Mortgages, consumer installment notes or similar advances of credit, the purchase of consumer installment contracts, or from a directly related field. A directly related field is something directly related to the lending or investing of funds in real estate Mortgages, not simply actions relating to real estate in general.

ii. Standard

A Nonsupervised Mortgagee must meet the general approval requirements set forth below and:

- meet FHA's principal activity requirement by deriving at least 50 percent of its gross revenue from:
  - its activities in lending or investing of funds in real estate Mortgages;
  - consumer installment notes or similar advances of credit;
  - the purchase of consumer installment contracts; or
  - a directly related field;
- have an acceptable business form;
- demonstrate creditworthiness; and
- have an acceptable funding program.

iii. Activities Authorized

A Nonsupervised Mortgagee may originate, underwrite, close, endorse, service, purchase, hold, or sell FHA-insured Mortgages.

c. Government Mortgagee

i. Definition

A Government Mortgagee is a federal, state, or municipal governmental agency, a Federal Reserve Bank, a Federal Home Loan Bank, the Federal Home Loan Mortgage Corporation (FHLMC, or Freddie Mac), or the Federal National Mortgage Association (FNMA, or Fannie Mae).

ii. Standard

A Government Mortgagee must meet the general approval requirements set forth below.

iii. Activities Authorized

A Government Mortgagee may originate, underwrite, close, endorse, service, purchase, hold, or sell FHA-insured Mortgages.

d. Investing Mortgagee

i. Definition

An Investing Mortgagee is an organization that invests funds under its own control.

ii. Standard

An Investing Mortgagee must meet the general approval requirements set forth below and:

- have staff capable of managing the Mortgagee's activities relating to its FHA-insured Mortgages;
- have an acceptable business form;
- demonstrate creditworthiness; and
- have an acceptable funding program.

iii. Activities Authorized

An Investing Mortgagee may purchase, hold, or sell FHA-insured Mortgages. An Investing Mortgagee may only service FHA-insured Mortgages if it receives prior approval.

iv. Activities Not Authorized

An Investing Mortgagee may not originate, underwrite, or close FHA-insured Mortgages in its own name or submit applications for FHA mortgage insurance.

3. Application and Eligibility Requirements for Approval

a. Title I and Title II Program Applications

An applicant for FHA approval may apply for Title I and Title II approval separately or in the same application.

b. Online Application

An applicant seeking FHA approval must submit an online application containing all information and documentation required to demonstrate eligibility for approval as provided in this section. Applicants must ensure that all information contained in and documentation submitted with the application is true, complete, and up to date as of the date of submission of the application.

i. Application Information

(A) Standard

The applicant must provide the following information as part of a completed application for FHA approval:
- general information (such as the applicant name, date the applicant was established, Taxpayer Identification Number (TIN), Nationwide Mortgage Licensing System and Registry Unique Identifier (NMLS ID), etc.);
- contact information (the primary contact information for all inquiries related to the application);
- addresses (the geographic and mailing addresses for the applicant's home office);
- Mortgagee type (the type of FHA Mortgagee approval being sought: Supervised, Nonsupervised, Government, or Investing);

Handbook 4000.1   5
Effective Date: 09/14/2015 | Last Revised: 07/10/2019
*Refer to the online version of SF Handbook 4000.1 for specific sections' effective dates

- Mortgagee function (the functions being sought: originate/underwrite, service, and/or hold);
- FHA program participation (the FHA program participation being sought: Title I, Title II Single Family, and/or Title II Multifamily);
- Corporate Officers (the names, titles, and Social Security Numbers (SSN) for all Corporate Officers who will be directly involved in managing, overseeing, or conducting FHA business and the designated Officer in Charge); and
- Principal Owners (the names, SSN or TIN, and percent ownership).

(B) Required Documentation

The applicant must submit all of the application information in the online application.

ii. Application Documentation

(A) Standard

The applicant must provide supporting documentation to demonstrate that it is eligible for FHA approval.

(B) Required Documentation

The applicant must submit all eligibility documentation listed in the table below that is required for the type of approval being sought. This documentation must be submitted in the online application.

Documents Required for Application	Supervised Mortgagee	Nonsupervised Mortgagee	Government Mortgagee	Investing Mortgagee	
				Federally Regulated[1]	Not Federally Regulated
Business Formation Documents		✓			✓
Commercial Credit Report of Mortgagee		✓			✓
Credit Reports of Principal Owners and Corporate Officers		✓			✓

---

[1]Federally regulated refers to an entity that is a member of the FRS or whose accounts are insured by the FDIC or the NCUA.

Documents Required for Application	Supervised Mortgagee	Nonsupervised Mortgagee	Government Mortgagee	Investing Mortgagee	
				Federally Regulated[1]	Not Federally Regulated
Resumes of Corporate Officers		✓	✓		✓
Resume of Officer in Charge	✓	✓	✓	✓	✓
State License or Registration	✓	✓		✓	✓
Financial Reports	✓	✓		✓	✓
Funding Program		✓			✓
Fidelity Bond	✓	✓	✓	✓	✓
Errors and Omissions Insurance	✓	✓	✓	✓	✓
Quality Control Plan	✓	✓	✓		

iii. Certification of Compliance

(A) Standard

As part of its application, the applicant, through a Corporate Officer, must complete a series of certification statements that address the applicant's compliance with FHA requirements.

(B) Required Documentation

The certification statements must be completed in the online application by a Corporate Officer of the applicant who has been included in the list of Corporate Officers in the online application.

(C) Unable to Certify

If an applicant is unable to certify to any of the certification statements, the applicant must submit a detailed explanation in the online application for each certification that it is unable to complete. The document must:
- explain in detail the reason(s) why the applicant is unable to certify;
- be on the applicant's letterhead;
- be dated;
- be signed by the Corporate Officer who signs the application; and

- contain language certifying that, if approved, the applicant will comply with all FHA requirements.

(D) FHA Review

FHA will review the applicant's explanation for being unable to certify and communicate to the applicant any additional information or documentation needed to render a final decision regarding the applicant's ability to complete the application process.

iv. Application Fee

(A) Standard

The applicant must pay a nonrefundable application fee when submitting an application for approval. Applicants applying for both Title I and Title II approval, whether simultaneously or separately, will only be assessed a single application fee.

(B) Exception

Applicants applying for approval as Government Mortgagees or applicants organized as nonprofits are not required to pay an application fee.

(C) Required Documentation

The application fee must be submitted as part of the online application.

c. Eligibility Requirements

i. Business Form

(A) Standard

A Nonsupervised or Investing Mortgagee must be organized in one of the following acceptable business forms. A sole proprietorship is not an acceptable business form.

(1) Corporation

(a) Definition

A Corporation is an Entity chartered in the United States or its territories.

(b) Standard

The corporation must be organized in accordance with federal and state laws regarding corporations and must provide for permanent succession.

(c) Required Documentation

The corporation must submit copies of its articles of incorporation and bylaws with its application.

(2) Limited Liability Company

(a) Definition

A Limited Liability Company (LLC) is organized under applicable state law which creates a legal Entity with a combination of the legal and tax attributes of corporations and partnerships.

(b) Standard

The LLC must:
- consist of two or more members, unless its single member is a corporation or LLC consisting of two or more persons or members;
- each natural person must be of legal age as recognized by the state of incorporation at the time such natural person becomes a member;
- have a minimum term of existence of 10 years from the date of application; and
- provide for succession and continuance in the event of the withdrawal or death of a member.

(c) Required Documentation

The LLC must submit its Articles of Organization and operating agreement with its application. The Articles of Organization and operating agreement must contain language addressing the requirements listed in the FHA LLC Standard section above.

The application must include the names and TINs of all members.

(3) Series Limited Liability Company

(a) Definition

A Series LLC is a specific type of LLC that is composed of separate membership interests, which are divided into individual series.

(b) Standard

The Series LLC must comply with all requirements for approval of an LLC. The Series LLC must be organized in accordance with state law that does not conflict with FHA requirements.

The Series LLC's operating agreement must stipulate that:
- no series may participate in FHA programs unless the approved Mortgagee owns 100 percent of the membership interests in that series; and
- the approved Mortgagee remains fully liable for the debts, liabilities, obligations and expenses of any and all series that participate in FHA programs.

(c) Required Documentation

The Series LLC must submit its Articles of Organization and operating agreement with its application.

The application must include the names and TINs of all series participating in FHA programs and of all members in the series participating in FHA programs.

(4) Partnership

(a) Definition

A Partnership is a for-profit business operation between two or more Entities that share ownership and management responsibilities.

(b) Standard

The partnership must:
1. be organized in accordance with relevant state law;
2. have a term of existence that continues for a minimum term of 10 years from the date of application; and
3. be structured to continue to exist even if a partner withdraws.

Each general partner must be a corporation or other chartered institution consisting of two or more individuals.

The partnership must designate a managing general partner, who:
- has as its principal activity the management of one or more partnerships, all of which are Mortgagees, lenders, or property improvement or Manufactured Housing loan lenders; and
- has exclusive authority to deal directly with the Secretary or its designee on behalf of each partnership.

(c) Required Documentation

The partnership must submit its partnership agreement. The partnership agreement must contain language addressing the requirements listed in the FHA Partnership Standard section above.

The partnership must submit the names and TINs of all general partners as well as the names and SSNs of all officers and directors of the managing general partner.

(5) Nonprofit

(a) Definition

A nonprofit is a charitable organization or corporation, civic league, social welfare organization, or local employee association organized for purposes other than profit.

(b) Standard

The nonprofit must be recognized as exempt from taxation by the Internal Revenue Service (IRS) under Internal Revenue Code (IRC) Section 501(a) as an entity described in Sections 501(c)(3) and (4).

A nonprofit organized as a corporation, LLC, or partnership must also comply with all requirements for the applicable business form.

(c) Required Documentation

The nonprofit must provide a copy of its IRS exemption letter. The nonprofit must submit all Business Formation Documents required of its business form.

(B) Required Documentation

The Mortgagee must submit its Business Formation Documents in the online application.

ii. Mortgagee Name

(A) Definitions

(1) Institution Name

The Mortgagee's Institution Name is the legally registered corporate name associated with the Mortgagee's home office.

(2) "Doing Business As" Name

The "Doing Business As" (DBA) name is any registered name or alias that the Mortgagee has a legal right to use.

(B) Standard

The Mortgagee must use as its institution or DBA name the name shown on its Business Formation Documents or for which it has received approval from its state of formation. The Mortgagee is prohibited from using any restricted word in, or as part of, its institution or DBA name in a manner that would violate the Helping Families Save Their Homes Act of 2009 (Pub.L. 111–22) or 18 U.S.C. § 709, which places restrictions on "federal," "government," or "national" and related words, unless the Mortgagee is exempt from these statutory prohibitions.

The Mortgagee's institution name and all DBA names used by a Mortgagee for conducting FHA business must be registered with FHA. The Mortgagee must use only those names that are registered with FHA in advertising and promotional materials related to FHA programs.

(C) Required Documentation

A Nonsupervised or Investing Mortgagee must submit its Business Formation Documents. A Supervised Mortgagee must submit a copy of the state license or registration for its home office as verification of its institution name.

The Mortgagee must submit documentation from the state showing it is legally approved to use its institution name or DBA name, if the name differs from that shown on its Business Formation Documents.

iii. Office Facilities

(A) Definitions

(1) Home Office

The Mortgagee's Home Office is the main office from which it manages its FHA business.

(2) Branch Offices

Branch Offices are all other offices from which a Mortgagee conducts FHA business.

(B) Standard

(1) Home Office

A Mortgagee must designate a headquarters or "home office" for its FHA business. A Mortgagee's home office does not have to be its corporate office.

The Mortgagee's home office must have a staff of at least two full-time employees. The Mortgagee may not rely on a shared receptionist to satisfy this full-time employee requirement.

A Mortgagee's home office facility must:
- be located in a commercial space that is separate from any other Entity (except for reception-type entrances or lobbies);
- be clearly identified, including having a permanently affixed business sign and other means of identification commonly used by businesses, so that the general public and other businesses will know, at all times, exactly which Entity is being represented and is conducting business; and
- display a fair housing poster if the Mortgagee deals with Borrowers and the general public.

(2) Branch Offices

Mortgagees must also register any branch offices that will conduct FHA business in accordance with the requirements set forth in the Branch Office requirements section of this *SF Handbook*. This includes any branches that will originate, underwrite, and/or service FHA-insured Mortgages.

The Mortgagee must ensure each registered branch office has at least one full-time employee. The Mortgagee may not rely on a shared receptionist or contractors to satisfy this full-time employee requirement.

The Mortgagee must display a fair housing poster in branch offices that deal with Borrowers and the general public.

(C) Required Documentation

FHA will verify compliance with the office facilities requirements through any onsite visits. The Mortgagee must maintain an up-to-date list of all offices meeting the standard.

iv. Ownership and Personnel

The Mortgagee must comply with the following requirements for its ownership and personnel.

(A) Principal Owners

(1) Definition

A Principal Owner is any individual or Entity meeting the following thresholds or roles for the applicable business form:

Business Form	Principal Owners
Publicly Traded Corporation	10% or more ownership
Private or Close Corporation	25% or more ownership
Limited Liability Company	All Members
Partnerships	All Partners

(2) Standard

The Mortgagee must ensure that none of its Principal Owners are suspended, debarred or otherwise excluded from participation in FHA programs (see Restricted Participation).

(3) Required Documentation

A Supervised, Nonsupervised, or Investing Mortgagee must identify all Principal Owners. The Mortgagee must submit this information in the online application.

(B) Personnel Requirements

(1) Corporate Officers

(a) Definitions

(i) Corporate Officers of Nonsupervised and Investing Mortgagees

A Corporate Officer is a natural person who serves as one of the following positions for a Nonsupervised or Investing Mortgagee:

- owner;
- President;
- Vice President in charge of managing or overseeing any aspect of the Mortgagee's FHA business;
- Chief Operating Officer (COO);
- Chief Financial Officer (CFO);
- Director;
- Corporate Secretary;
- Chief Executive Officer (CEO);
- General Counsel;
- Chairman of the Board;
- General Partner; or
- member or manager of an LLC.

(ii) Corporate Officers of Supervised and Government Mortgagees

A Corporate Officer is a natural person who serves as one of the following positions for a Supervised or Government Mortgagee:

- President;
- Vice President in charge of managing or overseeing any aspect of the Mortgagee's FHA business;
- Chief Operating Officer (COO);
- Chief Financial Officer (CFO);
- Director;
- Corporate Secretary;
- Chief Executive Officer (CEO);
- General Counsel;
- Chairman of the Board;
- General Partner; or
- specifically designated staff member(s) of a Government Mortgagee.

(b) Standard

The Mortgagee must ensure that no Corporate Officers are suspended, debarred or otherwise excluded from participation in FHA programs (see Restricted Participation).

The Mortgagee must ensure its Corporate Officers only represent a single Mortgagee, unless the following criteria are met:
- the Entities represented have some or all of the same Corporate Officers or Principal Owners; and
- there is a clear and effective separation of the Entities, and Borrowers know at all times exactly which Entity is being represented and with whom they are conducting business.

(c) Required Documentation

The Mortgagee must identify all Corporate Officers listed above who will be directly involved in managing, overseeing, or conducting FHA business. The Mortgagee must submit all of this information in the online application.

A Nonsupervised, Government, or Investing Mortgagee must submit a current resume covering the most recent seven-year period for each of these Corporate Officers.

(2) Officer in Charge

(a) Definition

The Officer in Charge is the Corporate Officer designated to manage and direct the Mortgagee's FHA operations.

(b) Standard

The Mortgagee must designate as the Officer in Charge a full-time Corporate Officer who is exclusively employed by the Mortgagee and has at least three years of experience in the specific Mortgagee functions or activities that the Mortgagee is approved to perform, including:

- originating or servicing Single Family or multifamily Mortgages;
- investing funds in real estate Mortgages; or
- managing other individuals performing these services.

A Corporate Officer's experience in real estate sales or brokerage does not qualify.

(c) Required Documentation

The Mortgagee must designate the Officer in Charge and submit a current resume covering the most recent seven-year period detailing the individual's relevant experience in the online application.

(3) Employees

(a) Definition

Employees are individuals under the direct supervision and control of the Mortgagee.

(b) Standard

(i) Eligibility of Employees

The Mortgagee must not employ any individual who will participate in FHA transactions if the individual is suspended, debarred, under a Limited Denial of Participation (LDP), or otherwise excluded from participation in FHA programs (see Restricted Participation).

(ii) Compensation

The Mortgagee must not compensate employees who perform underwriting or Quality Control (QC) activities on a commission basis.

The Mortgagee must report all employee compensation in accordance with IRS requirements.

(iii) SAFE Act Compliance

The Mortgagee must ensure that it and its employees comply with the requirements of the Secure and Fair Enforcement for Mortgage Licensing

Act of 2008 (SAFE Act) (12 U.S.C. § 1501 et seq.), including the licensing and registration of its employees in the NMLS.

(iv) Dual Employment

The Mortgagee must require its employees to be its employees exclusively, unless the Mortgagee has determined that the employee's other outside employment, including any self-employment, does not create a prohibited conflict of interest.

(v) Conflicts of Interest

Employees are prohibited from having multiple roles in a single FHA-insured transaction. Employees are prohibited from having multiple sources of compensation, either directly or indirectly, from a single FHA-insured transaction.

(vi) Underwriters

The Mortgagee must ensure that its underwriters are not managed by and do not report to any individual who performs mortgage origination activities.

The Mortgagee must ensure that its underwriters:
- meet basic eligibility requirements; and
- perform the underwriting function in a manner consistent with FHA guidelines.

(vii)   HECM Originators

The Mortgagee and any other party that participates in the origination of a HECM transaction must not participate in, be associated with, or employ any party that participates in or is associated with any other financial or insurance activity, unless the Mortgagee demonstrates that it or any other party maintains firewalls and other safeguards designed to ensure that:
- individuals participating in the origination of the HECM must have no involvement with, or incentive to provide the Borrower with, any other financial or insurance product; and
- the Borrower must not be required, directly or indirectly, as a condition of obtaining a HECM, to purchase any other financial or insurance product.

(c) Required Documentation

The Mortgagee must certify that it meets these requirements in the online application.

v. Creditworthiness

(A) Definitions

(1) Institutional Creditworthiness

A Creditworthy Institution is a Mortgagee with a credit background for the seven-year period preceding the FHA Mortgagee approval application or the lifespan of the institution if less than seven years that:

- reflects no delinquent accounts or collections and no legal actions; or
- reflects legal actions that have been adequately resolved, and/or delinquent accounts or collections that have been adequately resolved or that have an acceptable explanation.

(2) Individual Creditworthiness

A Creditworthy Individual is a person whose credit background for the seven-year period preceding the FHA Mortgagee approval application or for the length of the individual's credit history if less than seven years:

- reflects no delinquent accounts or collections, and reflects no legal actions that would impair the individual's credit, such as a foreclosure action, judgment, lien, or bankruptcy; or
- reflects legal actions that have been adequately resolved, and/or delinquent accounts or collections that have been adequately resolved or that have an acceptable explanation.

(B) Standard

A Nonsupervised or Investing Mortgagee must demonstrate that it is a creditworthy institution, and that its Principal Owners and Corporate Officers are creditworthy individuals.

(C) Required Documentation

A Nonsupervised or Investing Mortgagee must submit the following credit reports.

(1) Report on Mortgagee

A Nonsupervised or Investing Mortgagee must submit a commercial credit report not more than 90 Days old with its application. The Mortgagee must provide written explanations for all negative items disclosed on the credit report.

(2) Reports on Principal Owners and Corporate Officers

A Nonsupervised or Investing Mortgagee must submit a personal credit report for each of its Principal Owners and Corporate Officers with its application. The personal credit report must be a Residential Mortgage Credit Report (RMCR) or a Tri-Merged Credit Report (TRMCR) not more than 90 Days old.

The Mortgagee must submit a written explanation from the relevant Principal Owner or Corporate Officer for any negative item disclosed on the credit report.

vi. State License or Registration

Supervised, Nonsupervised, and Investing Mortgagees must meet the following licensing requirements.

(A) Business License or Registration

(1) Standard

The Mortgagee must have an active state license, registration, or equivalent approval to operate its business in the jurisdiction where the home office is located.

The Mortgagee must ensure that each branch office has all licenses, registrations, or approvals required for the types of Mortgagee functions or activities performed by such branch office for the jurisdiction in which that office is located.

A Mortgagee that has been refused a state license or been sanctioned by any state in which it will originate FHA Mortgages must disclose the circumstances of the refusal or sanction and the resolution to FHA.

(2) Required Documentation

The Mortgagee must submit a copy of its state license, registration or equivalent approval for the state in which the home office is located. The Mortgagee, through a Corporate Officer, must certify at application that it has not been refused a license or been sanctioned by any state in which it will originate FHA Mortgages.

If the Mortgagee has been subject to an action against its license, it is unable to certify. It must follow the unable to certify procedures and must submit documentation concerning the action that shows the nature of the action and evidence of an acceptable resolution (such as reinstatement or subsequent approval of a license, payment of sanctions or fines, or similar documentation).

(3) Exception for Mortgagees Exempt from State Licensing Requirements

If the Mortgagee is exempt from state licensing requirements, the Mortgagee must submit documentation of the applicable exemption.

(B) Personnel Licenses

(1) Standard

The Mortgagee must ensure that its Corporate Officers, employees, and Affiliates conducting FHA business for or on behalf of the Mortgagee have all state and federal licenses and registrations required for the Mortgagee functions or activities that such individuals or Affiliates will perform.

(2) Required Documentation

The Mortgagee must certify that it meets this requirement as part of the online application.

vii. Financial Requirements

(A) Standard

Supervised, Nonsupervised, and Investing Mortgagees must meet the following adjusted net worth and liquidity requirements at all times.

(1) Adjusted Net Worth

The Mortgagee must compute its adjusted net worth in accordance with the HUD OIG Handbook 2000.04, *Consolidated Audit Guide for Audits of HUD Programs*.

(a) Single Family Programs

The Mortgagee must have a minimum adjusted net worth of $1,000,000 plus 1 percent of the total volume in excess of $25,000,000 of FHA Single Family Mortgages originated, underwritten, serviced, and/or purchased during the prior fiscal year, up to a maximum required adjusted net worth of $2,500,000.

(b) Multifamily Programs

(i) With Servicing

The Mortgagee must have a minimum adjusted net worth of $1,000,000 plus an additional net worth of 1 percent of the total volume in excess of $25,000,000 of FHA multifamily Mortgages originated, purchased, and/or serviced during the prior fiscal year, up to a maximum required net worth of $2,500,000.

(ii) Without Servicing

The Mortgagee must have a minimum adjusted net worth of $1,000,000 plus an additional net worth of one-half of 1 percent of the total volume in excess of $25,000,000 of FHA multifamily Mortgages originated during the prior fiscal year, up to a maximum required net worth of $2,500,000.

(c) Dual Participation

A Mortgagee approved to participate in both Single Family and multifamily programs must have a minimum adjusted net worth of $1,000,000 plus an additional net worth of 1 percent of the total volume in excess of $25,000,000 of the aggregate of FHA Single Family and multifamily Mortgages originated, underwritten, purchased, and/or serviced during the prior fiscal year, up to a maximum required net worth of $2,500,000.

(2) Liquidity

Liquid assets must be computed in accordance with the HUD OIG Handbook 2000.04, *Consolidated Audit Guide for Audits of HUD Programs*.

The Mortgagee must hold no less than 20 percent of its required adjusted net worth in liquid assets.

(B) Exception for Government Mortgagees

The adjusted net worth and liquidity requirements do not apply to Government Mortgagees. Government Mortgagees are not required to submit financial information to FHA.

(C) Required Documentation

Supervised, Nonsupervised, and Investing Mortgagees must submit the computation of adjusted net worth, along with the documentation described below.

(1) Small Supervised Mortgagees

A Small Supervised Mortgagee must submit a copy of its Unaudited Regulatory Report (i.e., report of condition and income, also known as the "call report," which is submitted on the Federal Financial Institutions Examination Council Forms 031 and 041, or a consolidated or fourth quarter NCUA call report, submitted on NCUA Form 5300 or 5310) signed by a Corporate Officer that aligns with its fiscal year end.

(2) Large Supervised, Nonsupervised, and Investing Mortgagees

(a) Audit of Financial Statements

The Mortgagee must submit financial statements reported in accordance with the HUD OIG Handbook 2000.04, *Consolidated Audit Guide for Audits of HUD Programs*.

(b) Accounting and Auditing Standards

The Mortgagee must have prepared its financial statements in accordance with Generally Accepted Accounting Principles (GAAP) and had its audit performed in accordance with Generally Accepted Auditing Standards (GAAS).

(c) Audit Period Covered

A Mortgagee's audited financial statements must cover 12 months of operation. For companies operating for fewer than 12 months, the audited financial statements must cover all months of operation.

The end date of the audited financial statements must align with the applicant's fiscal year end period at the time of application:

- If the end date for the audited financial reports is more than six months old, the Mortgagee must also submit unaudited financial statements, signed by a Corporate Officer, for the most recent interim accounting period ending less than three months prior to submission of the application.
- If the Mortgagee is a new institution and has had no revenues or cash flow, the income statement and cash flow statement are not required as part of the audited financial statements.

viii. Principal Activity of Nonsupervised Mortgagees

(A) Standard

A Nonsupervised Mortgagee must derive at least 50 percent of its gross revenue from its activities in lending or investing of funds in real estate Mortgages, consumer installment notes or similar advances of credit, the purchase of consumer installment contracts, or from a directly related field. A directly related field is something directly related to the lending or investing of funds in real estate Mortgages, not simply actions relating to real estate in general.

(B) Required Documentation

The Nonsupervised Mortgagee must submit audited financial statements that reflect the sources of its revenue.

ix. Funding Program

(A) Nonsupervised Mortgagees

(1) Standard

A Nonsupervised Mortgagee that originates FHA Mortgages must maintain a warehouse line of credit or other mortgage-funding program acceptable to FHA.

Title I Mortgagees must have a minimum $500,000 warehouse line of credit or funding program.

Except for multifamily Mortgagees, Title II Mortgagees must have a minimum $1,000,000 warehouse line of credit or funding program, and must ensure the funding program or warehouse line of credit is sufficient to fund the Mortgagee's average 60-Day origination operations. The Mortgagee's average 60-Day origination operations refer to loans closed and funded, and/or purchased by the Mortgagee during the Mortgagee's highest 60-Day period by mortgage amount over the past 12 months.

(2) Required Documentation

The Mortgagee must submit documentation that it either 1) has a line of credit issued directly to the Mortgagee; or 2) has an agreement with a financial institution. The documentation must ensure the funding program or warehouse line of credit is sufficient to fund the Mortgagee's average 60-Day origination operations.

(B) Investing Mortgagees

(1) Standard

An Investing Mortgagee must have available, or have arranged for, funds or a line of credit sufficient to support a projected investment of at least $1,000,000 in property improvement, Manufactured Housing or real estate loans or Mortgages.

(2) Required Documentation

The Mortgagee must submit documentation that it either 1) has a line of credit issued directly to the Mortgagee; or 2) has an agreement to support the projected investment.

x. Fidelity Bond

(A) Standard

A Mortgagee must have fidelity bond coverage that meets the minimum coverage amount set by FHA. The Mortgagee must ensure that its fidelity bond coverage is in a form generally acceptable to one of the secondary mortgage market agencies, such as Freddie Mac, Fannie Mae, or the Government National Mortgage Association (GNMA, or Ginnie Mae).

A Government Mortgagee will meet this requirement if it maintains alternative insurance coverage that is approved by FHA and that ensures the faithful performance of the Mortgagee's responsibilities.

(B) Required Documentation

The Mortgagee must submit documentation evidencing that it has acceptable fidelity bond coverage.

xi. Errors and Omissions Insurance

(A) Standard

A Mortgagee must have errors and omissions insurance that meets the minimum coverage amount set by FHA. The Mortgagee must have errors and omissions insurance that is generally acceptable to one of the secondary market agencies, such as Freddie Mac, Fannie Mae, or Ginnie Mae.

A Government Mortgagee will meet this requirement if it maintains alternative insurance coverage that is approved by FHA and that ensures the faithful performance of the Mortgagee's responsibilities.

(B) Required Documentation

The Mortgagee must submit documentation evidencing that it has acceptable errors and omissions insurance.

xii. Quality Control Plan

(A) Standard

A Mortgagee that originates, underwrites, closes, endorses, or services FHA-insured Mortgages must have a QC Plan that meets FHA's requirements, as described in the Quality Control, Oversight and Compliance section of this *SF Handbook*. The Mortgagee must maintain and update its QC Plan as needed to ensure it is fully compliant with all applicable FHA requirements at all times.

(B) Required Documentation

The Mortgagee must submit a copy of its QC Plan.

d. Processing of Applications

FHA will review all completed applications for approval to determine if the applicant complies with all eligibility requirements. If FHA requires additional documentation or clarifying information, FHA may request such additional information and provide the applicant with a deadline for response. If the applicant does not submit a completed application or provide the additional information requested by the specified deadline, FHA may deny approval on this basis.

e. Application Approval

If FHA approves the application, FHA will provide notice via email and U.S. mail. This notice will include the Mortgagee's assigned FHA Lender Identification Number (FHA Lender ID), which must be used by the Mortgagee in all FHA computer systems and official correspondence with FHA.

f. Application Denial

If FHA denies the application, FHA will provide written notice to the applicant that includes an explanation of the reasons for the denial.

i. Appeal of Denial

The applicant may submit an appeal of the denial decision through the online application within 30 Days of the date of the denial.

If the denial is sustained, the applicant may submit a second appeal through the online application within 30 Days of the date the denial is sustained. If the denial of approval is sustained a second time, the applicant will be ineligible to apply for FHA approval for a period of 12 months.

ii. Reapplication

An applicant whose approval was denied may reapply after a period of 12 months. The applicant will be required to pay an application fee at the time it submits its subsequent application for approval.

4. Branch Offices

a. Registration

The Mortgagee must register all branch offices in which it conducts FHA business, including originating, underwriting, and/or servicing FHA-insured Mortgages. The Mortgagee must register each branch office and pay branch office registration fees through the Lender Electronic Assessment Portal (LEAP). A 10-digit FHA Lender ID will be assigned to each registered branch office.

The Mortgagee cannot register a new branch office within a HUD Field Office jurisdiction in which it has withdrawn a branch office in the last six months. The Mortgagee must instead make a request through LEAP to reassign the former office's 10-digit FHA Lender ID to the new branch and must pay the branch office registration fee.

b. Single Family Lending Area

i. Definition

An "Area Approved for Business" (AAFB) is the geographic area in which a Mortgagee's home or branch office is permitted to originate or underwrite FHA Mortgages. The AAFB is subdivided into HUD Field Office jurisdictions.

HUD Field Office jurisdictions can be verified on www.hud.gov/lenders under the Mortgage Origination tab.

ii. Standard

All branch offices registered by a Mortgagee will initially be granted a nationwide AAFB. The branch may only exercise its authority to originate or underwrite FHA Mortgages in those states where the Mortgagee fully complies with state origination and/or underwriting licensing and approval requirements.

c. Managers

i. Definitions

(A) Branch Manager

A Branch Manager is an onsite manager for a branch office who manages one branch office.

(B) Regional Manager

A Regional Manager is a manager who oversees the operation of multiple branch offices.

ii. Standard

The Mortgagee must have a branch and/or regional manager to oversee each of its branch offices.

iii. Required Documentation

The Mortgagee must provide the full names and titles of its branch and regional managers, along with their contact information, in LEAP.

d. Net Branching Prohibition

i. Standard

The Mortgagee must not engage an existing, legally separate mortgage company or broker to function as the Mortgagee's branch office or DBA name or to conduct FHA activities using the Mortgagee's FHA approval.

ii. Exception for Existing Leases

In cases where a Mortgagee acquires an existing office with the intent of operating it as a branch office, and the lease of the acquired office is not transferable to the Mortgagee, FHA will allow the Mortgagee to operate the acquired office as a branch office until the lease expires upon its own terms, so long as the Mortgagee can demonstrate that it has assumed financial liability for the payment of the lease. In such cases, the Mortgagee must document and maintain evidence that it has assumed financial liability for the payment of the lease and produce this documentation to FHA upon request.

5. Supplemental Mortgagee Authorities

After a Mortgagee is approved, the Mortgagee can apply for additional supplemental Mortgagee authorities in accordance with the following requirements.

a. Title II Direct Endorsement Authority

i. Scope of Authority

Approval to participate in FHA's Direct Endorsement (DE) Program permits a Mortgagee to underwrite Title II Single Family Mortgages without FHA's prior review and submit them directly for FHA insurance endorsement.

The Mortgagee must obtain separate DE approval for forward mortgage and Home Equity Conversion Mortgage (HECM) programs.

(A) Definitions

(1) Conditional Authority

Conditional Authority is the authority of a Mortgagee that has applied for and received basic FHA Mortgagee approval as a Supervised, Nonsupervised, or Government Mortgagee, and has not entered or completed the Test Case phase.

(2) Test Case Phase

The Test Case Phase is when a Mortgagee with conditional authority is approved by an FHA Homeownership Center (HOC) to submit one or more cases for FHA underwriting review.

(3) Unconditional DE Authority

Unconditional DE Authority permits a Mortgagee to underwrite and close Title II Single Family Mortgages prior to submitting them to FHA for FHA insurance endorsement.

(B) Standard

To obtain Unconditional DE authority, the Mortgagee must successfully complete the Test Case phase, which permits FHA to evaluate the Mortgagee's qualifications, experience, and expertise to underwrite Mortgages that satisfy FHA requirements.

(C) Exception

Unconditional DE authority may be granted, without the need for the Test Case phase, to the following categories of Mortgagees created by merger, acquisition, or reorganization:
- surviving FHA-approved Mortgagees; or
- new Mortgagees resulting in new FHA Lender IDs.

ii. Eligibility Requirements

A Mortgagee must meet the following requirements in order to apply for and participate in FHA's DE Program.

(A) Standard

(1) FHA Mortgagee Approval

A Mortgagee must have FHA approval as a Title II Supervised, Nonsupervised, or Government Mortgagee to be eligible to participate in the DE Program.

Mortgagees approved as Investing Mortgagees are not eligible to participate in the DE Program.

(2) Origination Experience

The Mortgagee must have:
- at least five years of experience in the origination of Single Family Mortgages; or
- a Principal Officer with at least five years of managerial experience in the origination of Single Family Mortgages. For the purposes of this *SF Handbook* a Principal Officer is the same as a Corporate Officer.

(3) Personnel Requirements

The Mortgagee must have an underwriter on its permanent staff.

(B) Exception for Certain Mortgagees Created by Merger, Acquisition, or Reorganization

Unconditional DE authority may be granted without the need for the Test Case phase following a merger, acquisition, or reorganization, so long as the following criteria are met:

- Either or both institutions, of the surviving FHA-Approved Mortgagee or the FHA-Approved Mortgagee resulting in a new FHA Lender ID, were unconditionally DE-approved prior to the merger, acquisition, or reorganization.
- If both institutions are unconditionally DE-approved, then the management and staff of at least one of the Mortgagees involved with the Mortgagee's Unconditional DE authority prior to the merger, acquisition, or reorganization must continue to exercise those responsibilities for the new Mortgagee. If only one institution is unconditionally DE-approved, then the management and staff involved with that Mortgagee's Unconditional DE authority prior to the merger, acquisition, or reorganization must continue to exercise those responsibilities for the new Mortgagee.
- Both Mortgagees have claim and default rates at or below the 150 percent national compare ratio. If only one institution is unconditionally DE-approved, then only that Mortgagee's claim and default rate is to be considered.

iii. Application and Approval

(A) First-Time Applicants

(1) Application

(a) Request to Enter into the Test Case Phase

The Mortgagee must submit a written application for Unconditional DE authority to the Jurisdictional HOC for the state where the Mortgagee's home office is located.

(b) Required Documentation

The Mortgagee's DE application must contain a letter signed by a Corporate Officer requesting entry into the Test Case phase that contains the Mortgagee's home office 10-digit FHA Lender ID and all underwriters' names and the four-character FHA-assigned identification numbers issued to these underwriters.

(2) Notification and Entrance Conference

If the Mortgagee meets the requirements for conditional authority and submits the required documentation, the Mortgagee will receive a Test Case phase approval letter from the HOC. The HOC will also provide reference materials and a list of the specific requirements that must be met for the Mortgagee to obtain Unconditional DE authority.

The Mortgagee must participate in an in-person or telephone entrance conference with the HOC before it will be eligible to submit Test Cases.

(3) Test Case Phase

The Mortgagee must submit Test Cases to FHA for review during the Test Case phase. FHA will review these cases for compliance with FHA's origination, underwriting, and closing requirements.

(a) Case Binder Submission [Text was deleted in this section.]

The Mortgagee must submit all Test Case files to the Jurisdictional HOC associated with the Mortgagee's home office.

Mortgagees who receive a DE program Test Case approval letter from HUD's HOC must submit all Test Case binders for review post-closing. The HOC will perform a review for compliance with FHA underwriting and closing guidelines. Review results will be documented in accordance with the Title II Loan Reviews/Findings section of this *SF Handbook*, and Mortgagees must respond to requests using the functions provided in the Loan Review System.

The HOC will issue either a Firm Commitment (approval) or Firm Reject (denial) via a Notice of Return (NOR). Once a Firm Commitment is issued, the HOC will process the case for endorsement. If a NOR is issued, the Mortgagee must make all necessary corrections and provide all required documentation to the HOC using the Loan Review System before the Mortgage can be endorsed.

(b) Test Case Underwriting Report [Text was deleted in this section.]

Mortgagees who receive a DE Program Test Case approval letter from HUD's HOC must review all Test Case results in the Loan Review System.

(c) Test Case Closing Documents

The Mortgagee must ensure that all required certifications are executed and included with each complete case binder that is submitted to the HOC for endorsement processing.

(4) Approval Decision

(a) Approval of Unconditional DE Authority

After the Mortgagee successfully completes the required Test Cases, FHA will grant the Mortgagee approval for Unconditional DE authority. The Mortgagee must receive a minimum of 15 Firm Commitments for forward mortgage authority or five Firm Commitments for HECM mortgage authority within a period of 12 consecutive months following the date of the DE Program Test Case approval letter in order to be granted Unconditional DE authority.

The Mortgagee will receive an approval letter and may then begin submitting Mortgages to FHA for endorsement without prior review by FHA.

(b) Denial of Unconditional DE Authority

The Mortgagee will be denied approval for Unconditional DE authority if, at any time during the Test Case phase, FHA determines that the Mortgagee's submissions demonstrate a lack of knowledge of FHA requirements, or if FHA identifies unacceptable practices.

(i) Denial Decision

FHA will provide the Mortgagee with written notice of a denial of Unconditional DE authority that specifies the reason for the denial.

(ii) Denial Appeal

The Mortgagee may appeal this denial by requesting an informal conference. The Mortgagee must submit its appeal in writing to the HOC that processed the Test Cases. The HOC must receive the appeal within 30 Days of the date of the notice of denial.

(iii) Informal Conference

FHA will conduct an informal conference with the Mortgagee and its counsel, if any, no later than 60 Days from the date of the denial.

(iv) Determination

FHA will issue a determination in writing following the informal conference stating whether Unconditional DE authority is approved or denied.

(v) Appeal Following Informal Conference

The Mortgagee may appeal a denial following the informal conference by submitting a written request to the Deputy Assistant Secretary (DAS) for Single Family Housing, or his or her designee, within 30 Days of the date of the denial determination.

The Mortgagee is not entitled to any meeting or informal conference with the DAS or the designee. The Mortgagee will be notified in writing of the decision of the DAS or the designee. The decision of the DAS or the designee constitutes final agency action.

(c) Reapplication Following Denial

Any Mortgagee who is denied Unconditional DE authority will not be permitted to reapply until it has:
- demonstrated appropriate remedial education or action;
- supplied evidence to support such action; and
- waited a minimum of 180 Days from the date of final agency action.

(B) Applications from Mortgagees Created by Merger, Acquisition or Reorganization

(1) Standard

The Mortgagee must submit a written application for Unconditional DE authority to the Jurisdictional HOC for the state where the Mortgagee's home office is located.

(2) Required Documentation

The Mortgagee's DE application must contain the following:
- a letter signed by a Corporate Officer requesting Unconditional DE authority that specifies:
  - o the FHA-approved and non-approved Entities involved in the merger, acquisition, or reorganization;
  - o which Entity is the surviving Entity; and
  - o the effective date of the merger, acquisition, or reorganization; and
- supporting documentation evidencing that the Mortgagee meets the exception criteria detailed above.

iv. Principal/Authorized Agent Relationship

(A) Definition

A Principal/Authorized Agent Relationship is one in which a Mortgagee with Unconditional DE authority permits another Unconditional DE-approved Mortgagee to underwrite Mortgages on its behalf.

(B) Standard

A Mortgagee with Unconditional DE authority (acting as the "principal") can designate another Unconditional DE-approved Mortgagee to act as its "authorized agent" for the purpose of underwriting Mortgages.

(1) Required Authorities

The authorized agent must have Unconditional DE authority to underwrite the type of Mortgage that is being underwritten. The Mortgagees must be approved as follows.

For a forward Mortgage:
- the principal may have Unconditional DE authority for either forward Mortgages or HECM; and
- the authorized agent *must* have Unconditional DE authority for forward Mortgages.

For a HECM:
- the principal may have Unconditional DE authority for either forward Mortgages or HECM; and
- the authorized agent *must* have Unconditional DE authority for HECM.

(2) Process

The principal must originate the Mortgage and the authorized agent must underwrite the Mortgage. The Mortgage may close in either Mortgagee's name, and either may submit the Mortgage for endorsement.

(C) Required Documentation

The relationship must be documented in LEAP by the authorized agent, and the principal's FHA Lender ID must be entered in the "Originator" field on the FHA case file and in FHAC.

v.   Sponsor/Sponsored Third-Party Originator Relationship

(A) Definition

A Sponsor/Sponsored Third-Party Originator (TPO) Relationship is one in which a Mortgagee (acting as the "sponsor") permits another entity to act as an originator and originate Mortgages on behalf of the Mortgagee.

(B) Standard

Only a Mortgagee with DE authority may use sponsored TPOs.

A Mortgagee must ensure its sponsored TPO meets all state license, registration, or equivalent approval requirements.

A Mortgagee is responsible for the actions of its sponsored TPOs under 24 CFR § 202.8(a)(3).

A Mortgagee must ensure its sponsored TPO and the TPO's officers, partners, directors, principals, managers, supervisors, loan processors, and loan originators are not ineligible under 24 CFR § 202.5(j).

A sponsored TPO is authorized to originate Mortgages for sale or transfer to a Mortgagee with DE authority. A Mortgagee must ensure its sponsored TPO does not close Mortgages in their own name.

Exception for Mortgagees Acting as a Sponsored Third-Party Originator

A Mortgagee may permit its sponsored TPO to close Mortgages in their own name if the TPO is also a Mortgagee.

(C) Required Documentation

A Mortgagee with Unconditional DE authority must confirm registration of its sponsored TPO on the Sponsored Originator Maintenance screen in FHAC. A Mortgagee must register its sponsored TPO on the Sponsored Originator Maintenance screen in FHAC if the sponsored TPO is not on the registry. The sponsored TPO's legal name and Employer Identification Number (EIN) must be included.

b.   Title II Single Family Lender Insurance Authority

i.   Scope of Authority

Approval to participate in FHA's Title II Single Family Lender Insurance (LI) Program permits a Mortgagee to endorse Mortgages for insurance with no prior review by FHA.

(A) Definitions

(1) LI Authority

LI Authority permits a Mortgagee with Title II Unconditional DE authority to endorse Single Family Mortgages for insurance without prior review by FHA.

(2) LI Compare Ratio

The LI Compare Ratio is the percentage of Mortgages underwritten by the Mortgagee that are in claim or default status compared with the percentage of Mortgages in claim or default status for all Mortgagees operating in the same state(s) over the preceding two-year period.

(B) Standard

To obtain Title II Single Family LI authority, the Mortgagee must meet the eligibility requirements as stated below and successfully complete the application and approval processes.

ii. Eligibility Requirements

(A) Standard

To obtain LI approval, the Mortgagee must:
- be an FHA-approved Mortgagee with Unconditional DE authority; and
- have an LI Compare Ratio that is at or below 150 percent.

(1) Exception for New Mortgagees Created by Merger, Acquisition, or Reorganization Resulting in New FHA Lender Identification Number

If the Mortgagee lacks an LI Compare Ratio because it was recently created by a merger, acquisition, or reorganization that resulted in the issuance of a new FHA Lender ID, it must:
- have Unconditional DE authority;
- have had one or more Mortgagees with LI authority at the time of the merger, acquisition, or reorganization, participate in the merger, acquisition, or reorganization;
- have had an acceptable LI Compare Ratio for all Mortgagees with LI authority participating in the merger, acquisition, or reorganization, at the time of the merger, acquisition, or reorganization;
- have an LI Compare Ratio that is derived from aggregating the claims and defaults of all formerly FHA-approved Mortgagees participating in the merger, acquisition, or reorganization that is not more than 150 percent; and
- ensure that the management and staff who were involved with LI processing for the FHA-approved Mortgagee prior to the merger,

acquisition, or reorganization will continue to exercise those responsibilities for the new Mortgagee.

iii. Application and Approval

(A) First-Time Applicants

(1) Standard

The Mortgagee must apply for LI authority through FHAC.

(2) Required Documentation

Before applying, the Mortgagee must make a written determination that it will participate in the LI Program. The Mortgagee's written determination to participate in the LI Program must be signed by a Principal Owner or Corporate Officer. The Mortgagee must retain a copy of such written determination and make it available to HUD upon request.

(3) Approval

FHAC will automatically approve or deny the Mortgagee's LI authority based on the Mortgagee's DE approval status and LI Compare Ratio.

(B) Application from Mortgagee Created by Merger, Acquisition, or Reorganization Resulting in New FHA Lender Identification Number

(1) Standard

Mortgagees created through mergers, acquisitions, or reorganizations that are issued a new FHA Lender ID must apply for LI authority through LEAP.

(2) Required Documentation

The Mortgagee's application must contain the following:
- a copy of the Acknowledgment of Terms and Conditions for LI screen in FHAC, printed and signed by a Corporate Officer;
- the name and contact information of the LI contact person and, at the discretion of the Mortgagee, the name and contact information for the back-up LI contact person;
- the name and FHA Lender ID of the new Mortgagee;
- the names and FHA Lender IDs of the Mortgagees participating in the merger, acquisition, or reorganization; and
- information identifying the management and staff experienced with LI processing employed by the new Mortgagee or transferring from a Mortgagee that previously held LI approval, and describing how the

management and staff will continue to exercise LI responsibilities for the new Mortgagee.

c. Title I Manufactured Housing Loan Direct Endorsement Authority

> ### RESERVED FOR FUTURE USE
>
> This section is reserved for future use, and until such time, FHA-Approved Mortgagees and Title I Manufactured Housing Mortgagees must continue to comply with all applicable law and existing Handbooks, Mortgagee Letters, Notices and outstanding guidance applicable to a Title I Manufactured Housing Mortgagee's participation in FHA programs.

d. Title II Multifamily Accelerated Processing Authority

Title II Multifamily Accelerated Processing (MAP) authority permits Mortgagees to underwrite and close multifamily Mortgages for FHA insurance without FHA's review prior to closing. The Office of Multifamily Housing grants this authority. Details on this authority are in the *Multifamily Accelerated Processing (MAP) Guide 4430.G*, which is available in HUD's Client Information and Policy System (HUDCLIPS).

6. Post-Approval Operations

a. Operating Requirements and Restrictions

A Mortgagee must comply with the following operating requirements and restrictions for its FHA business operations in addition to continuing to operate in full compliance with the eligibility requirements outlined in this *SF Handbook*.

b. Providing Information to FHA

Once approved, a Mortgagee must provide the following information to FHA using LEAP. The Mortgagee has an obligation to keep the information up to date.

i. Addresses for Correspondence

The Mortgagee must provide the following office addresses:
- Mailing - address of home office
- Geographic - street address(es) where its home and branch offices are physically located
- Administrative - street address to which HUD administrative notices from the HOC Quality Assurance and Processing and Underwriting Divisions, Office of Lender Activities and Program Compliance, Mortgagee Review Board (MRB), Office of General Counsel, and Office of Inspector General (OIG) are sent, including requests and/or demands for indemnification
- Premium - address to which FHA insurance premium correspondence is sent
- Payee - address to which FHA claim correspondence is sent

Handbook 4000.1
Effective Date: 09/14/2015 | Last Revised: 07/10/2019
*Refer to the online version of SF Handbook 4000.1 for specific sections' effective dates

37

- Servicing - street address of the main servicing office
- Computerized Homes Underwriting Management System (CHUMS) - address to which FHA originating, underwriting, endorsing, and closing correspondence is sent
- Endorsement - address to which all FHA mortgage endorsement correspondence is sent, including the Mortgage Insurance Certificate (MIC)

ii. Point of Contact

The Mortgagee must provide a primary administrative contact and an associated email address. The administrative contact is the point of contact associated with the Mortgagee's administrative address, and is the primary contact for all interaction between the Mortgagee and FHA. All HUD administrative notices from the HOC Quality Assurance and Processing and Underwriting Divisions, Office of Lender Activities and Program Compliance, MRB, Office of General Counsel, and OIG will be sent to the administrative contact, including requests and/or demands for indemnification.

Point of contact information is optional for all other addresses listed above.

iii. All Other Contact and Identification Information

The Mortgagee must provide all other required contact and identification information requested in LEAP, including phone, fax, email, and NMLS ID.

iv. Branch Office Information

For each registered branch office, the Mortgagee must provide the branch's address, phone number, email address, DBA name, and branch and regional managers.

v. Principal/Authorized Agent Relationships

The Mortgagee must identify its principal/authorized agent relationships in LEAP.

vi. Sponsor/Sponsored Third-Party Originator Relationships

The Mortgagee must identify its sponsored TPOs on the Sponsored Originator Maintenance screen in FHAC if the sponsored TPO is not on the registry. The sponsored TPO's legal name and EIN must be included.

vii. Cash Flow Accounts

The Mortgagee must use the Cash Flow Account Setup function in LEAP to provide its bank account information for the following payment types:
- Title I, Single Family Upfront Premiums
- Title I, Single Family (Periodic) Annual Premiums
- Title II, Single Family Upfront Premiums

- Title II, Single Family (Periodic) Monthly Premiums
- Title II, Single Family Claim Remittance Amounts

viii. Loan Review System Authorizations

The Mortgagee must grant the Loan Review System authorizations in FHAC to staff it deems qualified to perform the relevant function(s).

The Mortgagee must grant the Loan Review System Indemnification authorization to individuals authorized by the Mortgagee to sign indemnification agreements.

c. Compliance with Law

The Mortgagee must ensure that its operations are compliant with all applicable federal, state, and local laws.

d. Servicing of FHA-Insured Mortgages

The servicing of FHA-insured Mortgages must be performed by FHA-approved Mortgagees. FHA-approved Mortgagees that use a subservicer to service FHA-insured Mortgages must ensure the subservicer is also approved by FHA to service FHA-insured Mortgages. The servicing Mortgagee is responsible for the actions of their subservicers.

e. Employee Compensation

The Mortgagee must ensure its employees are compensated in accordance with the requirements for FHA approval.

f. Conflicts of Interest

The Mortgagee may not permit an employee to have multiple roles in a single FHA-insured transaction. Employees are prohibited from having multiple sources of compensation, either directly or indirectly, from a single FHA-insured transaction.

g. Payment of Operating Expenses

i. Definition

Operating Expenses are the costs associated with equipment, furniture, office rent, overhead, and employee compensation.

ii. Standard

The Mortgagee must pay all of its own operating expenses, including the expenses of its home office and any branch offices where it conducts FHA business.

The Mortgagee must maintain all accounts for operating expenses in its name.

h.   Prohibited Payments

The Mortgagee, or any of the Mortgagee's employees, must not pay or receive, or permit any other party involved in an FHA-insured mortgage transaction to pay or receive, any fee, kickback, compensation or thing of value to any person or Entity in connection with an FHA-insured mortgage transaction, except for services actually performed and permitted by HUD. The Mortgagee must not pay a referral fee to any person or Entity. The Mortgagee is not permitted to:

- advance funds to a real estate agent, real estate broker, mortgage broker, or packager as an advance of anticipated commissions on sales to be financed with an FHA-insured Mortgage to be provided by the Mortgagee;
- make low interest or no interest Mortgages to a real estate broker, real estate agent, mortgage broker, packager, builder or any other party from whom the Mortgagee accepts proposals involving FHA-insured Mortgages; or
- pay a gratuity or make a gift valued above items that are customarily distributed in the normal course of advertising, public relations, or as a general promotion device, to any person or Entity involved in the Mortgagee's FHA-insured mortgage transactions.

i.   Staffing

The Mortgagee must employ sufficient, experienced staff or engage, as permitted, the contract support necessary to carry out the Mortgagee's FHA business.

The Mortgagee is responsible for the actions of its staff that participate in FHA transactions. The Mortgagee must ensure that its Corporate Officers exercise control over the management and supervision of such staff, which must include regular and ongoing reviews of staff performance and of the work performed.

The Mortgagee is responsible for ensuring compliance with the licensing and registration requirements applicable to individual loan originators under the SAFE Act.

j.   Use of Contractors

i.   Permissible Use

The Mortgagee may use contract support for administrative, human resources, and clerical functions that include:
- clerical assistance;
- mortgage processing (typing of mortgage documents, mailing and collecting verification forms, ordering credit reports, and/or preparing for endorsement and shipping Mortgages to the Purchasing Mortgagee);
- ministerial tasks in mortgage servicing (processing of a foreclosure action, preservation and protection, and/or tax services);
- legal functions;
- Third Party Verification;

- Quality Control; and
- human resources services (payroll processing, payment of employment taxes and the provision of employee benefits) provided by a professional employer organization or a similar entity.

Third Party Verification refers to a process through which a Borrower's employment, income, and asset information is verified directly by the Mortgagee with a borrower's employer or financial institution, through the services of a third party vendor.

ii. Impermissible Use

The Mortgagee may not contract with any Entity or person that is suspended, debarred, under a Limited Denial of Participation (LDP), or who is otherwise excluded from participation in FHA transactions.

A Mortgagee must not contract out management or underwriting functions.

iii. Standard

The Mortgagee must ensure that the contracting out of certain functions does not and will not materially affect underwriting or servicing decisions or otherwise increase financial risk to FHA.

The Mortgagee remains responsible for the quality of its FHA-insured Mortgages and must ensure that its contractors fully comply with all applicable laws and FHA requirements.

The Mortgagee may own or have an ownership interest in a separate business Entity that offers such contract services.

Employees covered by a contract for human resources services described above must remain under the direct supervision and control of the Mortgagee. FHA considers the Mortgagee, the employer with respect to all activities related to FHA business, and the Mortgagee retains full responsibility and legal liability for the actions of employees covered by a contract for human resources services with regard to all HUD regulations and requirements.

iv. Required Documentation

The Mortgagee and its contractor must have a valid contractual agreement in place that specifies the roles and responsibilities of each party.

k. Affiliates

i. Definition

Affiliates are contractors, agents, vendors, subservicers, and sponsored TPOs who participate in FHA programs on behalf of an FHA-approved Mortgagee.

ii. Standard

The Mortgagee must ensure that its Affiliates are eligible and properly trained to participate in FHA programs.

The Mortgagee must ensure that each Affiliate of the Mortgagee adheres to FHA requirements when performing activities related to that Mortgagee's FHA business.

l. Branch Office Requirements

All branch offices must meet FHA's staffing, office facilities, and operating requirements, and all applicable licensing requirements.

m. Fair Housing Notice

The Mortgagee must prominently display a fair housing poster at each office that participates in activities related to Residential Real Estate-Related Transactions so as to be readily apparent to all persons seeking residential real estate or brokerage services. The Mortgagee must prominently display the Equal Housing Opportunity logo on documents, including both hard copy and electronic documents, distributed by the Mortgagee to the public.

n. Advertising

i. Definitions

(A) Advertising

Advertising is any communication made to an outside Entity or individual that describes or calls attention to a Mortgagee's FHA products or services.

(B) Advertising Device

An Advertising Device is a channel or instrument used to solicit, promote, or advertise FHA products or programs. Advertising Devices are present in the entire range of electronic and print media utilized by Mortgagees, including, but not limited to, websites, website addresses, business names, aliases, DBA names, domain names, email addresses, direct mail advertisements, solicitations, promotional materials and correspondence.

ii. Standard

(A) Advertising

A Mortgagee is solely responsible for the content of its advertising. This includes advertising abuses by employees of the approved Mortgagee, and any violations committed by employees of Affiliates or companies that advertise or generate FHA mortgage leads or other FHA business on behalf of the Mortgagee. The Mortgagee must ensure that all of its advertising communications and Advertising Devices, and the communications and Advertising Devices of its Affiliates, comply with all applicable state licensing and regulatory requirements.

(B) Advertising Device

A Mortgagee must not create the false impression that any of its Advertising Devices are official government forms, notices, or documents or that otherwise convey the false impression that an Advertising Device is authored, approved, or endorsed by HUD or FHA.

The Advertising Device must be written, formatted, and structured in a manner that clearly identifies the Mortgagee as the sole author and originator of the Advertising Device. The Advertising Device must reflect the Mortgagee's name, location, and appropriate contact information.

(1) HUD and FHA Names and Acronyms

The use of the words "federal," "government," "national," "U.S. Department of Housing and Urban Development," "Federal Housing Administration," and/or the letters "HUD" or "FHA," either alone or with other words or letters, by an FHA-approved Mortgagee, non-approved Mortgagee, or sponsored TPO in a manner that falsely represents that the Mortgagee's business services or products originate from HUD, FHA, the government of the United States, or any federal, state or local government agency is strictly prohibited.

(2) HUD and FHA Logos and Seals

Other than permissible use of the official FHA-Approved Lending Institution logo and the Equal Housing Opportunity logo, a Mortgagee must not use FHA or HUD logos or seals, any other official seal or logo of the U.S. Department of Housing and Urban Development, or any other insignia that imitates an official federal seal. No person, party, company, or firm, including FHA-approved Mortgagees, may use these logos or seals on any Advertising Device.

(a) FHA-Approved Lending Institution Logo User Restrictions

Only an FHA-approved Mortgagee may display the official FHA-Approved Lending Institution logo on an Advertising Device for the purpose of illustrating to the public the fact that the Mortgagee originates FHA-insured mortgage products.

The Mortgagee must not permit its sponsored TPOs to use the official FHA-Approved Lending Institution logo on any Advertising Device; unless the sponsored TPO is also an FHA-approved Mortgagee.

(b) FHA-Approved Lending Institution Logo Content Restrictions

The FHA-Approved Lending Institution logo must be displayed in a discreet manner. The Advertising Device, when taken as a whole, must emphasize the institution or DBA name of the Mortgagee, and not the federal government.

When using the FHA-Approved Lending Institution logo on an Advertising Device, the Mortgagee must include a conspicuous disclaimer that clearly informs the public that the Mortgagee displaying the Advertising Device is not acting on behalf of or at the direction of HUD, FHA, or the federal government. The disclaimer must be prominently displayed in a location proximate to where the FHA-Approved Lending Institution logo is displayed on each Advertising Device.

The Mortgagee may not alter or modify the FHA-Approved Lending Institution logo in any way.

(3) Advertising Devices of Sponsored Third-Party Originators

Advertising Devices used by sponsored TPOs must reflect the sponsored TPO's name, location, and appropriate contact information.

Sponsored TPOs are prohibited from engaging in any activity or authoring or distributing any Advertising Device that falsely advertises, represents, or otherwise conveys the impression that the sponsored TPO's business operations, products, or services either originate from or are expressly endorsed by HUD, FHA, the government of the United States, or any federal, state or local government agency.

iii. Required Documentation

The Mortgagee must retain copies of any Advertising Device it produces that is related to FHA programs for a period of two years from the date that the Advertising Device is circulated or used for advertisement, educational, or promotional purposes. Copies of Advertising Devices related to FHA programs may be kept in either electronic or print format and are to be provided to HUD upon request.

7.   Post-Approval Changes

The Mortgagee has an ongoing requirement to notify FHA of any changes to the information outlined in its application for FHA approval or in FHA's eligibility requirements.

a.   Requirements for All Post-Approval Changes

i.   Types of Notification

(A) Information Update

An Information Update is any change to a Mortgagee's basic institution or branch information in the FHA systems that can be directly managed by the Mortgagee.

(B) Notice of Material Event

A Notice of Material Event is the method of submitting a required notice to FHA of a change to the information provided by the Mortgagee at application as evidence of approval eligibility, or a change that affects the Mortgagee's standing as an FHA-approved Mortgagee.

(C) Change Request

A Change Request is the method of submitting information and/or business changes to FHA that requires FHA review and approval before acceptance. Any update or change that cannot be made by the Mortgagee directly is submitted as a Change Request.

ii.   Standard

The Mortgagee must submit all Information Updates, Notices of Material Event, and Change Requests to FHA using LEAP. All Information Updates, Notices of Material Event, and Change Requests must be submitted within 10 business days of the change, unless otherwise specified below.

Any change not specifically described in this *SF Handbook* that affects a Mortgagee's approval status or conduct of business with HUD must be reported to FHA with a detailed explanation and supporting documentation.

iii.   Required Documentation

The Mortgagee must:
- include a cover letter signed by a Corporate Officer summarizing the business change(s); and
- submit any required documents as specified in Application and Eligibility Requirements for Approval or as described in the LEAP User Manual.

b. Information Updates

The Mortgagee must submit Information Updates, as applicable, for the following information:

- addresses for correspondence
- point of contact
- all other contact and identification information
- branch office information
- principal/authorized agent relationships
- cash flow accounts

c. Change in Corporate Officer

The Mortgagee must submit a Change Request to FHA in order to add or remove a Corporate Officer.

d. Change in Partnership or Principal Owners

The Mortgagee must submit a Notice of Material Event to FHA if it experiences a change in partnership or Principal Owners. This includes the addition or removal of partners or Principal Owners.

e. "Doing Business As" Names

The Mortgagee must submit Information Updates, as applicable, for all DBA names or aliases that the Mortgagee has a legal right to use. If the Mortgagee has six or more DBA names, the Mortgagee must submit a Change Request through LEAP to add additional names.

f. Relocation to a Different State

i. Home Office

If the Mortgagee is changing the geographic address of its home office to a different state, the Mortgagee must submit a Change Request to FHA through LEAP.

ii. Branch Office

If the Mortgagee is changing the geographic address of a branch office to a different state, the Mortgagee must terminate the branch FHA Lender ID for the original office and register the new location as a new branch office. The branch FHA Lender ID for the original branch office will remain active for approximately 45 Days to allow for the completion of processing of Mortgages in process under that identification number.

Approved Mortgages that were approved before the branch office termination became effective may be endorsed. Cases at earlier stages of processing cannot be submitted for insurance by the terminated branch. However, the cases may be transferred for completion of processing and underwriting to another branch office or Mortgagee authorized to underwrite FHA-insured Mortgages in that area.

g. Liquid Assets or Net Worth Deficiency

If at any time a Mortgagee's adjusted net worth or liquidity falls below the required minimum, the Mortgagee must submit a Notice of Material Event to FHA within 30 business days of the deficiency. The Mortgagee must submit a Corrective Action Plan that outlines the steps taken to mitigate the deficiency and includes relevant information, such as contributions and efforts made to obtain additional capital.

h. Operating Loss

If a Mortgagee experiences an operating loss of 20 percent or greater of its adjusted net worth, the Mortgagee must submit a Notice of Material Event to FHA within 30 business days of the loss. The 20 percent threshold applies to losses in any quarter during the fiscal year or losses that exceed 20 percent on the financial statements submitted at recertification.

Following the initial notification, the Mortgagee must submit financial statements every quarter until it shows an operating profit for two consecutive quarters, or until it submits its financial reports as part of its recertification.

i. Fidelity Bond

The Mortgagee must submit a Notice of Material Event to FHA of any significant change(s) to its fidelity bond coverage. If a Mortgagee loses its fidelity bond coverage it must obtain a new policy within 30 Days.

j. Errors and Omissions Insurance

The Mortgagee must submit a Notice of Material Event to FHA of any significant change(s) to its errors and omissions insurance. If a Mortgagee loses its errors and omissions insurance it must obtain a new policy within 30 Days.

k. Principal Activity Change of Nonsupervised Mortgagee

If a Nonsupervised Mortgagee's activities change such that it no longer meets the principal activity requirement, the Mortgagee must submit a Notice of Material Event to FHA and submit a Corrective Action Plan detailing the steps it will take to meet the principal activity requirement to maintain its eligibility.

l. Servicing for Investing Mortgagees

In order to service FHA Mortgages, an Investing Mortgagee must submit a Change Request after it has received FHA Mortgagee approval. With its Change Request, the Mortgagee must:

- designate an <u>Officer in Charge</u> who meets the experience requirements for the Mortgagee's servicing function;
- provide a <u>resume</u> for the Officer in Charge;
- provide a <u>credit report</u> for the Officer in Charge; and
- provide an updated <u>QC Plan</u>.

FHA evaluates these requests on a case-by-case basis and reserves the right to request additional documents necessary to determine the Mortgagee's servicing capabilities.

m. Fiscal Year End Date

The Mortgagee must submit a Change Request to FHA in order to change its fiscal year end date.

Before approving the change, FHA may require the Mortgagee to submit interim financial reports to ensure the Mortgagee's next annual renewal financial reports cover no more than 18 months. Change Requests must be submitted at least 90 Days before the end of the Mortgagee's current fiscal year, as reported to FHA.

n. Supervision Change

If there is a change to a Supervised Mortgagee's supervising or regulatory agency, the Mortgagee must submit a Notice of Material Event to FHA and provide documentation of the change and the effective date.

o. Business Form

The Mortgagee must submit a Notice of Material Event to FHA if it reincorporates; changes its charter; changes the state where it is incorporated, organized or chartered; or completes any other equivalent business change.

i. Change Resulting in New Federal Taxpayer Identification Number

If a Mortgagee receives a different federal TIN as a result of a business change, the Mortgagee must submit a new <u>application</u> for FHA Mortgagee approval.

FHA will issue a new FHA Lender ID to the Mortgagee upon approval. When the new FHA Lender ID is issued, the old FHA Lender ID will remain active for approximately 45 Days to allow for completion of processing of Mortgages in process under that identification number.

ii. Change Not Resulting in New Federal Taxpayer Identification Number

If the Mortgagee does not receive a new federal TIN as a result of a business change, then the Mortgagee must submit the following documents to FHA:
- a Notice of Material Event in the form of a letter signed by a Corporate Officer containing the following provisions:

- providing a complete description of the business change;
- confirming that there has been no change in the federal TIN or depositor insurance (in the case of a Supervised Mortgagee);
- stipulating that the institution will continue to comply with all FHA approval and eligibility requirements; and
- stipulating that the newly chartered Entity will continue to be responsible for the assets and liabilities of the former Entity, including any problems found subsequently by HUD in the origination or servicing of any Mortgages originated or serviced by the Entity prior to the business change; and
- a copy of the Business Formation Documents.

p. Bankruptcy

i. Business

A Mortgagee that files a Chapter 7 bankruptcy petition must submit a Notice of Material Event to FHA.

A Mortgagee that files a bankruptcy petition under any other chapter of the United States Bankruptcy Code must submit a Notice of Material Event to FHA and submit with its notice, and quarterly thereafter, an internally prepared balance sheet and a statement of adjusted net worth for as long as the bankruptcy petition is active.

The Mortgagee must submit a Notice of Material Event to FHA of each change of status in the bankruptcy. FHA reserves the right to require the Mortgagee to submit additional information upon request in order to determine if the Mortgagee is eligible to maintain its FHA approval.

ii. Personal

The Mortgagee must submit a Notice of Material Event to FHA if any Corporate Officer or Principal Owner commences voluntary or involuntary bankruptcy. A current credit report for that Corporate Officer or Principal Owner must be submitted with the Notice of Material Event. FHA must be notified of each change of status in the bankruptcy proceedings.

q. Lending License(s)

The Mortgagee must submit a Notice of Material Event to FHA of any changes to its license(s). In the event of a lending license surrender or revocation, the Mortgagee must notify FHA which license(s) has been surrendered and provide an explanation of each action.

r. Mergers, Acquisitions, and Reorganizations

i. Merger or Consolidation

FHA's treatment of an FHA-approved Mortgagee for approval purposes following a merger will depend on the prior approval status of the surviving Entity.

(A) Duties of a Non-Surviving FHA-Approved Mortgagee

A non-surviving FHA-approved Mortgagee is required to do the following for any case in which they are merged or consolidated into another Entity.

(1) Standard

A non-surviving FHA-approved Mortgagee that holds a portfolio of FHA-insured Mortgages must transfer the Mortgages within 45 Days to a Mortgagee approved by FHA to service FHA Mortgages.

If a surviving FHA-approved Mortgagee acquires all of the non-surviving FHA-approved Mortgagee's outstanding FHA Mortgages, all of these Mortgages will be transferred in FHA systems to the surviving Entity when the merger is processed.

A non-surviving Mortgagee remains responsible for the payment of insurance premiums and compliance with all other obligations associated with the FHA Mortgages until the Mortgages are transferred and the mortgage record changes are reported accurately to HUD through FHAC, Electronic Data Interchange (EDI), or Business to Government (B2G).

Once the non-surviving Mortgagee ceases to exist or its approval is terminated, whichever comes first, the non-surviving Mortgagee must not:
- accept any new applications for FHA Mortgages;
- hold FHA Mortgages;
- service FHA Mortgages; or
- submit claims to HUD.

(2) Required Documentation

A non-surviving Mortgagee must submit a Change Request to FHA containing the following:
- a letter, signed by a Corporate Officer, that informs FHA of the merger. The letter must include information that:
  - indicates which Entity will survive;
  - provides the FHA Lender IDs for each FHA-approved Mortgagee involved;
  - provides the date the merger occurred or will occur; and

o requests the withdrawal of the non-surviving Mortgagee's FHA approval in accordance with FHA's voluntary withdrawal procedures;
- a copy of the legal document evidencing the merger;
- if a Supervised Mortgagee, a copy of the letter from the Federal Banking Agency that approved the merger; and
- if applicable, a letter describing how the non-surviving Mortgagee will dispose of the FHA-insured Mortgages that it held or serviced that have not been acquired by a surviving FHA-approved Mortgagee within 45 Days.

(B) Duties of a Surviving Entity

(1) FHA-Approved Mortgagee That Survives a Merger with a Non-Approved Entity

(a) Standard

An FHA-approved Mortgagee that is the surviving Entity in a merger with a non-approved Entity must notify FHA of the merger.

The surviving FHA-approved Mortgagee must register each of the non-surviving Entity's branch offices that will remain open under the auspices of the surviving Mortgagee and pay the branch office registration fee(s).

(b) Required Documentation

An FHA-approved Mortgagee that is the surviving Entity in a merger with a non-approved Entity must submit a Change Request to FHA containing the following:
- a letter, signed by a Corporate Officer, describing the merger;
- a copy of the legal document evidencing the merger; and
- if a Supervised Mortgagee, a copy of the letter from the Federal Banking Agency or other supervisory authority that approved the merger.

(2) Two or More FHA-Approved Mortgagees Merge

(a) Standard

An FHA-approved Mortgagee that is the surviving Entity in a merger with another FHA-approved Mortgagee must notify FHA of the merger.

The surviving Mortgagee must register each of the non-surviving Mortgagee's branch offices that will remain open under the auspices of the surviving Mortgagee and pay the branch office registration fee(s).

(b) Required Documentation

An FHA-approved Mortgagee that is the surviving Entity in a merger with another FHA-approved Mortgagee must submit a Change Request to FHA containing the following:

- a letter, signed by a Corporate Officer, describing the merger;
- a copy of the legal document evidencing the merger; and
- if a Supervised Mortgagee, a copy of the letter from the Federal Banking Agency or other supervisory authority that approved the merger.

(3) Non-Approved Entity That Survives a Merger with an FHA-Approved Mortgagee

(a) Standard

A non-approved surviving Entity must become an FHA-approved Mortgagee in order to originate, underwrite, close, endorse, service, purchase, hold, or sell FHA-insured Mortgages, or to submit claims on Mortgages to FHA, including those previously held by the non-surviving Mortgagee.

Immediately after becoming approved, the Mortgagee must register each of the non-surviving Entity's branch offices that will remain open under the auspices of the surviving Mortgagee and pay the branch office registration fee(s).

The FHA Lender IDs of the non-surviving Mortgagee's branch offices will remain active for up to 45 Days to allow for the completion of processing of Mortgages in process under these identification numbers. When new FHA Lender IDs for these branch offices are issued, the surviving Mortgagee must cease originating cases under the non-surviving Mortgagee's old FHA Lender ID numbers.

(b) Required Documentation

A non-approved surviving Entity must submit an online application for FHA approval containing all information and documentation required to demonstrate eligibility for approval. The Entity must also submit with its application a letter signed by a Corporate Officer that describes the merger, and, if applicable, the surviving Entity's intentions regarding the non-surviving Mortgagee's outstanding portfolio of FHA Mortgages and indemnifications.

ii. Sale, Acquisition, or Disassociation

FHA's treatment of a sale, acquisition, or disassociation of an FHA-approved Mortgagee depends on whether the FHA-approved Mortgagee dissolves, continues as a subsidiary or corporate affiliation of the acquiring Entity, or becomes an independent Entity.

(A) An FHA-Approved Mortgagee Is Acquired by Another Entity

(1) Dissolution of Acquired FHA-Approved Mortgagee

(a) Duties of Acquired FHA-Approved Mortgagee

(i) Standard

If an FHA-approved Mortgagee being acquired will be dissolved into another Entity, it must voluntarily withdraw its FHA approval. The acquired Mortgagee must transfer any FHA-insured Mortgages in its portfolio to a Mortgagee approved to service FHA-insured Mortgages.

The dissolving Mortgagee must continue to pay insurance premiums due and meet all other obligations associated with its FHA Mortgages until the Mortgages are transferred and the mortgage record changes are reported accurately to HUD in FHAC, EDI, or B2G.

(ii) Required Documentation

The FHA-approved Mortgagee being acquired must submit a Change Request to FHA in the form of a letter, signed by a Corporate Officer, that informs FHA of the details regarding the acquisition and requests the withdrawal of its FHA approval.

The Mortgagee must submit a copy of the articles of dissolution, a letter describing the acquisition, and, if applicable, how it will or has disposed of FHA Mortgages that it held or serviced.

(b) Duties of Acquiring Entity

(i) Standard

If a non-approved Entity is acquiring and dissolving an FHA-approved Mortgagee, the non-approved Entity must become an FHA-approved Mortgagee to originate, underwrite, close, endorse, service, purchase, hold, or sell FHA-insured Mortgages, or to submit claims on FHA Mortgages, including those previously held by the dissolved Mortgagee.

Immediately after becoming approved, the Mortgagee must register each of the dissolved Mortgagee's branch offices that will remain open under the auspices of the acquiring Entity.

(ii) Required Documentation

An FHA-approved Mortgagee that acquires and dissolves another FHA-approved Mortgagee is required to submit a Change Request to FHA through LEAP.

A non-approved Entity must submit an online application for FHA approval containing all information and documentation required to demonstrate eligibility for approval. The Entity must also submit with its application a letter signed by a Corporate Officer that describes the acquisition, and, if applicable, the acquiring Entity's intentions regarding the dissolved Mortgagee's outstanding portfolio of FHA Mortgages.

(2) Continuation as Subsidiary or Corporate Affiliation

(a) Acquisition by an FHA-Approved Mortgagee

(i) Standard

If the FHA-approved Mortgagee being acquired will continue to operate as a subsidiary or corporate affiliation of the acquiring FHA-approved Mortgagee, the acquired Mortgagee may continue to operate under its existing FHA Lender ID as a separately approved Mortgagee.

(ii) Required Documentation

Acquired FHA-Approved Mortgagee - The acquired Mortgagee must submit a Change Request to FHA in the form of a letter, signed by a Corporate Officer, informing FHA that it has been acquired and will continue to operate as a subsidiary or corporate affiliation of the acquiring FHA-approved Mortgagee.

Acquiring FHA-Approved Mortgagee - The acquiring FHA-approved Mortgagee must submit a Change Request to FHA in the form of a letter, signed by a Corporate Officer, that:
- describes the transaction;
- lists the names of all parties;
- lists the FHA Lender IDs of all parties;
- states the date of the acquisition; and
- stipulates that the acquired Mortgagee will continue as a subsidiary or corporate affiliation of the acquiring FHA-approved Mortgagee.

(b) Acquisition by a Non-Approved Entity

(i) Standard

If the acquired FHA-approved Mortgagee will continue to operate as a subsidiary or corporate affiliation of the acquiring Entity, it may continue to operate as an FHA-approved Mortgagee under its own name, whether or not the acquiring Entity becomes FHA-approved.

(ii) Required Documentation

The Mortgagee must submit a Change Request to FHA in the form of a letter, signed by a Corporate Officer, describing the acquisition and its future operating status.

(B) An FHA-Approved Mortgagee Acquires a Non-Approved Entity

(1) Standard

If an FHA-approved Mortgagee acquires a non-approved Entity the Mortgagee must notify FHA of the acquisition.

If an FHA-approved Mortgagee acquires a non-approved Entity and the acquired Entity will operate with a separate EIN as a subsidiary or corporate affiliation of the Mortgagee, the non-approved Entity must apply for separate approval in order to originate, underwrite, close, endorse, service, purchase, hold, or sell FHA-insured Mortgages.

(2) Required Documentation

If an FHA-approved Mortgagee acquires a non-approved Entity the Mortgagee is required to submit a Change Request to FHA in the form of a letter, signed by a Corporate Officer, describing the acquisition.

If an FHA-approved Mortgagee acquires a non-approved Entity and the acquired Entity intends to originate, underwrite, close, endorse, service, purchase, hold, or sell FHA-insured Mortgages operating with a separate EIN as a subsidiary or corporate affiliation of the Mortgagee, the non-approved Entity must submit an online application for FHA approval containing all information and documentation required to demonstrate eligibility for approval. The Entity must also submit with its application a letter signed by a Corporate Officer that describes the acquisition.

(C) An FHA-Approved Mortgagee Becomes Independent

(1) Standard

When an FHA-approved Mortgagee that has been a subsidiary or part of a larger Entity becomes independent, the Mortgagee must notify FHA of the disassociation.

If the disassociation results in changes to the Mortgagee's Corporate Officers or Principal Owners, the Mortgagee must submit the proper notifications to FHA as described in this *SF Handbook*.

(2) Required Documentation

When an FHA-approved Mortgagee that has been a subsidiary or part of a larger Entity becomes independent, the Mortgagee must submit a Change Request to FHA in the form of a letter, signed by a Corporate Officer, describing the details of the disassociation.

s.   Conservatorship, Receivership, or Transfer of Control

The Mortgagee must submit a Change Request to FHA if it goes into conservatorship, receivership, or is subject to a transfer of control to a federal or state supervisory agency.

The Mortgagee must submit a Change Request to FHA of a change of status in any of these situations and FHA reserves the right to require the Mortgagee to submit additional information in order to determine if the Mortgagee is eligible to maintain its FHA Mortgagee approval.

t.   Cease Operations

The Mortgagee must submit a Notice of Material Event to FHA if it ceases operations. If the Mortgagee ceases operations, it must also submit a Change Request for voluntary withdrawal of FHA approval.

u.   Unresolved Findings or Sanctions

A Mortgagee must submit a Notice of Material Event to FHA and provide relevant documentation if it or any officer, partner, director, principal, manager, supervisor, loan processor, loan underwriter, or loan originator employed or retained by the Mortgagee is subject to any Unresolved Findings or Sanctions.

A Mortgagee must submit a Notice of Material Event to FHA of a change of status in any Unresolved Finding or Sanction previously reported.

8. Annual Recertification

a. General Requirements

i. Standard

(A) Recertification Process

To retain its FHA approval, a Mortgagee must, unless otherwise noted, complete FHA's recertification process on an annual basis.

(B) Filing Deadline

Each Mortgagee must submit its recertification package within 90 Days after the Mortgagee's fiscal year end.

ii. Required Documentation

The Mortgagee must submit its annual recertification package through LEAP. The Mortgagee must submit the following to recertify its FHA approval:
- online certification
- recertification fee
- financial data

A Mortgagee that does not wish to retain its FHA approval must submit a Change Request for voluntary withdrawal of FHA approval.

iii. Exception for Recently Approved Mortgagees

(A) Standard

The Mortgagee is not required to submit audited financial statements or pay the recertification fee if the initial approval date of the Mortgagee is less than six months prior to the end of its fiscal year and the audited financial statements submitted for approval are for the period ending not more than six months prior to the end of its fiscal year.

However, the audited financial statements for the next recertification reporting period must cover the period from the date after the ending date of its audited financial statements submitted for approval to the end of its current fiscal year. The period covered by the renewal audit cannot exceed 18 months.

(B) Required Documentation

At the close of the first, full fiscal year following receipt of FHA approval, the Mortgagee must submit audited financial statements covering the period from the ending date of the financial statements used to obtain initial approval, and ending at the close of the Mortgagee's most recent fiscal year. Mortgagees may not submit financial statements that cover a period of more than 18 months.

b. Online Certification

i. Standard

The Mortgagee, through a Corporate Officer, must complete a series of annual certification statements that address the Mortgagee's compliance with FHA requirements over the Certification Period. The Certification Period is the one-year period beginning on the first day of the Mortgagee's prior fiscal year and ending on the last calendar day thereof.

ii. Required Documentation

The certification must be completed through LEAP by a Corporate Officer of the Mortgagee who has been granted the Certifying Official authorization in FHAC.

iii. Unable to Certify

(A) Standard

If a Mortgagee is unable to truthfully certify to one or more of the statements set forth in the online certification, the Mortgagee must not make the particular certification.

(B) Required Documentation

The Mortgagee must submit an explanation for each certification that it is unable to complete. The Mortgagee may submit supporting documentation with its explanation.

If additional information is required as a result of the Mortgagee's explanation, FHA will advise what additional information or documentation is required and provide a due date for the submission of the requested information or documentation.

(C) FHA Review

FHA will review the Mortgagee's explanation and request any additional information or documentation needed to render a final decision regarding the Mortgagee's ability to complete the annual recertification process.

iv. Repercussion of False Certification

If a Mortgagee submits a false certification to FHA, the Mortgagee and its certifying Corporate Officer may be referred for criminal, civil, or administrative actions, as appropriate.

Handbook 4000.1
Effective Date: 09/14/2015 | Last Revised: 07/10/2019
*Refer to the online version of SF Handbook 4000.1 for specific sections' effective dates

58

c. Annual Recertification Fee

i. Standard

The Mortgagee must pay an annual recertification fee after its online certification has been submitted and accepted. All fee payments must be made electronically. This recertification fee is non-refundable and will not be prorated.

ii. Calculation of Fee Amount

The Mortgagee will be assessed a fee for the Mortgagee's home office and for each branch office registered with FHA. Fees are calculated based on the Mortgagee's program approval(s), Mortgagee type, and the number of FHA-approved branch offices as of the last business day of the Mortgagee's Certification Period.

A Mortgagee that is terminating a branch office must do so on or before the last business day of the Certification Period in order to avoid paying the recertification fee for that branch office for the next Certification Period. Mortgagees attempting to terminate a branch office after the last day of their Certification Period will not be permitted to do so until the annual recertification fees have been paid in full.

iii. Exception for Government Mortgagees

Government Mortgagees are not required to pay a recertification fee.

d. Financial Data Submission

Supervised, Nonsupervised, and Investing Mortgagees must submit the financial data described below.

i. Small Supervised Mortgagees

A Small Supervised Mortgagee must submit a copy of its Unaudited Regulatory Report, signed by a Corporate Officer, that aligns with its fiscal year end.

ii. Large Supervised, Nonsupervised, and Investing Mortgagees

(A) Audit of Financial Statements

The Mortgagee must comply with the appropriate financial reporting procedures and requirements set forth in the HUD OIG Handbook 2000.04, *Consolidated Audit Guide for Audits of HUD Programs*.

(B) Accounting and Auditing Standards

The Mortgagee must have prepared its financial statements in accordance with GAAP and had its audit performed in accordance with the most currently effective

Government Accountability Office Generally Accepted Government Auditing Standards (GAGAS), also referred to as the "Yellow Book," and GAAS.

(C) Audit Related Questions

The Mortgagee must submit answers to FHA's Audit Related Questions. FHA's Audit Related Questions address information about the Mortgagee's financial data, the type of audit completed, and any Findings reported.

(D) Independent Public Accountant Attestation

The Mortgagee must submit its recertification package to an Independent Public Accountant (IPA) for review. The IPA must review the Mortgagee's financial data and Audit Related Questions, and complete the Agreed Upon Procedures. The Agreed Upon Procedures address compliance with required audit procedures.

iii. Exception for Government Mortgagees

Government Mortgagees are not required to submit financial information.

e. Rejection of a Mortgagee's Recertification Package

FHA may reject a Mortgagee's recertification package due to noncompliance. When this occurs, the Mortgagee must resubmit its financial data, and if applicable, the answers to FHA's Audit Related Questions along with an updated IPA attestation. All documents needed to cure deficiencies in the Mortgagee's recertification package must be submitted through LEAP.

f. Recertification Extension Requests

The Mortgagee may request an extension of its recertification package due date only as the result of a natural or catastrophic event resulting in a disruption of employee or mortgagee business operations. Extension requests must be submitted through LEAP prior to the Mortgagee's recertification package due date.

g. Failure to Recertify

A Mortgagee may be referred to the MRB for failing to timely and satisfactorily complete the annual recertification process.

9. Voluntary Withdrawal of FHA Mortgagee Approval

A Mortgagee that does not wish to retain its FHA approval must submit a Change Request for voluntary withdrawal of FHA approval.

a. Standard

The Mortgagee must satisfy all outstanding payable indemnification debts and Mortgage Insurance Premiums (MIP), and transfer the servicing and ownership of any FHA-insured Mortgages in its portfolio to an FHA-approved Mortgagee prior to its request being approved, and the Mortgagee will remain obligated on any outstanding indemnification agreements.

FHA will not honor a Mortgagee's request to withdraw while there is a pending administrative action or MRB action, or while the Mortgagee has unpaid indemnification claims or unsatisfied settlement agreement obligations owed to HUD.

b. Required Documentation

The Mortgagee must submit a Change Request for voluntary withdrawal in the form of a letter, signed by a Corporate Officer, and submitted through LEAP. If applicable, the request must be submitted within 10 business days of the change in the Mortgagee's eligibility status.

c. Reapplication

A Mortgagee whose approval is voluntarily withdrawn may reapply for FHA approval any time after its withdrawal.

B. OTHER PARTICIPANTS

1. Appraisers

a. FHA Appraiser Roster

i. Definition

Appraiser refers to an FHA Roster Appraiser who observes, analyzes, and reports the physical and economic characteristics of a Property and provides an opinion of value to FHA. An Appraiser's observation is limited to readily observable conditions and is not as comprehensive an inspection as one performed by a licensed home inspector.

ii. Standard

FHA requires Mortgagees to select qualified, competent and knowledgeable Appraisers.

FHA maintains a list of qualified Appraisers on the FHA Appraiser Roster. Only an Appraiser on the FHA Appraiser Roster and the Appraisal Subcommittee's (ASC) National Registry may be selected by the Mortgagee to conduct an appraisal for FHA-insured financing.

b. Application and Approval Process

i. Eligibility Requirements

(A) General

For placement on the FHA Appraiser Roster, the appraiser must:
- be a state-certified residential or state-certified general appraiser with credentials based on the minimum licensing/certification criteria issued by the Appraiser Qualifications Board (AQB) of the Appraisal Foundation;
- not be suspended, debarred, or otherwise excluded; and
- not be listed on HUD's Limited Denial of Participation (LDP) List, HUD's Credit Alert Verification Reporting System (CAIVRS), or subject to any current loss of standing or suspension as a certified appraiser in any state.

(B) Competency Requirement

The Appraiser must be knowledgeable of the Uniform Standards of Professional Appraisal Practice (USPAP) and FHA appraisal requirements. The Appraiser must meet the competency requirements defined in the USPAP prior to accepting an assignment. The Appraiser must be knowledgeable in the market where the assignment is located.

(C) Licensing Requirement

The Appraiser must be a state-certified residential or state-certified general Appraiser. The Appraiser must maintain and be able to prove certification in all states in which the Appraiser performs appraisals.

ii. Submitting the Application and Required Documentation

The appraiser must submit applications electronically through FHA Connection (FHAC) and follow the FHA Appraiser Roster Application Instructions.

(A) Form HUD-92563-A

The appraiser must complete form HUD-92563-A in FHAC. The appraiser must sign this form, scan it and save it in a PDF format for delivery to FHA.

The appraiser must certify that the appraiser has "read and fully understands and will comply with *FHA Single Family Housing Policy Handbook (SF Handbook), and FHA Single Family Housing Appraisal Report and Data Delivery Guide.*"

(B) State Certification

The appraiser must provide a PDF image of their current state-issued certification for each state in which the appraiser is certified.

(C) Pending or Settled Actions

The applicant must disclose all lawsuits, administrative complaints, Findings, or reports produced in connection with an investigation, audit, or review conducted by HUD, another federal, state, or local governmental agency, or by any other regulatory or oversight entity with jurisdiction over the appraiser, its officers, partners, directors, principals, managers, supervisors, and other agents, that are currently pending or were resolved within two years of the application, including any violations of the Fair Housing Act.

iii. Processing of Application

FHA will review all completed applications for approval to determine if the appraiser complies with all eligibility requirements. If FHA requires additional documentation or clarifying information, FHA may request such additional information and provide the appraiser with a deadline for response. If the appraiser does not submit a completed application or provide the additional information requested by the specified deadline, FHA may deny approval on this basis.

iv. Application Approval

If FHA approves the appraiser's application, the Appraiser's name will appear on the FHA Appraiser Roster.

v.   Application Rejection

Applicants deemed ineligible for placement on the FHA Appraiser Roster will be notified electronically and provided the reason(s) for denial.

c. Renewal

The Appraiser should renew expiring licenses at least 45 Days prior to expiration in order for state records to process the renewal to the ASC National Registry. FHA Appraiser Roster records are based on National Registry records. Failure of the Appraiser to renew in a timely manner may result in removal from the FHA Appraiser Roster.

d. Post-Approval Requirements

The Appraiser must comply with the following requirements and restrictions for its FHA business operations in addition to continuing to operate in full compliance with the eligibility requirements outlined in this *SF Handbook*.

i. Compliance with Law

The Appraiser's performance must comply with all applicable federal, state, and local laws. The Appraiser must adhere to all state and local laws relating to appraisal, licensing and certification requirements.

ii. Appraiser Competency Requirement

The Appraiser assigned to provide the appraisal must be able to complete an assignment for the property type, assignment type, and geographic location of the subject Property.

The Appraiser must comply with the USPAP, including the Competency Rule, when conducting appraisals of Properties intended as security for FHA-insured financing.

iii. Communications with Appraisers

An FHA Roster Appraiser must avoid conflicts of interest and the appearance of conflicts of interest. To avoid conflicts of interest and/or the appearance of conflicts of interest, the Appraiser must not be unduly influenced by:

- a member of a Mortgagee's loan production staff or any other person who is compensated based upon the successful completion of a loan; or
- anyone who reports ultimately to any officer of the Mortgagee not independent of the loan production staff and process.

The Appraiser is bound by the confidentiality provisions of the USPAP and may not discuss the value or conclusions of the appraisal with anyone other than the Direct Endorsement (DE) underwriter or FHA staff or their representatives. The Appraiser may discuss components of the appraisal that influence its quality and value with the DE underwriter who has responsibility for underwriting the case.

The Appraiser may interact with real estate agents and others, during the normal course of business, to provide property access, information and other market data.

iv. Appraisal Fees

The Appraiser and the Mortgagee or Mortgagee-designated third party will negotiate the appraisal fees and due date. FHA does not establish appraisal fees or due dates.

v. Obligation to Report to FHA

(A) Professional Appraisal Organizations

The Appraiser may be a member or hold designations in professional appraisal organizations. If the Appraiser is a member, candidate or associate of an appraisal organization, the Appraiser must report, by calling 1-800-CallFHA or sending an email to answers@hud.gov, any adjudicated actions resulting in a disciplinary action, or the suspension of the Appraiser, to FHA within 14 Days of such action. On disposition or adjudication of the action, the Appraiser must provide FHA with documentation and official Findings.

FHA may consider sanctions, including removal of an Appraiser found guilty of professional misconduct as adjudicated by a professional appraisal organization.

(B) Safeguards for Appraiser Independence

The Appraiser must report attempts to influence independence to answers@hud.gov or by calling 1-800-CallFHA. In addition, the appraiser must report the attempts to HUD OIG Hotline. Mortgagees, Appraisal Management Companies (AMC) and third parties are prohibited from influencing the independence of the Appraiser and the valuation process. Prohibited acts and attempts to influence the results of an appraisal include the following:

- withholding or threatening to withhold timely payment or partial payment for an appraisal report;
- withholding or threatening to withhold future business from an Appraiser, or demoting, terminating or threatening to demote or terminate an Appraiser;
- making expressed or implied promises of future business, promotions or increased compensation for an Appraiser;
- conditioning the ordering of an appraisal report or the payment of an appraisal fee, salary, or bonus on the opinion, conclusion or valuation to be reached, or on a preliminary value estimate requested from an Appraiser;
- requesting that an Appraiser provide an estimated, predetermined or desired valuation in an appraisal report prior to the completion of the appraisal report, or requesting that an Appraiser provide estimated values or comparable sales at any time prior to the Appraiser's completion of an appraisal report;
- providing the Appraiser with an anticipated, estimated, encouraged or desired value for a subject Property, or a proposed or target amount to be loaned to the Borrower, except for a copy of the sales contract for purchase and any addendum, which must be provided;
- providing the Appraiser, appraisal company, AMC or any Entity or person related to the Appraiser, with stock or other financial or non-financial benefits;
- allowing the removal of an Appraiser from a list of qualified Appraisers or the addition of an Appraiser to an exclusionary list of qualified appraisers, used by any Entity, without prompt written notice to the Appraiser that includes written evidence of the Appraiser's illegal conduct, violation of the USPAP or state licensing standards, improper or unprofessional behavior or other substantive reason for removal;
- ordering, obtaining, using, or paying for a second or subsequent appraisal or Automated Valuation Model (AVM) in connection with a mortgage financing transaction, unless:
  - there is a reasonable basis to believe that the initial appraisal was flawed or tainted and such appraisal is clearly and appropriately noted in the loan file; or
  - such appraisal or AVM was completed pursuant to a written, pre-established bona fide pre- or post-funding appraisal review, quality control process or underwriting guidelines and the Mortgagee adheres to a policy of selecting the most reliable appraisal, rather than the appraisal that states the highest value; and

- any other act or practice that impairs or attempts to impair an Appraiser's independence, objectivity, impartiality or violates law or regulation, including, the Truth in Lending Act (TILA), Regulation Z and the USPAP.

2. 203(k) Consultants

a. 203(k) Consultant Roster

The Standard 203(k) Rehabilitation Mortgage program requires the use of an FHA-approved 203(k) Consultant. FHA maintains a list of qualified Consultants on the FHA 203(k) Consultant Roster. Only a Consultant on the Roster may be selected by the Mortgagee to conduct Consultant functions in the 203(k) program.

b. Application and Approval Process

i. Eligibility Requirements

(A) Standard

To become an approved 203(k) Consultant, the prospective Consultant must be able to perform all duties outlined in 203(k) Consultant Requirements and fully understand the requirements of the 203(k) Rehabilitation Mortgage Insurance Program. The prospective Consultant must meet the qualifications for one or more of the following:
- be a state-licensed architect;
- be a state-licensed engineer;
- have at least three years of experience as a remodeling contractor or general contractor; or
- have at least three years of experience as a home inspector.

The prospective Consultant must not be listed on:
- the General Services Administration's (GSA) System for Award Management (SAM) (www.sam.gov);
- HUD's Limited Denial of Participation (LDP) List; or
- HUD's Credit Alert Verification Reporting System (CAIVRS).

(B) Required Documentation

(1) Narrative Description

The prospective Consultant must submit a narrative demonstrating that they fully understand the requirements of HUD's 203(k) Rehabilitation Mortgage Insurance Program, and describing their ability to:
- conduct Feasibility Studies;
- review or prepare architectural exhibits;
- prepare a Work Write-Up and Cost Estimate;

- complete <u>Draw Request Inspections</u>; and
- prepare <u>Change Order requests</u>.

(2) Location and Eligibility

The prospective Consultant must indicate the states in which they will be doing business and provide Consultant Eligibility Requirement documentation for each state. If the prospective Consultant will be doing business in more than one state, the Consultant must identify the state in which the Consultant will perform the majority of their business.

(3) State Licenses

(a) State-Licensed Architect

The prospective Consultant must submit proof of current license.

(b) State-Licensed Engineer

The prospective Consultant must submit proof of current license.

(c) Home Inspector

The prospective Consultant must submit:
- proof of current license if the applicant is located in a state, county, or other local jurisdiction that requires the licensing of home inspectors to perform the duties of a 203(k) Consultant; or
- if a current license is not required, a narrative description of their experience.

For the purposes of this requirement, FHA considers "located" to mean "doing business," and "license" to mean "license, certificate, registration, or approval."

(d) Remodeling or General Contractor

The prospective Consultant must submit:
- proof of current license if the applicant is located in a state, county, or other local jurisdiction that requires the licensing of contractors; or
- if a current license is not required, a narrative description of their experience.

For the purposes of this requirement, FHA considers "located" to mean "doing business," and "license" to mean "license, certificate, registration, or approval."

(4) Certification for Placement and Retention on the 203(k) Consultant Roster

Consultants and prospective Consultants must submit a 203(k) Consultant Roster Certification on their letterhead.

ii. Submitting the Application

The application documents must be submitted to the Jurisdictional Homeownership Center (HOC) based upon the state where the Consultant will perform a majority of their business. Applications must be submitted to the attention of the Processing and Underwriting Director.

iii. Incomplete Application

An applicant who submits an incomplete application package will receive notification indicating the information required to cure the deficiency. This notification letter will give the applicant 15 Days from the date on the letter to correct any deficiencies. If the applicant does not satisfy the outstanding requirement in its entirety and within the prescribed deadline, the approval will be denied and the applicant must wait an additional 90 Days before reapplying.

iv. Application Approval

FHA will inform the applicant if they are approved for placement on the FHA 203(k) Consultant Roster. Inclusion of a Consultant on the Roster means only that the Consultant has met the qualifications. It does not create or imply a warranty or endorsement by FHA of the Consultant, nor does it represent a warranty of any work performed by the Consultant.

Consultant Identification Number

Each prospective Consultant who is approved will be provided a Consultant Identification (ID) number and will be informed of their recertification due date. The Consultant ID number is required prior to doing any Consultant work associated with any 203(k) Mortgage and must be included on all documents that require the Consultant's signature.

v. Application Denial

Applicants deemed ineligible for placement on the FHA 203(k) Consultant Roster will be informed they are not approved for placement on the Roster and the reason the applicant has not met the qualifications. To request placement on the Roster, the applicant must submit a new application after resolving any issues.

vi. Biennial Recertification

To retain placement on the FHA 203(k) Consultant Roster, the Consultant must recertify every two years from the date of placement on the Roster. The Consultant is required to recertify that they are still in compliance with all laws, regulations, licensing, certification, registration or other approval requirements that govern their ability to perform as a 203(k) Consultant in the states where they do business.

Consultants must submit the required updated certification and attachments to either:
- email: answers@hud.gov
  Subject line: 203(k) Consultant Recertification; or
- regular mail:
  U.S. Dept. of HUD
  Attn: 203(k) Consultant Roster
  451 7th Street, SW, Ste. 9266
  Washington, DC 20410

203(k) Consultants who fail to meet the recertification requirements will be removed from the 203(k) Consultant Roster. To request reinstatement on the Roster, the Consultant must submit a new application after resolving the issue.

Phased Biennial Recertification for Existing 203(k) Consultants

Existing 203(k) Consultants who are on the FHA 203(k) Consultant Roster prior to March 14, 2016 must recertify every two years according to the following schedule.

203(k) Consultant ID begins with the letter:	Recertify every two years by:
A	October 1
D	January 1
P	April 1
S	July 1

3. Direct Endorsement Underwriters

a. Program Overview

The Direct Endorsement (DE) underwriter serves as the Mortgagee's subject matter expert for underwriting and must ensure compliance with all underwriting requirements in Origination through Post Closing/Endorsement for all manually underwritten Title II Forward Mortgages. Underwriting responsibilities include, but are not limited to, the following:
- calculation of maximum mortgage amounts;
- underwriting the Property; and
- underwriting of the Borrower.

The DE underwriter must also ensure compliance with all requirements for Underwriting the Property for all Title II Forward Mortgages underwritten using the Technology Open To Approved Lenders (TOTAL) Mortgage Scorecard.

The DE underwriter also serves as the Mortgagee's subject matter expert on the financial assessment requirements in Origination through Post Closing/Endorsement for all Home Equity Conversion Mortgages (HECM). Financial assessment requirements include, but are not limited to, the following:
- underwriting of the Property;
- analysis of the Borrower's credit history;
- analysis of the Borrower's property charge payment history;
- calculation of residual income; and
- determination of the need for and the amount of a Life Expectancy (LE) Set-Aside.

b. DE Underwriter Eligibility

i. Eligibility Requirements

The DE underwriter must meet the following requirements:
- have a minimum of three years full-time experience reviewing credit applications and one- to four-unit property appraisals, within the past five years; or,
- have a minimum of two years full-time experience reviewing credit applications and one- to four-unit property appraisals, within the past three years, combined with an additional three years of such full-time experience within the past ten years; and
- be a full-time employee of a single Mortgagee; and
- be authorized to bind the Mortgagee in matters involving origination of mortgages.

ii. Ineligible Participants

The DE underwriter **must not** be:
- listed on the General Services Administration's (GSA) System for Award Management (SAM) (www.sam.gov) or currently subject to a suspension, debarment, Limited Denial of Participation (LDP), or other restriction imposed under Part 24 of Title 24 of the Code of Federal Regulations, Part 180 of Title 2 of the Code of Federal Regulations as implemented by Part 2424 of Title 2, or any successor regulations to such parts, or under similar provisions of any other federal or state agency;
- under indictment for, or have been convicted of, an offense that reflects adversely upon the underwriter's integrity, competence or fitness to meet the responsibilities of a DE underwriter;
- subject to any Unresolved Findings made specifically against the underwriter as the result of any HUD or other governmental investigation or audit;
- engaged in business practices that do not conform to generally accepted practices of prudent underwriters or that demonstrate irresponsibility;

- convicted of, or have pled guilty or *nolo contendere* to, a felony related to participation in the real estate or mortgage industry:
  - ○ during the seven-year period preceding the date of registration in FHA Connection (FHAC); or
  - ○ at any time preceding the date of registration in FHAC, if such felony involved an act of fraud, dishonesty, or a breach of trust, or money laundering; or
- in violation of provisions of the Secure and Fair Enforcement for Mortgage Licensing Act of 2008 (SAFE Act) (12 U.S.C. § 5101 et seq.) or its equivalent under state law, including all Nationwide Mortgage Licensing System and Registry (NMLS) requirements.

Additionally, the DE underwriter must not have Dual Employment or Conflicts of Interest.

c. Mortgagee's Approval Process

The Mortgagee must register each of its underwriters in FHAC. By registering an underwriter in FHAC, the Mortgagee certifies that they meet the necessary qualifications described above.

d. Post-Approval Requirements

The Mortgagee must complete a series of annual certification statements that include the Mortgagee's review of underwriter compliance with eligibility requirements.

4. Nonprofits and Governmental Entities

a. Program Overview

FHA requires all nonprofits to obtain approval and be placed on the HUD Nonprofit Roster to participate in FHA's Single Family nonprofit programs.

Nonprofits participating in one of FHA's nonprofit programs must serve Low- to Moderate-Income individuals or families. Low- to Moderate-Income individuals or families refer to individuals or families whose household income does not exceed 115 percent of the median income for the area when adjusted for family size. The Jurisdictional Homeownership Center (HOC) may approve a higher percentage of up to 140 percent.

i. Types of Single Family Nonprofit Programs

(A) HUD Homes

(1) Discounted Purchase

Governmental Entities and HUD-approved Nonprofits are permitted to purchase homes from HUD at a discount.

I.   DOING BUSINESS WITH FHA
B.   Other Participants
4.   Nonprofits and Governmental Entities

(2) Exclusive Listing Period

Governmental Entities and HUD-approved Nonprofits are permitted to purchase Properties, without a discount, during the exclusive listing period for owner occupant purchasers.

(B) FHA Mortgagor

Governmental Entities and HUD-approved Nonprofits are eligible for the same FHA-insured financing as owner occupants.

After approval, nonprofits are still required to obtain credit qualification from a Mortgagee for each Mortgage originated.

(C) Secondary Financing

Governmental Entities and HUD-approved Nonprofits may provide secondary financing assistance to homebuyers utilizing FHA insurance on a first Mortgage when that assistance is secured with a second Mortgage or lien.

Additional information on Secondary Financing can be found in the Origination through Post-Closing/Endorsement section of this *SF Handbook*.

ii. Entities Requiring Approval to Participate in FHA Nonprofit Programs

(A) Nonprofits with 501(c)(3) Tax-Exempt Status

A nonprofit organization must have 501(c)(3) Internal Revenue Service (IRS) tax-exempt status.

When a nonprofit closes secondary financing in its own name, that nonprofit is required to be both FHA approved and placed on the HUD Nonprofit Roster even if the secondary financing will be held by the Governmental Entity.

(B) Nonprofit Instrumentalities of Government

(1) Definitions

A Nonprofit Instrumentality of Government (NPIOG) refers to a 501(c)(3) organization that was established by a governmental body or with governmental approval or under special law to serve a particular public purpose or designated as an instrumentality by law (statute or court opinion). FHA requires the unit of government that established the nonprofit to exercise Organizational Control, Operational Control or Financial Control of the nonprofit in its entirety or, at minimum, the specific homebuyer assistance program that is using FHA's credit enhancement.

Organizational Control refers to the majority of the governing board and/or Principal Officers that are named or approved by governmental body/officials.

Operational Control refers to the requirement that the government body approves all major decisions and/or expenditures.

Financial Control refers to the requirement that the government body provides funds through direct appropriations, grants, or Loans, with related controls applicable to all activities of the Entity.

HUD-approved NPIOGs will be included on FHA's Nonprofit Organization Roster.

(2) Permitted Level of Secondary Financing Assistance

FHA may approve an NPIOG to provide secondary financing for as much as 100 percent of the Borrower's Minimum Required Investment (MRI). If approved, FHA will issue the NPIOG an approval letter, and this approval will be reflected on the FHA Nonprofit Organization Roster and in FHAC. Interested Parties should check the Roster to ensure the approval status of an NPIOG.

(C) Section 115 Entities with 501(c)(3) Status

Section 115 Entities with 501(c)(3) status must meet the eligibility and application requirements for the HUD Homes and FHA Mortgagor programs.

iii. Entities Not Requiring FHA Approval to Participate in FHA Nonprofit Programs

FHA approval and placement on the HUD Nonprofit Roster are not required for federal, state, or local government agencies or their instrumentalities, provided those Entities are not organized as 501(c)(3) nonprofits.

(A) Governmental Entities and their Instrumentalities of Government

Governmental Entity refers to any federal, state, or local government agency or instrumentality. To be considered an Instrumentality of Government, the Entity must be established by a governmental body or with governmental approval or under special law to serve a particular public purpose or designated by law (statute or court opinion). HUD deems Section 115 Entities, as identified in Section 115 of the Internal Revenue Code, to be Instrumentalities of Government for the purpose of providing secondary financing.

FHA does not maintain a list of Governmental Entity program participants.

(B) Nonprofits with a Documented Agreement to Support Secondary Financing

When a Governmental Entity uses a nonprofit to assist in the operation of the Governmental Entity's secondary financing assistance programs, FHA approval and placement on the HUD Nonprofit Roster are not required so long as there is a documented agreement indicating (1) the functions performed include the Governmental Entity's secondary financing program and (2) the secondary financing legal documents (e.g., Note and deed of trust) name the Governmental Entity as the Mortgagee.

Governmental Entities that have nonprofits close the secondary financing in the name of the nonprofit must verify that the nonprofit is both FHA approved and on the HUD Nonprofit Roster.

Refer to Prohibited Sources of Minimum Cash Investment Under the National Housing Act - Interpretive Rule for additional guidance and clarification on the provision of downpayment assistance through secondary financing.

(C) Section 115 Entities

Section 115 Entities, as identified in Section 115 of the Internal Revenue Code, do not require approval to participate in FHA's Nonprofit Secondary Financing program. Section 115 Entities are not required to have voluntary board members. FHA considers Entities that have both 501(c)(3) and Section 115 status to be Instrumentalities of Government for purposes of secondary financing only.

iv. Ineligible Participants

The nonprofit or any officer, partner, director, principal or employee must not be:
- suspended, debarred, excluded from participation in FHA programs as listed in a Limited Denial of Participation (LDP), System for Award Management (SAM) (www.sam.gov) Excluded Parties List, or Credit Alert Verification Reporting System (CAIVRS), or otherwise excluded by similar procedures of any other federal or state agency;
- indicted for, or convicted of, an offense which reflects upon the responsibility, integrity, or ability of the nonprofit to participate in FHA activities;
- subject to Unresolved Findings as a result of HUD or other governmental investigation, audit, or review; or
- engaged in business practices that do not conform to generally accepted practices of prudent nonprofits or that demonstrate irresponsibility.

These requirements apply at the time that the nonprofit applies for approval and at all times while it is a HUD-approved Nonprofit.

b. Application and Approval Process

i. Initial Contact

Prospective applicants must submit an email to answers@HUD.gov identifying the nonprofit program(s) that the applicant would like to participate in. Prospective applicants must also identify the state where the program activities will take place.

ii. Submitting the Preliminary Information

The prospective applicant must submit the following information via email to the point of contact:

- the nonprofit's legal name and physical address of the main office;
- the name, phone number, and email address of the Executive Director;
- the name, title, phone number, and email address for all staff members requesting system access for application and reporting;
- the effective date of the nonprofit's 501(c)(3) tax-exempt status as reflected in the IRS Letter of Determination;
- the nonprofit's federal Employer Identification Number (EIN);
- the FHA nonprofit program(s) for which the nonprofit is seeking approval;
- indication of whether or not the nonprofit is an Instrumentality of Government; and
- confirmation that the nonprofit has two years of relevant housing experience within the last five years.

iii. Eligibility Requirements

A Complete Nonprofit Application refers to an application that satisfies all general application requirements and all program specific application requirements for the programs in which the nonprofit seeks approval.

In those instances when a nonprofit is applying to more than one program and the program specific application requirements request duplicate information, the nonprofit is only required to submit this information once.

A Complete Nonprofit Application must be submitted and approved in order for a nonprofit to participate in any one of FHA's nonprofit programs.

(A) General Application Requirements

Nonprofit applicants must satisfy all of FHA's general application requirements whether they are applying to one or all of FHA's nonprofit programs.

All certifications within the application must include the following language:

WARNING: HUD will prosecute false claims and statements. Conviction may result in criminal and/or civil penalties. (18 U.S.C. 1001, 1010, 1012; 31 U.S.C. 3729, 3802).

(1) IRS Tax-Exempt Status

(a) Standard

The nonprofit must have an effective date of exemption, as indicated by the IRS Letter of Determination, of at least two years prior to the FHA nonprofit application date.

(b) Required Documentation

(i) IRS Letter of Determination

The nonprofit must submit the IRS Letter of Determination verifying approval under Section 501(c)(3) as exempt from taxation under Section 501(a) of the Internal Revenue Code (IRC) of 1986, as amended.

(ii) Employer Identification Number

The nonprofit must provide its EIN and any subsidiary organization's EIN. Nonprofits may not assume the name and EIN of another dormant or defunct nonprofit.

(iii) Certification

The nonprofit must submit a document signed by an authorized representative of the nonprofit certifying the following:
- The nonprofit's approval for tax exemption has not been modified or revoked by the IRS.
- The program activities for which the nonprofit seeks FHA approval to participate in are consistent with the activities and purposes for which the IRS granted tax-exempt status.

The nonprofit has notified the IRS of any substantial and material changes in its character, purpose, or methods of operation.

(2) Board of Directors and Employees

(a) Standard

The nonprofit's Board of Directors must serve in a voluntary capacity for any service they provide in implementing the nonprofit's program and cannot receive compensation. Directors may receive reimbursement for expenses.

The nonprofit must operate in a manner so that no part of its net earnings is passed on to any individual board member, corporation, or other Entity affiliated with a board member. Board members cannot be employees of the nonprofit.

The occupational activities and obligations of board members cannot conflict with the work of the nonprofit.

It is a conflict of interest for a nonprofit to employ staff who also work for and receive financial benefits from an Entity that is providing the nonprofit with services.

(b) Required Documentation

(i) Voluntary Board Certification

The nonprofit must submit a certification signed by an authorized representative of the nonprofit agency confirming that the Board of Directors serves in a voluntary capacity.

(ii) Board of Directors Information

FHA requires information on the job responsibilities of all board members to ensure that their occupational activities and obligations do not conflict with the work of the nonprofit.

The nonprofit must provide the following information for each board member:
- name and board position;
- length of board term including expiration;
- Social Security Numbers (SSN) for all voting board members; and
- a description of outside employment that includes company name, title and nature of business.

(3) Principal Management and Staff Members

(a) Standard

(i) Conflict of Interest

Nonprofits must ensure that no conflicts of interest exist between their Boards of Directors, principal staff, or any other Entities that may participate in operating their Affordable Housing Programs (AHP).

It is a conflict of interest for a nonprofit to employ staff who also work for and receive financial benefits from an Entity that is providing the nonprofit with services related to the nonprofit's Affordable Housing Program Plan (AHPP).

(ii) Staff Experience

Principal staff and program managers must have experience in developing and administering housing programs. Hiring of experienced staff does not relieve the nonprofit agency of the relevant experience requirements.

(b) Required Documentation

The nonprofit must provide resumes and SSNs for principal management (Executive Director/President or Vice President, Project/Program Director, or similar position) and principal staff members.

The SSNs will be used only to assure HUD that no conflict-of-interest relationship exists, and the board and staff have no outstanding unpaid government Loans, sanctions, foreclosures, inappropriate transfers of Real Property, or Business Relationships.

(4) Relevant Experience

(a) Standard

The nonprofit must have a minimum of two consecutive years of relevant experience within the last five years as defined below:
- relevant experience for HUD Homes refers to the acquisition, rehabilitation, and resale of five Single Family Properties;
- relevant experience for FHA Mortgagor programs refers to the housing development or property management of Single Family Properties; and
- relevant experience for Secondary Financing refers to the acquisition, rehabilitation, and resale of five Single Family Properties or secondary financing experience.

Hiring of experienced staff does not relieve the nonprofit agency of the relevant experience requirements.

Exception

A nonprofit that does not meet this experience requirement may be able to obtain limited approval if it has at least one year of relevant experience as defined above and one year of other related housing experience. The nonprofit's "other related housing experience" must demonstrate that the organization has the financial and administrative capacity to purchase, rehabilitate and resell homes to serve Low- to Moderate-Income individuals or families.

(b) Required Documentation

The nonprofit must submit documentation to evidence relevant experience and other related housing experience, if applicable.

(5) Delegation of Signature Authority

Required Documentation

The nonprofit must provide organizational resolutions delegating signature authority to sign loan applications and/or sales contracts on behalf of the organization. These resolutions must be signed and dated by the appropriate persons under applicable state law, the Articles of Organization, and other governing documents.

(6) Quality Control Plan

(a) Standard

The nonprofit must have a Quality Control (QC) Plan that explains the organization's internal and external audit and monitoring procedures.

(b) Required Documentation

The nonprofit must provide a copy of the QC Plan that, at a minimum, includes the following elements:
- their system for maintaining records of QC Findings and actions;
- the process by which periodic reports that identify deficiencies are provided to senior management;
- the process by which prompt corrective measures are taken and documented by senior management, including time frames and any training provided when deficiencies are identified; and
- procedures to report any violation of law or regulation, any known false statement, fraud or program abuse to HUD, the HUD Office of Inspector General (OIG) and the appropriate federal, state or local law enforcement agency.

Although not required, nonprofit agencies are encouraged to include the following elements in their QC Plan:
- an impartial third-party Entity to conduct QC reviews on the nonprofit agencies' activities;
- procedures for expanding the scope of the QC review when fraud or patterns of deficiency may exist;
- procedures to identify revisions in FHA guidelines and inform staff of those revisions; and

Handbook 4000.1
Effective Date: 03/14/2016 | Last Revised: 07/10/2019
*Refer to the online version of SF Handbook 4000.1 for specific sections' effective dates

79

- procedures to hold nonprofit staff accountable for performance failures or errors.

(7) Administrative Capacity

(a) Standard

The nonprofit must demonstrate the capability to develop and carry out its homeownership program in a reasonable time frame and a successful manner.

Based on the level of administrative capacity, FHA may limit the number of Properties purchased at a discount and Mortgages insured by FHA.

(b) Required Documentation

The nonprofit must provide a narrative describing its past experience, if any, in acquisition, rehabilitation, property sales, counseling, and administration of a homeownership program or other AHPs.

(8) Financial Capacity

(a) Standard

The nonprofit must have the financial capacity to operate its homeownership program. FHA will assess the nonprofit's financial stability in terms of cash balances, assets and liabilities, annual expenses, and cash flow from operations.

Based on an analysis of submissions, FHA may limit the number of Properties a nonprofit may purchase at a discount and purchase with FHA-insured financing.

(b) Required Documentation [Text was deleted in this section.]

Documentation requirements differ based on the amount of a nonprofit's expended federal award, as defined by the Office of Management and Budget.

(i) Expended Federal Awards of $750,000 or More

The nonprofit must submit the three most recent year-end audited financial statements, profit and loss statements, and balance sheets. The audited financial statements must be provided by the applicant's Independent Public Accountant (IPA) certifying that the nonprofit:
- maintains internal controls over federal awards;
- complies with applicable laws, regulations, and contract or grant provisions; and
- prepares appropriate financial statements.

The nonprofit must also submit the most recent quarterly financial statement along with certification from a Certified Public Accountant (CPA) or other financial professional attesting that the information accurately represents the financial condition of the nonprofit agency.

(ii) Expended Federal Awards Less than $750,000

Nonprofits must submit two years of audited or unaudited financial statements, prepared in accordance with Generally Accepted Accounting Principles (GAAP) and reporting practices, and must include:
- an auditor's review report, if available;
- a treasurer's report; and
- any supplemental schedules.

The nonprofit must also submit the most recent quarterly financial statement along with certification from a CPA or other financial professional attesting that the information accurately represents the financial condition of the nonprofit agency.

(9) Other Business Partners

(a) Standard

A nonprofit agency must demonstrate that it maintains control over its homeownership program and cannot rely upon a business partner(s) to operate the program for which it seeks FHA approval.

(b) Required Documentation

The nonprofit must identify other business partners, such as real estate agents, Mortgagees, rehabilitation contractors and consultants providing administrative, financial, and management services. The nonprofit must identify the company by name and list staff with whom the nonprofit will work.

The nonprofit must explain the nature and cost of the services and how the nonprofit exercises control over its business partners.

(10) Consultant Services

(a) Standard

The nonprofit's operations must be independent of the influence, control, or direction of the consultant or any other outside party, particularly those seeking to derive profit or gain from a proposed project (including landowners, real estate brokers, bankers, contractors, builders, or consultants). Consultant services must be provided on an arm's length basis.

Consultant services – administrative, management, financial, or otherwise – provided under an independent contractor relationship (as opposed to an employer-employee relationship) must not constitute more than half of the nonprofit's activities throughout the duration of the approval period. This measurement will be calculated by evaluating the ratio of nonprofit staff to contracted or consultant staff; the ratio of hours devoted to the implementation of the AHPP by nonprofit staff versus contracted or consultant staff; and the funds devoted to paying nonprofit staff compared to those paying contracted or consultant staff. The nonprofit must have the in-house resources and capacity to operate its own programs, and contract for services only on a temporary and supplementary basis.

(b) Required Documentation

The nonprofit must explain the nature and cost of its consultant services and how the nonprofit exercises control over consultants; describe the work that will be performed by consultants for each program; and provide the percentage of work performed by consultants for each program.

The nonprofit must provide a disclosure and supporting documentation related to any agreements with other parties that may derive financial gain through the homeownership program. The disclosure must identify the name of the business Entity, the individuals from the company who will be working with the nonprofit, the terms of the relationship, and how the party will be compensated.

(11) Acting on Own Behalf Certification

The nonprofit must provide a certification signed by an authorized representative of the organization stating the following:

> *I certify that (Name of Nonprofit agency) is acting on its own behalf and is not under the influence, control, or direction of any party seeking to derive a profit or a gain from the proposed project, such as, but not limited to, a landowner, real estate broker, banker, contractor, builder, lender, or consultant.*

> *WARNING: HUD will prosecute false claims and statements. Conviction may result in criminal and/or civil penalties. (18 U.S.C. 1001, 1010, 1012; 31 U.S.C. 3729, 3802).*

The certification must include the date, and the authorized representative's printed name, signature, and title.

(12) FHA Approval Letter

If previously approved by FHA to participate in FHA's nonprofit programs, the nonprofit must submit a copy of its most recent approval letter.

(13) Adequate Facilities

(a) Standard

A nonprofit agency must have an office(s) located within a 200-mile radius of the geographical areas in which it plans to do business. For each office, nonprofits are required to have adequate office space, equipment and clerical assistance, so that employees may perform their duties in a responsible manner. A nonprofit's main office must be its designated facility to which FHA directs all communications about the management affairs of the nonprofit and from which the public obtains information about the activities of the nonprofit.

The nonprofit's facilities must be located in a space that is separate and apart from any other Entity. A nonprofit may share general reception-type entrances or lobbies with another business Entity or nonprofit. The facilities must be clearly defined to the public, so that visitors will know, at all times, exactly with which Entity they are doing business. This includes a sign and other common means of identification used by nonprofits and business Entities.

(b) Required Documentation

The nonprofit must submit the contact information and physical address of the agency's main office.

The nonprofit must also submit interior and exterior photographs of its office facilities and a copy of the floor plan identifying the nonprofit's work space.

(14) Lending Partner(s) Information

(a) Standard

A nonprofit must ensure that no conflicts of interest exist. Employees of the Lender cannot receive personal or financial benefit because of the Business Relationship with the nonprofit.

(b) Required Documentation

The nonprofit must provide the name, address, and contact of any lending institution, bank, or private party that has provided financing to the nonprofit.

(15) Application Certification

The nonprofit must submit a document signed by an authorized representative of the organization certifying to FHA that the information submitted in response to the application package is accurate.

The certification must include the date, and the authorized representative's printed name, signature, and title.

(B) Program Specific Eligibility Requirements

All general application requirements apply to participation in any of the three nonprofit programs. Refer to the programs below for additional program specific requirements.

(1) HUD Homes

(a) Name and Address Identification Number

(i) Standard

A nonprofit must obtain a Name and Address Identification Number (NAID) in order to bid on Real Estate Owned (REO) Properties.

(ii) Required Documentation

The nonprofit must submit IRS Form W-9, *Request for Taxpayer Identification Number (TIN) and Certification* and HUD form SAMS-1111, *Payee Name and Address*.

(b) Restrictions on Sale or Lease of Properties

FHA strictly prohibits the sale or lease of Properties acquired through the HUD Homes program to any of the nonprofit's officers, directors, elected or appointed officials, employees, or business associates, either during their tenure or for one year thereafter, or to any individual who is related by blood, marriage, or law to any of the above.

(c) Articles of Organization and Bylaws

(i) Standard

The nonprofit's mission statement, purpose, or goals stated in the nonprofit's Articles of Organization and bylaws must be consistent with those submitted in the application.

(ii) Required Documentation

Conformed Copy

The nonprofit must submit a Conformed Copy of its Articles of Organization, and bylaws if applicable. These documents must be signed and dated by the appropriate persons under applicable state law.

A Conformed Copy is a copy that agrees with the original and all amendments to it.

Written Declaration

A Conformed Copy of the Articles of Organization and bylaws must be accompanied by a written declaration signed by an authorized representative of the organization certifying the copy is a complete and accurate copy of the document.

As an alternative to the foregoing declaration, an organization may submit a Conformed Copy of its Articles of Organization approved and dated by the appropriate state authority.

(d) Affordable Housing Program Plan

(i) Definition

An Affordable Housing Program Plan (AHPP), also known as the Affordable Housing Program Narrative, is referred to as an AHPP for purposes of this *SF Handbook*.

AHPP refers to a program plan, as described in a written proposal submitted to FHA, operated by a nonprofit in specific geographical areas in which the nonprofit provides affordable homeownership opportunities for Low- to Moderate-Income buyers by purchasing, rehabilitating, and reselling HUD Homes to these buyers. The program can include other homeownership activities, such as counseling.

(ii) Standard

A nonprofit must adhere to its AHPP during its entire approval period. Any activity undertaken by a nonprofit that requires the use of their FHA nonprofit approval must be in accordance with the approved AHPP.

Unlike the application for approval, a separate AHPP must be submitted to every Jurisdictional HOC for the geographic areas in which the nonprofit agency wishes to do business.

If, at some point in the future, a nonprofit wants to engage in activities outside the scope of its approved AHPP, it must submit a revised AHPP to the Jurisdictional HOC(s) for approval prior to implementation.

Conflicts of Interest

No person who is an employee, officer, or elected or appointed official of the nonprofit agency, or who is in a position to participate in a decision making process pursuant to the AHPP or gain inside information with regard to the lease or purchase of the Property pursuant to the AHPP may obtain a personal or financial interest or benefit from the purchase of the Property, or have an interest in any contract, subcontract, or agreement with respect thereto, or the proceeds thereunder, either for themselves, or for those with whom they have family or business ties, during their tenure or for one year thereafter.

(iii) Required Documentation

Copy of the AHPP

The nonprofit must submit a copy of the AHPP for each local area in which the nonprofit agency intends to be active. If the nonprofit wants to expand its approval area, the Jurisdictional HOC may require additional information.

The AHPP must address the following:
- the areas, including state, city, county and zip code, in which the nonprofit plans to administer the program(s). The program must be operated within a 200-mile radius of the nonprofit's office;
- how Low- to Moderate-Income persons will benefit from participation in the program;
- how the nonprofit will transition families and individuals into homeownership;
- how the nonprofit's savings will be passed along to program recipients;
- how the nonprofit will locate the Low- to Moderate-Income persons who will participate;
- the type of homeownership counseling the nonprofit will provide to prospective homebuyers, if any. Provide a brief description of the administration of this counseling program;
- provide a list of all Properties the nonprofit currently owns and has owned within the last three years, all Properties the nonprofit has rehabilitated (include approximate cost of rehabilitation), and all Properties that the nonprofit manages. Indicate which Properties were financed directly or indirectly with FHA funds. Provide the date purchased and the purchase price, the date on which

rehabilitation was completed, the date the Property(ies) sold and its resale price. Include demographic information on Low- to Moderate- Income purchasers;

- the estimated developer fees as a dollar amount or percentage of the selling price for future transactions;
- the anticipated number and location of units the nonprofit expects to purchase;
- a time line for purchasing, rehabilitating, and selling (or placing in operation) Properties the nonprofit intends to purchase from HUD. Provide the number of Days for each phase of the development (actual dates are not necessary); and
- if the nonprofit agency intends to provide a lease-purchase program, the information relative to the manner in which rent is collected and applied, and whether repair reserves will be utilized to minimize repair costs after purchase.

Copy of the Board Resolution

The nonprofit must submit a copy of a board resolution that adopts the complete AHPP. This resolution must be signed and dated by the appropriate persons under applicable state law and as identified in the Articles of Organization and other governing documents.

(2) FHA Mortgagor

(a) Restrictions on Sale or Lease of Properties

FHA strictly prohibits the sale or lease of Properties acquired by the nonprofit with FHA-insured financing to any of the nonprofit's officers, directors, elected or appointed officials, employees, or business associates, either during their tenure or for one year thereafter, or to any individual who is related by blood, marriage, or law to any of the above.

(b) Articles of Organization and Bylaws

(i) Standard

The nonprofit's mission statement, purpose, or goals stated in the nonprofit's Articles of Organization and bylaws must be consistent with those submitted in the application.

(ii) Required Documentation

Conformed Copy

The nonprofit must submit a Conformed Copy of its Articles of Organization, and bylaws if applicable. These documents must be signed and dated by the appropriate persons under applicable state law.

A Conformed Copy is a copy that agrees with the original and all amendments to it.

Written Declaration

A Conformed Copy of the Articles of Organization and bylaws must be accompanied by a written declaration signed by an authorized representative of the organization certifying the copy is a complete and accurate copy of the document.

As an alternative to the foregoing declaration, an organization may submit a Conformed Copy of its Articles of Organization approved and dated by the appropriate state authority.

(c) Affordable Housing Program Plan

(i) Definition

An Affordable Housing Program Plan (AHPP), also known as the Affordable Housing Program Narrative, is referred to as an AHPP for purposes of this *SF Handbook*.

AHPP refers to a program plan, as described in a written proposal submitted to FHA, operated by a nonprofit in specific geographical areas in which the nonprofit provides affordable homeownership opportunities for Low- to Moderate-Income buyers by purchasing, rehabilitating, and reselling HUD Homes to these buyers. The program can include other homeownership activities, such as counseling.

(ii) Standard

A nonprofit must adhere to its AHPP. Any activity undertaken by a nonprofit that requires the use of their FHA nonprofit approval must be in accordance with the approved AHPP.

If a nonprofit wants to engage in activities outside the scope of their AHPP, it must submit for approval a revised AHPP to the Jurisdictional HOC(s).

If, at some point in the future, a nonprofit wants to engage in activities outside the scope of its approved AHPP, it must submit a revised AHPP to the Jurisdictional HOC(s) for approval prior to implementation.

Conflicts of Interest

No person who is an employee, officer, or elected or appointed official of the nonprofit agency or who is in a position to participate in a decision making process pursuant to the AHPP or gain inside information with regard to the lease or purchase of the Property pursuant to the AHPP may obtain a personal or financial interest or benefit from the purchase of the Property, or have an interest in any contract, subcontract, or agreement with respect thereto, or the proceeds thereunder, either for themselves, or for those with whom they have family or business ties, during their tenure or for one year thereafter.

(iii) Required Documentation

Copy of the AHPP

The nonprofit must submit a copy of the AHPP for each local area in which the nonprofit agency intends to be active. If the nonprofit wants to expand its approval area, the Jurisdictional HOC may require additional information.

The AHPP must address the following:
- the areas, including state, city, county and zip code, in which the nonprofit plans to administer the program(s). Program must be operated within a 200-mile radius of the nonprofit's office;
- how Low- to Moderate-Income persons will benefit from participation in the program;
- how the nonprofit will transition families and individuals into homeownership;
- how the nonprofit's savings will be passed along to program recipients;
- how the nonprofit will locate the Low- to Moderate-Income persons who will participate;
- the type of homeownership counseling the nonprofit will provide to prospective homebuyers, if any. Provide a brief description of the administration of this counseling program;
- provide a list of all Properties the nonprofit currently owns and has owned within the last three years, all Properties the nonprofit has rehabilitated (include approximate cost of rehabilitation), and all Properties that the nonprofit manages. Indicate which Properties were financed directly or indirectly with FHA funds. Obtain the date purchased and the purchase price, the date on which

rehabilitation was completed, the date the Property(ies) sold and its resale price. Include demographic information on Borrowers;

- the estimated developer fees or percentage of selling price for future transactions;
- the anticipated number and location of units the nonprofit expects to purchase;
- a time line for purchasing, rehabilitating, and selling (or placing in operation) Properties the nonprofit intends to purchase from FHA. Provide the number of Days for each phase of the development (actual dates are not necessary); and
- if the nonprofit agency intends to provide a lease-purchase program, the information relative to the manner in which rent is collected and applied, and whether repair reserves will be utilized to minimize repair costs after purchase.

Copy of the Board Resolution

The nonprofit must submit a copy of a board resolution that adopts the complete AHPP. This resolution must be signed and dated by the appropriate persons under applicable state law and as identified in the Articles of Organization and other governing documents.

(d) Past Mortgage Performance

The nonprofit must submit evidence of any past or current mortgage performance. If applicable, the nonprofit must include performance of FHA-insured Mortgages, including addresses and FHA case numbers; certification of completion for each 203(k) Property, including date sold, and sales price; and the full name and telephone number of the Borrower.

(3) Secondary Financing

(a) Affordable Housing Program Plan

(i) **Definition**

An Affordable Housing Program Plan (AHPP), also known as the Affordable Housing Program Narrative, is referred to as an AHPP for purposes of this *SF Handbook.*

AHPP refers to a program plan, as described in a written proposal submitted to FHA, operated by a nonprofit in specific geographical areas in which the nonprofit provides affordable homeownership opportunities for Low- to Moderate-Income buyers by purchasing, rehabilitating and reselling HUD Homes to these buyers. The program can include other homeownership activities, such as counseling.

(ii) Standard

A nonprofit must adhere to its AHPP. Any activity undertaken by a nonprofit that requires the use of their FHA nonprofit approval must be in accordance with the approved AHPP.

Unlike the application for approval, a separate AHPP must be submitted to every Jurisdictional HOC for the geographic areas in which the nonprofit agency wishes to do business.

If, at some point in the future, a nonprofit wants to engage in activities outside the scope of its approved AHPP, it must submit a revised AHPP to the Jurisdictional HOC(s) for approval prior to implementation.

(iii) Required Documentation

Copy of the AHPP

The nonprofit must submit a copy of the AHPP that meets the requirements above. If the nonprofit wants to expand its approval area, the Jurisdictional HOC may require additional information.

The AHPP must address the following:
- the areas, including state, city, county and zip code, in which the nonprofit plans to administer the program(s). The program must be operated within a 200-mile radius of the nonprofit's office;
- the source of current operating funds, and the long-term stability of these funding sources (include funding commitments from other organizations, if applicable). Provide documentation of the source(s) of funds for the secondary Loans to be provided;
- how Low- to Moderate-Income persons will benefit from participation in the program;
- how the nonprofit will locate the Low- to Moderate-Income persons who will participate;
- the type of homeownership counseling the nonprofit will provide to prospective homebuyers, if any. Provide a brief description of the administration of this counseling program;
- all fees and amounts charged to the Borrower, and whether they will be part of the secondary lien;
- the number of secondary financing Loans your nonprofit agency expects to provide per year;
- how the nonprofit will maintain control and oversight of the servicing of the nonprofit's Loans. If the nonprofit plans to use another Entity to service the subordinate lien, submit a copy of the agreement between the nonprofit and the servicing Entity;

- provide a description of the secondary financing program including eligibility requirements, restrictions on transferability and owner occupancy, and equity sharing if these features apply; and
- how the agency will ensure that the amount of assistance to be provided to homebuyers will conform with the restrictions in the approval letter and FHA underwriting guidelines.

Copy of the Board Resolution

The nonprofit must submit a copy of a board resolution that adopts the complete AHPP. This resolution must be signed and dated by the appropriate persons under applicable state law and as identified in the Articles of Organization and other governing documents.

(b) Restrictions on Conveyance

(i) Standard

Restrictions on conveyance must automatically terminate if title to the mortgaged Property is transferred by foreclosure or Deed-In-Lieu (DIL) of Foreclosure, or if the Mortgage is assigned to the Secretary.

(ii) Required Documentation

The nonprofit must submit copies of the legal instruments, such as the Mortgage and Note used by, or proposed to be used by, the nonprofit agency when providing secondary financing.

iv. Submitting the Application

The nonprofit applicant must submit applications electronically through the HUD Nonprofit Data Management System (NPDMS). NPDMS is an automated web-based system designed to allow for the electronic submission of application, recertification, and reporting documentation. NPDMS collects, stores, and provides web-based access to participant applications and property activity data.

After submitting the preliminary information and receiving confirmation of eligibility, the applicant will be provided with login instructions to access NPDMS. FHA will not accept paper applications.

The nonprofit must submit a completed application within 30 Days of receiving access to NPDMS. The application date refers to the date that the application package is electronically submitted through NPDMS.

v. Processing of Application

FHA will review all completed applications for approval to determine whether the nonprofit complies with all eligibility requirements. If FHA requires additional documentation or clarifying information, FHA may request such additional information and provide the nonprofit with a deadline for response. If the nonprofit does not provide the additional information requested by any specified deadline, FHA may deny approval on this basis.

vi. Incomplete Application

Nonprofit agencies that submit an incomplete application package will receive a letter indicating the information required to cure the deficiency. This letter will give nonprofit agencies 15 Days from the date on the letter to correct any deficiencies. If the new nonprofit applicant does not satisfy the outstanding requirement in its entirety and within the prescribed deadlines, the approval will be denied and the nonprofit must wait an additional 90 Days before reapplying.

vii. Application Approval

Nonprofit agencies that are approved for participation will be issued an approval letter from the Jurisdictional HOC describing which activities the nonprofit is approved for and any limitations associated with that approval. An approval is valid for a two-year period.

An approval granted by one HOC will be recognized and accepted by all other HOCs, with the exception of the AHPP. A nonprofit agency's AHPP must be separately approved by every Jurisdictional HOC for the geographic areas in which the nonprofit agency seeks to do business.

viii. Application Rejection

A nonprofit's application may be rejected due to deficiencies or for failure to submit a program that complies with applicable regulations and requirements of this *SF Handbook*. Nonprofit agencies that are not approved for participation will be issued a rejection letter from the Jurisdictional HOC describing the reasons for the application rejection.

The nonprofit must wait 90 Days to submit a new application.

ix. Recertification

(A) Standard

(1) Recertification Process

To retain FHA approval, nonprofits must complete FHA's recertification process prior to their two-year approval expiration. Recertification of nonprofit agencies is not automatic.

Nonprofit agencies must demonstrate that they have created affordable housing opportunities in a fiscally responsible way. Nonprofit agencies must demonstrate that they met the following standards, if applicable, during the approval period:
- ability to meet HUD's and the nonprofit agency's goals to expand affordable housing opportunities for Low- to Moderate-Income individuals;
- acceptable Default and foreclosure rate(s) on FHA-insured Properties;
- ability to complete rehabilitation within approved time frames as identified in the AHPP;
- minimal change in staff and the nonprofit agency's experience;
- adherence to HUD resale requirements; and
- maintenance of an acceptable accounting system to report on property-specific costs related to purchase, rehabilitation, rental, and resale.

(2) Filing Deadline

The required documentation must be submitted to the Jurisdictional HOC at least 90 Days prior to the end of the approval period. The HOC must be notified of any changes that impact the recertification application after it has been submitted.

(B) Required Documentation

The recertification process is similar to that of the initial application process. Nonprofits must submit the following recertification documents through the NPDMS:
- a Complete Nonprofit Application; and
- a detailed description of the FHA program activities for which the nonprofit was approved during the approval period. Nonprofits must provide the following information where applicable:
  o property address;
  o FHA case number (on acquisition);
  o FHA case number (on resale, if applicable);
  o date of acquisition;
  o indication of whether the nonprofit utilized a 203(b) or 203(k) Mortgage for acquisition;
  o Net Development Costs (NDC);
  o mortgage amounts;

o   name of the first Mortgagee;
o   name of any additional Mortgagees (if applicable);
o   name of the ultimate Borrower;
o   household size and income;
o   discount amount;
o   resale price and date;
o   date of delinquency; and
o   date of Default.

Additional Required Documentation for FHA Mortgagor

The nonprofit must also submit evidence of any past or current mortgage performance. If applicable, the nonprofit must include performance of FHA-insured Mortgages, including addresses and FHA case numbers; certification of completion for each 203(k) Property, including date sold, and sales price; and the full name and telephone number of Borrower.

(C) Incomplete Recertification Application

Nonprofit agencies that submit incomplete recertification applications will receive a letter indicating the information required to cure the deficiency. This letter will give nonprofit agencies 15 Days from the date on the letter to correct any deficiencies. If the nonprofit applicant does not satisfy the outstanding requirement in its entirety and within the prescribed deadlines, the approval for recertification will be denied.

If the nonprofit does not submit an acceptable recertification application before the expiration of the two year approval period, the nonprofit will be removed from the HUD Nonprofit Roster.

(D) Failure to Recertify

Failure to recertify will result in the nonprofit's removal from the program and the HUD Nonprofit Roster.

The nonprofit must comply with all program requirements for any program activity that was not finalized at the time of removal.

(E) Recertification Application Approval

Nonprofit agencies that are recertified for participation will be issued an approval letter from the Jurisdictional HOC describing which activities the nonprofit is approved for and any limitations associated with that approval. An approval is valid for a two year period.

An approval granted by one HOC will be recognized and accepted by all other HOCs, with the exception of the AHPP. A nonprofit agency's AHPP must be separately approved by every Jurisdictional HOC for the geographic areas in which the nonprofit agency seeks to do business.

(F) Recertification Application Rejection

A nonprofit's recertification application may be rejected due to deficiencies or for failure to submit a program that complies with applicable regulations and requirements of this *SF Handbook*.

Nonprofit agencies that are not approved for recertification will be issued a rejection letter from the Jurisdictional HOC describing the reasons for the rejection of the recertification application and will be removed from the HUD Nonprofit Roster.

c. Post-Approval Requirements

Governmental Entities and HUD-approved Nonprofits must comply with the following requirements and restrictions for its FHA business operations in addition to continuing to operate in full compliance with the eligibility requirements outlined in this *SF Handbook*.

i. Consultant Services

Consultant services provided under an independent contractor relationship (as opposed to an employer-employee relationship) must not constitute more than half of the nonprofit's activities in the operation of its FHA-approved programs. This measurement will be calculated by evaluating the ratio of nonprofit staff to contracted or consultant staff; the ratio of hours devoted to the implementation of the AHPP by nonprofit staff versus contracted or consultant staff; and the funds devoted to paying nonprofit staff compared to those paying contracted or consultant staff. The nonprofit must have the in-house resources and capacity to run its own programs, and contract for services on a temporary and supplementary basis.

Therefore, to ensure that the consultant services are provided on an arm's length basis, the nonprofit must disclose any written and/or side agreements with parties that may derive financial gain through the homeownership program. Disclosure must identify the name of the business Entity, and the individuals from the company who will be working with the nonprofit, the terms of the relationship and how the party will be compensated. Failure to adequately disclose may result in a conflict-of-interest determination.

The nonprofit must contact the Program Support Division (PSD) immediately at the Jurisdictional HOC if more than half of the nonprofit's activities are provided by consultants under an independent contractor relationship at any time during the approval period.

ii. Limitation on the Number of 203(k) FHA-Insured Mortgages

A nonprofit is prohibited from further borrowing under its FHA Mortgagor approval if the nonprofit has 10 or more incomplete 203(k) developments at any given time.

Exceptional Performance Waiver

Nonprofit agencies with an exceptional performance record of successfully completing 203(k) developments (defined as those agencies that have successfully completed 20 or more 203(k) developments) may apply to the HOC for a waiver of the limitation on 203(k) Mortgages. This waiver request must contain a narrative describing the nonprofit agency's homeownership or long-term rental program; current audited financial statements with an unqualified opinion from a CPA for the prior three years; a listing of all Properties currently owned by the nonprofit agency (both conventional and government financed); a record of performance on **all** 203(k) Mortgages (current as well as previous Loans); as well as the evidence to support the sale or rental of these Properties. Nonprofit agencies that are approved for this waiver, for financing for more than 10 203(k) Mortgages at one time, will have it stated in their approval letter from the HOC.

iii. HUD Homes – Individual Property Files

(A) Definition

Individual Property Files refer to files that Governmental Entities and HUD-approved Nonprofits participating in the HUD Homes program must maintain for each Property purchased, sold, or leased when a discount of 10 percent or greater is obtained at the time of purchase.

(B) Standard

Governmental Entities and HUD-approved Nonprofits must submit the Individual Property Files to FHA through the NPDMS no later than 60 Days after the resale of a Property to a subsequent homebuyer. Governmental Entities and HUD-approved Nonprofits must send an e-mail to the appropriate point of contact within the PSD, in the Jurisdictional HOC, notifying them when an Individual Property File is ready for review. Individual Property Files are ready for review once all data has been entered and supporting documentation has been uploaded.

The Individual Property File must be maintained for a minimum of three years after the Property is sold by the nonprofit.

(C) Required Documentation

The Individual Property File must include all supporting documentation for NDCs.

The supporting documentation includes the following:
- copies of the fully executed Closing Disclosures or similar legal documents for the nonprofit's purchase from HUD and from the nonprofit's resale of the Property to the new purchaser;
- a copy of a signed Land Use Restriction Addendum (LURA);

- income verification for the purchaser who bought from the nonprofit. This may be in the form of a W-2, pay stubs, Verification of Employment (VOE), or tax returns. Nonprofits must also provide a certification that the resale purchaser's income was at or below 115 percent of HUD's determination of median income for their area when adjusted for family size;
- appraisal reports if the Property was purchased as a 203(k) or financed with 203(b) or other FHA insurance funds;
- rehabilitation documents must include:
  o   Work Write-Up/contractor estimate of repair costs
  o   change orders
  o   inspection of repairs by nonprofit
  o   invoices from contractors
  o   copies of payments to contractors
- additional rehabilitation documents for 203(k) must include:
  o   draw requests
  o   Lien Waivers
  o   Final Release Notice
- if the Property is leased under an approved lease/purchase program:
  o   copies of executed lease
  o   income verification
  o   evidence of proactive work of nonprofit to move tenants into homeownership
  o   appraisal or document from independent third party to determine fair market rent
  o   list of other program costs, including developer's fees

Accounting records must be maintained in a property-specific format so that cost calculations can be made for all expenses related to each specific Property.

In addition, Governmental Entities and HUD-approved Nonprofits must submit a list of all business partners participating in the acquisition, rehabilitation and resale of the Property. The list must include the name of the company, the name of the principals, the name and title of all staff with whom the nonprofit is working, a description of the services provided by the company, and an accounting of the costs and fees associated with those services. This information must be reported for all real estate agents, Lenders, and contractors involved in the acquisition, rehabilitation and sale of the HUD Homes Property.

(D) HUD Homes – Net Development Costs

The NDCs are composed of the allowable property Acquisition Costs plus allowable rehabilitation, holding, and selling costs which Governmental Entities and HUD-approved Nonprofits incur when purchasing HUD Homes at discounted prices, redeveloping the Properties for resale, and selling those Properties. The NDC calculation applies to all HUD Homes sold to nonprofit organizations and Governmental Entities at a 10 percent or greater discount regardless of the source of the financing (FHA, conventional Mortgage, or cash), except for discounted REO homes purchased through the Dollar Home Sales to Local Governments, Asset Control Areas (ACA), and Good Neighbor Next Door (GNND) programs.

The purpose of these discounts and the limits on development costs is to make housing affordable to Low- to Moderate-Income families. HUD limits the costs that are eligible to be included in the NDC calculation and prohibits the nonprofit organization or Governmental Entity from reselling the repaired or improved Properties at prices in excess of 110 percent of the NDC calculation. If the nonprofit organization's or Governmental Entity's resale price of the HUD Home exceeds 110 percent of the NDC, or if non-allowable items that are included in the NDC result in an excessive sales price, the HUD-approved Nonprofit or Governmental Entity must use the excess profit to pay down the existing Mortgage associated with that particular resale.

(1) Costs Allowed in Calculating the Net Development Costs

Only the costs specifically included in the following list, within the prescribed limitations and/or conditions, may be included in calculating the NDCs:
- the discounted purchase price paid to HUD;
- upon the purchase of the Property from HUD, prepaid items and financing and closing costs actually incurred, which must be reasonable and customary for the area in which the Property is located, is limited to the following:
  o actual loan origination fee, not to exceed 1 percent;
  o supplemental loan origination fee (203(k) Mortgages only);
  o credit report fee;
  o net tax and insurance escrow deposit;
  o settlement fee (purchaser's portion);
  o discount points;
  o hazard insurance premiums;
  o Mortgagee's title insurance policy premium;
  o Owner's title insurance policy premium;
  o notary fees;
  o recording fees;
  o appraisal fee;
  o courier fees;
  o document preparation fees;
  o attorney fees for services performed in connection with the mortgage closing, such as review of abstract or preparation of closing documents; and
  o flood plain certification and fee for determination of flood zone;
- for the time period the nonprofit organization or Governmental Entity holds title, the following costs, limited to amounts that are reasonable and customary for the area in which the Property is located, may be included:

- o fees paid to an approved 203(k) Consultant for Work Write-Ups, Cost Estimates, and inspections only;
- o property management, but only if related to periodic inspection and/or minor maintenance of the Property;
- o architectural fees, but only if the services are provided by a licensed architectural firm or individual architect;
- o rehabilitation costs, which are the total verifiable contractor and vendor expenditures incurred in the actual reconstruction, repair, restoration and physical improvement of the Property. Rehabilitation costs are limited to the actual price paid to the contractor for completing each repair or improvement, and may also include expenditures for mechanical systems inspections, sewer and well inspections, repair inspections, foundation certifications for Manufactured Housing obtained from a licensed engineer, and roof inspections from a licensed contractor. HUD may require canceled checks and corresponding receipts as proof of rehabilitation costs. When calculating the NDC, Governmental Entities or HUD-approved Nonprofits using grant funds for the rehabilitation of HUD Homes acquired at a discount, cannot include the cost of the rehabilitation that is paid for by those grant funds;
- o cost of public and municipal services and utilities and real property taxes for the subject premises, except for delinquent interest or penalty charges incurred as a result of failure of program participant to pay these expenses in a timely manner;
- o cost of termite inspection and extermination services;
- o Homeowners' Association (HOA) or Condominium Fees;
- o permits and other fees paid to units of state and local governments that are required by rule, law, regulation or other legally binding mandate that must be paid before initiating or completing the rehabilitation or property improvement;
- o survey costs;
- o hazard and liability insurance premiums; and
- o interest portion of Mortgage Payments limited to a maximum of six months interest payments, less any and all rents received. If the Property is resold in less than 180 Days, the interest payment credit must be prorated on the basis of the actual payments made – rent received and interest paid would be allowable costs but not the principal; and
- • upon the resale of the Property to a new purchaser, only the following seller closing costs that are actually incurred, limited to amounts that are reasonable and customary for the area in which the Property is located, may be included:
  - o 1/2 of closing agent fee (seller's portion);
  - o electronic wiring fees;
  - o courier and mailing fees (seller's documents only);
  - o title insurance premium (owner's policy only);

- o state, county, or city tax stamps, if local law requires the seller to pay these costs;
- o homeowners warranty premium;
- o environmental hazard certification;
- o document preparation fee (seller's documents only);
- o recording (deed only) and re-conveyance fees;
- o sales commissions for real estate broker/agent services; and
- o condominium transfer fee

(2) Costs Not Allowed in Calculating the Net Development Costs

Costs not listed in Costs Allowed in Calculating the Net Development Costs are ineligible and cannot be included in the NDC calculation. Ineligible costs include:

- general administration cost of the nonprofit organization's or Governmental Entity's AHPP and homeownership programs, including overhead and staffing costs;
- housing developer fees and/or real estate consultant fees;
- sales bonuses and sales incentives (other than sales commissions) for selling or listing real estate brokers/agents;
- gifts to the Low- to Moderate-Income purchaser for downpayment, financing or closing costs, prepaid items, and any other purchaser-related expenses associated with their purchase of the Property;
- development, maintenance and management costs related to other Properties in the nonprofit organization's or Governmental Entity's inventory;
- delinquent property tax or utility penalties and interest;
- Mortgage Payment late fees, prepayment penalties, pay-off quote fees and fax charges; and
- any development costs that are paid from local, state, or federal grant funds that would otherwise be allowable in the NDC calculation.

(E) HUD Homes – Land Use Restriction Addendum

(1) Definition

The Land Use Restriction Addendum (LURA) is a legally binding contractual agreement between HUD and the Governmental Entities or nonprofits imposing restrictions on the resale of a HUD Home that the nonprofit organization or Governmental Entity purchased at a discount of 10 percent or greater.

(2) Standard

Governmental Entities and HUD-approved Nonprofits participating in the HUD Homes program must execute the LURA as part of the FHA sales contract for any Property purchased at a 10 percent or greater discount. The LURA terminates five years from the date of execution.

I.   **DOING BUSINESS WITH FHA**
B.   **Other Participants**
5.   **Real Estate Brokers**

The LURA requires the purchaser to expand affordable housing opportunities by complying with the following requirements:

- The purchaser must complete needed repairs to bring the Property into compliance with local housing code followed by resale, lease, or lease purchase only to a person who intends to occupy the Property as their Principal Residence and whose income is at or below 115 percent of the median income in the area, when adjusted for family size, or state, Governmental Entity, tribe, or agency thereof.
- If sold, the purchaser must resell the Property for an amount not in excess of 110 percent of the NDCs. The NDCs are the total HUD-allowable costs to purchase, rehabilitate, and resell the Property.
- The Property may not be occupied by or resold to any of the purchaser's officers, directors, elected or appointed officials, employees, or business associates, either during their tenure or for one year thereafter, or to any individual who is related by blood, marriage, or law to any of the above.
- There may be no conflict of interest with individuals or firms that may provide acquisition or rehabilitation funding; management, sales or rehabilitation services; or other services associated with the Property.

The Governmental Entity or HUD-approved Nonprofit must provide periodic reports, in the format and frequency specified in the HUD Homes – Individual Property Files section.

Exception

Discounted homes purchased through the Dollar Homes Sales to Local Governments, GNND and ACA programs are not subject to the LURA restrictions.

5.   Real Estate Brokers

a.   Definition

A HUD-Registered Real Estate Broker is a real estate listing or selling broker approved by HUD to list or sell HUD Real Estate Owned (REO) Properties.

A Listing Broker is a HUD-Registered Real Estate Broker who lists HUD-owned Properties for sale.

A Selling Broker is a HUD-Registered Real Estate Broker who submits bids on behalf of prospective buyers.

Handbook 4000.1   102
Effective Date: 03/14/2016 | Last Revised: 07/10/2019
*Refer to the online version of SF Handbook 4000.1 for specific sections' effective dates

b. Requirements

i. Program Overview

HUD must approve any real estate broker wishing to list Properties or represent buyers in sales transactions of HUD REO Properties.

ii. Use of Name and Address Identification Numbers

Each real estate broker wishing to list Properties or represent buyers in sales transactions of HUD REO Properties must have an active Name and Address Identification Number (NAID) issued by HUD; all agents conducting business in that real estate broker's office may use that broker's active NAID. For brokerages with several offices, each with a different real estate broker, each office may apply for a separate NAID.

c. Application and Registration Process

i. Real Estate Broker's Application

Real estate brokers must submit the following to the Jurisdictional Homeownership Center (HOC) for the area in which the broker's office is located:
- form SAMS-1111, *Payee Name and Address*;
- form SAMS-1111-A, *Real Estate Broker Certification*;
- IRS Letter 147C or other official Internal Revenue Service (IRS) document reflecting their business name and Employer Identification Number (EIN) or, if operating under a Social Security Number (SSN), a copy of their Social Security card;
- a copy of their active real estate broker's license with an expiration date;
- a copy of their current driver's license with an expiration date; and
- a recent utility bill or bank statement that lists the address and company or broker name shown on form SAMS-1111.

ii. HUD Registration

HUD will issue an NAID to HUD-Registered Real Estate Brokers via HUD Home Store.

d. Annual Recertification

HUD-Registered Real Estate Brokers must be recertified by HUD each year. NAID certifications for brokers are valid for only one year from the date they are issued. HUD-Registered Real Estate Brokers must submit the completed form SAMS-1111 and supporting documentation to the Jurisdictional HOC for the area in which the broker's office is located.

Failure to timely submit annual recertification may result in deactivation of the NAID by HUD in accordance with 24 CFR § 291.100(i).

6. Closing Agents

a. Requirements

Closing Agents must meet all of the following requirements in order to conduct a closing on a sales transaction of a HUD REO Property.

i. Licensure or Ability to Do Business in State where Property is Located

The Closing Agent must be an attorney, title company, or escrow company that meets all State and local requirements for eligibility to conduct closings as follows:
- An attorney or law firm may act as Closing Agent if they are duly licensed to practice law in the State where the Property is located and state law allows an attorney to facilitate closings.
- A title company may act as Closing Agent if they are duly licensed to do business in the State where the Property is located and are regulated by the state insurance commission, or similar regulatory agency recognized by the State.
- An escrow company may act as Closing Agent if they are duly licensed to do business in the State where the Property is located and meet all state legal and regulatory requirements as a recognized and registered escrow company.

ii. Errors and Omissions Insurance

The Closing Agent is covered by errors and omissions insurance of at least $1,000,000.

iii. Debarment or Suspension

A Closing Agent must not, and cannot, participate in any aspect of the closing or title clearance process if they are currently debarred, suspended, or otherwise excluded from participating in HUD's programs.

b. Application and Approval Process

i. Title Identification Number

(A) Definition

A Title Identification (ID) Number is a number identifying a Closing Agent registered to perform closings on HUD REO sales transactions.

(B) Standard

The Closing Agent must complete a one-time registration to receive a HUD-issued Title ID Number. The Closing Agent must provide to the Asset Manager (AM):
- a copy of the Closing Agent's state license; and
- a Closing Protection Letter (CPL) evidencing errors and omissions insurance coverage.

HUD will review the Closing Agent's documentation and, if HUD approves, will issue a Title ID Number. The AM will notify the Closing Agent of the issuance of the Title ID Number.

ii. P260 Access

Once the Closing Agent has received a HUD-issued Title ID Number, the Closing Agent must contact the AM to request access to P260.

7. Additional Other Participants

RESERVED FOR FUTURE USE

This section is reserved for future use, and until such time, FHA-approved Mortgagees and Other Participants must continue to comply with all applicable law and existing Handbooks, Mortgagee Letters, Notices and outstanding guidance applicable to their participation in FHA programs.

II. ORIGINATION THROUGH POST-CLOSING/ENDORSEMENT

A. TITLE II INSURED HOUSING PROGRAMS FORWARD MORTGAGES

The Title II Insured Housing Programs Forward Mortgages, Origination through Post-Closing/Endorsement section in this *FHA Single Family Housing Policy Handbook (SF Handbook)* provides the origination, underwriting, closing, post-closing, and endorsement standards and procedures applicable to all Single Family (one- to four-units) Mortgages insured under Title II of the National Housing Act, except for Home Equity Conversion Mortgages (HECM). The Mortgagee must fully comply with all of the following standards and procedures in originating, underwriting, and closing for obtaining Federal Housing Administration (FHA) mortgage insurance on a Mortgage. If there are any exceptions or program-specific standards or procedures that differ from those set forth below, the exceptions or alternative program or product specific standards and procedures are explicitly stated. Terms and acronyms used in this *SF Handbook* have their meanings defined in the Glossary and Acronyms and in the specific section of the *SF Handbook* in which the definitions are located.

1. Origination/Processing

a. Applications and Disclosures

The Mortgagee must obtain a completed <u>Fannie Mae Form 1003</u>/<u>Freddie Mac Form 65, Uniform Residential Loan Application (URLA)</u> from the Borrower and provide all required federal and state disclosures in order to begin the origination process. The Mortgagee is responsible for using the most recent version of all forms as of the date of completion of the form.

i. Contents of the Mortgage Application Package

The Mortgagee must maintain all information and documentation that is relevant to its approval decision in the mortgage file. All information and documentation that is required in this *SF Handbook*, and any incidental information or documentation related to those requirements, is relevant to the Mortgagee's approval decision.

If after obtaining all documentation required below, the Mortgagee has reason to believe it needs additional support of the approval decision, the Mortgagee must obtain additional explanation and documentation, consistent with information in the mortgage file to clarify or supplement the information and documentation submitted by the Borrower.

(A) General Requirements

(1) Maximum Age of Mortgage Documents

(a) General Document Age

Documents used in the origination and underwriting of a Mortgage may not be more than 120 Days old at the Disbursement Date. Documents whose validity for underwriting purposes is not affected by the passage of time, such as divorce decrees or tax returns, may be more than 120 Days old at the Disbursement Date.

For purposes of counting Days for periods provided in this *SF Handbook*, Day one is the Day after the effective or issue date of the document, whichever is later.

(b) Appraisal Validity

(i) Initial Appraisal Validity

The 120 Day validity period for an appraisal (see <u>Ordering Appraisals</u>) may be extended for 30 Days at the option of the Mortgagee if (1) the Mortgagee approved the Borrower or HUD issued the Firm Commitment before the expiration of the original appraisal; or (2) the Borrower signed a valid sales contract prior to the expiration date of the appraisal.

(ii) Appraisal Update

An appraisal update must be performed before the initial appraisal, with no extension, has expired. Where the initial appraisal is subsequently updated, the updated appraisal is valid for a period of 240 Days after the effective date of the initial appraisal report that is being updated.

(2) Handling of Documents

Mortgagees must not accept or use documents relating to the employment, income, assets, or credit of Borrowers that have been handled by, or transmitted from or through the equipment of unknown parties, or Interested Parties. Mortgagees may not accept or use any third party verifications that have been handled by, or transmitted from or through any Interested Party, or the Borrower.

(a) Information Sent to the Mortgagee Electronically

The Mortgagee must authenticate all documents received electronically by examining the source identifiers (e.g., the fax banner header or the sender's email address) or contacting the source of the document by telephone to verify the document's validity. The Mortgagee must document the name and telephone number of the individual with whom the Mortgagee verified the validity of the document.

(b) Information Obtained via Internet

The Mortgagee must authenticate documents obtained from an internet website and examine portions of printouts downloaded from the internet including the Uniform Resource Locator (URL) address, as well as the date and time the documents were printed. The Mortgagee must visit the URL or the main website listed in the URL if the page is password protected to verify the website exists and print out evidence documenting the Mortgagee's visit to the URL and website.

Documentation obtained through the internet must contain the same information as would be found in an original hard copy of the document.

(c) Confidentiality Policy for Credit Information

Mortgagees must not divulge sources of credit information, except as required by a contract or by law. All personnel with access to credit information must ensure that the use and disclosure of information from a credit report complies with:
- Title VIII of the Civil Rights Act of 1968 (Fair Housing Act);
- the Fair Credit Reporting Act, Public Law 91-508;
- the Right to Privacy Act, Public Law 93-579;

- the Financial Privacy Act, Public Law 95-630; and
- the Equal Credit Opportunity Act, Public Law 94-239 and 12 CFR Part 202.

(3) Signature Requirements for all Application Forms

All Borrowers must sign and date the initial and final Fannie Mae Form 1003/Freddie Mac Form 65, *Uniform Residential Loan Application* (URLA). All Borrowers must sign and date page two of the initial form HUD-92900-A, *HUD/VA Addendum to Uniform Residential Loan Application,* and sign and date the complete final form HUD-92900-A. The application may not be signed by any party who will not be on the Note.

- For Borrowers that are Entities, the signatory must be a representative who is duly authorized to bind the Entity.
- A Power of Attorney (POA) may not be used unless the Mortgagee verifies and documents that all of the following requirements have been satisfied:
  - For military personnel, a POA may only be used for one of the applications (initial or final), but not both:
    - when the service member is on overseas duty or on an unaccompanied tour;
    - when the Mortgagee is unable to obtain the absent Borrower's signature on the application by mail or via fax; and
    - where the attorney-in-fact has specific authority to encumber the Property and to obligate the Borrower. Acceptable evidence includes a durable POA specifically designed to survive incapacity and avoid the need for court proceedings.
  - For incapacitated Borrowers, a POA may only be used where:
    - a Borrower is incapacitated and unable to sign the mortgage application;
    - the incapacitated individual will occupy the Property to be insured, or the Property is being underwritten as an eligible Investment Property; and
    - the attorney-in-fact has specific authority to encumber the Property and to obligate the Borrower. Acceptable evidence includes a durable POA specifically designed to survive incapacity and avoid the need for court proceedings.

For guidance on use of POA on closing documents refer to Use of Power of Attorney at Closing.

Prohibition on Documents Signed in Blank

Mortgagees are not permitted to have Borrowers sign documents in blank, incomplete documents, or blank sheets of paper.

(4) Policy on Use of Electronic Signatures

(a) Definition

An Electronic Signature refers to any electronic sound, symbol, or process attached to or logically associated with a contract or record and executed or adopted by a person with the intent to sign the record. FHA does not accept an electronic signature that is solely voice or audio. Digital signatures are a subset of electronic signatures.

(b) Use of Electronic Signatures

An electronic signature conducted in accordance with the Electronic Signature Performance Standards (Performance Standards) is accepted on FHA documents requiring signatures to be included in the case binder for mortgage insurance, unless otherwise prohibited by law.

Electronic Signatures meeting the Performance Standards are treated as equivalent to handwritten signatures.

(c) Electronic Signature Performance Standards

The Performance Standards are the set of guidelines that govern FHA acceptance of an electronic signature. The use of electronic signatures is voluntary. However, Mortgagees choosing to use electronic signatures must fully comply with the Performance Standards.

(i) The Electronic Signatures in Global and National Commerce Act (E-SIGN Act) Compliance and Technology

A Mortgagee's electronic signature technology must comply with all requirements of the E-SIGN Act, including those relating to disclosures, consent, signature, presentation, delivery, retention and any state law applicable to the transaction.

(ii) Third Party Documents

Third Party Documents are those documents that are originated and signed outside of the control of the Mortgagee, such as the sales contract. FHA will accept electronic signatures on Third Party Documents included in the case binder for mortgage insurance endorsement in accordance with the E-SIGN Act and the Uniform Electronic Transactions Act (UETA). An indication of the electronic signature and date should be clearly visible when viewed electronically and in a paper copy of the electronically signed document.

(iii) Authorized Documents

Authorized Documents refer to the documents on which FHA accepts electronic signatures provided that the Mortgagee complies with the Performance Standards.

- **Mortgage Insurance Endorsement Documents:** Electronic signatures will be accepted on all documents requiring signatures included in the case binder for mortgage insurance except the Note. FHA will accept electronic signatures on the Note for forward Mortgages only. FHA will not accept electronic signatures on HECM Notes.

- **Servicing and Loss Mitigation Documentation:** Electronic signatures will be accepted on any documents associated with servicing or loss mitigation services for FHA-insured Mortgages.

- **FHA Insurance Claim Documentation:** Electronic signatures will be accepted on any documents associated with the filing of a claim for FHA insurance benefits, including form HUD-27011, *Single Family Application for Insurance Benefits*.

- **HUD Real Estate Owned (REO) Documents:** Electronic signatures will be accepted on the HUD REO Sales Contract and related addenda.

(iv) Associating an Electronic Signature with the Authorized Document

The Mortgagee must ensure that the process for electronically signing authorized documents provide for the document to be presented to the signatory before an electronic signature is obtained. The Mortgagee must ensure that the electronic signature is attached to, or logically associated with, the document that has been electronically signed.

(v) Intent to Sign

The Mortgagee must be able to prove that the signer certified that the document is true, accurate, and correct at the time signed. Electronic signatures are only valid under the E-SIGN Act if they are "executed or adopted by a person with the intent to sign the record." Establishing intent includes:

- identifying the purpose for the Borrower signing the electronic record;
- being reasonably certain that the Borrower knows which electronic record is being signed; and

Handbook 4000.1   111
Effective Date: 09/14/2015 | Last Revised: 07/10/2019
*Refer to the online version of SF Handbook 4000.1 for specific sections' effective dates

- providing notice to the Borrower that their electronic signature is about to be applied to, or associated with, the electronic record.

Intent to use an electronic signature may be established by, but is not limited to:

- an online dialog box or alert advising the Borrower that continuing the process will result in an electronic signature;
- an online dialog box or alert indicating that an electronic signature has just been created and giving the Borrower an opportunity to confirm or cancel the signature; or
- a click-through agreement advising the Borrower that continuing the process will result in an electronic signature.

(vi) Single Use of Signature

Mortgagees must require a separate action by the signer, evidencing intent to sign, in each location where a signature or initials are to be applied.

This provision does not apply to documents signed by Mortgagee employees or Mortgagee contractors provided the Mortgagee obtains the consent of the individual for the use of their electronic signature. The Mortgagee must document the employee's or contractor's consent.

(vii) Authentication

Definition

Authentication refers to the process used to confirm a signer's identity as a party in a transaction.

Standard for Authentication

Before a Mortgagee submits the case for endorsement, the Mortgagee must confirm the identity of the signer by authenticating data provided by the signer with information maintained by an independent source. Independent sources include, but are not limited to:

- national commercial credit bureaus;
- commercially available data sources or services;
- state motor vehicle agencies; or
- government databases.

The Mortgagee must verify a signer's name and date of birth, and either their Social Security Number (SSN) or driver's license number.

(viii) Attribution

Definition

Attribution is the process of associating the identity of a signer with their signature.

Standard for Attribution

The Mortgagee must maintain evidence sufficient to establish that the electronic signature may be attributed to the individual purported to have signed.

The Mortgagee must use one of the following methods, or combinations of methods, to establish attribution:

- selection by or assignment to the individual of a Personal Identification Number (PIN), password, or other shared secret, that the individual uses as part of the signature process;
- delivery of a credential to the individual by a trusted third party, used either to sign electronically or to prevent undetected alteration after the electronic signature using another method;
- knowledge base authentication using "out of band/wallet" information;
- measurement of some unique biometric attribute of the individual and creation of a computer file that represents the measurement, together with procedures to protect against disclosure of the associated computer file to unauthorized parties; or
- public key cryptography.

(ix) Credential Loss Management

Mortgagees must have a system in place to ensure the security of all issued credentials. One or a combination of the following loss management controls is acceptable:

- maintaining the uniqueness of each combined identification code and password, such that no two individuals have the same combination of identification code and password;
- ensuring that identification code and password issuances are periodically checked, recalled, or revised;
- following loss management procedures to electronically de-authorize lost, stolen, missing, or otherwise compromised identification code or password information, and to issue temporary or permanent replacements using suitable, rigorous controls;
- using transaction safeguards to prevent unauthorized use of passwords or identification codes; or

- detecting and reporting any attempts at unauthorized use of the password or identification code to the system security unit.

(d) Required Documentation and Integrity of Records

Mortgagees must ensure that they employ industry-standard encryption to protect the signer's signature and the integrity of the documents to which it is affixed. Mortgagees must ensure that their systems will detect and record any tampering with the electronically signed documents. FHA will not accept documents that show evidence of tampering.

If changes to the document are made, the electronic process must be designed to provide an "audit trail" showing all alterations, the date and time they were made, and identify who made them.

The Mortgagee's system must be designed so that the signed document is designated as the Authoritative Copy. The Authoritative Copy of an electronically signed document refers to the electronic record that is designated by the Mortgagee or holder as the controlling reference copy.

(B) Mortgage Application and Initial Supporting Documentation

(1) URLA and HUD/VA Addendum to the URLA

Unless otherwise noted, *URLA* and *HUD/VA Addendum to the URLA* refer to both initial and final applications.

The Mortgagee must obtain the Borrower's initial complete, signed *URLA* (Fannie Mae Form 1003/Freddie Mac Form 65) and page two of form HUD-92900-A before underwriting the mortgage application.

The Mortgagee must also include the debt of a non-borrowing spouse on the *URLA* if the Borrower resides in or the Property to be purchased is located in a community property state.

The loan originator identified on the *URLA* must be the actual licensed loan originator regardless of whether the loan originator is employed by a sponsored Third-Party Originator (TPO) or the Mortgagee. The *URLA* must contain the loan originator's name, Nationwide Mortgage Licensing System and Registry (NMLS) identification number, telephone number, and signature.

(2) Mortgage Application Name Requirements

(a) Standard

All mortgage applications must be executed in the legal names of all parties.

All mortgage applications must be executed in the name of one or more individuals.

Mortgage applications from a corporation, partnership, sole proprietorship, or trust must be in the name of the Entity and also be in the name of one or more individuals.

Exception

Mortgage applications for Governmental Entities and HUD-approved Nonprofits that provide assistance to low or moderate income families may be solely in the corporation's name.

(b) Required Documentation

The Mortgagee must include a statement that it has verified the Borrower's identity using valid government-issued photo identification prior to endorsement of the Mortgage or the Mortgagee may choose to include a copy of such photo identification as documentation.

For nonprofit Borrowers, the Mortgagee must obtain a copy of the FHA approval letter from the nonprofit. The Mortgagee must also verify that the nonprofit is eligible to be a Borrower as indicated on the U.S. Department of Housing and Urban Development (HUD) Nonprofit Agency Roster.

(C) Borrower Authorization for Verification Information

(1) Borrower's Authorization

(a) Standard

The Mortgagee must obtain the Borrower's authorization to verify the information needed to process the mortgage application. The Mortgagee must obtain a non-borrowing spouse's consent and authorization where necessary to verify specific information required to process the mortgage application, including the non-borrowing spouse's consent for the Mortgagee to verify their SSN with the Social Security Administration (SSA).

(b) Required Documentation

For each individual or Entity, Borrower authorization may be accomplished through a blanket authorization form.

(2) Form HUD-92900-A Part IV: Borrower Consent for Social Security Administration to Verify Social Security Number

The Mortgagee must obtain the Borrower's signature on Part IV of form HUD-92900-A to verify the Borrower's SSN with the SSA.

(3) Tax Verification Form or Equivalent

The Mortgagee must obtain the Borrower's signature on the appropriate Internal Revenue Service (IRS) form to obtain tax returns directly from the IRS for all credit-qualifying Mortgages at the time the final *URLA* is executed.

(D) Borrower's Authorization for Use of Information Protected under the Privacy Act

(1) Standard

The Mortgagee must obtain the Borrower's consent for use of the Borrower's information for any purpose relating to the origination, servicing, loss mitigation, and disposition of the Mortgage or Property securing the Mortgage, and relating to any insurance claim and ultimate resolution of such claims by the Mortgagee and FHA.

(2) Required Documentation

The Mortgagee must obtain a signed statement from the Borrower that clearly expresses the Borrower's consent for the use of the Borrower's information as required above.

(E) Sales Contract and Supporting Documentation

(1) Sales Contract

(a) Standard

The Mortgagee must not originate an insured Mortgage for the purchase of a Property if any provision of the sales contract violates FHA requirements.

The Mortgagee must ensure that (1) all purchasers listed on the sales contract are Borrowers, and (2) only Borrowers sign the sales contract.

An addendum or modification may be used to remove or correct any provisions of the sales contract that do not conform to these requirements.

The Family Member of a purchaser, who is not a borrower, may be listed on the sales contract without modification or removal.

Family Member is defined as follows, regardless of actual or perceived sexual orientation, gender identity, or legal marital status:

- child, parent, or grandparent;
    - a child is defined as a son, stepson, daughter, or stepdaughter;
    - a parent or grandparent includes a step-parent/grandparent or foster parent/grandparent;
- spouse or domestic partner;
- legally adopted son or daughter, including a child who is placed with the Borrower by an authorized agency for legal adoption;
- foster child;
- brother, stepbrother;
- sister, stepsister;
- uncle;
- aunt; or
- son-in-law, daughter-in-law, father-in-law, mother-in-law, brother-in-law, or sister-in-law of the Borrower.

(i) Amendatory Clause

If the Borrower does not receive form HUD-92800.5B, *Conditional Commitment Direct Endorsement Statement of Appraised Value,* before signing the sales contract, the sales contract must be amended before closing to include an amendatory clause that contains the following language:

> "It is expressly agreed that notwithstanding any other provisions of this contract, the purchaser shall not be obligated to complete the purchase of the property described herein or to incur any penalty by forfeiture of earnest money deposits or otherwise, unless the purchaser has been given, in accordance with HUD/FHA or VA requirements, a written statement by the Federal Housing Commissioner, Department of Veterans Affairs, or a Direct Endorsement lender setting forth the appraised value of the property of not less than $_____*. The purchaser shall have the privilege and option of proceeding with consummation of the contract without regard to the amount of the appraised valuation. The appraised valuation is arrived at to determine the maximum mortgage the Department of Housing and Urban Development will insure. HUD does not warrant the value or condition of the property. The purchaser should satisfy himself/herself that the price and condition of the property are acceptable."

* Mortgagees must ensure the actual dollar amount of the sales price stated in the contract has been inserted in the amendatory clause. Increases to the sale price require a revised amendatory clause.

An amendatory clause is not required in connection with:

- HUD REO sales;
- FHA's 203(k) mortgage program;
- sales in which the seller is:
  - o Fannie Mae;
  - o Freddie Mac;
  - o U.S. Department of Veterans Affairs (VA);
  - o United States Department of Agriculture (USDA) Rural Housing Services;
  - o other federal, state, and local government agencies;
  - o a Mortgagee disposing of REO assets; or
  - o a seller at a foreclosure sale; or
- sales in which the Borrower will not be an owner-occupant (for example, sales to nonprofit agencies).

(ii) Real Estate Certification

The Borrower, seller, and the real estate agent or broker involved in the sales transaction must certify, to the best of their knowledge and belief, that (1) the terms and conditions of the sales contract are true and (2) any other agreement entered into by any parties in connection with the real estate transaction is part of, or attached to, the sales agreement.

A separate certification is not needed if the sales contract contains a statement that (1) there are no other agreements between parties and the terms constitute the entire agreement between the parties, and (2) all parties are signatories to the sales contract submitted at the time of underwriting.

(iii) Property Assessed Clean Energy

Where the subject Property is encumbered with a Property Assessed Clean Energy (PACE) obligation, the sales contract must include a clause specifying that the PACE obligation will be satisfied by the seller at, or prior to, closing.

(b) Required Documentation

The Mortgagee must obtain all signed copies of sales contract(s), including a complete copy of the final sales contract with any modifications or revisions agreed upon by Borrower and seller.

(2) Statement of Appraised Value

The Borrower must receive a copy of form HUD-92800.5B.

A statement of appraised value is not required in connection with:
- HUD REO sales;

- FHA's 203(k) mortgage program;
- sales in which the seller is:
    - Fannie Mae;
    - Freddie Mac;
    - the VA;
    - USDA Rural Housing Services;
    - other federal, state, and local government agencies;
    - a Mortgagee disposing of REO assets; or
    - a seller at a foreclosure sale; or
- sales in which the Borrower will not be an owner-occupant (for example, sales to nonprofit agencies).

ii. Disclosures and Legal Compliance

(A) HUD Required Disclosures

The Mortgagee must provide or ensure the Borrower is provided with any disclosure required by FHA, including the following disclosures.

(1) Informed Consumer Choice Disclosure

The Mortgagee must provide the Borrower with an Informed Consumer Choice Disclosure (FHA INFO 13-32) in accordance with the requirements of 24 CFR § 203.10 if the Borrower may qualify for similar non FHA-insured mortgage products offered by the Mortgagee.

(2) Form HUD-92900-B, Important Notice to Homebuyers

The Mortgagee must provide the Borrower with a copy of form HUD-92900-B, *Important Notice to Homebuyers*, signed by the Borrower and provide the Borrower with a copy to keep for the Borrower's records when the Borrower applies for the Mortgage. The Mortgagee must retain the original form HUD-92900-B signed by the Borrower.

(3) Lead-Based Paint

If the Property was built before 1978, the seller must disclose any information known about lead-based paint and lead-based paint hazards before selling the house, in accordance with the HUD-EPA Lead Disclosure Rule (24 CFR 35, subpart A, and the identical 40 CFR 745, subpart F). For such Properties, the Mortgagee must ensure that:

- the Borrower has been provided the EPA-approved information pamphlet on identifying and controlling lead-based paint hazards ("Protect Your Family From Lead In Your Home");
- the Borrower was given a 10-Day period before becoming obligated to purchase the home to conduct a lead-based paint inspection or risk

assessment to determine the presence of lead-based paint or lead-based paint hazards, or waived the opportunity;
- the sales contract contains an attachment in the language of the contract (e.g., English, Spanish), signed and dated by both the seller and purchaser:
  - o containing a lead warning statement as set forth in 24 CFR § 35.92(a)(1).
  - o providing the seller's disclosure of the presence of any known lead-based paint and/or lead-based paint hazards in the target housing being sold, or indication of no knowledge of such presence;
  - o listing any records or reports available to the seller pertaining to lead-based paint and/or lead-based paint hazards in property housing being sold, or indication by the seller that no such records or reports exist; and
  - o affirming that the Borrower received the pamphlet, disclosure, and records or reports, above; and
- when any agent is involved in the transaction on behalf of the seller, the sales contract includes a statement that the agent has informed the seller of the seller's Lead Disclosure Rule obligations, the agent is aware of his/her duty to ensure compliance with the requirements of the Rule, and the agent has signed and dated the contract.

(4) Form HUD-92564-CN, For Your Protection: Get a Home Inspection

Mortgagees are required to provide form HUD-92564-CN, *For Your Protection: Get a Home Inspection,* to prospective homebuyers at first contact, be it for pre-qualification, pre-approval, or initial application.

(B) Compliance with all Applicable Laws, Rules and Requirements

The Mortgagee is required to comply with all federal, state and local laws, rules, and requirements applicable to the mortgage transaction, including all applicable disclosure requirements and the requirements of the Consumer Financial Protection Bureau (CFPB), including those related to:
- Truth in Lending Act (TILA); and
- Real Estate Settlement Procedure Act (RESPA).

(C) Nondiscrimination Policy

The Mortgagee must fully comply with all applicable provisions of:
- Title VIII of the Civil Rights Act of 1968 (Fair Housing Act);
- the Fair Credit Reporting Act, Public Law 91-508; and
- the Equal Credit Opportunity Act, Public Law 94-239 and 12 CFR Part 202.

The Mortgagee must make all determinations with respect to the adequacy of the Borrower's income in a uniform manner without regard to race, color, religion, sex, national origin, familial status, handicap, marital status, actual or perceived sexual orientation, gender identity, source of income of the Borrower, or location of the Property.

iii. Application Document Processing

(A) Mortgagee Responsibilities

The Mortgagee must order the FHA case number and perform any associated tasks in FHA Connection (FHAC). The Mortgagee may use non-employees in connection with its origination of FHA-insured Mortgages only as described below. The Mortgagee ultimately remains responsible for the quality of the Mortgage and for strict compliance with all applicable FHA requirements, regardless of the Mortgagee's relationship to the person or Entity performing any particular service or task.

(1) Sponsored Third-Party Originator

The Mortgagee is responsible for dictating the specific application and processing tasks to be performed by the sponsored TPO. Only HUD-approved Mortgagees acting in the capacity of a sponsored TPO may have direct access to FHAC.

(2) Housing Counseling Services

Mortgagees must ensure that Borrowers receive all required counseling, and that all counseling is provided by HUD-approved housing counseling agencies.

(3) Other Contract Service Providers

The Mortgagee may utilize Eligible Contractors to perform the following administrative and clerical functions: typing of mortgage documents, mailing out and collecting verification forms, ordering credit reports, and/or preparing for endorsement and shipping Mortgages to investors.

(4) Excluded Parties

The Mortgagee may not contract with Entities or persons that are suspended, debarred, or otherwise excluded from participation in HUD programs, or under a Limited Denial of Participation (LDP) that excludes their participation in FHA programs. The Mortgagee must ensure that no sponsored TPO or contractor engages such an Entity or person to perform any function relating to the origination of an FHA-insured Mortgage. The Mortgagee must check the System for Award Management (SAM) (www.sam.gov) and must follow appropriate procedures defined by that system to confirm eligibility for participation.

(B) Initial Document Processing

The Mortgagee begins processing the Mortgage by obtaining an initial *URLA* (Fannie Mae Form 1003/Freddie Mac Form 65) and Part V of form HUD-92900-A.

(1) Ordering Case Numbers

The Mortgagee must use FHAC to order FHA case numbers. A case number can be obtained only when the Mortgagee has an active mortgage application for the subject Borrower and Property.

In order to obtain a case number, the Mortgagee must:
- provide the subject Borrower's name, SSN, and date of birth;
- provide the property address; and
- certify that the Mortgagee has an active mortgage application for the subject Borrower and Property.

The Mortgagee is not required to input appraiser information at the time the case number is ordered.

(a) Automated Data Processing Codes

FHA Automated Data Processing (ADP) Codes are derived from the section of the National Housing Act under which the Mortgage is to be insured. The Mortgagee must select the correct ADP code for each Mortgage in FHAC.

(b) Case Numbers on Sponsored Originations

The Mortgagee will not be able to order case numbers for sponsored originations unless their sponsored TPO has been registered in FHAC.

(2) Holds Tracking

If FHAC detects that a case number currently exists for the Property, a case number will not be assigned. The Mortgagee will receive notification that the case number assignment has been placed in Holds Tracking. The Mortgagee must review the Holds Tracking screen in FHAC to determine the necessary actions to obtain a case number.

(3) Canceling and Reinstating Case Numbers

(a) Canceling a Case Number

The Mortgagee may request cancellation of a case number by submitting a request to HUD. A case number will be canceled only if:
- an appraisal has not been completed and the Borrower will not close the Mortgage as an FHA-insured Mortgage;

- the FHA mortgage insurance will not be sought; or
- the appraisal has already expired.

The Mortgagee must submit a request for cancellation to the FHA Resource Center at answers@hud.gov using the Case Cancellation Request Template.

(b) Automatic Case Number Cancellations

Case numbers are automatically canceled after six months if one of the following actions is not performed as a last action:
- appraisal information entered;
- Firm Commitment issued by FHA;
- insurance application received and subsequent updates; or
- Notices of Return (NOR) or resubmissions.

Updates to the Borrower's name and/or property address, an appraisal update, or a transmission of the Upfront Mortgage Insurance Premium (UFMIP) do not constitute Last Action Taken.

(c) Reinstatement of Case Numbers

The Mortgagee may request reinstatement of canceled case numbers by submitting a request to the FHA Resource Center using the Case Reinstatement Request Template.

Case numbers that were automatically canceled will be reinstated only if the Mortgagee provides evidence that the subject Mortgage closed prior to cancellation of the case number, such as a Closing Disclosure or similar legal document.

(4) Transferring Case Numbers

(a) Requirements for the Transferring Mortgagee

The original Mortgagee must assign the case number to the new Mortgagee using the Case Transfer function in FHAC immediately upon the Borrower's request.

The original Mortgagee may provide processing documents but is not required to do so.

The original Mortgagee may not charge the Borrower for the transfer of any documents, but the original Mortgagee may negotiate a fee with the new Mortgagee for providing the processing documents. The original Mortgagee is never entitled to a fee for the transfer of processing documents for a Streamline Refinance.

(b) Case Number Transfer Involving a Rejected Mortgage

If the transfer involves a rejected Mortgage, the original Mortgagee must complete the Mortgage Credit Reject function in FHAC prior to transferring the Mortgage.

(c) Case Number Transfer Involving a Sponsored Third-Party Originator

Where a case number is transferred to a new approved Mortgagee or sponsored TPO, the original Mortgagee, its authorized agent, or sponsored TPO that is also an FHA-approved Mortgagee must complete the appropriate sections in FHAC as described in the FHAC Guide – Case Processing Support Functions.

(5) Ordering Title Commitments

The Mortgagee must order a title commitment to ensure the Property will be properly titled and the Mortgage secured in accordance with FHA requirements.

(6) Ordering Appraisals

The Mortgagee must order a new appraisal for each case number assignment and may not reuse an appraisal that was performed under another case number, even if the prior appraisal is not yet more than 120 Days old.

(a) Appraisal Integrity

The Mortgagee is responsible for identifying any problems or potential problems with the integrity, accuracy and thoroughness of an appraisal submitted to FHA for mortgage insurance purposes.

Appraisers must comply with the Uniform Standards of Professional Appraisal Practice (USPAP), including the Competency Rule, when conducting appraisals of Properties intended as security for FHA-insured financing. In appraising any Property for the purpose of obtaining FHA mortgage insurance, the Appraiser must certify that they are capable of performing the appraisal because they have the necessary qualifications and access to all necessary data.

The Mortgagee must ensure that FHA is listed on the appraisal report as an Intended User of the appraisal.

(b) Selection of a Qualified Appraiser

The Mortgagee must order an appraisal from an Appraiser who is listed on the FHA Appraiser Roster and is qualified and knowledgeable in the specific market area in which the Property is located. The Mortgagee must evaluate the Appraiser's education, training and actual field experience to determine whether the Appraiser has sufficient qualifications to perform the appraisal before assignment.

The Mortgagee may not discriminate on the basis of race, color, religion, national origin, sex, age, disability, or actual or perceived sexual orientation and gender identity in the selection of an Appraiser.

(c) Use of Appraisal Management Company or Third-Party Contractors

The Mortgagee may engage an Appraisal Management Company (AMC) to perform services related to the obtaining of an appraisal. The Mortgagee remains responsible for the acts of its AMC or third-party contractors.

The Mortgagee may not pay the AMC and other third-party contractors fees in excess of what is customary and reasonable for such services in the market area where the Property being appraised is located. Any management fees must be for actual services related to the ordering process, or review of appraisal for FHA financing.

(d) Appraiser Independence

The Mortgagee must ensure it does not compromise the Appraiser's independence.

The Mortgagee may not allow the Appraiser to be selected, retained, managed, or compensated by a mortgage broker or any member of a Mortgagee's staff who is compensated on a commission basis tied to the successful completion of a Mortgage or who is not independent of the Mortgagee's mortgage production staff or processes.

The Mortgagee must ensure that it does not:
- compensate the Appraiser at a rate that is not commensurate in the market area of the Property being appraised with the assignment type, complexity and scope of work required for the appraisal services performed;
- withhold or threaten to withhold timely payment or partial payment for an appraisal report;
- prohibit the Appraiser from recording the fee paid for the performance of the appraisal in the appraisal report;
- condition the ordering of an appraisal report or the payment of an appraisal fee, salary, or bonus on the opinion, conclusion or valuation to be reached, or on a preliminary value estimate requested from an Appraiser;

- provide to the Appraiser, appraisal company, AMC or any Entity or person related to the Appraiser, appraisal company or AMC, stock or other financial or non-financial benefits;
- order, obtain, use, or pay for a second or subsequent appraisal or Automated Valuation Model (AVM) in connection with a Mortgage financing transaction unless:
  - there is a reasonable basis to believe that the initial appraisal was flawed or tainted and such belief is clearly and appropriately noted in the mortgage file; or
  - such appraisal or AVM was completed pursuant to written, pre-established bona fide pre- or post-Disbursement appraisal review or quality control process or underwriting guidelines and the Mortgagee adheres to a policy of selecting the most reliable appraisal, rather than the appraisal that states the highest value;
- withhold or threaten to withhold future business from an Appraiser, or demote or terminate or threaten to demote or terminate an Appraiser in order to influence an Appraiser to arrive at a predetermined or desired value;
- make expressed or implied promises of future business, promotions or increased compensation for an Appraiser in order to influence an Appraiser to arrive at a predetermined or desired value;
- allow the removal of an Appraiser from a list of qualified Appraisers or the addition of an Appraiser to an exclusionary list of qualified Appraisers, used by any Entity, without prompt written notice to such Appraiser. The notice must include written evidence of the Appraiser's illegal conduct, violation of USPAP or state licensing standards, improper or unprofessional behavior or other substantive reason for removal;
- request that an Appraiser provide an estimated, predetermined or desired valuation in an appraisal report prior to the completion of the appraisal report, or request that an Appraiser provide estimated values or comparable sales at any time prior to the Appraiser's completion of an appraisal report;
- provide to the Appraiser an anticipated, estimated, encouraged or desired value for a subject Property or a proposed, or target amount to be loaned to the Borrower, except that a copy of the sales contract for purchase and any addendum must be provided; or
- perform any other act or practice that impairs or attempts to impair an Appraiser's independence, objectivity, or impartiality, or that violates any applicable law, regulation, or requirement.

(e) Additional Requirements When Ordering an Appraisal

The Mortgagee must provide to the selected Appraiser the FHA case number and a complete copy of the subject sales contract including all addendums, land lease, surveys and other legal documents contained in the mortgage file necessary to analyze the Property.

The Mortgagee must disclose all known information regarding any environmental hazard that is in or on the subject Property, or in the vicinity of the Property, whether obtained from the Borrower, the real estate broker, or any other party to the transaction.

Where the Mortgagee determines that the Property is subject to a PACE obligation, it must notify the Appraiser that the PACE obligation will be paid off as a condition of loan approval.

(7) Appraisal Effective Date

(a) Standard

The effective date of the appraisal cannot be before the FHA case number assignment date unless the Mortgagee certifies, via the certification field in the Appraisal Logging Screen in FHAC, that the appraisal was ordered for conventional lending or government-guaranteed loan purposes and was performed by a FHA Roster Appraiser.

The Mortgagee must ensure that the appraisal was performed in accordance with FHA appraisal reporting instructions as detailed in this *SF Handbook* and the Appraisal Report and Data Delivery Guide. The intended use of the appraisal must indicate that it is solely to assist FHA in assessing the risk of the Property securing the FHA-insured Mortgage. Additionally, FHA and the Mortgagee must be indicated as the intended users of the appraisal report.

(b) Required Documentation

The Mortgagee must retain documentation in the case binder substantiating conversion of the Mortgage to FHA.

(8) Transferring Existing Appraisals

In cases where a Borrower has switched Mortgagees, the first Mortgagee must, at the Borrower's request, transfer the appraisal to the second Mortgagee within five business days. The Appraiser is not required to provide the appraisal to the new Mortgagee. The client name on the appraisal does not need to reflect the new Mortgagee. If the original Mortgagee has not been reimbursed for the cost of the appraisal, the Mortgagee is not required to transfer the appraisal until it is reimbursed.

The second Mortgagee may not request the Appraiser to re-address the appraisal. If the second Mortgagee finds deficiencies in the appraisal, the Mortgagee must order a new appraisal.

Where a Mortgagee uses an existing appraisal for a different Borrower, the Mortgagee must enter the new Borrower's information in FHAC. The Mortgagee must collect an appraisal fee from the new Borrower and refund the fee to the original Borrower.

If a Case Transfer is involved, the new Mortgagee must enter the Borrower's information in FHAC. The new Mortgagee must collect an appraisal fee from the Borrower, and send the fee to the original Mortgagee, who, in turn, must refund the fee to the original Borrower.

(9) Ordering Second Appraisal

The Mortgagee is prohibited from ordering an additional appraisal to achieve an increase in value for the Property and/or the elimination or reduction of deficiencies and/or repairs required.

The Mortgagee may order a second appraisal for Mortgages that are in accordance with requirements on Property Flipping.

(a) Second Appraisal by Original Mortgagee

A second appraisal may only be ordered if the Direct Endorsement (DE) underwriter (underwriter) determines the first appraisal is materially deficient and the Appraiser is unable or uncooperative in resolving the deficiency. The Mortgagee must fully document the deficiency and status of the appraisal in the mortgage file. The Mortgagee must pay for the second appraisal.

Material deficiencies on appraisals are those deficiencies that have a direct impact on value and marketability. Material deficiencies include, but are not limited to:
- failure to report readily observable defects that impact the health and safety of the occupants and/or structural soundness of the house;
- reliance upon outdated or dissimilar comparable sales when more recent and/or comparable sales were available as of the effective date of the appraisal; and
- fraudulent statements or conclusions when the Appraiser had reason to know or should have known that such statements or conclusions compromise the integrity, accuracy and/or thoroughness of the appraisal submitted to the client.

(b) Second Appraisal by Second Mortgagee

A second appraisal may only be ordered by the second Mortgagee under the following limited circumstances:
- the first appraisal contains material deficiencies as determined by the underwriter for the second Mortgagee;

- the Appraiser performing the first appraisal is prohibited from performing appraisals for the second Mortgagee; or
- the first Mortgagee fails to provide a copy of the appraisal to the second Mortgagee in a timely manner, and the failure would cause a delay in closing and harm to the Borrower, including loss of interest rate lock, violation of purchase contract deadline, occurrence of foreclosure proceedings and imposition of late fees.

(c) Use of Second Appraisal

For the first two cases outlined above, the Mortgagee must rely only on the second appraisal and ensure that copies of both appraisals are retained in the case binder. For the third case above, the first appraisal must be added to the case binder if it is received.

(d) Required Documentation

The Mortgagee must document why a second appraisal was ordered and retain the explanation and all appraisal reports in the case binder.

(10) Ordering an Update to an Appraisal

The Mortgagee may only order an update if (1) it is a Mortgagee listed as an Intended User of the original appraisal or (2) it has received permission from the original client and the Appraiser. The Appraiser incorporates the original report being updated by attachment rather than by reference per Advisory Opinion 3 of the USPAP.

The Mortgagee may use an update of appraisal only if:
- it is performed by the FHA Appraiser who performed the original appraisal, who is currently in good standing on the FHA Appraiser Roster;
- the Property has not declined in value;
- the building improvements that contribute value to the Property can be observed from the street or a public way;
- the exterior inspection of the Property reveals no deficiencies or other significant changes;
- the update of appraisal was ordered by the Mortgagee and completed by the Appraiser prior to the expiration of the initial 120-Day period; and
- the original appraisal report was not previously updated.

(11) Appraisal Delivery – Electronic Appraisal Delivery Portal

(a) Definition

The Electronic Appraisal Delivery (EAD) portal is a web-based platform where Mortgagees or their designated third-party service providers electronically deliver FHA Single Family appraisal reports prior to endorsement.

(b) Standard

Mortgagees or their designated third-party service providers must deliver appraisals through the EAD portal.

(c) Required Documentation

Appraisals submitted through the EAD are the appraisal of record for endorsement.

b. General Mortgage Insurance Eligibility

i. Mortgage Purpose

FHA offers various mortgage insurance programs which insure approved Mortgagees against losses on Mortgages. FHA-insured Mortgages may be used to purchase housing, improve housing, or refinance existing Mortgages.

(A) Purchase/Construction to Permanent

The Borrower may finance the purchase of an existing one- to four-unit residence, and may also finance construction of a one- to four-unit residence through a Construction to Permanent Mortgage.

Properties to be acquired through an unrecorded land contract must be treated as a purchase.

(B) Rehabilitation

(1) 203(k) Standard and Limited Rehabilitation Mortgages

The Section 203(k) Rehabilitation Mortgage Insurance is used to:
- rehabilitate an existing one- to four-unit Structure, which will be used primarily for residential purposes;
- rehabilitate such a Structure and refinance the outstanding indebtedness on the Structure and the Real Property on which the Structure is located; or
- purchase and rehabilitate the Structure and purchase the Real Property on which the Structure is located.

(2) 203(h) and 203(k) for Disaster Victims

The Section 203(h) Mortgage Insurance for Disaster Victims program allows FHA to insure Mortgages made by qualified Mortgagees to victims of a Presidentially-Declared Major Disaster Area (PDMDA) who have lost their housing, or whose housing was damaged and are in the process of rebuilding or buying another house.

(C) Refinance

A refinance transaction is used to pay off the existing debt or to withdraw equity from the Property with the proceeds of a new Mortgage for a Borrower with legal title to the subject Property.

Types of Refinances

FHA insures several different types of refinance transactions:
1. Cash-out refinances are designed to pull equity out of the Property.
2. No cash-out refinances of FHA-insured and non FHA-insured Mortgages are designed to pay existing liens. These include: Rate and Term refinance, Simple Refinance, and Streamline Refinance.
3. Refinances of non FHA-insured Mortgages are available for qualified Borrowers in negative equity positions (Short Refi).
4. Refinances for rehabilitation or repair (Section 203(k)).

ii. Borrower Eligibility

(A) General Borrower Eligibility Requirements

In order to obtain FHA-insured financing, all Borrowers must meet the eligibility criteria in this section.

A party who has a financial interest in the mortgage transaction, such as the seller, builder or real estate agent, may not be a co-Borrower or a Cosigner. Exceptions may be granted when the party with the financial interest is a Family Member.

(1) Social Security Number

(a) Standard

Each Borrower must provide evidence of their valid SSN to the Mortgagee.

Exception

Individuals employed by the World Bank, a foreign embassy or equivalent employer identified by HUD, state and local government agencies, Instrumentalities of Government, and HUD-approved Nonprofit organizations are not required to provide an SSN.

(b) Required Documentation

The Mortgagee must:

- validate and document an SSN for each Borrower, co-Borrower, or Cosigner on the Mortgage by:
  - entering the Borrower's name, date of birth, and SSN in the Borrower/address validation screen through FHAC; and
  - examining the Borrower's original pay stubs, W-2 forms, valid tax returns obtained directly from the IRS, or other document relied upon to underwrite the Mortgage; and
- resolve any inconsistencies or multiple SSNs for individual Borrowers that are revealed during Mortgage processing and underwriting using a service provider to verify the SSN with the SSA.

(2) Borrower Age Limits

The Borrower must be old enough to enter into a mortgage Note that can be legally enforced in the state, or other jurisdiction, where the Property is located ("State Law"). There is no maximum age limit for a Borrower.

(3) Borrower Minimum Decision Credit Score

(a) Definition

The Minimum Decision Credit Score (MDCS) refers to the credit score reported on the Borrower's credit report when all reported scores are the same. Where three scores are reported, the median score is the MDCS. Where two differing scores are reported, the MDCS is the lowest score. Where only one score is reported, that score is the MDCS.

An MDCS is determined for each Borrower. Where the Mortgage involves multiple Borrowers, the Mortgagee must determine the MDCS for each Borrower, and then select the lowest MDCS for all Borrowers.

Where the Mortgage involves multiple Borrowers and one or more of the Borrowers do not have a credit score (non-traditional or insufficient credit), the Mortgagee must select the lowest MDCS of the Borrower(s) with credit score(s).

(b) Eligibility Standard

The Borrower is not eligible for FHA-insured financing if the MDCS is less than 500.

(4) Borrower and Co-Borrower Ownership and Obligation Requirements

To be eligible, all occupying and non-occupying Borrowers and co-Borrowers must take title to the Property in their own name or a Living Trust at settlement, be obligated on the Note or credit instrument, and sign all security instruments.

In community property states, the Borrower's spouse is not required to be a Borrower or a Cosigner. However, the Mortgage must be executed by all parties necessary to make the lien valid and enforceable under State Law.

(5) Cosigner Requirements

Cosigners are liable for the debt and therefore, must sign the Note. Cosigners do not hold an ownership interest in the subject Property and therefore, do not sign the security instrument.

(6) Principal Residence in the United States

Non-occupying co-Borrowers or Cosigners must either be United States (U.S.) citizens or have a Principal Residence in the U.S.

(7) Military Personnel Eligibility

(a) Standard

Borrowers who are military personnel, who cannot physically reside in a Property because they are on Active Duty, are still considered owner occupants and are eligible for maximum financing if a Family Member of the Borrower will occupy the subject Property as their Principal Residence, or the Borrower intends to occupy the subject Property upon discharge from military service.

(b) Required Documentation

The Mortgagee must obtain a copy of the Borrower's military orders evidencing the Borrower's Active Duty status and that the duty station is more than 100 miles from the subject Property.

The Mortgagee must obtain the Borrower's intent to occupy the subject Property upon discharge from military service, if a Family Member will not occupy the subject Property as their Principal Residence.

(8) Citizenship and Immigration Status

U.S. citizenship is not required for Mortgage eligibility.

(9) Residency Requirements

The Mortgagee must determine the residency status of the Borrower based on information provided on the mortgage application and other applicable documentation. In no case is a Social Security card sufficient to prove immigration or work status.

(a) Lawful Permanent Resident Aliens

(i) Standard

A Borrower with lawful permanent resident alien status may be eligible for FHA-insured financing provided the Borrower satisfies the same requirements, terms and conditions as those for U.S. citizens.

(ii) Required Documentation

The mortgage file must include evidence of the permanent residency and indicate that the Borrower is a lawful permanent resident alien on the *URLA*.

The U.S. Citizenship and Immigration Services (USCIS) within the Department of Homeland Security provides evidence of lawful, permanent residency status.

(b) Non-Permanent Resident Aliens

A Borrower who is a non-permanent resident alien may be eligible for FHA-insured financing provided:
- the Property will be the Borrower's Principal Residence;
- the Borrower has a valid SSN, except for those employed by the World Bank, a foreign embassy, or equivalent employer identified by HUD;
- the Borrower is eligible to work in the United States, as evidenced by the Employment Authorization Document issued by the USCIS; and
- the Borrower satisfies the same requirements, terms and conditions as those for U.S. citizens.

The Employment Authorization Document is required to substantiate work status. If the Employment Authorization Document will expire within one year and a prior history of residency status renewals exists, the Mortgagee may assume that continuation will be granted. If there are no prior renewals, the Mortgagee must determine the likelihood of renewal based on information from the USCIS.

A Borrower residing in the U.S. by virtue of refugee or asylee status granted by the USCIS is automatically eligible to work in this country. The Employment Authorization Document is not required, but documentation substantiating the refugee or asylee status must be obtained.

(c) Non-U.S. Citizens without Lawful Residency

Non-U.S. citizens without lawful residency in the U.S. are not eligible for FHA-insured Mortgages.

(10) Borrower Ineligibility Due to Delinquent Federal Non-Tax Debt

(a) Standard

Mortgagees are prohibited from processing an application for an FHA-insured Mortgage for Borrowers with delinquent federal non-tax debt, including deficiency Judgments and other debt associated with past FHA-insured Mortgages. Mortgagees are required to determine whether the Borrowers have delinquent federal non-tax debt. Mortgagees may obtain information on delinquent Federal Debts from public records, credit reports or equivalent, and must check all Borrowers against the Credit Alert Verification Reporting System (CAIVRS).

(b) Verification

If a delinquent Federal Debt is reflected in a public record, credit report or equivalent, or CAIVRS or an Equivalent System, the Mortgagee must verify the validity and delinquency status of the debt by contacting the creditor agency to whom the debt is owed. If the debt was identified through CAIVRS, the Mortgagee must contact the creditor agency using the contact phone number and debt reference number reflected in the Borrower's CAIVRS report.

If the creditor agency confirms that the debt is valid and in delinquent status as defined by the Debt Collection Improvement Act, then the Borrower is ineligible for an FHA-insured Mortgage until the Borrower resolves the debt with the creditor agency.

The Mortgagee may not deny a Mortgage solely on the basis of CAIVRS information that has not been verified by the Mortgagee. If resolved either by determining that the information in CAIVRS is no longer valid or by resolving the delinquent status as stated above, the Mortgagee may continue to process the mortgage application.

(c) Resolution

In order for a Borrower with verified delinquent Federal Debt to become eligible, the Borrower must resolve their federal non-tax debt in accordance with the Debt Collection Improvement Act.

The creditor agency that is owed the debt can verify that the debt has been resolved in accordance with the Debt Collection Improvement Act.

(d) Required Documentation

The Mortgagee must include documentation from the creditor agency to support the verification and resolution of the debt. For debt reported through

CAIVRS, the Mortgagee may obtain evidence of resolution by obtaining a clear CAIVRS report.

(11) Eligibility Period for Borrowers Delinquent on FHA-Insured Mortgages

If a Borrower is currently delinquent on an FHA-insured Mortgage, they are ineligible for a new FHA-insured Mortgage unless the delinquency is resolved.

(12) Delinquent Federal Tax Debt

(a) Standard

Borrowers with delinquent Federal Tax Debt are ineligible.

Tax liens may remain unpaid if the Borrower has entered into a valid repayment agreement with the federal agency owed to make regular payments on the debt and the Borrower has made timely payments for at least three months of scheduled payments. The Borrower cannot prepay scheduled payments in order to meet the required minimum of three months of payments.

The Mortgagee must include the payment amount in the agreement in the calculation of the Borrower's Debt-to-Income (DTI) ratio.

(b) Verification

Mortgagees must check public records and credit information to verify that the Borrower is not presently delinquent on any Federal Debt and does not have a tax lien placed against their Property for a debt owed to the federal government.

(c) Required Documentation

The Mortgagee must include documentation from the IRS evidencing the repayment agreement and verification of payments made, if applicable.

(13) Valid First Liens

The Mortgagee must ensure that the mortgaged Property will be free and clear of all liens, except the insured Mortgage and any secondary liens permitted by FHA regulations at 24 CFR §§ 203.32 and 203.41.

(a) Consent of Non-Borrowing Spouses

If necessary to perfect a valid first lien under state law, the Mortgagee must require a non-borrowing spouse to execute either the security instrument or documentation indicating that they are relinquishing all rights to the Property.

(b) Tax Liens

Tax liens may remain unpaid if the Borrower has entered into a valid repayment agreement with the lien holder to make regular payments on the debt and the Borrower has made timely payments for at least three months of scheduled payments. The Borrower cannot prepay scheduled payments in order to meet the required minimum of three months of payments. Except for federal tax liens, the lien holder must subordinate the tax lien to the FHA-insured Mortgage.

(14) Additional Eligibility Requirements for Nonprofit Organizations and State and Local Government Agencies

(a) Eligibility Criteria for a Mortgage for Nonprofit Organizations

(i) Standard

HUD-approved Nonprofit organizations may be eligible for FHA-insured Mortgages. Nonprofits are not eligible for cash-out refinances.

HUD-approved Nonprofit organizations are eligible for the same percentage of financing that is available to an owner-occupant on their Principal Residence.

HUD-approved Nonprofit organizations may only obtain FHA-insured fixed rate Mortgages.

(ii) Required Documentation

A HUD-approved Nonprofit must be listed on the HUD Nonprofit Agency Roster and intend to sell or lease the Property to Low- to Moderate-Income families.

(b) Eligibility Criteria for a Mortgage for State and Local Government Agencies

(i) Standard

State and local government agencies and instrumentalities of government may obtain FHA-insured financing provided:
- the agency has the legal authority to become the Borrower;
- the particular state or local government is not in bankruptcy; and
- there is no legal prohibition on obtaining a deficiency Judgment based solely on its status as a state and local government.

State and local government agencies are eligible for the same percentage of financing that is available to an owner-occupant on their Principal

Residence. State and local government agencies are not eligible for cash-out refinances.

State and local government agencies may only obtain FHA-insured fixed rate Mortgages.

(ii) Required Documentation

The Mortgagee must obtain an opinion from counsel verifying the legal status requirements of the agency.

State and local government agencies are not required to be listed on the HUD-approved Nonprofit roster.

(15) Eligibility Requirements for Living Trusts

(a) Property Held in Living Trusts

The Mortgagee may originate a Mortgage for a living trust for a Property held by the living trust, provided the beneficiary of the living trust is a Cosigner and will occupy the Property as their Principal Residence, and the trust provides reasonable means to assure that the Mortgagee will be notified of any changes to the trust, including transfer of beneficial interest and any changes in occupancy status of the Property.

(b) Living Trusts and Security Instruments

(i) Standard

The name of the living trust must appear on the security instrument, such as the Mortgage, deed of trust, or security deed.

The name of the individual Borrower must appear on the security instrument when required to create a valid lien under state law. The names of the owner-occupant and other Borrowers, if any, must also appear on the Note with the trust.

The name of the individual Borrower is not required to appear on the property deed or title.

(ii) Required Documentation

The Mortgagee must obtain a copy of the trust documentation.

(B) Excluded Parties

The Mortgagee must establish that no participants are Excluded Parties and document the determination on form HUD-92900-LT, *FHA Loan Underwriting and Transmittal Summary*.

(1) Borrower

(a) Standard

A Borrower is not eligible to participate in FHA-insured mortgage transactions if they are suspended, debarred, or otherwise excluded from participating in HUD programs.

(b) Required Documentation

The Mortgagee must check the HUD LDP list to confirm the Borrower's eligibility to participate in an FHA-insured mortgage transaction.

The Mortgagee must check SAM (www.sam.gov) and follow appropriate procedures defined by that system to confirm eligibility for participation.

The Mortgagee must check the "Yes" box on form HUD-92900-LT if the Borrower appears on either the LDP or SAM list.

(2) Other Parties to the Transaction

(a) Standard

A Mortgage is not eligible for FHA insurance if anyone participating in the mortgage transaction is listed on HUD's LDP list or in SAM as being excluded from participation in HUD transactions. This may include but is not limited to:
- seller (except where selling the Principal Residence)
- listing and selling real estate agent
- loan originator
- loan processor
- underwriter
- Appraiser
- 203(k) Consultant
- Closing Agent
- title company

(b) Required Documentation

The Mortgagee must check the HUD LDP list and SAM (www.sam.gov) and follow appropriate procedures defined by that system to confirm eligibility for all participants involved in the transaction.

iii. Occupancy Types

(A) Principal Residence

(1) Definition

A Principal Residence refers to a dwelling where the Borrower maintains or will maintain their permanent place of abode, and which the Borrower typically occupies or will occupy for the majority of the calendar year. A person may have only one Principal Residence at any one time.

(2) Standard

(a) FHA Requirement for Owner Occupancy

At least one Borrower must occupy the Property within 60 Days of signing the security instrument and intend to continue occupancy for at least one year.

203(k) Rehabilitation products may have different requirements for the length of time to occupy the Property.

(b) FHA-Insured Mortgages on Principal Residences

FHA will not insure more than one Property as a Principal Residence for any Borrower, except as noted below. FHA will not insure a Mortgage if it is determined that the transaction was designed to use FHA mortgage insurance as a vehicle for obtaining Investment Properties, even if the Property to be insured will be the only one owned using FHA mortgage insurance.

Properties previously acquired as Investment Properties are not subject to these restrictions.

(c) Exceptions to the FHA Policy Limiting the Number of Mortgages per Borrower

The table below describes the only circumstances in which a Borrower with an existing FHA-insured Mortgage for a Principal Residence may obtain an additional FHA-insured Mortgage on a new Principal Residence.

Policy Exceptions	Eligibility Requirements
Relocation	A Borrower may be eligible to obtain another FHA-insured Mortgage without being required to sell an existing Property covered by an FHA-insured Mortgage if the Borrower is: • relocating or has relocated for an employment-related reason; and • establishing or has established a new Principal Residence in an area more than 100 miles from the Borrower's current Principal Residence. If the Borrower moves back to the original area, the Borrower is not required to live in the original house and may obtain a new FHA-insured Mortgage on a new Principal Residence, provided the relocation meets the two requirements above.
Increase in family size	A Borrower may be eligible for another house with an FHA-insured Mortgage if the Borrower provides satisfactory evidence that: • the Borrower has had an increase in legal dependents and the Property now fails to meet family needs; and • the Loan-to-Value (LTV) ratio on the current Principal Residence is equal to or less than 75% or is paid down to that amount, based on the outstanding Mortgage balance and a current residential appraisal.
Vacating a jointly-owned Property	A Borrower may be eligible for another FHA-insured Mortgage if the Borrower is vacating (with no intent to return) the Principal Residence which will remain occupied by an existing co-Borrower.
Non-occupying co-Borrower	A non-occupying co-Borrower on an existing FHA-insured Mortgage may qualify for another FHA-insured Mortgage on a new Property to be their own Principal Residence. A Borrower with an existing FHA-insured Mortgage on their own Principal Residence may qualify as a non-occupying co-Borrower on other FHA-insured Mortgages.

(3) Required Documentation

The Borrower must indicate on the *URLA* (Fannie Mae Form 1003/Freddie Mac Form 65) that the Property will be the Borrower's Principal Residence and certify to that fact on form HUD-92900-A, *HUD/VA Addendum to URLA*.

(B) Secondary Residence

(1) Definition

Secondary Residence refers to a dwelling that a Borrower occupies in addition to their Principal Residence, but less than a majority of the calendar year. A Secondary Residence does not include a Vacation Home.

(2) Standard

Secondary Residences are only permitted with written approval from the Jurisdictional HOC after a determination that:
- the Borrower has no other Secondary Residence;
- the Secondary Residence will not be a Vacation Home or be otherwise used primarily for recreational purposes;
- the commuting distance to the Borrower's workplace creates an undue hardship on the Borrower and there is no affordable rental housing meeting the Borrower's needs within 100 miles of the Borrower's workplace; and
- the maximum mortgage amount is 85 percent of the lesser of the appraised value or sales price.

(3) Required Documentation

The Mortgagee must demonstrate the lack of affordable rental housing, and include:
- a satisfactory explanation of the need for a Secondary Residence and the lack of available rental housing; and
- written evidence from local real estate professionals who verify a lack of acceptable housing in the area.

(C) Investment Property

(1) Definition

An Investment Property refers to a Property that is not occupied by the Borrower as a Principal or Secondary Residence.

(2) Standard

Investment Properties are not eligible for FHA insurance.

Exception

Investment Properties are eligible if the borrower is a HUD-approved Nonprofit Borrower, or a state and local government agency, or an Instrumentality of Government.

Investment Properties are eligible for insurance under the HUD Real Estate Owned (REO) Purchasing product, except under the 203(k) program.

iv. Property Eligibility and Acceptability Criteria

(A) General Property Eligibility

The Property must be located within the U.S., Puerto Rico, Guam, the Virgin Islands, the Commonwealth of the Northern Mariana Islands, or American Samoa.

(1) Special Flood Hazard Areas

The Mortgagee must determine if a Property is located in a Special Flood Hazard Area (SFHA) as designated by the Federal Emergency Management Agency (FEMA). The Mortgagee must obtain flood zone determination services, independent of any assessment made by the Appraiser to cover the Life of the Loan Flood Certification.

A Property is not eligible for FHA insurance if:
- a residential building and related improvements to the Property are located within SFHA Zone A, a Special Flood Zone Area, or Zone V, a Coastal Area, and insurance under the National Flood Insurance Program (NFIP) is not available in the community; or
- the improvements arc, or arc proposed to be, located within a Coastal Barrier Resources System (CBRS).

(a) Eligibility for Proposed or New Construction in SFHAs

If any portion of the dwelling, related Structures or equipment essential to the value of the Property and subject to flood damage is located within an SFHA, the Property is not eligible for FHA mortgage insurance unless the Mortgagee:
- obtains from FEMA a final Letter of Map Amendment (LOMA) or final Letter of Map Revision (LOMR) that removes the Property from the SFHA; or
- obtains a FEMA National Flood Insurance Program Elevation Certificate (FEMA Form 086-0-33) prepared by a licensed engineer or surveyor. The elevation certificate must document that the lowest floor including the basement of the residential building, and all related improvements/equipment essential to the value of the Property, is built at or above the 100-year flood elevation in compliance with the NFIP criteria, and insurance under the NFIP is obtained.

(b) Eligibility for Existing Construction in SFHAs

When any portion of the residential improvements is determined to be located within an SFHA, insurance under the NFIP must be obtained.

(c) Eligibility for Condominiums in SFHAs

The Mortgagee must ensure the Homeowners' Association (HOA) obtains insurance under the NFIP on buildings located within the SFHA. The flood insurance coverage must protect the interest of the Borrowers who hold title to an individual unit, as well as the common areas of the Condominium Project.

(d) Eligibility for Manufactured Housing in SFHAs

The finished grade level beneath the Manufactured Home must be at or above the 100-year return frequency flood elevation. If any portion of the dwelling, related Structures or equipment essential to the Property Value and subject to flood damage for both new and existing Manufactured Homes are located within an SFHA, the Property is not eligible for FHA mortgage insurance unless the Mortgagee obtains:

- a FEMA issued LOMA or LOMR that removes the Property from the SFHA; or
- a FEMA National Flood Insurance Program (NFIP) Elevation Certificate (FEMA Form 086-0-33) prepared by a licensed engineer or surveyor stating that the finished grade beneath the Manufactured Home is at or above the 100-year return frequency flood elevation, and insurance under the NFIP is obtained.

(e) Required Flood Insurance Amount

For Properties located within an SFHA, flood insurance must be maintained for the life of the Mortgage in an amount at least equal to the lesser of:

- the outstanding balance of the Mortgage, less estimated land costs; or
- the maximum amount of the NFIP insurance available with respect to the property improvements.

(f) Required Documentation

The Mortgagee must obtain a Life of Loan Flood Certification for all Properties. If applicable, the Mortgagee must also obtain a:

- FEMA Letter of Map Amendment;
- FEMA Letter of Map Revision; or
- FEMA National Flood Insurance Program Elevation Certificate (FEMA Form 086-0-33).

(g) Restrictions on Property Locations within Coastal Barrier Resources System

In accordance with the Coastal Barrier Resources Act, a Property is not eligible for FHA mortgage insurance if the improvements are or are proposed to be located within the Coastal Barrier Resources System.

Handbook 4000.1 144

Effective Date: 09/14/2015 | Last Revised: 07/10/2019
*Refer to the online version of SF Handbook 4000.1 for specific sections' effective dates

(2) Seller Must Be Owner of Record

(a) Standard

To be eligible for a mortgage insured by FHA, a Property must be purchased from the owner of record. The transaction may not involve any sale or assignment of the sales contract.

(b) Required Documentation

The Mortgagee must obtain documentation verifying that the seller is the owner of record.

Such documentation may include, but is not limited to:
- a property sales history report;
- a copy of the recorded deed from the seller; or
- other documentation, such as a copy of a property tax bill, title commitment, or binder, demonstrating the seller's ownership of the Property and the date it was acquired.

This requirement applies to all FHA purchase money Mortgages, regardless of the time between resales.

(3) Restrictions on Property Flipping

Property Flipping is indicative of a practice whereby recently acquired Property is resold for a considerable profit with an artificially inflated value.

(a) Definition

Property Flipping refers to the purchase and subsequent resale of a Property in a short period of time.

(b) Standard

(i) Time Restriction on Transfers of Title

The eligibility of a Property for a Mortgage insured by FHA is determined by the time that has elapsed between the date the seller has acquired title to the Property and the date of execution of the sales contract that will result in the FHA-insured Mortgage.

FHA defines the seller's date of acquisition as the date the seller acquired legal ownership of that Property. FHA defines the resale date as the date of execution of the sales contract by all parties intending to finance the Property with an FHA-insured Mortgage.

(ii) Restriction on Resales Occurring 90 Days or Fewer After Acquisition

A Property that is being resold 90 Days or fewer following the seller's date of acquisition is not eligible for an FHA-insured Mortgage.

(iii) Resales Occurring Between 91 Days and 180 Days After Acquisition

A Mortgagee must obtain a second appraisal by another Appraiser if:
- the resale date of a Property is between 91 and 180 Days following the acquisition of the Property by the seller; and
- the resale price is 100 percent or more over the price paid by the seller to acquire the Property.

If the second appraisal supports a value of the Property that is more than 5 percent lower than the value of the first appraisal, the lower value must be used as the Property Value in determining the Adjusted Value.

The cost of the second appraisal may not be charged to the Borrower.

(iv) Exceptions to Time Restrictions on Resale

Exceptions to time restrictions on resale are:
- Properties acquired by an employer or relocation agency in connection with the relocation of an employee;
- resales by HUD under its REO program;
- sales by other U.S. government agencies of Single Family Properties pursuant to programs operated by these agencies;
- sales of Properties by nonprofits approved to purchase HUD owned Single Family Properties at a discount with resale restrictions;
- sales of Properties that are acquired by the seller by inheritance;
- sales of Properties by state and federally-chartered financial institutions and Government-Sponsored Enterprises (GSE);
- sales of Properties by local and state government agencies; and
- sales of Properties within PDMDAs, only upon issuance of a notice of an exception from HUD.

The restrictions listed above and those in 24 CFR § 203.37a do not apply to a builder selling a newly built house or building a house for a Borrower planning to use FHA-insured financing.

(c) Required Documentation

The Mortgagee must obtain a 12 month chain of title documenting compliance with time restrictions on resales.

(4) Restriction on Investment Properties for Hotel and Transient Use

(a) Standard

The Mortgagee must obtain the Borrower's agreement that Investment Properties using FHA-insured financing will not be used for hotel or transient purposes, or otherwise rented for periods of less than 30 Days.

(b) Required Documentation

The Mortgagee must obtain a completed form HUD-92561, *Borrower's Contract with Respect to Hotel and Transient Use of Property,* for each Mortgage secured by:
- a two- to four-unit dwelling; or
- a Single Family dwelling that is one of a group of five or more dwellings owned by the Borrower within a two block radius.

(5) Mixed Use of Property

Mixed Use refers to a Property suitable for a combination of uses including any of the following: commercial, residential, retail, office or parking space. Mixed Use one- to four-unit Single Family Properties are eligible for FHA insurance, provided:
- a minimum of 51 percent of the entire building square footage is for residential use; and
- the commercial use will not affect the health and safety of the occupants of the residential Property.

(6) Property Assessed Clean Energy

Property Assessed Clean Energy (PACE) refers to an alternative means of financing energy and other PACE-allowed improvements for residential properties using financing provided by private enterprises in conjunction with state and local governments. Generally, the repayment of the PACE obligation is collected in the same manner as a special assessment tax; it is collected by the local government rather than paid directly by the Borrower to the party providing the PACE financing.

Generally, the PACE obligation is also secured in the same manner as a special assessment tax against the Property. In the event of a sale, including a foreclosure sale, of the Property with outstanding PACE financing, the obligation will continue with the Property causing the new homeowner to be responsible for the payments on the outstanding PACE amount. In cases of foreclosure, priority collection of delinquent payments for the PACE assessment may be waived or relinquished.

Properties which will remain encumbered with a PACE obligation are not eligible for FHA mortgage insurance.

(7) Dwelling Unit Limitation

(a) Standard

If the Mortgage will be secured by an Investment Property, including Mortgages for Governmental Entities or nonprofit Borrowers, the Borrower may not have a financial interest, regardless of the ownership or financing type, in more than seven Dwelling Units within a two block radius. In determining the number of Dwelling Units owned by the Borrower, the Mortgagee must count each Dwelling Unit in a two-, three-, and four-family Property.

(b) Required Documentation

If the Borrower owns six or more units within a two block radius, a map must be provided disclosing the locations of the units as evidence of compliance with FHA's seven unit limitation.

(B) Property Types

FHA's programs differ from one another primarily in terms of what types of Properties and financing are eligible. Except as otherwise stated in this *SF Handbook*, FHA's Single Family programs are limited to one- to four-family Properties that are owner-occupied Principal Residences. FHA insures Mortgages on Real Property secured by:
- detached or semi-detached dwellings
- Manufactured Housing
- townhouses or row houses
- individual units within FHA-approved Condominium Projects

FHA will not insure Single Family Mortgages secured by:
- commercial enterprises
- boarding houses
- hotels, motels and condotels
- tourist houses
- private clubs
- bed and breakfast establishments
- other transient housing

- Vacation Homes
- fraternity and sorority houses

(1) One Unit

A one-unit Property is a one-family dwelling.

(2) Two Unit

A two-unit Property is a Single Family residential Property with two individual dwellings.

The Mortgagee must obtain a completed form HUD-92561, *Borrower's Contract with Respect to Hotel and Transient Use of Property.*

(3) Three to Four Unit

A three- to four-unit Property is a Single Family residential Property with three to four individual dwellings.

The Mortgagee must obtain a completed form HUD-92561.

Self-Sufficiency Rental Income Eligibility

(a) Definition

Net Self-Sufficiency Rental Income refers to the Rental Income produced by the subject Property over and above the Principal, Interest, Taxes, and Insurance (PITI).

(b) Standard

The PITI divided by the monthly Net Self-Sufficiency Rental Income may not exceed 100 percent for three- to four-unit Properties.

(c) Calculation

Net Self-Sufficiency Rental Income is calculated by using the Appraiser's estimate of fair market rent from all units, including the unit the Borrower chooses for occupancy, and subtracting the greater of the Appraiser's estimate for vacancies and maintenance, or 25 percent of the fair market rent.

(4) Condominium Unit

A Condominium Unit is a Property contained in a multi-unit project that has individually-owned Dwelling units, which may be either attached in one or more Structures or detached from each other, and is primarily residential in use.

(a) Standard

A condominium development is created by state or local law and is characterized by fee-simple ownership of a unit, which is defined in the condominium documents, together with common areas. The property interest in these areas is both common and undivided on the part of all unit owners, each of whom belongs to the HOA that typically maintains the Property and collects assessments or dues from each unit owner.

A Condominium Project must be FHA approved before a Mortgage on an individual condominium unit can be insured.

(b) Site Condominiums

Site Condominiums are Single Family detached dwellings encumbered by a declaration of condominium covenants or condominium form of ownership and do not need to be FHA-approved.

Manufactured Housing condominium units may not be processed as Site Condominiums.

(5) Manufactured Housing

(a) Definition

Manufactured Housing is a Structure that is transportable in one or more sections. It may be part of a Condominium Project, provided the project meets applicable FHA requirements.

(b) Standard

To be eligible for FHA mortgage insurance as a Single Family Title II Mortgage, all Manufactured Housing must:
- be designed as a one-family dwelling;
- have a floor area of not less than 400 square feet;
- have the HUD Certification Label affixed or have obtained a letter of label verification issued on behalf of HUD, evidencing the house was constructed on or after June 15, 1976, in compliance with the Federal Manufactured Home Construction and Safety Standards;
- be classified as real estate (but need not be treated as real estate for purposes of state taxation);
- be built and remain on a permanent chassis;
- be designed to be used as a dwelling with a permanent foundation built in accordance with the Permanent Foundations Guide for Manufactured Housing (PFGMH); and

- have been directly transported from the manufacturer or the dealership to the site.

(c) Required Documentation

(i) HUD Certification Label

If the appraisal indicates the HUD Certification Label is missing from the Manufactured Housing unit, the Mortgagee must obtain label verification from the Institute for Building Technology and Safety (IBTS).

(ii) PFGMH Certification

The Mortgagee must obtain a certification by an engineer or architect, who is licensed/registered in the state where the Manufactured Home is located, attesting to compliance with the PFGMH.

The Mortgagee may obtain a copy of the foundation certification from a previous FHA-insured Mortgage, showing that the foundation met the guidelines published in the PFGMH that were in effect at the time of certification, provided there are no alterations and/or observable damage to the foundation since the original certification.

If the Appraiser notes additions or alterations to the Manufactured Housing unit, the Mortgagee must ensure the addition was addressed in the foundation certification.

If the additions or alterations were not addressed in the foundation certification, the Mortgagee must obtain:
- an inspection by the state administrative agency that inspects Manufactured Housing for compliance; or
- certification of the structural integrity from a licensed structural engineer if the state does not employ inspectors.

(C) Property Valuation

The Mortgagee is responsible for obtaining an appraisal to verify the value of the Property and the Property's compliance with HUD's Minimum Property Standards (MPS).

(1) Integrity of Valuation Process: Communications with Mortgagees

The Mortgagee must ensure the integrity of the valuation process by ensuring the valuation process is free from conflicts of interest and the appearance of conflicts of interest.

(a) Standard

The Mortgagee must prevent its staff, or any person who is compensated on a commission basis upon the successful completion of a Mortgage, or who reports, ultimately, to any officer of the Mortgagee not independent of the mortgage production staff and process, from having substantive communications with an Appraiser relating to or having an impact on valuation, including ordering or managing an appraisal assignment. Normal communications necessary to processing of a case is permissible, but cannot attempt to influence the Appraiser.

The underwriter who has responsibility for the quality of the appraisal report is allowed to request clarifications and discuss with the Appraiser components of the appraisal that influence its quality.

(b) Exception for Smaller Mortgagees

When absolute lines of independence cannot be achieved because of the Mortgagee's small size and limited staff, the Mortgagee must clearly demonstrate that it has prudent safeguards to isolate its collateral evaluation process from influence or interference from its mortgage production process.

(2) Communications with Third Parties

The underwriter may request a clarification or reconsideration of value from the Appraiser, following the requirements in Reconsideration of Value. The Mortgagee may not discuss the contents of an appraisal with anyone other than the Borrower.

(3) Verifying HUD's Minimum Property Standards/Minimum Property Requirements

As the on-site representative for the Mortgagee, the Appraiser provides preliminary verification that a Property meets the Property Acceptability Criteria, which include HUD's Minimum Property Requirements (MPR) or Minimum Property Standards (MPS).

When examination of a Property reveals noncompliance with the Property Acceptability Criteria, the Appraiser must note all repairs necessary to make the Property comply with HUD's Property Acceptability Criteria, together with the estimated cost to cure.

v. Legal Restrictions on Conveyance (Free Assumability)

The Mortgagee must determine that any legal restrictions on conveyance conform with the requirements in 24 CFR § 203.41.

In accordance with 24 CFR § 203.41 (d)(1)(ii), FHA considers a reasonable share of appreciation to be at least 50 percent. HUD does not object to affordable housing programs whereby the homeowner's share of appreciation is on a sliding scale beginning at zero, provided that within two years the homeowner would be permitted to retain 50 percent of the appreciation. If the program sets a maximum sales price restriction, the Borrower must be permitted to retain 100 percent of the appreciation.

A Property that contains leased equipment, or operates with a leased energy system or Power Purchase Agreement (PPA), may be eligible for FHA-insured financing but only when such agreements are free of restrictions that prevent the Borrower from freely transferring the Property.

Such agreements are acceptable, provided they do not cause a conveyance (ownership transfer) of the insured Property by the Borrower to:
- be void, or voidable by a third party;
- be the basis of contractual liability of the Borrower (including rights of first refusal, pre-emptive rights or options related to a Borrower's efforts to convey);
- terminate or be subject to termination all or part of the interest held by the Borrower;
- be subject to the consent of a third party;
- be subject to limits on the amount of sales proceeds a Borrower can retain (e.g., due to a lien, "due on sale" clause, etc.);
- be grounds for accelerating the insured Mortgage; or
- be grounds for increasing the interest rate of the insured Mortgage.

Any restrictions resulting from provisions of the lease or PPA do not conflict with FHA regulations unless they include provisions encumbering the Real Property or restricting the transfer of the Real Property.

Legal restrictions on conveyance of Real Property (i.e., the house) that could require the consent of a third party (e.g., energy provider, system owner, etc.), include but are not limited to, credit approval of a new purchaser before the seller can convey the Real Property, unless such provisions may be terminated at the option of, and with no cost to, the owner.

If an agreement for an energy system lease or PPA could cause restriction upon transfer of the house, the Property is subject to impermissible legal restrictions and is generally ineligible for FHA insurance.

2. Allowable Mortgage Parameters

This section provides the basic underwriting standards for Single Family (one to four units) Mortgages insured under the National Housing Act. When underwriting a Mortgage, the Mortgagee must determine the Borrower's creditworthiness, capacity to repay, and available capital to support the Mortgage. The Mortgagee must also examine the Property to ensure it provides sufficient collateral for the Mortgage.

For each Mortgage the Federal Housing Administration (FHA) insures, the Mortgagee must fully comply with the following underwriting procedures.

a. Maximum Mortgage Amounts

A Mortgage that is to be insured by FHA cannot exceed the Nationwide Mortgage Limits, the nationwide area mortgage limit, or the maximum Loan-to-Value (LTV) ratio. The maximum LTV ratios vary depending upon the type of Borrower, type of transaction (purchase or refinance), program type, and stage of construction.

Under most programs, the maximum Mortgage is the lesser of the Nationwide Mortgage Limit for the area, or a percentage of the Adjusted Value.

For purchase transactions, the Adjusted Value is the lesser of:
- purchase price less any inducements to purchase; or
- the Property Value.

For refinance transactions:
- For Properties acquired by the Borrower within 12 months of the case number assignment date, the Adjusted Value is the lesser of:
  - the Borrower's purchase price, plus any documented improvements made subsequent to the purchase; or
  - the Property Value.
- Properties acquired by the Borrower within 12 months of case number assignment by inheritance or through a gift from a Family Member may utilize the calculation of Adjusted Value for properties purchased 12 months or greater.
- For properties acquired by the Borrower greater than or equal to 12 months prior to the case number assignment date, the Adjusted Value is the Property Value.

i. National Housing Act's Statutory Limits

The National Housing Act establishes the maximum Mortgage limits and the mortgage amounts for all FHA mortgage insurance programs.

ii. Nationwide Mortgage Limits

Mortgage limits are calculated based on the median house prices in accordance with the statute. FHA's Single Family mortgage limits are set by Metropolitan Statistical Area and county and will be published periodically. FHA's Single Family mortgage limits are available by MSA and county, or by downloading a complete listing. FHA publishes updated limits effective for each calendar year.

These limits will be set at or between the low cost area and high cost area limits based on the median house prices for the area.

(A) Requests for Local Increases

Any requests to change high-cost area Mortgage limits determined by HUD must be received by FHA's Santa Ana Homeownership Center (HOC) at the address below no later than 30 Days from the publication of the limits each year. Any changes in area Mortgage limits as a result of valid appeals will be retroactively in effect for case numbers assigned on or after January 1 of each year.

Each request to change Mortgage limits must contain sufficient housing sales price data, listing one-family Properties sold in an area within the look-back period, January through August of the previous year. Requests should differentiate between Single Family residential Properties, and condominiums or cooperative housing units. Ideally, data provided should also distinguish between distressed and non-distressed sales. Requests for a change will only be considered for counties for which HUD does not already have home sales transaction data for the calculation of Mortgage limits.

All requests for local area increases in all areas will be handled exclusively by FHA's Santa Ana HOC:

> Attn: Program Support/Loan Limits
> U.S. Department of Housing and Urban Development
> Santa Ana Homeownership Center
> Santa Ana Federal Building
> 34 Civic Center Plaza, Room 7015
> Santa Ana, CA 92701-4003

(B) Low Cost Area

The FHA national low cost area mortgage limits, which are set at 65 percent of the national conforming limit of $424,100 for a one-unit Property, are, by property unit number, as follows:
- One-unit: $275,665
- Two-unit: $352,950
- Three-unit: $426,625
- Four-unit: $530,150

(C) High Cost Area

The FHA national high cost area mortgage limits, which are set at 150 percent of the national conforming limit of $424,100 for a one-unit Property, are, by property unit number, as follows:
- One-unit: $636,150
- Two-unit: $814,500
- Three-unit: $984,525
- Four-unit: $1,223,475

(D) Special Exceptions for Alaska, Hawaii, Guam, and the Virgin Islands

FHA adjusts mortgage limit ceilings for the special exception areas of Alaska (AK), Hawaii (HI), Guam (GU) and the Virgin Islands (VI) to account for higher costs of construction. These Special Exception Area limit ceilings are set at 150 percent of FHA's High Cost Area mortgage limits, rounded down to the nearest $25. These four special exception areas have a higher ceiling as follows:
- One-unit: $954,225
- Two-unit: $1,221,750
- Three-unit: $1,476,775
- Four-unit: $1,835,200

iii. Financing of Upfront Mortgage Insurance Premium

Unless otherwise stated in this section (Origination through Post-Closing/Endorsement), restrictions to mortgage amounts and LTVs are based upon the amount prior to the financing of the Upfront Mortgage Insurance Premium (UFMIP) (Base Loan Amount). The total mortgage amount may be increased by the financed UFMIP amount.

iv. Calculating Maximum Mortgage Amounts on Purchases

The maximum mortgage amount that FHA will insure on a specific purchase is calculated by multiplying the appropriate LTV percentage by the Adjusted Value.

In order for FHA to insure this maximum mortgage amount, the Borrower must make a Minimum Required Investment (MRI) of at least 3.5 percent of the Adjusted Value.

v. Additions to the Mortgage Amount for Repair and Improvement

(A) Appraiser Required Repairs

A Mortgagee may add repair costs to the sales price before calculating the mortgage amount if:
- the repairs are required by the Appraiser to meet HUD's MPR;
- the repairs are paid for by the Borrower; and

- the sales contract or addendum identifies the Borrower as the party responsible for payment and completion of the repairs.

The maximum amount of repair costs that may be added to the sales price is the lesser of:

- the amount by which the value of the Property exceeds the sales price;
- the Appraiser's estimate of repairs; or
- the amount of the contractor's bid.

(B) Energy-Related Weatherization Repairs and Improvements

A Mortgagee may add energy-related weatherization costs, to be paid for by the Borrower, in accordance with Weatherization policies.

(C) Solar Energy Systems

A Mortgagee may add the cost of a solar energy system (including active and passive solar- and wind-driven systems) to the Mortgage in accordance with Solar and Wind Technologies policies.

When adding the cost of a solar energy system to the mortgage amount, the maximum insurable mortgage limit may be exceeded by up to 20 percent.

b. Loan-to-Value Limits

The determination of the maximum LTV percentage available is influenced by:
- the particular mortgage insurance program (See Programs and Products); and
- the transaction type.

The Mortgagee must apply the lowest applicable LTV percentage as determined under the requirements in this section.

i. LTV Limitations Based on Borrower's Credit Score (Applies to All Transactions)

The Mortgagee must review the credit report to determine the Borrower's Minimum Decision Credit Score (MDCS), except for Mortgages to be insured under Section 247, Section 248, Streamline Refinances, and Assumptions.

The MDCS will be used to determine the maximum insured financing available to a Borrower with traditional credit.

The table below describes the relationship between the Borrower's MDCS and the LTV ratio for which they are eligible. Borrowers with non-traditional or insufficient credit histories are eligible for maximum financing, but must be underwritten using the procedures in Manual Underwriting.

If the Borrower's Minimum Decision Credit Score is...	Then the Borrower is...
at or above 580	eligible for maximum financing.
between 500 and 579	limited to a maximum LTV of 90%.

ii. Purchase

For purchase transactions, the maximum LTV is 96.5 percent of the Adjusted Value.

For special programs and products including refinances, the maximum LTV is determined in accordance with requirements listed in this *SF Handbook's* Programs and Products section.

(A) LTV Limitations Based on Identities of Interest

(1) Definitions

An Identity-of-Interest Transaction is a sale between parties with an existing Business Relationship or between Family Members.

Business Relationship refers to an association between individuals or companies entered into for commercial purposes.

(2) Maximum LTV for Identity-of-Interest and Tenant/Landlord Transactions

The maximum LTV percentage for Identity-of-Interest transactions on Principal Residences is restricted to 85 percent.

The maximum LTV percentage for a transaction where a tenant-landlord relationship exists at the time of contract execution is restricted to 85 percent.

(3) Exceptions to the Maximum LTV

The 85 percent maximum LTV restriction does not apply for Identity-of-Interest transactions under the following circumstances.

(a) Family Member Transactions

The 85 percent LTV restriction may be exceeded if a Borrower purchases as their Principal Residence:
- the Principal Residence of another Family Member; or
- a Property owned by another Family Member in which the Borrower has been a tenant for at least six months immediately predating the sales contract. A lease or other written evidence to verify occupancy is required.

(b) Builder's Employee Purchase

The 85 percent LTV restriction may be exceeded if an employee of a builder, who is not a Family Member, purchases one of the builder's new houses or models as a Principal Residence.

(c) Corporate Transfer

The 85 percent LTV restriction may be exceeded if a corporation transfers an employee to another location, purchases the employee's house, and sells the house to another employee.

(d) Tenant Purchase

The 85 percent LTV restriction may be exceeded if the current tenant purchases the Property where the tenant has rented the Property for at least six months immediately predating the sales contract.

A lease or other written evidence to verify occupancy is required.

(B) LTV Limitations Based on Non-Occupying Borrower Status

(1) Definition

A Non-Occupying Borrower Transaction refers to a transaction involving two or more Borrowers in which one or more of the Borrower(s) will not occupy the Property as their Principal Residence.

(2) Maximum LTV for Non-Occupying Borrower Transaction

For Non-Occupying Borrower Transactions, the maximum LTV is 75 percent. The LTV can be increased to a maximum of 96.5 percent if the Borrowers are Family Members, provided the transaction does not involve:
- a Family Member selling to a Family Member who will be a non-occupying co-Borrower; or
- a transaction on a two- to four-unit Property.

iii. Refinance

For refinance transactions, the maximum LTV is determined in accordance with Refinance program specific requirements.

iv. New Construction

For New Construction transactions, the maximum LTV is determined in accordance with New Construction program specific requirements.

c. **Required Investment**

i. **Total Required Investment**

Total Required Investment refers to the amount the Borrower must contribute to the transaction including the Borrower's downpayment and the Borrower-paid transaction costs. The Total Required Investment includes the Minimum Required Investment (MRI).

ii. **Minimum Required Investment**

Minimum Required Investment (MRI) refers to the Borrower's contribution in cash or its equivalent required by Section 203(b)(9) of the National Housing Act, which represents at least 3.5 percent of the Adjusted Value of the Property.

d. **Maximum Mortgage Term**

The maximum mortgage term may not exceed 30 years from the date that amortization begins. FHA does not require that mortgage terms be in five year multiples.

e. **Mortgage Insurance Premiums**

FHA collects a one-time Upfront Mortgage Insurance Premium (UFMIP) and an annual insurance premium, also referred to as the periodic or monthly MIP, which is collected in monthly installments.

i. **Upfront Mortgage Insurance Premium**

(A) **Upfront Mortgage Insurance Premium Amount**

Most FHA mortgage insurance programs require the payment of UFMIP, which may be financed into the Mortgage. The UFMIP is not considered when calculating the area-based Nationwide Mortgage Limits and LTV limits.

The UFMIP charged for all amortization terms is 175 Basis Points (bps), unless otherwise stated in the applicable Programs and Products or in the MIP chart.

The UFMIP must be entirely financed into the Mortgage or paid entirely in cash. Any UFMIP amounts paid in cash are added to the total cash settlement requirements. However, if the UFMIP is financed into the Mortgage, the entire amount is to be financed except for any amount less than $1.00.

The mortgage amount must be rounded down to the nearest whole dollar amount, regardless of whether the UFMIP is financed or paid in cash.

(B) **Refund and Credit of Upfront Mortgage Insurance Premium**

The UFMIP is not refundable, except in connection with the refinancing to a new FHA-insured Mortgage. See the Refinances Section.

ii. Annual (or Periodic) Mortgage Insurance Premium

The periodic MIP is an annual MIP that is payable monthly. The amount of the annual MIP is based on the LTV ratio, Base Loan Amount and the term of the Mortgage.

Calculation of the MIP

The MIP rate and duration of the MIP assessment period vary by mortgage term, Base Loan Amount, and LTV ratio for the Mortgage, as shown in the MIP chart.

3. Underwriting the Property

The Mortgagee must underwrite the completed appraisal report to determine if the Property provides sufficient collateral for the FHA-insured Mortgage. The appraisal and Property must comply with the requirements in Appraiser and Property Requirements for Title II Forward and Reverse Mortgages. The appraisal must be reported in accordance with Acceptable Appraisal Reporting Forms and Protocols.

a. Property Acceptability Criteria

The Mortgagee must evaluate the appraisal and any supporting documentation to determine if the Property complies with HUD's Property Acceptability Criteria. Existing and New Construction Properties must comply with Application of Minimum Property Requirements and Minimum Property Standards by Construction Status.

i. Defective Conditions

The Mortgagee must evaluate the appraisal in accordance with Defective Conditions to determine if the Property is eligible for an FHA-insured Mortgage. If defective conditions exist and correction is not feasible, the Mortgagee must reject the Property.

ii. Minimum Property Requirements and Minimum Property Standards

As the on-site representative for the Mortgagee, the Appraiser provides preliminary verification that a Property meets the Property Acceptability Criteria, which includes HUD's Minimum Property Requirements (MPR) and Minimum Property Standards (MPS).

Minimum Property Requirements refer to general requirements that all homes insured by FHA be safe, sound, and secure.

Minimum Property Standards refer to regulatory requirements relating to the safety, soundness and security of New Construction.

When examination of a Property reveals noncompliance with the Property Acceptability Criteria, the Appraiser must note all repairs necessary to make the Property comply with HUD's Property Acceptability Criteria, together with the estimated cost to cure. If the Appraiser cannot determine that a Property meets HUD's MPR or MPS, the Mortgagee may obtain an inspection from a qualified Entity to make the determination. Mortgagees must use professional judgment in determining when inspections are necessary to determine that a property meets MPR or MPS. Mortgagees must also use professional judgment in determining when a Property condition poses a threat to the health and safety of the occupant and/or jeopardizes the soundness and structural integrity of the Property, such that additional inspections and/or repairs are necessary.

The Mortgagee must confirm that the Property complies with the following eligibility criteria. If the Mortgage is to be insured under the 203(k) program, the Mortgagee must confirm that the Property will comply with the following eligibility criteria upon completion of repairs and improvements.

(A) Encroachment

The Mortgagee must ensure the subject's dwelling, garage, or other improvements do not encroach onto an adjacent Property, right-of-way, utility Easement, or building restriction line. The Mortgagee must also ensure a neighboring dwelling, garage, or other improvements do not encroach onto the subject Property. Encroachment by the subject or adjacent Property fences is acceptable provided such Encroachment does not affect the marketability of the subject Property.

(B) Overhead Electric Power

The Mortgagee must confirm that any Overhead Electric Power Transmission Lines do not pass directly over any dwelling, Structure or related property improvement, including pools. The power line must be relocated for a Property to be eligible for FHA-insured financing.

The residential service drop line may not pass directly over any pool, spa or water feature.

If the dwelling or related property improvements are located within the Easement area, the Mortgagee must obtain a certification from the appropriate utility company or local regulatory agency stating that the relationship between the improvements and Local Distribution Lines conforms to local standards and is safe.

(C) Access to Property

The Mortgagee must confirm that the Property is provided with a safe pedestrian access and Adequate Vehicular Access from a public or private street. Streets must either be dedicated to public use and maintenance, or retained as private streets protected by permanent recorded Easements.

Private streets, including shared driveways, must be protected by permanent recorded Easements, ownership interest, or be owned and maintained by an HOA. Shared driveways do not require a joint maintenance agreement.

(D) Onsite Hazards and Nuisances

The Mortgagee must require corrective work to mitigate potential adverse effects from any onsite hazards or nuisances reported by the Appraiser.

(E) Abandoned Gas and Oil Well

If the Property contains any abandoned gas or oil wells, the Mortgagee must obtain a letter from the local jurisdiction or appropriate state agency stating that the subject well was permanently abandoned in a safe manner.

If the Property contains any abandoned petroleum product wells, the Mortgagee must ensure that a qualified petroleum engineer has inspected the Property and assessed the risk, and that the appropriate state authorities have concurred on clearance recommendations.

(F) Requirements for Living Unit

The Mortgagee must confirm that each living unit contains:
- a continuing and sufficient supply of safe and potable water under adequate pressure and of appropriate quality for all household uses;
- sanitary facilities and a safe method of sewage disposal. Every living unit must have at least one bathroom, which must include, at a minimum, a water closet, lavatory, and a bathtub or shower;
- adequate space for healthful and comfortable living conditions;
- heating adequate for healthful and comfortable living conditions;
- domestic hot water; and
- electricity adequate for lighting, cooking and for mechanical equipment used in the living unit.

The Mortgagee must ensure that appliances that are to remain and that contribute to the market value opinion are operational.

FHA does not have a minimum size requirement for one- to four-family dwellings and condominium units. For Manufactured Housing requirements, see the Manufactured Housing section.

(G) Swimming Pools

The Mortgagee must confirm that any swimming pools comply with all local ordinances.

(H) Structural Conditions

The Mortgagee must confirm that the Structure of the Property will be serviceable for the life of the Mortgage.

The Mortgagee must confirm that all foundations will be serviceable for the life of the Mortgage and adequate to withstand all normal loads imposed.

(I) Economic Life/Section 223(e)

The Mortgagee must confirm that the term of the Mortgage is less than or equal to the remaining economic life of the Property.

If the Property is located in an older, declining urban area and the remaining economic life produces an unreasonably short mortgage term by reason of its location, the Property may be acceptable under Section 223(e), provided:
- the area is reasonably able to support adequate housing and living conditions for families of lower income levels;
- the location features adversely affecting the desirability and usefulness of the Property do not endanger the health and safety of its occupants;
- the Property is marketable to the typical occupant of the area;
- the physical life of the Property is greater than or equal to the term of the Mortgage; and
- the Mortgage represents an overall acceptable risk as determined by the Jurisdictional HOC.

All Mortgages to be insured under Section 223(e) must be submitted to the Jurisdictional HOC for prior approval.

(J) Environmental

The Mortgagee must confirm that the Property is frcc of all known environmental and safety hazards and adverse conditions that may affect the health and safety of the occupants, the Property's ability to serve as collateral, and the structural soundness of the improvements.

(K) Lead-Based Paint

The Mortgagee must confirm that the Property is free of lead paint hazards.

(L) Methamphetamine Contamination

If the Mortgagee or the Appraiser identifies a Property as contaminated by the presence of methamphetamine (meth), either by its manufacture or by consumption, the Property is ineligible due to this environmental hazard until the Property is certified safe for habitation.

(M) Repair Requirements

The Mortgagee must determine which repairs must be made for an existing Property to be eligible for FHA-insured financing.

(N) Utility Services

If utilities are not located on Easements that have been permanently dedicated to the local government or appropriate public utility body, the Mortgagee must confirm that this information is recorded on the deed record.

(O) Water Supply Systems

(1) Public Water Supply System

The Mortgagee must confirm that a connection is made to a public or Community Water System whenever feasible and available at a reasonable cost. If connection costs to the public or community system are not reasonable, the existing onsite systems are acceptable, provided they are functioning properly and meet the requirements of the local health department.

When a public water supply system is present, the water quality is considered to be safe and potable and to meet the requirements of the health authority with jurisdiction unless:
- the Appraiser indicates deficiencies with the water or notifies the Mortgagee that the water is unsafe; or
- the health authority with jurisdiction issues a public notice indicating that the water is unsafe.

(2) Individual Water Supply Systems (Wells) [Text was deleted in this section.]

When an Individual Water Supply System is present, the Mortgagee must ensure that the water quality meets the requirements of the health authority with jurisdiction.

If there are no local (or state) water quality standards, then water quality must meet the standards set by the EPA, as presented in the National Primary Drinking Water regulations in 40 CFR §§ 141 and 142.

(a) Requirements for Well Water Testing

A well water test is required for, but not limited to, Properties:
- that are newly constructed;
- where an Appraiser has reported deficiencies with a well or the well water;
- where water is reported to be unsafe or known to be unsafe;
- located in close proximity to dumps, landfills, industrial sites, farms (pesticides) or other sites that could contain hazardous wastes; or
- where the distance between the well and septic system is less than 100 feet.

All testing must be performed by a disinterested third party. This includes the collection and transport of the water sample collected at the water supply source. The sample must be collected and tested by the local health authority, a commercial testing laboratory, a licensed sanitary engineer, or other party that is acceptable to the local health authority. At no time will the Borrower/owner or other Interested Party collect and/or transport the sample.

Requirements for the location of wells for FHA-insured Properties are located in 24 CFR § 200.926d (f) (3).

The following tables provide the minimum distance required between wells and sources of pollution for Existing Construction:

	Individual Water Supply System for Minimum Property Requirements for Existing Construction*
1	Property line/10 feet
2	Septic tank/50 feet
3	Drain field/100 feet
4	Septic tank drain field reduced to 75 feet if allowed by local authority
5	If the subject Property line is adjacent to residential Property then local well distance requirements prevail. If the subject Property is adjacent to non-residential Property or roadway, there needs to be a separation distance of at least 10 feet from the property line.
* distance requirements of local authority prevail if greater than stated above	

The following provides the minimum requirements for water wells:

	Water Wells Minimum Property Standards for New Construction 24 CFR § 200.926d(f)(1)
1	Lead-free piping
2	If no local chemical and bacteriological water standards, state standards apply
3	Connection of public water whenever feasible
4	Wells must deliver water flow of five gallons per minute over at least a four-hour period

	Water Wells Minimum Property Requirements for Existing Construction
1	Existing wells must deliver water flow of three to five gallons per minute
2	No exposure to environmental contamination
3	Continuing supply of safe and potable water
4	Domestic hot water
5	Water quality must meet requirements of local jurisdiction or the EPA if no local standard

(b) Required Documentation

The Mortgagee must obtain a valid water test from the local health authority or a lab qualified to conduct water testing in the jurisdictional state or local authority.

(3) Shared Wells

The Mortgagee must confirm that a Shared Well:
- serves existing Properties that cannot feasibly be connected to an acceptable public or Community Water supply System;
- is capable of providing a continuous supply of water to involved Dwelling Units so that each existing Property simultaneously will be assured of at least three gallons per minute (five gallons per minute for Proposed Construction) over a continuous four-hour period. (The well itself may have a lesser yield if pressurized storage is provided in an amount that will make 720 gallons of water available to each connected existing dwelling during a continuous four-hour period or 1,200 gallons of water available to each proposed dwelling during a continuous four-hour period. The shared well system yield must be demonstrated by a certified pumping test or other means acceptable to all agreeing parties.);
- provides safe and potable water. An inspection is required under the same circumstances as an individual well. This may be evidenced by a letter from the health authority having jurisdiction or, in the absence of local health department standards, by a certified water quality analysis demonstrating that the well water complies with the EPA's National Interim Primary Drinking Water Regulations;
- has a valve on each dwelling service line as it leaves the well so that water may be shut off to each served dwelling without interrupting service to the other Properties; and
- serves no more than four living units or Properties.

(a) Requirements for Well Water Testing

A well water test is required for, but not limited to, Properties:
- that are newly constructed;
- where an Appraiser has reported deficiencies with a well or the well water;
- where water is reported to be unsafe or known to be unsafe;
- located in close proximity to dumps, landfills, industrial sites, farms (pesticides) or other sites that could contain hazardous wastes; or
- where the distance between the well and septic system is less than 100 feet.

All testing must be performed by a disinterested third party. This includes the collection and transport of the water sample collected at the water supply source. The sample must be collected and tested by the local health authority, a commercial testing laboratory, a licensed sanitary engineer, or other party that is acceptable to the local health authority. At no time will the Borrower/owner or other Interested Party collect and/or transport the sample.

For both proposed and existing Properties, the Mortgagee must ensure that the shared well agreement complies with the guidance provided in the following table.

Item	Provisions that must be reflected in any acceptable shared well agreement include the following:
1	Require that the agreement is binding upon signatory parties and their successors in title, recorded in local deed records when executed and recorded, and reflects joiner by any Mortgagee holding a Mortgage on any Property connected to the Shared Well.
2	Permit well water sampling and testing by the local authority at the request of any party at any time.
3	Require that corrective measures be implemented if testing reveals a significant water quality deficiency, but only with the consent of a majority of all parties.
4	Ensure continuity of water service to "supplied" parties if the "supplying" party has no further need for the shared well system. ("Supplied" parties normally should assume all costs for their continuing water supply.)
5	Prohibit well water usage by any party for other than bona fide domestic purposes.
6	Prohibit connection of any additional living unit to the shared well system without: • the consent of all parties; • the appropriate amendment of the agreement; and • compliance with item 3.
7	Prohibit any party from locating or relocating any element of an individual sewage disposal system within 75 feet (100 feet for Proposed Construction) of the Shared Well.
8	Establish Easements for all elements of the system, ensuring access and necessary working space for system operation, maintenance, improvement, inspection and testing.
9	Specify that no party may install landscaping or improvements that will impair use of the Easements.

Item	Provisions that must be reflected in any acceptable shared well agreement include the following:
10	Specify that any removal and replacement of preexisting site improvements, necessary for system operation, maintenance, replacement, improvement, inspection or testing, will be at the cost of their owner, except for costs to remove and replace common boundary fencing or walls, which must be shared equally between or among parties.
11	Establish the right of any party to act to correct an emergency in the absence of the other parties onsite. An emergency must be defined as failure of any shared portion of the system to deliver water upon demand.
12	Permit an agreement amendment to ensure equitable readjustment of shared costs when there may be significant changes in well pump energy rates or the occupancy or use of an involved Property.
13	Require the consent of a majority of all parties upon cost sharing, except in emergencies, before actions are taken for system maintenance, replacement or improvement.
14	Require that any necessary replacement or improvement of a system element(s) will at least restore original system performance.
15	Specify required cost sharing for: • the energy supply for the well pump; • system maintenance, including repairs, testing, inspection and disinfection; • system component replacement due to wear, obsolescence, incrustation or corrosion; and • system improvement to increase the service life of a material or component to restore well yield or to provide necessary system protection.
16	Specify that no party is responsible for unilaterally incurred shared well debts of another party, except for correction of emergency situations. Emergency correction costs must be equally shared.
17	Require that each party be responsible for: • prompt repair of any detected leak in this water service line or plumbing system; • repair costs to correct system damage caused by a resident or guest at their Property; and • necessary repair or replacement of the service line connecting the system to the dwelling.
18	Require equal sharing of repair costs for system damage caused by persons other than a resident or guest at a Property sharing the well.
19	Ensure equal sharing of costs for abandoning all or part of the shared system so that contamination of ground water or other hazards will be avoided.

Item	Provisions that must be reflected in any acceptable shared well agreement include the following:
20	Ensure prompt collection from all parties and prompt payment of system operation, maintenance, replacement or improvement costs.
21	Specify that the recorded agreement may not be amended during the term of a federally-insured or -guaranteed Mortgage on any Property served, except as provided in items 5 and 11 above.
22	Provide for binding arbitration of any dispute or impasse between parties with regard to the system or terms of agreement. Binding arbitration must be through the American Arbitration Association or a similar body and may be initiated at any time by any party to the agreement. Parties to the agreement must equally share arbitration costs.

(b) Required Documentation

The Mortgagee must obtain a valid water test from the local health authority or a lab qualified to conduct water testing in the jurisdictional state or local authority.

(P) Individual Residential Water Purification Systems

(1) Definition

An Individual Residential Water Purification System refers to equipment, either point-of-entry or point-of-use, installed on Properties that otherwise do not have access to a continuous supply of safe and potable water.

(2) Standard

If a Property does not have access to a continuous supply of safe and potable water without the use of a water purification system, the Mortgagee must ensure that the Property has an individual residential water purification system as well as a service contract for the ongoing maintenance of the Property, a plan approved by the local or state health authority, and an escrow account.

(a) Approved Equipment for Individual Residential Water Purification Systems

Water purification equipment must be approved by a nationally recognized testing laboratory acceptable to the local or state health authority. The Mortgagee must obtain a certification from a local or state health authority which certifies that:

- A point-of-entry or point-of-use water purification system is on the Property. If the system employs point-of use equipment, the purification system must be employed on each water supply source (faucet) serving the Property. Where point-of-entry systems are used, separate water supply systems carrying untreated water for flushing toilets may be constructed.

- The system is sufficient to ensure an uninterrupted supply of safe and potable water adequate to meet household needs.
- The water supply, when treated by the equipment, meets the requirements of the local or state health authority, and has been determined to meet local or state quality standards for drinking water. If neither state nor local standards are applicable, then quality must be determined in accordance with standards set by the Environmental Protection Agency (EPA) pursuant to the Safe Drinking Water Act in 40 CFR Parts 141 and 142.
- A plan exists that provides for the monitoring, servicing, maintenance, and replacement of the water equipment, and the plan meets the service contract requirements.

(b) Borrower Notice of Water Purification System

The Mortgagee must provide written notification to the Borrower that the Property has a hazardous water supply that requires treatment in order to remain safe and acceptable for human consumption. The notification to the Borrower must identify specific contaminants in the water supply serving the Property, and the related health hazard arising from the presence of those contaminants.

The Mortgagee must ensure that the Borrower has received a written estimate of the maintenance and replacement costs of the equipment necessary to ensure continuous safe drinking water.

(c) Service Contract for Individual Residential Water Purification Systems

Before mortgage closing, the Mortgagee must ensure that the Borrower has entered into a service contract with an organization or individual specifically approved by the local or state health authority to carry out the provisions of the required plan for the servicing, maintenance, repair, and replacement of the water purification equipment.

(d) Approved Plan for Individual Residential Water Purification Systems

An approved plan is a contract entered into by the Borrower and Mortgagee and approved by the local or state health authority, and that sets out conditions as described below that must be met by the parties as a condition to insurance of the Mortgage by HUD.

The plan must set forth the respective responsibilities to be assumed by the Borrower and the Mortgagee, as well as the other entities who will implement the plan, such as the health authority and the service contractor. In particular:

- The plan must set out the responsibilities of the health authority for monitoring and enforcing the performance of the service contractor, including any successor contractor that the health authority may later have occasion to name. By its approval of the plan, the health authority documents its acceptance of these responsibilities, and the plan should so indicate.

- The plan must provide for the monitoring of the operation of the water purification equipment, as well as for servicing (including disinfecting) and repairing and replacing the system as frequently as necessary, taking into consideration the system's design, anticipated use, and the type and level of contaminants present. Installation, servicing, repair, and replacement of the water purification system must be performed by an individual or organization approved for this purpose by the local or state health authority and identified in the plan. The plan must refer to specific terms and conditions of the required service contract.

- Under the plan, responsibility for monitoring the performance of the service contractor and for ensuring that the water purification system is properly serviced, repaired, and replaced rests with the local or state health authority that approved the plan. The plan must confer on the health authority all powers necessary to effect compliance by the service contractor. The health authority's powers must include the authority to notify the Borrower of any noncompliance by the service contractor. The plan must provide that upon any notification of noncompliance received from the health authority, the Borrower may discharge the service contractor for cause and appoint a successor organization or individual as service contractor.

- The Mortgagee must ensure that any plan developed in accordance with this section must provide that an analysis of the water supply must be obtained from the local or state health authority no less frequently than annually, but more frequently if determined at any time to be necessary by the health authority or by the service contractor.

The plan must provide that if the dwelling served by the water purification system is refinanced, or is sold or otherwise transferred with a HUD-insured Mortgage, the plan will:

- continue in full force and effect;
- impose an obligation on the Borrower to notify any subsequent purchaser or transferee of the necessity for the water purification system and for its proper maintenance, and of the obligation to make escrow payments; and

- require the Borrower to furnish the purchaser with a copy of the plan before any sales contract is signed.

(e) Escrow for Maintenance and Replacement of Individual Residential Water Purification Systems

The Mortgagee must establish and maintain an escrow account to ensure proper servicing, maintenance, repair, and replacement of the water purification equipment. To the extent permitted under RESPA, the amount to be collected and escrowed by the Mortgagee must be based upon information provided by the manufacturer for the maintenance and replacement of the water purification equipment and for other charges anticipated by the service contractor. The initial monthly escrow amount must be stated in the plan. Disbursements from the account will be limited to costs associated with the normal servicing, maintenance, repair, or replacement of the water purification equipment. Disbursements may only be made to the service contractor or its successor, to equipment suppliers, to the local or state health authority for the performance of testing or other required services, or to another entity approved by the health authority. The Mortgagee must maintain the escrow account as long as water purification remains necessary and the Mortgage is insured by HUD.

The Mortgagee must provide the Borrower with the Water Purification Equipment Rider for signature.

(3) Required Documentation

(a) Borrower Notice of Water Purification System

A copy of the notification statement (including cost estimates), dated before the date of the sales contract and signed by the prospective Borrower to acknowledge its receipt, must accompany the submission for insurance endorsement. If a sales contract is signed in advance of the disclosure required by this paragraph, an addendum must be executed after the information is provided to the prospective Borrower and after they have acknowledged receipt of the disclosure.

(b) Borrower's Certification of Water Purification System

At the time the application is signed, the Borrower must sign a certification acknowledging that the Property has a water purification system that must be maintained.

(c) Approved Plan for Individual Residential Water Purification Systems

The Mortgagee must ensure a copy of the approved plan is provided to HUD.

(d) Service Contract for Individual Residential Water Purification Systems

The Mortgagee must ensure a copy of the service contract signed by the Borrower is provided to HUD.

(e) Water Purification Equipment Rider for Individual Residential Water Purification Systems

The Mortgagee must ensure a copy of the Water Purification Equipment Rider is provided to HUD.

(Q) Sewage System

The Mortgagee must confirm that a connection is made to a public or community sewage disposal system whenever feasible and available at a reasonable cost. If connection costs to the public or community system are not reasonable, the existing Onsite Sewage Disposal Systems are acceptable provided they are functioning properly and meet the requirements of the local health department

When the Onsite Sewage Disposal System is not sufficient and an off-site system is available, the Mortgagee must confirm connection to an off-site sewage system. When the Onsite Sewage Disposal System is not sufficient and an off-site system is not available, the Mortgagee must reject the Property unless the Onsite Sewage Disposal System is repaired or replaced and complies with local health department standards.

(R) Termites

For existing Properties, the Mortgagee must confirm that the Property is free of wood destroying insects and organisms. If the appraisal is made subject to inspection by a qualified pest control specialist, the Mortgagee must obtain such inspection and evidence of any required treatment to confirm the Property is free of wood destroying insects and organisms.

Soil poisoning is an unacceptable method for treating termites unless the Mortgagee obtains satisfactory assurance that the treatment will not endanger the quality of the water supply.

iii. Minimum Required Repairs

When the appraisal report or inspection from a qualified Entity indicates that repairs are required to make the Property meet HUD's MPR or MPS, the Mortgagee must comply with Repair Requirements.

If repairs for Existing Construction cannot be completed prior to closing, the Mortgagee may establish an escrow account in accordance with Repair Completion Escrow Requirements.

iv. Leased Equipment

The Mortgagee must ensure that the Property Value does not include the value of any equipment, including an energy system, that is not fully owned by the Borrower. The Mortgagee must review the terms of the lease on any equipment to ensure they do not contain any Legal Restrictions on Conveyance (Free Assumability).

Appraisal Review

The Mortgagee must review the appraisal and ensure that it is complete, accurate, and provides a credible analysis of the marketability and value of the Property.

v.   Quality of Appraisal

The Mortgagee must evaluate the appraisal and ensure it complies with the requirements in Valuation and Reporting Protocols, and any additional appraisal requirements that are specific to the subject Property.

vi. Chain of Title

The Mortgagee must review the appraisal to determine if the subject Property was sold within 12 months prior to the case number assignment date. If the subject Property was sold within the previous 12 months the Mortgagee must review evidence of prior ownership and determine if there are any undisclosed Identity-of-Interest transactions, and for compliance with Restrictions on Property Flipping.

vii. Opinion of Market Value

The Mortgagee must ensure the Market Value of the Property is sufficient to adequately secure the FHA-insured Mortgage.

viii.   Reconsideration of Value

The underwriter may request a reconsideration of value when the Appraiser did not consider information that was relevant on the effective date of the appraisal. The underwriter must provide the Appraiser with all relevant data that is necessary for a reconsideration of value.

The Appraiser may charge an additional fee if the relevant data was not available on the effective date of the appraisal. If the unavailability of data is not the fault of the Borrower, the Borrower must not be held responsible for the additional costs. The effective date of the appraisal is the date the Appraiser inspected the Property.

b. Required Documentation for Underwriting the Property

If additional inspections, repairs or certifications are noted by the appraisal or are required to demonstrate compliance with Property Acceptability Criteria, the Mortgagee must obtain evidence of completion of such inspections, repairs or certifications.

c. Conditional Commitment Direct Endorsement Statement of Appraised Value

The Conditional Commitment Direct Endorsement Statement of Appraised Value (form HUD-92800.5B) provides the terms upon which the commitment/direct endorsement statement of appraised value is made and the specific conditions that must be met before HUD can endorse a Firm Commitment for mortgage insurance. The underwriter must complete form HUD-92800.5B as directed in the form instructions.

Where a Statement of Appraised Value is required, the Mortgagee must provide the Borrower with a copy of the completed form HUD-92800.5B.

4. Underwriting the Borrower Using the TOTAL Mortgage Scorecard (TOTAL)

a. Underwriting with an Automated Underwriting System

FHA's Technology Open To Approved Lenders (TOTAL) Mortgage Scorecard is not an Automated Underwriting System (AUS) but a scorecard that must interface through a system-to-system connection with an AUS.

Each AUS using TOTAL Mortgage Scorecard provides a Feedback Certificate/Finding Report, which documents results of the credit risk evaluation, and identifies the credit report utilized for the scoring event. The Feedback Certificate/Finding Report upon which the Mortgagee makes its underwriting decision prior to endorsement must be included in the case binder.

i. Use of TOTAL Mortgage Scorecard

All transactions must be scored through TOTAL Mortgage Scorecard, except Streamline Refinance transactions, assumptions, and Mortgages made to nonprofit/Governmental Entity Borrowers.

If the Mortgage involves a HUD employee, the Mortgagee must score the transaction through TOTAL. If the file receives an Accept, the Mortgagee must underwrite the transaction in accordance with the guidance in this Underwriting the Borrower Using the TOTAL Mortgage Scorecard section. The Mortgagee must submit the underwritten mortgage application to the Processing and Underwriting Division Director at the Jurisdictional HOC for final underwriting approval.

Mortgagees using TOTAL remain solely responsible for prudent underwriting practices and the Final Underwriting Decision.

ii. Requirements for the Submission of Data through TOTAL Mortgage Scorecard

The Mortgagee must submit data to TOTAL Mortgage Scorecard through an approved AUS vendor in a data format acceptable to the AUS vendor, to meet the requirements described in the TOTAL Mortgage Scorecard Developer's Guide.

iii. Function of TOTAL Mortgage Scorecard

TOTAL Mortgage Scorecard evaluates the overall credit risk posed by the Borrower, based on a number of credit variables, when combined with the functionalities of an AUS.

The Mortgagee may not accept or deny an FHA-insured Mortgage based solely on a risk assessment generated by TOTAL Mortgage Scorecard.

The Mortgagee must ensure full compliance with all FHA eligibility requirements, and all requirements of this section. The Mortgagee must verify the information used to score the Mortgage through TOTAL but does not need to analyze the credit history, unless otherwise stated in this section, if an Accept or Approve recommendation is received.

The underwriter must still underwrite all appraisals according to standard FHA requirements.

The underwriter must fully underwrite those applications where TOTAL issues a Refer.

(A) Automated Underwriting System Data Entry Requirements

(1) Mortgagees

The Mortgagee must verify the integrity of all data elements entered into the AUS to ensure the outcome of the Mortgage credit risk evaluation is valid including:
- Borrower's Credit Report
- Borrower's Liabilities/Debt
- Borrower's Effective Income
- Borrower's Assets/Reserves
- Adjusted Value
- Borrower's total Mortgage Payment including Principal, Interest, Taxes, and Insurance (PITI)

The Borrower's total Mortgage Payment includes:
- Principal and Interest (P&I);
- real estate taxes;
- hazard insurance;
- flood insurance as applicable;
- Mortgage Insurance Premium;
- HOA or condominium association fees or expenses;
- Ground Rent;
- special assessments;
- payments for any acceptable secondary financing; and
- any other escrow payments.

The Mortgagee may deduct the amount of the Mortgage Credit Certificate or Section 8 Homeownership Voucher if it is paid directly to the Servicer. Where real estate taxes are abated, Mortgagees may use the abated amount provided that (1) the Mortgagee can document the abated amount with the taxing authority and (2) the abatement will remain in place for at least the first three years of the Mortgage.

(2) Sponsored Third-Party Originators

The Mortgagee may permit a sponsored TPO to enter data into the AUS. Both the Mortgagee and its sponsored TPO must ensure and verify all data entered into the

AUS. The Mortgagee remains ultimately responsible for ensuring the data entered into the AUS is correct.

The Mortgagee must ensure the Employer Identification Number (EIN) of its sponsored TPO is entered into the AUS. If the Mortgagee is using an AUS that is unable to transmit the sponsored TPO EIN, the Mortgagee must enter "6999609996" in the Lender ID field.

(B) New Versions of TOTAL Mortgage Scorecard

From time to time, FHA will release new versions of TOTAL Mortgage Scorecard. FHA will announce the date that the new version will be available. All Mortgages being scored for the first time will be scored using the new version. For Mortgages with a case number, the Mortgages will be scored using the version that was effective when the case number was assigned. Existing Mortgages scored without a case number will be scored according to the version number tag that is provided in the TOTAL file by the AUS provider (if none, then the current version will be used). All Mortgages without a case number will be scored using the new version 90 Days after the new version is implemented.

iv. Feedback Certificates: Risk Classification and Related Responsibilities (TOTAL)

If the Feedback Certificate/Finding Report shows an Accept or Approve, it will be referred to as Accept.

(A) Accept/Eligible

If the Feedback Certificate/Finding Report shows an Accept/Eligible recommendation, the Mortgage may be eligible for FHA's insurance endorsement provided the Mortgagee verified that data entered into the AUS is accurate and complete and that the entire mortgage application complies with all FHA requirements.

The Mortgagee must verify that all supporting documentation and information entered into TOTAL Mortgage Scorecard is consistent with the final underwriting decision if the Mortgage receives an Accept/Eligible.

(B) Accept/Ineligible

If the Feedback Certification/Finding Report shows an Accept/Ineligible recommendation, the Borrower's credit and capacity would meet the threshold for approval, but the Mortgage does not fully comply with FHA's eligibility requirements. The Feedback Certificate will identify the specific eligibility requirement that the Mortgage does not meet.

The Mortgagee must analyze the Feedback Certificate and determine if the reason for the ineligibility is one that can be resolved in a manner that complies with FHA underwriting requirements. If the Mortgagee can correct the reason for ineligibility, the Mortgagee may rescore the Mortgage in the AUS.

When the reason for ineligibility cannot be corrected in the AUS, the Mortgagee may underwrite the Mortgage using the following requirements for an Accept Mortgage, but must resolve the reason for ineligibility in accordance with FHA requirements and must provide an explanation of the resolution in the remarks section of form HUD-92900-LT, *FHA Loan Underwriting and Transmittal Summary*.

(C) Refer

The underwriter must manually underwrite any mortgage application for which the Feedback Certificate shows a Refer recommendation or any result other than those described above.

v. Accept Risk Classifications Requiring a Downgrade to Manual Underwriting (TOTAL)

The Mortgagee must downgrade and manually underwrite any Mortgage that received an Accept recommendation if:
- the mortgage file contains information or documentation that cannot be entered into or evaluated by TOTAL Mortgage Scorecard;
- additional information, not considered in the AUS recommendation affects the overall insurability of the Mortgage;
- the Borrower has $1,000 or more collectively in Disputed Derogatory Credit Accounts;
- the date of the Borrower's bankruptcy discharge as reflected on bankruptcy documents is within two years from the date of case number assignment;
- the case number assignment date is within three years of the date of the transfer of title through a Pre-Foreclosure Sale (Short Sale);
- the case number assignment date is within three years of the date of the transfer of title through a foreclosure sale;
- the case number assignment date is within three years of the date of the transfer of title through a Deed-in-Lieu (DIL) of foreclosure;
- the Mortgage Payment history, for any mortgage trade line reported on the credit report used to score the application, requires a downgrade as defined in Housing Obligations/Mortgage Payment History;
- the Borrower has undisclosed mortgage debt that requires a downgrade; or
- business income shows a greater than 20 percent decline over the analysis period.

vi. Applicability of Automated Underwriting System Rules (TOTAL)

If a determination is made that the Mortgage must be downgraded to manual underwriting, the Mortgagee must cease its use of the AUS and comply with all requirements for manual underwriting when underwriting a downgraded Mortgage.

vii. TOTAL Mortgage Scorecard Tolerance Levels for Rescoring

The Mortgagee must rescore a Mortgage when any data element of the Mortgage change and/or new Borrower information becomes available.

The Mortgagee is not required to rescore a Mortgage if the following data elements change from the last scoring event within the described tolerance levels:

When assessing...	Rescore is not required if:
Cash Reserves	Cash Reserves verified are not less than 10% below the previously scored amount
Income	Income verified is not less than 5% below the previously scored amount
Tax and Insurance Escrow	The cumulative monthly tax and insurance escrow does not result in more than a 2% increase in the Total Mortgage Payment to Effective Income Ratio (PTI)

b. Credit Requirements (TOTAL)

i. General Credit Review Requirements (TOTAL)

The Mortgagee must obtain a credit report for each Borrower who will be obligated on the mortgage Note. The Mortgagee may obtain a joint report for individuals with joint accounts.

The Mortgagee must obtain a credit report for a non-borrowing spouse who resides in a community property state, or if the subject Property is located in a community property state.

The credit report must indicate the non-borrowing spouse's SSN, where an SSN exists, was matched with the SSA, or the Mortgagee must either provide separate documentation indicating that the SSN was matched with the SSA or provide a statement that the non-borrowing spouse does not have an SSN. Where an SSN does not exist for a non-borrowing spouse, the credit report must contain, at a minimum, the non-borrowing spouse's full name, date of birth, and previous addresses for the last two years.

ii. Credit Reports (TOTAL)

The Mortgagee must use a traditional credit report. If a traditional credit report is not available or the traditional credit report is insufficient, the Feedback Certificate will show a Refer recommendation, and the Mortgagee must manually underwrite the Mortgage.

The Mortgagee must obtain a Tri-Merged Credit Report (TRMCR) from an independent consumer reporting agency.

(A) Requirements for the Credit Report (TOTAL)

Credit reports must contain all information from at least two credit repositories pertaining to credit, residence history, and public records information; be in an easy to read and understandable format; and not require code translations. The credit report may not contain whiteouts, erasures, or alterations. The Mortgagee must retain copies of all credit reports.

The credit report must include:
- the name of the Mortgagee ordering the report;
- the name, address, and telephone number of the consumer-reporting agency;
- the name and SSN of each Borrower; and
- the primary repository from which any particular information was pulled, for each account listed.

A truncated SSN is acceptable for FHA mortgage insurance purposes provided that the mortgage application captures the full nine-digit SSN.

The credit report must also include:
- all inquiries made within the last 90 Days
- all credit and legal information not considered obsolete under the Fair Credit Reporting Act (FCRA), including information for the last seven years, which consumer reporting agencies have reported as verified and currently accurate, regarding:
  - bankruptcies
  - Judgments
  - lawsuits
  - foreclosures
  - tax liens
- for each Borrower debt listed:
  - the date the account was opened
  - high credit amount
  - required payment amount
  - unpaid balance
  - payment history

(B) New Credit Report (TOTAL)

The Mortgagee must obtain a new credit report and rescore the Mortgage through TOTAL if the underwriter identifies inconsistencies between any information in the mortgage file and the original credit report.

iii. Evaluating Credit History (TOTAL)

The Mortgagee must analyze the Borrower's credit history in accordance with the Accept Risk Classifications Requiring a Downgrade to Manual Underwriting section.

If a determination is made that the Mortgage must be downgraded to manual underwriting, the Mortgagee must cease its use of the AUS and comply with all requirements for manual underwriting when underwriting a downgraded Mortgage.

(A) Collection Accounts, Charge Off Accounts, Accounts with Late Payments in the Previous 24 Months, and Judgments (TOTAL)

The Mortgagee is not required to obtain an explanation of collection accounts, Charge Off Accounts, accounts with late payments, Judgments or other derogatory information.

(B) Disputed Derogatory Credit Accounts (TOTAL)

(1) Definition

Disputed Derogatory Credit Account refers to disputed Charge Off Accounts, disputed collection accounts, and disputed accounts with late payments in the last 24 months.

Exclusions from cumulative balance include:
- disputed medical accounts; and
- disputed derogatory credit resulting from identity theft, credit card theft or unauthorized use. To exclude these balances, the Mortgagee must include a copy of the police report or other documentation from the creditor to support the status of the accounts.

(2) Standard

If the credit report utilized by TOTAL Mortgage Scorecard indicates that the Borrower has $1,000 or more collectively in Disputed Derogatory Credit Accounts, the Mortgage must be downgraded to a Refer and manually underwritten.

Disputed Derogatory Credit Accounts of a non-borrowing spouse in a community property state are not included in the cumulative balance for determining if the mortgage application is downgraded to a Refer.

(C) Non-Derogatory Disputed Accounts and Disputed Accounts Not Indicated on the Credit Report (TOTAL)

(1) Definition

Non-Derogatory Disputed Accounts include the following types of accounts:
- disputed accounts with zero balance
- disputed accounts with late payments aged 24 months or greater
- disputed accounts that are current and paid as agreed

(2) Required Documentation and Standard

If a Borrower is disputing non-derogatory accounts, or is disputing accounts which are not indicated on the credit report as being disputed, the Mortgagee is not required to downgrade the application to a Refer. However, the Mortgagee must analyze the effect of the disputed accounts on the Borrower's ability to repay the Mortgage. If the dispute results in the Borrower's monthly debt payments utilized in computing the Debt-to-Income (DTI) ratio being less than the amount indicated on the credit report, the Borrower must provide documentation of the lower payments.

Non-derogatory disputed accounts are excluded from the $1,000 cumulative balance limit.

(D) Judgments (TOTAL)

(1) Definition

Judgment refers to any debt or monetary liability of the Borrower, and the Borrower's spouse in a community property state unless excluded by state law, created by a court, or other adjudicating body.

(2) Standard

The Mortgagee must verify that court-ordered Judgments are resolved or paid off prior to or at closing.

Judgments of a non-borrowing spouse in a community property state must be resolved or paid in full, with the exception of obligations excluded by state law.

Exception

A Judgment is considered resolved if the Borrower has entered into a valid agreement with the creditor to make regular payments on the debt, the Borrower has made timely payments for at least three months of scheduled payments and the Judgment will not supersede the FHA-insured mortgage lien. The Borrower cannot prepay scheduled payments in order to meet the required minimum of three months of payments.

The Mortgagee must include the payment amount in the agreement in the Borrower's monthly liabilities and debt.

The Mortgagee must obtain a copy of the agreement and evidence that payments were made on time in accordance with the agreement.

(3) Required Documentation

The Mortgagee must provide the following documentation:
- evidence of payment in full, if paid prior to settlement;
- the payoff statement, if paid at settlement; or
- the payment arrangement with creditor, if not paid prior to or at settlement, and a subordination agreement for any liens existing on title.

(E) Inaccuracy in Debt Considered (TOTAL)

When an inaccuracy in the amount or type of debt or obligation is revealed during the application process and the correct information was not considered by the AUS, the Mortgagee must:
- verify the actual monthly payment amount;
- re-submit the Mortgage for evaluation by TOTAL if the cumulative change in the amount of the liabilities that must be included in the Borrower's debt increases by more than $100 per month; and
- determine that the additional debt was not/will not be used for the Borrower's Minimum Required Investment (MRI).

(F) Bankruptcy (TOTAL)

(1) Standard

The Mortgagee must document the passage of two years since the discharge date of any bankruptcy. If the bankruptcy was discharged within two years from the date of case number assignment, the Mortgage must be downgraded to a Refer and manually underwritten.

(2) Required Documentation

If the credit report does not verify the discharge date or additional documentation is necessary to determine if any liabilities were discharged in the bankruptcy, the Mortgagee must obtain the bankruptcy and discharge documents.

(G) Pre-Foreclosure Sales (Short Sales) (TOTAL)

(1) Definition

Pre-Foreclosure Sales, also known as Short Sales, refer to the sales of real estate that generate proceeds that are less than the amount owed on the Property and the lien holders agree to release their liens and forgive the deficiency balance on the real estate.

(2) Standard

The Mortgagee must document the passage of three years since the date of the Short Sale. If the Short Sale occurred within three years of the case number assignment date, the Mortgage must be downgraded to a Refer and manually underwritten.

This three-year period begins on the date of transfer of title by Short Sale.

(3) Required Documentation

If the credit report does not verify the date of the transfer of title by Short Sale, the Mortgagee must obtain the Short Sale documents.

(H) Foreclosure (TOTAL)

(1) Standard

The Mortgagee must manually downgrade to a Refer if the Borrower had a foreclosure in which title transferred from the Borrower within three years of case number assignment.

(2) Required Documentation

If the credit report does not verify the date of the transfer of title through the foreclosure, the Mortgagee must obtain the foreclosure documents.

(I) Deed-in-Lieu of Foreclosure (TOTAL)

(1) Standard

The Mortgagee must manually downgrade to a Refer if the Borrower had a DIL of foreclosure in which title transferred from the Borrower within three years of case number assignment.

(2) Required Documentation

If the credit report does not verify the date of the transfer of title by DIL of foreclosure, the Mortgagee must obtain a copy of the DIL of foreclosure.

(J) Credit Counseling/Payment Plan (TOTAL)

Participating in a consumer credit counseling program does not require a downgrade to a manual underwriting.

No explanation or other documentation is needed.

(K) Housing Obligations/Mortgage Payment History (TOTAL)

(1) Definition

Housing Obligation/Mortgage Payment refers to the monthly payment due for rental or Properties owned.

A Mortgage Payment is considered delinquent if not paid within the month due.

(2) Late Mortgage Payments for Purchase and No Cash-Out Refinance

The Mortgage must be downgraded to a Refer and manually underwritten if any mortgage trade line, including mortgage line-of-credit payments, during the most recent 12 months reflects:
- three or more late payments of greater than 30 Days;
- one or more late payments of 60 Days plus one or more 30-Day late payments; or
- one payment greater than 90 Days late.

A Mortgage that has been modified must utilize the payment history in accordance with the modification agreement for the time period of modification in determining late housing payments.

(3) Cash-Out Refinance Transactions

The Mortgage must be downgraded to a Refer and manually underwritten if any mortgage trade line, including mortgage line-of-credit payments, reflects:
- a current delinquency; or
- any delinquency within 12 months of the case number assignment date.

A Mortgage that has been modified must utilize the payment history in accordance with the modification agreement for the time period of modification in determining late housing payments.

iv. Evaluating Liabilities and Debts (TOTAL)

The Mortgagee must review all credit report inquiries to ensure that all debts, including any new debt payments resulting from material inquiries listed on the credit report, are used to calculate the debt ratios. The Mortgagee must also determine that any recent debts were not incurred to obtain any part of the Borrower's required funds to close on the Property being purchased.

Material Inquiries refer to inquires which may potentially result in obligations incurred by the Borrower for other Mortgages, auto loans, leases, or other Installment Loans. Inquiries from department stores, credit bureaus, and insurance companies are not considered material inquiries.

(A) General Liabilities and Debts (TOTAL)

The Mortgagee must determine the Borrower's monthly liabilities by reviewing all debts listed on the credit report, *Uniform Residential Loan Application (URLA)*, and required documentation.

All applicable monthly liabilities must be included in the qualifying ratio. Closed-end debts do not have to be included if they will be paid off within 10 months and the cumulative payments of all such debts are less than or equal to 5 percent of the Borrower's gross monthly income. The Borrower may not pay down the balance in order to meet the 10-month requirement.

Accounts for which the Borrower is an authorized user must be included in a Borrower's DTI ratio unless the Mortgagee can document that the primary account holder has made all required payments on the account for the previous 12 months. If less than three payments have been required on the account in the previous 12 months, the payment amount must be included in the Borrower's DTI.

Loans secured against deposited funds, where repayment may be obtained through extinguishing the asset and these funds are not included in calculating the Borrower's assets, do not require consideration of repayment for qualifying purposes.

The Mortgagee must document that the funds used to pay off debts prior to closing came from an acceptable source, and the Borrower did not incur new debts that were not included in the DTI ratio.

Negative income must be subtracted from the Borrower's gross monthly income, and not treated as a recurring monthly liability unless otherwise noted.

(B) Undisclosed Debt Other Than a Mortgage (TOTAL)

When a debt or obligation (other than a Mortgage) not listed on the mortgage application and/or credit report and not considered by the AUS is revealed during the application process, the Mortgagee must:
- verify the actual monthly payment amount;
- re-submit the Mortgage for evaluation by TOTAL if the cumulative change in the amount of the liabilities that must be included in the Borrower's debt increases by more than $100 per month; and

- determine that any funds borrowed were not/will not be used for the Borrower's MRI.

(C) Undisclosed Mortgage Debt (TOTAL)

When an existing debt or obligation that is secured by a Mortgage but is not listed on the credit report and not considered by the AUS is revealed during the application process, the Mortgagee must obtain a verification of Mortgage directly from the Servicer.

The Mortgage must be downgraded to a Refer and manually underwritten if the mortgage history reflects:
- a current delinquency;
- any delinquency within 12 months of the case number assignment date; or
- more than two 30 Day late payments within 24 months of the case number assignment date.

A Mortgage that has been modified must utilize the payment history in accordance with the modification agreement for the time period of modification in determining late Mortgage Payments.

(D) Federal Debt (TOTAL)

(1) Definition

Federal Debt refers to debt owed to the federal government for which regular payments are being made.

(2) Standard

The Mortgagee must include the debt. The amount of the required payment must be included in the calculation of the Borrower's total debt to income.

(3) Required Documentation

The Mortgagee must include documentation from the federal agency evidencing the repayment agreement and verification of payments made, if applicable.

(E) Alimony, Child Support, and Maintenance (TOTAL)

(1) Definition

Alimony, Child Support, and Maintenance are court-ordered or otherwise agreed upon payments.

(2) Standard

For Alimony, if the Borrower's income was not reduced by the amount of the monthly alimony obligation in the Mortgagee's calculation of the Borrower's gross income, the Mortgagee must include the monthly obligation in the calculation of the Borrower's debt.

Child Support and Maintenance are to be treated as a recurring liability and the Mortgagee must include the monthly obligation in the Borrower's liabilities and debt.

(3) Required Documentation

The Mortgagee must verify and document the monthly obligation by obtaining the official signed divorce decree, separation agreement, maintenance agreement, or other legal order.

The Mortgagee must also obtain the Borrower's pay stubs covering no less than 28 consecutive Days to verify whether the Borrower is subject to any order of garnishment relating to the Alimony, Child Support, and Maintenance.

(4) Calculation of Monthly Obligation

The Mortgagee must calculate the Borrower's monthly obligation from the greater of:
- the amount shown on the most recent decree or agreement establishing the Borrower's payment obligation; or
- the monthly amount of the garnishment.

(F) Non-Borrowing Spouse Debt in Community Property States (TOTAL)

(1) Definition

Non-Borrowing Spouse Debt refers to debts owed by a spouse that are not owed by, or in the name of the Borrower.

(2) Standard

If the Borrower resides in a community property state or the Property being insured is located in a community property state, debts of the non-borrowing spouse must be included in the Borrower's qualifying ratios, except for obligations specifically excluded by state law.

The non-borrowing spouse's credit history is not considered a reason to deny a mortgage application.

(3) Required Documentation

The Mortgagee must verify and document the debt of the non-borrowing spouse.

The Mortgagee must make a note in the file referencing the specific state law that justifies the exclusion of any debt from consideration.

The Mortgagee must obtain a credit report for the non-borrowing spouse in order to determine the debts that must be included in the liabilities. The credit report for the non-borrowing spouse is for the purpose of establishing debt only, and is not submitted to TOTAL Mortgage Scorecard for the purpose of credit evaluation. The credit report for the non-borrowing spouse may be traditional or non-traditional.

(G) Deferred Obligations (TOTAL)

(1) Definition

Deferred Obligations (excluding Student Loans) refer to liabilities that have been incurred but where payment is deferred or has not yet commenced, including accounts in forbearance.

(2) Standard

The Mortgagee must include deferred obligations in the Borrower's liabilities.

(3) Required Documentation

The Mortgagee must obtain written documentation of the deferral of the liability from the creditor and evidence of the outstanding balance and terms of the deferred liability. The Mortgagee must obtain evidence of the actual monthly payment obligation, if available.

(4) Calculation of Monthly Obligation

The Mortgagee must use the actual monthly payment to be paid on a deferred liability, whenever available.

If the actual monthly payment is not available for installment debt, the Mortgagee must utilize the terms of the debt or 5 percent of the outstanding balance to establish the monthly payment.

(H) Student Loans (TOTAL)

(1) Definition

Student Loan refers to liabilities incurred for educational purposes.

(2) Standard

The Mortgagee must include all Student Loans in the Borrower's liabilities, regardless of the payment type or status of payments.

(3) Required Documentation

If the payment used for the monthly obligation is:
- less than 1 percent of the outstanding balance reported on the Borrower's credit report; and
- less than the monthly payment reported on the Borrower's credit report;

the Mortgagee must obtain written documentation of the actual monthly payment, the payment status, and evidence of the outstanding balance and terms from the creditor.

(4) Calculation of Monthly Obligation

Regardless of the payment status, the Mortgagee must use either:
- the greater of:
  - 1 percent of the outstanding balance on the loan; or
  - the monthly payment reported on the Borrower's credit report; or
- the actual documented payment, provided the payment will fully amortize the loan over its term.

(I) Installment Loans (TOTAL)

(1) Definition

Installment Loans (excluding Student Loans) refer to loans, not secured by real estate, that require the periodic payment of P&I. A loan secured by an interest in a timeshare must be considered an Installment Loan.

(2) Standard

The Mortgagee must include the monthly payment shown on the credit report, loan agreement or payment statement to calculate the Borrower's liabilities.

If the credit report does not include a monthly payment for the loan, the Mortgagee must use the amount of the monthly payment shown in the loan agreement or payment statement and enter it into TOTAL Mortgage Scorecard.

(3) Required Documentation

If the monthly payment shown on the credit report is utilized to calculate the monthly debts, no further documentation is required.

If the credit report does not include a monthly payment for the loan, or the payment reported on the credit report is greater than the payment on the loan agreement or payment statement, the Mortgagee must obtain a copy of the loan agreement or payment statement documenting the amount of the monthly payment. If the credit report, loan agreement or payment statement shows a deferred payment arrangement for an Installment Loan, refer to the Deferred Obligations section.

(J) Revolving Charge Accounts (TOTAL)

(1) Definition

A Revolving Charge Account refers to a credit arrangement that requires the Borrower to make periodic payments but does not require full repayment by a specified point of time.

(2) Standard

The Mortgagee must include the monthly payment shown on the credit report for the Revolving Charge Account. Where the credit report does not include a monthly payment for the account, the Mortgagee must use the payment shown on the current account statement or 5 percent of the outstanding balance.

(3) Required Documentation

The Mortgagee must use the credit report to document the terms, balance and payment amount on the account, if available.

Where the credit report does not reflect the necessary information on the charge account, the Mortgagee must obtain a copy of the most recent charge account statement or use 5 percent of the outstanding balance to document the monthly payment.

(K) 30-Day Accounts (TOTAL)

(1) Definition

A 30-Day Account refers to a credit arrangement that requires the Borrower to pay off the outstanding balance on the account every month.

(2) Standard

The Mortgagee must verify the Borrower paid the outstanding balance in full on every 30-Day Account each month for the past 12 months. 30-Day Accounts that are paid monthly are not included in the Borrower's DTI. If the credit report reflects any late payments in the last 12 months, the Mortgagee must utilize 5 percent of the outstanding balance as the Borrower's monthly debt to be included in the DTI.

(3) Required Documentation

The Mortgagee must use the credit report to document that the Borrower has paid the balance on the account monthly for the previous 12 months. The Mortgagee must use the credit report to document the balance, and must document that funds are available to pay off the balance in excess of the funds and Reserves required to close the Mortgage.

(L) Contingent Liabilities (TOTAL)

(1) Definition

A Contingent Liability refers to a liability that may result in the obligation to repay only when a specific event occurs. For example, a contingent liability exists when an individual can be held responsible for the repayment of a debt if another legally obligated party defaults on the payment. Contingent liabilities may include Cosigner liabilities and liabilities resulting from a mortgage assumption without release of liability.

(2) Standard

The Mortgagee must include monthly payments on contingent liabilities in the calculation of the Borrower's monthly obligations unless the Mortgagee verifies and documents that there is no possibility that the debt holder will pursue debt collection against the Borrower should the other party default or the other legally obligated party has made 12 months of timely payments.

(3) Calculation of Monthly Obligation

The Mortgagee must calculate the monthly payment on the contingent liability based on the terms of the agreement creating the contingent liability.

(4) Required Documentation

(a) Mortgage Assumptions

The Mortgagee must obtain the agreement creating the contingent liability or assumption agreement and deed showing transfer of title out of the Borrower's name.

(b) Cosigned Liabilities

If the cosigned liability is not included in the monthly obligation, the Mortgagee must obtain documentation to evidence that the other party to the debt has been making regular on-time payments during the previous 12 months, and does not have a history of delinquent payments on the loan.

(c) Court Ordered Divorce Decree

The Mortgagee must obtain a copy of the divorce decree ordering the spouse to make payments.

(M) Collection Accounts (TOTAL)

(1) Definition

A Collection Account refers to a Borrower's loan or debt that has been submitted to a collection agency by a creditor.

(2) Standard

If the credit reports used in the TOTAL Mortgage Scorecard analysis show cumulative outstanding collection account balances of $2,000 or greater, the Mortgagee must:
- verify that the debt is paid in full at the time of or prior to settlement using acceptable sources of funds;
- verify that the Borrower has made payment arrangements with the creditor and include the monthly payment in the Borrower's DTI; or
- if a payment arrangement is not available, calculate the monthly payment using 5 percent of the outstanding balance of each collection and include the monthly payment in the Borrower's DTI.

Collection accounts of a non-borrowing spouse in a community property state must be included in the $2,000 cumulative balance and analyzed as part of the Borrower's ability to pay all collection accounts, unless excluded by state law.

(3) Required Documentation

The Mortgagee must provide the following documentation:
- evidence of payment in full, if paid prior to settlement;
- the payoff statement, if paid at settlement; or
- the payment arrangement with creditor, if not paid prior to or at settlement.

If the Mortgagee uses 5 percent of the outstanding balance, no documentation is required.

(N) Charge Off Accounts (TOTAL)

(1) Definition

Charge Off Account refers to a Borrower's loan or debt that has been written off by the creditor.

(2) Standard

Charge Off Accounts do not need to be included in the Borrower's liabilities or debt.

(O) Private Savings Clubs (TOTAL)

(1) Definition

Private Savings Club refers to a non-traditional method of saving by making deposits into a member-managed resource pool.

(2) Standard

If the Borrower is obligated to continue making ongoing contributions under the pooled savings agreement, this obligation must be counted in the Borrower's total debt.

The Mortgagee must verify and document the establishment and duration of the Borrower's membership in the club and the amount of the Borrower's required contribution to the club.

(3) Required Documentation

The Mortgagee must also obtain the club's account ledgers and receipts, and verification from the club treasurer that the club is still active.

(P) Business Debt in Borrower's Name (TOTAL)

(1) Definition

Business Debt in Borrower's Name refers to liabilities reported on the Borrower's personal credit report, but payment for the debt is attributed to the Borrower's business.

(2) Standard

When business debt is reported on the Borrower's personal credit report, the debt must be included in the DTI calculation, unless the Mortgagee can document that the debt is being paid by the Borrower's business, and the debt was considered in the cash flow analysis of the Borrower's business. The debt is considered in the cash flow analysis where the Borrower's business tax returns reflect a business expense related to the obligation, equal to or greater than the amount of payments documented as paid out of company funds. Where the Borrower's business tax returns show an interest expense related to the obligation, only the interest portion of the debt is considered in the cash flow analysis.

(3) Required Documentation

When a self-employed Borrower states debt appearing on their personal credit report is being paid by their business, the Mortgagee must obtain documentation that the debt is paid out of company funds and that the debt was considered in the cash flow analysis of the Borrower's business.

(Q)Obligations Not Considered Debt (TOTAL)

Obligations not considered debt include:
- medical collections
- federal, state, and local taxes, if not delinquent and no payments are required
- automatic deductions from savings, when not associated with another type of obligation
- Federal Insurance Contributions Act (FICA) and other retirement contributions, such as 401(k) accounts
- collateralized loans secured by depository accounts
- utilities
- child care
- commuting costs
- union dues
- insurance, other than property insurance
- open accounts with zero balances
- voluntary deductions, when not associated with another type of obligation

c. Income Requirements (TOTAL)

Definition of Effective Income (TOTAL)

Effective Income refers to income that may be used to qualify a Borrower for a Mortgage. Effective Income must be reasonably likely to continue through at least the first three years of the Mortgage, and meet the specific requirements described below.

i. General Income Requirements (TOTAL)

The Mortgagee must document the Borrower's income and employment history, verify the accuracy of the amounts of income being reported, and determine if the income can be considered as Effective Income in accordance with the requirements listed below.

The Mortgagee may only consider income if it is legally derived and, when required, properly reported as income on the Borrower's tax returns.

Negative income must be subtracted from the Borrower's gross monthly income, and not treated as a recurring monthly liability unless otherwise noted.

If FHA requires tax returns as required documentation for any type of Effective Income, the Mortgagee must also analyze the tax returns in accordance with Appendix 2.0 – Analyzing IRS Forms.

ii. Employment Related Income (TOTAL)

(A) Definition

Employment Income refers to income received as an employee of a business that is reported on IRS Form W-2.

(B) Standard

The Mortgagee may use Employment related Income as Effective Income in accordance with the standards provided for each type of Employment related Income.

(C) Required Documentation

For all Employment related Income, the Mortgagee must verify the Borrower's most recent two years of employment and income, and document using one of the following methods.

(1) Traditional Current Employment Documentation

The Mortgagee must obtain one of the following to verify current employment:
- the most recent pay stub and a written Verification of Employment (VOE) covering two years; or
- direct electronic verification of employment by a TPV vendor covering two years, subject to the following requirements:
  - the Borrower has authorized the Mortgagee to verify income and employment; and
  - the date of the data contained in the completed verification conforms with FHA requirements in Maximum Age of Mortgage Documents.

Re-verification of employment must be completed within 10 Days prior to the date of the Note. Verbal or electronic re-verification of employment is acceptable. Electronic re-verification employment data must be current within 30 days of the date of the verification.

(2) Alternative Current Employment Documentation

If using alternative documentation, the Mortgagee must:
- obtain copies of the most recent pay stub that shows the Borrower's year-to-date earnings;
- obtain copies of the original IRS W-2 forms from the previous two years; and
- document current employment by telephone, sign and date the verification documentation, and note the name, title, and telephone number of the person with whom employment was verified.

Re-verification of employment must be completed within 10 Days prior to the date of the Note. Verbal or electronic re-verification of employment is acceptable. Electronic re-verification employment data must be current within 30 days of the date of the verification.

(3) Past Employment Documentation

Direct verification of the Borrower's employment history for the previous two years is not required if all of the following conditions are met:
- The current employer confirms a two year employment history, or a paystub reflects a hiring date.
- Only base pay is used to qualify (no Overtime, Bonus or Tip Income).
- The Borrower executes IRS Form 4506, *Request for Copy of Tax Return,* IRS Form 4506-T, *Request for Transcript of Tax Return,* or IRS Form 8821, *Tax Information Authorization,* for the previous two tax years.

If the applicant has not been employed with the same employer for the previous two years and/or not all conditions immediately above can be met, then the Mortgagee must obtain one or a combination of the following for the most recent two years to verify the applicant's employment history:
- W-2(s)
- VOE(s)
- direct electronic verification by a TPV vendor, subject to the following requirements:
  - the Borrower has authorized the Mortgagee to verify income and employment; and
  - the date of the data contained in the completed verification conforms with FHA requirements in Maximum Age of Mortgage Documents
- evidence supporting enrollment in school or the military during the most recent two full years

iii. Primary Employment (TOTAL)

(A) Definition

Primary Employment is the Borrower's principal employment, unless the income falls within a specific category identified below. Primary employment is generally full-time employment and may be either salaried or hourly.

(B) Standard

The Mortgagee may use primary Employment Income as Effective Income.

(C) Calculation of Effective Income

(1) Salary

For employees who are salaried and whose income has been and will likely be consistently earned, the Mortgagee must use the current salary to calculate Effective Income.

(2) Hourly

For employees who are paid hourly, and whose hours do not vary, the Mortgagee must consider the Borrower's current hourly rate to calculate Effective Income.

For employees who are paid hourly and whose hours vary, the Mortgagee must average the income over the previous two years. If the Mortgagee can document an increase in pay rate the Mortgagee may use the most recent 12-month average of hours at the current pay rate.

iv. Part-Time Employment (TOTAL)

(A) Definition

Part-Time Employment refers to employment that is not the Borrower's primary employment and is generally performed for less than 40 hours per week.

(B) Standard

The Mortgagee may use Employment Income from Part-Time Employment as Effective Income if the Borrower has worked a part-time job uninterrupted for the past two years and the current position is reasonably likely to continue.

(C) Calculation of Effective Income

The Mortgagee must average the income over the previous two years. If the Mortgagee can document an increase in pay rate the Mortgagee may use a 12-month average of hours at the current pay rate.

v. Overtime, Bonus or Tip Income (TOTAL)

(A) Definition

Overtime, Bonus or Tip Income refers to income that the Borrower receives in addition to the Borrower's normal salary.

(B) Standard

The Mortgagee may use Overtime, Bonus or Tip Income as Effective Income if the Borrower has received this income for the past two years and it is reasonably likely to continue.

Periods of Overtime, Bonus or Tip Income less than two years may be considered Effective Income if the Mortgagee documents that the Overtime, Bonus or Tip Income has been consistently earned over a period of not less than one year and is reasonably likely to continue.

(C) Calculation of Effective Income

For employees with Overtime, Bonus or Tip Income, the Mortgagee must calculate the Effective Income by using the lesser of:
- the average Overtime, Bonus or Tip Income earned over the previous two years or, if less than two years, the length of time Overtime, Bonus or Tip Income has been earned; or
- the average Overtime, Bonus or Tip Income earned over the previous year.

vi. Seasonal Employment (TOTAL)

(A) Definition

Seasonal Employment refers to employment that is not year round, regardless of the number of hours per week the Borrower works on the job.

(B) Standard

The Mortgagee may consider Employment Income from Seasonal Employment as Effective Income if the Borrower has worked the same line of work for the past two years and is reasonably likely to be rehired for the next season. The Mortgagee may consider unemployment income as Effective Income for those with Effective Income from Seasonal Employment.

(C) Required Documentation

For seasonal employees with unemployment income, the Mortgagee must document the unemployment income for two full years and there must be reasonable assurance that this income will continue.

(D) Calculation of Effective Income

For employees with Employment Income from Seasonal Employment, the Mortgagee must average the income earned over the previous two full years to calculate Effective Income.

vii. Employer Housing Subsidy (TOTAL)

(A) Definition

Employer Housing Subsidy refers to employer-provided mortgage assistance.

(B) Standard

The Mortgagee may utilize Employer Housing Subsidy as Effective Income.

(C) Required Documentation

The Mortgagee must verify and document the existence and the amount of the housing subsidy.

(D) Calculation of Effective Income

For employees receiving an Employer Housing Subsidy, the Mortgagee may add the Employer Housing Subsidy to the total Effective Income, but may not use it to offset the Mortgage Payment.

viii. Employed by Family-Owned Business (TOTAL)

(A) Definition

Family-Owned Business Income refers to Employment Income earned from a business owned by the Borrower's family, but in which the Borrower is not an owner.

(B) Standard

The Mortgagee may consider Family-Owned Business Income as Effective Income if the Borrower is not an owner in the family-owned business.

(C) Required Documentation

The Mortgagee must verify and document that the Borrower is not an owner in the family-owned business by using official business documents showing the ownership percentage.

Official business documents include corporate resolutions or other business organizational documents, business tax returns or Schedule K-1(IRS Form 1065),

U.S. Return of Partnership Income, or an official letter from a certified public accountant on their business letterhead.

In addition to traditional or alternative documentation requirements, the Mortgagee must obtain copies of signed personal tax returns or tax transcripts.

(D) Calculation of Effective Income

(1) Salary

For employees who are salaried and whose income has been and will likely continue to be consistently earned, the Mortgagee must use the current salary to calculate Effective Income.

(2) Hourly

For employees who are paid hourly, and whose hours do not vary, the Mortgagee must consider the Borrower's current hourly rate to calculate Effective Income.

For employees who are paid hourly and whose hours vary, the Mortgagee must average the income over the previous two years. If the Mortgagee can document an increase in pay rate the Mortgagee may use the most recent 12-month average of hours at the current pay rate.

ix. Commission Income (TOTAL)

(A) Definition

Commission Income refers to income that is paid contingent upon the conducting of a business transaction or the performance of a service.

(B) Standard

The Mortgagee may use Commission Income as Effective Income if the Borrower earned the income for at least one year in the same or similar line of work and it is reasonably likely to continue.

(C) Required Documentation [Text was deleted in this section.]

For all Commission Income, the Mortgagee must use traditional or alternative employment documentation.

(D) Calculation of Effective Income [Text was deleted in this section.]

The Mortgagee must calculate Effective Income for commission by using the lesser of:

- either, (i) the average Commission Income earned over the previous two years for Commission Income earned for two years or more, or (ii) the length of time Commission Income has been earned if less than two years; or
- the average Commission Income earned over the previous year.

x. Self-Employment Income (TOTAL)

(A) Definition

Self-Employment Income refers to income generated by a business in which the Borrower has a 25 percent or greater ownership interest.

There are four basic types of business structures. They include:
- sole proprietorships;
- corporations;
- limited liability or "S" corporations; and
- partnerships.

(B) Standard

(1) Minimum Length of Self-Employment

The Mortgagee may consider Self-Employment Income if the Borrower has been self-employed for at least two years.

If the Borrower has been self-employed between one and two years, the Mortgagee may only consider the income as Effective Income if the Borrower was previously employed in the same line of work in which the Borrower is self-employed or in a related occupation for at least two years.

(2) Stability of Self-Employment Income

Income obtained from businesses with annual earnings that are stable or increasing is acceptable. If the income from businesses shows a greater than 20 percent decline in Effective Income over the analysis period, the Mortgagee must downgrade and manually underwrite.

(C) Required Documentation

(1) Individual and Business Tax Returns

The Mortgagee must obtain complete individual federal income tax returns for the most recent two years, including all schedules.

The Mortgagee must obtain the Borrower's business tax returns for the most recent two years unless the following criteria are met:

- individual federal income tax returns show increasing Self-Employment Income over the past two years;
- funds to close are not coming from business accounts; and
- the Mortgage to be insured is not a cash-out refinance.

In lieu of signed individual or business tax returns from the Borrower, the Mortgagee may obtain a signed IRS Form 4506, *Request for Copy of Tax Return*, IRS Form 4506-T, *Request for Transcript of Tax Return*, or IRS Form 8821, *Tax Information Authorization*, and tax transcripts directly from the IRS.

(2) Profit & Loss Statements and Balance Sheets

The Mortgagee must obtain a year-to-date Profit and Loss (P&L) statement and balance sheet if more than a calendar quarter has elapsed since date of most recent calendar or fiscal year-end tax return was filed by the Borrower. A balance sheet is not required for self-employed Borrowers filing Schedule C income.

If income used to qualify the Borrower exceeds the two year average of tax returns, an audited P&L or signed quarterly tax return must be obtained from the IRS.

(D) Calculation of Effective Income

The Mortgagee must analyze the Borrower's tax returns to determine gross Self-Employment Income. Requirements for analyzing self-employment documentation are found in Analyzing IRS Forms.

The Mortgagee must calculate gross Self-Employment Income by using the lesser of:
- the average gross Self-Employment Income earned over the previous two years; or
- the average gross Self-Employment Income earned over the previous one year.

xi. Additional Required Analysis of Stability of Employment Income (TOTAL)

(A) Frequent Changes in Employment

If the Borrower has changed employers more than three times in the previous 12-month period, or has changed lines of work, the Mortgagee must take additional steps to verify and document the stability of the Borrower's Employment Income. Additional analysis is not required for fields of employment that regularly require a Borrower to work for various employers (such as Temp Companies or Union Trades). The Mortgagee must obtain:
- transcripts of training and education demonstrating qualification for a new position; or
- employment documentation evidencing continual increases in income and/or benefits.

(B) Addressing Gaps in Employment

For Borrowers with gaps in employment of six months or more (an extended absence), the Mortgagee may consider the Borrower's current income as Effective Income if it can verify and document that:
- the Borrower has been employed in the current job for at least six months at the time of case number assignment; and
- a two year work history prior to the absence from employment using standard or alternative employment verification.

(C) Addressing Temporary Reduction in Income

For Borrowers with a temporary reduction of income due to a short-term disability or similar temporary leave, the Mortgagee may consider the Borrower's current income as Effective Income, if it can verify and document that:
- the Borrower intends to return to work;
- the Borrower has the right to return to work; and
- the Borrower qualifies for the Mortgage taking into account any reduction of income due to the circumstance.

For Borrowers returning to work before or at the time of the first Mortgage Payment due date, the Mortgagee may use the Borrower's pre-leave income.

For Borrowers returning to work after the first Mortgage Payment due date, the Mortgagee may use the Borrower's current income plus available surplus liquid asset Reserves, above and beyond any required Reserves, as an income supplement up to the amount of the Borrower's pre-leave income. The amount of the monthly income supplement is the total amount of surplus Reserves divided by the number of months between the first payment due date and the Borrower's intended date of return to work.

Required Documentation

The Mortgagee must provide the following documentation for Borrowers on temporary leave:
- a written statement from the Borrower confirming the Borrower's intent to return to work, and the intended date of return;
- documentation generated by current employer confirming the Borrower's eligibility to return to current employer after temporary leave; and
- documentation of sufficient liquid assets, in accordance with Sources of Funds, used to supplement the Borrower's income through intended date of return to work with current employer.

xii. Other Sources of Effective Income (TOTAL)

(A) Disability Benefits (TOTAL)

(1) Definition

Disability Benefits are benefits received from the Social Security Administration (SSA), Department of Veterans Affairs (VA), other public agencies, or a private disability insurance provider.

(2) Required Documentation

The Mortgagee must verify and document the Borrower's receipt of benefits from the SSA, VA, or private disability insurance provider. The Mortgagee must obtain documentation that establishes award benefits to the Borrower.

If any disability income is due to expire within three years from the date of mortgage application, that income cannot be used as Effective Income.

If the Notice of Award or equivalent document does not have a defined expiration date, the Mortgagee may consider the income effective and reasonably likely to continue. The Mortgagee may not rely upon a pending or current re-evaluation of medical eligibility for benefit payments as evidence that the benefit payment is not reasonably likely to continue.

Under no circumstance may the Mortgagee inquire into or request documentation concerning the nature of the disability or the medical condition of the Borrower.

(a) Social Security Disability

For Social Security Disability income, including Supplemental Security Income (SSI), the Mortgagee must obtain a copy of the last Notice of Award letter, or an equivalent document that establishes award benefits to the Borrower, and one of the following documents:
- federal tax returns;
- the most recent bank statement evidencing receipt of income from the SSA;
- a Proof of Income Letter, also known as a "Budget Letter" or "Benefits Letter" that evidences income from the SSA; or
- a copy of the Borrower's form SSA-1099/1042S, *Social Security Benefit Statement*.

(b) VA Disability

For VA disability benefits, the Mortgagee must obtain from the Borrower a copy of the veteran's last Benefits Letter showing the amount of the assistance, and one of the following documents:

- federal tax returns; or
- the most recent bank statement evidencing receipt of income from the VA.

If the Benefits Letter does not have a defined expiration date, the Mortgagee may consider the income effective and reasonably likely to continue for at least three years.

(c) Private Disability

For private disability benefits, the Mortgagee must obtain documentation from the private disability insurance provider showing the amount of the assistance and the expiration date of the benefits, if any, and one of the following documents:
- federal tax returns; or
- the most recent bank statement evidencing receipt of income from the insurance provider.

(3) Calculation of Effective Income

The Mortgagee must use the most recent amount of benefits received to calculate Effective Income.

(B) Alimony, Child Support, and Maintenance Income (TOTAL)

(1) Definition

Alimony, Child Support, and Maintenance Income refers to income received from a former spouse or partner or from a non-custodial parent of the Borrower's minor dependent.

(2) Required Documentation

The Mortgagee must obtain a fully executed copy of the Borrower's final divorce decree, legal separation agreement, court order, or voluntary payment agreement with documented receipt.

When using a final divorce decree, legal separation agreement or court order, the Mortgagee must obtain evidence of receipt using deposits on bank statements; canceled checks; or documentation from the child support agency for the most recent three months that supports the amount used in qualifying.

The Mortgagee must document the voluntary payment agreement with 12 months of canceled checks, deposit slips, or tax returns.

The Mortgagee must provide evidence that the claimed income will continue for at least three years. The Mortgagee may use the front and pertinent pages of the divorce decree/settlement agreement and/or court order showing the financial details.

(3) Calculation of Effective Income

When using a final divorce decree, legal separation agreement or court order, if the Borrower has received consistent Alimony, Child Support and Maintenance Income for the most recent three months, the Mortgagee may use the current payment to calculate Effective Income.

When using evidence of voluntary payments, if the Borrower has received consistent Alimony, Child Support and Maintenance Income for the most recent six months, the Mortgagee may use the current payment to calculate Effective Income.

If the Alimony, Child Support and Maintenance Income have not been consistently received for the most recent six months, the Mortgagee must use the average of the income received over the previous two years to calculate Effective Income. If Alimony, Child Support and Maintenance Income have been received for less than two years, the Mortgagee must use the average over the time of receipt.

(C) Military Income (TOTAL)

(1) Definition

Military Income refers to income received by military personnel during their period of active, Reserve, or National Guard service, including:
- base pay
- Basic Allowance for Housing
- clothing allowances
- flight or hazard pay
- Basic Allowance for Subsistence
- proficiency pay

The Mortgagee may not use military education benefits as Effective Income.

(2) Required Documentation

The Mortgagee must obtain a copy of the Borrower's military Leave and Earnings Statement (LES). The Mortgagee must verify the Expiration Term of Service date on the LES. If the Expiration Term of Service date is within the first 12 months of the Mortgage, Military Income may only be considered Effective Income if the Borrower represents their intent to continue military service.

(3) Calculation of Effective Income

The Mortgagee must use the current amount of Military Income received to calculate Effective Income.

(D) Mortgage Credit Certificates (TOTAL)

(1) Definition

Mortgage Credit Certificates refer to government Mortgage Payment subsidies other than Section 8 Homeownership Vouchers.

(2) Required Documentation

The Mortgagee must verify and document that the Governmental Entity subsidizes the Borrower's Mortgage Payments either through direct payments or tax rebates.

(3) Calculating Effective Income

Mortgage Credit Certificate income that is not used to directly offset the Mortgage Payment before calculating the qualifying ratios may be included as Effective Income. The Mortgagee must use the current subsidy rate to calculate the Effective Income.

(E) Section 8 Homeownership Vouchers (TOTAL)

(1) Definition

Section 8 Homeownership Vouchers refer to housing subsidies received under the Housing Choice Voucher homeownership option from a Public Housing Agency (PHA).

(2) Required Documentation

The Mortgagee must verify and document the Borrower's receipt of the Housing Choice Voucher homeownership subsidies. The Mortgagee may consider that this income is reasonably likely to continue for three years.

(3) Calculation of Effective Income

The Mortgagee may only use Section 8 Homeownership Voucher subsidies as Effective Income if it is not used as an offset to the monthly Mortgage Payment. The Mortgagee must use the current subsidy rate to calculate the Effective Income.

(F) Other Public Assistance (TOTAL)

(1) Definition

Public Assistance refers to income received from government assistance programs.

(2) Required Documentation

Mortgagees must verify and document the income received from the government agency.

If any Public Assistance income is due to expire within three years from the date of mortgage application, that income cannot be used as Effective Income. If the documentation does not have a defined expiration date, the Mortgagee may consider the income effective and reasonably likely to continue.

(3) Calculation of Effective Income

The Mortgagee must use the current rate of Public Assistance received to calculate Effective Income.

(G) Automobile Allowances (TOTAL)

(1) Definition

Automobile Allowance refers to the funds provided by the Borrower's employer for automobile related expenses.

(2) Required Documentation [Text was deleted in this section.]

The Mortgagee must verify and document the Automobile Allowance received from the employer for the previous two years.

(3) Calculation of Effective Income

The Mortgagee must use the full amount of the Automobile Allowance to calculate Effective Income.

(H) Retirement Income (TOTAL)

Retirement Income refers to income received from Pensions, 401(k) distributions, and Social Security.

(1) Social Security Income (TOTAL)

(a) Definition

Social Security Income or Supplemental Security Income (SSI) refers to income received from the SSA other than disability income.

(b) Required Documentation

The Mortgagee must verify and document the Borrower's receipt of income from the SSA and that it is likely to continue for at least a three year period from the date of case number assignment.

For SSI, the Mortgagee must obtain any one of the following documents:
- federal tax returns;
- the most recent bank statement evidencing receipt of income from the SSA;
- a Proof of Income Letter, also known as a "Budget Letter" or "Benefits Letter" that evidences income from the SSA; or
- a copy of the Borrower's form SSA-1099/1042S, *Social Security Benefit Statement*.

In addition to verification of income, the Mortgagee must document the continuance of this income by obtaining from the Borrower (1) a copy of the last Notice of Award letter which states the SSA's determination on the Borrower's eligibility for SSA income or (2) an equivalent document that establishes award benefits to the Borrower (equivalent document). If any income from the SSA is due to expire within three years from the date of case number assignment, that income may not be used for qualifying.

If the Notice of Award or equivalent document does not have a defined expiration date, the Mortgagee must consider the income effective and reasonably likely to continue. The Mortgagee may not request additional documentation from the Borrower to demonstrate continuance of Social Security Administration income.

If the Notice of Award letter or equivalent document specifies a future start date for receipt of income, this income may only be considered effective on the specified start date.

(c) Calculation of Effective Income

The Mortgagee must use the current amount of Social Security Income received to calculate Effective Income.

(2) Pension (TOTAL)

(a) Definition

Pension refers to income received from the Borrower's former employer(s).

(b) Required Documentation

The Mortgagee must verify and document the Borrower's receipt of periodic payments from the Borrower's Pension and that the payments are likely to continue for at least three years.

The Mortgagee must obtain any one of the following documents:
- federal tax returns;
- the most recent bank statement evidencing receipt of income from the former employer; or
- a copy of the Borrower's Pension/retirement letter from the former employer.

(c) Calculation of Effective Income

The Mortgagee must use the current amount of Pension income received to calculate Effective Income.

(3) Individual Retirement Account and 401(k) (TOTAL)

(a) Definition

Individual Retirement Account (IRA)/401(k) Income refers to income received from an IRA.

(b) Required Documentation

The Mortgagee must verify and document the Borrower's receipt of recurring IRA/401(k) distribution Income and that it is reasonably likely to continue for three years.

The Mortgagee must obtain the most recent IRA/401(k) statement and any one of the following documents:
- federal tax returns; or
- the most recent bank statement evidencing receipt of income.

(c) Calculation of Effective Income

For Borrowers with IRA/401(k) Income that has been and will be consistently received, the Mortgagee must use the current amount of IRA Income received to calculate Effective Income. For Borrowers with fluctuating IRA/401(k)

Income, the Mortgagee must use the average of the IRA/401(k) Income received over the previous two years to calculate Effective Income. If IRA/401(k) Income has been received for less than two years, the Mortgagee must use the average over the time of receipt.

(I) Rental Income (TOTAL)

(1) Definition

Rental Income refers to income received or to be received from the subject Property or other real estate holdings.

(2) Rental Income Received from the Subject Property (TOTAL)

(a) Standard

The Mortgagee may consider Rental Income from existing and prospective tenants if documented in accordance with the following requirements.

Rental Income from the subject Property may be considered Effective Income when the Property is a two- to four-unit dwelling, or an acceptable one- to four-unit Investment Property.

(b) Required Documentation

Documentation varies depending upon the length of time the Borrower has owned the Property.

(i) Limited or No History of Rental Income

Where the Borrower does not have a history of Rental Income from the subject since the previous tax filing:

Two- to Four-Units

The Mortgagee must verify and document the proposed Rental Income by obtaining an appraisal showing fair market rent (use Fannie Mae Form 1025/Freddie Mac Form 72, *Small Residential Income Property Appraisal Report*) and, if available, the prospective leases.

One Unit

The Mortgagee must verify and document the proposed Rental Income by obtaining a Fannie Mae Form 1004/Freddie Mac Form 70, *Uniform Residential Appraisal Report*; Fannie Mae Form 1007/Freddie Mac Form 1000, *Single Family Comparable Rent Schedule*; and Fannie Mae Form 216/Freddie Mac Form 998, *Operating Income Statement*, showing fair market rent and, if available, the prospective lease.

(ii) History of Rental Income

Where the Borrower has a history of Rental Income from the subject since the previous tax filing, the Mortgagee must verify and document the existing Rental Income by obtaining the Borrower's most recent tax returns, including Schedule E, from the previous two years.

For Properties with less than two years of Rental Income history, the Mortgagee must document the date of acquisition by providing the deed, Closing Disclosure or similar legal document.

(c) Calculation of Effective Income

The Mortgagee must add the net subject property Rental Income to the Borrower's gross income to calculate Effective Income. The Mortgagee may not reduce the Borrower's total Mortgage Payment by the net subject property Rental Income.

(i) Limited or No History of Rental Income

To calculate the Effective Income from the subject Property where the Borrower does not have a history of Rental Income from the subject Property since the previous tax filing, the Mortgagee must use the lesser of:
- the monthly operating income reported on Fannie Mae Form 216/Freddie Mac Form 998; or
- 75 percent of the lesser of:
  o fair market rent reported by the Appraiser; or
  o the rent reflected in the lease or other rental agreement.

(ii) History of Rental Income

The Mortgagee must calculate the Rental Income by averaging the amount shown on Schedule E.

Depreciation, mortgage interest, taxes, insurance and any HOA dues shown on Schedule E may be added back to the net income or loss.

If the Property has been owned for less than two years, the Mortgagee must annualize the Rental Income for the length of time the Property has been owned.

(3) Rental Income from Other Real Estate Holdings (TOTAL)

(a) Standard

Rental Income from other real estate holdings may be considered Effective Income if the documentation requirements listed below are met. If Rental Income is being derived from the Property being vacated by the Borrower, the Borrower must be relocating to an area more than 100 miles from the Borrower's current Principal Residence. The Mortgagee must obtain a lease agreement of at least one year's duration after the Mortgage is closed and evidence of the payment of the security deposit or first month's rent.

(b) Required Documentation

(i) Limited or No History of Rental Income

Where the Borrower does not have a history of Rental Income for the Property since previous tax filing, including Property being vacated by the Borrower, the Mortgagee must obtain an appraisal evidencing market rent and that the Borrower has at least 25 percent equity in the Property. The appraisal is not required to be completed by an FHA Roster Appraiser.

Two- to Four-Units

The Mortgagee must verify and document the proposed Rental Income by obtaining an appraisal showing fair market rent (use Fannie Mae Form 1025/Freddie Mac Form 72, *Small Residential Income Property Appraisal Report*) and, if available, the prospective leases.

One Unit

The Mortgagee must verify and document the proposed Rental Income by obtaining a Fannie Mae Form 1004/Freddie Mac Form 70, *Uniform Residential Appraisal Report*, Fannie Mae Form 1007/Freddie Mac Form 1000, *Single Family Comparable Rent Schedule*, and Fannie Mae Form 216/Freddie Mac Form 998, *Operating Income Statement*, showing fair market rent and, if available, the prospective lease.

(ii) History of Rental Income

The Mortgagee must obtain the Borrower's last two years' tax returns with Schedule E.

(c) Calculation of Effective Net Rental Income

(i) Limited or No History of Rental Income

To calculate the effective net Rental Income from other real estate holdings where the Borrower does not have a history of Rental Income since the previous tax filing, the Mortgagee must deduct the Principal, Interest, Taxes, and Insurance (PITI) from the lesser of:

- the monthly operating income reported on Fannie Mae Form 216/Freddie Mac Form 998; or
- 75 percent of the lesser of:
  - o fair market rent reported by the Appraiser; or
  - o the rent reflected in the lease or other rental agreement.

(ii) History of Net Rental Income

The Mortgagee must calculate the net Rental Income by averaging the amount shown on the Schedule E provided the Borrower continues to own all Properties included on the Schedule E.

Depreciation shown on Schedule E may be added back to the net income or loss.

If the Property has been owned for less than two years, the Mortgagee must annualize the Rental Income for the length of time the Property has been owned.

For Properties with less than two years of Rental Income history, the Mortgagee must document the date of acquisition by providing the deed, Closing Disclosure or similar legal document.

Positive net Rental Income must be added to the Borrower's Effective Income. Negative net Rental Income must be included as a debt/liability.

(4) Boarders of the Subject Property (TOTAL)

(a) Definition

Boarder refers to an individual renting space inside the Borrower's Dwelling Unit.

(b) Standard

Rental Income from Boarders is only acceptable if the Borrower has a two-year history of receiving income from Boarders that is shown on the tax return and the Borrower is currently receiving Boarder income.

(c) Required Documentation

The Mortgagee must obtain two years of the Borrower's tax returns evidencing income from Boarders and the current lease.

For purchase transactions, the Mortgagee must obtain a copy of the executed written agreement documenting their intent to continue boarding with the Borrower.

(d) Calculation of Effective Income

The Mortgagee must calculate the Effective Income by using the lesser of the two year average or the current lease.

(J) Investment Income (TOTAL)

(1) Definition

Investment Income refers to interest and dividend income received from assets such as certificates of deposits, mutual funds, stocks, bonds, money markets, and savings and checking accounts.

(2) Required Documentation

The Mortgagee must verify and document the Borrower's Investment Income by obtaining tax returns for the previous two years and the most recent account statement.

(3) Calculation of Effective Income

The Mortgagee must calculate Investment Income by using the lesser of:
- the average Investment Income earned over the previous two years; or
- the average Investment Income earned over the previous one year.

The Mortgagee must subtract any of the assets used for the Borrower's required funds to close to purchase the subject Property from the Borrower's liquid assets prior to calculating any interest or dividend income.

(K) Capital Gains and Losses (TOTAL)

(1) Definition

Capital Gains refer to a profit that results from a disposition of a capital asset, such as a stock, bond or real estate, where the amount realized on the disposition exceeds the purchase price.

Capital Losses refer to a loss that results from a disposition of a capital asset, such as a stock, bond or real estate, where the amount realized on the disposition is less than the purchase price.

(2) Standard

Capital gains or losses must be considered when determining Effective Income, when the individual has a constant turnover of assets resulting in gains or losses.

(3) Required Documentation

Three years' tax returns are required to evaluate an earnings trend. If the trend:
- results in a gain, it may be added as Effective Income; or
- consistently shows a loss, it must be deducted from the total income.

(L) Expected Income (TOTAL)

(1) Definition

Expected Income refers to income from cost-of-living adjustments, performance raises, a new job, or retirement that has not been, but will be received within 60 Days of mortgage closing.

(2) Standard

The Mortgagee may consider Expected Income as Effective Income except when Expected Income is to be derived from a family-owned business.

(3) Required Documentation

The Mortgagee must verify and document the existence and amount of Expected Income with the employer in writing and that it is guaranteed to begin within 60 Days of mortgage closing. For expected Retirement Income, the Mortgagee must verify the amount and that it is guaranteed to begin within 60 Days of the mortgage closing.

(4) Calculation of Effective Income

Income is calculated in accordance with the standards for the type of income being received. The Mortgagee must also verify that the Borrower will have sufficient income or cash Reserves to support the Mortgage Payment and any other obligations between mortgage closing and the beginning of the receipt of the income.

(M) Trust Accounts (TOTAL)

(1) Definition

Trust Income refers to income that is regularly distributed to a Borrower from a trust.

(2) Required Documentation

The Mortgagee must verify and document the existence of the Trust Agreement or other trustee statement. The Mortgagee must also verify and document the frequency, duration, and amount of the distribution by obtaining a bank statement or transaction history from the bank.

The Mortgagee must verify that regular payments will continue for at least the first three years of the mortgage term.

(3) Calculation of Effective Income

The Mortgagee must use the income based on the terms and conditions in the Trust Agreement or other trustee statement to calculate Effective Income.

(N) Annuities or Similar (TOTAL)

(1) Definition

Annuity Income refers to a fixed sum of money periodically paid to the Borrower from a source other than employment.

(2) Required Documentation

The Mortgagee must verify and document the legal agreement establishing the annuity and guaranteeing the continuation of the annuity for the first three years of the Mortgage. The Mortgagee must also obtain a bank statement or a transaction history from a bank evidencing receipt of the annuity.

(3) Calculation of Effective Income

The Mortgagee must use the current rate of the annuity to calculate Effective Income.

The Mortgagee must subtract any of the assets used for the Borrower's required funds to close to purchase the subject Property from the Borrower's liquid assets prior to calculating any Annuity Income.

(O) Notes Receivable Income (TOTAL)

(1) Definition

Notes Receivable Income refers to income received by the Borrower as payee or holder in due course of a promissory Note or similar credit instrument.

(2) Required Documentation

The Mortgagee must verify and document the existence of the Note. The Mortgagee must also verify and document that payments have been consistently received for the previous 12 months by obtaining tax returns, deposit slips or canceled checks and that such payments are guaranteed to continue for the first three years of the Mortgage.

(3) Calculation of Effective Income

For Borrowers who have been and will be receiving a consistent amount of Notes Receivable Income, the Mortgagee must use the current rate of income to calculate Effective Income. For Borrowers whose Notes Receivable Income fluctuates, the Mortgagee must use the average of the Notes Receivable Income received over the previous year to calculate Effective Income.

(P) Non-Taxable Income (Grossing Up) (TOTAL)

(1) Definition

Non-Taxable Income refers to types of income not subject to federal taxes, which includes, but is not limited to:
- some portion of Social Security Income;
- some federal government employee Retirement Income;
- Railroad Retirement benefits;
- some state government Retirement Income;
- certain types of disability and Public Assistance payments;
- Child Support;
- military allowances; and
- other income that is documented as being exempt from federal income taxes.

(2) Required Documentation

The Mortgagee must document and support the amount of income to be Grossed Up for any Non-Taxable Income source and the current tax rate applicable to the Borrower's income that is being Grossed Up.

(3) Calculation of Effective Income

The amount of continuing tax savings attributed to Non-Taxable Income may be added to the Borrower's gross income.

The percentage of Non-Taxable Income that may be added cannot exceed the greater of 15 percent or the appropriate tax rate for the income amount, based on the Borrower's tax rate for the previous year. If the Borrower was not required to file a federal tax return for the previous tax reporting period, the Mortgagee may Gross Up the Non-Taxable Income by 15 percent.

The Mortgagee may not make any additional adjustments or allowances based on the number of the Borrower's dependents.

d. Asset Requirements (TOTAL)

i. General Asset Requirements (TOTAL)

The Mortgagee may only consider assets derived from acceptable sources in accordance with the requirements outlined below.

Closing costs, prepaid items and other fees may not be applied towards the Borrower's MRI.

(A) Earnest Money Deposit (TOTAL)

The Mortgagee must verify and document the deposit amount and source of funds if the amount of the earnest money deposit exceeds 1 percent of the sales price or is excessive based on the Borrower's history of accumulating savings, by obtaining:
- a copy of the Borrower's canceled check;
- certification from the deposit-holder acknowledging receipt of funds;
- a Verification of Deposit (VOD) or bank statement showing that the average balance was sufficient to cover the amount of the earnest money deposit at the time of the deposit; or
- direct electronic verification by a TPV vendor, subject to the following requirements:
  - the Borrower has authorized the Mortgagee to verify assets;
  - the date of the completed verification conforms with FHA requirements in Maximum Age of Mortgage Documents; and
  - the information shows that the average balance was sufficient to cover the amount of the earnest money deposit at the time of the deposit.

If the source of the earnest money deposit was a gift, the Mortgagee must verify that the gift is in compliance with Gifts (Personal and Equity) (TOTAL).

(B) Cash to Close (TOTAL)

The Mortgagee must document all funds that are used for the purpose of qualifying for or closing a Mortgage, including those to satisfy debt or pay costs outside of closing.

The Mortgagee must verify and document that the Borrower has sufficient funds from an acceptable source to facilitate the closing.

(1) Determining the Amount Needed for Closing

For a purchase transaction, the amount of cash needed by the Borrower to close an FHA-insured Mortgage is the difference between the total cost to acquire the Property and the total mortgage amount.

For a refinance transaction, the amount of cash needed by the Borrower to close an FHA-insured Mortgage is the difference between the total payoff requirements of the Mortgage being refinanced and the total mortgage amount.

(2) Mortgagee Responsibility for Estimating Settlement Requirements

In addition to the MRI, additional Borrower expenses must be included in the total amount of cash that the Borrower must provide at mortgage settlement.

(a) Origination Fees and Other Closing Costs

The Mortgagee or sponsored TPO may charge a reasonable origination fee.

The Mortgagee or sponsored TPO may charge and collect from Borrowers those customary and reasonable closing costs and prepaid items necessary to close the Mortgage. Charges may not exceed the actual costs.

The Mortgagee must comply with HUD's Qualified Mortgage Rule at 24 CFR § 203.19.

(b) Discount Points

Discount Points refer to a charge from the Mortgagee for the interest rate chosen. They are paid by the Borrower and become part of the total cash required to close.

(c) Types of Prepaid Items (Including Per Diem Interest)

Prepaid items may include flood and hazard insurance premiums, MIPs, real estate taxes, and per diem interest. They must comply with the requirements of the CFPB.

(d) Non-Realty or Personal Property

Non-Realty or Personal Property items (chattel) that the Borrower agrees to pay for separately, including the amount subtracted from the sales price when determining the maximum Mortgage, are included in the total cash requirements for the Mortgage.

(e) Upfront Mortgage Insurance Premium Amounts

Any UFMIP amounts paid in cash are added to the total cash settlement requirements. The UFMIP must be entirely financed into the Mortgage or paid entirely in cash. However, if the UFMIP is financed into the Mortgage, the entire amount is to be financed except for any amount less than $1.00.

(f) Real Estate Agent Fees

If a Borrower is represented by a real estate agent and must pay any fee directly to the agent, that expense must be included in the total of the Borrower's settlement requirements.

(g) Repairs and Improvements

Repairs and improvements, or any portion paid by the Borrower that cannot be financed into the Mortgage, are part of the Borrower's total cash requirements.

(h) Premium Pricing on FHA-Insured Mortgages

Premium Pricing refers to the aggregate credits from a Mortgagee or TPO at the interest rate chosen.

Premium Pricing may be used to pay a Borrower's actual closing costs and prepaid items. Premium Pricing is not included as part of the Interested Party limitation unless the Mortgagee or TPO is the property seller, real estate agent, builder or developer.

The funds derived from a premium priced Mortgage:
- must be disclosed in accordance with RESPA;
- must be used to reduce the principal balance if the credit amount exceeds the actual dollar amount for closing costs and prepaid items; and
- may not be used for payment of debts, collection accounts, escrow shortages or missed Mortgage Payments, or Judgments.

(i) Interested Party Contributions on the Closing Disclosure

The Mortgagee may apply Interested Party credits to the closing costs and prepaid items including any items Paid Outside Closing (POC).

The refund of the Borrower's POCs may be used toward the Borrower's MRI if the Mortgagee documents that the POCs were paid with the Borrower's own funds.

The Mortgagee must identify the total Interested Party credits on the front page of the Closing Disclosure or similar legal document or in an addendum. The Mortgagee must identify each item paid by Interested Party Contributions.

(j) Real Estate Tax Credits

Where real estate taxes are paid in arrears, the seller's real estate tax credit may be used to meet the MRI, if the Mortgagee documents that the Borrower had sufficient assets to meet the MRI and the Borrower paid closing costs and other prepaid items at the time of underwriting.

This permits the Borrower to bring a portion of their MRI to the closing and combine that portion with the real estate tax credit for their total MRI.

(C) Reserves (TOTAL)

The Mortgagee must verify and document all assets submitted to the AUS.

Reserves refer to the sum of the Borrower's verified and documented liquid assets minus the total funds the Borrower is required to pay at closing.

Reserves do not include:
- the amount of cash taken at settlement in cash-out transactions;
- incidental cash received at settlement in other loan transactions;
- equity in another Property; or
- borrowed funds from any source.

Required Reserves for Three- to Four-Unit Properties

The Mortgagee must verify and document Reserves equivalent to three months' PITI after closing for three- to four-unit Properties.

ii. Source Requirements for the Borrower's Minimum Required Investment (TOTAL)

(A) Definition

Minimum Required Investment (MRI) refers to the Borrower's contribution in cash or its equivalent required by Section 203(b)(9) of the National Housing Act, which represents at least 3.5 percent of the Adjusted Value of the Property.

(B) Standard

The Mortgagee may only permit the Borrower's MRI to be provided by a source permissible under Section 203(b)(9)(C) of the National Housing Act, which means the funds for the Borrower's MRI must not come from:
  (1) the seller of the Property;
  (2) any other person or Entity who financially benefits from the transaction (directly or indirectly); or
  (3) anyone who is or will be reimbursed, directly or indirectly, by any party included in (1) or (2) above.

While additional funds to close may be provided by one of these sources if permitted under the relevant requirements above, none of the Borrower's MRI may come from these sources. The Mortgagee must document permissible sources for the full MRI in accordance with special requirements noted above.

Additionally, in accordance with Prohibited Sources of Minimum Cash Investment Under the National Housing Act -Interpretive Rule, HUD does not interpret Section 203(b)(9)(C) of the National Housing Act to prohibit Governmental Entities, when acting in their governmental capacity, from providing the Borrower's MRI where the Governmental Entity is originating the insured Mortgage through one of its homeownership programs.

(C) Required Documentation

Where the Borrower's MRI is provided by someone other than the Borrower, the Mortgagee must also obtain documentation to support the permissible nature of the source of those funds.

To establish that the Governmental Entity provided the Borrower's MRI in a manner consistent with HUD's Interpretive Rule, the Mortgagee must document that the Governmental Entity incurred prior to or at closing an enforceable legal liability or obligation to fund the Borrower's MRI. It is not sufficient to document that the Governmental Entity has agreed to reimburse the Mortgagee for the use of funds legally belonging to the Mortgagee to fund the Borrower's MRI.

The Mortgagee must obtain:

- a canceled check, evidence of wire transfer or other draw request showing that prior to or at the time of closing the Governmental Entity had authorized a draw of the funds provided towards the Borrower's MRI from the Governmental Entity's account; or
- a letter from the Governmental Entity, signed by an authorized official, establishing that the funds provided towards the Borrower's MRI were funds legally belonging to the Governmental Entity, when acting in their governmental capacity, at or before closing.

Where a letter from the Governmental Entity is submitted, the precise language of the letter may vary, but must demonstrate that the funds provided for the Borrower's MRI legally belonged to the Governmental Entity at or before closing, by stating, for example:

- the Governmental Entity has, at or before closing, incurred a legally enforceable liability as a result of its agreement to provide the funds towards the Borrower's MRI;
- the Governmental Entity has, at or before closing, incurred a legally enforceable obligation to provide the funds towards the Borrower's MRI; or
- the Governmental Entity has, at or before closing, authorized a draw on its account to provide the funds towards the Borrower's MRI.

While the Mortgagee is not required to document the actual transfer of funds in satisfaction of the obligation or liability, the failure of the Governmental Entity to satisfy the obligation or liability may result in a determination that the funds were provided by a prohibited source.

iii. Sources of Funds (TOTAL)

The Mortgagee must verify liquid assets for cash to close and Reserves as indicated.

(A) Checking and Savings Accounts (TOTAL)

(1) Definition

Checking and Savings Accounts refer to funds from Borrower-held accounts in a financial institution that allows for withdrawals and deposits.

(2) Standard

The Mortgagee must verify and document the existence of and amounts in the Borrower's checking and savings accounts.

For recently opened accounts and recent individual deposits of more than 1 percent of the Adjusted Value, the Mortgagee must obtain documentation of the deposits. The Mortgagee must also verify that no debts were incurred to obtain part, or all, of the MRI.

(3) Required Documentation

If the Borrower does not hold the deposit account solely, all non-Borrower parties on the account must provide a written statement that the Borrower has full access and use of the funds.

(a) Traditional Documentation

The Mortgagee must obtain:
- a written VOD and the Borrower's most recent statement for each account; or
- direct verification by a TPV vendor of the Borrower's account covering activity for a minimum of the most recent available month, subject to the following requirements:
  - the Borrower has authorized the Mortgagee to use a TPV vendor to verify assets; and
  - the date of the data contained in the completed verification is current within 30 days of the date of the verification.

(b) Alternative Documentation

If a VOD is not obtained, a statement showing the previous month's ending balance for the most recent month is required. If the previous month's balance is not shown, the Mortgagee must obtain statement(s) for the most recent two months.

(B) Cash on Hand (TOTAL)

(1) Definition

Cash on Hand refers to cash held by the Borrower outside of a financial institution.

(2) Standard

The Mortgagee must verify that the Borrower's Cash on Hand is deposited in a financial institution or held by the escrow/title company.

(3) Required Documentation

The Mortgagee must verify and document the Borrower's Cash on Hand by obtaining an explanation from the Borrower describing how the funds were accumulated and the amount of time it took to accumulate the funds.

The Mortgagee must also determine the reasonableness of the accumulation based on the time period during which the funds were saved and the Borrower's:
- income stream;

- spending habits;
- documented expenses; and
- history of using financial institutions.

(C) Retirement Accounts (TOTAL)

(1) Definition

Retirement Accounts refer to assets accumulated by the Borrower for the purpose of retirement.

(2) Standard

The Mortgagee may include up to 60 percent of the value of assets, less any existing loans, from the Borrower's retirement accounts, such as IRAs, thrift savings plans, 401(k) plan, and Keogh accounts, unless the Borrower provides conclusive evidence that a higher percentage may be withdrawn after subtracting any federal income tax and withdrawal penalties.

The portion of the assets not used to meet closing requirements, after adjusting for taxes and penalties, may be counted as Reserves.

(3) Required Documentation

The Mortgagee must obtain the most recent monthly or quarterly statement to verify and document the existence and amounts in the Borrower's retirement accounts, the Borrower's eligibility for withdrawals, and the terms and conditions for withdrawal from any retirement account.

If any portion of the asset is required for funds to close, evidence of liquidation is required.

(D) Stocks and Bonds (TOTAL)

(1) Definition

Stocks and Bonds are investment assets accumulated by the Borrower.

(2) Standard

The Mortgagee must determine the value of the stocks and bonds from the most recent monthly or quarterly statement.

If the stocks and bonds are not held in a brokerage account, the Mortgagee must determine the current value of the stocks and bonds through third party verification. Government-issued savings bonds are valued at the original purchase price, unless the Mortgagee verifies and documents that the bonds are eligible for redemption when cash to close is calculated.

(3) Required Documentation

The Mortgagee must verify and document the existence of the Borrower's stocks and bonds by obtaining brokerage statement(s) for each account for the most recent two months. Evidence of liquidation is not required.

For stocks and bonds not held in a brokerage account the Mortgagee must obtain a copy of each stock or bond certificate.

(E) Private Savings Clubs (TOTAL)

(1) Definition

Private Savings Club refers to a non-traditional method of saving by making deposits into a member-managed resource pool.

(2) Standard

The Mortgagee may consider Private Savings Club funds that are distributed to and received by the Borrower as an acceptable source of funds.

The Mortgagee must verify and document the establishment and duration of the club, and the Borrower's receipt of funds from the club. The Mortgagee must also determine that the received funds were reasonably accumulated, and not borrowed.

(3) Required Documentation

The Mortgagee must obtain the club's account ledgers and receipts, and a verification from the club treasurer that the club is still active.

(F) Gifts (Personal and Equity) (TOTAL)

(1) Definition

Gifts refer to the contributions of cash or equity with no expectation of repayment.

(2) Standards for Gifts

(a) Acceptable Sources of Gifts Funds

Gifts may be provided by:
- the Borrower's Family Member;
- the Borrower's employer or labor union;

- a close friend with a clearly defined and documented interest in the Borrower;
- a charitable organization;
- a governmental agency or public Entity that has a program providing homeownership assistance to:
  - low or moderate income families; or
  - first-time homebuyers.

Any gift of the Borrower's MRI must also comply with the additional requirements set forth in Source Requirements for the Borrower's MRI.

(b) Donor's Source of Funds

Cash on Hand is not an acceptable source of donor gift funds.

(3) Required Documentation

The Mortgagee must obtain a gift letter signed and dated by the donor and Borrower that includes the following:
- the donor's name, address, and telephone number;
- the donor's relationship to the Borrower;
- the dollar amount of the gift; and
- a statement that no repayment is required.

Documenting the Transfer of Gifts

The Mortgagee must verify and document the transfer of gift funds from the donor to the Borrower in accordance with the requirements below.

a. If the gift funds have been verified in the Borrower's account, obtain the donor's bank statement showing the withdrawal and evidence of the deposit into the Borrower's account.

b. If the gift funds are not verified in the Borrower's account, obtain the certified check or money order or cashier's check or wire transfer or other official check evidencing payment to the Borrower or settlement agent, and the donor's bank statement evidencing sufficient funds for the amount of the gift.

If the gift funds are being borrowed by the donor and documentation from the bank or other savings account is not available, the Mortgagee must have the donor provide written evidence that the funds were borrowed from an acceptable source, not from a party to the transaction.

The Mortgagee and its Affiliates are prohibited from providing the loan of gift funds to the donor unless the terms of the loan are equivalent to those available to the general public.

Regardless of when gift funds are made available to a Borrower or settlement agent, the Mortgagee must be able to make a reasonable determination that the gift funds were not provided by an unacceptable source.

(4) Standards for Gifts of Equity

(a) Who May Provide Gifts of Equity

Only Family Members may provide equity credit as a gift on Property being sold to other Family Members.

(b) Required Documentation

The Mortgagee must obtain a gift letter signed and dated by the donor and Borrower that includes the following:
- the donor's name, address, and telephone number;
- the donor's relationship to the Borrower;
- the dollar amount of the gift; and
- a statement that no repayment is required.

(G) Interested Party Contributions (TOTAL)

(1) Definition

Interested Parties refer to sellers, real estate agents, builders, developers, Mortgagees, Third Party Originators (TPO), or other parties with an interest in the transaction.

Interested Party Contribution refers to a payment by an Interested Party, or combination of parties, toward the Borrower's origination fees, other closing costs, prepaid items and discount points.

(2) Standard

Interested Parties may contribute up to 6 percent of the sales price toward the Borrower's origination fees, other closing costs, prepaid items and discount points. The 6 percent limit also includes:
- Interested Party payment for permanent and temporary interest rate buydowns, and other payment supplements;
- payments of mortgage interest for fixed rate Mortgages;
- Mortgage Payment protection insurance; and
- payment of the UFMIP.

Interested Party Contributions that exceed actual origination fees, other closing costs, prepaid items and discount points are considered an inducement to purchase. Interested Party Contributions exceeding 6 percent are considered an inducement to purchase.

Interested Party Contributions may not be used for the Borrower's MRI.

Exceptions

Premium Pricing credits from the Mortgagee or TPO are excluded from the 6 percent limit, provided the Mortgagee or TPO is not the seller, real estate agent, builder, or developer.

Payment of real estate agent commissions or fees, typically paid by the seller under local or state law, or local custom, is not considered an Interested Party Contribution. The satisfaction of a PACE lien or obligation against the Property by the property owner is not considered an Interested Party Contribution.

(3) Required Documentation

The Mortgagee must document the total Interested Party Contributions on the sales contract or applicable legally binding document, form HUD-92900-LT, and Closing Disclosure or similar legal document. When a legally binding document other than the sales contract is used to document the Interested Party Contributions, the Mortgagee must provide a copy of this document to the assigned Appraiser.

(H) Inducements to Purchase (TOTAL)

Inducements to Purchase refer to certain expenses paid by the seller and/or another Interested Party on behalf of the Borrower and result in a dollar-for-dollar reduction to the purchase price when computing the Adjusted Value of the Property before applying the appropriate Loan-to-Value (LTV) percentage.

These inducements include, but are not limited to:
- contributions exceeding 6 percent of the purchase price;
- contributions exceeding the origination fees, other closing costs, prepaid items and discount points;
- decorating allowances;
- repair allowances;
- excess rent credit;
- moving costs;
- paying off consumer debt;
- Personal Property;
- sales commission on the Borrower's present residence; and

- below-market rent, except for Borrowers who meet the Identity-of-Interest exception for Family Members.

(1) Personal Property (TOTAL)

Replacement of existing Personal Property items listed below are not considered an inducement to purchase, provided the replacement is made prior to settlement and no cash allowance is given to the Borrower. The inclusion of the items below in the sales agreement is also not considered an inducement to purchase if inclusion of the item is customary for the area:

- range
- refrigerator
- dishwasher
- washer
- dryer
- carpeting
- window treatment
- other items determined appropriate by the HOC

(2) Sales Commission (TOTAL)

An inducement to purchase exists when the seller and/or Interested Party agrees to pay any portion of the Borrower's sales commission on the sale of the Borrower's present residence.

An inducement to purchase also exists when a Borrower is not paying a real estate commission on the sale of their present residence, and the same real estate broker or agent is involved in both transactions, and the seller is paying a real estate commission on the Property being purchased by the Borrower that exceeds what is typical for the area.

(3) Rent Below Fair Market (TOTAL)

A reduced rent is an inducement to purchase when the sales contract includes terms permitting the Borrower to live in the Property rent-free or has an agreement to occupy the Property at a rental amount greater than 10 percent below the Appraiser's estimate of fair market rent. When such an inducement exists, the amount of inducement is the difference between the rent charged and the Appraiser's estimate of fair market rent prorated over the period between execution of the sales contract and execution of the Property sale.

Rent below fair market is not considered an inducement to purchase when a builder fails to deliver a Property at an agreed-upon time, and permits the Borrower to occupy an existing or other unit for less than market rent until construction is complete.

(I) Downpayment Assistance Programs (TOTAL)

FHA does not "approve" downpayment assistance programs administered by charitable organizations, such as nonprofits. FHA also does not allow nonprofit entities to provide gifts to pay off:

- Installment Loans
- credit cards
- collections
- Judgments
- liens
- similar debts

The Mortgagee must ensure that a gift provided by a charitable organization meets the appropriate FHA requirements, and that the transfer of funds is properly documented.

(1) Gifts from Charitable Organizations that Lose or Give Up Their Federal Tax-Exempt Status

If a charitable organization makes a gift that is to be used for all, or part, of a Borrower's downpayment, and the organization providing the gift loses or gives up its federal tax-exempt status, FHA will recognize the gift as an acceptable source of the downpayment provided that:

- the gift is made to the Borrower;
- the gift is properly documented; and
- the Borrower has entered into a contract of sale (including any amendments to purchase price) on or before the date the IRS officially announces that the charitable organization's tax-exempt status is terminated.

(2) Mortgagee Responsibility for Ensuring that Downpayment Assistance Provider is a Charitable Organization

The Mortgagee is responsible for ensuring that an Entity providing downpayment assistance is a charitable organization as defined by Section 501(a) of the Internal Revenue Code (IRC) of 1986 pursuant to Section 501(c) (3) of the IRC.

One resource for this information is the IRS Exempt Organization Select Check, which contains a list of organizations eligible to receive tax-deductible charitable contributions.

(J) Secondary Financing (TOTAL)

Secondary Financing is any financing other than the first Mortgage that creates a lien against the Property. Any such financing that does create a lien against the Property is not considered a gift or a grant even if it does not require regular payments or has other features forgiving the debt.

(1) Secondary Financing Provided by Governmental Entities and HOPE Grantees (TOTAL)

(a) Definitions

A Governmental Entity refers to any federal, state, or local government agency or instrumentality.

To be considered an Instrumentality of Government, the Entity must be established by a governmental body or with governmental approval or under special law to serve a particular public purpose or designated by law (statute or court opinion) and does not have 501(c)(3) status. HUD deems Section 115 Entities to be Instrumentalities of Government for the purpose of providing secondary financing.

Homeownership and Opportunity for People Everywhere (HOPE) Grantee refers to an Entity designated in the homeownership plan submitted by an applicant for an implementation grant under the HOPE program.

(b) Standard

FHA will insure a first Mortgage on a Property that has a second Mortgage or lien made or held by a Governmental Entity, provided that:
- the secondary financing is disclosed at the time of application;
- no costs associated with the secondary financing are financed into the FHA-insured first Mortgage;
- the insured first Mortgage does not exceed the FHA Nationwide Mortgage Limit for the area in which the Property is located;
- the secondary financing payments are included in the total Mortgage Payment;
- any secondary financing of the Borrower's MRI fully complies with the additional requirements set forth in Source Requirements for the Borrower's MRI;
- the secondary financing does not result in cash back to the Borrower except for refund of earnest money deposit or other Borrower costs paid outside of closing; and
- the second lien does not provide for a balloon payment within 10 years from the date of execution.

Nonprofits assisting a Governmental Entity in the operation of its secondary financing programs must have HUD approval and placement on the Nonprofit Organization Roster unless there is a documented agreement that:

- the functions performed are limited to the Governmental Entity's secondary financing program; and
- the secondary financing legal documents (Note and Deed of Trust) name the Governmental Entity as the Mortgagee.

Secondary financing that will close in the name of the nonprofit and be held by a Governmental Entity must be made by a HUD-approved Nonprofit.

The Mortgagee must enter information on HUD-approved Nonprofits into FHA Connection (FHAC), as applicable.

Secondary financing provided by Governmental Entities or HOPE grantees may be used to meet the Borrower's MRI. Any loan of the Borrower's MRI must also comply with the additional requirements set forth in Source Requirements for the Borrower's MRI.

There is no maximum Combined Loan-to-Value (CLTV) for secondary financing loans provided by Governmental Entities or HOPE grantees.

Any secondary financing meeting this standard is deemed to have prior approval in accordance with 24 CFR § 203.32.

(c) Required Documentation

The Mortgagee must obtain from the provider of any secondary financing:
- documentation showing the amount of funds provided to the Borrower for each transaction;
- copies of the Mortgage and Note; and
- a letter from the Governmental Entity on their letterhead evidencing the relationship between them and the nonprofit for each FHA-insured Mortgage, signed by an authorized official and containing the following information:
  - the FHA case number for the first Mortgage;
  - the complete property address;
  - the name, address and Tax ID for the nonprofit;
  - the name of the Borrower(s) to whom the nonprofit is providing secondary financing;
  - the amount and purpose for the secondary financing provided to the Borrower; and
  - a statement indicating whether the secondary financing:
    - will close in the name of the Governmental Entity; or
    - will be closed in the name of the nonprofit and held by the Governmental Entity.

Where a nonprofit assisting a Governmental Entity with its secondary financing programs is not a HUD-approved Nonprofit, a documented agreement must be provided that:

- the functions performed by the nonprofit are limited to the Governmental Entity's secondary financing program; and
- the secondary financing legal documents (Note and Deed of Trust) name the Governmental Entity as the Mortgagee.

(2) Secondary Financing Provided by HUD-Approved Nonprofits (TOTAL)

(a) Definition

A HUD-approved Nonprofit is a nonprofit agency approved by HUD to act as a mortgagor using FHA mortgage insurance, purchase the Department's Real Estate Owned (REO) Properties (HUD Homes) at a discount, and provide secondary financing.

HUD-approved Nonprofits appear on the HUD Nonprofit Roster.

(b) Standard

FHA will insure a first Mortgage on a Property that has a second Mortgage or lien held by a HUD-approved Nonprofit, provided that:

- the secondary financing is disclosed at the time of application;
- no costs associated with the secondary financing are financed into the FHA-insured first Mortgage;
- the secondary financing payments must be included in the total Mortgage Payment;
- the secondary financing must not result in cash back to the Borrower except for refund of earnest money deposit or other Borrower costs paid outside of closing;
- the secondary financing may not be used to meet the Borrower's MRI;
- there is no maximum CLTV for secondary financing loans provided by HUD-approved Nonprofits; and
- the second lien may not provide for a balloon payment within 10 years from the date of execution.

Secondary financing provided by Section 115 Entities must follow the guidance in Secondary Financing Provided by Governmental Entities and HOPE Grantees.

Any secondary financing meeting this standard is deemed to have prior approval in accordance with 24 CFR § 203.32.

(c) Required Documentation

The Mortgagee must obtain from the provider of any secondary financing:
- documentation showing the amount of funds provided to the Borrower for each transaction; and
- copies of the Mortgage and Note.

The Mortgagee must enter information into FHAC on the nonprofit and the Governmental Entity as applicable. If there is more than one nonprofit, enter information on all nonprofits.

(3) Family Members (TOTAL)

(a) Standard

FHA will insure a first Mortgage on a Property that has a second Mortgage or lien held by a Family Member, provided that:
- the secondary financing is disclosed at the time of application;
- no costs associated with the secondary financing are financed into the FHA-insured first Mortgage;
- the secondary financing payments must be included in the total Mortgage Payment;
- the secondary financing must not result in cash back to the Borrower except for refund of earnest money deposit or other Borrower costs paid outside of closing;
- the secondary financing may be used to meet the Borrower's MRI;
- the CLTV ratio of the Base Loan Amount and secondary financing amount must not exceed 100 percent of the Adjusted Value;
- the second lien may not provide for a balloon payment within 10 years from the date of execution;
- any periodic payments are level and monthly;
- there is no prepayment penalty;
- if the Family Member providing the secondary financing borrows the funds, the lending source may not be an Entity with an Identity of Interest in the sale of the Property, such as the:
  - seller;
  - builder;
  - loan originator; or
  - real estate agent;
- mortgage companies with retail banking Affiliates may have the Affiliate lend the funds to the Family Member. However, the terms and conditions of the loan to the Family Member cannot be more favorable than they would be for any other Borrowers;
- if funds loaned by the Family Member are borrowed from an acceptable source, the Borrower may not be a co-Obligor on the Note;

- if the loan from the Family Member is secured by the subject Property, only the Family Member provider may be the Note holder; and
- the secondary financing provided by the Family Member must not be transferred to another Entity at or subsequent to closing.

Any secondary financing meeting this standard is deemed to have prior approval in accordance with 24 CFR § 203.32.

(b) Required Documentation

The Mortgagee must obtain from the provider of any secondary financing:
- documentation showing the amount of funds provided to the Borrower for each transaction and source of funds; and
- copies of the Mortgage and Note.

If the secondary financing funds are being borrowed by the Family Member and documentation from the bank or other savings account is not available, the Mortgagee must have the Family Member provide written evidence that the funds were borrowed from an acceptable source, not from a party to the transaction, including the Mortgagee.

(4) Private Individuals and Other Organizations (TOTAL)

(a) Definition

Private Individuals and Other Organizations refer to any individuals or Entities providing secondary financing which are not covered elsewhere in this Secondary Financing section.

(b) Standard

FHA will insure a first Mortgage on a Property that has a second Mortgage or lien held by private individuals and other organizations, provided that:
- the secondary financing is disclosed at the time of application;
- no costs associated with the secondary financing are financed into the FHA-insured first Mortgage;
- the secondary financing payments must be included in the total Mortgage Payment;
- the secondary financing must not result in cash back to the Borrower except for refund of earnest money deposit or other Borrower costs paid outside of closing;
- the secondary financing may not be used to meet the Borrower's MRI;
- the CLTV ratio of the Base Loan Amount and secondary financing amount must not exceed the applicable FHA LTV limit;
- the Base Loan Amount and secondary financing amount must not exceed the Nationwide Mortgage Limits;

- the second lien may not provide for a balloon payment within 10 years from the date of execution;
- any periodic payments are level and monthly; and
- there is no prepayment penalty, after giving the Mortgagee 30 Days advance notice.

Any secondary financing meeting this standard is deemed to have prior approval in accordance with 24 CFR § 203.32.

(c) Required Documentation

The Mortgagee must obtain from the provider of any secondary financing:
- documentation showing the amount of funds provided to the Borrower for each transaction; and
- copies of the Mortgage and Note.

(K) Loans (TOTAL)

A Loan refers to an arrangement in which a lender gives money or Property to a Borrower and the Borrower agrees to return the Property or repay the money.

(1) Collateralized Loans (TOTAL)

(a) Definition

A Collateralized Loan is a loan that is fully secured by a financial asset of the Borrower, such as deposit accounts, certificates of deposit, investment accounts, or Real Property. These assets may include stocks, bonds, and real estate other than the Property being purchased.

(b) Standard

Loans secured against deposited funds, where repayment may be obtained through extinguishing the asset, do not require consideration of repayment for qualifying purposes. The Mortgagee must reduce the amount of the corresponding asset by the amount of the collateralized loan.

(c) Who May Provide Collateralized Loans

Only an independent third party may provide the borrowed funds for collateralized loans.

The seller, real estate agent or broker, lender, or other Interested Party may not provide such funds. Unacceptable borrowed funds include:
- unsecured signature loans;
- cash advances on credit cards;

- borrowing against household goods and furniture; and
- other similar unsecured financing.

Any loan of the Borrower's MRI must also comply with the additional requirements set forth in Source Requirements for the Borrower's MRI.

(d) Required Documentation

The Mortgagee must verify and document the existence of the Borrower's assets used to collateralize the loan, the promissory Note securing the asset, and the loan proceeds.

(2) Retirement Account Loans (TOTAL)

(a) Definition

A Retirement Account Loan is a loan that is secured by the Borrower's retirement assets.

(b) Standard

The Mortgagee must reduce the amount of the retirement account asset by the amount of the outstanding balance of the retirement account loan.

(c) Required Documentation

The Mortgagee must verify and document the existence and amounts in the Borrower's retirement accounts and the outstanding loan balance.

(3) Disaster Relief Loans (TOTAL)

(a) Definition

Disaster Relief Loans refer to loans from a Governmental Entity that provide immediate housing assistance to individuals displaced due to a natural disaster.

(b) Standard

Secured or unsecured disaster relief loans administered by the Small Business Administration (SBA) may also be used. If the SBA loan will be secured by the Property being purchased, it must be clearly subordinate to the FHA-insured Mortgage, and meet the requirements for Secondary Financing provided by Governmental Entities.

Any loan of the Borrower's MRI must also comply with the additional requirements set forth in Source Requirements for the Borrower's MRI.

Any monthly payment arising from this type of loan must be included in the qualifying ratios.

(c) Required Documentation

The Mortgagee must verify and document the promissory Note.

(L) Grants (TOTAL)

(1) Disaster Relief Grants (TOTAL)

(a) Definition

Disaster Relief Grants refer to grants from a Governmental Entity that provide immediate housing assistance to individuals displaced due to a natural disaster. Disaster relief grants may be used for the Borrower's MRI.

(b) Required Documentation

The Mortgagee must verify and document the Borrower's receipt of the grant and terms of use.

Any grant of the Borrower's MRI must also comply with the additional requirements set forth in Source Requirements for the Borrower's MRI.

(2) Federal Home Loan Bank Homeownership Set-Aside Grant Program (TOTAL)

(a) Definition

The Federal Home Loan Bank's (FHLB) Affordable Housing Program (AHP) Homeownership Set-Aside Grant Program is an acceptable source of downpayment assistance and may be used in conjunction with FHA-insured financing. Secondary financing that creates a lien against the Property is not considered a gift or grant even if it does not require regular payments or has other features forgiving the debt.

(b) Standard

Any AHP Set-Aside funds used for the Borrower's MRI must also comply with the additional requirements set forth in Source Requirements for the Borrower's MRI.

(c) Required Documentation

The Mortgagee must verify and document the Borrower's receipt of the grant and terms of use.

The Mortgagee must also verify and document that the Retention Agreement required by the FHLB is recorded against the Property and results in a Deed Restriction, and not a second lien. The Retention Agreement must:

- provide that the FHLB will have ultimate control over the AHP grant funds if the funds are repaid by the Borrower;
- include language terminating the legal restrictions on conveyance if title to the Property is transferred by foreclosure or DIL, or assigned to the Secretary of HUD; and
- comply with all other FHA regulations.

(M) Employer Assistance (TOTAL)

(1) Definition

Employer Assistance refers to benefits provided by an employer to relocate the Borrower or assist in the Borrower's housing purchase, including closing costs, prepaid items, MIP, or any portion of the MRI. Employer Assistance does not include benefits provided by an employer through secondary financing.

A salary advance cannot be considered as assets to close.

(2) Standard

(a) Relocation Guaranteed Purchase

The Mortgagee may allow the net proceeds (relocation guaranteed purchase price minus the outstanding liens and expenses) to be used as cash to close.

(b) Employer Assistance Plans

The amount received under Employer Assistance Plans may be used as cash to close.

(3) Required Documentation

(a) Relocation Guaranteed Purchase

If the Borrower is being transferred by their company under a guaranteed sales plan, the Mortgagee must obtain an executed buyout agreement signed by all parties and receipt of funds indicating that the employer or relocation service takes responsibility for the outstanding mortgage debt.

The Mortgagee must verify and document the agreement guaranteeing employer purchase of the Borrower's previous residence and the net proceeds from sale.

(b) Employer Assistance Plans

The Mortgagee must verify and document the Borrower's receipt of assistance. If the employer provides this benefit after settlement, the Mortgagee must verify and document that the Borrower has sufficient cash for closing.

(N) Sale of Personal Property (TOTAL)

(1) Definition

Personal Property refers to tangible property, other than Real Property, such as cars, recreational vehicles, stamps, coins or other collectibles.

(2) Standard

The Mortgagee must use the lesser of the estimated value or actual sales price when determining the sufficiency of assets to close.

(3) Required Documentation

Borrowers may sell Personal Property to obtain cash for closing.

The Mortgagee must obtain a satisfactory estimate of the value of the item, a copy of the bill of sale, evidence of receipt, and deposit of proceeds. A value estimate may take the form of a published value estimate issued by organizations such as automobile dealers, philatelic or numismatic associations, or a separate written appraisal by a qualified Appraiser with no financial interest in the mortgage transaction.

(O) Trade-In of Manufactured Housing (TOTAL)

(1) Definition

Trade-In of Manufactured Housing refers to the Borrower's sale or trade-in of another Manufactured Home that is not considered real estate to a Manufactured Housing dealer or an independent third party.

(2) Standard

The net proceeds from the Trade-In of a Manufactured Home may be utilized as the Borrower's source of funds.

Trade-ins cannot result in cash back to the Borrower from the dealer or independent third party.

(3) Required Documentation

The Mortgagee must verify and document the installment sales contract or other agreement evidencing a transaction and value of the trade-in or sale. The Mortgagee must obtain documentation to support the Trade Equity.

(P) Sale of Real Property (TOTAL)

(1) Definition

The Sale of Real Property refers to the sale of Property currently owned by the Borrower.

(2) Standard

Net proceeds from the Sale of Real Property may be used as an acceptable source of funds.

(3) Required Documentation

The Mortgagee must verify and document the actual sale and the Net Sale Proceeds by obtaining a fully executed Closing Disclosure or similar legal document.

The Mortgagee must also verify and document that the transaction was arms-length, and that the Borrower is entitled to the Net Sale Proceeds.

(Q) Real Estate Commission from Sale of a Subject Property (TOTAL)

(1) Definition

Real Estate Commission from Sale of Subject Property refers to the Borrower's (i.e., buyer's) portion of a real estate commission earned from the sale of the Property being purchased.

(2) Standard

Mortgagees may consider Real Estate Commissions from the Sale of Subject Property as part of the Borrower's acceptable source of funds if the Borrower is a licensed real estate agent.

A Family Member entitled to the commission may also provide it as a gift, in compliance with standard gift requirements.

(3) Required Documentation

The Mortgagee must verify and document that the Borrower, or Family Member giving the commission as a gift, is a licensed real estate agent, and is entitled to a Real Estate Commission from Sale of Subject Property being purchased.

(R) Sweat Equity (TOTAL)

(1) Definition

Sweat Equity refers to labor performed, or materials furnished, by or on behalf of the Borrower before closing on the Property being purchased.

(2) Standard

The Mortgagee may consider the reasonable estimated cost of the work or materials as an acceptable source of funds.

Sweat Equity provided by anyone other than the Borrower can only be used as an MRI if it meets the Source Requirements for the Borrower's MRI.

The Mortgagee may consider any amount as Sweat Equity that has not already been included in the mortgage amount. The Mortgagee may not consider clean up, debris removal, and other general maintenance, and work to be performed using repair escrow as Sweat Equity.

Cash back to the Borrower is not permitted in Sweat Equity transactions.

(3) Required Documentation

For materials furnished, the Mortgagee must obtain evidence of the source of funds and the Market Value of the materials.

For labor, the Mortgagee must verify and document that the work will be completed in a satisfactory manner. The Mortgagee must also obtain evidence of Contributory Value of the labor either through an Appraiser's estimate, or a cost-estimating service.

- For labor on Existing Construction, the Mortgagee must also obtain an appraisal indicating the repairs or improvements to be performed. (Any work completed or materials provided before the appraisal are not eligible.)
- For labor on Proposed Construction, the Mortgagee must also obtain the sales contract indicating the tasks to be performed by the Borrower during construction.

(S) Trade Equity (TOTAL)

(1) Definition

Trade Equity refers to when a Borrower trades their Real Property to the seller as part of the cash investment.

(2) Standard

The amount of the Borrower's equity contribution is determined by:
- using the lesser of the Property's appraised value or sales price; and
- subtracting all liens against the Property being traded, along with any real estate commission.

If the Property being traded has an FHA-insured Mortgage, assumption processing requirements and restrictions apply.

(3) Required Documentation

The Mortgagee must obtain a residential appraisal report complying with FHA appraisal policy to determine the Property's value. The Mortgagee must also obtain the Closing Disclosure or similar legal document to document the sale of the Property.

(T) Rent Credits (TOTAL)

(1) Definition

Rent Credits refer to the amount of the rental payment that exceeds the Appraiser's estimate of fair market rent.

(2) Standard

The Mortgagee may use the cumulative amount of rental payments that exceeds the Appraiser's estimate of fair market rent towards the MRI.

(3) Required Documentation

The Mortgagee must obtain the rent with option to purchase agreement, the Appraiser's estimate of market rent, and evidence of receipt of payments.

e. Final Underwriting Decision (TOTAL)

The Mortgagee may approve the Mortgage as eligible for FHA insurance endorsement if:
- TOTAL Mortgage Scorecard rated the mortgage application as Accept;
- the underwriter underwrote the appraisal according to standard FHA requirements;

- the Mortgagee reviewed the TOTAL Mortgage Scorecard findings, and verified that all information entered into TOTAL Mortgage Scorecard is consistent with mortgage documentation, and is true, complete, and accurate; and
- the Mortgage meets all FHA requirements applicable to Mortgages receiving a rating of Accept from TOTAL Mortgage Scorecard.

While TOTAL Mortgage Scorecard is available for Mortgagees to use in their pre-qualification process of mortgage applicants, the Mortgagee must score the Mortgage at least once after assignment of an FHA case number. FHA will not recognize the risk assessment nor will information be carried from TOTAL Mortgage Scorecard to FHAC for endorsement processing, without an FHA case number. It is imperative that the Mortgagees make certain that they enter the FHA case number into their Loan Origination System or AUS as soon as it is known. This will ensure a more efficient endorsement process.

i. Documentation of Final Underwriting Review Decision (TOTAL)

The Mortgagee must complete the following documents to evidence their final underwriting decision.

(A) Form HUD-92900-LT, FHA Loan Underwriting and Transmittal Summary

On form HUD-92900-LT, the Mortgagee must:
- indicate the CHUMS ID of the underwriter who reviewed the appraisal;
- complete the Risk Assessment; and
- enter the identification of "ZFHA" in the CHUMS ID.

When the Feedback Certificate indicates "Accept/Ineligible," the Mortgagee must document the circumstances or other reasons that were evaluated in making the decision to approve the Mortgage in the Remarks section.

(B) Form HUD-92800.5B, Conditional Commitment Direct Endorsement Statement of Appraised Value

The underwriter must confirm that form HUD-92800.5B is completed as directed in the form instructions.

(C) Form HUD-92900-A, HUD/VA Addendum to Uniform Residential Loan Application

The Mortgagee must complete form HUD-92900-A as directed in the form instructions.

An authorized officer of the Mortgagee, the Borrower, and the underwriter must execute form HUD-92900-A, as indicated in the instructions.

ii. Conditional Approval (TOTAL)

The Mortgagee must condition the approval of the Borrower on the completion of the final *URLA* (Fannie Mae Form 1003/Freddie Mac Form 65) and form HUD-92900-A.

iii. HUD Employee Mortgages (TOTAL)

If the Mortgage involves a HUD employee, the Mortgagee must condition the Mortgage on its approval by HUD. The Mortgagee must submit the case binder to the Processing and Underwriting Division Director at the Jurisdictional HOC for final underwriting approval.

iv. Notification of Borrower of Approval and Term of the Approval (TOTAL)

The Mortgagee must timely notify the Borrower of their approval. The underwriter's approval or the Firm Commitment is valid for the greater of 90 Days or the remaining life of the:
- Conditional Commitment issued by HUD; or
- the underwriter's approval date of the Property, indicated as Action Date on form HUD-92800.5B.

5. Manual Underwriting of the Borrower

The Mortgagee must manually underwrite those applications where the AUS issues a Refer or applications which were downgraded to a manual underwrite.

If a Mortgage receiving the AUS Refer or downgrade to manual processing involves a HUD employee, the Mortgagee must underwrite the transaction in accordance with the guidance in this Manual Underwriting section. The Mortgagee must submit the underwritten mortgage application to the Processing and Underwriting Division Director at the Jurisdictional HOC for final underwriting approval.

a. Credit Requirements (Manual)

i. General Credit Requirements (Manual)

FHA's general credit policy requires Mortgagees to analyze the Borrower's credit history, liabilities, and debts to determine creditworthiness.

The Mortgagee must either obtain a Tri-Merged Credit Report (TRMCR) or a Residential Mortgage Credit Report (RMCR) from an independent consumer reporting agency.

The Mortgagee must utilize the same credit report and credit scores sent to TOTAL.

The Mortgagee must obtain a credit report for each Borrower who will be obligated on the mortgage Note. The Mortgagee may obtain a joint report for individuals with joint accounts.

The Mortgagee must obtain a credit report for a non-borrowing spouse who resides in a community property state, or if the subject Property is located in a community property state. The credit report must indicate the non-borrowing spouse's SSN, where an SSN exists, was matched with the SSA, or the Mortgagee must either provide separate documentation indicating that the SSN was matched with the SSA or provide a statement that the non-borrowing spouse does not have an SSN. Where an SSN does not exist for a non-borrowing spouse, the credit report must contain, at a minimum, the non-borrowing spouse's full name, date of birth, and previous addresses for the last two years.

The Mortgagee is not required to obtain a credit report for non-credit qualifying Streamline Refinance transactions.

ii. Types of Credit History (Manual)

If a traditional credit report is available, the Mortgagee must use a traditional credit report. However, if a traditional credit report is not available, the Mortgagee must develop the Borrower's credit history using the requirements for Non-Traditional and Insufficient Credit.

(A) Traditional Credit (Manual)

If the TRMCR or RMCR generates a credit score, the Mortgagee must utilize traditional credit history.

(1) Requirements for the Credit Report

Credit reports must obtain all information from at least two credit repositories pertaining to credit, residence history, and public records information; be in an easy to read and understandable format; and not require code translations. The credit report may not contain whiteouts, erasures, or alterations. The Mortgagee must retain copies of all credit reports.

The credit report must include:
- the name of the Mortgagee ordering the report;
- the name, address, and telephone number of the consumer-reporting agency;
- the name and SSN of each Borrower; and
- the primary repository from which any particular information was pulled, for each account listed.

A truncated SSN is acceptable for FHA mortgage insurance purposes provided that the mortgage application captures the full nine-digit SSN.

The credit report must also include:
- all inquiries made within the last 90 Days;
- all credit and legal information not considered obsolete under the Fair Credit Reporting Act (FCRA), including information for the last seven years, which consumer reporting agencies have reported as verified and currently accurate, regarding:
  - bankruptcies;
  - Judgments;
  - lawsuits;
  - foreclosures; and
  - tax liens; and
- for each Borrower debt listed:
  - the date the account was opened;
  - high credit amount;
  - required monthly payment amount;
  - unpaid balance; and
  - payment history.

(2) Updated Credit Report or Supplement to the Credit Report

The Mortgagee must obtain an updated credit report or supplement if the underwriter identifies inconsistencies between any information in the mortgage file and the original credit report.

(3) Credit Information Not Listed on Credit Report

A Mortgagee must develop credit information separately for any open debt listed on the mortgage application but not referenced in the credit report by using the procedures for Independent Verification of Non-Traditional Credit Providers.

(4) Specific Requirements for Residential Mortgage Credit Report

In addition to meeting the general credit report requirements, the RMCR must:
- provide a detailed account of the Borrower's employment history;
- verify each Borrower's current employment and income through an interview with the Borrower's employer or explain why such an interview was not completed;
- contain a statement attesting to the certification of employment for each Borrower and the date the information was verified; and
- report a credit history for each trade line within 90 Days of the credit report for each account with a balance.

(B) Non-Traditional and Insufficient Credit (Manual)

For Borrowers without a credit score, the Mortgagee must either obtain a Non-Traditional Mortgage Credit Report (NTMCR) from a credit reporting company or independently develop the Borrower's credit history using the requirements outlined below.

(1) Non-Traditional Mortgage Credit Report

(a) Definition

An NTMCR is designed to access the credit history of a Borrower who does not have the types of trade references that appear on a traditional credit report and used either as:
- a substitute for a TRMCR or an RMCR; or
- a supplement to a traditional credit report that has an insufficient number of trade items reported to generate a credit score.

(b) Standard

Mortgagees may use a NTMCR developed by a credit reporting agency that verifies the following information for all non-traditional credit references:
- the existence of the credit providers;

- that the credit was actually extended to the Borrower; and
- the creditor has a published address or telephone number.

The NTMCR must not include subjective statements such as "satisfactory" or "acceptable," must be formatted in a similar fashion to traditional references, and provide the:
- creditor's name;
- date of opening;
- high credit;
- current status of the account;
- 12-month history of the account;
- required monthly payment;
- unpaid balance; and
- payment history in the delinquency categories (for example, 0x30 and 0x60).

(2) Independent Verification of Non-Traditional Credit Providers

The Mortgagee may independently verify the Borrower's credit references by documenting the existence of the credit provider and that the provider extended credit to the Borrower.

a. To verify the existence of each credit provider, the Mortgagee must review public records from the state, county, or city or other documents providing a similar level of objective information.
b. To verify credit information, the Mortgagee must:
  - use a published address or telephone number for the credit provider and not rely solely on information provided by the applicant; and
  - obtain the most recent 12 months of canceled checks, or equivalent proof of payment, demonstrating the timing of payment to the credit provider.
c. To verify the Borrower's rental payment history, the Mortgagee must obtain a rental reference from the appropriate rental management company, provided the Borrower is not renting from a Family Member, demonstrating the timing of payment of the most recent 12 months in lieu of 12 months of canceled checks or equivalent proof of payment.

(3) Sufficiency of Credit References

To be sufficient to establish the Borrower's credit, the credit history must include three credit references, including at least one of the following:
- rental housing payments (subject to independent verification if the Borrower is a renter);
- telephone service; or

- utility company reference (if not included in the rental housing payment), including:
  - gas;
  - electricity;
  - water;
  - television service; or
  - internet service.

If the Mortgagee cannot obtain all three credit references from the list above, the Mortgagee may use the following sources of unreported recurring debt:

- insurance premiums not payroll deducted (for example, medical, auto, life, renter's insurance);
- payment to child care providers made to businesses that provide such services;
- school tuition;
- retail store credit cards (for example, from department, furniture, appliance stores, or specialty stores);
- rent-to-own (for example, furniture, appliances);
- payment of that part of medical bills not covered by insurance;
- a documented 12-month history of savings evidenced by regular deposits resulting in an increased balance to the account that:
  - were made at least quarterly;
  - were not payroll deducted, and;
  - caused no insufficient funds (NSF) checks;
- an automobile lease;
- a personal loan from an individual with repayment terms in writing and supported by canceled checks to document the payments; or
- a documented 12-month history of payment by the Borrower on an account for which the Borrower is an authorized user.

iii. Evaluating Credit History (Manual)

(A) General Credit (Manual)

The underwriter must examine the Borrower's overall pattern of credit behavior, not just isolated unsatisfactory or slow payments, to determine the Borrower's creditworthiness.

The Mortgagee must not consider the credit history of a non-borrowing spouse.

(B) Types of Payment Histories (Manual)

The underwriter must evaluate the Borrower's payment histories in the following order: (1) previous housing expenses and related expenses, including utilities; (2) installment debts; and (3) Revolving Charge Accounts.

(1) Satisfactory Credit

The underwriter may consider a Borrower to have an acceptable payment history if the Borrower has made all housing and installment debt payments on time for the previous 12 months and has no more than two 30-Day late Mortgage Payments or installment payments in the previous 24 months.

The underwriter may approve the Borrower with an acceptable payment history if the Borrower has no major derogatory credit on Revolving Charge Accounts in the previous 12 months.

Major derogatory credit on Revolving Charge Accounts must include any payments made more than 90 Days after the due date, or three or more payments more than 60 Days after the due date.

(2) Payment History Requiring Additional Analysis

If a Borrower's credit history does not reflect satisfactory credit as stated above, the Borrower's payment history requires additional analysis.

The Mortgagee must analyze the Borrower's delinquent accounts to determine whether late payments were based on a disregard for financial obligations, an inability to manage debt, or extenuating circumstances. The Mortgagee must document this analysis in the mortgage file. Any explanation or documentation of delinquent accounts must be consistent with other information in the file.

The underwriter may only approve a Borrower with a credit history not meeting the satisfactory credit history above if the underwriter has documented the delinquency was related to extenuating circumstances.

(C) Payment History on Housing Obligations (Manual)

The Mortgagee must determine the Borrower's Housing Obligation payment history through:
- the credit report;
- verification of rent received directly from the landlord (for landlords with no Identity of Interest with the Borrower);
- verification of Mortgage received directly from the Servicer; or
- a review of canceled checks that cover the most recent 12-month period.

The Mortgagee must verify and document the previous 12 months' housing history. For Borrowers who indicate they are living rent-free, the Mortgagee must obtain verification from the property owner where they are residing that the Borrower has been living rent-free and the amount of time the Borrower has been living rent free.

A Mortgage that has been modified must utilize the payment history in accordance with the modification agreement for the time period of modification in determining late housing payments.

(D) Collection Accounts (Manual)

(1) Definition

A Collection Account is a Borrower's loan or debt that has been submitted to a collection agency through a creditor.

(2) Standard

The Mortgagee must determine if collection accounts were a result of:
- the Borrower's disregard for financial obligations;
- the Borrower's inability to manage debt; or
- extenuating circumstances.

(3) Required Documentation

The Mortgagee must document reasons for approving a Mortgage when the Borrower has any collection accounts.

The Borrower must provide a letter of explanation, which is supported by documentation, for each outstanding collection account. The explanation and supporting documentation must be consistent with other credit information in the file.

(E) Charge Off Accounts (Manual)

(1) Definition

Charge Off Account refers to a Borrower's loan or debt that has been written off by the creditor.

(2) Standard

The Mortgagee must determine if Charge Off Accounts were a result of:
- the Borrower's disregard for financial obligations;
- the Borrower's inability to manage debt; or
- extenuating circumstances.

(3) Required Documentation

The Mortgagee must document reasons for approving a Mortgage when the Borrower has any Charge Off Accounts.

The Borrower must provide a letter of explanation, which is supported by documentation, for each outstanding Charge Off Account. The explanation and supporting documentation must be consistent with other credit information in the file.

(F) Disputed Derogatory Credit Accounts (Manual)

(1) Definition

Disputed Derogatory Credit Account refers to disputed Charge Off Accounts, disputed collection accounts, and disputed accounts with late payments in the last 24 months.

(2) Standard

The Mortgagee must analyze the documentation provided for consistency with other credit information to determine if the derogatory credit account should be considered in the underwriting analysis.

The following items may be excluded from consideration in the underwriting analysis:
- disputed medical accounts; and
- disputed derogatory credit resulting from identity theft, credit card theft or unauthorized use provided the Mortgagee includes a copy of the police report or other documentation from the creditor to support the status of the account in the mortgage file.

(3) Required Documentation

If the credit report indicates that the Borrower is disputing derogatory credit accounts, the Borrower must provide a letter of explanation and documentation supporting the basis of the dispute.

If the disputed derogatory credit resulted from identity theft, credit card theft or unauthorized use balances, the Mortgagee must obtain a copy of the police report or other documentation from the creditor to support the status of the accounts.

(G) Judgments (Manual)

(1) Definition

Judgment refers to any debt or monetary liability of the Borrower, and the Borrower's spouse in a community property state unless excluded by state law, created by a court, or other adjudicating body.

(2) Standard

The Mortgagee must verify that court-ordered Judgments are resolved or paid off prior to or at closing.

Judgments of a non-borrowing spouse in a community property state must be resolved or paid in full, with the exception of obligations excluded by state law.

Regardless of the amount of outstanding Judgments, the Mortgagee must determine if the Judgment was a result of:
- the Borrower's disregard for financial obligations;
- the Borrower's inability to manage debt; or
- extenuating circumstances.

Exception

A Judgment is considered resolved if the Borrower has entered into a valid agreement with the creditor to make regular payments on the debt, the Borrower has made timely payments for at least three months of scheduled payments and the Judgment will not supersede the FHA-insured mortgage lien. The Borrower cannot prepay scheduled payments in order to meet the required minimum of three months of payments.

The Mortgagee must include the payment amount in the agreement in the calculation of the Borrower's Debt-to-Income (DTI) ratio.

The Mortgagee must obtain a copy of the agreement and evidence that payments were made on time in accordance with the agreement.

(3) Required Documentation

The Mortgagee must provide the following documentation:
- evidence of payment in full, if paid prior to settlement;
- the payoff statement, if paid at settlement; or
- the payment arrangement with creditor, if not paid prior to or at settlement, and a subordination agreement for any liens existing on title.

(H) Bankruptcy (Manual)

(1) Standard: Chapter 7

A Chapter 7 bankruptcy (liquidation) does not disqualify a Borrower from obtaining an FHA-insured Mortgage if, at the time of case number assignment, at least two years have elapsed since the date of the bankruptcy discharge. During this time, the Borrower must have:
- re-established good credit; or
- chosen not to incur new credit obligations.

An elapsed period of less than two years, but not less than 12 months, may be acceptable, if the Borrower:

- can show that the bankruptcy was caused by extenuating circumstances beyond the Borrower's control; and
- has since exhibited a documented ability to manage their financial affairs in a responsible manner.

(2) Standard: Chapter 13

A Chapter 13 bankruptcy does not disqualify a Borrower from obtaining an FHA-insured Mortgage, if at the time of case number assignment at least 12 months of the pay-out period under the bankruptcy has elapsed.

The Mortgagee must determine that during this time, the Borrower's payment performance has been satisfactory and all required payments have been made on time; and the Borrower has received written permission from bankruptcy court to enter into the mortgage transaction.

(3) Required Documentation

If the credit report does not verify the discharge date or additional documentation is necessary to determine if any liabilities were discharged in the bankruptcy, the Mortgagee must obtain the bankruptcy and discharge documents.

The Mortgagee must also document that the Borrower's current situation indicates that the events which led to the bankruptcy are not likely to recur.

(I) Foreclosure and Deed-in-Lieu of Foreclosure (Manual)

(1) Standard

A Borrower is generally not eligible for a new FHA-insured Mortgage if the Borrower had a foreclosure or a DIL of foreclosure in the three-year period prior to the date of case number assignment.

This three-year period begins on the date of the DIL or the date that the Borrower transferred ownership of the Property to the foreclosing Entity/designee.

Exceptions

The Mortgagee may grant an exception to the three-year requirement if the foreclosure was the result of documented extenuating circumstances that were beyond the control of the Borrower, such as a serious illness or death of a wage earner, and the Borrower has re-established good credit since the foreclosure.

Divorce is not considered an extenuating circumstance. An exception may, however, be granted where a Borrower's Mortgage was current at the time of the

Borrower's divorce, the ex-spouse received the Property, and the Mortgage was later foreclosed.

The inability to sell the Property due to a job transfer or relocation to another area does not qualify as an extenuating circumstance.

(2) Required Documentation

If the credit report does not indicate the date of the foreclosure or DIL of foreclosure, the Mortgagee must obtain the Closing Disclosure, deed or other legal documents evidencing the date of property transfer.

If the foreclosure or DIL of foreclosure was the result of a circumstance beyond the Borrower's control, the Mortgagee must obtain an explanation of the circumstance and document that the circumstance was beyond the Borrower's control.

(J) Pre-Foreclosure Sales (Short Sales) (Manual)

(1) Definition

Pre-Foreclosure Sales, also known as Short Sales, refer to the sales of real estate that generate proceeds that are less than the amount owed on the Property and the lien holders agree to release their liens and forgive the deficiency balance on the real estate.

(2) Standard

A Borrower is generally not eligible for a new FHA-insured Mortgage if they relinquished a Property through a Short Sale within three years from the date of case number assignment.

This three-year period begins on the date of transfer of title by Short Sale.

(a) Exception for Borrower Current at the Time of Short Sale

A Borrower is considered eligible for a new FHA-insured Mortgage if, from the date of case number assignment for the new Mortgage:
- all Mortgage Payments on the prior Mortgage were made within the month due for the 12-month period preceding the Short Sale; and
- installment debt payments for the same time period were also made within the month due.

(b) Exception for Extenuating Circumstances

The Mortgagee may grant an exception to the three-year requirement if the Short Sale was the result of documented extenuating circumstances that were beyond the control of the Borrower, such as a serious illness or death of a wage earner, and the Borrower has re-established good credit since the Short Sale.

Divorce is not considered an extenuating circumstance. An exception may, however, be granted where a Borrower's Mortgage was current at the time of the Borrower's divorce, the ex-spouse received the Property, and there was a subsequent Short Sale.

The inability to sell the Property due to a job transfer or relocation to another area does not qualify as an extenuating circumstance.

(3) Required Documentation

If the credit report does not indicate the date of the Short Sale, the Mortgagee must obtain the Closing Disclosure, deed or other legal documents evidencing the date of property transfer.

If the Short Sale was the result of a circumstance beyond the Borrower's control, the Mortgagee must obtain an explanation of the circumstance and document that the circumstance was beyond the Borrower's control.

(K) Credit Counseling/Payment Plan

Participating in a consumer credit counseling program does not disqualify a Borrower from obtaining an FHA-insured Mortgage, provided the Mortgagee documents that:
* one year of the pay-out period has elapsed under the plan;
* the Borrower's payment performance has been satisfactory and all required payments have been made on time; and
* the Borrower has received written permission from the counseling agency to enter into the mortgage transaction.

iv. Evaluating Liabilities and Debts (Manual)

(A) General Liabilities and Debts (Manual)

(1) Standard

The Mortgagee must determine the Borrower's monthly liabilities by reviewing all debts listed on the credit report, *URLA*, and required documentation.

All applicable monthly liabilities must be included in the qualifying ratio. Closed-end debts do not have to be included if they will be paid off within 10 months and the cumulative payments of all such debts are less than or equal to 5 percent of the Borrower's gross monthly income. The Borrower may not pay down the balance in order to meet the 10-month requirement.

Accounts for which the Borrower is an authorized user must be included in a Borrower's DTI ratio unless the Mortgagee can document that the primary account holder has made all required payments on the account for the previous 12 months. If less than three payments have been required on the account in the previous 12 months, the payment amount must be included in the Borrower's DTI.

Negative income must be subtracted from the Borrower's gross monthly income, and not treated as a recurring monthly liability unless otherwise noted.

Loans secured against deposited funds, where repayment may be obtained through extinguishing the asset and these funds are not included in calculating the Borrower's assets, do not require consideration of repayment for qualifying purposes.

(2) Required Documentation

The Mortgagee must document that the funds used to pay off debts prior to closing came from an acceptable source, and the Borrower did not incur new debts that were not included in the DTI ratio.

(B) Undisclosed Debt and Inquiries (Manual)

(1) Standard

When a debt or obligation is revealed during the application process that was not listed on the mortgage application and/or credit report, the Mortgagee must:
- verify the actual monthly payment amount;
- include the payment amount in the agreement in the Borrower's monthly liabilities and debt; and
- determine that any unsecured funds borrowed were not/will not be used for the Borrower's MRI.

The Mortgagee must obtain a written explanation from the Borrower for all inquiries shown on the credit report that were made in the last 90 Days.

(2) Required Documentation

The Mortgagee must document all undisclosed debt and support for its analysis of the Borrower's debt.

(C) Federal Debt (Manual)

(1) Definition

Federal Debt refers to debt owed to the federal government for which regular payments are being made.

(2) Standard

The Mortgagee must include the debt. The amount of the required payment must be included in the calculation of the Borrower's total debt to income.

(3) Required Documentation

The Mortgagee must include documentation from the federal agency evidencing the repayment agreement and verification of payments made, if applicable.

(D) Alimony, Child Support, and Maintenance (Manual)

(1) Definition

Alimony, Child Support, and Maintenance are court-ordered or otherwise agreed upon payments.

(2) Standard

For Alimony, if the Borrower's income was not reduced by the amount of the monthly alimony obligation in the Mortgagee's calculation of the Borrower's gross income, the Mortgagee must verify and include the monthly obligation in its calculation of the Borrower's debt.

Child Support and Maintenance are to be treated as a recurring liability and the Mortgagee must include the monthly obligation in the Borrower's liabilities and debt.

(3) Required Documentation

The Mortgagee must obtain the official signed divorce decree, separation agreement, maintenance agreement, or other legal order.

The Mortgagee must also obtain the Borrower's pay stubs covering no less than 28 consecutive Days to verify whether the Borrower is subject to any order of garnishment relating to the Alimony, Child Support, and Maintenance.

(4) Calculation of Monthly Obligation

The Mortgagee must calculate the Borrower's monthly obligation from the greater of:
- the amount shown on the most recent decree or agreement establishing the Borrower's payment obligation; or
- the monthly amount of the garnishment.

(E) Non-Borrowing Spouse Debt in Community Property States (Manual)

(1) Definition

Non-Borrowing Spouse Debt refers to debts owed by a spouse that are not owed by, or in the name of the Borrower.

(2) Standard

If the Borrower resides in a community property state or the Property being insured is located in a community property state, debts of the non-borrowing spouse must be included in the Borrower's qualifying ratios, except for obligations specifically excluded by state law.

The non-borrowing spouse's credit history is not considered a reason to deny a mortgage application.

(3) Required Documentation

The Mortgagee must verify and document the debt of the non-borrowing spouse.

The Mortgagee must make a note in the file referencing the specific state law that justifies the exclusion of any debt from consideration.

The Mortgagee must obtain a credit report for the non-borrowing spouse in order to determine the debts that must be counted in the DTI ratio.

(F) Deferred Obligations (Manual)

(1) Definition

Deferred Obligations (excluding Student Loans) refer to liabilities that have been incurred but where payment is deferred or has not yet commenced, including accounts in forbearance.

(2) Standard

The Mortgagee must verify and include deferred obligations in the calculation of the Borrower's liabilities.

(3) Required Documentation

The Mortgagee must obtain written documentation of the deferral of the liability from the creditor and evidence of the outstanding balance and terms of the deferred liability. The Mortgagee must obtain evidence of the actual monthly payment obligation, if available.

(4) Calculation of Monthly Obligation

The Mortgagee must use the actual monthly payment to be paid on a deferred liability, whenever available.

If the actual monthly payment is not available for installment debt, the Mortgagee must utilize the terms of the debt or 5 percent of the outstanding balance to establish the monthly payment.

(G) Student Loans (Manual)

(1) Definition

Student Loan refers to liabilities incurred for educational purposes.

(2) Standard

The Mortgagee must include all Student Loans in the Borrower's liabilities, regardless of the payment type or status of payments.

(3) Required Documentation

If the payment used for the monthly obligation is:
- less than 1 percent of the outstanding balance reported on the Borrower's credit report; and
- less than the monthly payment reported on the Borrower's credit report;

the Mortgagee must obtain written documentation of the actual monthly payment, the payment status, and evidence of the outstanding balance and terms from the creditor.

(4) Calculation of Monthly Obligation

Regardless of the payment status, the Mortgagee must use either:
- the greater of:
  - 1 percent of the outstanding balance on the loan; or
  - the actual documented payment; or
- if the actual documented payment is less than 1 percent of the outstanding balance, the Mortgagee may use the lower payment only if it will fully amortize the loan over its term.

(H) Installment Loans (Manual)

(1) Definition

Installment Loans (excluding Student Loans) refer to loans, not secured by real estate, that require the periodic payment of P&I. A loan secured by an interest in a timeshare must be considered an Installment Loan.

(2) Standard

The Mortgagee must include the monthly payment shown on the credit report, loan agreement or payment statement to calculate the Borrower's liabilities.

If the credit report does not include a monthly payment for the loan, the Mortgagee must use the amount of the monthly payment shown in the loan agreement or payment statement.

(3) Required Documentation

If the monthly payment shown on the credit report is utilized to calculate the monthly debts, no further documentation is required.

If the credit report does not include a monthly payment for the loan, or the payment reported on the credit report is greater than the payment on the loan agreement or payment statement, the Mortgagee must obtain a copy of the loan agreement or payment statement documenting the amount of the monthly payment. If the credit report, loan agreement or payment statement shows a deferred payment arrangement for an Installment Loan, refer to the Deferred Obligations section.

(I) Revolving Charge Accounts (Manual)

(1) Definition

A Revolving Charge Account refers to a credit arrangement that requires the Borrower to make periodic payments but does not require full repayment by a specified point of time.

(2) Standard

The Mortgagee must include the monthly payment shown on the credit report for the Revolving Charge Account. Where the credit report does not include a monthly payment for the account, the Mortgagee must use the payment shown on the current account statement or 5 percent of the outstanding balance.

(3) Required Documentation

The Mortgagee must use the credit report to document the terms, balance and payment amount on the account, if available.

Where the credit report does not reflect the necessary information on the charge account, the Mortgagee must obtain a copy of the most recent charge account statement or use 5 percent of the outstanding balance to document the monthly payment.

(J) 30-Day Accounts (Manual)

(1) Definition

A 30-Day Account refers to a credit arrangement that requires the Borrower to pay off the outstanding balance on the account every month.

(2) Standard

The Mortgagee must verify the Borrower paid the outstanding balance in full on every 30-Day Account each month for the past 12 months. 30-Day Accounts that are paid monthly are not included in the Borrower's DTI. If the credit report reflects any late payments in the last 12 months, the Mortgagee must utilize 5 percent of the outstanding balance as the Borrower's monthly debt to be included in the DTI.

(3) Required Documentation

The Mortgagee must use the credit report to document that the Borrower has paid the balance on the account monthly for the previous 12 months. The Mortgagee must use the credit report to document the balance, and must document that funds are available to pay off the balance, in excess of the funds and Reserves required to close the Mortgage.

(K) Business Debt in Borrower's Name (Manual)

(1) Definition

Business Debt in Borrower's Name refers to liabilities reported on the Borrower's personal credit report, but payment for the debt is attributed to the Borrower's business.

(2) Standard

When business debt is reported on the Borrower's personal credit report, the debt must be included in the DTI calculation, unless the Mortgagee can document that the debt is being paid by the Borrower's business, and the debt was considered in the cash flow analysis of the Borrower's business. The debt is considered in the cash flow analysis where the Borrower's business tax returns reflect a business expense related to the obligation, equal to or greater than the amount of payments documented as paid out of company funds. Where the Borrower's business tax returns show an interest expense related to the obligation, only the interest portion of the debt is considered in the cash flow analysis.

(3) Required Documentation

When a self-employed Borrower states debt appearing on their personal credit report is being paid by their business, the Mortgagee must obtain documentation that the debt is paid out of company funds and that the debt was considered in the cash flow analysis of the Borrower's business.

(L) Disputed Derogatory Credit Accounts (Manual)

(1) Definition

Disputed Derogatory Credit Accounts refer to disputed Charge Off Accounts, disputed collection accounts, and disputed accounts with late payments in the last 24 months.

(2) Standard

If the Borrower has $1,000 or more collectively in Disputed Derogatory Credit Accounts, the Mortgagee must include a monthly payment in the Borrower's debt calculation.

The following items are excluded from the cumulative balance:
- disputed medical accounts; and
- disputed derogatory credit resulting from identity theft, credit card theft or unauthorized use.

Disputed Derogatory Credit Accounts of a non-borrowing spouse in a community property state are not included in the cumulative balance.

(M) Non-derogatory Disputed Account and Disputed Accounts Not Indicated on the Credit Report (Manual)

(1) Definition

Non-Derogatory Disputed Accounts include the following types of accounts:
- disputed accounts with zero balance;
- disputed accounts with late payments aged 24 months or greater; or
- disputed accounts that are current and paid as agreed.

(2) Standard

If a Borrower is disputing non-derogatory accounts, or is disputing accounts which are not indicated on the credit report as being disputed, the Mortgagee must analyze the effect of the disputed accounts on the Borrower's ability to repay the loan. If the dispute results in the Borrower's monthly debt payments utilized in computing the DTI ratio being less than the amount indicated on the credit report, the Borrower must provide documentation of the lower payments.

(N) Contingent Liabilities (Manual)

(1) Definition

A Contingent Liability is a liability that may result in the obligation to repay only where a specific event occurs. For example, a contingent liability exists when an individual can be held responsible for the repayment of a debt if another legally obligated party defaults on the payment. Contingent liabilities may include Cosigner liabilities and liabilities resulting from a mortgage assumption without release of liability.

(2) Standard

The Mortgagee must include monthly payments on contingent liabilities in the calculation of the Borrower's monthly obligations unless the Mortgagee verifies that there is no possibility that the debt holder will pursue debt collection against the Borrower should the other party default or the other legally obligated party has made 12 months of timely payments.

(3) Required Documentation

(a) Mortgage Assumptions

The Mortgagee must obtain the agreement creating the contingent liability or assumption agreement and deed showing transfer of title out of the Borrower's name.

(b) Cosigned Liabilities

If the cosigned liability is not included in the monthly obligation, the Mortgagee must obtain documentation to evidence that the other party to the debt has been making regular on-time payments during the previous 12 months, and does not have a history of delinquent payments on the loan.

(c) Court Ordered Divorce Decree

The Mortgagee must obtain a copy of the divorce decree ordering the spouse to make payments.

(4) Calculation of Monthly Obligation

The Mortgagee must calculate the monthly payment on the contingent liability based on the terms of the agreement creating the contingent liability.

(O) Collection Accounts (Manual)

(1) Definition

A Collection Account refers to a Borrower's loan or debt that has been submitted to a collection agency by a creditor.

(2) Standard

If the credit reports used in the analysis show cumulative outstanding collection account balances of $2,000 or greater, the Mortgagee must:
- verify that the debt is paid in full at the time of or prior to settlement using an acceptable source of funds;
- verify that the Borrower has made payment arrangements with the creditor; or
- if a payment arrangement is not available, calculate the monthly payment using 5 percent of the outstanding balance of each collection and include the monthly payment in the Borrower's DTI ratio.

Collection accounts of a non-borrowing spouse in a community property state must be included in the $2,000 cumulative balance and analyzed as part of the Borrower's ability to pay all collection accounts, unless specifically excluded by state law.

(3) Required Documentation

The Mortgagee must provide the following documentation:
- evidence of payment in full, if paid prior to settlement;
- the payoff statement, if paid at settlement; or
- the payment arrangement with creditor, if not paid prior to or at settlement.

If the Mortgagee uses 5 percent of the outstanding balance, no documentation is required.

(P) Charge Off Accounts (Manual)

(1) Definition

Charge Off Account refers to a Borrower's loan or debt that has been written off by the creditor.

(2) Standard

Charge Off Accounts do not need to be included in the Borrower's liabilities or debt.

(Q)Private Savings Clubs (Manual)

(1) Definition

Private Savings Club refers to a non-traditional method of saving by making deposits into a member-managed resource pool.

(2) Standard

If the Borrower is obligated to continue making ongoing contributions under the pooled savings agreement, this obligation must be counted in the Borrowers' total debt.

The Mortgagee must verify and document the establishment and duration of the Borrower's membership in the club and the amount of the Borrower's required contribution to the club.

(3) Required Documentation

The Mortgagee must also obtain the club's account ledgers and receipts, and verification from the club treasurer that the club is still active.

(R)Obligations Not Considered Debt

Obligations not considered debt include:
- medical collections
- federal, state, and local taxes, if not delinquent and no payments required
- automatic deductions from savings, when not associated with another type of obligation
- Federal Insurance Contributions Act (FICA) and other retirement contributions, such as 401(k) accounts
- collateralized loans secured by depository accounts
- utilities
- child care
- commuting costs
- union dues
- insurance, other than property insurance
- open accounts with zero balances
- voluntary deductions, when not associated with another type of obligation

b. Income Requirements (Manual)

Effective Income Definition

Effective Income refers to income that may be used to qualify a Borrower for a Mortgage. Effective Income must be reasonably likely to continue through at least the first three years of the Mortgage, and meet the specific requirements described below.

i. General Income Requirements (Manual)

The Mortgagee must document the Borrower's income and employment history, verify the accuracy of the amounts of income being reported, and determine if the income can be considered as Effective Income in accordance with the requirements listed below.

The Mortgagee may only consider income if it is legally derived and, when required, properly reported as income on the Borrower's tax returns.

Negative income must be subtracted from the Borrower's gross monthly income and not treated as a recurring monthly liability unless otherwise noted.

If FHA requires tax returns as required documentation for any type of Effective Income, the Mortgagee must also analyze the tax returns in accordance with Appendix 2.0 – Analyzing IRS Forms.

ii. Employment Related Income (Manual)

(A) Definition

Employment Income refers to income received as an employee of a business that is reported on IRS Form W-2.

(B) Standard

The Mortgagee may use Employment related Income as Effective Income in accordance with the standards provided for each type of Employment related Income.

(C) Required Documentation

For all Employment related Income, the Mortgagee must verify the Borrower's most recent two years of employment and income, and document using one of the following methods.

(1) Traditional Current Employment Documentation

The Mortgagee must obtain one of the following to verify current employment:
- the most recent pay stubs covering a minimum of 30 consecutive Days (if paid weekly or bi-weekly, pay stubs must cover a minimum of 28

consecutive Days) that show the Borrower's year-to-date earnings, and a written Verification of Employment (VOE) covering two years; or

- direct verification by a TPV vendor covering two years, subject to the following requirements:
  - o the Borrower has authorized the Mortgagee to verify income and employment; and
  - o the date of the data contained in the completed verification conforms with FHA requirements in Maximum Age of Mortgage Documents.

Re-verification of employment must be completed within 10 Days prior to the date of the Note. Verbal or electronic re-verification of employment is acceptable. Electronic re-verification employment data must be current within 30 days of the date of the verification.

(2) Alternative Current Employment Documentation

If using alternative documentation, the Mortgagee must:
- obtain copies of the most recent pay stub that shows the Borrower's year-to-date earnings;
- obtain copies of the original IRS W-2 forms from the previous two years; and
- document current employment by telephone, sign and date the verification documentation, and note the name, title, and telephone number of the person with whom employment was verified.

Re-verification of employment must be completed within 10 Days prior to the date of the Note. Verbal or electronic re-verification of employment is acceptable. Electronic re-verification employment data must be current within 30 days of the date of the verification.

(3) Past Employment Documentation

Direct verification of the Borrower's employment history for the previous two years is not required if all of the following conditions are met:
- The current employer confirms a two year employment history, or a paystub reflects a hiring date.
- Only base pay is used to qualify (no Overtime, Bonus or Tip Income).
- The Borrower executes IRS Form 4506, *Request for Copy of Tax Return,* IRS Form 4506-T, Request for Transcript of Tax Return, or IRS Form 8821, *Tax Information Authorization,* for the previous two tax years.

If the applicant has not been employed with the same employer for the previous two years and/or not all conditions immediately above can be met, then the Mortgagee must obtain one or a combination of the following for the most recent two years to verify the applicant's employment history:
- W-2(s)

- VOE(s)
- direct verification of employment by a TPV vendor, subject to the following requirements:
  - the Borrower has authorized the Mortgagee to verify income and employment; and
  - the date of the data contained in the completed verification conforms with FHA requirements in Maximum Age of Mortgage Documents
- evidence supporting enrollment in school or the military during the most recent two full years

iii. Primary Employment (Manual)

(A) Definition

Primary Employment is the Borrower's principal employment, unless the income falls within a specific category identified below. Primary employment is generally full-time employment and may be either salaried or hourly.

(B) Standard

The Mortgagee may use primary Employment Income as Effective Income.

(C) Calculation of Effective Income

(1) Salary

For employees who are salaried and whose income has been and will likely be consistently earned, the Mortgagee must use the current salary to calculate Effective Income.

(2) Hourly

For employees who are paid hourly, and whose hours do not vary, the Mortgagee must consider the Borrower's current hourly rate to calculate Effective Income.

For employees who are paid hourly and whose hours vary, the Mortgagee must average the income over the previous two years. If the Mortgagee can document an increase in pay rate the Mortgagee may use the most recent 12-month average of hours at the current pay rate.

iv. Part-Time Employment (Manual)

(A) Definition

Part-Time Employment refers to employment that is not the Borrower's primary employment and is generally performed for less than 40 hours per week.

(B) Standard

The Mortgagee may use Employment Income from Part-Time Employment as Effective Income if the Borrower has worked a part-time job uninterrupted for the past two years and the current position is reasonably likely to continue.

(C) Calculation of Effective Income

The Mortgagee must average the income over the previous two years. If the Mortgagee can document an increase in pay rate the Mortgagee may use a 12-month average of hours at the current pay rate.

v. Overtime, Bonus or Tip Income (Manual)

(A) Definition

Overtime, Bonus or Tip Income refers to income that the Borrower receives in addition to the Borrower's normal salary.

(B) Standard

The Mortgagee may use Overtime, Bonus or Tip Income as Effective Income if the Borrower has received this income for the past two years and it is reasonably likely to continue.

Periods of Overtime, Bonus or Tip Income less than two years may be considered Effective Income if the Mortgagee documents that the Overtime, Bonus or Tip Income has been consistently earned over a period of not less than one year and is reasonably likely to continue.

(C) Calculation of Effective Income

For employees with Overtime, Bonus or Tip Income, the Mortgagee must calculate Effective Income by using the lesser of:
- the average Overtime, Bonus or Tip Income earned over the previous two years or, if less than two years, the length of time Overtime, Bonus or Tip Income has been earned; or
- the average Overtime, Bonus or Tip Income earned over the previous year.

vi. Seasonal Employment (Manual)

(A) Definition

Seasonal Employment refers to employment that is not year round, regardless of the number of hours per week the Borrower works on the job.

(B) Standard

The Mortgagee may consider Employment Income from Seasonal Employment as Effective Income if the Borrower has worked the same line of work for the past two years and is reasonably likely to be rehired for the next season. The Mortgagee may consider unemployment income as Effective Income for those with Effective Income from Seasonal Employment.

(C) Required Documentation

For seasonal employees with unemployment income, the Mortgagee must document the unemployment income for two full years and there must be reasonable assurance that this income will continue.

(D) Calculation of Effective Income

For employees with Employment Income from Seasonal Employment, the Mortgagee must average the income earned over the previous two full years to calculate Effective Income.

vii. Employer Housing Subsidy (Manual)

(A) Definition

Employer Housing Subsidy refers to employer-provided mortgage assistance.

(B) Standard

The Mortgagee may utilize Employer Housing Subsidy as Effective Income.

(C) Required Documentation

The Mortgagee must verify and document the existence and the amount of the housing subsidy.

(D) Calculation of Effective Income

For employees receiving an Employer Housing Subsidy, the Mortgagee may add the Employer Housing Subsidy to the total Effective Income, but may not use it to offset the Mortgage Payment.

viii. Employed by Family-Owned Business (Manual)

(A) Definition

Family-Owned Business Income refers to Employment Income earned from a business owned by the Borrower's family, but in which the Borrower is not an owner.

(B) Standard

The Mortgagee may consider Family-Owned Business Income as Effective Income if the Borrower is not an owner in the family-owned business.

(C) Required Documentation

The Mortgagee must verify and document that the Borrower is not an owner in the family-owned business by using official business documents showing the ownership percentage.

Official business documents include corporate resolutions or other business organizational documents, business tax returns or Schedule K-1(IRS Form 1065), *U.S. Return of Partnership Income*, or an official letter from a certified public accountant on their business letterhead.

In addition to traditional or alternative documentation requirements, the Mortgagee must obtain copies of signed personal tax returns or tax transcripts.

(D) Calculation of Effective Income

(1) Salary

For employees who are salaried and whose income has been and will likely continue to be consistently earned, the Mortgagee must use the current salary to calculate Effective Income.

(2) Hourly

For employees who are paid hourly, and whose hours do not vary, the Mortgagee must consider the Borrower's current hourly rate to calculate Effective Income.

For employees who are paid hourly and whose hours vary, the Mortgagee must average the income over the previous two years. If the Mortgagee can document an increase in pay rate the Mortgagee may use the most recent 12-month average of hours at the current pay rate.

ix. Commission Income (Manual)

(A) Definition

Commission Income refers to income that is paid contingent upon the conducting of a business transaction or the performance of a service.

(B) Standard

The Mortgagee may use Commission Income as Effective Income if the Borrower earned the income for at least one year in the same or similar line of work and it is reasonably likely to continue.

(C) Required Documentation [Text was deleted in this section.]

For all Commission Income, the Mortgagee must use traditional or alternative employment documentation.

(D) Calculation of Effective Income

The Mortgagee must calculate Effective Income for commission by using the lesser of:
- either, (i) the average Commission Income earned over the previous two years for Commission Income earned for two years or more, or (ii) the length of time Commission Income has been earned if less than two years; or
- the average Commission Income earned over the previous year.

x. Self-Employment Income (Manual)

(A) Definition

Self-Employment Income refers to income generated by a business in which the Borrower has a 25 percent or greater ownership interest.

There are four basic types of business structures. They include:
- sole proprietorship;
- corporations;
- limited liability or "S" corporations; and
- partnerships.

(B) Standard

(1) Minimum Length of Self-Employment

The Mortgagee may consider Self-Employment Income if the Borrower has been self-employed for at least two years.

If the Borrower has been self-employed between one and two years, the Mortgagee may only consider the income as Effective Income if the Borrower was previously employed in the same line of work in which the Borrower is self-employed or in a related occupation for at least two years.

(2) Stability of Self-Employment Income

Income obtained from businesses with annual earnings that are stable or increasing is acceptable. If the income from businesses shows a greater than 20 percent decline in Effective Income over the analysis period, the Mortgagee must document that the business income is now stable.

A Mortgagee may consider income as stable after a 20 percent reduction if the Mortgagee can document the reduction in income was the result of an extenuating circumstance, the Borrower can demonstrate the income has been stable or increasing for a minimum of 12 months, and the Borrower qualifies utilizing the reduced income.

(C) Required Documentation

(1) Individual and Business Tax Returns

The Mortgagee must obtain signed, completed individual and business federal income tax returns for the most recent two years, including all schedules.

In lieu of signed individual or business tax returns from the Borrower, the Mortgagee may obtain a signed IRS Form 4506, *Request for Copy of Tax Return*, IRS Form 4506-T, *Request for Transcript of Tax Return*, or IRS Form 8821, *Tax Information Authorization*, and tax transcripts directly from the IRS.

(2) Profit & Loss Statements and Balance Sheets

The Mortgagee must obtain a year-to-date Profit and Loss (P&L) statement and balance sheet if more than a calendar quarter has elapsed since date of most recent calendar or fiscal year-end tax return was filed by the Borrower. A balance sheet is not required for self-employed Borrowers filing Schedule C income.

If income used to qualify the Borrower exceeds the two year average of tax returns, an audited P&L or signed quarterly tax return obtained from the IRS is required.

(3) Business Credit Reports

The Mortgagee must obtain a business credit report for all corporations and "S" corporations.

(D) Calculation of Effective Income

The Mortgagee must analyze the Borrower's tax returns to determine gross Self-Employment Income. Requirements for analyzing self-employment documentation are found in Analyzing IRS Forms.

The Mortgagee must calculate gross Self-Employment Income by using the lesser of:
- the average gross Self- Employment Income earned over the previous two years; or
- the average gross Self-Employment Income earned over the previous one year.

xi. Additional Required Analysis of Stability of Employment Income

(A) Frequent Changes in Employment

If the Borrower has changed employers more than three times in the previous 12-month period, or has changed lines of work, the Mortgagee must take additional steps to verify and document the stability of the Borrower's Employment Income. Additional analysis is not required for fields of employment that regularly require a Borrower to work for various employers (such as Temp Companies or Union Trades). The Mortgagee must obtain:
- transcripts of training and education demonstrating qualification for a new position; or
- employment documentation evidencing continual increases in income and/or benefits.

(B) Addressing Gaps in Employment

For Borrowers with gaps in employment of six months or more (an extended absence), the Mortgagee may consider the Borrower's current income as Effective Income if it can verify and document that:
- the Borrower has been employed in the current job for at least six months at the time of case number assignment; and
- a two year work history prior to the absence from employment using standard or alternative employment verification.

(C) Addressing Temporary Reduction in Income

For Borrowers with a temporary reduction of income due to a short-term disability or similar temporary leave, the Mortgagee may consider the Borrower's current income as Effective Income, if it can verify and document that:
- the Borrower intends to return to work;
- the Borrower has the right to return to work; and
- the Borrower qualifies for the Mortgage taking into account any reduction of income due to the circumstance.

For Borrowers returning to work before or at the time of the first Mortgage Payment due date, the Mortgagee may use the Borrower's pre-leave income.

For Borrowers returning to work after the first Mortgage Payment due date, the Mortgagee may use the Borrower's current income plus available surplus liquid asset Reserves, above and beyond any required Reserves, as an income supplement up to the amount of the Borrower's pre-leave income. The amount of the monthly income supplement is the total amount of surplus Reserves divided by the number of months between the first payment due date and the Borrower's intended date of return to work.

Required Documentation

The Mortgagee must provide the following documentation for Borrowers on temporary leave:

- a written statement from the Borrower confirming the Borrower's intent to return to work, and the intended date of return;
- documentation generated by current employer confirming the Borrower's eligibility to return to current employer after temporary leave; and
- documentation of sufficient liquid assets, in accordance with Sources of Funds, used to supplement the Borrower's income through intended date of return to work with current employer.

xii. Other Sources of Effective Income (Manual)

(A) Disability Benefits (Manual)

(1) Definition

Disability Benefits refer to benefits received from the Social Security Administration (SSA), Department of Veterans Affairs (VA), or a private disability insurance provider.

(2) Required Documentation

The Mortgagee must verify and document the Borrower's receipt of benefits from the SSA, VA, or private disability insurance provider. The Mortgagee must obtain documentation that establishes award benefits to the Borrower.

If any disability income is due to expire within three years from the date of mortgage application, that income cannot be used as Effective Income. If the Notice of Award or equivalent document does not have a defined expiration date, the Mortgagee may consider the income effective and reasonably likely to continue. The Mortgagee may not rely upon a pending or current re-evaluation of medical eligibility for benefit payments as evidence that the benefit payment is not reasonably likely to continue.

Under no circumstance may the Mortgagee inquire into or request documentation concerning the nature of the disability or the medical condition of the Borrower.

(a) Social Security Disability (Manual)

For Social Security Disability income, including Supplemental Security Income (SSI), the Mortgagee must obtain a copy of the last Notice of Award letter, or an equivalent document that establishes award benefits to the Borrower, and one of the following documents:
- federal tax returns;
- the most recent bank statement evidencing receipt of income from the SSA;
- a Proof of Income Letter, also known as a "Budget Letter" or "Benefits Letter" that evidences income from the SSA; or
- a copy of the Borrower's form SSA-1099/1042S, *Social Security Benefit Statement*.

(b) VA Disability

For VA disability benefits, the Mortgagee must obtain from the Borrower a copy of the veteran's last Benefits Letter showing the amount of the assistance, and one of the following documents:
- federal tax returns; or
- the most recent bank statement evidencing receipt of income from the VA.

If the Benefits Letter does not have a defined expiration date, the Mortgagee may consider the income effective and reasonably likely to continue for at least three years.

(c) Private Disability

For private disability benefits, the Mortgagee must obtain documentation from the private disability insurance provider showing the amount of the assistance and the expiration date of the benefits, if any, and one of the following documents:
- federal tax returns; or
- the most recent bank statement evidencing receipt of income from the insurance provider.

(3) Calculation of Effective Income

The Mortgagee must use the most recent amount of benefits received to calculate Effective Income.

(B) Alimony, Child Support, and Maintenance Income (Manual)

(1) Definition

Alimony, Child Support, and Maintenance Income refers to income received from a former spouse or partner or from a non-custodial parent of the Borrower's minor dependent.

(2) Required Documentation

The Mortgagee must obtain a fully executed copy of the Borrower's final divorce decree, legal separation agreement, court order, or voluntary payment agreement with documented receipt.

When using a final divorce decree, legal separation agreement or court order, the Mortgagee must obtain evidence of receipt using deposits on bank statements; canceled checks; or documentation from the child support agency for the most recent three months that supports the amount used in qualifying.

The Mortgagee must document the voluntary payment agreement with 12 months of canceled checks, deposit slips, or tax returns.

The Mortgagee must provide evidence that the claimed income will continue for at least three years. The Mortgagee may use the front and pertinent pages of the divorce decree/settlement agreement and/or court order showing the financial details.

(3) Calculation of Effective Income

When using a final divorce decree, legal separation agreement or court order, if the Borrower has received consistent Alimony, Child Support and Maintenance Income for the most recent three months, the Mortgagee may use the current payment to calculate Effective Income.

When using evidence of voluntary payments, if the Borrower has received consistent Alimony, Child Support and Maintenance Income for the most recent six months, the Mortgagee may use the current payment to calculate Effective Income.

If the Alimony, Child Support and Maintenance Income have not been consistently received for the most recent six months, the Mortgagee must use the average of the income received over the previous two years to calculate Effective Income. If Alimony, Child Support and Maintenance Income have been received for less than two years, the Mortgagee must use the average over the time of receipt.

(C) Military Income (Manual)

(1) Definition

Military Income refers to income received by military personnel during their period of active, Reserve, or National Guard service, including:
- base pay
- Basic Allowance for Housing
- clothing allowances
- flight or hazard pay
- Basic Allowance for Subsistence
- proficiency pay

The Mortgagee may not use education benefits as Effective Income.

(2) Required Documentation

The Mortgagee must obtain a copy of the Borrower's military Leave and Earnings Statement (LES). The Mortgagee must verify the Expiration Term of Service date on the LES. If the Expiration Term of Service date is within the first 12 months of the Mortgage, Military Income may only be considered Effective Income if the Borrower represents their intent to continue military service.

(3) Calculation of Effective Income

The Mortgagee must use the current amount of Military Income received to calculate Effective Income.

(D) Mortgage Credit Certificates (Manual)

(1) Definition

Mortgage Credit Certificates refer to government Mortgage Payment subsidies other than Section 8 Homeownership Vouchers.

(2) Required Documentation

The Mortgagee must verify and document that the Governmental Entity subsidizes the Borrower's Mortgage Payments either through direct payments or tax rebates.

(3) Calculating Effective Income

Mortgage Credit Certificate income that is not used to directly offset the Mortgage Payment before calculating the qualifying ratios may be included as Effective Income. The Mortgagee must use the current subsidy rate to calculate the Effective Income.

(E) Section 8 Homeownership Vouchers (Manual)

(1) Definition

Section 8 Homeownership Vouchers refer to housing subsidies received under the Housing Choice Voucher homeownership option from a Public Housing Agency (PHA).

(2) Required Documentation

The Mortgagee must verify and document the Borrower's receipt of the Housing Choice Voucher homeownership subsidies. The Mortgagee may consider that this income is reasonably likely to continue for three years.

(3) Calculation of Effective Income

The Mortgagee may only use Section 8 Homeownership Voucher subsidies as Effective Income if it is not used as an offset to the monthly Mortgage Payment. The Mortgagee must use the current subsidy rate to calculate the Effective Income.

(F) Other Public Assistance (Manual)

(1) Definition

Public Assistance refers to income received from government assistance programs.

(2) Required Documentation

Mortgagees must verify and document the income received from the government agency.

If any Public Assistance income is due to expire within three years from the date of mortgage application, that income cannot be used as Effective Income. If the documentation does not have a defined expiration date, the Mortgagee may consider the income effective and reasonably likely to continue.

(3) Calculation of Effective Income

The Mortgagee must use the current rate of Public Assistance received to calculate Effective Income.

(G) Automobile Allowances (Manual)

(1) Definition

Automobile Allowance refers to the funds provided by the Borrower's employer for automobile related expenses.

(2) Required Documentation [Text was deleted in this section.]

The Mortgagee must verify and document the Automobile Allowance received from the employer for the previous two years.

(3) Calculation of Effective Income

The Mortgagee must use the full amount of the Automobile Allowance to calculate Effective Income.

(H) Retirement Income (Manual)

Retirement Income refers to income received from Pensions, 401(k) distributions, and Social Security.

(1) Social Security Income (Manual)

(a) Definition

Social Security Income or Supplemental Security Income (SSI) refers to income received from the SSA other than disability income.

(b) Required Documentation

The Mortgagee must verify and document the Borrower's receipt of income from the SSA and that it is likely to continue for at least a three year period from the date of case number assignment.

For SSI, the Mortgagee must obtain any one of the following documents:
- federal tax returns;
- the most recent bank statement evidencing receipt of income from the SSA;
- a Proof of Income Letter, also known as a "Budget Letter" or "Benefits Letter" that evidences income from the SSA; or
- a copy of the Borrower's SSA Form-1099/1042S, *Social Security Benefit Statement*.

In addition to verification of income, the Mortgagee must document the continuance of this income by obtaining from the Borrower (1) a copy of the last Notice of Award letter which states the SSA's determination on the

Borrower's eligibility for SSA income, or (2) equivalent documentation that establishes award benefits to the Borrower (equivalent document). If any income from the SSA is due to expire within three years from the date of case number assignment, that income may not be used for qualifying.

If the Notice of Award or equivalent document does not have a defined expiration date, the Mortgagee must consider the income effective and reasonably likely to continue. The Mortgagee may not request additional documentation from the Borrower to demonstrate continuance of Social Security Income.

If the Notice of Award letter or equivalent document specifies a future start date for receipt of income, this income may only be considered effective on the specified start date.

(c) Calculation of Effective Income

The Mortgagee must use the current amount of Social Security Income received to calculate Effective Income.

(2) Pension (Manual)

(a) Definition

Pension refers to income received from the Borrower's former employer(s).

(b) Required Documentation

The Mortgagee must verify and document the Borrower's receipt of periodic payments from the Borrower's Pension and that the payments are likely to continue for at least three years.

The Mortgagee must obtain any one of the following documents:
- federal tax returns;
- the most recent bank statement evidencing receipt of income from the former employer; or
- a copy of the Borrower's Pension/retirement letter from the former employer.

(c) Calculation of Effective Income

The Mortgagee must use the current amount of Pension income received to calculate Effective Income.

(3) Individual Retirement Account and 401(k) (Manual)

(a) Definition

Individual Retirement Account (IRA)/401(k) Income refers to income received from an IRA.

(b) Required Documentation

The Mortgagee must verify and document the Borrower's receipt of recurring IRA/401(k) distribution Income and that it is reasonably likely to continue for three years.

The Mortgagee must obtain the most recent IRA/401(k) statement and any one of the following documents:
- federal tax returns; or
- the most recent bank statement evidencing receipt of income.

(c) Calculation of Effective Income

For Borrowers with IRA/401(k) Income that has been and will be consistently received, the Mortgagee must use the current amount of IRA Income received to calculate Effective Income. For Borrowers with fluctuating IRA/401(k) Income, the Mortgagee must use the average of the IRA/401(k) Income received over the previous two years to calculate Effective Income. If IRA/401(k) Income has been received for less than two years, the Mortgagee must use the average over the time of receipt.

(I) Rental Income (Manual)

(1) Definition

Rental Income refers to income received or to be received from the subject Property or other real estate holdings.

(2) Rental Income Received from the Subject Property (Manual)

(a) Standard

The Mortgagee may consider Rental Income from existing and prospective tenants if documented in accordance with the following requirements.

Rental Income from the subject Property may be considered Effective Income when the Property is a two- to four-unit dwelling, or an acceptable one- to four-unit Investment Property.

(b) Required Documentation

Required documentation varies depending upon the length of time the Borrower has owned the Property.

(i) Limited or No History of Rental Income

Where the Borrower does not have a history of Rental Income from the subject since the previous tax filing:

Two-to Four-Units

The Mortgagee must verify and document the proposed Rental Income by obtaining an appraisal showing fair market rent (use Fannie Mae Form 1025/Freddie Mac Form 72, *Small Residential Income Property Appraisal Report*) and the prospective leases if available.

One Unit

The Mortgagee must verify and document the proposed Rental Income by obtaining a Fannie Mae Form 1004/Freddie Mac Form 70, *Uniform Residential Appraisal Report*, Fannie Mae Form 1007/Freddie Mac Form 1000, *Single Family Comparable Rent Schedule*, and Fannie Mae Form 216/Freddie Mac Form 998, *Operating Income Statement*, showing fair market rent and, if available, the prospective lease.

(ii) History of Rental Income

Where the Borrower has a history of Rental Income from the subject since the previous tax filing, the Mortgagee must verify and document the existing Rental Income by obtaining the existing lease, rental history over the previous 24 months that is free of unexplained gaps greater than three months (such gaps could be explained by student, seasonal or military renters, or property rehabilitation), and the Borrower's most recent tax returns, including Schedule E, from the previous two years.

For Properties with less than two years of Rental Income history, the Mortgagee must document the date of acquisition by providing the deed, Closing Disclosure or other legal document.

(c) Calculation of Effective Income

The Mortgagee must add the net subject property Rental Income to the Borrower's gross income. The Mortgagee may not reduce the Borrower's total Mortgage Payment by the net subject property Rental Income.

(i) Limited or No History of Rental Income

To calculate the Effective Income from the subject Property where the Borrower does not have a history of Rental Income from the subject Property since the previous tax filing, the Mortgagee must use the lesser of:

- the monthly operating income reported on Fannie Mae Form 216/Freddie Mac Form 998; or
- 75 percent of the lesser of:
  - o fair market rent reported by the Appraiser; or
  - o the rent reflected in the lease or other rental agreement.

(ii) History of Rental Income

The Mortgagee must calculate the Rental Income by averaging the amount shown on the Schedule E.

Depreciation, mortgage interest, taxes, insurance and any HOA dues shown on Schedule E may be added back to the net income or loss.

If the Property has been owned for less than two years, the Mortgagee must annualize the Rental Income for the length of time the Property has been owned.

(3) Rental Income from Other Real Estate Holdings (Manual)

(a) Standard

Rental Income from other real estate holdings may be considered Effective Income if the documentation requirements listed below are met. If Rental Income is being derived from the Property being vacated by the Borrower, the Borrower must be relocating to an area more than 100 miles from the Borrower's current Principal Residence. The Mortgagee must obtain a lease agreement of at least one year's duration after the Mortgage is closed and evidence of the payment of the security deposit or first month's rent.

(b) Required Documentation

(i) Limited or No History of Rental Income

Where the Borrower does not have a history of Rental Income for the Property since the previous tax filing, including Property being vacated by the Borrower, the Mortgagee must obtain an appraisal evidencing market rent and that the Borrower has at least 25 percent equity in the Property. The appraisal is not required to be completed by an FHA Roster Appraiser.

Two- to Four-Units

The Mortgagee must verify and document the proposed Rental Income by obtaining an appraisal showing fair market rent (use Fannie Mae Form 1025/Freddie Mac Form 72, *Small Residential Income Property Appraisal Report*) and the prospective leases if available.

One Unit

The Mortgagee must verify and document the proposed Rental Income by obtaining a Fannie Mae Form 1004/Freddie Mac Form 70, *Uniform Residential Appraisal Report*, Fannie Mae Form 1007/Freddie Mac Form 1000, *Single Family Comparable Rent Schedule*, and Fannie Mae Form 216/Freddie Mac Form 998, *Operating Income Statement,* showing fair market rent and, if available, the prospective lease.

(ii) History of Rental Income

The Mortgagee must obtain the Borrower's last two years' tax returns with Schedule E.

(c) Calculation of Effective Net Rental Income

(i) Limited or No History of Rental Income

To calculate the effective net Rental Income from other real estate holdings where the Borrower does not have a history of Rental Income since the previous tax filing, the Mortgagee must deduct the PITI from the lesser of:

- the monthly operating income reported on Fannie Mae Form 216/Freddie Mac Form 998, or
- 75 percent of the lesser of:
  - fair market rent reported by the Appraiser; or
  - the rent reflected in the lease or other rental agreement.

(ii) History of Net Rental Income

The Mortgagee must calculate the net Rental Income by averaging the amount shown on the Schedule E provided the Borrower continues to own all Properties included on the Schedule E.

Depreciation shown on Schedule E may be added back to the net income or loss.

If the Property has been owned for less than two years, the Mortgagee must annualize the Rental Income for the length of time the Property has been owned.

For Properties with less than two years of Rental Income history, the Mortgagee must document the date of acquisition by providing the deed, Closing Disclosure or other legal document.

Positive net Rental Income must be added to the Borrower's Effective Income. Negative net Rental Income must be included as a debt/liability.

(4) Boarders of the Subject Property (Manual)

(a) Definition

Boarder refers to an individual renting space inside the Borrower's Dwelling Unit.

(b) Standard

Rental Income from Boarders is only acceptable if the Borrower has a two-year history of receiving income from Boarders that is shown on the tax return and the Borrower is currently receiving Boarder income.

(c) Required Documentation

The Mortgagee must obtain two years of the Borrower's tax returns evidencing income from Boarders and the current lease.

For purchase transactions, the Mortgagee must obtain a copy of the executed written agreement documenting their intent to continue boarding with the Borrower.

(d) Calculation of Effective Income

The Mortgagee must calculate the Effective Income by using the lesser of the two-year average or the current lease.

(J) Investment Income (Manual)

(1) Definition

Investment Income refers to interest and dividend income received from assets such as certificates of deposits, mutual funds, stocks, bonds, money markets, and savings and checking accounts.

(2) Required Documentation

The Mortgagee must verify and document the Borrower's Investment Income by obtaining tax returns for the previous two years and the most recent account statement.

(3) Calculation of Effective Income

The Mortgagee must calculate Investment Income by using the lesser of:
- the average Investment Income earned over the previous two years; or
- the average Investment Income earned over the previous one year.

The Mortgagee must subtract any of the assets used for the Borrower's required funds to close to purchase the subject Property from the Borrower's liquid assets prior to calculating any interest or dividend income.

(K) Capital Gains and Losses (Manual)

(1) Definition

Capital Gains refer to a profit that results from a disposition of a capital asset, such as a stock, bond or real estate, where the amount realized on the disposition exceeds the purchase price.

Capital Losses refer to a loss that results from a disposition of a capital asset, such as a stock, bond or real estate, where the amount realized on the disposition is less than the purchase price.

(2) Standard

Capital gains or losses must be considered when determining Effective Income, when the individual has a constant turnover of assets resulting in gains or losses.

(3) Required Documentation

Three years' tax returns are required to evaluate an earnings trend. If the trend:
- results in a gain, it may be added as Effective Income; or
- consistently shows a loss, it must be deducted from the total income.

(L) Expected Income (Manual)

(1) Definition

Expected Income refers to income from cost-of-living adjustments, performance raises, a new job, or retirement that has not been, but will be received within 60 Days of mortgage closing.

(2) Standard

The Mortgagee may consider Expected Income as Effective Income except when Expected Income is to be derived from a family-owned business.

(3) Required Documentation

The Mortgagee must verify and document the existence and amount of Expected Income with the employer in writing and that it is guaranteed to begin within 60 Days of mortgage closing. For expected Retirement Income, the Mortgagee must verify the amount and that it is guaranteed to begin within 60 Days of the mortgage closing.

(4) Calculation of Effective Income

Income is calculated in accordance with the standards for the type of income being received. The Mortgagee must also verify that the Borrower will have sufficient income or cash Reserves to support the Mortgage Payment and any other obligations between mortgage closing and the beginning of the receipt of the income.

(M) Trust Accounts (Manual)

(1) Definition

Trust Income refers to income that is regularly distributed to a Borrower from a trust.

(2) Required Documentation

The Mortgagee must verify and document the existence of the Trust Agreement or other trustee statement. The Mortgagee must also verify and document the frequency, duration, and amount of the distribution by obtaining a bank statement or transaction history from the bank.

The Mortgagee must verify that regular payments will continue for at least the first three years of the mortgage term.

(3) Calculation of Effective Income

The Mortgagee must use the income based on the terms and conditions in the Trust Agreement or other trustee statement to calculate Effective Income.

(N) Annuities or Similar (Manual)

(1) Definition

Annuity Income refers to a fixed sum of money periodically paid to the Borrower from a source other than employment.

(2) Required Documentation

The Mortgagee must verify and document the legal agreement establishing the annuity and guaranteeing the continuation of the annuity for the first three years of the Mortgage. The Mortgagee must also obtain a bank statement or a transaction history from a bank evidencing receipt of the annuity.

(3) Calculation of Effective Income

The Mortgagee must use the current rate of the annuity to calculate Effective Income.

The Mortgagee must subtract any of the assets used for the Borrower's required funds to close to purchase the subject Property from the Borrower's liquid assets prior to calculating any Annuity Income.

(O) Notes Receivable Income (Manual)

(1) Definition

Notes Receivable Income refers to income received by the Borrower as payee or holder in due course of a promissory Note or similar credit instrument.

(2) Required Documentation

The Mortgagee must verify and document the existence of the Note. The Mortgagee must also verify and document that payments have been consistently received for the previous 12 months by obtaining tax returns, deposit slips or canceled checks and that such payments are guaranteed to continue for the first three years of the Mortgage.

(3) Calculation of Effective Income

For Borrowers who have been and will be receiving a consistent amount of Notes Receivable Income, the Mortgagee must use the current rate of income to calculate Effective Income. For Borrowers whose Notes Receivable Income fluctuates, the Mortgagee must use the average of the Notes Receivable Income received over the previous year to calculate Effective Income.

(P) Non-Taxable Income (Grossing Up) (Manual)

(1) Definition

Non-Taxable Income refers to types of income not subject to federal taxes, which includes, but is not limited to:
- some portion of Social Security Income;
- some federal government employee Retirement Income;

Handbook 4000.1
Effective Date: 09/14/2015 | Last Revised: 07/10/2019
*Refer to the online version of SF Handbook 4000.1 for specific sections' effective dates

297

- Railroad Retirement benefits;
- some state government Retirement Income;
- certain types of disability and Public Assistance payments;
- Child Support;
- military allowances; and
- other income that is documented as being exempt from federal income taxes.

(2) Required Documentation

The Mortgagee must document and support the amount of income to be Grossed Up for any Non-Taxable Income source and the current tax rate applicable to the Borrower's income that is being Grossed Up.

(3) Calculation of Effective Income

The amount of continuing tax savings attributed to Non-Taxable Income may be added to the Borrower's gross income.

The percentage of Non-Taxable Income that may be added cannot exceed the greater of 15 percent or the appropriate tax rate for the income amount, based on the Borrower's tax rate for the previous year. If the Borrower was not required to file a federal tax return for the previous tax reporting period, the Mortgagee may Gross Up the Non-Taxable Income by 15 percent.

The Mortgagee may not make any additional adjustments or allowances based on the number of the Borrower's dependents.

c. Asset Requirements (Manual)

i. General Asset Requirements (Manual)

The Mortgagee may only consider assets derived from acceptable sources in accordance with the requirements outlined below.

Closing costs, prepaid items and other fees may not be applied towards the Borrower's MRI.

(A) Earnest Money Deposit (Manual)

The Mortgagee must verify and document the deposit amount and source of funds if the amount of the earnest money deposit exceeds 1 percent of the sales price or is excessive based on the Borrower's history of accumulating savings, by obtaining:
- a copy of the Borrower's canceled check;
- certification from the deposit-holder acknowledging receipt of funds;

- a Verification of Deposit (VOD) or bank statement showing that the average balance was sufficient to cover the amount of the earnest money deposit at the time of the deposit; or
- direct verification by a TPV vendor, subject to the following requirements:
  - the Borrower has authorized the Mortgagee to verify assets;
  - the date of the completed verification conforms with FHA requirements in Maximum Age of Mortgage Documents; and
  - the information shows that the average balance was sufficient to cover the amount of the earnest money deposit at the time of the deposit.

If the source of the earnest money deposit was a gift, the Mortgagee must verify that the gift is in compliance with Gifts (Personal and Equity).

(B) Cash to Close (Manual)

The Mortgagee must document all funds that are used for the purpose of qualifying for or closing a Mortgage, including those to satisfy debt or pay costs outside of closing.

The Mortgagee must verify and document that the Borrower has sufficient funds from an acceptable source to facilitate the closing.

(1) Determining the Amount Needed for Closing

For a purchase transaction, the amount of cash needed by the Borrower to close an FHA-insured Mortgage is the difference between the total cost to acquire the Property and the total mortgage amount.

For a refinance transaction, the amount of cash needed by the Borrower to close an FHA-insured Mortgage is the difference between the total payoff requirements of the Mortgage being refinanced and the total mortgage amount.

(2) Mortgagee Responsibility for Estimating Settlement Requirements

In addition to the MRI, additional Borrower expenses must be included in the total amount of cash that the Borrower must provide at mortgage settlement.

(a) Origination Fees and Other Closing Costs

The Mortgagee or sponsored TPO may charge a reasonable origination fee.

The Mortgagee or sponsored TPO may charge and collect from Borrowers those customary and reasonable closing costs and prepaid items necessary to close the Mortgage. Charges may not exceed the actual costs.

The Mortgagee must comply with HUD's Qualified Mortgage Rule at 24 CFR § 203.19.

(b) Discount Points

Discount Points refer to a charge from the Mortgagee for the interest rate chosen. They are paid by the Borrower and become part of the total cash required to close.

(c) Types of Prepaid Items (Including Per Diem Interest)

Prepaid items may include flood and hazard insurance premiums, MIP, real estate taxes, and per diem interest. They must comply with the requirements of the CFPB.

(d) Non-Realty or Personal Property

Non-Realty or Personal Property items (chattel) that the Borrower agrees to pay for separately, including the amount subtracted from the sales price when determining the maximum Mortgage, are included in the total cash requirements for the Mortgage.

(e) Upfront Mortgage Insurance Premium Amounts

Any UFMIP amounts paid in cash are added to the total cash settlement requirements. The UFMIP must be entirely financed into the Mortgage or paid entirely in cash. However, if the UFMIP is financed into the Mortgage, the entire amount is to be financed except for any amount less than $1.00.

(f) Real Estate Agent Fees

If a Borrower is represented by a real estate agent and must pay any fee directly to the agent, that expense must be included in the total of the Borrower's settlement requirements.

(g) Repairs and Improvements

Repairs and improvements, or any portion paid by the Borrower that cannot be financed into the Mortgage, are part of the Borrower's total cash requirements.

(h) Premium Pricing on FHA-Insured Mortgages

Premium Pricing refers to the aggregate credits from a Mortgagee or TPO at the interest rate chosen.

Premium Pricing may be used to pay a Borrower's actual closing costs and prepaid items. Premium Pricing is not included as part of the Interested Party limitation unless the Mortgagee or TPO is the property seller, real estate agent, builder or developer.

The funds derived from a premium priced Mortgage:
- must be disclosed in accordance with RESPA;
- must be used to reduce the principal balance if the credit amount exceeds the actual dollar amount for closing costs and prepaid items; and
- may not be used for payment of debts, collection accounts, escrow shortages or missed Mortgage Payments, or Judgments.

(i) Interested Party Contributions on the Closing Disclosure

The Mortgagee may apply Interested Party credits to the origination fees, other closing costs, prepaid items and discount points including any items Paid Outside Closing (POC).

The refund of the Borrower's POCs may be used toward the Borrower's MRI if the Mortgagee documents that the POCs were paid with the Borrower's own funds.

The Mortgagee must identify the total Interested Party credits on the front page of the Closing Disclosure or similar legal document or in an addendum. The Mortgagee must identify each item paid by Interested Party Contributions.

(j) Real Estate Tax Credits

Where real estate taxes are paid in arrears, the seller's real estate tax credit may be used to meet the MRI, if the Mortgagee documents that the Borrower had sufficient assets to meet the MRI and the Borrower paid closing costs at the time of underwriting.

This permits the Borrower to bring a portion of their MRI to the closing and combine that portion with the real estate tax credit for their total MRI.

(C) Reserves (Manual)

Reserves refer to the sum of the Borrower's verified and documented liquid assets minus the total funds the Borrower is required to pay at closing.

Reserves do not include:
- the amount of cash taken at settlement in cash-out transactions;
- incidental cash received at settlement in other loan transactions;
- gift funds;
- equity in another Property; or
- borrowed funds from any source.

Handbook 4000.1
Effective Date: 09/14/2015 | Last Revised: 07/10/2019
*Refer to the online version of SF Handbook 4000.1 for specific sections' effective dates

301

(1) Reserves for One- to Two-Unit Properties

The Mortgagee must verify and document Reserves equivalent to one month's PITI after closing for one- to two-unit Properties.

(2) Reserves for Three- to Four-Unit Properties

The Mortgagee must verify and document Reserves equivalent to three months' PITI after closing for three- to four-unit Properties.

ii. Source Requirements for the Borrower's Minimum Required Investment (Manual)

(A) Definition

Minimum Required Investment (MRI) refers to the Borrower's contribution in cash or its equivalent required by Section 203(b)(9) of the National Housing Act, which represents at least 3.5 percent of the Adjusted Value of the Property.

(B) Standard

The Mortgagee may only permit the Borrower's MRI to be provided by a source permissible under Section 203(b)(9)(C) of the National Housing Act, which means the funds for the Borrower's MRI must not come from:
   (1) the seller of the Property;
   (2) any other person or Entity who financially benefits from the transaction (directly or indirectly); or
   (3) anyone who is or will be reimbursed, directly or indirectly, by any party included in (1) or (2) above.

While additional funds to close may be provided by one of these sources if permitted under the relevant requirements above, none of the Borrower's MRI may come from these sources. The Mortgagee must document permissible sources for the full MRI in accordance with special requirements noted above.

Additionally, in accordance with Prohibited Sources of Minimum Cash Investment Under the National Housing Act -Interpretive Rule, HUD does not interpret Section 203(b)(9)(C) of the National Housing Act to prohibit Governmental Entities, when acting in their governmental capacity, from providing the Borrower's MRI where the Governmental Entity is originating the insured Mortgage through one of its homeownership programs.

(C) Required Documentation

Where the Borrower's MRI is provided by someone other than the Borrower, the Mortgagee must also obtain documentation to support the permissible nature of the source of those funds.

To establish that the Governmental Entity provided the Borrower's MRI in a manner consistent with HUD's Interpretive Rule, the Mortgagee must document that the Governmental Entity incurred prior to or at closing an enforceable legal liability or obligation to fund the Borrower's MRI. It is not sufficient to document that the Governmental Entity has agreed to reimburse the Mortgagee for the use of funds legally belonging to the Mortgagee to fund the Borrower's MRI.

The Mortgagee must obtain:
- a canceled check, evidence of wire transfer or other draw request showing that prior to or at the time of closing the Governmental Entity had authorized a draw of the funds provided towards the Borrower's MRI from the Governmental Entity's account; or
- a letter from the Governmental Entity, signed by an authorized official, establishing that the funds provided towards the Borrower's MRI were funds legally belonging to the Governmental Entity, when acting in their governmental capacity, at or before closing.

Where a letter from the Governmental Entity is submitted, the precise language of the letter may vary, but must demonstrate that the funds provided for the Borrower's MRI legally belonged to the Governmental Entity at or before closing, by stating, for example:
- the Governmental Entity has, at or before closing, incurred a legally enforceable liability as a result of its agreement to provide the funds towards the Borrower's MRI;
- the Governmental Entity has, at or before closing, incurred a legally enforceable obligation to provide the funds towards the Borrower's MRI; or
- the Governmental Entity has, at or before closing, authorized a draw on its account to provide the funds towards the Borrower's MRI.

While the Mortgagee is not required to document the actual transfer of funds in satisfaction of the obligation or liability, the failure of the Governmental Entity to satisfy the obligation or liability may result in a determination that the funds were provided by a prohibited source.

iii. Sources of Funds (Manual)

The Mortgagee must verify liquid assets for cash to close and Reserves as indicated.

(A) Checking and Savings Accounts (Manual)

(1) Definition

Checking and Savings Accounts refer to funds from Borrower-held accounts in a financial institution that allows for withdrawals and deposits.

(2) Standard

The Mortgagee must verify and document the existence of and amounts in the Borrower's checking and savings accounts.

For recently opened accounts and recent individual deposits of more than 1 percent of the Adjusted Value, the Mortgagee must obtain documentation of the deposits. The Mortgagee must also verify that no debts were incurred to obtain part, or all, of the MRI.

(3) Required Documentation

If the Borrower does not hold the deposit account solely, all non-Borrower parties on the account must provide a written statement that the Borrower has full access and use of the funds.

(a) Traditional Documentation

The Mortgagee must obtain:
- a written VOD and the Borrower's most recent statement for each account; or
- direct verification by a TPV vendor of the Borrower's account covering activity for a minimum of the most recent available month activity for a minimum of one month, subject to the following requirements:
  - the Borrower has authorized the Mortgagee to use a TPV vendor to verify assets; and
  - the date of the data contained in the completed verification is current within 30 days of the date of the verification.

(b) Alternative Documentation

If a VOD is not obtained, a statement showing the previous month's ending balance for the most recent month is required. If the previous month's balance is not shown, the Mortgagee must obtain statement(s) for the most recent two months.

(B) Cash on Hand (Manual)

(1) Definition

Cash on Hand refers to cash held by the Borrower outside of a financial institution.

(2) Standard

The Mortgagee must verify that the Borrower's Cash on Hand is deposited in a financial institution or held by the escrow/title company.

(3) Required Documentation

The Mortgagee must verify and document the Borrower's Cash on Hand by obtaining an explanation from the Borrower describing how the funds were accumulated and the amount of time it took to accumulate the funds.

The Mortgagee must also determine the reasonableness of the accumulation based on the time period during which the funds were saved and the Borrower's:
- income stream;
- spending habits;
- documented expenses; and
- history of using financial institutions.

(C) Retirement Accounts (Manual)

(1) Definition

Retirement Accounts refer to assets accumulated by the Borrower for the purpose of retirement.

(2) Standard

The Mortgagee may include up to 60 percent of the value of assets, less any existing loans, from the Borrower's retirement accounts, such as IRAs, thrift savings plans, 401(k) plan, and Keogh accounts, unless the Borrower provides conclusive evidence that a higher percentage may be withdrawn after subtracting any federal income tax and withdrawal penalties.

The portion of the assets not used to meet closing requirements, after adjusting for taxes and penalties, may be counted as Reserves.

(3) Required Documentation

The Mortgagee must obtain the most recent monthly or quarterly statement to verify and document the existence and amounts in the Borrower's retirement accounts, the Borrower's eligibility for withdrawals, and the terms and conditions for withdrawal from any retirement account.

If any portion of the asset is required for funds to close, evidence of liquidation is required.

(D) Stocks and Bonds (Manual)

(1) Definition

Stocks and Bonds are investment assets accumulated by the Borrower.

(2) Standard

The Mortgagee must determine the value of the stocks and bonds from the most recent monthly or quarterly statement.

If the stocks and bonds are not held in a brokerage account, the Mortgagee must determine the current value of the stocks and bonds through third party verification. Government-issued savings bonds are valued at the original purchase price, unless the Mortgagee verifies and documents that the bonds are eligible for redemption when cash to close is calculated.

(3) Required Documentation

The Mortgagee must verify and document the existence of the Borrower's stocks and bonds by obtaining brokerage statement(s) for each account for the most recent two months. Evidence of liquidation is not required.

For stocks and bonds not held in a brokerage account the Mortgagee must obtain a copy of each stock or bond certificate.

(E) Private Savings Clubs (Manual)

(1) Definition

Private Savings Club refers to a non-traditional method of saving by making deposits into a member-managed resource pool.

(2) Standard

The Mortgagee may consider Private Savings Club funds that are distributed to and received by the Borrower as an acceptable source of funds.

The Mortgagee must verify and document the establishment and duration of the club, and the Borrower's receipt of funds from the club. The Mortgagee must also determine that the received funds were reasonably accumulated, and not borrowed.

(3) Required Documentation

The Mortgagee must obtain the club's account ledgers and receipts, and a verification from the club treasurer that the club is still active.

(F) Gifts (Personal and Equity) (Manual)

(1) Definition

Gifts refer to the contributions of cash or equity with no expectation of repayment.

(2) Standards for Gifts

(a) Acceptable Sources of Gifts Funds

Gifts may be provided by:
- the Borrower's Family Member;
- the Borrower's employer or labor union;
- a close friend with a clearly defined and documented interest in the Borrower;
- a charitable organization;
- a governmental agency or public Entity that has a program providing homeownership assistance to:
  - low or moderate income families; or
  - first-time homebuyers.

Any gift of the Borrower's MRI must also comply with the additional requirements set forth in Source Requirements for the Borrower's MRI.

(b) Reserves

Surplus gift funds may not be considered as cash Reserves.

(c) Donor's Source of Funds

Cash on Hand is not an acceptable source of donor gift funds.

(3) Required Documentation

The Mortgagee must obtain a gift letter signed and dated by the donor and Borrower that includes the following:
- the donor's name, address, telephone number;
- the donor's relationship to the Borrower;
- the dollar amount of the gift; and
- a statement that no repayment is required.

Documenting the Transfer of Gifts

The Mortgagee must verify and document the transfer of gift funds from the donor to the Borrower in accordance with the requirements below.

> *a.* If the gift funds have been verified in the Borrower's account, obtain the donor's bank statement showing the withdrawal and evidence of the deposit into the Borrower's account.
>
> *b.* If the gift funds are not verified in the Borrower's account, obtain the certified check or money order or cashier's check or wire transfer or other official check evidencing payment to the Borrower or settlement agent, and the donor's bank statement evidencing sufficient funds for the amount of the gift.

If the gift funds are being borrowed by the donor and documentation from the bank or other savings account is not available, the Mortgagee must have the donor provide written evidence that the funds were borrowed from an acceptable source, not from a party to the transaction.

The Mortgagee and its Affiliates are prohibited from providing the loan of gift funds to the donor unless the terms of the loan are equivalent to those available to the general public.

Regardless of when gift funds are made available to a Borrower or settlement agent, the Mortgagee must be able to make a reasonable determination that the gift funds were not provided by an unacceptable source.

(4) Standards for Gifts of Equity

(a) Who May Provide Gifts of Equity

Only Family Members may provide equity credit as a gift on Property being sold to other Family Members.

(b) Required Documentation

The Mortgagee must obtain a gift letter signed and dated by the donor and Borrower that includes the following:
- the donor's name, address, telephone number;
- the donor's relationship to the Borrower;
- the dollar amount of the gift; and
- a statement that no repayment is required.

(G) Interested Party Contributions (Manual)

(1) Definition

Interested Parties refer to sellers, real estate agents, builders, developers, Mortgagees, Third Party Originators (TPO), or other parties with an interest in the transaction.

Interested Party Contribution refers to a payment by an Interested Party, or combination of parties, toward the Borrower's origination fees, other closing costs, prepaid items and discount points.

(2) Standard

Interested Parties may contribute up to 6 percent of the sales price toward the Borrower's origination fees, other closing costs, prepaid items and discount points. The 6 percent limit also includes:

- Interested Party payment for permanent and temporary interest rate buydowns, and other payment supplements;
- payments of mortgage interest for fixed rate Mortgages;
- Mortgage Payment protection insurance; and
- payment of the UFMIP.

Interested Party Contributions that exceed actual origination fees, other closing costs, prepaid items and discount points are considered an inducement to purchase. Interested Party Contributions exceeding 6 percent are considered an inducement to purchase.

Interested Party Contributions may not be used for the Borrower's MRI.

Exceptions

Premium Pricing credits from the Mortgagee or TPO are excluded from the 6 percent limit provided the Mortgagee or TPO is not the seller, real estate agent, builder or developer.

Payment of real estate agent commissions or fees, typically paid by the seller under local or state law, or local custom, is not considered an Interested Party Contribution. The satisfaction of a PACE lien or obligation against the Property by the property owner is not considered an Interested Party Contribution.

(3) Required Documentation

The Mortgagee must document the total Interested Party Contributions on the sales contract or applicable legally binding document, form HUD-92900-LT, and Closing Disclosure or similar legal document. When a legally binding document other than the sales contract is used to document the Interested Party Contributions, the Mortgagee must provide a copy of this document to the assigned Appraiser.

(H) Inducements to Purchase (Manual)

Inducements to Purchase refer to certain expenses paid by the seller and/or another Interested Party on behalf of the Borrower and result in a dollar-for-dollar reduction to the purchase price when computing the Adjusted Value of the Property before applying the appropriate Loan-to-Value (LTV) percentage.

These inducements include, but are not limited to:
- contributions exceeding 6 percent of the purchase price;
- contributions exceeding the origination fees, other closing costs, prepaid items and discount points;
- decorating allowances;
- repair allowances;
- excess rent credit;
- moving costs;
- paying off consumer debt;
- Personal Property;
- sales commission on the Borrower's present residence; and
- below-market rent, except for Borrowers who meet the Identity-of-Interest exception for Family Members.

(1) Personal Property (Manual)

Replacement of existing Personal Property items listed below are not considered an inducement to purchase, provided the replacement is made prior to settlement and no cash allowance is given to the Borrower. The inclusion of the items below in the sales agreement is also not considered an inducement to purchase if inclusion of the item is customary for the area:
- range
- refrigerator
- dishwasher
- washer
- dryer
- carpeting
- window treatment
- other items determined appropriate by the HOC

(2) Sales Commission (Manual)

An inducement to purchase exists when the seller and/or Interested Party agrees to pay any portion of the Borrower's sales commission on the sale of the Borrower's present residence.

An inducement to purchase also exists when a Borrower is not paying a real estate commission on the sale of their present residence, and the same real estate broker or agent is involved in both transactions, and the seller is paying a real estate commission on the Property being purchased by the Borrower that exceeds what is typical for the area.

(3) Rent Below Fair Market (Manual)

A reduced rent is an inducement to purchase when the sales contract includes terms permitting the Borrower to live in the Property rent-free or has an agreement to occupy the Property at a rental amount greater than 10 percent below the Appraiser's estimate of fair market rent. When such an inducement exists, the amount of inducement is the difference between the rent charged and the Appraiser's estimate of fair market rent prorated over the period between execution of the sales contract and execution of the Property sale.

Rent below fair market is not considered an inducement to purchase when a builder fails to deliver a Property at an agreed-upon time, and permits the Borrower to occupy an existing or other unit for less than market rent until construction is complete.

(I) Downpayment Assistance Programs (Manual)

FHA does not "approve" downpayment assistance programs administered by charitable organizations, such as nonprofits. FHA also does not allow nonprofit entities to provide gifts to pay off:
- Installment Loans
- credit cards
- collections
- Judgments
- liens
- similar debts

The Mortgagee must ensure that a gift provided by a charitable organization meets the appropriate FHA requirements, and that the transfer of funds is properly documented.

(1) Gifts from Charitable Organizations that Lose or Give Up Their Federal Tax-Exempt Status

If a charitable organization makes a gift that is to be used for all, or part, of a Borrower's downpayment, and the organization providing the gift loses or gives up its federal tax-exempt status, FHA will recognize the gift as an acceptable source of the downpayment provided that:
- the gift is made to the Borrower;
- the gift is properly documented; and
- the Borrower has entered into a contract of sale (including any amendments to purchase price) on or before the date the IRS officially announces that the charitable organization's tax-exempt status is terminated.

(2) Mortgagee Responsibility for Ensuring that Downpayment Assistance Provider is a Charitable Organization

The Mortgagee is responsible for ensuring that an Entity providing downpayment assistance is a charitable organization as defined by Section 501(a) of the Internal Revenue Code (IRC) of 1986 pursuant to Section 501(c) (3) of the IRC.

One resource for this information is the IRS Exempt Organization Select Check, which contains a list of organizations eligible to receive tax-deductible charitable contributions.

(J) Secondary Financing (Manual)

Secondary Financing is any financing other than the first Mortgage that creates a lien against the Property. Any such financing that does create a lien against the Property is not considered a gift or a grant even if it does not require regular payments or has other features forgiving the debt.

(1) Secondary Financing Provided by Governmental Entities and HOPE Grantees (Manual)

(a) Definitions

A Governmental Entity refers to any federal, state, or local government agency or instrumentality.

To be considered an Instrumentality of Government, the Entity must be established by a governmental body or with governmental approval or under special law to serve a particular public purpose or designated by law (statute or court opinion) and does not have 501(c)(3) status. HUD deems Section 115 Entities to be Instrumentalities of Government for the purpose of providing secondary financing.

Homeownership and Opportunity for People Everywhere (HOPE) Grantee refers to an Entity designated in the homeownership plan submitted by an applicant for an implementation grant under the HOPE program.

(b) Standard

FHA will insure a first Mortgage on a Property that has a second Mortgage or lien made or held by a Governmental Entity, provided that:
- the secondary financing is disclosed at the time of application;
- no costs associated with the secondary financing are financed into the FHA-insured first Mortgage;
- the insured first Mortgage does not exceed the FHA Nationwide Mortgage Limit for the area in which the Property is located;

- the secondary financing payments are included in the total Mortgage Payment;
- any secondary financing of the Borrower's MRI fully complies with the additional requirements set forth in Source Requirements for the Borrower's MRI;
- the secondary financing does not result in cash back to the Borrower except for refund of earnest money deposit or other Borrower costs paid outside of closing; and
- the second lien does not provide for a balloon payment within 10 years from the date of execution.

Nonprofits assisting a Governmental Entity in the operation of its secondary financing programs must have HUD approval and placement on the Nonprofit Organization Roster unless there is a documented agreement that:

- the functions performed are limited to the Governmental Entity's secondary financing program; and
- the secondary financing legal documents (Note and Deed of Trust) name the Governmental Entity as the Mortgagee.

Secondary financing that will close in the name of the nonprofit and be held by a Governmental Entity must be made by a HUD-approved Nonprofit.

The Mortgagee must enter information on HUD-approved Nonprofits into FHAC, as applicable.

Secondary financing provided by Governmental Entities or HOPE grantees may be used to meet the Borrower's MRI. Any loan of the Borrower's MRI must also comply with the additional requirements set forth in Source Requirements for the Borrower's MRI.

There is no maximum Combined Loan-to-Value (CLTV) for secondary financing loans provided by Governmental Entities or HOPE grantees.

Any secondary financing meeting this standard is deemed to have prior approval in accordance with 24 CFR § 203.32.

(c) Required Documentation

The Mortgagee must obtain from the provider of any secondary financing:

- documentation showing the amount of funds provided to the Borrower for each transaction;
- copies of the Mortgage and Note; and
- a letter from the Governmental Entity on their letterhead evidencing the relationship between them and the nonprofit for each FHA-insured Mortgage, signed by an authorized official and containing the following information:

o   the FHA case number for the first Mortgage;
o   the complete property address;
o   the name, address and Tax ID for the nonprofit;
o   the name of the Borrower(s) to whom the nonprofit is providing secondary financing;
o   the amount and purpose for the secondary financing provided to the Borrower; and
o   a statement indicating whether the secondary financing:
   ▪   will close in the name of the Governmental Entity; or
   ▪   will be closed in the name of the nonprofit and held by the Governmental Entity.

Where a nonprofit assisting a Governmental Entity with its secondary financing programs is not a HUD-approved Nonprofit, a documented agreement must be provided that:
- the functions performed by the nonprofit are limited to the Governmental Entity's secondary financing program; and
- the secondary financing legal documents (Note and Deed of Trust) name the Governmental Entity as the Mortgagee.

(2) Secondary Financing Provided by HUD-Approved Nonprofits (Manual)

(a) Definition

A HUD-approved Nonprofit is a nonprofit agency approved by HUD to act as a mortgagor using FHA mortgage insurance, purchase the Department's Real Estate Owned (REO) Properties (HUD Homes) at a discount, and provide secondary financing.

HUD-approved Nonprofits appear on the HUD Nonprofit Roster.

(b) Standard

FHA will insure a first Mortgage on a Property that has a second Mortgage or lien held by a HUD-approved Nonprofit, provided that:
- the secondary financing is disclosed at the time of application;
- no costs associated with the secondary financing are financed into the FHA-insured first Mortgage;
- the secondary financing payments must be included in the total Mortgage Payment;
- the secondary financing must not result in cash back to the Borrower except for refund of earnest money deposit or other Borrower costs paid outside of closing;
- the secondary financing may not be used to meet the Borrower's MRI;
- there is no maximum CLTV for secondary financing loans provided by HUD-approved Nonprofits; and

- the second lien may not provide for a balloon payment within 10 years from the date of execution.

Secondary financing provided by Section 115 Entities must follow the guidance in Secondary Financing Provided by Governmental Entities and HOPE Grantees.

Any secondary financing meeting this standard is deemed to have prior approval in accordance with 24 CFR § 203.32.

(c) Required Documentation

The Mortgagee must obtain from the provider of any secondary financing:
- documentation showing the amount of funds provided to the Borrower for each transaction; and
- copies of the Mortgage and Note.

The Mortgagee must enter information into FHAC on the nonprofit and the Governmental Entity as applicable. If there is more than one nonprofit, enter information on all nonprofits.

(3) Family Members (Manual)

(a) Standard

FHA will insure a first Mortgage on a Property that has a second Mortgage or lien held by a Family Member, provided that:
- the secondary financing is disclosed at the time of application;
- no costs associated with the secondary financing are financed into the FHA-insured first Mortgage;
- the secondary financing payments must be included in the total Mortgage Payment;
- the secondary financing must not result in cash back to the Borrower except for refund of earnest money deposit or other Borrower costs paid outside of closing;
- the secondary financing may be used to meet the Borrower's MRI;
- the CLTV ratio of the Base Loan Amount and secondary financing amount must not exceed 100 percent of the Adjusted Value;
- the second lien may not provide for a balloon payment within 10 years from the date of execution;
- any periodic payments are level and monthly;
- there is no prepayment penalty;
- if the Family Member providing the secondary financing borrows the funds, the lending source may not be an Entity with an Identity of Interest in the sale of the Property, such as the:
  - seller;

- o builder;
- o loan originator; or
- o real estate agent;
- mortgage companies with retail banking Affiliates may have the Affiliate lend the funds to the Family Member. However, the terms and conditions of the loan to the Family Member cannot be more favorable than they would be for any other Borrowers;
- if funds loaned by the Family Member are borrowed from an acceptable source, the Borrower may not be a co-Obligor on the Note;
- if the loan from the Family Member is secured by the subject Property, only the Family Member provider may be the Note holder; and
- the secondary financing provided by the Family Member must not be transferred to another Entity at or subsequent to closing.

Any secondary financing meeting this standard is deemed to have prior approval in accordance with 24 CFR § 203.32.

(b) Required Documentation

The Mortgagee must obtain from the provider of any secondary financing:
- documentation showing the amount of funds provided to the Borrower for each transaction and source of funds; and
- copies of the Mortgage and Note.

If the secondary financing funds are being borrowed by the Family Member and documentation from the bank or other savings account is not available, the Mortgagee must have the Family Member provide written evidence that the funds were borrowed from an acceptable source, not from a party to the transaction, including the Mortgagee.

(4) Private Individuals and Other Organizations (Manual)

(a) Definition

Private Individuals and Other Organizations refer to any individuals or Entities providing secondary financing which are not covered elsewhere in this Secondary Financing section.

(b) Standard

FHA will insure a first Mortgage on a Property that has a second Mortgage or lien held by private individuals and other organizations, provided that:
- the secondary financing is disclosed at the time of application;
- no costs associated with the secondary financing are financed into the FHA-insured first Mortgage;

- the secondary financing payments must be included in the total Mortgage Payment;
- the secondary financing must not result in cash back to the Borrower except for refund of earnest money deposit or other Borrower costs paid outside of closing;
- the secondary financing may not be used to meet the Borrower's MRI;
- the CLTV ratio of the Base Loan Amount and secondary financing amount must not exceed the applicable FHA LTV limit;
- the Base Loan Amount and secondary financing amount must not exceed the Nationwide Mortgage Limits.
- the second lien may not provide for a balloon payment within 10 years from the date of execution;
- any periodic payments are level and monthly; and
- there is no prepayment penalty, after giving the Mortgagee 30 Days advance notice.

Any secondary financing meeting this standard is deemed to have prior approval in accordance with 24 CFR § 203.32.

(c) Required Documentation

The Mortgagee must obtain from the provider of any secondary financing:
- documentation showing the amount of funds provided to the Borrower for each transaction; and
- copies of the Mortgage and Note.

(K) Loans (Manual)

A Loan refers to an arrangement in which a lender gives money or Property to a Borrower and the Borrower agrees to return the Property or repay the money.

(1) Collateralized Loans (Manual)

(a) Definition

A Collateralized Loan is a loan that is fully secured by a financial asset of the Borrower, such as deposit accounts, certificates of deposit, investment accounts, or Real Property. These assets may include stocks, bonds, and real estate other than the Property being purchased.

(b) Standard

Loans secured against deposited funds, where repayment may be obtained through extinguishing the asset, do not require consideration of repayment for qualifying purposes. The Mortgagee must reduce the amount of the corresponding asset by the amount of the collateralized loan.

(c) Who May Provide Collateralized Loans

Only an independent third party may provide the borrowed funds for collateralized loans.

The seller, real estate agent or broker, lender, or other Interested Party may not provide such funds. Unacceptable borrowed funds include:
- unsecured signature loans;
- cash advances on credit cards;
- borrowing against household goods and furniture; and
- other similar unsecured financing.

Any loan of the Borrower's MRI must also comply with the additional requirements set forth in Source Requirements for the Borrower's MRI.

(d) Required Documentation

The Mortgagee must verify and document the existence of the Borrower's assets used to collateralize the loan, the promissory Note securing the asset, and the loan proceeds.

(2) Retirement Account Loans (Manual)

(a) Definition

A Retirement Account Loan is a loan that is secured by the Borrower's retirement assets.

(b) Standard

The Mortgagee must reduce the amount of the retirement account asset by the amount of the outstanding balance of the retirement account loan.

(c) Required Documentation

The Mortgagee must verify and document the existence and amounts in the Borrower's retirement accounts and the outstanding loan balance.

(3) Disaster Relief Loans (Manual)

(a) Definition

Disaster Relief Loans refer to loans from a Governmental Entity that provide immediate housing assistance to individuals displaced due to a natural disaster.

(b) Standard

Secured or unsecured disaster relief loans administered by the Small Business Administration (SBA) may also be used. If the SBA loan will be secured by the Property being purchased, it must be clearly subordinate to the FHA-insured Mortgage, and meet the requirements for Secondary Financing Provided by Governmental Entities and HOPE Grantees.

Any loan of the Borrower's MRI must also comply with the additional requirements set forth in Source Requirements for the Borrower's MRI.

Any monthly payment arising from this type of loan must be included in the qualifying ratios.

(c) Required Documentation

The Mortgagee must verify and document the promissory Note.

(L) Grants (Manual)

(1) Disaster Relief Grants (Manual)

(a) Definition

Disaster Relief Grants refer to grants from a Governmental Entity that provide immediate housing assistance to individuals displaced due to a natural disaster. Disaster relief grants may be used for the Borrower's MRI.

(b) Required Documentation

The Mortgagee must verify and document the Borrower's receipt of the grant and terms of use.

Any grant of the Borrower's MRI must also comply with the additional requirements set forth in Source Requirements for the Borrower's MRI.

(2) Federal Home Loan Bank Homeownership Set-Aside Grant Program (Manual)

(a) Definition

The Federal Home Loan Bank's (FHLB) Affordable Housing Program (AHP) Homeownership Set-Aside Grant Program is an acceptable source of downpayment assistance and may be used in conjunction with FHA-insured financing. Secondary financing that creates a lien against the Property is not considered a gift or grant even if it does not require regular payments or has other features forgiving the debt.

(b) Standard

Any AHP Set-Aside funds used for the Borrower's MRI must also comply with the additional requirements set forth in Source Requirements for the Borrower's MRI.

(c) Required Documentation

The Mortgagee must verify and document the Borrower's receipt of the grant and terms of use.

The Mortgagee must also verify and document that the Retention Agreement required by the FHLB is recorded against the Property and results in a Deed Restriction, and not a second lien. The Retention Agreement must:

- provide that the FHLB will have ultimate control over the AHP grant funds if the funds are repaid by the Borrower;
- include language terminating the legal restrictions on conveyance if title to the Property is transferred by foreclosure or DIL, or assigned to the Secretary of HUD; and
- comply with all other FHA regulations.

(M) Employer Assistance (Manual)

(1) Definition

Employer Assistance refers to benefits provided by an employer to relocate the Borrower or assist in the Borrower's housing purchase, including closing costs, prepaid items, MIP, or any portion of the MRI. Employer Assistance does not include benefits provided by an employer through secondary financing.

A salary advance cannot be considered as assets to close.

(2) Standard

(a) Relocation Guaranteed Purchase

The Mortgagee may allow the net proceeds (relocation guaranteed purchase price minus the outstanding liens and expenses) to be used as cash to close.

(b) Employer Assistance Plans

The amount received under Employer Assistance Plans may be used as cash to close.

(3) Required Documentation

(a) Relocation Guaranteed Purchase

If the Borrower is being transferred by their company under a guaranteed sales plan, the Mortgagee must obtain an executed buyout agreement signed by all parties and receipt of funds indicating that the employer or relocation service takes responsibility for the outstanding mortgage debt.

The Mortgagee must verify and document the agreement guaranteeing employer purchase of the Borrower's previous residence and the net proceeds from sale.

(b) Employer Assistance Plans

The Mortgagee must verify and document the Borrower's receipt of assistance. If the employer provides this benefit after settlement, the Mortgagee must verify and document that the Borrower has sufficient cash for closing.

(N) Sale of Personal Property (Manual)

(1) Definition

Personal Property refers to tangible property, other than Real Property, such as cars, recreational vehicles, stamps, coins or other collectibles.

(2) Standard

The Mortgagee must use the lesser of the estimated value or actual sales price when determining the sufficiency of assets to close.

(3) Required Documentation

Borrowers may sell Personal Property to obtain cash for closing.

The Mortgagee must obtain a satisfactory estimate of the value of the item, a copy of the bill of sale, evidence of receipt, and deposit of proceeds. A value estimate may take the form of a published value estimate issued by organizations such as automobile dealers, philatelic or numismatic associations, or a separate written appraisal by a qualified Appraiser with no financial interest in the mortgage transaction.

(O) Trade-In of Manufactured Housing (Manual)

(1) Definition

Trade-In of Manufactured Housing refers to the Borrower's sale or trade-in of another Manufactured Home that is not considered real estate to a Manufactured Housing dealer or an independent third party.

(2) Standard

The net proceeds from the Trade-In of a Manufactured Home may be utilized as the Borrower's source of funds.

Trade-ins cannot result in cash back to the Borrower from the dealer or independent third party.

(3) Required Documentation

The Mortgagee must verify and document the installment sales contract or other agreement evidencing a transaction and value of the trade-in or sale. The Mortgagee must obtain documentation to support the Trade Equity.

(P) Sale of Real Property (Manual)

(1) Definition

The Sale of Real Property refers to the sale of Property currently owned by the Borrower.

(2) Standard

Net proceeds from the Sale of Real Property may be used as an acceptable source of funds.

(3) Required Documentation

The Mortgagee must verify and document the actual sale and the Net Sale Proceeds by obtaining a fully executed Closing Disclosure or similar legal document.

The Mortgagee must also verify and document that the transaction was arms-length, and that the Borrower is entitled to the Net Sale Proceeds.

(Q) Real Estate Commission from Sale of a Subject Property (Manual)

(1) Definition

Real Estate Commission from Sale of Subject Property refers to the Borrower's (i.e., buyer's) portion of a real estate commission earned from the sale of the Property being purchased.

(2) Standard

Mortgagees may consider Real Estate Commissions from Sale of Subject Property as part of the Borrower's acceptable source of funds if the Borrower is a licensed real estate agent.

A Family Member entitled to the commission may also provide it as a gift, in compliance with standard gift requirements.

(3) Required Documentation

The Mortgagee must verify and document that the Borrower, or Family Member giving the commission as a gift, is a licensed real estate agent, and is entitled to a real estate commission from the sale of the Property being purchased.

(R) Sweat Equity (Manual)

(1) Definition

Sweat Equity refers to labor performed, or materials furnished, by or on behalf of the Borrower before closing on the Property being purchased.

(2) Standard

The Mortgagee may consider the reasonable estimated cost of the work or materials as an acceptable source of funds.

Sweat Equity provided by anyone other than the Borrower can only be used as an MRI if it meets the Source Requirements for the Borrower's MRI.

The Mortgagee may consider any amount as Sweat Equity that has not already been included in the mortgage amount. The Mortgagee may not consider clean up, debris removal, and other general maintenance, and work to be performed using repair escrow as Sweat Equity.

Cash back to the Borrower is not permitted in Sweat Equity transactions.

(3) Required Documentation

For materials furnished, the Mortgagee must obtain evidence of the source of funds and the Market Value of the materials.

For labor, the Mortgagee must verify and document that the work will be completed in a satisfactory manner. The Mortgagee must also obtain evidence of Contributory Value of the labor either through an Appraiser's estimate, or a cost-estimating service.

- For labor on Existing Construction, the Mortgagee must also obtain an appraisal indicating the repairs or improvements to be performed. (Any work completed or materials provided before the appraisal are not eligible)
- For labor on Proposed Construction, the Mortgagee must also obtain the sales contract indicating the tasks to be performed by the Borrower during construction.

(S) Trade Equity (Manual)

(1) Definition

Trade Equity refers to when a Borrower trades their Real Property to the seller as part of the cash investment.

(2) Standard

The amount of the Borrower's equity contribution is determined by:

- using the lesser of the Property's appraised value or sales price; and
- subtracting all liens against the Property being traded, along with any real estate commission.

If the Property being traded has an FHA-insured Mortgage, assumption processing requirements and restrictions apply.

(3) Required Documentation

The Mortgagee must obtain a residential appraisal report complying with FHA appraisal policy to determine the Property's value. The Mortgagee must also obtain the Closing Disclosure or similar legal document to document the sale of the Property.

(T) Rent Credits (Manual)

(1) Definition

Rent Credits refer to the amount of the rental payment that exceeds the Appraiser's estimate of fair market rent.

(2) Standard

The Mortgagee may use the cumulative amount of rental payments that exceeds the Appraiser's estimate of fair market rent towards the MRI.

(3) Required Documentation

The Mortgagee must obtain the rent with option to purchase agreement, the Appraiser's estimate of market rent, and evidence of receipt of payments.

d. Final Underwriting Decision (Manual)

The Direct Endorsement (DE) underwriter is ultimately responsible for making an underwriting decision on behalf of their DE Mortgagee in compliance with HUD requirements.

i. Duty of Care/Due Diligence (Manual)

The underwriter must exercise the same level of care that would be used in underwriting a Mortgage entirely dependent on the Property as security. Compliance with FHA requirements is deemed to be the minimum standard of due diligence required in originating and underwriting an FHA-insured Mortgage.

ii. Specific Underwriter Responsibilities (Manual)

The underwriter must review each Mortgage as a separate and unique transaction, recognizing that there may be multiple factors that demonstrate a Borrower's ability and willingness to make timely Mortgage Payments to make an underwriting decision on behalf of their DE Mortgagee in compliance with HUD requirements. The underwriter must evaluate the totality of the Borrower's circumstances and the impact of layering risks on the probability that a Borrower will be able to repay the mortgage obligation according to the terms of the Mortgage.

As the responsible party, the underwriter must:
- review appraisal reports, compliance inspections, and credit analyses to ensure reasonable conclusions, sound reports, and compliance with HUD requirements regardless of who prepared the documentation;
- determine the acceptability of the appraisal, the inspections, the Borrower's capacity to repay the Mortgage, and the overall acceptability of the Mortgage for FHA insurance;
- identify any inconsistencies in information obtained by the Mortgagee in the course of reviewing the Borrower's application regardless of the materiality of such information to the origination and underwriting of a Mortgage; and
- resolve all inconsistencies identified before approving the Borrower's application, and document the inconsistencies and their resolutions of the inconsistencies in the file.

The underwriter must identify and report any misrepresentations, violations of HUD requirements, and fraud to the appropriate party within their organization.

iii. Underwriting of Credit and Debt (Manual)

The underwriter must determine the creditworthiness of the Borrower, which includes analyzing the Borrower's overall pattern of credit behavior and the credit report (see Credit Requirements).

The lack of traditional credit history or the Borrower's decision to not use credit may not be used as the sole basis for rejecting the mortgage application.

Compensating factors cannot be used to compensate for any derogatory credit.

The underwriter must ensure that there are no other unpaid obligations incurred in connection with the mortgage transaction or the purchase of the Property.

iv. Underwriting of Income (Manual)

The underwriter must review the income of a Borrower and verify that it has been supported with the proper documentation (see Income Requirements).

v. Underwriting of Assets (Manual)

The underwriter must review the assets of a Borrower and verify that they have been supported with the proper documentation (see Asset Requirements).

vi. Verifying Mortgage Insurance Premium and Mortgage Amount (Manual)

The underwriter must review the MIP and mortgage amount and verify that they have been supported with the proper documentation (see Underwriting).

vii. Calculating Qualifying Ratios (Manual)

(A) General Information about Qualifying Ratios

For all transactions, except non-credit qualifying Streamline Refinances, the underwriter must calculate the Borrower's Total Mortgage Payment to Effective Income Ratio (PTI) and the Total Fixed Payment to Effective Income ratio, or DTI, and verify compliance with the ratio requirements listed in the Approvable Ratio Requirements Chart.

The Mortgagee must exclude any obligation that is wholly secured by existing assets of the Borrower from the calculation of the Borrower's debts, provided the assets securing the debt are also not considered in qualifying the Borrower.

(B) Calculating Total Mortgage Payment

The total Mortgage Payment includes:
- P&I;
- real estate taxes;
- hazard insurance;
- flood insurance as applicable;
- MIP;
- HOA or condominium association fees or expenses;
- Ground Rent;
- special assessments;
- payments for any acceptable secondary financing; and
- any other escrow payments.

The Mortgagee may deduct the amount of the Mortgage Credit Certificate or Section 8 Homeownership Voucher if it is paid directly to the Servicer.

(1) Estimating Real Estate Taxes

The Mortgagee must use accurate estimates of monthly tax escrows when calculating the total Mortgage Payment.

In New Construction cases and Manufactured Homes converting to real estate, property tax estimates must be based on the land and improvements.

Where real estate taxes are abated, Mortgagees may use the abated amount provided that (1) the Mortgagee can document the abated amount with the taxing authority and (2) the abatement will remain in place for at least the first three years of the Mortgage.

(2) Condominium Utility Expenses

The portion of a condominium fee that is clearly attributable to utilities may be subtracted from the HOA fees before computing qualifying ratios, provided the Borrower provides proper documentation, such as statements from the utility company.

(3) Temporary Interest Rate Buydowns

The Mortgagee must use the Note rate when calculating principal and interest for Mortgages that involve a temporary interest rate buydown.

(C) Calculating Total Fixed Payment

The total fixed payment includes:

- the total Mortgage Payment; and
- monthly obligations on all debts and liabilities.

viii. Approvable Ratio Requirements (Manual)

The maximum Total Mortgage Payment to Effective Income Ratio (PTI) and Total Fixed Payments to Effective Income Ratio, or DTI, applicable to manually underwritten Mortgages are summarized in the matrix below.

The qualifying ratios for Borrowers with no credit score are computed using income only from Borrowers occupying the Property and obligated on the Mortgage. Non-occupant co-Borrower income may not be included.

Lowest Minimum Decision Credit Score	Maximum Qualifying Ratios (%)	Acceptable Compensating Factors
500-579 or No Credit Score	31/43	Not applicable. Borrowers with Minimum Decision Credit Scores below 580, or with no credit score may not exceed 31/43 ratios. Energy Efficient Homes may have stretch ratios of 33/45.
580 and above	31/43	No compensating factors required. Energy Efficient Homes may have stretch ratios of 33/45.
580 and above	37/47	**One** of the following: • verified and documented cash Reserves; • minimal increase in housing payment; or • residual income.
580 and above	40/40	No discretionary debt.
580 and above	40/50	**Two** of the following: • verified and documented cash Reserves; • minimal increase in housing payment; • significant additional income not reflected in Effective Income; and/or • residual income.

ix. Documenting Acceptable Compensating Factors (Manual)

The following describes the compensating factors and required documentation that may be used to justify approval of manually underwritten Mortgages with qualifying ratios as described above.

(A) Energy Efficient Homes

(1) Standard

For Mortgages on New Construction, the Borrower is eligible for the EEH stretch ratios when the Property meets or exceeds the higher of:
- the latest energy code standard that has been adopted by HUD through a Federal Register notice; or
- the applicable International Energy Conservation Code (IECC) year used by the state or local building code.

For Mortgages on Existing Construction, the Borrower is eligible for the EEH stretch ratios when the property meets either of the following conditions:
- Homes that *currently* score a **"6" or higher** on the Home Energy Score scale; or
- Homes where documented cost-effective energy improvements, as identified in the Home Energy Score Report, would increase a home's score to a **"6" or higher** are completed prior to closing, or in association with FHA's 203(k), Weatherization, EEM or Solar and Wind programs.

(2) Required Documentation

The following documents must be included in the case binder submitted for endorsement:
- For Mortgages on Existing Construction, a copy of the Home Energy Score Report.
- For Mortgages on New Construction, a copy of the Builder's Certification, form HUD-92541, to evidence the IECC code, successor code or local/state building code used.

(B) Verified and Documented Cash Reserves

Verified and documented cash Reserves may be cited as a compensating factor subject to the following requirements.
- Reserves are equal to or exceed three total monthly Mortgage Payments (one and two units); or
- Reserves are equal to or exceed six total monthly Mortgage Payments (three and four units).

Reserves are calculated as the Borrower's total assets as described in Asset Requirements less:
- the total funds required to close the Mortgage;
- gifts;
- borrowed funds; and
- cash received at closing in a cash-out refinance transaction or incidental cash received at closing in the mortgage transaction.

(C) Minimal Increase in Housing Payment

A minimal increase in housing payment may be cited as a compensating factor subject to the following requirements:

- the new total monthly Mortgage Payment does not exceed the current total monthly housing payment by more than $100 or 5 percent, whichever is less; and
- there is a documented 12 month housing payment history with no more than one 30 Day late payment. In cash-out transactions all payments on the Mortgage being refinanced must have been made within the month due for the previous 12 months.
- If the Borrower has no current housing payment Mortgagees may not cite this compensating factor.

The Current Total Monthly Housing Payment refers to the Borrower's current total Mortgage Payment or current total monthly rent obligation.

(D) No Discretionary Debt

No discretionary debt may be cited as a compensating factor subject to the following requirements:

- the Borrower's housing payment is the only open account with an outstanding balance that is not paid off monthly;
- the credit report shows established credit lines in the Borrower's name open for at least six months; and
- the Borrower can document that these accounts have been paid off in full monthly for at least the past six months.

Borrowers who have no established credit other than their housing payment, no other credit lines in their own name open for at least six months, or who cannot document that all other accounts are paid off in full monthly for at least the past six months, do not qualify under this criterion. Credit lines not in the Borrower's name but for which they are an authorized user do not qualify under this criterion.

(E) Significant Additional Income Not Reflected in Effective Income

Additional income from Overtime, Bonuses, Part-Time or Seasonal Employment that is not reflected in Effective Income can be cited as a compensating factor subject to the following requirements:

- the Mortgagee must verify and document that the Borrower has received this income for at least one year, and it will likely continue; and
- the income, if it were included in gross Effective Income, is sufficient to reduce the qualifying ratios to not more than 37/47.

Income from non-borrowing spouses or other parties not obligated for the Mortgage may not be counted under this criterion.

This compensating factor may be cited only in conjunction with another compensating factor when qualifying ratios exceed 37/47 but are not more than 40/50.

(F) Residual Income

Residual income may be cited as a compensating factor provided it can be documented and it is at least equal to the applicable amounts for household size and geographic region found on the Table of Residual Incomes By Region found in the Department of Veterans Affairs (VA) *Lenders Handbook - VA Pamphlet 26-7*, Chapter 4.9 b and e.

(1) Calculating Residual Income

Residual income is calculated as total Effective Income of all occupying Borrowers less:

- state income taxes;
- federal income taxes;
- municipal or other income taxes;
- retirement or Social Security;
- total fixed payment;
- estimated maintenance and utilities;
- job related expenses (e.g., child care); and
- the amount of the Gross Up of any Non-Taxable Income.

If available, Mortgagees must use federal and state tax returns from the most recent tax year to document state and local taxes, retirement, Social Security and Medicare. If tax returns are not available, Mortgagees may rely upon current pay stubs.

For estimated maintenance and utilities, Mortgagees must multiply the Gross Living Area of the Property by the maintenance and utility factor found in the *Lenders Handbook - VA Pamphlet 26-7*.

(2) Using Residual Income as a Compensating Factor

To use residual income as a compensating factor, the Mortgagee must count all members of the household of the occupying Borrower without regard to the nature of their relationship and without regard to whether they are joining on title or the Note to determine "family size."

Exception

The Mortgagee may omit any individuals from "family size" who are fully supported from a source of verified income which is not included in Effective

Income in the mortgage analysis. These individuals must voluntarily provide sufficient documentation to verify their income to qualify for this exception.

From the table provided in *Lenders Handbook - VA Pamphlet 26-7*, select the applicable mortgage amount, region and household size. If residual income equals or exceeds the corresponding amount on the table, it may be cited as a compensating factor.

x. Borrower Approval or Denial (Manual)

(A) Re-Underwriting

The Mortgagee must re-underwrite a Mortgage when any data element of the Mortgage changes and/or new Borrower information becomes available.

(B) Documentation of Final Underwriting Review Decision [Text was deleted in this section.]

The underwriter must complete the following documents to evidence their final underwriting decision.

For cases involving Mortgages to HUD employees, the Mortgagee completes the following and then submits the complete underwritten mortgage application to FHA for review and issuance of a Firm Commitment or Rejection Notice prior to closing.

For cases involving Mortgagees that receive a DE program Test Case phase approval letter from HUD's HOC, the Mortgagee completes the following and then submits the complete underwritten mortgage application post-closing to FHA for review and issuance of a Firm Commitment or Rejection Notice.

(1) Form HUD-92900-LT, FHA Loan Underwriting and Transmittal Summary

The underwriter must record the following items on form HUD-92900-LT:
- their decision;
- any compensating factors;
- any modification of the mortgage amount and approval conditions under "Underwriter Comments"; and
- their DE Identification Number and signature.

(2) Form HUD-92800.5B, Conditional Commitment Direct Endorsement Statement of Appraised Value

The underwriter must confirm that form HUD-92800.5B is completed as directed in the form instructions.

(3) Form HUD-92900-A, HUD/VA Addendum to Uniform Residential Loan Application

The underwriter must complete form HUD-92900-A as directed in the form instructions.

An authorized officer of the Mortgagee, the Borrower, and the underwriter must execute form HUD-92900-A, as indicated in the instructions.

(C) Conditional Approval

The underwriter must condition the approval of the Borrower on the completion of the final *URLA* (Fannie Mae Form 1003/Freddie Mac Form 65) and form HUD-92900-A at or before closing if the underwriter relied on an initial *URLA* and form HUD-92900-A in underwriting the Mortgage.

(D) HUD Employee Mortgages

If the Mortgage involves a HUD employee, the Mortgagee must condition the loan on the approval of the Mortgage by HUD. The Mortgagee must submit the case binder to the Processing and Underwriting Division Director at the Jurisdictional HOC for final underwriting approval.

(E) Notification of Borrower of Approval and Term of the Approval

The Mortgagee must timely notify the Borrower of their approval. The underwriter's approval or the Firm Commitment is valid for the greater of 90 Days or the remaining life of the:
- Conditional Commitment issued by HUD; or
- the underwriter's approval date of the Property, indicated as Action Date on form HUD-92800.5B.

(F) Responsibilities upon Denial

When a Mortgage is denied, the Mortgagee must comply with all requirements of the FCRA, and the Equal Credit Opportunity Act (ECOA), as implemented by Regulation B (12 CFR Part 1002). The Mortgagee must complete the Mortgage Credit Reject in FHAC.

xi. Back to Work - Extenuating Circumstances (Manual) [Expired for case numbers assigned on or after October 1, 2016]

The Back to Work – Extenuating Circumstances Policy guidance allows Borrowers who have experienced an Economic Event resulting in loss of employment and household income to use an alternative manner for credit qualification for purchase money Mortgages.

(A) Definitions

For the purpose of the Back to Work – Extenuating Circumstances Policy only:

Economic Event refers to any occurrence beyond the Borrower's control that results in loss of employment, loss of income, or a combination of both, which causes a reduction in the Borrower's household income of 20 percent or more for a period of at least six months.

Onset of an Economic Event refers to the month of loss of employment/income.

Recovery from an Economic Event refers to the re-establishment of Satisfactory Credit.

Satisfactory Credit refers to when a Borrower's credit history is clear of late housing payments, installment debt payments, and major derogatory credit issues on Revolving Charge Accounts for a period of 12 months. Any open Mortgages must be current with a 12 month satisfactory payment history. Mortgages may have been brought current through a Loan Modification, "temporary" or "permanent," as long as all payments are documented as being received in accordance with the modification agreement.

Borrower Household Income refers to the gross income of the Borrower and all household members.

Household Member refers to the Borrower and any individual residing at the Borrower's Principal Residence at the time of the Economic Event, and who was a co-Borrower on the Borrower's previous Mortgage.

(B) General Eligibility

Mortgagees must use the Back to Work – Extenuating Circumstances guidance when manually underwriting a purchase money mortgage application from a Borrower who has experienced an Economic Event resulting in a foreclosure, Short Sale/Pre-Foreclosure Sale, bankruptcy, or other negative impact on credit.

The Mortgagee must verify and document the existence of an Economic Event that reduced household income by 20 percent or more for a period of at least six months.

The Mortgagee must obtain the necessary authorization to verify the loss of income of the household member that experienced the Economic Event, even if the household member is not an applicant on the current Mortgage.

(C) Underwriting and Documentation Requirements

(1) Consideration of Derogatory Credit

(a) Standard

The Mortgagee must determine that the Borrower exhibited satisfactory credit prior to the Onset of an Economic Event, the Borrower's derogatory credit occurred after the Onset of an Economic Event, and the Borrower has re-established satisfactory credit for a minimum of 12 months as of the date of case number assignment.

The Mortgagee must analyze and document all delinquent accounts and all derogatory credit, including collections and Judgments, bankruptcies, foreclosures, deeds-in-lieu, and Short Sales/Pre-Foreclosure Sales, to determine whether credit deficiencies were the result of an Economic Event.

(b) Required Documentation

The Borrower's credit must be documented with their credit report per standard FHA requirements.

The Borrower's income must be documented in accordance with the general FHA requirements for household members.

The Mortgagee must verify and document event-related collections and Judgments that were the result of the Economic Event. For Borrowers with open collection accounts or Judgments, the Mortgagee must also meet the requirements for Evaluating Liabilities and Debt and Evaluating Credit History.

(c) Economic Event-Related Chapter 7 Bankruptcy

The Mortgagee must verify and document that the bankruptcy was the result of an Economic Event and a minimum of 12 months have elapsed since the date of discharge of the bankruptcy.

(d) Economic Event-Related Chapter 13 Bankruptcy

The Mortgagee must verify and document that the bankruptcy was the result of an Economic Event and all required bankruptcy payments were made on time, or a minimum of 12 months of the pay-out period under the bankruptcy has elapsed at the time of case number assignment and all required bankruptcy payments were made on time.

If the Chapter 13 Bankruptcy was not discharged prior to mortgage application, the Mortgagee must also verify and document that the Borrower has received written permission from the Bankruptcy Court to enter into the subject mortgage transaction.

(e) Economic Event-Related Mortgage Foreclosure

The Mortgagee must verify and document that the foreclosure or DIL was the result of the Economic Event and a minimum of 12 months have elapsed since the date of foreclosure or DIL.

(f) Economic Event-Related Pre-foreclosure Sale (Short Sale)

The Mortgagee must verify and document that the Short Sale was the result of the Economic Event and a minimum of 12 months have elapsed since the date of sale.

(g) Evaluating Non-Traditional Credit

The Mortgagee may deem a Borrower to have satisfactory credit if the Borrower's non-traditional credit history covering at least 12 months in duration has no history of delinquency on rental housing payments, no more than one 30-Day delinquency on payments due to other creditors, and no collection accounts/court records reporting (other than medical and/or identity theft).

(2) Loss of Employment

The Mortgagee must verify and document the loss of employment by obtaining a written Verification of Employment (VOE) evidencing the termination date. In cases where the prior employer is no longer in business, the Mortgagee must obtain a written termination notice or other publicly available documentation of the business closure. They must also document receipt of unemployment income.

(3) Loss of Income

The Mortgagee must verify and document the Borrower's household income prior to loss of income by obtaining a written VOE evidencing prior income, or tax transcripts, or W-2s.

For a loss of income based on Seasonal Employment, the Mortgagee must verify and document a two-year history of Seasonal Employment in the same field immediately prior to the loss of income, in addition to meeting the documentation requirement above.

For a loss of income based on Part-Time Employment, the Mortgagee must verify and document a two-year history of continuous Part-Time Employment immediately prior to the loss of income in addition to meeting the documentation requirements above.

(4) Post Economic Event Income

Only the income of Borrowers who were household members at the time of the Economic Event may be used as Effective Income for the purpose of establishing a 20 percent reduction in income.

(D) Housing Counseling

To qualify for purposes of establishing satisfactory credit following the Economic Event, the Borrower must receive homeownership counseling or a combination of homeownership education and counseling.

Housing counseling may be conducted in person, via telephone, via internet, or other methods approved by HUD, and mutually agreed upon by the Borrower and housing counseling agency as provided for in the Housing Counseling Program Handbook.

A list of HUD-approved housing counseling agencies can be obtained online at http://www.hud.gov/ or by calling 1-(800)-569-4287.

All housing counseling and education must be completed a minimum of 30 Days but no more than six months prior to the Borrower submitting a mortgage application to a Mortgagee.

(1) One-on-One Counseling

Each Borrower must receive one hour of one-on-one counseling from a HUD-approved counseling agency. The counseling must address the cause of the Economic Event and the actions taken to overcome the Economic Event to reduce the likelihood of reoccurrence.

(2) Housing Education

The housing education may be provided by HUD-approved housing counseling agencies, state housing finance agencies, approved intermediaries or their sub-grantees, or through an online course.

(3) Required Documentation

The Mortgagee must obtain a copy of the Borrower's letter from the housing counseling agency evidencing completion of the required pre-purchase counseling. The letter must be on the housing counseling agency's letterhead, must display the agency's Tax Identification Number (TIN), must state that counseling was delivered in accordance with Back to Work requirements, verify the date counseling was completed, and signed by the Borrower and authorized official of the agency.

The Mortgagee must also obtain copies of all required housing counseling disclosures as follows:

- an explicit description of any financial relationships between the agency and the Mortgagee;
- a statement that the Borrower is not obligated to pursue a Mortgage with a Mortgagee; and
- a statement that "Completion of this housing counseling program and receipt of a letter of completion of counseling do not qualify you (the borrower) for an FHA-insured mortgage. A mortgagee will have to determine if you (the borrower) qualify for a mortgage. You understand that you may not be approved for a mortgage."

The Mortgagee must place the documentation of the pre-purchase housing counseling and housing counseling agency disclosures in the FHA case binder immediately after the Borrower's credit report.

(E) Insurance Application Processing

The Mortgagee must indicate the application has been underwritten in accordance with Back to Work – Extenuating Circumstances in the insurance application screen on FHA Connection (FHAC).

The Mortgagee must also complete the housing counseling information in the insurance application screen on FHAC.

(F) Expiration of Guidance

This guidance expires on September 30, 2016.

xii. Underwriting Nonprofit Borrowers (Manual)

(A) General Eligibility

Nonprofit agencies must be HUD-approved as a Borrower prior to case number assignment. The Jurisdictional HOC approves or denies the nonprofit agency's participation in FHA activities. The approval is valid for a two year period.

(B) Borrower Eligibility

The Mortgagee must review the Nonprofit List in FHAC, and ensure the maximum case load limitation is not exceeded for nonprofit Borrowers.

The Mortgagee must ensure that Additional Eligibility Requirements for Nonprofit Organizations and State and Local Government Agencies are met.

The Mortgagee must verify that the nonprofit organization remains eligible under Section 501(c)(3) as exempt from taxation under Section 501(a) of the Internal Revenue Code of 1986, as amended.

(1) Employer Identification Number (EIN)

The Mortgagee must obtain the Employer Identification Number (EIN) of the nonprofit Borrower and enter it into the SSN field in FHAC.

(2) Credit Alert and Limited Denial of Participation Screening

The Mortgagee must screen nonprofit Borrowers through the Credit Alert Verification Reporting System (CAIVRS) and the Limited Denial of Participation List using the nonprofit Borrower's EIN.

(C) Program and Product Limitations

Nonprofit Borrowers are eligible only for fixed rate Mortgages.

Nonprofit Borrowers are eligible only for FHA-to-FHA refinances.

(D) Maximum Loan-to-Value Limits

Mortgages for nonprofit Borrowers are subject to the same LTV limitations as Mortgages secured by a Principal Residence.

(E) Underwriting

The Mortgagee must underwrite nonprofit Borrowers in accordance with the guidance provided in this section. The Underwriting the Borrower Using the TOTAL Mortgage Scorecard and Manual Underwriting of the Borrower sections are not applicable to nonprofit Borrowers.

The Mortgagee must obtain documentation to determine the nonprofit Borrower's actual financial capacity and demonstrate that it has stability and proper cash management.

(1) Standard

(a) Funding Stream Analysis

The Mortgagee must consider the reliability and duration of the funding stream, and whether the primary sources of funding are competitive, whether the nonprofit Borrower's funding stream is from a mix of private and public sources, or only from public funds, and if other sources of funding are available should one or more be curtailed.

Handbook 4000.1
Effective Date: 09/14/2015 | Last Revised: 07/10/2019
*Refer to the online version of SF Handbook 4000.1 for specific sections' effective dates

339

The Mortgagee must also consider whether those funding sources permit overhead and administrative allowances as well as the amount of the nonprofit Borrower's assets that will be encumbered by the downpayments on the Mortgages.

(b) Financial Capacity Analysis

The Mortgagee must analyze the year-to-date and previous two years' financial statements, balance sheets, statements of activity and statements of cash flow to determine the financial stability and capacity of the nonprofit Borrower, including all mortgage applications in process.

(i) Unrestricted Cash Balance

The Mortgagee must determine if the nonprofit Borrower has an unrestricted cash balance exclusive of lines of credit and Rental Income from the financed Properties that is stable or increasing and supports a six month reserve meeting the greater of:
- 10 percent of the total Mortgage Payments due each month on all Mortgages; or
- total Mortgage Payments for the single largest Mortgage.

(ii) Liquidity Ratio

The Mortgagee must determine if the nonprofit Borrower has a liquidity ratio (current assets divided by current liabilities) of 2.00 or greater. Lines of credit are not to be considered in this ratio.

(iii) Total Net Assets (Equity)

The Mortgagee must determine that the total net assets are:
- stable or increasing; and
- equal to or greater than 25 percent of the proposed mortgage debt.

(iv) Unrestricted Net Assets

The Mortgagee must determine that the unrestricted net assets are stable or increasing.

(v) Total Assets and Liabilities

The Mortgagee must determine that:
- the total assets are stable or increasing; and
- the trend of liabilities is stable or increasing at the same rate as the total assets.

(vi) Support and Revenue Accounts

Definition

Support and Revenue Accounts refer to operating income and other non-debt income sources.

Standard

The Mortgagee must determine that:
- the support and revenue accounts are stable or increasing; and
- the trend of operating expenses is stable or increasing at the same rate as the support and revenue accounts.

(vii) Cash Flow

The Mortgagee must determine that the trend of cash flow from operating activities is positive.

(viii) Working Capital

Definition

Working Capital refers to the liquid assets less short-term liabilities.

Standard

The Mortgagee must determine that the trend of working capital is stable or increasing.

(2) Required Documentation

The Mortgagee must obtain:
- the two most recent years':
  - audited financial statements (balance sheet, statement of activity, statement of cash flow); and
  - Form IRS 990, *Return of Organization Exempt from Income Tax*;
- most recent audited 90-Day year-to-date financial statement;
- credit reports on the nonprofit agency; and
- corporate resolution delegating signatory authority.

(F) Final Underwriting Decision

The Mortgagee must analyze the nonprofit Borrower's financial capacity for each Mortgage being considered in accordance with the standards above.

If the nonprofit Borrower does not meet all of the standards above, the Mortgagee must document acceptable compensating factors.

The Mortgagee must describe how it arrived at the conclusion that the nonprofit Borrower was an acceptable mortgage risk and met FHA's eligibility criteria. The analysis must consider the effect of the proposed mortgage debt(s) on the nonprofit agency's financial condition.

6. Closing

a. Mortgagee Closing Requirements

i. Chain of Title

The Mortgagee must obtain evidence of prior ownership when a Property was sold within 12 months of the case number assignment date. The Mortgagee must review the evidence of prior ownership to determine any undisclosed Identity-of-Interest transactions.

ii. Title

The Mortgagee must ensure that all objections to title have been cleared and any discrepancies have been resolved to ensure that the FHA-insured Mortgage is in first lien position.

(A) Good and Marketable Title

The Mortgagee must determine if there are any exceptions to good and marketable title not covered by the General Waiver (see Section General Eligibility and 24 CFR § 203.389).

The Mortgagee must review any exceptions discovered during the title search and decide whether such title exceptions affect the Property's value and/or marketability.

If the Mortgagee determines that any exception affects the Property's value and/or marketability, the Mortgagee must request a waiver.

(B) Requests for Title Exceptions Not Covered by the General Waiver

The Mortgagee must submit a request for a waiver when the Title Exception is not covered by the General Waiver, to the attention of the Processing and Underwriting Division Director at the Jurisdictional HOC prior to endorsement. The request must include the case number, the specific guideline and the reason the Mortgagee is asking for the waiver. If the Jurisdictional HOC grants the requested waiver, the HOC will notify the Mortgagee in writing. The Mortgagee must place the notice of approval in the mortgage file.

If the waiver request is denied and good and marketable title is not obtained, the Mortgage is not eligible for FHA insurance.

(C) Manufactured Housing

Good and marketable title showing the Manufactured Home and land are classified as real estate at the time of closing is required.

If there were two existing titles at the time the housing unit was purchased, the Mortgagee must ensure that all state or local requirements for proper purging of the title (chattel or equivalent debt instrument) have been met, and the subject Property is classified as real estate prior to endorsement. The Manufactured Home need not be taxed as Real Property.

iii. Legal Restrictions on Conveyance (Free Assumability)

The Mortgagee must determine if there are any legal restrictions on conveyance in accordance with 24 CFR § 203.41.

iv. Closing in Compliance with Mortgage Approval

The Mortgagee must instruct the settlement agent to close the Mortgage in the same manner in which it was underwritten and approved.

The Mortgagee must ensure that the conditions listed on form HUD-92900-A and/or form HUD-92800.5B are satisfied.

v. Closing in the Mortgagee's Name

A Mortgage may close in the name of the Mortgagee or the sponsoring Mortgagee, the principal or the authorized agent. TPOs that are not FHA-approved Mortgagees may not close in their own names or perform any functions in FHA Connection (FHAC).

vi. Required Forms

The Mortgagee must use the forms and/or language prescribed by FHA in the legal documents used for closing the Mortgage.

vii. Certifications

(A) Borrower Certification

The Borrower must sign the certification on form HUD-92900-A for all transactions and the Settlement Certification for purchase transactions in accordance with the instructions provided on the form.

(B) Seller Certification

The seller must sign the certification on the Settlement Certification for purchase transactions.

(C) Settlement Agent Certification

The settlement agent must sign the certification on the Settlement Certification for purchase transactions.

(D) Lender Certification

The Mortgagee must sign the certifications on the form HUD-92900-A in accordance with the instructions provided on the form.

viii. Projected Escrow

The Mortgagee must establish the escrow account in accordance with the regulatory requirements in 24 CFR § 203.550 and RESPA.

(A) Monthly Escrow Obligations

The Mortgagee must collect a monthly amount from the Borrower that will enable it to pay all escrow obligations in accordance with 24 CFR § 203.23. The escrow account must be sufficient to meet the following obligations when they become due:
- hazard insurance premiums;
- real estate taxes;
- Mortgage Insurance Premiums (MIP);
- special assessments;
- flood insurance premiums if applicable;
- Ground Rents if applicable;
- servicing, maintenance, repair and replacement of water purification equipment; and
- any item that would create liens on the Property positioned ahead of the FHA-insured Mortgage, other than condominium or Homeowners' Association (HOA) fees.

(B) Repair Completion Escrow Requirement

The Mortgagee may establish a repair escrow for incomplete construction, or for alterations and repairs that cannot be completed prior to loan closing, provided the housing is habitable and safe for occupancy at the time of loan closing.

Repair escrow funds must be sufficient to cover the cost of the repairs or improvements. The cost for Borrower labor may not be included in the repair escrow account.

The Mortgagee must execute form HUD-92300, *Mortgagee's Assurance of Completion*, to indicate that the repair escrow has been established.

The Mortgagee must certify on form HUD-92051, *Compliance Inspection Report*, that the incomplete construction, alterations and repairs have been satisfactory completed.

Effective for case numbers assigned on or after October 31, 2016, after the repair escrow account is closed, the Mortgagee must complete the Escrow Closeout Certification screen in FHAC within 30 Days after the escrow account is closed.

ix. Temporary Interest Rate Buydown Escrow Requirements

The Mortgagee must establish an escrow for temporary interest rate buydowns.

The escrow agreement must not:
- permit reversion of undistributed escrow funds to the provider if the Property is sold or the Mortgage is prepaid in full; nor
- allow unexpended escrow funds to be provided to the Borrower in cash, unless the borrower funds were used to establish the escrow account.

Payments must be made by the escrow agent to the Mortgagee or servicing agent. If escrow payments are not received for any reason, the Borrower is responsible for making the total payment as described in the mortgage Note.

x. Closing Costs and Fees

The Mortgagee must ensure that all fees charged to the Borrower comply with all applicable federal, state and local laws and disclosure requirements.

The Mortgagee is not permitted to use closing costs to help the Borrower meet the Minimum Required Investment (MRI).

(A) Collecting Customary and Reasonable Fees

The Mortgagee may charge the Borrower reasonable and customary fees that do not exceed the actual cost of the service provided.

The Mortgagee must ensure that the aggregate charges do not violate FHA's Tiered Pricing rules.

(B) Other Fees and Charges

The Mortgagee or sponsored TPO may charge the Borrower discount points, and lock-in and rate lock fees consistent with FHA and CFPB requirements.

(1) Origination Fees

The Mortgagee may charge an origination fee in accordance with RESPA.

(2) Discount Points

The Mortgagee may charge the Borrower discount points.

(3) Lock-in and Rate Lock Fees

The Mortgagee may charge the Borrower lock-in and rate lock fees only if the Mortgagee provides a lock-in or commitment agreement guaranteeing the interest rate and/or discount points for a period of not less than 15 Days prior to the anticipated closing.

(C) Qualified Mortgage

The Mortgagee must ensure the points and fees charged are in compliance with FHA's Qualified Mortgage Rule.

(D) Tiered Pricing

The Mortgagee must ensure that the aggregate fees and charges do not violate the following Tiered Pricing rule.

(1) Definitions for Tiered Pricing

Area refers to a metropolitan statistical area as established by the Office of Management and Budget.

Mortgage Charge refers to the interest rate, discount points, origination fee, and any other amount charged to the Borrower for an insured Mortgage.

Mortgage Charge Rate refers to the total amount of Mortgage Charges for a Mortgage expressed as a percentage of the initial principal of the Mortgage.

Tiered Pricing refers to any variance in Mortgage Charge Rates of more than two percentage points from the Mortgagee's reasonable and customary rate for insured Mortgages for dwellings located within the area.

(2) Required Documentation

The Mortgagee must document that any variation in the Mortgage Charge Rate is based on actual variations in fees or costs to the Mortgagee to make the Mortgage.

(3) Standard

The Mortgagee may not make a Mortgage with a Mortgage Charge Rate that varies more than two percentage points from the Mortgagee's reasonable and customary rate for insured Mortgages for dwellings located within the area.

To determine whether a Mortgage exceeds the two percentage point variation limit, the Mortgagee must compare Mortgage Charge Rates for Mortgages of the same type, from the same area, and made on the same day or during some other reasonably limited period.

See Section 203(u) of the National Housing Act (12 U.S.C. § 1709(u)), 24 CFR § 200.12.

xi. Disbursement Date

Disbursement Date refers to the date the proceeds of the Mortgage are made available to the Borrower.

The Disbursement Date must occur before the expiration of the FHA-issued Firm Commitment or DE approval and credit documents.

xii. Per Diem Interest and Interest Credits

The Mortgagee may collect per diem interest from the Disbursement Date to the date amortization begins.

Alternatively, the Mortgagee may begin amortization up to 7 Days prior to the Disbursement Date and provide a per diem interest credit. Any per diem interest credit may not be used to meet the Borrower's MRI.

Per diem interest must be computed using a factor of 1/365th of the annual rate.

xiii.   Signatures

The Mortgagees must ensure that the Mortgage, Note, and all closing documents are signed by all required parties in accordance with the Borrower Eligibility.

The Mortgagee must ensure that the signatures block on the Mortgage follows the Fannie Mae/Freddie Mac format, with the following exceptions: witness signatures are only required if witnesses are required by state law, and the Borrower's Social Security Number (SSN) may be omitted.

(A) Use of Power of Attorney at Closing

A Borrower may designate an attorney-in-fact to use a Power of Attorney (POA) to sign documents on their behalf at closing, including page 4 of the final HUD-92900-A, *HUD/VA Addendum to Uniform Residential Loan Application* and the final Fannie Mae Form 1003/Freddie Mac Form 65, *Uniform Residential Loan Application (URLA)*.

Unless required by applicable state law, or as stated in the Exception below, or they are the Borrower's Family Member, none of the following persons connected to the transaction may sign the security instrument or Note as the attorney-in-fact under a POA:
- Mortgagee, or any employee or Affiliate;
- loan originator, or employer or employee;
- title insurance company providing the title insurance policy, the title agent closing the Mortgage, or any of their Affiliates; or
- any real estate agent or any person affiliated with such real estate agent.

Exception

Closing documents may be signed by an attorney-in-fact who is connected to the transaction if the POA expressly authorizes the attorney-in-fact to execute the required documents on behalf of a Borrower, only if the Borrower, to the satisfaction of the attorney-in-fact in a recorded interactive session conducted via the internet has:

- confirmed their identity; and
- reaffirmed, after an opportunity to review the required mortgage documents, their agreement to the terms and conditions of the required mortgage documents evidencing such transaction and to the execution of such required Mortgage by such attorney-in-fact.

The Mortgagee must obtain copies of the signed initial *URLA* and initial form HUD 92900-A signed by the Borrower or POA in accordance with Signature Requirements for all Application Forms.

(B) Electronic Signatures

See Policy on Use of Electronic Signatures.

b. Mortgage and Note

i. Definitions

Mortgage refers to any form of security instrument that is commonly used in a jurisdiction in connection with a loan secured by a one- to four-family residential Property and the land on which it is situated, such as a deed of trust or security deed or land contract.

Note refers to any form of credit instrument commonly used in a jurisdiction to evidence a Mortgage.

ii. Standard

The Mortgagee must develop or obtain a separate Mortgage and Note that conforms generally to the Freddie Mac and Fannie Mae forms in both form and content, but that includes the specific modification required by FHA set forth in the applicable Model Note and Mortgage.

The Mortgagee must ensure that the Mortgage and Note comply with all applicable state and local requirements for creating a recordable and enforceable Mortgage, and an enforceable Note.

c. Disbursement of Mortgage Proceeds

i. Standard for Disbursement of Mortgage Proceeds

The Mortgagee must verify that Mortgage proceeds are disbursed in the proper amount to the Borrower and the seller, or in the case of a refinance transaction, to the debt holder. At closing, the Mortgage proceeds disbursed by the Mortgagee and the cash from the Borrower must equal the total Acquisition Cost or refinance cost.

ii. Required Documentation for Disbursement of Mortgage Proceeds

The Mortgagee must obtain the final Closing Disclosure or similar legal document from the settlement agent. If the seller's Closing Disclosure or similar legal document is provided separately, the Mortgagee must obtain from the Closing Agent a copy of the final disclosure provided to the seller to keep in the case binder.

7. Post-Closing and Endorsement

a. Pre-Endorsement Review

The Mortgagee must complete a pre-endorsement review of the mortgage file to ensure all applicable documents as described in the Uniform Case Binder Stacking Order are included in the endorsement submission. The Mortgagee must exercise due diligence in performing its pre-endorsement responsibilities. This review must be conducted by staff not involved in the originating, processing, or underwriting of the Mortgage. The case binder must contain all documentation relied upon by the Mortgagee to justify its decision to approve the Mortgage.

b. Mortgagee Pre-Endorsement Review Requirements

When conducting the pre-endorsement review, the Mortgagee must review and verify the following items, as applicable. All documents must be legible.

i. Late Submission Letter

ii. Form HUD-92900-LT, FHA Loan Underwriting and Transmittal Summary

Confirm that the form is completed. The form must be signed and dated by the underwriter, as applicable.

iii. Note (Including Any Secondary Mortgage) [Text was deleted in this section.]

Confirm that the Note is the Authoritative Copy, the Borrower name on the Note matches form HUD-92900-LT, and the required language from the Model Note is present. The Mortgagee must also confirm that:
- the Note has been executed;
- the mortgage amount is not higher than approved by the underwriter on form HUD-92900-LT or form HUD-92900-A;
- the term of the Mortgage is the same as on the *Uniform Residential Loan Application* (*URLA*, Fannie Mae Form 1003/Freddie Mac Form 65); and
- all applicable allonges, agreements, and riders are properly executed.

For Test Cases and HUD employee Mortgages, the Mortgagee must ensure that the Borrower's name on the Note matches form HUD-92900.4, *Firm Commitment*.

iv. Security Instrument

Confirm that the security instrument:
- is the Authoritative Copy;
- has been executed (along with all riders indicated on the last page of the security instrument);
- includes the principal balance that is not higher than, and maturity date that is not different than, that approved by the underwriter; and

- lists the same property address as the URAR (Fannie Mae Form 1003/Freddie Mac Form 65).

v. Closing Disclosure and Settlement Certification

Confirm that the Closing Disclosure or similar legal document is complete and signed by all required parties, and the Settlement Certification is complete and signed by the Borrower, seller (as applicable, except in case of HUD Real Estate Owned (REO) Sales), and settlement agent. The Settlement Certification is not required for refinance transactions. If the seller's Closing Disclosure or similar legal document is provided separately, the Mortgagee must obtain from the Closing Agent a copy of the final disclosure provided to the seller to keep in the case binder.

vi. Final Uniform Residential Loan Application

Confirm the *URLA* (Fannie Mae Form 1003/Freddie Mac Form 65) is signed and dated by the Mortgagee and all Borrowers. If the final *URLA* is not signed by the Mortgagee, the initial application signed by the Mortgagee is acceptable.

vii. Form HUD-92900-A, HUD/VA Addendum to Uniform Residential Loan Application

Confirm that form HUD-92900-A, *HUD/VA Addendum to Uniform Residential Loan Application,* is completed as instructed on the form.

viii. Credit Report(s)

Confirm that the mortgage file contains a credit report for each Borrower; if the Property or the Borrower is located in a community property state confirm that the mortgage file contains a credit report for a non-borrowing spouse. If there are multiple credit reports, all credit reports must be submitted in the case binder.

ix. CAIVRS Report

Confirm that the mortgage file contains a clear Credit Alert Verification Reporting System (CAIVRS) report or documentation from the creditor agency to support the verification and resolution of the debt.

x. Asset Verification

Confirm that the mortgage file contains the Verification of Deposit (VOD) and/or bank statements.

xi. Gift Letter

Confirm that the mortgage file contains a gift letter if a gift is shown on form HUD-92900-LT.

xii. Secondary Financing Documentation

The Mortgagee must confirm that the mortgage file contains a copy of the Mortgage and Note, if applicable.

xiii. Income Verification

Confirm that the mortgage file contains verification of the Borrower's income.

xiv. Evidence of the Social Security Number

Confirm that the mortgage file contains evidence of the Borrower's Social Security Number (SSN).

xv. Form HUD-92300, Mortgagee's Assurance of Completion

Confirm that form HUD-92300, *Mortgagee's Assurance of Completion*, is completed and signed, if applicable.

xvi. Form HUD-92051, Compliance Inspection Report or Fannie Mae Form 1004D, Appraisal Update and/or Completion Report

Confirm that form HUD-92051, *Compliance Inspection Report*, or Fannie Mae Form 1004D/Freddie Mac Form 442, *Appraisal Update and/or Completion Report, Part B*, is completed, signed and dated by an approved inspector. Local government inspection with the underwriter certification may be accepted.

xvii. Form NPMA-33, Wood Destroying Insect Inspection Report

Confirm that the file contains the National Pest Management Association (NPMA) form NPMA-33, *Wood Destroying Insect Inspection Report,* or the state mandated infestation report, as applicable.

xviii. Local Health Authority's Approval for Individual Water and Sewer Systems

Confirm that the file contains the Local Health Authority's approval for Individual Water Supply Systems and sewer systems, if applicable.

xix. New Construction Exhibits

For New Construction, confirm that the documentation requirements found in the New Construction Product Sheet are in the mortgage file.

xx. Form HUD-92800.5b, Conditional Commitment and Direct Endorsement Statement of Appraised Value

xxi. Appraisal Report

Confirm that the original Fannie Mae Form 1004/Freddie Mac Form 70, *Uniform Residential Appraisal Report* (URAR), or other appropriate appraisal form, is complete and contains the Appraiser's signature and date.

xxii. Specialized Eligibility Documents

Confirm that the mortgage file contains all required program-specific documents.

xxiii. Purchase Contract and Addenda

Confirm that the Sales/Purchase Contract, addenda, and the Amendatory Clause are signed by all Borrowers and sellers. The Amendatory Clause is not required on REO Sales, or 203(k) Mortgages.

Confirm that Real Estate Certification is signed by Borrowers, sellers, and selling real estate agent or broker if their signature is not contained within the purchase agreement.

c. Inspection and Repair Escrow Requirements for Mortgages Pending Closing or Endorsement in Presidentially-Declared Major Disaster Areas

All Properties with pending Mortgages or endorsements in areas under a Presidentially-Declared Major Disaster Areas (PDMDA) designated for individual assistance must have a damage inspection report that identifies and quantifies any dwelling damage. The damage inspection report must be completed by an FHA Roster Appraiser even if the inspection shows no damage to the Property, and the report must be dated after the Incident Period (as defined by FEMA) or 14 Days from the Incident Period start date, whichever is earlier. If the effective date of the appraisal is on or after the date required above for an inspection, a separate damage inspection report is not necessary.

Streamline Refinances are allowed to proceed to closing and/or endorsement without any additional requirements.

FHA does not require the Appraiser to ensure utilities are on at the time of this inspection if they have not yet been restored for the area.

Damage inspections should be completed by the original Appraiser. However, if the original Appraiser is not available, another FHA Roster Appraiser in good standing with geographic competence in the affected market may be used. If the Mortgagee uses a different Appraiser to inspect the Property, the Appraiser performing the damage inspection must be provided with a complete copy of the original appraisal.

All damages must be repaired by licensed contractors or per local jurisdictional requirements. All damages, regardless of amount, must be repaired and the Property restored to pre-loss condition with appropriate and applicable documentation.

i. Mortgages Pending Closing

The following table shows inspection and repair escrow requirements that apply to Mortgages on Properties that have not yet been closed:

Pending Mortgage Closure	
If...	**Then...**
The Mortgage is not closed,	Inspect the Property to determine damage exists. Provide on-site inspection with interior/exterior photographs.
No damage exists,	Close Mortgage and document inspection.
Damage exists but is below $5,000 and Property is habitable,	Complete repairs and close Mortgage or establish repair escrow and close Mortgage.
Damage exists and is above $5,000 or the Property is not habitable,	Do not close Mortgage. Repairs must be complete prior to closing.
When...	**Then...**
Repairs above $5,000 are completed and inspected with interior/exterior photographs,	Document inspection and close Mortgage.

ii. Mortgages Pending Endorsement

The following table shows inspection and escrow requirements that apply to Mortgages on Properties that have closed but are not yet endorsed:

Pending Mortgage Endorsement	
If...	**Then...**
The Mortgage is closed but not yet endorsed,	Inspect the Property to determine if damage exists. Provide drive-by inspection with exterior photographs.
No damage exists,	Endorse Mortgage and document inspection.
Damage exists but is below $5,000 and Property is habitable,	Complete repairs and endorse Mortgage or establish repair escrow and endorse Mortgage.
Damage exists and is above $5,000 or the Property is not habitable,	Do not endorse Mortgage.
When...	**Then...**

Pending Mortgage Endorsement	
If...	**Then...**
Repairs above $5,000 are completed and inspected with interior/exterior photographs,	Document inspection and endorse Mortgage.

iii. Pre-Closing Appraisal Validity in Disaster Areas

For Mortgages that are not closed prior to the Incident Period, as defined by FEMA, in PDMDAs where a damage inspection report reveals property damage, the appraisal validity period is extended from 120 Days to a maximum of one year from the effective date of the original appraisal.

In no instance will an appraisal be acceptable for a mortgage closing that has an effective date beyond one year. Mortgages with appraisals having effective dates in excess of one year require a new appraisal.

d. Procedures for Endorsement

To initiate the insurance endorsement process, the Mortgagee must complete the Insurance Application function in FHAC and compile the uniform case binder, with all of the necessary documents.

Instructions for specific requirements for data format and delivery to FHAC are found in the FHA Connection Guide.

The Mortgage must be current to be eligible for endorsement.

Either the sponsoring Mortgagee, principal or authorized agent must:
- complete the Mortgage Insurance Premium (MIP) Transmittal via FHAC or by batch;
- pay the Upfront MIP (UFMIP) to FHA in a lump sum within 10 Days after mortgage closing or the Disbursement Date, whichever is later;
- send the MIP to FHA, and receive payment status through FHAC or email communications;
- submit evidence of assignment of the case for endorsement in the name of the originating Mortgagee; and
- transfer the case number to another Mortgagee prior to closing, complete the Lender Transfer screen in FHAC, and complete the assignment of the Mortgage after endorsement to a new holding or servicing Mortgagee via FHAC.

i. Late UFMIP Payments

(A) 10-30 Days Late

A one-time late charge of 4 percent is assessed on an UFMIP payment received more than 10 Days after the mortgage closing or Disbursement Date, whichever is later.

The Mortgagee must pay the late fee before FHA will endorse the Mortgage for insurance.

(B) More than 30 Days Late

If the UFMIP is paid more than 30 Days after mortgage closing or Disbursement Date, whichever is later, the Mortgagee will be assessed the late fee plus interest. The interest rate is the U.S. Department of the Treasury's Current Value of Funds Rate in effect when the UFMIP payment is received. The Mortgagee must pay both charges before FHA will endorse the Mortgage for insurance.

ii. Assembly of Case Binder

The Mortgagee must prepare and submit a uniform case binder to the Jurisdictional HOC.

(A) Uniform Case Binder Requirements

The Mortgagee must ensure that all case binders are complete, meet FHA specifications, and contain all required documents arranged in the correct stacking order.

(B) Uniform Case Binder Format [Text was deleted in this section.]

The uniform case binder must be color coded as follows:
- Yellow – Cases submitted for Mortgagees with Lender Insurance authority
- Manila – Cases submitted for Mortgagees without Lender Insurance authority
- Blue – Test Cases submitted for Mortgagees who receive a DE program Test Case phase approval letter from HUD's HOC

The Mortgagee must complete the front of the binder and write the case number on the side and bottom tabs of the binder.

(C) Uniform Case Binder Stacking Order [Text was deleted in this section.]

The Mortgagee must ensure that all required documents, as applicable, are arranged in the stacking order chart below.

All appraisals must be submitted through FHA's EAD portal prior to endorsement. Complete instructions and data delivery format requirements for each appraisal form are found in the Appraisal Report and Data Delivery Guide.

Left Side	
Appraisal and Related Documents	
Conditional Commitment Direct Endorsement Statement of Appraised Value	HUD-92800.5B
Compliance Inspection Report	HUD-92051
Mortgagee Assurance of Completion	HUD-92300

Appraisal Update and/or Completion Report *(Not required for appraisals submitted through the Electronic Appraisal Delivery Portal (EAD))*	Fannie Mae Form 1004D
Appraisal Report, including all attachments and endorsements (*Uniform Residential Appraisal Report, Individual Condominium Unit Appraisal Report, Manufactured Homes Appraisal Report*, or *Small Residential Income Property Appraisal Report*) *(Not required for appraisals submitted through the Electronic Appraisal Delivery Portal (EAD))*	Fannie Mae Form 1004 Fannie Mae Form 1073 Fannie Mae Form 1004C Fannie Mae Form 1025
Life of Loan Flood Certification	
Evidence of Flood Insurance (required if Property is in flood zone A or V.)	
Evidence of hazard insurance	
Wood Destroying Insect Infestation Report or state mandated report	NPMA-33
Waivers – Property specific issued by HOC	
Borrower's Contract with Respect to Hotel and Transient Use of Property	HUD-92561
New Construction Exhibits (for all Properties built or proposed in the last 12 months)	
Builder's Certification	HUD-92541
Warranty of Completion of Construction	HUD-92544
Certificate of Occupancy and Building Permit	
Final Inspection	
Early Start Letter & 3 FHA Inspections	
Local Health Authority Approval for Individual Water and Sewer Systems	
Subterranean Termite Protection Builder's Guarantee	NPMA-99A
New Construction Subterranean Termite Service Record	NPMA-99B
LOMR, LOMA, Elevation Certificate	
Manufactured Housing	
Engineer's Certification for Manufactured Housing Foundation	
LOMR, LOMA, Elevation Certificate (if not included with New Construction Docs)	
Condominiums	
Certification for Individual Unit Financing	
Specialized Eligibility Documents	
Hawaiian Home Land	
Presidentially-Declared Disaster Area	
Energy Efficient Documents & Home Energy Rating System (HERS) Report	

203(k) Documents	
Borrower's Acknowledgement	HUD-92700-A
Borrower Identity of Interest Certification	
Rehabilitation Self-help Agreement	
Homeowner/Contractor Agreement	
Contractor & Borrower Cost Estimates	
Rehabilitation Loan Agreement	
Rehabilitation Loan Rider	
Consultant Work Write-Up	
Consultant Identity of Interest Certification	
Draw Request	HUD-9746-A
Purchase Transactions	
Purchase Contract	
Amendatory Clause	
Real Estate Certification	
Other contract addendums or short sale approval	
Chain of Title and Evidence of Good and Marketable Title	
Right Side	
Underwriting Documentation	
Late Endorsement Letter	
FHA Connection Screen Prints	
FHA Loan Underwriting and Transmittal Summary	HUD-92900-LT
Underwriter Memos, Clarifications, or Attachments	
Automated Underwriting System (AUS) Feedback Certificate	
Mortgage Note for new first lien	
Security Instrument for new first lien	
Mortgage Riders & Allonges	
Secondary Lien Exhibits	
All Closing Disclosures or similar legal documents with Addendums	
Loan Estimate	
FHA/RESPA/TILA Required Disclosures including Affiliated Business Arrangement Disclosure Statement if applicable	
Buydown Agreement	
Power of Attorney	
Uniform Residential Loan Application (URLA) – Initial and Final	Fannie Mae Form 1003
HUD/VA Addendum to Uniform Residential Loan Application – Initial and Final	HUD-92900-A
Borrower Authorization for Verification	

Borrower Authorization for Use of Information Protected under Privacy Act	
Refinance Documentation	
Refinance Authorization Screen Printout	
Payoff Statement(s) for all liens to be satisfied with Mortgage proceeds	
Borrower Certification for Refinance of Borrowers in Negative Equity Position	HUD-92918
Borrower Identification Documentation	
Evidence of Social Security Number (SSN) or Tax Identification Number (TIN)	
Legal residency status documents for non-U.S. citizens – Employment Authorization Document	
Credit and Capacity Documentation	
Credit report(s)	
Verification of Mortgage or rent	
Credit related documentation and explanations	
Housing Counseling Certificate(s)	
Source of Funds Verification	
Verification of non-gift source of funds	
Verification of gift source of funds	
Income and Employment Documentation	
All required documentation grouped by Borrower	

iii. Case Binder Submission – Direct Endorsement Non-Lender Insurance

The case binder must be received by the Jurisdictional HOC no later than 60 Days after the Disbursement Date.

(A) Late Submission

If the case binder is submitted more than 60 Days after the Disbursement Date, the Mortgagee must submit a late endorsement request, certifying that:
- no Mortgage Payment is currently unpaid;
- all escrow accounts for taxes, hazard insurance and MIPs are current and intact, except for Disbursements that may have been made to cover payments for which the accounts were specifically established; and
- neither the Mortgagee nor its agents provided the funds to bring and/or keep the Mortgage current or to bring about the appearance of an acceptable payment history.

Each late endorsement request must:
- list the FHA case number;
- list the Borrower's name;
- be dated and signed by the Mortgagee's representative; and

- be printed on company letterhead with the Mortgagee's address and telephone number.

(B) Assignee Mortgagee

The assignee Mortgagee of a Mortgage may submit the Mortgage for endorsement in its name or the name of the originating Mortgagee. The assignee must also notify the Jurisdictional HOC of the assignment, and verify that the originating Mortgagee completed all certifications.

The Purchasing Mortgagee may pay any required MIP, late charges, and interest.

(C) After Receipt of a Notice of Return

Notice of Return (NOR) refers to a notification to the Mortgagee specifying the reason a Mortgage is not currently eligible for endorsement.

If the Jurisdictional HOC issues an NOR, the Mortgagee may request reconsideration for insurance endorsement. All requests for reconsideration must be received by the Jurisdictional HOC within the 60-Day endorsement submission period or within 30 Days of the issuance of the NOR, whichever is longer. If the request for reconsideration is submitted after this time period, the Mortgagee must follow the guidelines for late submission.

Mortgagees submitting paper case binders must submit the original case binder with any request for reconsideration.

iv. Ineligible for Endorsement – Non-Lender Insurance

(A) Notice of Return

If the Mortgage is ineligible for insurance endorsement, FHAC issues an electronic NOR, which states the reasons for non-endorsement and any corrective actions that the Mortgagee must take.

If the Mortgage is permanently rejected for insurance endorsement, the Mortgagee must notify the Borrower that they do not have an FHA-insured Mortgage and of the circumstances that made the Mortgage ineligible for FHA insurance.

(B) Additional Requirements for Permanently Rejected Mortgages

The Mortgagee must obtain a refund of both the UFMIP and any periodic MIP paid by or on behalf of the Borrower, and apply the refund to the principal balance of the Mortgage.

(C) Excessive Mortgage Amounts

An excessive mortgage amount occurs when the Mortgagee closes a Mortgage in an amount higher than what is permitted by FHA requirements. The Mortgage is not eligible for insurance until the amount is reduced to within permissible limits. The Mortgagee may choose to either pay down the principal balance, or re-close the Mortgage to an insurable amount.

The Mortgagee must provide a copy of the payment ledger showing that the principal balance has been paid down to an insurable amount.

v. Endorsement Processing – Lender Insurance

Once the Mortgagee has completed the entry of all required data, completed the pre-endorsement review, and satisfied itself that the Mortgage meets HUD requirements, it will click "yes" in the Insurance Decision field, enter the FHA Connection ID of the individual insuring the Mortgage, enter the insurance date on the Insurance Application screen and click "send."

The Mortgagee must endorse the Mortgage no later than 60 Days after the Disbursement Date.

Late Submission

If the Mortgage is endorsed more than 60 Days after the Disbursement Date, the Mortgagee must complete a late endorsement certification stating:
- no Mortgage Payment is currently unpaid;
- all escrow accounts for taxes, hazard insurance and MIPs are current and intact, except for Disbursements that may have been made to cover payments for which the accounts were specifically established; and
- neither the Mortgagee nor its agents provided the funds to bring and/or keep the Mortgage current or to bring about the appearance of an acceptable payment history.

Each late endorsement certification must:
- list the FHA case number;
- list the Borrower's name;
- be dated and signed by the Mortgagee's representative; and
- be printed on company letterhead with the Mortgagee's address and telephone number.

The Mortgagee must retain the certification in the case binder.

Handbook 4000.1

Effective Date: 09/14/2015 | Last Revised: 07/10/2019
*Refer to the online version of SF Handbook 4000.1 for specific sections' effective dates

362

vi. Case Warnings – Lender Insurance

Case warnings are issued by FHAC based on system edits. They identify issues that must be addressed before the Mortgage can be insured. There are two kinds of case warnings: non-severe and severe.

(A) Severe Case Warnings

Severe case warnings are case warnings that make the Mortgage ineligible for Lender Insurance (LI), which include:

- a Borrower failed or is pending SSN validation;
- a Borrower has a record in CAIVRS;
- the pre-endorsement delinquency status is delinquent; or
- a deficiency exists causing risks to HUD. The requesting HOC will add text to the case warning message screen identifying the reasons requiring submission of the case binder to the HOC for a pre-endorsement review.

Once the severe case warning is corrected, documentation in support of clearing the case warning and the case binder must be submitted to the Jurisdictional HOC for pre-endorsement review and endorsement processing.

(B) Non-severe Case Warnings

Non-severe case warnings are warnings to provide guidance to the Mortgagee that conditions have been detected and must be researched before the Mortgage can be endorsed. If, after researching the matter, the Mortgagee determines that HUD requirements have not been violated, the Mortgagee may re-submit the Mortgage for insurance.

By re-submitting the information, the Mortgagee is representing that the warning has been reviewed and the Mortgage is eligible for insurance endorsement. FHAC will then allow the Mortgage to be insured by the Mortgagee.

vii. Mortgagee with Conditional Direct Endorsement Approval (Test Case) [Text was deleted in this section.]

For Mortgagees who receive a DE program Test Case phase approval letter from HUD's HOC, the Mortgagee must ensure that:

- all required certifications are executed;
- a complete case file post-closing is submitted that includes all required origination, underwriting and closing documents in the order specified in the Case Binder Documents Requirements Checklist that is provided to the Mortgagee during the Entrance Conference; and
- the documents are placed in a blue folder with a completed front cover, the FHA case number written on the side and bottom tab of the folder, and "TEST CASE" written in large letters on the front of the folder.

e. Endorsement and Post-Endorsement

i. Endorsement

Upon successful completion of a pre-endorsement review either by FHA or the LI Mortgagee, an electronic Mortgage Insurance Certificate (MIC) will be issued.

The Mortgage becomes insured on the date the MIC is issued.

ii. Post-Endorsement

(A) Confirming Status of the Mortgage Insurance Certificate

The Mortgagee can confirm the endorsement status of a Mortgage using FHAC or FHA Connection Business to Government (FHAC-B2G) application.

(B) Obtaining the Mortgage Insurance Certificate

When requesting the MIC, the Mortgagee must specify whether it is to be prepared in the name of the originator (principal), or authorized agent, as it appears in HUD Systems.

The MIC will be issued electronically. The Mortgagee can download and print copies of the MIC as needed.

(C) Corrections to the Mortgage Insurance Certificate

To obtain a correction to the MIC, the Mortgagee must submit the MIC Correction Request Template to the FHA Resource Center. This form may be used to correct the property address, Borrower name, ADP Code, maturity and first payments dates, P&I, interest rate, SSN, FHA case number, mortgage amount or other information contained in the MIC, or to add a co-Borrower.

(D) Corrections to Original Instruments

The Mortgagee must follow applicable local law when making corrections to the original instruments.

If new instruments are executed as required by local law, the Mortgagee must submit the new instruments prior to insurance endorsement.

(E) Partial Release of Security

FHA approval for partial release of security is required except in limited circumstances. See FHA Servicing Policy for more information.

iii. Case Binder Submission – Lender Insurance Mortgagees

LI Mortgagees must submit the case binder to the Jurisdictional HOC (or other HUD office as identified in the notice) when requested by FHA.

FHA will request the case binder through a daily email notification to the Mortgagee's contact person.

If requested, the LI Mortgagee must submit the case binder within 10 business days of request.

If approved to submit electronic Case Binders (eCBs) to FHA, the LI Mortgagee must submit the eCB through FHAC through the Insuring, Underwriting Report, and Lender Letter screens.

iv. Mortgage File Retention

The Mortgagee must maintain their mortgage file, including the case binder, in either hard copy or electronic format for a period of two years from the date of endorsement.

Mortgagees retaining eCBs are not required to maintain a separate version of the eCB indexed for electronic submission to HUD.

If HUD requests a case binder that is maintained electronically, the Mortgagee must follow the requirements in the eCB Developer's Guide.

8. Programs and Products

a. 203(k) Rehabilitation Mortgage Insurance Program

i. Overview

The Section 203(k) Rehabilitation Mortgage Insurance Program is used to:
- rehabilitate an existing one- to four-unit Structure, which will be used primarily for residential purposes;
- rehabilitate such a Structure and refinance outstanding indebtedness on the Structure and the Real Property on which the Structure is located; or
- purchase and rehabilitate a Structure and purchase the Real Property on which the Structure is located.

Structure refers to a building that has a roof and walls, and stands permanently in one place that contains single or multiple housing units that are used for human habitation.

Mortgages to be insured under Section 203(k) must be processed and underwritten in accordance with the requirements in Origination Through Post-Closing/Endorsement, except where noted otherwise in this appendix.

(A) Types of 203(k) Rehabilitation Mortgages

There are two types of 203(k) Rehabilitation Mortgages: Standard 203(k) and Limited 203(k), as described below. The guidance in this appendix is applicable to both Standard 203(k) and Limited 203(k) Mortgages unless noted otherwise.

(1) Standard 203(k)

The Standard 203(k) Mortgage may be used for remodeling and repairs. There is a minimum repair cost of $5,000 and the use of a 203(k) Consultant is required.

(2) Limited 203(k)

The Limited 203(k) may only be used for minor remodeling and non-structural repairs. The Limited 203(k) does not require the use of a 203(k) Consultant, but a Consultant may be used. The total rehabilitation cost must not exceed $35,000. There is no minimum rehabilitation cost.

(B) Eligible Supplemental Programs and Products

A 203(k) Mortgage may be used in conjunction with the following:
- Section 203(h) Mortgage Insurance for Disaster Victims
- Energy Efficient Mortgages
- Solar and Wind Technologies

ii. Borrower Eligibility

The Borrower must meet the eligibility requirements found in the <u>Borrower Eligibility</u> section, and the additional guidance provided here related to nonprofit agency Borrowers.

The Mortgagee must verify and document the nonprofit agency Borrower's caseload. The Mortgagee must review the Nonprofit List in FHA Connection (<u>FHAC</u>), and ensure the maximum 203(k) case load limitation is not exceeded for nonprofit Borrowers.

iii. Property Eligibility

The Property must be an existing Property that has been completed for at least one year prior to the case number assignment date. If the Mortgagee is unsure whether the Property has been completed for at least one year, the Mortgagee must request a copy of the Certificate of Occupancy (CO) or equivalent.

A Property that is not eligible for a 203(b) Mortgage due to health and safety or security issues may be eligible under 203(k) if the rehabilitation or repair work performed will correct such issues.

A Property with an existing 203(k) Mortgage is not eligible to be refinanced until all repairs are completed and the case has been electronically closed out.

The following property types may be financed:
- a one- to four-unit Single Family Structure;
- an individual condominium unit, meeting the following requirements:
  - the unit must be located in an FHA-approved Condominium Project and must comply with all other requirements for condominiums;
  - rehabilitation or improvements are limited to the interior of the unit, except for the installation of firewalls in the attic for the unit;
  - no more than five units per condominium association, or 25 percent of the total number of units, whichever is less, can undergo rehabilitation at any time; and
  - after rehabilitation is complete, the unit is located in a Structure containing no more than four units. For townhouse style condominiums, each townhouse is considered as one Structure, provided each unit is separated by a one and one-half hour firewall from foundation to roof;
- a Site Condominium unit;
- Manufactured Housing where the rehabilitation does not affect the structural components of the Structure that were designed and constructed in conformance with the <u>Federal Manufactured Home Construction and Safety Standards</u> and must comply with all other requirements for <u>Manufactured Housing</u>;
- a Mixed Use Property with one- to four-residential units, provided:
  - 51 percent of the Gross Building Area (GBA) is for residential use; and
  - commercial use will not affect the health and safety of the occupants of the residential Property; and

- a HUD Real Estate Owned (REO) Property:
  - the Property is identified as eligible for 203(k) financing as evidenced in the sales contract or addendum. Investor purchases of HUD REO Properties are not eligible for 203(k) financing.

(A) Dwelling Unit Limitation

A Mortgagee may determine that units in a neighborhood are not subject to the Dwelling Unit Limitation of no more than seven Dwelling Units within a two block radius when:
- the neighborhood has been targeted by a state or local government for redevelopment or revitalization;
- the state or local government has approved and submitted a plan to HUD describing the program of neighborhood redevelopment and revitalization, including the geographic area targeted for redevelopment, and the nature and proportion of public or private commitments that have been made in support of the redevelopment;
- the nonprofit agency borrower will own no more than 10 percent of the Dwelling Units (regardless of financing type) in the designated redevelopment area; and
- the nonprofit agency borrower will have no more than eight Dwelling Units on adjacent lots.

The Mortgagee must review the approved redevelopment plan to ensure that the units in which the nonprofit agency has or will have a financial interest are located within the targeted geographic area. The Mortgagee must also review public records to determine that the agency does not exceed the limitations on the number of units that they may own in the redevelopment area, and that they have no more than eight adjacent units.

(B) Required Documentation

The Mortgagee must obtain the following documentation:
- a copy of the redevelopment plan; and
- evidence that the state or local government approved the plan.

The Mortgagee must submit the documentation to HUD in the case binder.

iv. Application Requirements

The Mortgagee must provide the Borrower with the form HUD-92700-A, *203(k) Borrower's Acknowledgment*.

v. Case Number Assignment Data Entry Requirements

In order to request a case number for a 203(k) Mortgage, the Mortgagee must enter the following information:

(A) 203(k) Program Type Indicator

The Mortgagee must select either Standard 203(k) or Limited 203(k) as the program type.

(B) Consultant Identification Number

The Mortgagee must enter the Consultant identification number into the "Consultant ID" field on the Case Number Assignment screen in FHAC. For a Limited 203(k) with no Consultant, the Mortgagee must enter "203KS" in the "Consultant ID" field.

(C) Automated Data Processing Code

The Mortgagee must enter the appropriate 203(k) Automated Data Processing (ADP) code.

(D) Construction Code

The Mortgagee must enter "Substantial Rehabilitation" in the drop-down menu labeled "Construction Code."

(E) Refinance Type

For a refinance transaction, the Mortgagee must select "Not Streamlined" in the drop-down menu labeled "All Refinances."

(F) Converting From a Non-203(k) to a 203(k) Mortgage

If the Mortgagee had originally requested the case number assignment for a non-203(k) Mortgage, the Mortgagee must update the existing case data in the Case Number Assignment screen, changing the ADP Code to a valid 203(k) ADP Code and the "Construction Code" to "Substantial Rehabilitation."

vi. Standard 203(k) Transactions

(A) Standard 203(k) Eligible Improvements

The Standard 203(k) requires a minimum of $5,000 in eligible improvements.

(1) Types of Improvements

Types of eligible improvements include, but are not limited to:

- converting a one-family Structure to a two-, three- or four-family Structure;
- decreasing an existing multi-unit Structure to a one- to four-family Structure;
- reconstructing a Structure that has been or will be demolished, provided the complete existing foundation system is not affected and will still be used;
- repairing, reconstructing or elevating an existing foundation where the Structure will not be demolished;
- purchasing an existing Structure on another site, moving it onto a new foundation and repairing/renovating it;
- making structural alterations such as the repair or replacement of structural damage, additions to the Structure, and finished attics and/or basements;
- rehabilitating, improving or constructing a garage;
- eliminating health and safety hazards that would violate HUD's Minimum Property Requirements (MPR);
- installing or repairing wells and/or septic systems;
- connecting to public water and sewage systems;
- repairing/replacing plumbing, heating, AC and electrical systems;
- making changes for improved functions and modernization;
- making changes for aesthetic appeal;
- repairing or adding roofing, gutters and downspouts;
- making energy conservation improvements;
- creating accessibility for persons with disabilities;
- installing or repairing fences, walkways, and driveways;
- installing a new refrigerator, cooktop, oven, dishwasher, built-in microwave oven, and washer/dryer;
- repairing or removing an in-ground swimming pool;
- installing smoke detectors;
- making site improvements;
- landscaping;
- installing or repairing exterior decks, patios, and porches;
- constructing a windstorm shelter; and
- covering lead-based paint stabilization costs, if the Structure was built before 1978, in accordance with the Single Family mortgage insurance lead-based paint rule (24 CFR 200.805 and 200.810(c)) and the U.S. Environmental Protection Agency's (EPA) Renovation, Repair, and Painting Rule (40 CFR 745, especially subparts E and Q).

(2) Improvements Standards

(a) General Improvement Standards

All improvements to existing Structures must comply with HUD's MPR and meet or exceed local building codes. For a newly constructed addition to the existing Structure, the energy improvements must meet or exceed local codes and the requirements of the latest energy code standard that has been adopted by HUD through a Federal Register notice.

(b) Specific Improvement Standards

Any addition of a Structure unit must be attached to the existing Structure. Site improvements, landscaping, patios, decks and terraces must increase the As-Is Property Value equal to the dollar amount spent on the improvements or be necessary to preserve the Property from erosion.

(B) Standard 203(k) Ineligible Improvements/Repairs

The 203(k) mortgage proceeds **may not** be used to finance costs associated with the purchase or repair of any luxury item, any improvement that does not become a permanent part of the subject Property, or improvements that solely benefit commercial functions within the Property, including:
- recreational or luxury improvements, such as:
  - swimming pools (existing swimming pools can be repaired)
  - an exterior hot tub, spa, whirlpool bath, or sauna
  - barbecue pits, outdoor fireplaces or hearths
  - bath houses
  - tennis courts
  - satellite dishes
  - tree surgery (except when eliminating an endangerment to existing improvements)
  - photo murals
  - gazebos; or
- additions or alterations to support commercial use or to equip or refurbish space for commercial use.

(C) Standard 203(k) Establishing Repairs and Improvements

The Mortgagee must select an FHA-approved 203(k) Consultant from the FHA 203(k) Consultant Roster in FHAC. The Mortgagee must not use the services of a Consultant who has demonstrated previous poor performance based on reviews performed by the Mortgagee. The Consultant must inspect the Property and prepare the Work Write-Up and Cost Estimate.

The Work Write-Up refers to the report prepared by a 203(k) Consultant that identifies each Work Item to be performed and the specifications for completion of the repair.

Cost Estimate refers to a breakdown of the cost for each proposed Work Item, prepared by a 203(k) Consultant.

Work Item refers to a specific repair or improvement that will be performed.

Exception for Borrowers Doing Own Work

For Borrowers performing their own work under a Rehabilitation Self-Help Agreement, the Consultant must identify on the Work Write-Up each Work Item to be performed by the Borrower. The Borrower must not be reimbursed for labor costs.

(D) Standard 203(k) Financeable Repair and Improvement Costs and Fees

The following repair and improvement costs and fees may be financed:
- costs of construction, repairs and rehabilitation;
- architectural/engineering professional fees;
- the 203(k) Consultant fee subject to the limits in the 203(k) Consultant Fee Schedule section;
- inspection fees performed during the construction period, provided the fees are reasonable and customary for the area;
- title update fees;
- permits; and
- a Feasibility Study, when necessary to determine if the rehabilitation is feasible.

Any costs for Energy Efficient Mortgages and Solar Energy Systems must not be included in financeable repair and improvement costs.

For Borrowers performing their own work, the Mortgagee must include the costs for labor and materials for each Work Item to be completed by the Borrower under a Rehabilitation (Self-Help) Loan Agreement.

(E) Standard 203(k) Financeable Contingency Reserve

Contingency Reserve refers to funds that are set aside to cover unforeseen project costs.

The Mortgagee must refer to the following chart to determine when a Contingency Reserve is required. The minimum and maximum Contingency Reserve is established as a percentage of the Financeable Repair and Improvement Costs.

For Structures with an actual age of less than 30 years:

	Minimum	Maximum
Required when evidence of termite damage	10%	20%
Discretionary	No Minimum	20%

For Structures with an actual age of 30 years or more:

	Minimum	Maximum
Required	10%	20%
Required when utilities are not operable as referenced in the Work Write-Up	15%	20%

The Borrower may provide their own funds to establish the Contingency Reserves. Where the Borrower has provided their own funds for Contingency Reserves, they must be noted under a separate category in the Repair Escrow Account.

(F) Standard 203(k) Financeable Mortgage Payment Reserves

A Mortgage Payment Reserve refers to an amount set aside to make Mortgage Payments when the Property cannot be occupied during rehabilitation.

A Mortgagee may establish a financeable Mortgage Payment Reserve, not to exceed six months of Mortgage Payments. The Mortgage Payment Reserve may include Mortgage Payments only for the period during which the Property cannot be occupied. The number of Mortgage Payments cannot exceed the completion time frame required in the Rehabilitation Loan Agreement.

For multi-unit properties, if one or more units are occupied, the Mortgage Payment Reserve may only include the portion of the Mortgage Payment attributable to the units that cannot be occupied. To calculate the amount that can be included in the Mortgage Payment Reserve, the Mortgagee will divide the monthly Mortgage Payment by the number of units in the Property, and multiply that figure by the number of units that cannot be occupied. The resulting figure is the amount of the Mortgage Payment that will be paid through the Mortgage Payment Reserve. The Borrower is responsible for paying the servicing Mortgagee the portion of the Mortgage not covered by the Mortgage Payment Reserve.

(G) Standard 203(k) Financeable Mortgage Fees

The Mortgagee may finance the following fees and charges.

(1) Origination Fee

The Mortgagee may finance a portion of the Borrower-paid origination fee not to exceed the greater of $350, or 1.5 percent of the total of the Financeable Repair and Improvement Costs and Fees, Financeable Contingency Reserves and Financeable Mortgage Payment Reserves.

(2) Discount Points

The Mortgagee may finance a portion of the Borrower-paid discount points not to exceed an amount equal to the discount point percentage multiplied by the total of Financeable Repair and Improvement Costs and Fees, Financeable Contingency Reserves and Financeable Mortgage Payment Reserves.

(H) Standard 203(k) Required Documentation and Review

(1) Review of Contractor Qualifications

Prior to closing, the Mortgagee must ensure that a qualified general or specialized contractor has been hired and, by contract, has agreed to complete the work described in the Work Write-Up for the amount of the Cost Estimate and within the allotted time frame. To determine whether the contractor is qualified, the Mortgagee must review the contractor's credentials, work experience and client references, and ensure that the contractor meets all jurisdictional licensing and bonding requirements.

(2) Consultant's Work Write-Up and Cost Estimate

The Mortgagee must obtain the Consultant's Work Write-Up and Cost Estimate for all Standard 203(k) Mortgages. The Mortgagee must ensure the Work Write-Up/Cost Estimate specifies the type of repair and cost of each Work Item. The Mortgagee must review the Work Write-Up and ensure that all health and safety issues identified were addressed before, including additional Work Items.

(3) Architectural Exhibits

The Mortgagee must obtain and review all applicable architectural exhibits.

(4) Sales Contract

The Mortgagee must ensure the sales contract includes a provision that the Borrower has applied for Section 203(k) financing, and that the contract is contingent upon mortgage approval and the Borrower's acceptance of additional required improvements as determined by the Mortgagee.

When the Borrower is financing a HUD REO Property, the Mortgagee must ensure that the first block on Line 4 of form HUD-9548, *Instructions for Sales Contract,* is checked, as well as the applicable block for 203(k).

vii. Limited 203(k) Transactions

(A) Limited 203(k) Eligible Improvements

The Limited 203(k) may only be used for minor remodeling and non-structural repairs. The total rehabilitation cost may not exceed $35,000. There is no minimum repair cost.

(1) Types of Improvements

Eligible improvement types include, but are not limited to:
- eliminating health and safety hazards that would violate HUD's MPR;
- repairing or replacing wells and/or septic systems;
- connecting to public water and sewage systems;
- repairing/replacing plumbing, heating, AC and electrical systems;
- making changes for improved functions and modernization;
- eliminating obsolescence;
- repairing or installing new roofing, provided the structural integrity of the Structure will not be impacted by the work being performed; siding; gutters; and downspouts;
- making energy conservation improvements;
- creating accessibility for persons with disabilities;
- installing or repairing fences, walkways, and driveways;
- installing a new refrigerator, cooktop, oven, dishwasher, built-in microwave oven and washer/dryer;
- repairing or removing an in-ground swimming pool;
- installing smoke detectors;
- installing, replacing or repairing exterior decks, patios, and porches; and
- covering lead-based paint stabilization costs (above and beyond what is paid for by HUD when it sells REO properties) if the Structure was built before 1978, in accordance with the Single Family mortgage insurance lead-based paint rule and EPA's Renovation, Repair, and Painting Rule.

(2) Improvements Standards

(a) General Improvement Standards

All improvements to existing Structures must comply with HUD's MPR and meet or exceed local building codes.

(b) Specific Improvement Standards

Patios and decks must increase the As-Is Property Value equal to the dollar amount spent on the improvements.

(B) Limited 203(k) Ineligible Improvements/Repairs

The Limited 203(k) mortgage proceeds **may not** be used to finance major rehabilitation or major remodeling. FHA considers a repair to be "major" when any of the following are applicable:

- the repair or improvements are expected to require more than six months to complete;
- the rehabilitation activities require more than two payments per specialized contractor;
- the required repairs arising from the appraisal:
  - o necessitate a Consultant to develop a specification of repairs/Work Write-Up; or
  - o require plans or architectural exhibits; or
- the repair prevents the Borrower from occupying the Property for more than 15 Days during the rehabilitation period.

Additionally, the Limited 203(k) mortgage proceeds **may not** be used to finance the following specific repairs:

- converting a one-family Structure to a two-, three- or four-family Structure;
- decreasing an existing multi-unit Structure to a one- to four-family Structure;
- reconstructing a Structure that has been or will be demolished;
- repairing, reconstructing or elevating an existing foundation;
- purchasing an existing Structure on another site and moving it onto a new foundation;
- making structural alterations such as the repair of structural damage and New Construction, including room additions;
- landscaping and site improvements;
- constructing a windstorm shelter;
- making additions or alterations to support commercial use or to equip or refurbish space for commercial use; and/or
- making recreational or luxury improvements, such as:
  - o new swimming pools;
  - o an exterior hot tub, spa, whirlpool bath, or sauna;
  - o barbecue pits, outdoor fireplaces or hearths;
  - o bath houses;
  - o tennis courts;
  - o satellite dishes;
  - o tree surgery (except when eliminating an endangerment to existing improvements);

- o photo murals; or
- o gazebos.

(C) Limited 203(k) Establishing Repair and Improvement Costs

The Borrower must submit a work plan to the Mortgagee and use one or more contractors to provide the Cost Estimate and complete the required improvements and repairs. The contractors must be licensed and bonded if required by the local jurisdiction. The Borrower must provide the contractors' credentials and bids to the Mortgagee.

The Mortgagee must review the contractors' credentials, work experience and client references and ensure that the contractors meet all jurisdictional licensing and bonding requirements. The Mortgagee must examine the work plan and the contractors' bids and determine if they fall within the usual and customary range for similar work.

The Mortgagee may require the Borrower to provide additional Cost Estimates if necessary.

Exception for Borrowers Doing Own Work

For Borrowers performing their own work under a Rehabilitation Self-Help Agreement, the Borrower must submit a work plan detailing the Work Items to be performed by the Borrower and a Cost Estimate from a contractor other than the Borrower that provides a breakdown of the cost for labor and materials for each Work Item. The contractor must be licensed and bonded if required by the local jurisdiction. The Borrower must not be reimbursed for labor costs.

(D) Limited 203(k) Financeable Repair and Improvement Costs and Fees

The following costs and fees may be financed:
- costs of construction, repairs and rehabilitation;
- inspection fees performed during the construction period, provided the fees are reasonable and customary for the area;
- title update fees; and
- permits.

Any costs for Energy Efficient Mortgages and Solar Energy Systems must not be included in financeable repair and improvement costs.

For Borrowers performing their own work, the Mortgagee must include the costs for labor and materials for each Work Item to be completed by the Borrower under a Rehabilitation (Self-Help) Loan Agreement.

(E) Limited 203(k) Financeable Contingency Reserves

A Contingency Reserve is not mandated; however, at the Mortgagee's discretion, a Contingency Reserve account may be established and may be financed. The Contingency Reserve account may not exceed 20 percent of the Financeable Repair and Improvement Costs.

The Borrower may provide their own funds to establish the Contingency Reserves. Where the Borrower has provided their own funds for Contingency Reserves, they must be noted under a separate category in the Repair Escrow Account.

(F) Limited 203(k) Financeable Mortgage Fees

The Mortgagee may include the following fees and charges in the rehabilitation Cost Estimates.

(1) Origination Fee

The Mortgagee may include a portion of the Borrower-paid origination fee not to exceed the greater of $350, or 1.5 percent of the total of the Financeable Repair and Improvement Costs and Fees and Financeable Contingency Reserves.

(2) Discount Points

The Mortgagee may include a portion of the Borrower-paid discount points not to exceed an amount equal to the discount point percentage multiplied by total of Financeable Repair and Improvement Costs and Fees and Financeable Contingency Reserves.

(G) Limited 203(k) Ineligible Fees and Costs

The following fees and costs **may not** be financed under the Limited 203(k):
- Mortgage Payment Reserves
- architectural/engineering professional fees
- 203(k) Consultant fee
- a Feasibility Study

(H) Limited 203(k) Required Documentation

The following documentation is required for the Limited 203(k).

(1) Work Plan

The Mortgagee must obtain a work plan from the Borrower detailing the proposed repairs or improvements. The Borrower may develop the work plan themselves or engage an outside party, including a Contractor or a 203(k) Consultant, to assist. There is no required format for the work plan.

(2) Written Proposal and Cost Estimates

The Mortgagee must obtain a written proposal and Cost Estimate from a contractor for each specialized repair or improvement. The Mortgagee must ensure that the selected contractor meets all jurisdictional licensing and bonding requirements. The written proposal must indicate Work Items that require permits and state that repairs are non-structural. The Cost Estimate must state the nature and type of repair and cost for each Work Item, broken down by labor and materials.

The Mortgagee must obtain written Cost Estimates for each Work Item, broken down by labor and materials, to be performed by the Borrower under a self-help agreement.

(3) Sales Contract

The Mortgagee must obtain a copy of the sales contract and ensure that the sales contract includes a provision that the Borrower has applied for Section 203(k) financing, and that the contract is contingent upon mortgage approval and the Borrower's acceptance of additional required improvements as determined by the Mortgagee.

When the Borrower is financing a HUD REO Property, the Mortgagee must ensure that the first block on Line 4 of the form HUD-9548, *Instructions for Sales Contract* is checked, as well as the applicable block for 203(k).

viii. Appraisals for Standard 203(k) and Limited 203(k)

(A) Establishing Value

The Mortgagee must establish both an Adjusted As-Is Value and an After Improved Value of the Property.

(1) Appraisal Reports

An appraisal by an FHA Roster Appraiser is always required to establish the After Improved Value of the Property. Except as described below in cases of Property Flipping and refinance transactions, the Mortgagee is not required to obtain an as-is appraisal and may use alternate methods mentioned below to establish the Adjusted As-Is Value. If an as-is appraisal is obtained, the Mortgagee must use it in establishing the Adjusted As-Is Value.

(2) Adjusted As-Is Value

The Mortgagee must establish the Adjusted As-Is Value as described below.

Handbook 4000.1   379
Effective Date: 09/14/2015 | Last Revised: 07/10/2019
*Refer to the online version of SF Handbook 4000.1 for specific sections' effective dates

(a) Purchase Transactions

For purchase transactions, the Adjusted As-Is Value is the lesser of:
- the purchase price less any inducements to purchase; or
- the As-Is Property Value.

The As-Is Property Value refers to the as-is value as determined by an FHA Roster Appraiser, when an as-is appraisal is obtained.

In the case of Property Flipping, the Mortgagee must obtain an as-is appraisal if needed to comply with the Property Flipping guidelines.

(b) Refinance Transactions

(i) Properties Acquired Greater Than or Equal to 12 Months Prior to the Case Assignment Date

The Mortgagee must obtain an as-is appraisal to determine the Adjusted As-Is Value when the existing debt on the Property plus the following items exceeds the After Improved Value:
- Financeable Repairs and Improvement Costs;
- Financeable Mortgage Fees;
- Financeable Contingency Reserves; and
- Financeable Mortgage Payment Reserves (for Standard 203(k) only).

When an appraisal is obtained, the Adjusted As-Is Value is the As-Is Property Value.

The Mortgagee has the option of using the existing debt plus fees associated with the new Mortgage or obtaining an as-is appraisal to determine the Adjusted As-Is Value when the existing debt on the Property plus the following items does not exceed the After Improved Value:
- Financeable Repairs and Improvement Costs;
- Financeable Mortgage Fees;
- Financeable Contingency Reserves; and
- Financeable Mortgage Payment Reserves (for Standard 203(k) only).

Existing debt includes:
- the unpaid principal balance of the first Mortgage as of the month prior to mortgage Disbursement;
- the unpaid principal balance of any purchase money junior Mortgage as of the month prior to mortgage Disbursement;

- the unpaid principal balance of any junior liens over 12 months old as of the date of mortgage Disbursement. If the balance or any portion of an equity line of credit in excess of $1,000 was advanced within the past 12 months and was for purposes other than repairs and rehabilitation of the Property, that portion above and beyond $1,000 of the line of credit is not eligible for inclusion in the new Mortgage;
- interest due on the existing Mortgage(s);
- Mortgage Insurance Premium (MIP) due on existing Mortgage;
- any prepayment penalties assessed;
- late charges; and
- escrow shortages.

(ii) Properties Acquired Less Than 12 Months Prior to the Case Assignment Date

For properties acquired by the Borrower within 12 months of the case number assignment date, an as-is appraisal must be obtained.

The Adjusted As-Is Value is the As-Is Property Value.

For properties acquired by the Borrower within 12 months of the case assignment date by inheritance or through a gift from a Family Member, the Mortgagee may utilize the calculation of Adjusted As-Is Value for properties acquired greater than or equal to 12 months prior to the case assignment date.

(3) After Improved Value

To establish the After Improved Value, the Mortgagee must obtain an appraisal of the Property subject to the repairs and improvements.

(B) Documents to be Provided to the Appraiser at Assignment

The Mortgagee must provide the Appraiser with a copy of the Consultant's Work Write-Up and Cost Estimate for a Standard 203(k), or the work plan, contractor's proposal and Cost Estimates for a Limited 203(k).

ix. Maximum Mortgage Amount for Purchase

The maximum mortgage amount that FHA will insure on a 203(k) purchase is the lesser of:
- the appropriate Loan-to-Value (LTV) ratio from the Purchase Loan-to-Value Limits, multiplied by the lesser of:
  - the Adjusted As-Is Value, plus:

- Financeable Repair and Improvement Costs, for Standard 203(k) or Limited 203(k);
- Financeable Mortgage Fees, for Standard 203(k) or Limited 203(k);
- Financeable Contingency Reserves, for Standard 203(k) or Limited 203(k); and
- Financeable Mortgage Payment Reserves, for Standard 203(k) only; or
  - 110 percent of the After Improved Value (100 percent for condominiums); or
- the Nationwide Mortgage Limits.

For a HUD REO 203(k) purchase utilizing the Good Neighbor Next Door (GNND) or $100 Down sales incentive, the Mortgagee must calculate the maximum mortgage amount that FHA will insure in accordance with HUD REO Purchasing.

x. Maximum Mortgage Amount for Refinance

The maximum mortgage amount that FHA will insure on a 203(k) refinance is the lesser of:

1. the existing debt and fees associated with the new Mortgage, plus:
   - Financeable Repair and Improvement Costs, for Standard 203(k) or Limited 203(k);
   - Financeable Mortgage Fees, for Standard 203(k) or Limited 203(k);
   - Financeable Contingency Reserves, for Standard 203(k) or Limited 203(k); and
   - Financeable Mortgage Payment Reserves, for Standard 203(k) only; or
2. the appropriate LTV ratio below, multiplied by the lesser of:
   - the Adjusted As-Is Value, plus:
     - Financeable Repair and Improvement Costs, for Standard 203(k) or Limited 203(k);
     - Financeable Mortgage Fees, for Standard 203(k) or Limited 203(k);
     - Financeable Contingency Reserves, for Standard 203(k) or Limited 203(k); and
     - Financeable Mortgage Payment Reserves, for Standard 203(k) only); or
   - 110 percent of the After Improved Value (100 percent for condominiums); or
3. the Nationwide Mortgage Limits.

(A) Loan-to-Value Ratios for Refinance

The table below describes the relationship between the Borrower's Minimum Decision Credit Score and the LTV ratio for which they are eligible.

If the Borrower's Minimum Decision Credit Score is:	Then the Borrower is:
at or above 580	eligible for maximum financing of 97.75%.
between 500 and 579	limited to a maximum LTV of 90%.

For Secondary Residences, the maximum LTV is 85 percent.

(B) Required Documentation

The Mortgagee must obtain the mortgage payoff statement for existing debt.

xi. Maximum Mortgage Amounts for Energy Efficient Mortgages, Weatherization Items, and Solar Energy Systems

The Mortgagee must calculate the maximum mortgage amount without factoring in the cost of Energy Efficient Mortgage (EEM) items, weatherization items, and solar energy systems. The Mortgagee may then add the cost of these improvements to determine the Base Loan Amount. The Base Loan Amount may not exceed 110 percent of the After Improved Value of the Property (100 percent for condominiums).

For Limited 203(k) transactions, the costs for energy improvements can be in addition to the $35,000 limit on total rehabilitation cost.

xii. Combined Loan-to-Value

(A) Secondary Financing Provided by Governmental Entities, Homeownership and Opportunity for People Everywhere Grantees, and HUD-Approved Nonprofits

There is no maximum Combined Loan-to-Value (CLTV) for secondary financing meeting the requirements found in Governmental Entities, Homeownership and Opportunity for People Everywhere (HOPE) Grantees, and HUD-Approved Nonprofits.

(B) Secondary Financing Provided by Family Members

There is no maximum CLTV for secondary financing meeting the requirements found in Family Members.

(C) Secondary Financing Provided by Private Individuals and Other Organizations

The maximum CLTV for secondary financing provided by private individuals and other organizations is 110 percent of the After Improved Value. Secondary financing provided by private individuals and other organizations may not be used to meet the Borrower's minimum downpayment requirement.

xiii. Mortgage Insurance Premium

The Mortgagee must comply with the MIP requirements found in the MIP Chart.

For the purpose of calculating the LTV for application of the MIP, the Mortgagee must divide the Base Loan Amount by the After Improved Value.

xiv. Underwriting

The Mortgagee must comply with the underwriting requirements found in Origination Through Post-Closing/Endorsement and the additional guidance provided below.

(A) Required Documentation Standard 203(k) and Limited 203(k)

(1) Identity-of-Interest Certification

Identity of Interest refers to a transaction between Family Members, business partners or other business affiliates.

Conflict of interest refers to any party to the transaction who has a direct or indirect personal, business, or financial relationship sufficient to appear that may cause partiality and influence the transaction.

Sales transactions between Family Members are permitted. The Mortgagee must ensure there are no other instances of Identity of Interest or conflict of interest between parties in the 203(k) transaction. The Borrower and the 203(k) Consultant must each sign an Identity-of-Interest certification that is placed in the case binder.

If the Borrower selected a 203(k) Consultant to perform a Feasibility Study, the Mortgagee may select the same 203(k) Consultant for the project without creating an Identity of Interest.

(a) Borrower's Certification

The Borrower must sign a certification stating the following:

> *"I hereby certify to the Department of Housing and Urban Development (HUD) and (Mortgagee), that I/We ___ do or ___ do not have an identity-of-interest with the seller. I/We do not have an identity-of-interest with the 203(k) Consultant of the property. I also certify that I/We do not have a conflict-of-interest with any other party to the transaction, including the real estate agent, mortgagee, contractor, 203(k) Consultant and/or the appraiser. In addition, I certify that I am not obtaining any source of funds or acting as a buyer for another individual, partnership, company or investment club and I/We ___will or ___will not occupy the residence I/We are purchasing or refinancing."*

> *Warning: HUD will prosecute false claims and statements. Conviction may result in criminal and/or civil penalties. (18 U.S.C. 1001, 1010, 1012; 31 U.S.C. 3729, 3802).*

_____   _____
Borrower's Signature   *Date*

_____   _____
Co-borrower's Signature   *Date*

(b) 203(k) Consultant's Certification

All 203(k) Consultants are required to sign the following certification after preparing/reviewing the Work Write-Up and Cost Estimate, stating:

> *"I hereby certify that I have carefully inspected this property for compliance with the general acceptability requirements (including health and safety) in HUD's Minimum Property Requirements or Minimum Property Standards. I have required as necessary and reviewed the architectural exhibits, including any applicable engineering and termite reports, and the estimated rehabilitation cost and they are acceptable for the rehabilitation of this property. I have no personal interest, present or prospective, in the property, applicant, or proceeds of the mortgage. I also certify that I have no identity-of-interest or conflict-of-interest with the borrower, seller, mortgagee, real estate agent, appraiser, plan reviewer, contractor, subcontractor or any party with a financial interest in the transaction. To the best of my knowledge, I have reported all items requiring correction and that the rehabilitation proposal now meets all HUD requirements for 203(k) Rehabilitation Mortgage Insurance."*

> *Warning: HUD will prosecute false claims and statements. Conviction may result in criminal and/or civil penalties. (18 U.S.C 1001, 1010, 1012; 31 U.S.C 3729, 3802).*

_____   _____
Consultant's Signature   *Date*

(2) Borrower Acting as General Contractor or Doing Own Work (Self-Help)

The Mortgagee must document approval for the Borrower to act as the general contractor or to complete their own work.

- The Mortgagee must verify and document that the Borrower is either a licensed general contractor or can document experience in completing rehabilitation projects.
- The Mortgagee must ensure the Borrower demonstrates the necessary expertise and experience to perform the specific repair competently and timely.
- The Mortgagee must instruct the Borrower of the requirement to maintain complete records showing the actual cost of rehabilitation, including paid receipts for materials and Lien Waivers from any subcontractors.
- The Mortgagee must ensure all permits are obtained prior to commencement of work.

- The Mortgagee must obtain Cost Estimates that clearly state the cost for completion of each Work Item, including the cost of labor and materials; however, only materials cost will be reimbursed.
- The Mortgagee must obtain a signed Rehabilitation (Self-Help) Loan Agreement from the Borrower.

(3) Repairs Noted by the Appraiser

When an appraisal report identifies the need for health and safety repairs that were not included in the Consultant's Work Write-Up, Borrower's work plan, or contractor's proposal, the Mortgagee must ensure the repairs are included in the Consultant's final Work Write-Up or the Borrower's final work plan.

(4) 203(k) Borrower's Acknowledgment (Form HUD-92700-A)

The Mortgagee must obtain an executed form HUD-92700-A, *203(k) Borrower's Acknowledgment*.

(5) Feasibility Study

If a Feasibility Study was performed to determine if the project is financially feasible, the Mortgagee must obtain a copy of the study.

(6) Borrower Contractor Agreement

The Mortgagee must obtain a written agreement between the Borrower and the general contractor, or if there is no general contractor, for each contractor. The contractor must agree in writing to complete the work for the amount of the Cost Estimate and within the allotted time frame.

(B) Required Documentation for Standard 203(k) Only

(1) Consultant Final Work Write-Up and Cost Estimate

The Mortgagee must obtain the final Work Write-Up and Cost Estimate from the Consultant. The final Work Write-Up must include all required repairs and improvements to meet HUD's Minimum Property Standards (MPS) and MPR (as applicable) and the Borrower's electives.

The Cost Estimate must state the nature and type of repair and cost for each Work Item, broken down by labor and materials. Lump sum costs are permitted only in line items where a lump sum estimate is reasonable and customary.

(2) Architectural Exhibits

The Mortgagee must obtain and review all required architectural exhibits included in the Consultant's final Work Write-Up.

(3) Consultant/Borrower Agreement

The Mortgagee must obtain a written agreement between the Consultant and the Borrower that fully explains the services to be performed and the fees to be charged for each service. The written agreement must disclose to the Borrower that any inspection performed by the Consultant is not a "Home Inspection," as detailed in the disclosure form HUD-92564-CN, *For Your Protection Get a Home Inspection.*

(C) Required Documentation for Limited 203(k) Only

Contractor's Cost Estimate

The Mortgagee must obtain the final contractor's itemized estimate of the repairs and improvements to be completed for all Work Items.

xv. Closing

(A) Standard

The Mortgagee must comply with requirements found in the Closing section and the additional guidance provided below.

There is only one closing that includes the rehabilitation funds. The rehabilitation funds are escrowed and disbursed as the work is satisfactorily completed.

(1) Establishing the Rehabilitation Escrow Account

(a) Standard 203(k)

The Mortgagee must establish an interest bearing rehabilitation escrow account to include, as applicable:
- Standard 203(k) Financeable Repair and Improvement Costs and Fees;
- Standard 203(k) Financeable Contingency Reserves;
- Standard 203(k) Financeable Mortgage Payment Reserves;
- the cost of EEM, weatherization or solar energy systems improvements; and
- the Borrower's own funds for Contingency Reserves.

(b) Limited 203(k)

The Mortgagee must establish an interest bearing rehabilitation escrow account to include, as applicable:
- Limited 203(k) Financeable Repair and Improvement Costs and Fees;
- Limited 203(k) Financeable Contingency Reserves;

- the cost of EEM, weatherization or solar energy systems improvements; and
- the Borrower's own funds for Contingency Reserves.

(c) Escrow Closeout Certification Screen

The Mortgagee must complete all applicable fields on the Escrow Closeout Certification screen in FHAC.

(2) Initial Draw at Closing

The Mortgagee must document the amount and purpose of an initial draw at closing on the form HUD-92900-LT, *FHA Loan Underwriting and Transmittal Summary.*

(a) Standard 203(k)

For Standard 203(k) transactions, Mortgagees may disburse the following at closing:
- permit fees (the permit must be obtained before work commences);
- prepaid architectural or engineering fees;
- prepaid Consultant fees;
- origination fees;
- discount points;
- materials costs for items, prepaid by the Borrower in cash or by the contractor, where a contract is established with the supplier and an order is placed with the manufacturer for delivery at a later date; and
- up to 50 percent of materials costs for items, not yet paid for by the Borrower or contractor, where a contract is established with the supplier and an order is placed with the manufacturer for delivery at a later date.

For any Disbursements paid to the contractor, the Mortgagee must hold back 10 percent of the draw request in the Contingency Reserve.

(b) Limited 203(k)

For Limited 203(k) transactions, Mortgagees may disburse the following at closing:
- permit fees (the permit must be obtained before work commences);
- origination fees;
- discount points; and
- up to 50 percent of the estimated materials and labor costs before beginning construction only when the contractor is not willing or able to defer receipt of payment until completion of the work, or the

payment represents the cost of materials incurred prior to construction. A statement from the contractor is sufficient to document.

(B) Required Documentation

(1) Rehabilitation Loan Agreement

The Mortgagee and Borrower must execute the Rehabilitation Loan Agreement, which establishes the conditions under which the Mortgagee will disburse the rehabilitation escrow account funds.

The Rehabilitation Loan Agreement is incorporated by reference and made a part of the security instrument.

(a) Standard 203(k) Rehabilitation Period

The Mortgagee must review the 203(k) Consultant's Work Write-Up to determine the time frame for completion of repairs not to exceed six months.

(b) Limited 203(k) Rehabilitation Period

The Mortgagee must consult the Borrower Contractor Agreement to determine the time frame for completion of repairs not to exceed six months.

(2) Security Instrument and Rehabilitation Loan Rider

If the Mortgage involves releases from the rehabilitation escrow account, the following language must be placed in the security instrument:

"Provisions pertaining to releases are contained in the Rehabilitation Loan Rider, which is attached to this mortgage and made a part hereof."

The Rehabilitation Loan Rider is a required modification to a security instrument.

xvi. Data Delivery/203(k) Calculator

The 203(k) Calculator enables Mortgagees to calculate the Maximum Mortgage amount, LTV for MIP, and the amount to establish a repair escrow when required for all 203(k) transactions.

Mortgagees may begin to use the 203(k) Calculator in FHAC when the functionality becomes available, but must use the 203(k) Calculator prior to endorsement for all 203(k) transactions with case numbers assigned on and after October 31, 2016.

Required data for the 203(k) Calculator are:
- 203(k) Program Type (Standard 203(k) or Limited 203(k));
- As-Is Property Value;
- Adjusted As-Is Value;

- After Improved Value;
- existing debt on the Property for a refinance;
- credit for lead-based paint stabilization per HUD REO contract (if applicable);
- Financeable Repair and Improvement Costs, for Standard 203(k) or Limited 203(k);
- Financeable Contingency Reserves, for Standard 203(k) or Limited 203(k);
- Financeable Mortgage Payment Reserves, for Standard 203(k) only;
- Financeable Mortgage Fees, for Standard 203(k) or Limited 203(k);
- cost of EEM or solar energy systems improvements; and
- principal balance of secondary financing provided by private individuals and other organizations.

For applications to be endorsed prior to the availability of data delivery functionality in FHAC, the Mortgagee must detail the data delivery requirements shown above on form HUD-92900-LT, or include the applicable 203(k) Maximum Mortgage Calculation Worksheet.

xvii. Post-Closing and Endorsement

The Mortgagee must comply with requirements in Post-Closing and Endorsement.

203(k) Mortgages are eligible for endorsement after the initial mortgage proceeds are disbursed and a rehabilitation escrow account is established.

(A) Rehabilitation Period

The rehabilitation period starts when the Mortgage is funded.

The rehabilitation period is specified in the Rehabilitation Loan Agreement.

(B) Extension Requests

If the work is not completed within the rehabilitation period specified in the Rehabilitation Loan Agreement, the Borrower may request an extension of time and must submit adequate documentation to justify the extension. The Mortgagee may grant an extension at its discretion only if the Mortgage Payments are current.

(1) Required Documentation

The Mortgagee must obtain:
- evidence that the Mortgage is current;
- an explanation for the delay from the Borrower, contractor, or Consultant; and
- a new estimated completion date.

(2) Escrow Closeout Certification Screen

The Mortgagee must complete the required fields on the Escrow Closeout Certification screen in FHAC to document the approval or the denial for the extension request of the rehabilitation period specified in the Rehabilitation Loan Agreement.

(C) Failure to Start or Complete Work

As stated in the Rehabilitation Loan Agreement, the Mortgagee may consider the Mortgage to be in default if work:
- has not started within 30 Days of the Disbursement Date;
- ceases for more than 30 consecutive Days; or
- has not been completed within the established time frame, or an extended time frame approved by the Mortgagee.

If the Mortgagee considers the Mortgage to be in default for failure to start or complete work, and the Mortgage is not in payment default, the Mortgagee must apply any unused rehabilitation funds towards the principal amount.

xviii. Rehabilitation Escrow Account

When the Mortgage closes, the Mortgagee must place all proceeds designated for the rehabilitation, including the Contingency Reserve, inspection fees and any Mortgage Payments, in an interest bearing escrow account.

- The Mortgagee must pay the net income earned by the rehabilitation escrow account to the Borrower through an agreed upon method of payment.
- The Mortgagee may allow net income to accumulate and be paid in one lump sum after completion of the rehabilitation.
- The Mortgagee that is the custodian of the repair escrow funds is responsible for ensuring all funds from the escrow account are properly distributed.

(A) Accounting of 203(k) Rehabilitation Funds

The Mortgagee must utilize an accounting system that records all transactions from the rehabilitation escrow account and which documents the amount escrowed for each of these categories:
- repairs
- Contingency Reserve
- inspection fees
- title update fees
- Mortgage Payments
- other fees (i.e., architectural and engineering fees, Consultant fees, permits, supplemental origination fee and discount points on repair costs)

The accounting system must provide:
- the Borrower's name and property address
- the FHA case number
- the Closing Date
- the scheduled completion date
- the amount of funds in the rehabilitation escrow account
- the interest rate provided on the escrow account

For each draw on the escrow account, the accounting system must record:
- a list of Disbursements
- the number of Days in escrow
- the amount of money in the account
- the interest earned for the applicable time period
- the balance of interest remaining in the account

(B) Project Management

Mortgagees must ensure work is completed on schedule and workmanship is acceptable.

When notified of an issue, Mortgagees must intercede in disagreements among Borrowers, contractors, or Consultants.

(1) Health and Safety

The Mortgagee must ensure that all health and safety items not in the original Work Write-Up or work plan that are discovered during the rehabilitation period are addressed by completion of a change order.

(2) Change Order Request

The Mortgagee must obtain form HUD-92577, *Request for Acceptance of Changes in Approved Drawings and Specifications*, from the Consultant or inspector if there are any deviations from the Work Write-Up. The Mortgagee must approve the change order before any work can be done.

(C) Escrow Administration

The Mortgagee is fully responsible for authorizing draw inspections, managing the rehabilitation escrow account, and approving the associated draws from the account.

It is the Mortgagee's responsibility to ensure that any inspections are completed in a quality and timely manner, regardless of who performs the inspections.

(1) Release of Funds

The Mortgagee may release funds only when repairs and improvements per the draw request, whether made by the contractor or Borrower, meet all federal, state, and local laws, codes and ordinances, including any required permits and inspections.

The Mortgagee may release funds for lead-based paint stabilization only when a state- or EPA-certified lead-based paint inspector, certified risk assessor or sampling technician, independent of the firm that performed the stabilization, performs the clearance examination and clearance is obtained.

For an existing Structure moved to a new foundation or a Structure that will be elevated, the Mortgagee must not release mortgage proceeds for the existing Structure on the non-mortgaged Property until the new foundation has been properly inspected and the Structure has been properly placed and secured to the new foundation.

The Mortgagee must obtain Lien Waivers, or equivalent, at the time of any Disbursement of funds to ensure the validity of the first lien on the Property. If all Work Items performed by a contractor have not been completed at the time of draw request, the Mortgagee must obtain a partial conditional Lien Waiver for the Work Items that have been completed for each draw request.

For repairs made by the Borrower under a self-help agreement, the Mortgagee is permitted to release funds for materials only.

When the rehabilitation escrow account includes Mortgage Payment Reserves, the Mortgagee must make monthly Mortgage Payments directly from the interest bearing reserve account. Once the Property is able to be occupied, application of the Mortgage Payment Reserves will cease. Mortgage Payment Reserves remaining in the reserve account after occupancy of the Property must be used to reduce the mortgage principal.

(a) Draw Request

The Mortgagee must obtain an executed form HUD-9746-A, *Draw Request Section 203(k)*, from the 203(k) Consultant, or from the Borrower when there is no 203(k) Consultant, requesting the release of escrow funds for completed Work Items.

The Mortgagee must review and approve each draw request to ensure that the work for which funds are being requested has been completed satisfactorily and that the form has been properly executed by the Borrower, contractor and Consultant, if any.

The Mortgagee may not approve a draw request for work that is not yet complete.

The Mortgagee may not approve draw requests for materials for work that is not completed, except for:

- materials costs for items prepaid by the Borrower in cash or by the contractor, where a contract is established with the supplier and an order is placed with the manufacturer for delivery at a later date; and
- up to 50 percent of materials costs for items, not yet paid for by the Borrower or contractor, where a contract is established with the supplier and an order is placed with the manufacturer for delivery at a later date.

(b) Change Orders

Work must be 100 percent complete on each change order item before the release of funds for the Work Items from the rehabilitation escrow account.

(c) Holdbacks

The Mortgagee must hold back 10 percent of each draw request prior to release of funds from the rehabilitation escrow account.

Exception

When a subcontractor is 100 percent complete with a Work Item, the work completed is acceptable to the inspector, and the contractor and subcontractor provide the necessary Lien Waivers, or equivalent, the Mortgagee is not required to hold back funds; the Mortgagee has discretion to hold back funds if not required.

(d) Timeliness of Release

The Mortgagee must release funds within five business days after receipt of a properly executed draw request and title update when necessary.

(i) Standard 203(k) Release of Funds

Maximum Draw Requests

The Mortgagee may approve a maximum of five draw requests (four intermediate and one final).

Contingency Reserve

To allow use of contingency funds for improvements other than health and safety when rehabilitation is incomplete, the Mortgagee must determine that it is unlikely that any health or safety deficiency will be discovered, and that the Mortgage will not exceed 95 percent of the appraised value.

When the rehabilitation is complete, the Borrower may use the Contingency Reserve account to fund additional improvements not included in the original Work Write-Up.

The Mortgagee must obtain a change order detailing the additional improvements, including the costs of labor and materials.

The Mortgagee must inform the Borrower in writing of the approval or rejection of the request to use funds from the Contingency Reserve account for additional improvements within five business days.

Method of Payment

The Mortgagee will release escrow funds upon completion of the rehabilitation in compliance with the Work Write-Up.

The Mortgagee must issue checks to both the Borrower and contractors as co-payees, unless the Borrower provides written authorization, at each draw, to issue the check directly to the contractor.

The Mortgagee may issue the check directly to the Borrower alone if the release is for:
- materials for work performed under a self-help agreement; or
- materials for items prepaid by the Borrower under contract with the supplier.

(ii) Limited 203(k) Release of Funds

Maximum Number of Draw Requests

The Mortgagee may approve a maximum of two draw requests per contractor or the Borrower (if acting as the contractor).

When necessary, the Mortgagee may arrange a payment schedule, not to exceed two releases, per specialized contractor (an initial release plus a final release).

Total Repair Costs Less Than or Equal to $15,000

The Mortgagee must ensure that the repairs and/or improvements have been completed by obtaining contractor's receipts or a signed Borrower's Letter of Completion. The Mortgagee is not required to perform or have others perform inspections of the completed work.

The Mortgagee may choose to obtain or perform inspections if they believe such actions are necessary for program compliance or risk mitigation. If the Mortgagee determines that an inspection by a third party is necessary to ensure proper completion of the proposed repair or improvement item, the Mortgagee may charge the Borrower for the costs of no more than two inspections per contractor.

Total Repair Costs Exceeding $15,000

The Mortgagee must ensure that the repairs and/or improvements have been completed by performing an inspection or by obtaining an inspection by a third party to determine that the repairs have been satisfactorily completed. The Mortgagee must obtain a signed Borrower's Letter of Completion.

Contingency Reserve

The Mortgagee must ensure funds escrowed in the Contingency Reserve are used solely to pay for the proposed repairs or improvements and any unforeseen items related to these repair items.

Method of Payment

The Mortgagee will release rehabilitation escrow funds upon completion of the rehabilitation in compliance with the work plan.

The Mortgagee may issue checks solely to the contractor, or issue checks to the Borrower and the contractor as co-payees.

The Mortgagee may issue the check directly to the Borrower alone if the release is for:
- materials for work performed under a self-help agreement; or
- materials for items prepaid by the Borrower under contract with the supplier.

(2) Final Escrow Closeout

The Mortgagee must include the interest earned in the final payment on the rehabilitation escrow account and may include the total of all holdbacks. However, if it is required to protect the priority of the security instrument, the Mortgagee may retain the holdback for a period not to exceed 35 Days (or the time period required by law to file a lien, whichever is longer), to ensure compliance with state Lien Waiver laws or other state requirements.

(a) Standard

(i) Standard 203(k)

Before final release of rehabilitation escrow funds, the Mortgagee must approve the final inspection and draw request signed by the Consultant, contractor, and Borrower.

(ii) Limited 203(k)

Before a final release is made to any contractor, the Mortgagee must determine that all work by the contractor has been completed, is acceptable by the Borrower, and all necessary inspections have been made with acceptable documentation.

(b) Required Documentation for both Standard 203(k) and Limited 203(k)

The Mortgagee must:
- obtain the Borrower's Letter of Completion signed by the Borrower indicating satisfaction with the completed work and requesting a final inspection and final release of funds;
- obtain a CO, or equivalent, if required by the local jurisdiction;
- obtain all inspections required by the local jurisdiction;
- complete the Final Release Notice authorizing the final payment;
- provide the Mortgagee's extension approval if applicable; and
- obtain a release of any and all liens arising out of the contract or submission of receipts, or other evidence of payment covering all subcontractors or suppliers who could file a legal claim.

(3) Contingency Release

The Mortgagee must inform the Borrower of its approval or rejection of the Borrower's request for funds to be made available from the Contingency Reserve account for the purpose of improvements.

A Borrower who established the Contingency Funds with their own funds may receive a refund of their funds, or may request the remaining funds be applied towards the principal balance.

For Standard 203(k), the Mortgagee must either make funds available for additional improvements or apply the funds towards the principal balance if the Contingency Reserve was financed.

For Limited 203(k), the Mortgagee must apply the funds towards the principal balance if the Contingency Reserve was financed.

(4) Mortgage Payment Reserve

Mortgage Payment Reserves remaining in the reserve account after the Final Release Notice is issued must be used to reduce the mortgage principal.

(5) Escrow Closeout Certification

(a) Standard

After the rehabilitation escrow account is closed, the Mortgagee must complete the Escrow Closeout Certification screen in FHAC within 30 Days after the escrow account is closed.

(b) Required Documentation

The Mortgagee must certify that the following documents were reviewed and verified for accuracy:
- Final Release Notice
- Borrower's Letter of Completion
- title update/Lien Waivers
- draw request forms and inspection reports
- change orders
- Mortgagee accounting of the rehabilitation escrow account and payment ledgers
- contingency release letters

xix.   Quality Control

HUD will hold Mortgagees and 203(k) Consultants fully accountable for the mortgage proceeds.

Mortgagees must exercise due diligence with regard to the full scope of the 203(k) Consultant's services. Standards for the 203(k) Consultant's performance must be clearly defined in the Mortgagee's Quality Control Plan and should be provided to each Consultant that the Mortgagee relies on in the 203(k) program. Mortgagees must evaluate and document the performance of these Consultants on at least an annual basis, to include a review of the Consultant's actual work product.

xx. Servicing

(A) Delinquencies

If the Mortgage is delinquent, the Mortgagee may refuse to make further releases from the rehabilitation escrow account.

(B) Payment Default

The project must stop if the Mortgage is in payment default. The Mortgagee must obtain an inspection of all repairs that have been completed up until this point by the 203(k) Consultant for a Standard 203(k), or for a Limited 203(k) by a third party. The Mortgagee may approve a release of funds for Work Items that have already been completed as of the date the work was stopped.

The inspection obtained by the Mortgagee must also note any items that are required to be completed to protect the interest of the collateral from deteriorating, such as a roof, and health and safety items for a Property that is occupied. The Mortgagee must ensure the completion of any Work Item that the inspection determines is necessary to protect the occupants and/or the collateral. The Mortgagee may use the services of the mortgagor's contractor, if appropriate, or may engage the services of another qualified contractor to complete the Work Item. The Mortgagee may approve a subsequent release of funds for that Work Item.

The Mortgagee has the option to call the Mortgage due and payable.

If the default is cured, the project may resume.

(C) Bankruptcy

The Mortgagee may not approve further advances if the Borrower declares bankruptcy unless otherwise required by law or as needed to protect FHA's first lien position. The Mortgagee must obtain an inspection of all repairs that have been completed by the 203(k) Consultant for a Standard 203(k), or for a Limited 203(k) by a third party. The Mortgagee may approve a release of funds for Work Items that have already been completed as of the date the work was stopped.

(D) Foreclosure of Mortgage during Rehabilitation Period

In the event of a foreclosure during rehabilitation, the Mortgagee must obtain a final inspection to determine the amount of work that has been completed since the start of construction and the cost for the work.

Using a format similar to the Final Release Notice, the Mortgagee will authorize release of rehabilitation escrow funds for the completed work and holdbacks on any previous Disbursements.

If funds remain in the rehabilitation escrow account, the Mortgagee will reduce the amount of claim (unpaid mortgage principal balance) by the unexpended funds in the rehabilitation escrow account.

The Mortgagee must submit a copy of the Final Release Notice with any insurance claim.

Handbook 4000.1
Effective Date: 09/14/2015 | Last Revised: 07/10/2019
*Refer to the online version of SF Handbook 4000.1 for specific sections' effective dates

399

b. Disasters and 203(h) Mortgage Insurance for Disaster Victims

i. Definition

Section 203(h) of the National Housing Act authorizes FHA to insure Mortgages to victims of a Presidentially-Declared Major Disaster Area (PDMDA) for the purchase or reconstruction of a Single Family Property.

Mortgages to be insured under Section 203(h) must be processed and underwritten in accordance with the regulations and requirements applicable to the 203(b) program. Where 203(b) program guidance conflicts with the specific requirements on Section 203(h) Mortgages provided below, this specific guidance controls.

ii. Eligibility Requirements

(A) Borrower Eligibility

(1) Application Deadline

The FHA case number must be assigned within one year of the date the PDMDA is declared, unless an additional period of eligibility is provided.

(2) Principal Residence

The mortgaged Property must be the Borrower's Principal Residence.

(3) Credit Score

The Borrower must have a minimum credit score of 500.

(B) Property Eligibility

The previous residence (owned or rented) must have been located in a PDMDA and destroyed or damaged to such an extent that reconstruction or replacement is necessary. A list of the specified affected counties and cities and corresponding disaster declarations are provided by the Federal Emergency Management Agency (FEMA).

The purchased or reconstructed Property must be a Single Family Property or a unit in an FHA-approved Condominium Project.

(C) Minimum Required Investment/Maximum Loan-to-Value

The Borrower is not required to make the Minimum Required Investment (MRI). The maximum Loan-to-Value (LTV) ratio limit is 100 percent of the Adjusted Value. If a 203(k) is used in conjunction with a 203(h), the 203(k) LTV applies.

(D) Underwriting

The Mortgagee should be as flexible as prudent decision making permits.

The Mortgagee is required to make every effort to obtain traditional documentation regarding employment, assets, and credit, and must document their attempts. Where traditional documentation is unavailable, the Mortgagee may use alternative documentation as outlined below. Where specific requirements are not provided below, the Mortgagee may use alternative documentation that is reasonable and prudent to rely upon in underwriting a Mortgage.

(1) Credit

For Borrowers with derogatory credit, the Mortgagee may consider the Borrower a satisfactory credit risk if the credit report indicates satisfactory credit prior to a disaster, and any derogatory credit subsequent to the date of the disaster is related to the effects of the disaster.

(2) Income

If prior employment cannot be verified because records were destroyed by the disaster, and the Borrower is in the same/similar field, then FHA will accept W-2s and tax returns from the Internal Revenue Service (IRS) to confirm prior employment and income.

The Mortgagee may also include short-term employment obtained following the disaster in the calculation of Effective Income.

(3) Liabilities

When a Borrower is purchasing a new house, the Mortgagee may exclude the Mortgage Payment on the destroyed residence located in a PDMDA from the Borrower's liabilities. To exclude the Mortgage Payments from the liabilities, the Mortgagee must:
- obtain information that the Borrower is working with the servicing Mortgagee to appropriately address their mortgage obligation; and
- apply any property insurance proceeds to the Mortgage of the damaged house.

(4) Assets

If traditional asset documentation is not available, the Mortgagee may use statements downloaded from the Borrower's financial institution website to confirm the Borrower has sufficient assets to close the Mortgage.

(5) Housing Payment History

The Mortgagee may disregard any late payments on a previous obligation on a Property that was destroyed or damaged in the disaster where the late payments were a result of the disaster and the Borrower was not three or more months delinquent on their Mortgage at the time of the disaster.

The Mortgagee may justify approval if the Borrower was three or more months delinquent if extenuating circumstances are documented by the Mortgagee.

iii. Eligibility Documentation Requirements

The Mortgagee must document and verify that the Borrower's previous residence was in the disaster area, and was destroyed or damaged to such an extent that reconstruction or replacement is necessary. Documentation attesting to the damage of the previous house must accompany the mortgage application. If purchasing a new house, the house need not be located in the area where the previous house was located.

iv. Refinancing Policy

Refinancing is permitted in conjunction with rehabilitation.

v. Using Section 203(k) with 203(h) for Rehabilitation

Damaged residences located in a PDMDA are eligible for Section 203(k) mortgage insurance regardless of the age of the Property. The residence only needs to have been completed and ready for occupancy for eligibility under Section 203(k). All other Section 203(k) policy must be followed.

c. Energy Efficient Mortgages

i. Definitions

The Energy Efficient Mortgage (EEM) program allows the Mortgagee to offer financing for cost-effective energy efficient improvements to an existing Property at the time of purchase or refinancing, or for upgrades above the established residential building code for New Construction.

Cost-Effective refers to the costs of the energy efficiency improvements that are less than the present value of the energy saved over the estimated useful life of those improvements.

ii. Eligibility

(A) Eligible Property Types

EEM may be used with:
- New Construction Properties (one- to four-units);
- Existing Construction Properties (one- to four-units);
- condominiums (one unit); or
- Manufactured Housing.

(B) Eligible Programs and Transactions Types

The EEM program can be used in conjunction with any mortgage insurance under Title II, including:
- 203(b)
  - Purchase
  - No cash-out refinance
- 203(h) Mortgage Insurance for Disaster Victims
- 203(k) (Standard and Limited)
- Weatherization Policy (Existing Construction only)

iii. Standard

Energy Package

The energy package is the set of improvements agreed to by the Borrower based on recommendations and analysis performed by a qualified home energy rater. The improvements can include energy-saving equipment, and active and passive solar and wind technologies. The energy package can include materials, labor, inspections, and the home energy assessment by a qualified energy rater. If the Borrower desires, labor may include the cost of an EEM Facilitator (project manager).

(A) Cost-Effective Test

The financed portion of an energy package must be cost-effective. A cost-effective energy package is one where the cost of the improvements, including maintenance and repair, is less than the value of the energy saved over the estimated useful life of those improvements.

(B) Cost-effective Test for New Construction

For New Construction, the financed portion of an energy package includes only those cost-effective energy improvements over and above the greater of the following:
- the latest energy code standard that has been adopted by HUD through a Federal Register notice; or
- the applicable IECC year used by the state or local building code for New Construction.

More information on this energy code can be obtained from the Department of Energy or the International Code Council.

(C) Changes to the Energy Package after Mortgage Closing

If the work that is done differs from the approved energy package, a change order along with a revised home energy audit must be submitted to the Direct Endorsement (DE) underwriter for approval. If the changes still meet the cost-effective test, no further analysis is required. If not, the funds for the work not included in the approval energy package must be used to pay down the mortgage principal.

iv. Home Energy Report/Assessment

The Borrower must obtain a home energy assessment. The purpose of the energy assessment under the EEM program is to identify opportunities for improving the energy efficiency of the home and their cost-effectiveness. The assessment must be conducted by a qualified energy rater, assessor, or auditor using whole-home assessment standards, protocols and procedure.

(A) Qualifications of Energy Raters/Assessors

Qualified home energy raters/assessors must be trained and certified as one of the following:
- Building Performance Institute Building Analyst Professional;
- Building Performance Institute Home Energy Professional Energy Auditor;
- Residential Energy Services Network Home Energy Rater; or
- energy rater, assessor or auditor who meets local or state jurisdictional requirements for conducting residential energy audits or assessments, including training, certification, licensure and insurance requirements.

The home energy report must reflect one of the above professional credentials by the rater/assessor.

(B) Home Energy Report

The home energy report reflects recommendations of energy-saving improvements for the Borrower's consideration. Included with the recommendations are estimates of energy savings and cost-effective analysis for each of the suggested improvements. These estimates consider energy costs in today's dollars (present value). The Mortgagee must use the energy-savings information from the home energy report to determine that the cost-effective test is met for the financed energy package.

(C) Home Energy Report for New Construction

On newly constructed housing, the home energy report must identify improvements that are over and above the greater of the following:
- the requirements of the latest energy code standard that has been adopted by HUD through a Federal Register notice; or
- the applicable IECC year used by the state or local building code for New Construction.

(D) Required Documentation

The Mortgagee must obtain a copy of the home energy report. This report must not be greater than 120 Days old.

The Mortgagee must submit two forms HUD-92900-LT, *FHA Loan Underwriting and Transmittal Summary* as described in the Underwriting Section below.

v. Maximum Financeable Energy Package

The maximum amount of the energy package that can be added to the Base Loan Amount is the lesser of:
- the dollar amount of a cost-effective energy package as determined by the home energy audit; or
- the lesser of 5 percent of:
  o the Adjusted Value;
  o 115 percent of the median area price of a Single Family dwelling; or
  o 150 percent of the national conforming mortgage limit.

Energy Efficient Mortgage Calculator Tool

The Mortgagee must calculate the dollar amount of a cost-effective energy package as determined by the home energy audit, as shown in Energy Package. The EEM Calculator, located in FHA Connection (FHAC) on the Case Processing screen, will perform the calculation of Maximum Financeable Energy Package. The EEM Calculator uses data entered for the Mortgage to calculate the maximum energy package.

Handbook 4000.1   405
Effective Date: 09/14/2015 | Last Revised: 07/10/2019
*Refer to the online version of SF Handbook 4000.1 for specific sections' effective dates

For a Streamline Refinance, the EEM Calculator uses the appraised value from the initial transaction, contained within FHA Connection records, as the Adjusted Value.

vi. Maximum Mortgage Amount

The maximum final Base Loan Amount is determined by adding the maximum financeable energy package amount to the initial maximum Base Loan Amount. For New Construction, the cost of the financeable energy package must be subtracted from the sales price when computing the Adjusted Value.

When utilizing an EEM in conjunction with a 203(k) or Weatherization, the items included in the maximum financeable energy package must be excluded from the items included when calculating the initial maximum Base Loan Amount under these programs.

The maximum FHA Nationwide Mortgage Limit for an area may be exceeded by the maximum financeable energy package.

vii. Underwriting

The Mortgagee must calculate the Borrower's debt ratios using the initial Base Loan Amount plus the portion of the Upfront Mortgage Insurance Premium (UFMIP) attributable to the initial Base Loan Amount.

(A) TOTAL Mortgage Scorecard

For purposes of submission to the Technology Open To Approved Lenders (TOTAL) Mortgage Scorecard, the Mortgagee must utilize the initial Base Loan Amount prior to the addition of the financeable energy package.

If the Mortgagee obtains an Accept or Approve on a mortgage application that does not include the financeable energy package, FHA will recognize the risk rating from TOTAL Mortgage Scorecard and permit the increase to the Mortgage Payment without re-underwriting or rescoring. The Mortgagee must provide a form HUD-92900-LT, *FHA Loan Underwriting and Transmittal Summary*, without the financeable energy package, showing the qualifying ratios in the case binder. A second form HUD-92900-LT must be completed by the underwriter showing mortgage amount calculation that includes the financeable energy package, as reflected in FHAC. The second form must also be included in the case binder.

The underwriter must attest on the second form HUD-92900-LT that they have reviewed the calculations associated with the energy efficient improvements and found the Mortgage and the Property to be in compliance with FHA's underwriting instructions.

(B) Manual Underwriting

The Mortgagee must provide a form HUD-92900-LT, without the financeable energy package, showing the qualifying ratios in the case binder. A second form HUD-92900-LT must be completed by the underwriter showing mortgage amount calculation that includes the financeable energy package, as reflected in FHAC. The second form must also be included in the case binder.

The underwriter must attest on the second form HUD-92900-LT that they have reviewed the calculations associated with the energy efficient improvements and found the Mortgage and the Property to be in compliance with FHA's underwriting instructions.

viii. Appraisals

For Existing and New Construction, the appraisal does not need to reflect the value of the energy package that will be added to the Property. If the appraisal does include the value of the energy package, the value must be subtracted from the Property Value when computing the Adjusted Value.

On the 203(k) program, the After Improved Value is to be used for the EEM process.

ix. Cash-Out

The Borrower may not receive cash back from the mortgage transaction. If an excess exists, funds must be applied to the principal Mortgage balance.

x. Energy Efficient Mortgage Escrows

For all Mortgages on existing Properties, except 203(k), if the energy package items are not complete by the time of closing, the Mortgagee must establish an escrow account for the remaining cost of the energy improvements in accordance with the Repair Completion Escrow Requirements.

(A) 203(k)

If the energy package is part of a Section 203(k) Rehabilitation Mortgage, then the escrowed amounts of the energy package must be included in the rehabilitation escrow account.

(B) Borrower Labor

Escrows may not include costs for labor or work performed by the Borrower (Sweat Equity).

(C) Form HUD-92300, Mortgagee's Assurance of Completion

When funds to complete the energy package are escrowed, the Mortgagee must execute form HUD-92300, *Mortgagee's Assurance of Completion*, to indicate that the escrow for the energy package improvements has been established.

xi. Completion Requirements for Energy Efficient Mortgages

With the exception of 203(k), the energy package is to be installed within 90 Days of the mortgage Disbursement. If the work is not completed within 90 Days, the Mortgagee must apply the EEM funds to a prepayment of the mortgage principal.

For 203(k) Mortgages, the Mortgagee must follow the 203(k) Escrow Guidance.

xii. Inspection

The Mortgagee, the rater, or an International Code Council (ICC) Residential Combination Inspector (RCI) or Combination Inspector (CI) may inspect the installation of the improvements. The Borrower may be charged an inspection fee.

d. Refinances

i. Overview

(A) Definition

A Refinance Transaction is used to pay off the existing debt or to withdraw equity from the Property with the proceeds of a new Mortgage for a Borrower with legal title to the subject Property.

(B) Types of Refinances

(1) Cash-Out

A Cash-Out Refinance is a refinance of any Mortgage or a withdrawal of equity where no Mortgage currently exists, in which the mortgage proceeds are not limited to specific purposes.

(2) No Cash-Out

A No Cash-Out Refinance is a refinance of any Mortgage in which the mortgage proceeds are limited to the purpose of extinguishing the existing debt and costs associated with the transaction. FHA offers three types of no cash-out refinances:

(a) Rate and Term

Rate and Term refers to a no cash-out refinance of any Mortgage in which all proceeds are used to pay existing mortgage liens on the subject Property and costs associated with the transaction.

(b) Simple Refinance

Simple Refinance refers to a no cash-out refinance of an existing FHA-insured Mortgage in which all proceeds are used to pay the existing FHA-insured mortgage lien on the subject Property and costs associated with the transaction.

(c) Streamline Refinance

Streamline Refinance refers to the refinance of an existing FHA-insured Mortgage requiring limited Borrower credit documentation and underwriting. There are two different streamline options available.

(i) Credit Qualifying

The Mortgagee must perform a credit and capacity analysis of the Borrower, but no appraisal is required.

(ii) Non-Credit Qualifying

The Mortgagee does not need to perform credit or capacity analysis or obtain an appraisal.

(3) Refinance of Borrowers in Negative Equity Positions (also known as Short Refinance)

A Borrower who is current on their non FHA-insured Mortgage may qualify for an FHA-insured refinance Mortgage provided that the Mortgagee or investor writes off at least 10 percent of the unpaid principal balance of the existing first lien Mortgage. (See Refinance of Borrowers in Negative Equity Positions Program (Short Refi)).

(4) Refinances for the Purpose of Rehabilitation or Repair

A Borrower may refinance existing debts and obtain additional financing for purposes of rehabilitation and repair. Refer to 203(k) Rehabilitation Mortgage Insurance Program for guidelines for refinances under FHA's Section 203(k) program.

(5) Refinancing of an Existing Section 235 Mortgage

An existing Section 235 Mortgage may be refinanced as any no cash-out refinance.

In refinancing a Section 235 Mortgage, the Mortgagee is required to repay to FHA any amount of excess subsidy. The outstanding principal balance on a Section 235 is calculated by adding back to the balance any amount of the excess subsidy paid to FHA.

If FHA has a junior lien that was part of the original Section 235 financing, FHA will subordinate the junior lien to the Section 203(b) Mortgage that refinances the Section 235 Mortgage.

ii. General Eligibility

(A) FHA-Insured to FHA-Insured Refinances (FHA-to-FHA)

FHA-to-FHA refinances may be used with any refinance type. The Mortgagee must obtain a Refinance Authorization Number from FHA Connection (FHAC) for all FHA-to-FHA refinances.

FHA will not issue a new case number for any FHA to FHA Refinance where the existing Mortgage to be paid off has a repair or rehabilitation escrow account that the Escrow Closeout Certification has not been completed in FHAC.

(B) General Borrower Eligibility

At least one Borrower on the refinancing Mortgage must hold title to the Property being refinanced prior to case number assignment.

(C) General Property Eligibility

For a transaction involving a Manufactured Home to be considered a refinance, the Manufactured Home must have been permanently erected on a site for more than twelve months prior to case number assignment.

(D) General Mortgage Eligibility

(1) Standard [Text was deleted in this section.]

The Mortgagee must not approve any Mortgage that refinances or otherwise replaces a Mortgage that has been subject to eminent domain condemnation or seizure, by a state, municipality, or any other political subdivision of a state.

(2) Required Documentation

If the Mortgage to be insured is located in an area where a state, municipality, or other political subdivision has exercised eminent domain condemnation or seizure of a Mortgage, the Mortgagee must obtain a certification from the Borrower stating the Mortgage being refinanced was not subject to eminent domain condemnation or seizure.

iii. Temporary Interest Rate Buydowns

Temporary interest rate buydowns are not permitted with refinance transactions.

iv. Upfront Mortgage Insurance Premium Refunds

If the Borrower is refinancing their current FHA-insured Mortgage to another FHA-insured Mortgage within 3 years, a refund credit is applied to reduce the amount of the Upfront Mortgage Insurance Premium (UFMIP) paid on the refinanced Mortgage, according to the refund schedule shown in the table below:

Upfront Mortgage Insurance Premium Refund Percentages											
Month of Year											
Year	1	2	3	4	5	6	7	8	9	10	11	12
1	80	78	76	74	72	70	68	66	64	62	60	58
2	56	54	52	50	48	46	44	42	40	38	36	34
3	32	30	28	26	24	22	20	18	16	14	12	10

Handbook 4000.1
Effective Date: 09/14/2015 | Last Revised: 07/10/2019
*Refer to the online version of SF Handbook 4000.1 for specific sections' effective dates

411

v. Cash-Out Refinances

(A) Borrower Eligibility

Nonprofit agencies, state and local government agencies and Instrumentalities of Government are not eligible for cash-out refinances. Income from a non-occupant co-Borrower may not be used to qualify for a cash-out refinance.

(1) Occupancy Requirements

(a) Standard

Cash-out refinance transactions are only permitted on owner-occupied Principal Residences.

The Property securing the cash-out refinance must have been owned and occupied by the Borrower as their Principal Residence for the 12 months prior to the date of case number assignment.

Exception

In the case of inheritance, a Borrower is not required to occupy the Property for a minimum period of time before applying for a cash-out refinance, provided the Borrower has not treated the subject Property as an Investment Property at any point since inheritance of the Property. If the Borrower rents the Property following inheritance, the Borrower is not eligible for cash-out refinance until the Borrower has occupied the Property as a Principal Residence for at least 12 months.

(b) Required Documentation

The Mortgagee must review the Borrower's employment documentation or obtain utility bills to evidence the Borrower has occupied the subject Property as their Principal Residence for the 12 months prior to case number assignment.

(2) Payment History Requirements

(a) Standard

The Mortgagee must document that the Borrower has made all payments for all their Mortgages within the month due for the previous 12 months or since the Borrower obtained the Mortgages, whichever is less.

Additionally, the payments for all Mortgages secured by the subject Property must have been paid within the month due for the month prior to mortgage Disbursement.

Properties with Mortgages must have a minimum of six months of Mortgage Payments. Properties owned free and clear may be refinanced as cash-out transactions.

(b) Required Documentation

If the Mortgage on the subject Property is not reported in the Borrower's credit report or is not in the name of the Borrower, the Mortgagee must obtain a verification of Mortgage, bank statements or other documentation to evidence that all payments have been made by the Borrower in the month due for the previous 12 months.

(B) Maximum Mortgage Amounts

(1) Standard

(a) Maximum Loan-to-Value

The maximum LTV is 85 percent of the Adjusted Value.

(b) Maximum Combined Loan-to-Value

The maximum CLTV is 85 percent of the Adjusted Value.

(c) Nationwide Mortgage Limit

The combined mortgage amount of the first Mortgage and any subordinate liens cannot exceed the Nationwide Mortgage Limit described in National Housing Act's Statutory Limits.

(2) Required Documentation

The Mortgagee must obtain the payoff statement for all existing Mortgages.

vi. No Cash-Out Refinances

(A) Rate and Term

(1) Borrower Eligibility

(a) Occupancy Requirements

(i) Standard

Rate and Term refinance transactions are only permitted on owner-occupied Principal Residences and HUD-approved Secondary Residences.

(ii) Required Documentation

The Mortgagee must review the Borrower's employment documentation or obtain utility bills to evidence the Borrower currently occupies the Property and determine the length of time the Borrower has occupied the subject Property as their Principal Residence.

(b) Payment History Requirements (Manually Underwritten)

(i) Standard

For all mortgages on all properties with less than six months of Mortgage Payment history, the Borrower must have made all payments within the month due.

For all mortgages on all properties with greater than six months history, the Borrower must have made all Mortgage Payments within the month due for the six months prior to case number assignment and have no more than one 30-Day late payment for the previous six months for all mortgages.

The Borrower must have made the payments for all Mortgages secured by the subject Property for the month prior to mortgage Disbursement.

(ii) Required Documentation

If the Mortgage on the subject Property is not reported in the Borrower's credit report, the Mortgagee must obtain a verification of Mortgage to evidence payment history for the previous 12 months.

(2) Maximum Mortgage Amount

(a) Maximum Loan-to-Value Ratio

The maximum LTV for a Rate and Term refinance is:
- 97.75 percent for Principal Residences that have been owner-occupied for previous 12 months, or owner-occupied since acquisition if acquired within 12 months, at case number assignment;
- 85 percent for a Borrower who has occupied the subject Property as their Principal Residence for fewer than 12 months prior to the case number assignment date; or if owned less than 12 months, has not occupied the Property for that entire period of ownership; or
- 85 percent for all HUD-approved Secondary Residences.

(b) Calculating Maximum Mortgage Amount

(i) Standard

The maximum mortgage amount for a Rate and Term refinance is:
- the lesser of:
  - the Nationwide Mortgage Limit;
  - the maximum LTV based on the Maximum LTV Ratio from above; or
  - the sum of existing debt and costs associated with the transaction as follows:
    - existing debt includes:
      - the unpaid principal balance of the first Mortgage as of the month prior to mortgage Disbursement;
      - the unpaid principal balance of any purchase money junior Mortgage as of the month prior to mortgage Disbursement;
      - the unpaid principal balance of any junior liens over 12 months old as of the date of mortgage Disbursement. If the balance or any portion of an equity line of credit in excess of $1,000 was advanced within the past 12 months and was for purposes other than repairs and rehabilitation of the Property, that portion above and beyond $1,000 of the line of credit is not eligible for inclusion in the new Mortgage;
      - ex-spouse or co-Borrower equity, as described in "Refinancing to Buy out Title Holder Equity" below;
      - interest due on the existing Mortgage(s);
      - the unpaid principal balance of any unpaid PACE obligation;
      - Mortgage Insurance Premium (MIP) due on existing Mortgage;
      - any prepayment penalties assessed;
      - late charges; and
      - escrow shortages;
    - allowed costs include all Borrower paid costs associated with the new Mortgage; and
    - any Borrower-paid repairs required by the appraisal;
- less any refund of the Upfront Mortgage Insurance Premium (UFMIP).

Short Payoffs

The Mortgagee may approve a Rate and Term refinance where the maximum mortgage amount is insufficient to extinguish the existing mortgage debt, provided the existing Note holder writes off the amount of the indebtedness that cannot be refinanced into the new FHA-insured Mortgage.

Refinancing to Buy Out Title-Holder Equity

When the purpose of the new Mortgage is to refinance an existing Mortgage to buy out an existing title-holder's equity, the specified equity to be paid is considered property-related indebtedness and eligible to be included in the new mortgage calculation. The Mortgagee must obtain the divorce decree, settlement agreement, or other legally enforceable equity agreement to document the equity awarded to the title-holder.

Refinancing to Pay off Recorded Land Contracts

When the purpose of the new Mortgage is to pay off an outstanding recorded land contract, the unpaid principal balance will be deemed to be the outstanding balance on the recorded land contract.

Use of Estimates in Calculating Maximum Mortgage Amount

The Mortgagee may utilize estimates of existing debts and costs in calculating the maximum mortgage amount to the extent that the actual debts and costs do not result in the Borrower receiving greater than $500 cash back at mortgage Disbursement.

Cash to the Borrower resulting from the refund of Borrowers unused escrow balance from the previous Mortgage must not be considered in the $500 cash back limit whether received at or subsequent to mortgage Disbursement.

Excess Cash Back

When the estimated costs utilized in calculating the maximum mortgage amount result in greater than $500 cash back to the Borrower at mortgage Disbursement, Mortgagees may reduce the Borrower's outstanding principal balance to satisfy the $500 cash back requirement. The Mortgagee must submit the Mortgage for endorsement at the reduced principal amount.

(ii) Required Documentation

The Mortgagee must obtain the payoff statement on all existing Mortgages.

(c) Maximum Combined Loan-to-Value Ratio

The maximum CLTV ratio for a Rate and Term refinance is 97.75 percent. For open-end line of credit, the Mortgagee must utilize the maximum accessible credit limit of the subordinate lien to calculate the CLTV ratio.

(3) Refinance of HOPE for Homeowners Mortgages

If the Mortgage being refinanced is a HOPE for Homeowners Mortgage, the Mortgagee must refer to the requirements in the HOPE for Homeowners Servicing Section.

(B) Simple Refinance

(1) Borrower Eligibility

(a) Occupancy Requirements

(i) Standard

Simple Refinance is only permissible for owner-occupied Principal or HUD-approved Secondary Residences.

(ii) Required Documentation

The Mortgagee must review the Borrower's employment documentation or obtain utility bills to evidence the Borrower currently occupies the Property as their Principal Residence.

The Mortgagee must obtain evidence that the Secondary Residence has been approved by the Jurisdictional HOC.

(b) Payment History Requirements (Manually Underwritten)

(i) Standard

For all mortgages on all properties with less than six months of Mortgage Payment history, the Borrower must have made all payments within the month due.

For all mortgages on all properties with greater than six months history, the Borrower must have made all Mortgage Payments within the month due for the six months prior to case number assignment and have no more than one 30-Day late payment for the previous six months for all mortgages.

The Borrower must have made the payments for all Mortgages secured by the subject Property for the month prior to mortgage Disbursement.

(ii) Required Documentation

If the Mortgage on the subject Property is not reported in the Borrower's credit report, the Mortgagee must obtain a verification of Mortgage to evidence payment history for the previous 12 months.

(2) Maximum Mortgage Amount

(a) Maximum LTV

The maximum LTV ratio for a Simple Refinance is:
- 97.75 percent for Principal Residences; and
- 85 percent for HUD-approved Secondary Residences.

(b) Maximum CLTV

The maximum CLTV for a Simple Refinance is:
- 97.75 percent for Principal Residences; and
- 85 percent for HUD-approved Secondary Residences.

(3) Calculating Maximum Mortgage Amount for Simple Refinance Transactions

(a) Standard

The maximum mortgage amount for a Simple Refinance is:
- the lesser of:
  - the Nationwide Mortgage Limit;
  - the Maximum LTV ratio from above; or
  - the sum of existing debt and costs associated with the transaction as follows:
    - existing debt includes:
      - unpaid principal balance of the FHA-insured first Mortgage as of the month prior to mortgage Disbursement;
      - interest due on the existing Mortgage;
      - the unpaid principal balance of any PACE obligation;
      - MIP due on existing Mortgage;
      - late charges; and
      - escrow shortages;
    - allowed costs include all Borrower paid costs associated with the new Mortgage; and
    - Borrower-paid repairs required by the appraisal;
- less any refund of UFMIP.

(b) Use of Estimates in Calculating Maximum Mortgage Amount

The Mortgagee may utilize estimates of existing debts and costs in calculating the maximum mortgage amount to the extent that the actual debts and costs do not result in the Borrower receiving greater than $500 cash back at mortgage Disbursement.

Cash to the Borrower resulting from the refund of Borrower's unused escrow balance from the previous Mortgage must not be considered in the $500 cash back limit whether received at or subsequent to mortgage Disbursement.

(c) Excess Cash Back

When the estimated costs utilized in calculating the maximum mortgage amount resulted in greater than $500 cash back to the Borrower at mortgage Disbursement, Mortgagees may reduce the Borrower's outstanding principal balance to satisfy the $500 cash back requirement.

(d) Required Documentation

The Mortgagee must obtain the payoff statement for the existing Mortgage being refinanced.

(4) Upfront and Annual Mortgage Insurance Premium

See Appendix 1.0 – Mortgage Insurance Premiums for assessing upfront and annual MIP.

(C) Streamline Refinances

Streamline Refinance may be used when the proceeds of the Mortgage are used to extinguish an existing FHA-insured first mortgage lien. Mortgagees must manually underwrite all Streamline Refinances in accordance with the guidance provided in this section.

(1) Streamline Refinance Exemptions

(a) Non-Credit Qualifying Exemptions

Unless otherwise stated in this section, the following sections of Origination through Post-Closing/ Endorsement do not apply to non-credit qualifying Streamline Refinances:
- Ordering Appraisal
- Transferring Existing Appraisal
- Ordering Second Appraisal
- Ordering an Update to an Appraisal
- Borrower Minimum Decision Credit Score

- Borrower and Co-Borrower Ownership and Obligation Requirements
- Cosigner Requirements
- Principal Residence in the United States
- Military Personnel Eligibility
- Citizenship and Immigration Status
- Residency Requirements
- Borrower Ineligibility Due to Delinquent Federal Non-Tax Debt
- Delinquent Federal Tax Debt
- Property Eligibility and Acceptability Criteria
- National Housing Act's Statutory Limits
- Nationwide Mortgage Limits
- LTV Limitations Based on Borrower's Credit Score
- Underwriting the Property
- Underwriting the Borrower Using the TOTAL Mortgage Scorecard
- Credit Requirements (Manual)
- Income Requirements (Manual)
- Asset Requirements (Manual)
- Underwriting of Credit and Debt (Manual)
- Underwriting of Income (Manual)
- Underwriting of Assets (Manual)
- Calculating Qualifying Ratios (Manual)
- Approvable Ratio Requirements (Manual)
- Documenting Acceptable Compensating Factors (Manual)

(b) Credit Qualifying Exemptions

The following sections of Origination through Post-Closing/ Endorsement do not apply to credit qualifying Streamline Refinances:
- Ordering Appraisal
- Transferring Existing Appraisal
- Ordering Second Appraisal
- Ordering an Update to an Appraisal
- Borrower Ineligibility Due to Delinquent Federal Non-Tax Debt
- Delinquent Federal Tax Debt
- Property Eligibility and Acceptability Criteria
- National Housing Act's Statutory Limits
- Nationwide Mortgage Limits
- LTV Limitations Based on Borrower's Credit Score
- Underwriting the Property
- Underwriting the Borrower Using the TOTAL Mortgage Scorecard

(2) Borrower Eligibility

(a) Occupancy Requirements

(i) Standard

Streamline Refinances may be used for Principal Residences, HUD-approved Secondary Residences, or non-owner occupied Properties.

(ii) Required Documentation

The Mortgagee must review the Borrower's employment documentation or obtain utility bills to evidence that the Borrower currently occupies the Property as their Principal Residence.

The Mortgagee must obtain evidence that the Secondary Residence has been approved by the Jurisdictional HOC.

The Mortgagee must process the Streamline Refinance as a non-owner occupied Property if the Mortgagee cannot obtain evidence that the Borrower occupies the Property either as a Principal or Secondary Residence.

(b) Payment History Requirements

(i) Standard

Non-Credit Qualifying

The Borrower must have made all Mortgage Payments for all Mortgages on the subject Property within the month due for the six months prior to case number assignment and have no more than one 30-Day late payment for the previous six months for all Mortgages on the subject Property. The Borrower must have made the payments for all Mortgages secured by the subject Property within the month due for the month prior to mortgage Disbursement.

Credit Qualifying

For all mortgages on all properties with less than six months of Mortgage Payment history, the Borrower must have made all payments within the month due.

For all mortgages on all properties with greater than six months of Mortgage Payment history, the Borrower must have made all Mortgage Payments within the month due for the six months prior to case number assignment and have no more than one 30-Day late payment for the previous six months.

The Borrower must have made the payments for all Mortgages secured by the subject Property within the month due for the month prior to mortgage Disbursement.

(ii) Required Documentation

If the Mortgage on the subject Property is not reported in the Borrower's credit report, the Mortgagee must obtain a verification of Mortgage to evidence payment history for the previous 12 months.

(3) Non-owner Occupied Properties and HUD-Approved Secondary Residences

Non-owner occupied Properties and HUD-approved Secondary Residences are only eligible for Streamline Refinancing into a fixed rate Mortgage.

(4) General Information Applicable to All Streamline Refinances

(a) Mortgage Seasoning Requirements

On the date of the FHA case number assignment:
- the Borrower must have made at least six payments on the FHA-insured Mortgage that is being refinanced;
- at least six full months must have passed since the first payment due date of the Mortgage that is being refinanced;
- at least 210 Days must have passed from the Closing Date of the Mortgage that is being refinanced; and
- if the Borrower assumed the Mortgage that is being refinanced, they must have made six payments since the time of assumption.

(b) Use of TOTAL Mortgage Scorecard on Streamline Refinances

The Mortgagee must manually underwrite all Streamline Refinances. The Mortgagee may score the Mortgage through TOTAL Mortgage Scorecard but the findings are invalid.

(c) Net Tangible Benefit of Streamline Refinances

(i) Definitions

A Net Tangible Benefit is a reduced Combined Rate, a change from an ARM to a fixed rate Mortgage, and/or a reduced term that results in a financial benefit to the Borrower.

Combined Rate refers to the interest rate on the Mortgage plus the Mortgage Insurance Premium (MIP) rate.

Reduction in Term refers to the reduction of the remaining amortization period of the existing Mortgage.

(ii) Standard for Refinances without a Term Reduction

The Mortgagee must determine that there is a net tangible benefit to the Borrower meeting the standards in the chart below for all Streamline Refinance transactions without a reduction in term.

From	To		
	Fixed Rate New Combined Rate	**One-Year ARM New Combined Rate**	**Hybrid ARM New Combined Rate**
Fixed Rate	At least 0.5 percentage points below the prior Combined Rate.	At least 2 percentage points below the prior Combined Rate.	At least 2 percentage points below the prior Combined Rate.
Any ARM With Less Than 15 Months to Next Payment Change Date	No more than 2 percentage points above the prior Combined Rate.	At least 1 percentage point below the prior Combined Rate.	At least 1 percentage point below the prior Combined Rate.
Any ARM With Greater Than or Equal to 15 Months to Next Payment Change Date	No more than 2 percentage points above the prior Combined Rate.	At least 2 percentage points below the prior Combined Rate.	At least 1 percentage point below the prior Combined Rate.

(iii) Standard for Refinances with a Term Reduction

The Mortgagee must determine that there is a net tangible benefit to the Borrower meeting the standards in the chart below for all Streamline Refinance transactions with a reduction in term.

Additionally, the combined principal, interest, and MIP payment of the new Mortgage must not exceed the combined principal, interest, and MIP payment of the refinanced Mortgage by more than $50.

From	To		
	Fixed Rate New Combined Rate	**One-Year ARM New Combined Rate**	**Hybrid ARM New Combined Rate**
Fixed Rate	Below the prior Combined Rate.	N/A	N/A

From	To		
	Fixed Rate New Combined Rate	**One-Year ARM New Combined Rate**	**Hybrid ARM New Combined Rate**
Any ARM With Less Than 15 Months to Next Payment Change Date	No more than 2 percentage points above the prior Combined Rate.	N/A	N/A
Any ARM With Greater Than or Equal to 15 Months to Next Payment Change Date	No more than 2 percentage points above the prior Combined Rate.	N/A	N/A

(d) HUD Employee Mortgage

For non-credit qualifying Streamline Refinances only, any HUD employee may have their Mortgage underwritten and approved/denied by the Mortgagee.

(e) Reviewing Limited Denial Participation and SAM Exclusion Lists

The Mortgagee must check the HUD Limited Denial of Participation (LDP) list to confirm the Borrower's eligibility to participate in an FHA-insured mortgage transaction.

The Mortgagee must check the System for Award Management (SAM) (www.sam.gov) and must follow appropriate procedures defined by that system to confirm eligibility for participation.

(f) Borrower Additions to Title

Individuals may be added to the title and Mortgage on a non-credit qualifying Streamline Refinance without a creditworthiness review.

(g) Borrower Credit Reports

FHA does not require a credit report on the non-credit qualifying Streamline Refinance. The Mortgagee must obtain a credit report for the credit qualifying Streamline Refinance.

If the Mortgagee obtains a credit score, the Mortgagee must enter it into FHAC. If more than one credit score is obtained, the Mortgagee must enter all available credit scores into FHAC.

Handbook 4000.1   424
Effective Date: 09/14/2015 | Last Revised: 07/10/2019
*Refer to the online version of SF Handbook 4000.1 for specific sections' effective dates

(h) Funds to Close

The Mortgagee must verify Borrower's funds to close, in excess of the total Mortgage Payment of the new Mortgage, in accordance with the applicable sections of Sources of Funds.

Additionally, the Mortgagee may provide an unsecured interest-free loan to establish a new escrow account in an amount not to exceed the present escrow balance on the existing Mortgage.

(i) Maximum Mortgage Amortization Period

The maximum amortization period of a Streamline Refinance is limited to the lesser of:
- the remaining amortization period of the existing Mortgage plus 12 years; or
- 30 years.

(j) Maximum Mortgage Calculation for Streamline Refinances

(i) Standard

For owner-occupied Principal Residences and HUD-approved Secondary Residences, the maximum Base Loan Amount for Streamline Refinances is:
- the lesser of:
  - the outstanding principal balance of the existing Mortgage as of the month prior to mortgage Disbursement; plus:
    - interest due on the existing Mortgage; and
    - MIP due on existing Mortgage; or
  - the original principal balance of the existing Mortgage (including financed UFMIP);
- less any refund of UFMIP.

For Investment Properties, the maximum Base Loan Amount for Streamline Refinances is:
- the lesser of:
  - the outstanding principal balance of the existing Mortgage as of the month prior to mortgage Disbursement; or
  - the original principal balance of the existing Mortgage (including financed UFMIP);
- less any refund of UFMIP.

Use of Estimates in Calculating Maximum Mortgage Amount

The Mortgagee may utilize estimates in calculating the maximum mortgage amount to the extent that the total mortgage amount does not result in the Borrower receiving greater than $500 cash back at mortgage Disbursement.

Cash to the Borrower resulting from the refund of Borrowers unused escrow balance from the previous Mortgage must not be considered in the $500 cash back limit whether received at or subsequent to mortgage Disbursement.

Excess Cash Back

When the estimates utilized in calculating the maximum mortgage amount resulted in greater than $500 cash back to the Borrower at mortgage Disbursement, Mortgagees may reduce the Borrower's outstanding principal balance to satisfy the $500 cash back requirement.

(ii) Required Documentation

The Mortgagee must obtain the payoff statement on the existing Mortgage.

(k) Maximum CLTV Ratio and Subordinate Financing

Existing Subordinate financing, in place at the time of case number assignment, must be resubordinated to the Streamline Refinance. New Subordinate financing is permitted only where the proceeds of the subordinate financing are used to:
- reduce the principal amount of the existing FHA-insured Mortgage; or
- finance the origination fees, other closing costs, prepaid items, or discount points associated with the refinance.

There is no maximum CLTV.

Mortgagees must contact the National Servicing Center for processing of any HUD held lien subordination.

(l) Appraisal and Inspection Requirements on Streamline Refinances

Appraisals are not required on Streamline Refinances. The receipt or possession of an appraisal by the Mortgagee does not affect the eligibility or maximum mortgage amount on Streamline Refinances.

(m) Assessing Upfront and Annual MIP

See Appendix 1.0 – Mortgage Insurance Premiums for assessing upfront and annual MIP.

For the purpose of calculating the MIP, FHA uses the original value of the Property to calculate the LTV.

(n) HOPE for Homeowners Mortgages

HOPE for Homeowners Mortgages may not be refinanced using the FHA streamline process.

(5) Streamline Refinance Non-Credit Qualifying

(a) Borrower Eligibility

A Borrower is eligible for a Streamline Refinance without credit qualification if all Borrowers on the existing Mortgage remain as Borrowers on the new Mortgage. Mortgages that have been assumed are eligible provided the previous Borrower was released from liability.

Exception

A Borrower on the Mortgage to be paid may be removed from title and new Mortgage in cases of divorce, legal separation or death when:
- the divorce decree or legal separation agreement awarded the Property and responsibility for payment to the remaining Borrower, if applicable; and
- the remaining Borrower can demonstrate that they have made the Mortgage Payments for a minimum of six months prior to case number assignment.

(b) Special Documentation and Procedures for Non-Credit Qualifying Streamline Refinances

Mortgagees may use an abbreviated *Uniform Residential Loan Application* (*URLA*, Fannie Mae Form 1003/Freddie Mac Form 65) on non-credit qualifying Streamline Refinances only. Mortgagees are not required to complete sections IV, V, VI, and VIII (a-k) on an abbreviated *URLA*, provided all other required information is captured.

(6) Streamline Refinance Credit Qualifying

(a) Borrower Eligibility

At least one Borrower from the existing Mortgage must remain as a Borrower on the new Mortgage.

(b) Credit Underwriting

In addition to the requirements in this section, credit qualifying Streamline Refinances must meet all requirements of Manual Underwriting, except for any requirements for Appraisals or LTV Calculations.

e. Refinance of Borrowers in Negative Equity Positions Program (Short Refi) [EXPIRED]

i. Definition

The Short Refi program allows the Mortgagee to refinance a non FHA-insured Mortgage in which the Borrower is in a negative equity position.

ii. General Eligibility Criteria

The existing first lien holder must write off at least 10 percent of the unpaid principal balance.

The Borrower must be in a negative equity position and may not have an existing FHA-insured Mortgage. The Borrower must be current for the month due or have successfully completed a three month trial payment plan on the existing Mortgage to be refinanced.

The Mortgagee is not permitted to use Premium Pricing to pay off existing debt obligations to qualify the Borrower for the new Mortgage.

The Mortgagee is not permitted to make Mortgage Payments on behalf of the Borrower or otherwise bring the existing Mortgage current to make it eligible for FHA insurance.

The refinanced FHA-insured first Mortgage must have a Loan-to-Value (LTV) ratio of no more than 97.75 percent and any new or re-subordinated Mortgages must not result in a Combined Loan-to-Value (CLTV) ratio greater than 115 percent.

There is no maximum CLTV ratio for second liens held by Governmental Entities or Instrumentalities of Government.

All Mortgages under the program must close on or before December 31, 2016.

(A) Borrower Certification

(1) Standard

The Borrower must certify on form HUD-92918, *FHA Refinance of Borrowers in Negative Equity Positions Borrower Certification,* that they have not been convicted within the last 10 years, in connection with a real estate or mortgage transaction, of any of the following: (a) felony larceny, theft, fraud, or forgery; (b) money laundering; or (c) tax evasion from receiving assistance authorized or funded by the Emergency Economic Stabilization Act of 2008 (EESA).

(2) Required Documentation

The executed Borrower certification must be included in the FHA case binder submitted for insurance endorsement.

(B) Trial Payment Plan

(1) Standard

A Borrower who is delinquent on their current Mortgage must successfully make three on-time payments on a trial payment plan before closing.

At the time of underwriting the new FHA-insured Mortgage, the new total monthly Mortgage Payment amount cannot increase by more than 6 percent over the trial payment amount on the existing Mortgage.

(2) Required Documentation

The Mortgagee must document in the case binder the Borrower's successful completion of the most recent trial payment plan.

(C) Secondary Financing

New or re-subordinated secondary financing that permits the Borrower to comply with the eligibility requirements of the program is permitted, subject to the following limitations:

- the terms of the subordinate lien(s) must not provide for a balloon payment before 10 years, unless the Property is sold or refinanced;
- the terms must permit prepayment by the Borrower, without penalty, after giving 30 Days advance notice;
- periodic payments, if any, must be collected monthly; and
- if payments on subordinate financing are required, they must be included in the qualifying ratios unless payments are deferred until at least 36 months after Disbursement.

iii. Underwriting

The Borrower must qualify for the new Mortgage under the applicable TOTAL Underwriting or Manual Underwriting requirements, except for the credit, debt-to-income and new mortgage requirements below.

(A) Credit Requirements

The existing Mortgage to be refinanced may not have been brought current by the existing first lien holder, except through an acceptable trial payment plan.

(B) Debt-to-Income Ratios

For Mortgages that receive a Refer risk classification from FHA's Technology Open To Approved Lenders (TOTAL) Mortgage Scorecard and/or are manually underwritten, the homeowner's total monthly Mortgage Payment, including the first and any subordinate Mortgage(s), cannot be greater than 31 percent of gross monthly income; and total debt, including all recurring debts, cannot be greater than 50 percent of the gross monthly income.

Exception

The Borrower's monthly total Mortgage Payment may be up to 35 percent of gross monthly income if their total debt does not exceed 48 percent of the gross monthly income.

(C) New Mortgage

(1) Write-off

The existing first lien holder must write off at least 10 percent of the unpaid principal balance of the Mortgage that is being refinanced.

(2) Mortgage Type and Automated Data Processing Codes

The Mortgagee must enter the Mortgage as a "conventional to FHA refinance non delinquent" in FHA Connection (FHAC).

The Mortgagee must refer to the FHAC ADP Codes for Short Refinance codes.

f. Section 251 Adjustable Rate Mortgages

i. Definition

An Adjustable Rate Mortgage (ARM) refers to a Mortgage in which the interest rate can change annually based on an index plus a margin.

ii. Required Disclosures

The Borrower must sign a disclosure that explains the terms of the ARM at mortgage application.

iii. ARM Types

The Mortgagee must establish the initial interest rate and the margin. The margin must be constant for the entire term of the Mortgage.

The interest rate must remain constant for an initial period of 1, 3, 5, 7, or 10 years, depending on the ARM program chosen by the Borrower, and then may change annually for the remainder of the mortgage term.

A 1- and 3-year ARM may increase by one percentage point annually after the initial fixed interest rate period, and five percentage points over the life of the Mortgage.

A 5-year ARM may either allow for increases of one percentage point annually, and five percentage points over the life of the Mortgage; or increases of two percentage points annually, and six points over the life of the Mortgage.

A 7- and 10-year ARM may only increase by two percentage points annually after the initial fixed interest rate period, and six percentage points over the life of the Mortgage.

iv. Initial Interest Rate Adjustments

The first interest rate adjustment must occur in accordance with the following chart:

If the ARM is initially at a fixed interest rate for ...	Then the first adjustment rate change may occur no sooner than ...	And no later than ...
1 year	12 months	18 months.
3 years	36 months	42 months.
5 years	60 months	66 months.
7 years	84 months	90 months.
10 years	120 months	126 months.

v. Indices

The interest rate governing index may be the 1-Year Constant Maturity Treasury (CMT) or 1-Year London Interbank Offered Rate (LIBOR).

The 1-Year CMT is the weekly average yield on U.S. Treasury Securities, adjusted to a constant maturity of one year published in the Federal Reserve Board's Statistical Release H.15(519).

The 1-Year LIBOR is the London Interbank Offered Rate as published in the Wall Street Journal on the first business day of each week.

vi. Temporary Interest Rate Buydowns

Temporary interest rate buydowns are not permitted with ARM transactions.

vii. Underwriting Requirements

The Mortgagee must underwrite the Mortgage based on payments calculated using the initial interest rate.

1-year ARMs

If the Loan-to-Value (LTV) is 95 percent or more, the Mortgagee must underwrite the Mortgage based on payments calculated using the initial interest rate plus one percent.

If the Mortgage is less than 95 percent, the Mortgagee must underwrite the Mortgage based on payments calculated using the initial interest rate.

viii. Mortgage Term

The ARM must be fully amortizing over a period of no more than 30 years.

ix. Required Documentation

(A) Model Note

The Mortgagee must use the Model ARM Note for all ARMs. Paragraph 1 of this form must be adapted or additional paragraphs may be added to provide a full description of the adjustable rate feature of the Mortgage to the extent required by state or local law to create an enforceable agreement.

The Mortgagee must ensure that the ARM Note contains amortization provisions that allow for annual adjustments in the rate of interest charged.

(B) Mortgage Document

The mortgage documents for an ARM must specify the:

- initial interest rate;
- margin;
- date of the first adjustment to the interest rate; and
- frequency of adjustments.

g. Section 248 Mortgages on Indian Land

i. Definitions

A Section 248 Mortgage on Indian Land refers to a purchase or refinance Mortgage covering one- to four-family dwellings on Indian Lands.

Indian Land refers to those lands that are held by or for the benefit of Indian Tribes under some restriction or with some attribute peculiar to the legal status of its owners.

Indian Tribe refers to any Indian or Alaskan native tribe, band, nation, or other organized group or community of Indians or Alaskan natives recognized as eligible for the services provided to Indians or Alaskan natives by the Secretary of Interior because of its status as such an Entity, or that was an eligible recipient under Chapter 67 of title 31, United States Code, prior to the repeal of this section.

ii. Eligibility

(A) Standard

The Mortgagee must obtain documentation from the Indian/Native American that the Indian Land/reservation has adopted eviction procedures acceptable to HUD.

(B) Required Documentation

The Mortgagee must obtain a certification from the Indian Tribe confirming the Indian Land/reservations compliance with HUD's requirements. The Mortgagee must include the certification in the mortgage file and take the following measures:
- certify to HUD that it has adopted eviction procedures and will enforce them;
- permit HUD access to tribal lands for the purpose of servicing Properties;
- agree to the lease form that HUD prescribes; and
- enact a law that grants the tribal government's court the jurisdiction to hear evictions and foreclosures so that FHA-insured and FHA-held Mortgages can be assured a first lien or provides that the law of the state in which the Property is located determines the priority of liens against the Property. If the reservation spans two or more states, the state in which the Property is located is the applicable state law.

(C) Borrower Eligibility

Only an Indian Tribe or a member of the Indian Tribe may be a Borrower. Where there is a co-Borrower, at least one Borrower must be an Indian Tribe or a member of the Indian Tribe. The Borrower must occupy the Property as their Principal Residence.

(D) Property Eligibility

The Property must be located on land held by the Indian Tribe or held by the United States government for the benefit of the Indian Tribe.

Units in cooperatives are not eligible.

The Borrower must hold a Residential Lease for the Property.

(E) First Lien Status

The Mortgages must be secured by a first lien on the Property that has been filed with the state recording system and with the Bureau of Indian Affairs, U.S. Department of the Interior.

(F) Assumptions

The Mortgagee cannot approve an assumption of a Mortgage secured by a Property located on an Indian Land/reservation unless the Indian Tribe has approved the assumption or sale of the rights to the Property securing the Mortgage. The Mortgagee must comply with all requirements for assumptions.

(G) Lease and Mortgage

The model Lease and model Mortgage Rider must be used in connection with any Section 248 Mortgages. Modifications may be made to the Section 248 rider with the approval of the Jurisdictional HOC.

The term of the lease must be 25 years with a provision for an automatic extension of an additional 25 years.

The lease must prohibit termination by either or both parties while the Leasehold is mortgaged under Section 248.

iii. Underwriting

(A) Tribal Leasehold and Taxes

The Mortgagee must obtain tax information on the Leasehold from the tribe and include the payment of such taxes in the calculation of the Borrower's Mortgage Payment as is done with local property taxes.

(B) Mortgage Insurance Premiums

The Section 248 program does not require an Upfront Mortgage Insurance Premium (UFMIP). Annual premiums are found in Appendix 1.0 – Mortgage Insurance Premiums.

iv. Valuation

The Mortgagee must ensure that the appraisal of the Property meets the requirements specified in the <u>Appraisal of Single Family Housing on Indian Lands</u> section of the Appraiser requirements.

h. Section 247 Single Family Mortgage Insurance on Hawaiian Home Lands

i. Definition

FHA insures Mortgages made to Native Hawaiians to purchase or refinance one- to four-family dwellings located on Hawaiian Home Lands, which are owned by the State of Hawaii, Department of Hawaiian Home Lands (DHHL) and leased to Native Hawaiians for 99 year lease terms.

ii. Eligibility Requirements

(A) Borrower Eligibility

(1) Native Hawaiian

A Borrower must be a native Hawaiian who is at least 18 years of age and certified as eligible to hold a Hawaiian Home Lands Lease, or possesses a lease of Hawaiian Home Lands issued under Section 207(a) of the Hawaiian Homes Commission Act, 1920, that has been certified by DHHL as being a valid current lease, and not in default.

Native Hawaiian means a descendant of not less than 50 percent part of the blood of the races inhabiting the Hawaiian Islands before January 1, 1778 (or, in the case of an individual who succeeds a spouse or parent in an interest in a lease of Hawaiian Home Lands, such lower percentage as may be established for such succession under Section 209 of the Hawaiian Homes Commission Act, 1920, or under the corresponding provision of the constitution of the State of Hawaii adopted under Section 4 of the Act entitled, "An Act to provide for the admission of the State of Hawaii into the Union," approved March 18, 1959). 12 U.S.C. § 1715z-12(d)(1).

(2) Principal Residence

The Property must be the Borrower's Principal Residence (leased land condominiums and townhomes are allowed).

(3) Co-Borrower

DHHL may be a co-Borrower on the Mortgage.

(B) Mortgaged Property Location

The mortgaged Property must be located within the Hawaiian Home Lands covered under a homestead lease issued under Section 207(a) of Hawaiian Homes Commission Act, 1920, or under the corresponding provision of the Constitution of the State of Hawaii adopted under Section 4 of the Act entitled "An Act to provide for the admission of the State of Hawaii into the Union," approved March 18, 1959 (73 Stat. 5).

iii. Required Documentation

(A) Certificate of Eligibility

Certificates of Eligibility are issued by DHHL and certify that the Borrower possesses a homestead lease in good standing (not canceled or in default).

The Mortgagee must verify and obtain documentation that the Borrower has a Certificate of Eligibility for an existing Hawaiian Home Land lease issued by DHHL, or possesses a lease of Hawaiian Home Lands issued under Section 207(a) of the Hawaiian Homes Commission Act, 1920 (42 Stat. 110).

Obtaining a Certificate of Eligibility

To obtain a Certificate of Eligibility, the Mortgagee must submit a Request for Certification of Eligibility form to the DHHL. DHHL will issue the Certification of Eligibility to the Mortgagee.

(B) Copy of Homestead Lease

The Mortgagee must obtain a recorded copy of either (1) the original homestead lease issued by DHHL that identifies the proposed Borrower as the lessee; or (2) the original homestead lease plus documentation of the chain of succession or assignment of the homestead lease to the Borrower and DHHL's consent to each and every transfer of the homestead lease. If the lease was issued prior the development of the Hawaii State recording system, the Mortgagee must provide written confirmation from DHHL or provide other evidence that the lease was validly issued to the lessee.

The Mortgagee must document all amendments to the original homestead lease. All homestead lease documents must bear evidence of having been recorded at the DHHL.

(C) DHHL Mortgage Insurance Program Rider

The Mortgagee must obtain an executed copy of the DHHL Mortgage Insurance Program Rider. This rider must be recorded in DHHL's recording system.

(D) DHHL Mortgage Form

The Mortgagee must use the DHHL Mortgage Form. The Mortgagee must certify and document that the Mortgage has been recorded with DHHL.

(E) DHHL Consent to Mortgage

The Mortgagee must obtain a "Consent to Mortgage" executed by the Chairman of the Hawaiian Homes Commission and recorded with DHHL. Mortgagees can obtain this form by writing to the Department of Hawaiian Home Lands, Attn: Loan Services Branch.

iv. Appraisal

Mortgagees are required to obtain only a Cost Approach Appraisal for both Existing and Proposed Construction. The Market and Sales Comparison Approaches are not required.

The following statement may be included on the Uniform Standards of Professional Appraisal Practices (USPAP): "The final value stated in this appraisal is not 'market value' as defined in USPAP. This appraisal has been completed for FHA mortgage insurance purposes, per HUD instructions for DHHL Properties." For more information on appraisal requirements, refer to the Appraiser section.

v. Origination

(A) Loan-to-Value Limits for Cash-Out Refinances

The maximum LTV ratio for refinance loans is 75 percent.

The maximum LTV may be increased to 85 percent when the Borrower is paying off an existing Mortgage and all remaining proceeds are used for documented home improvements.

Cash-out refinancing for the purpose of debt consolidation is not allowed.

(B) Mortgage Insurance Premium

The Mortgage Insurance Premium (MIP) payment on a Section 247 Mortgage is a one-time upfront MIP of 380 Basis Points (bps).

Annual or periodic MIPs are not assessed on Section 247 Mortgages.

vi. Underwriting

For refinance transactions, for the purpose of consolidating debt, the Mortgagee must include all debt, including those being paid off through the refinance, when calculating the Borrower's debt ratio.

vii. Closing

(A) Lien Position

The Section 247 Mortgage must give rise to a valid and secured interest in the mortgaged Property. However, the lien is not required to be in first position.

(B) Recordation

The Mortgage must be recorded in DHHL's recording system upon closing of the Mortgage. The documents must **not** be recorded at the State of Hawaii Bureau of Conveyances or filed with the Office of Assistant Registrar of the Land Court. Recordation at either of these offices does not effectuate a lien on the Hawaiian Home Lands lease.

i. New Construction

i. Definitions

New Construction refers to Proposed Construction, Properties Under Construction, and Properties Existing Less than One Year as defined below:

- Proposed Construction refers to a Property where no concrete or permanent material has been placed. Digging of footing is not considered permanent.
- Under Construction refers to the period from the first placement of permanent material to 100 percent completion with no Certificate of Occupancy (CO) or equivalent.
- Existing Less than One Year refers to a Property that is 100 percent complete and has been completed less than one year from the date of the issuance of the CO or equivalent. The Property must have never been occupied.

FHA treats the sale of an occupied Property that has been completed less than one year from the issuance of the CO or equivalent as an existing Property.

Pre-Approval refers to Properties that are less than one year old and meet one of the following requirements:

- the Property was appraised and the Mortgagee issued form HUD-92800.5B, *Conditional Commitment Direct Endorsement Statement of Appraised Value*, before construction started;
- a building permit or its equivalent has been issued by a local jurisdiction (not applicable to Manufactured Housing); or
- the Mortgagee issued an Early Start Letter.

Early Start Letter refers to the document issued by the Mortgagee in response to a builder's request to start construction before the appraisal is completed. The Early Start Letter indicates the Mortgagee's approval of the Property before issuance of form HUD 92800.5B and without affecting the maximum mortgage amount. The Mortgagee can issue the Early Start Letter if local jurisdiction has issued a building permit, in jurisdictions that require building permits, and a case number has been assigned. The Mortgagee can issue the Early Start Letter in jurisdictions that do not require building permits if a case number has been assigned.

ii. Inspections or Warranties for Maximum Financing

(A) Site Built Housing and Condominiums (By Construction Status at Time of Appraisal)

(1) Proposed Construction

The Mortgagee must obtain one of the following:

- copies of the building permit and CO (or equivalent);

- three inspections (footing, framing and final) performed by an ICC RCI or CI on form HUD-92051, *Compliance Inspection Report* (for Modular Housing, footing and final only); or
- three inspections (footing, framing and final) performed by the local authority with jurisdiction over the Property (for Modular Housing, footing and final only).

(2) Under-Construction

The Mortgagee must obtain:
- copies of the building permit and CO (or equivalent); or
- a final inspection issued by the local authority with jurisdiction over the Property or an ICC RCI or CI.

(3) Existing for Less than One Year (100 Percent Complete)

The Mortgagee must obtain:
- a copy of the CO (or equivalent); or
- a final inspection issued by the local authority with jurisdiction over the Property or an ICC RCI or CI.

(B) Manufactured Housing (By Construction Status at Time of Appraisal) Inspection Requirements for Maximum Financing

(1) Proposed Construction

The Mortgagee must obtain:
- two inspections (initial and final) performed by an ICC RCI or CI; or
- two inspections (initial and final) performed by the certifying engineer or architect.

(2) Under Construction

The Mortgagee must obtain a final inspection issued by the ICC RCI or CI or certifying engineer or architect.

(3) Existing for Less than One Year (100 Percent Complete)

The Mortgagee must obtain a final inspection issued by the ICC RCI or CI or certifying engineer or architect.

HUD will only accept inspections by a local building authority on Manufactured Housing Properties with jurisdiction over the Property if there are no ICC RCIs or CIs or certifying engineers or architects available to perform these inspections.

iii. Required Documentation for Maximum Financing

The Mortgagee must obtain and include the following documents in the case binder:
- form HUD-92541, *Builder's Certification of Plans, Specifications, and Site;*
- form HUD-92544, *Warranty of Completion of Construction;*
- evidence that the Property was pre-approved, with an Early Start Letter or copy of building permit issued by local authority prior to start of construction;
- required inspections, as applicable;
- Wood Infestation Report, unless the Property is located in an area of no to slight infestation as indicated on HUD's "Termite Treatment Exception Areas" list:
  - Form HUD-NPMA-99-A, *Subterranean Termite Protection Builder's Guarantee,* is required for all New Construction. If the building is constructed with steel, masonry or concrete building components with only minor interior wood trim and roof sheathing, no treatment is needed. The Mortgagee must ensure that the builder notes on the form that the construction is masonry, steel, or concrete.
  - Form HUD-NPMA-99-B, *New Construction Subterranean Termite Service Record,* is required when the proposed Property is treated with a soil chemical termiticide. The Mortgagee must reject the use of post construction soil treatment when the termiticide is applied only around the perimeter of the foundation.
- local Health Authority well water analysis and/or septic report, where required by the local jurisdictional authority.

iv. Financing LTV Limit

Properties that are Under Construction or Existing for Less than One Year are limited to a 90 percent LTV unless they meet the Pre-Approval requirements and the Required Documentation for Maximum Financing.

For a Mortgage with an LTV of 90 percent or less, the Mortgagee must obtain:
- form HUD-92541, *Builder's Certification of Plans, Specifications, and Site;*
- final inspection or appraisal, if the Property is 100 percent complete;
- Wood Infestation Report, unless the Property is located in an area of no to slight infestation as indicated on HUD's "Termite Treatment Exception Areas" list:
  - Form HUD-NPMA-99-A, *Subterranean Termite Protection Builder's Guarantee,* is required for all New Construction. If the building is constructed with steel, masonry or concrete building components with only minor interior wood trim and roof sheathing, no treatment is needed. The Mortgagee must ensure that the builder notes on the form that the construction is masonry, steel, or concrete.
  - Form HUD-NPMA-99-B, *New Construction Subterranean Termite Service Record,* is required when the proposed Property is treated with a soil chemical termiticide. The Mortgagee must reject the use of post construction soil treatment when the termiticide is applied only around the perimeter of the foundation.

- local Health Authority well water analysis and/or septic report, where required by the local jurisdictional authority.

v. Documents to be Provided to Appraiser at Assignment

The Mortgagee must provide the Appraiser with a fully executed form HUD-92541, signed and dated no more than 30 Days prior to the date the appraisal was ordered.

For Properties 90 percent completed or less, the Mortgagee must provide a copy of the floor plan, plot plan, and any other exhibits necessary to allow the Appraiser to determine the size and level of finish of the house they are appraising.

For Properties greater than 90 percent but less than 100 percent completed, the Mortgagee must provide the Appraiser with a list of components to be installed or completed after the date of inspection.

vi. Property Considerations

New Construction must meet HUD's Minimum Property Requirements (MPR) and Minimum Property Standards (MPS).

vii. Mortgagee Review of Appraisal

(A) Site Considerations

(1) Environmental

The Mortgagee must require corrective work to mitigate any condition that arises during construction that may affect the health and safety of the occupants, the Property's ability to serve as collateral, or the structural soundness of the improvements.

(2) Operating Oil or Gas Wells

If a proposed or newly constructed dwelling is located within 75 feet of an operating oil or gas well, the Mortgagee must reject the Property unless mitigation measures are completed.

(3) Slush Pits

If a Property is Proposed Construction near an active or abandoned Slush Pit, the Appraiser must require a survey to locate the pit. The Mortgagee is to assess any impact on the subject Property.

(4) Special Airport Hazards

If a proposed or newly constructed Property is located within Runway Clear Zones (also known as Runway Protection Zones) at civil airports or within Clear Zones at military airfields, the Mortgagee must reject the Property for insurance.

A proposed or newly constructed Property located in Accident Potential Zone I at military airfields may be eligible for FHA mortgage insurance provided that the Mortgagee determines that the Property complies with Department of Defense guidelines.

(5) Flood Hazard Areas

If any portion of the property improvements (the dwelling and related Structures/equipment essential to the value of the Property and subject to flood damage) is located within a Special Flood Hazard Area (SFHA), the Mortgagee must reject the Property, unless:

- a final Letter of Map Amendment (LOMA) or final Letter of Map Revision (LOMR) that removes the Property from the SFHA is obtained from the Federal Emergency Management Agency (FEMA); or
- the Mortgagee obtains a FEMA National Flood Insurance Program (NFIP) Elevation Certificate (FEMA Form 086-0-33), that documents that the lowest floor (including the basement) of the residential building and all related improvements/equipment essential to the value of the Property, is built at or above the 100-year flood elevation in compliance with the NFIP criteria. The Mortgagee must ensure that the flood elevation certificate is prepared by a licensed engineer or surveyor and completed based on finished construction.

The Mortgagee must include the LOMA, LOMR, or flood elevation certificate with the case when it is submitted for endorsement.

The Mortgagee must ensure that insurance under the NFIP is obtained when a flood elevation certificate documents that the Property remains located within an SFHA.

(6) Individual Water Supply Systems (Wells)

The Mortgagee must ensure that new wells are drilled and are no less than 20 feet deep and cased. Casing should be steel or other casing material that is durable, leak-proof, and acceptable to either the local health authority or the trade or profession licensed to drill and repair wells in the local jurisdiction.

A well located within the foundation walls of New Construction is not acceptable except in arctic or sub-arctic regions.

(a) Requirements for Well Water Testing

A well water test is required for all newly constructed Properties.

All testing must be performed by a disinterested third party. This includes the collection and transport of the water sample collected at the water supply source. The sample must be collected and tested by the local health authority, a commercial testing laboratory, a licensed sanitary engineer, or other party that is acceptable to the local health authority. At no time will the Borrower/owner or other Interested Party collect and/or transport the sample.

The following tables provide the minimum distance required between wells and sources of pollution:

Water Well Location Minimum Property Standards for New Construction 24 CFR § 200.926d(f)(3)(iv)*	
1	Property line/10 feet
2	Septic tank/50 feet
3	Absorption field/100 feet
4	Seepage pit or cesspool/100 feet
5	Sewer lines with permanent water tight joints/10 feet
6	Other sewer lines/50 feet
7	Chemically poisoned soil/25 feet (reduced to 15 feet where ground surface is protected by impervious strata of clay, hardpan or rock)
8	Dry well/50 feet
9	Other – refer to local health authority minimums
* distance requirements of local authority prevail if greater than stated above	

The following provides the minimum standards for Individual Water Supply Systems (wells):

Individual Water System Minimum Property Standards for New Construction 24 CFR § 200.926d(f)(1) and (2)	
1	Lead-free piping
2	If no local chemical and bacteriological water standards, state standards apply
3	Connection of public water whenever feasible
4	Wells must deliver water flow of five gallons per minute over at least a four-hour period

(b) Required Documentation

The Mortgagee must submit a valid water test from the local health authority or qualified lab.

(7) Shared Well

A Shared Well is permitted only if the Mortgagee obtains evidence that:
- it is not feasible to serve the housing by an acceptable public or Community Water System; and
- the housing is located in an area other than in an area where local officials have certified that installation of public or adequate Community Water Systems and sewer systems are economically feasible.

(B) Sales Comparison Approach: Comparable Selection

For Properties in new subdivisions, the selected comparable sales must include at least one sale outside the subdivision or project and at least one sale from within the subdivision or project.

viii. Completion of Construction

Regardless of the inspection process used, the Mortgagee must certify on form HUD-92900-A, *HUD/VA Addendum to Uniform Residential Loan Application,* that the Property is 100 percent complete and meets HUD's MPR and MPS.

j. Construction to Permanent

i. Definition

Construction to Permanent (CP) refers to the construction of a dwelling on land owned or being purchased by the Borrower. The CP program combines the features of a construction loan with that of a traditional long-term permanent residential Mortgage using a single mortgage closing prior to the start of construction.

A construction loan refers to a short-term interim loan for financing the cost of construction.

ii. General Eligibility

The Borrower must have contracted with a builder to construct the dwelling. The builder must be a licensed general contractor.

The Borrower may act as the general contractor, only if the Borrower is also a licensed general contractor.

iii. Property Eligibility

The Borrower must either be purchasing the land at the closing of the construction loan, or already own the land.

iv. Calculating Maximum Mortgage Amount

The Mortgagee must use the lesser of the appraised value or the documented Acquisition Cost to determine the Adjusted Value.

The maximum mortgage amount is calculated using the appropriate purchase Loan-to-Value (LTV) percentage of the lesser of the appraised value or the documented Acquisition Cost.

The documented Acquisition Cost of the Property includes:
- the builder's price (includes cost of land if being purchased from builder), or the sum of all subcontractor bids and materials (if land is already owned by the Borrower);
- Borrower-paid options and construction costs not included in the builder's price to build;
- closing costs associated with any interim financing of the land, and
- either of the following:
  - the lesser of the cost of the land, or appraised value of the land, if the land is owned six months or less at case number assignment; **or**
  - the appraised value of the land if the land has been owned for greater than six months at case number assignment, or was received as an acceptable gift.

For Manufactured Housing, the builder's price to build includes the sum of the cost of the unit(s), the cost to transport the unit from the dealer's lot to the installation site, and all on-site installation costs.

v. Minimum Required Investment

(A) Standard

The Borrower may utilize any cash investment in the Acquisition Cost of the Property or land equity to satisfy the Minimum Required Investment (MRI) in accordance with Calculating Maximum Mortgage Amount.

(B) Required Documentation

The Mortgagee must document the cash investment was from an acceptable source of funds in accordance with TOTAL or Manual Underwriting requirements as applicable.

vi. Required Documentation

The Mortgagee must obtain the Closing Disclosure or similar legal document showing the cost of the land and the date of purchase.

The Mortgagee must obtain evidence that the funds used to pay Borrower-paid options were derived from an acceptable source. The Mortgagee must obtain an itemization of the options and expenses, and cost of each item.

The Mortgagee must comply with New Construction requirements.

vii. Mortgage Interest Rate

During the construction period, the interest rate may be variable. The Mortgagee and the Borrower must enter into an agreement that:
- documents the range in which the interest rate may float during construction;
- documents the point of interest rate lock-in;
- specifies that the permanent Mortgage will not exceed a specific maximum interest rate; and
- permits the Borrower to lock in at a lower rate, if available and they have not already locked in a rate.

The Mortgagee must qualify the Borrower for the Mortgage at the maximum rate at which the permanent Mortgage may be set.

viii. Required Documentation for Closing

In addition to standard FHA documents, the following documents must be used:

(A) A Construction Rider to the Note, and Construction Loan Agreement. These construction documents may be in any form acceptable to the Mortgagee, but they must provide that all special construction terms end when the construction loan converts to a permanent Mortgage. After conversion, only the permanent mortgage terms (based on standard documents) continue to be effective, making the permanent Mortgage eligible for FHA mortgage insurance.

(B) A disclosure issued to the Borrower explaining that the Mortgage is not eligible for FHA mortgage insurance until after a final inspection, or the issuance of a certificate of occupancy by the local governmental jurisdiction, whichever is later.

(C) Either, a fully executed contract agreement between the builder and the Borrower, which includes the contractor's price to build; or documentation of the actual costs of construction where the Borrower is acting as the general contractor.

(D) Documentation of land acquisition or land ownership.

(E) A payoff statement and evidence of the actual payoff if mortgage proceeds are used to purchase or pay off debt on the land.

ix. Escrow Account

At closing, after funds are disbursed to cover the purchase of the land, the balance of the mortgage proceeds must be placed in an escrow account to be disbursed as construction progresses.

The Mortgagee must obtain the Borrower's written authorization for each draw prior to disbursing funds to the contractor.

After completion of construction, the construction escrow account must be fully extinguished, and any remaining funds must be applied to the outstanding principal balance of the permanent Mortgage.

x. Required Documentation for Endorsement

If the LTV exceeds 90 percent, the Mortgagee must comply with Inspections or Warranties for Maximum Financing and Required Documentation for Maximum Financing.

If the LTV is 90 percent or less, the Mortgagee must comply with the documentation requirements found in the New Construction Financing LTV Limit.

The following documentation is required for Mortgage endorsement:

- The Mortgagee must obtain a title update after conversion to the permanent Mortgage to show that the mortgaged Property is free and clear of all liens other than the Mortgage.
- The Mortgagee must verify and document that the construction was fully drawn down and that any remaining funds were used to pay down the principal balance on the permanent Mortgage.

xi. Endorsement

The Mortgage must be endorsed within 60 Days of the final inspection or issuance of the Certificate of Occupancy (CO), whichever is later.

xii. Start of Amortization

Amortization of the permanent Mortgage must begin no later than the first of the month following 60 Days from the date of the final inspection or issuance of the CO.

k. Building on Own Land

i. Definition

Building on Own Land refers to the permanent financing of a newly constructed dwelling on land owned by the Borrower and may include the extinguishing of any construction loans.

ii. Eligibility

The Borrower must have contracted with a builder to construct the dwelling. The builder must be a licensed general contractor.

The Borrower may act as the general contractor, only if the Borrower is also a licensed general contractor.

iii. Calculating Maximum Mortgage Amount

The Mortgagee must use the lesser of the appraised value or the documented Acquisition Cost to determine the Adjusted Value.

The maximum mortgage amount is calculated using the appropriate purchase Loan-to-Value (LTV) percentage of the lesser of the appraised value or the documented Acquisition Cost.

The documented Acquisition Cost of the Property includes:
- the builder's price or the sum of all subcontractor bids and materials;
- Borrower-paid options and construction costs not included in the builder's price to build;
- interest and other costs associated with a construction loan obtained by the Borrower to fund construction, if applicable; and
- either of the following:
  - the lesser of the cost of the land, or appraised value of the land, if the land is owned six months or less at case number assignment; **or**
  - the appraised value of the land if the land has been owned for greater than six months at case number assignment or was received as an acceptable gift.

For Manufactured Housing, the builder's price to build includes the sum of the cost of the unit(s), the cost to transport the unit from the dealer's lot to the installation site, and all on-site installation costs.

iv. Minimum Required Investment

(A) Standard

The Borrower may utilize any cash investment in the Acquisition Cost of the Property or land equity to satisfy the MRI in accordance with Calculating Maximum Mortgage Amount.

(B) Required Documentation

The Mortgagee must document that the cash investment was from an acceptable source of funds in accordance with TOTAL or Manual Underwriting requirements as applicable.

If the land was given as a gift to the Borrower, the Mortgagee must verify that the donor was not a prohibited source.

The Mortgagee must obtain standard gift documentation for any gift of land.

v. Borrower's Additional Equity in the Property

The Borrower may not receive cash back from the additional equity in the Property, but the Borrower may replenish their own cash expenditures for any Borrower-paid extras over and above the contract specifications and any out-of-pocket expenses not included in the builder's price. The Mortgagee must obtain an itemization of the extras and expenses and the cost of each item.

vi. Required Documentation

The Mortgagee must document the date of purchase of the land by obtaining the Closing Disclosure or similar legal document.

The Mortgagee must obtain evidence that the funds used to pay Borrower paid options were derived from an acceptable source. The Mortgagee must obtain an itemization of the options, expenses, and cost of each item.

The Mortgagee must comply with New Construction requirements.

l. Weatherization

The weatherization product permits the Borrower to finance the cost of eligible energy-related weatherization improvements, in conjunction with a purchase or refinance.

i. Eligibility

(A) Eligible Programs and Transaction Types

Weatherization improvements may be financed in conjunction with the following:
- Section 203(b)
  - purchase transaction
  - no cash-out refinance transaction
- Section 203(h) Mortgage Insurance for Disaster Victims
- Energy Efficient Mortgages (EEM)

For financing of weatherization under the 203(k) Rehabilitation Mortgage Insurance Program, refer to 203(k) Rehabilitation Mortgage Insurance Program.

(B) Eligible Property Types

Weatherization improvements may be used on the following property types:
- existing Properties (one- to four-units)
- condominiums (one unit)
- Manufactured Housing (single unit)

(C) Eligible Weatherization Items

Eligible energy-related weatherization items include the following measures:
- air sealing (including weather-stripping doors, caulking window and plumbing penetrations)
- insulation (attic, floors, walls, basement)
- duct sealing and insulation
- smart thermostats and equipment controls
- windows and doors
- low flow water fixtures
- carbon monoxide monitors and other combustion appliance safety measures

(D) Maximum Dollar Amount

The maximum allowable cost of energy-related weatherization items that can be financed is:
- $2,000 (not to exceed actual cost) without a separate value determination;
- $3,500 (not to exceed actual cost) if supported by a value determination made by an FHA Roster Appraiser; or
- no limit (not to exceed actual cost) if:

- o supported by a value determination made by an FHA Roster Appraiser; and
- o a separate on-site inspection is made by an ICC RCI or CI.

(E) Required Documentation

The Mortgagee must document the cost of work including the weatherization materials and labor.

(F) Maximum Mortgage Amount Calculation

When determining the Adjusted Value, the dollar limit of the energy-related weatherization items may be added to both the sales price and the Property Value.

(G) Weatherization Combined with Energy Efficient Mortgage

For existing Properties, energy-related weatherization items may be combined with the EEM.

(H) Cash-Out

The Borrower may not receive cash back from the mortgage transaction. If an excess exists, funds must be applied to the principal Mortgage balance.

(I) Escrows

The Mortgagee must establish an escrow account for the remaining costs of the energy improvements if the installation of weatherization items is not complete by the time of closing for all Mortgages on existing Properties, except 203(k). The Mortgagee must establish an escrow account for the remaining cost of the energy improvements in accordance with the Repair Completion Escrow Requirements.

If the costs of the energy improvements and weatherization items are part of a 203(k) Rehabilitation Mortgage, then the escrowed amounts of the energy improvements and weatherization items must be included in the rehabilitation escrow account.

Escrows may not include costs for labor or work performed by the Borrower (Sweat Equity).

(J) Form HUD-92300, Mortgagee's Assurance of Completion

When funds to complete weatherization improvements are escrowed, the Mortgagee must execute form HUD-92300, *Mortgagee's Assurance of Completion*, to indicate that the escrow for weatherization improvements has been established.

ii. Completion Requirements for Weatherization Measures

(A) Time of Completion

Installation of weatherization improvements must be completed within:
- 30 Days of the mortgage Disbursement; or
- 90 Days of the mortgage Disbursement if the improvements are part of an energy package for an EEM.

The Mortgagee must apply the remaining weatherization escrow funds to a prepayment of the mortgage principal if the work is not completed within the required time frames.

Any funds remaining in the escrow account at the end of the improvement period must be applied to pay down the mortgage principal.

(B) Escrow Closeout Certification

After the repair or rehabilitation escrow account is closed, the Mortgagee must complete the Escrow Closeout Certification screen in FHAC within 30 Days after the escrow account is closed.

(C) Inspection

The Mortgagee or their agent must inspect the weatherization items or obtain evidence from a local authority that the system was installed in accordance with local requirements.

m. Solar and Wind Technologies

The solar and wind technologies policy allows the Mortgagee to increase the Base Loan Amount to cover the cost and installation of new solar or wind energy system improvements made, or to be made, to the Property at the time of a purchase or refinance.

i. Eligibility

(A) Eligible Property Types

The following property types are eligible for the solar and wind technologies policy:
- one- to four-unit Properties
- Manufactured Housing (one unit)

Condominium units are ineligible for solar and wind technologies.

(B) Eligible Programs and Transaction Types

Costs for new solar and wind energy systems may be added to an FHA-insured base Mortgage, for the following programs:
- Section 203(b)
  - purchase transaction
  - Rate and Term refinance and Simple Refinance
- Section 203(h) Mortgage Insurance for Disaster Victims
- Section 203(k) Rehabilitation Mortgage Insurance Program

ii. Eligible Solar and Wind Technologies

Active and passive solar systems, as well as wind-driven systems, are acceptable.

(A) Photovoltaic Systems

Photovoltaic systems must provide electricity for the residence, and must meet applicable fire and electrical code requirement.

(B) Wind Turbine for Residential Properties

A wind turbine must:
- have a nameplate capacity of no more than 100 kilowatts;
- have a performance and safety certification from:
  - the International Electrotechnical Commission (IEC) standards from an accredited product certification body; or
  - the American Wind Energy Association (AWEA) standards from the Small Wind Certification Council (SWCC) or a Nationally Recognized Testing Laboratory (NRTL); and

- be installed by an installer who has received either a North American Board of Certified Energy Practitioners Small Wind Installer Certification or small wind turbine installation training from an accredited training organization.

iii. Title to Systems

The Borrower must own, not lease, solar or wind energy systems for the systems to be considered eligible improvements. Leased equipment and Solar Power Purchase Agreements (SPPA) may not be financed under any FHA Title II programs.

iv. Maximum Mortgage Amount Calculation

(A) Maximum Mortgage Amount - Purchase

The Mortgagee must compute the Adjusted Value by using the purchase price excluding the cost and installation of the solar or wind technology system and the Property Value excluding the cost and installation of the solar or wind technology system.

The Mortgagee must add the lesser of:
- the cost and installation of the solar or wind technology system; or
- 20% of the Property Value to the Base Loan Amount.

The Mortgagee must exclude any rebates identified in the contract and assigned to the contractor in determining the cost and installation of the solar or wind technology system.

(B) Maximum Mortgage Amount - Refinance

The Mortgagee must compute the Adjusted Value by using the Property Value without the cost and installation of the solar or wind technology system.

The Mortgagee must add the lesser of:
- the cost and installation of the solar or wind technology system; or
- 20% of the Property Value to the Base Loan Amount.

The Mortgagee must exclude any rebates identified in the contract and assigned to the contractor in determining the cost and installation of the solar or wind technology system.

(C) Nationwide Mortgage Limit – Purchase and Refinance

The Base Loan Amount may exceed the Nationwide Mortgage Limit for the geographical area (see Maximum Mortgage Amounts) by no more than 20 percent.

v. Required Documentation

The Mortgagee must document the cost of work, including the energy systems' materials and labor.

vi. Cash-Out

The Borrower may not receive cash back from the mortgage transaction. If an excess exists, the Mortgagee must apply these funds to the principal Mortgage balance.

vii. Escrows

The Mortgagee must establish an escrow account in accordance with the Repair Completion Escrow Requirements for the remaining cost of the energy improvements if the installation of solar or wind energy systems is not complete by the time of closing.

If the energy package is part of a 203(k) Rehabilitation Mortgage, then the escrowed amounts of the energy package must be included in the rehabilitation escrow account.

Any funds remaining in the escrow account at the end of the improvement period must be applied to pay down the mortgage principal.

(A) Borrower Labor

Escrows may not include costs for labor or work performed by the Borrower (Sweat Equity).

(B) Required Documentation: Form HUD-92300, Mortgagee's Assurance of Completion

When funds to complete the solar or wind energy systems are escrowed, the Mortgagee must execute form HUD-92300, *Mortgagee's Assurance of Completion*, to indicate that the escrow for the solar or wind improvements has been established.

viii. Completion Requirements for Solar and Wind Technology Installation

(A) Time of Completion

Installations of solar and wind energy systems must be completed within 120 Days of the mortgage Disbursement.

The Mortgagee must apply the remaining solar and wind escrow funds to a prepayment of the mortgage principal, if the work is not completed within the required time frames.

(B) Inspection

The Mortgagee or their agent must inspect the solar and wind improvement or obtain evidence from a local authority that the system was installed in accordance with local code.

(C) Escrow Closeout Certification

After the repair or rehabilitation escrow account is closed, the Mortgagee must complete the Escrow Closeout Certification screen in FHAC within 30 Days after the escrow account is closed.

n. Assumptions

i. Definition

Assumption refers to the transfer of an existing mortgage obligation from an existing Borrower to the assuming Borrower.

ii. Occupancy Eligibility Requirements

If the original Mortgage was closed on or after December 15, 1989, the assuming Borrower must intend to occupy the Property as a Principal Residence or HUD-approved Secondary Residence.

If the original Mortgage was closed prior to December 15, 1989, the assuming Borrower may assume the Mortgage as a Principal Residence, HUD-approved Secondary Residence or Investment Property.

iii. Restrictions on Loan-to-Value Ratio

(A) Investment Property

The maximum Loan-to-Value (LTV) for an Investment Property assumption is 75%.

Either the original appraised value or new Property Value may be used to determine compliance with the 75% LTV limitation.

(B) HUD-Approved Secondary Residence

The maximum LTV for a HUD-approved Secondary Residence assumption is 85%.

Either the original appraised value or new Property Value may be used to determine compliance with the 85% LTV limitation.

iv. Processing of an Assumption

(A) Initiating Processing

The Mortgagee must notify HUD via FHA Connection (FHAC) of assumptions:
- within 15 Days of any change of Borrower; or
- within 15 Days of the date the Mortgagee receives actual or constructive knowledge of the transfer of ownership.

This notification does not formally release the original Borrower from personal liability for the mortgage Note.

(B) Release of Liability

The Mortgagee must prepare form HUD-92210.1, *Approval of Purchaser and Release of Seller*, thereby releasing the original owner when they sell by assumption to the assuming Borrower who executes an agreement to assume the Mortgage and to pay the debt.

v. Underwriting Review

Assuming Borrowers must be underwritten in accordance with Origination through Post-Closing/Endorsement, except for the following sections:

- Ordering Case Numbers
- Ordering Appraisal
- Transferring Existing Appraisal
- Ordering Second Appraisal
- Ordering an Update to an Appraisal
- Property Eligibility and Acceptability Criteria
- National Housing Act's Statutory Limits
- Nationwide Mortgage Limits
- Underwriting the Property
- Underwriting the Borrower Using the TOTAL Mortgage Scorecard

(A) Exceptions in Case of Transfer by Devise or Descent

The Mortgagee may process an assumption without credit review of the assuming Borrower if the transfer is by devise or descent, or other circumstances in which the transfer cannot legally lead to exercise of the due-on-sale, such as a divorce in which the party remaining on title retains occupancy, and the assuming Borrower can demonstrate that they have made the Mortgage Payments for a minimum of six months prior to the date of application of the assumption.

(B) Exception to Minimum Required Investment

The assuming Borrower is not required to make a cash investment in the Property. The assuming Borrower may assume 100% of the outstanding principal balance of the Mortgage, subject to the restrictions on LTV ratio for Investment Properties and HUD-approved Secondary Residences.

(C) Responsibility of Direct Endorsement Underwriter

The holding or servicing Mortgagee is responsible for the underwriting review. The review must be completed by a Direct Endorsement (DE) underwriter registered by the Mortgagee in FHAC. Where the holding or servicing Mortgagee does not originate Mortgages or is not approved under the DE program, it may have an Authorized Agent perform the review.

(D) Use of TOTAL Mortgage Scorecard for Assumptions

The TOTAL Mortgage Scorecard must not be used for assumptions. The DE underwriter must manually underwrite the assumption.

vi. Allowable Fees and Charges

(A) Processing Fee and Other Costs

Mortgagees may charge the assuming Borrower a processing fee that is reasonable and customary not to exceed a maximum of $900.

The Mortgagee may charge the assuming Borrower other costs in accordance with Allowable Charges Separate from Assumption Processing Fees.

(B) Interested Party Contributions

The seller or other Interested Parties may make contributions toward the assuming Borrower's actual closing costs consistent with the requirements in Interested Party Contributions.

o. HUD Real Estate Owned Purchasing

i. Definition

(A) HUD REO Property

A HUD Real Estate Owned (REO) Property, also known as a HUD Home or a HUD-owned home, refers to a one- to four-unit residential Property acquired by HUD as a result of a foreclosure or other means of acquisition on an FHA-insured Mortgage, whereby the Secretary of HUD becomes the property owner and offers it for sale to recover the mortgage insurance claim that HUD paid to the Mortgagee.

(B) Insured HUD REO Property Purchase

An Insured HUD REO Property Purchase refers to the purchase of a HUD REO Property by a Borrower with a new FHA-insured Mortgage.

(C) Insured HUD REO Property Purchase Programs

(1) Section 203(b)

The HUD REO Property meets HUD's Minimum Property Requirements (MPR) in its as-is condition with no repairs, alterations, or inspections required.

(2) Section 203(b) With Repair Escrow

The HUD REO Property does not meet HUD's MPR in its as-is condition, but if repairs of no more than $10,000 are completed, the HUD REO Property would meet HUD's MPR. An escrow account to complete the repairs necessary to meet MPR after closing is required.

Effective for case numbers assigned on or after October 31, 2016, the Mortgagee must comply with the Repair Completion Escrow Requirement.

(3) Section 203(k)

The HUD REO Property does not qualify for Section 203(b) or Section 203(b) with Repair Escrow, and is eligible for FHA-insured financing only under Section 203(k).

(D) Special Sales Incentives

(1) Good Neighbor Next Door

The Good Neighbor Next Door (GNND) sales incentive permits an Owner-Occupant Borrower who is a full-time law enforcement officer, teacher, firefighter, or emergency medical technician who meets HUD requirements to purchase a specifically designated HUD REO Property located in a HUD-designated Revitalization Area with FHA-insured financing at a 50 percent discount from the purchase price. When using FHA-insured financing, the Borrower may purchase the HUD REO Property with a minimum downpayment of $100. In addition, the Borrower may include in the mortgage amount customary and reasonable closing costs.

GNND purchases may be processed as Section 203(b), Section 203(b) with Repair Escrow, or Section 203(k).

(2) $100 Down

The $100 Down sales incentive permits a Borrower to purchase a HUD REO Property with FHA-insured financing with a minimum downpayment of $100.

$100 Down purchases may be processed as Section 203(b), Section 203(b) with Repair Escrow, or Section 203(k).

ii. Sales Contract

(A) General

The Mortgagee must obtain form HUD-9548, *Sales Contract Property Disposition Program*, and any applicable addenda, which will establish the purchase price, price discount, eligibility for GNND and eligibility for $100 Down, and meet the requirements for the Sales Contract.

(B) Contract Sales Terms

Line 4 of the sales contract will specify the Insured HUD REO Property Purchase Program under which the Borrower is applying, the downpayment, and the mortgage amount.

Regardless of the Insured HUD REO Property Purchase Program entered on Line 4 of form HUD-9548, the Mortgagee must determine the eligibility of the Property, the eligibility of the Borrower, and the specific Insured HUD REO Property Purchase Program that must be used to finance the purchase.

(C) Good Neighbor Next Door

Where the Borrower is approved for the GNND sales incentive, Line 8 will specify the discount that will be applied to the purchase price on Line 3. The amount of the cash downpayment specified on Line 4 will be $100.

(D) Eligible Nonprofit or State or Local Government Agency Borrower

Under certain circumstances, eligible nonprofit or state and local government agency Borrowers may purchase Properties at a discount from the stated listing price. Line 8 will specify the discount that will be applied to the purchase price on Line 3.

(E) $100 Down

Where the Borrower has been approved for the $100 Down sales incentive, the amount of the cash downpayment specified on Line 4 will be $100.

(F) Closing Costs and Sales Commissions Paid by HUD

The amount on Line 5 specifies the amount of closing costs that HUD will pay on behalf of the Borrower. The amounts on Line 6a and 6b represent the sales commissions HUD will pay to the selling and listing broker.

Contributions by HUD toward the Borrower's closing costs are not defined as Interested Party Contributions (TOTAL or Manual) or Inducements to Purchase (TOTAL or Manual).

iii. Ordering Case Numbers

(A) Section 203(b) and Section 203(b) With Repair Escrow

Mortgagees must order case numbers for Insured HUD REO Property Purchases in accordance with Ordering Case Numbers.

Mortgagees must select "Real Estate Owned w/Appraisal" for Processing Type and enter the case number of the HUD REO Property in the Prior Case Number field. The HUD REO Property case number can be found on the top right-hand corner of form HUD-9548.

(B) Section 203(k)

Mortgagees must order case numbers for Insured HUD REO Property Purchases in accordance with Case Number Assignment Data Entry Requirements.

Mortgagees must select "Real Estate Owned w/Appraisal" for Processing Type and enter the case number of the HUD REO Property in the Prior Case Number field. The HUD REO Property case number can be found on the top right-hand corner of form HUD-9548.

iv. Appraisals

(A) Ordering Appraisals

(1) Section 203(b) and Section 203(b) With Repair Escrow

Mortgagees must order appraisals in accordance with the requirements of Ordering Appraisals.

(2) Section 203(k)

Mortgagees must order appraisals in accordance with the requirements of Ordering Appraisals and Appraisals for Standard 203(k) and Limited 203(k).

(B) Appraisal Review and Property Acceptability

The Mortgagee must review the appraisal and property conditions in accordance with the requirements of Underwriting the Property.

v. Occupancy Types

(A) Principal Residence

An Owner-Occupant Borrower may purchase HUD REO Properties using Section 203(b), Section 203(b) with Repair Escrow, and Section 203(k).

(B) Investment Property

(1) Eligible Nonprofit or State or Local Government Agency Borrower

An eligible nonprofit or state or local government agency Borrower may purchase HUD REO Properties using Section 203(b), Section 203(b) with Repair Escrow, and Section 203(k).

(2) Investor Buyer

A Borrower may purchase HUD REO Properties as Investment Properties using Section 203(b) or Section 203(b) with Repair Escrow.

vi. Maximum Mortgage Amounts

(A) Section 203(b)

Mortgagees must calculate the maximum mortgage amounts in accordance with the requirements of Calculating Maximum Mortgage Amounts for Purchases, using the applicable Loan-To-Value ratio (LTV) from this section, subject to LTV Limitations Based on Borrower's Credit Score.

(1) Owner-Occupant Borrower

The maximum LTV is 96.5 percent.

(2) Eligible Nonprofit or State or Local Government Agency Borrower

The maximum LTV is 96.5 percent.

Where the eligible nonprofit or state or local government agency Borrower purchases the HUD REO Property at a discount, Mortgagees must calculate the discounted purchase price in accordance with the requirements for calculating the discounted purchase price for GNND transactions. The discounted purchase price must be used when determining the Adjusted Value.

(3) Investor Buyer

The maximum LTV is 75.0 percent.

(B) Section 203(b) With Repair Escrow

Mortgagees must initially calculate the mortgage amount in accordance with the requirements for Section 203(b) above. Mortgagees must add to the amount resulting from that calculation the amount of an escrow account for the completion of repairs after closing.

The maximum escrow amount must be based on the sum of the repairs required to meet the intent of HUD's MPR, plus a 10 percent contingency. The total escrow amount, including the 10 percent contingency, must not exceed $11,000.

Effective for case numbers assigned on or after October 31, 2016, the Mortgagee must comply with the Repair Completion Escrow Requirement.

(C) Good Neighbor Next Door

(1) Discounted Purchase Price

Mortgagees must calculate the discounted purchase price and use that amount as the purchase price in determining the Adjusted Value for a 203(b) transaction or the Adjusted As-Is Value for a 203(k) transaction.

The discounted purchase price is calculated by reducing the contract sales price on Line 3 of form HUD-9548 by the discount percentage on Line 8 of form HUD-9548. To that amount the Mortgagee must add:
- sales commissions from Line 6 of form HUD-9548; and
- any Borrower-paid closing costs (including prepaid items).

(2) Section 203(b)

Mortgagees must calculate the maximum mortgage amount by subtracting $100 from the Adjusted Value.

(3) Section 203(b) With Repair Escrow

Mortgagees must calculate the maximum mortgage amount by subtracting $100 from the sum of the Adjusted Value plus 110 percent of the estimated cost of repairs, not to exceed $11,000.

(D) $100 Down

(1) Section 203(b)

Mortgagees must calculate the maximum mortgage amount by subtracting $100 from the Adjusted Value.

(2) Section 203(b) With Repair Escrow

Mortgagees must calculate the maximum mortgage amount by subtracting $100 from the sum of the Adjusted Value plus 110 percent of the estimated cost of repairs, not to exceed $11,000.

(E) Section 203(k)

(1) Owner-Occupant Borrower

Mortgagees must calculate the maximum mortgage amount in accordance with the requirements of Section 203(k) Maximum Mortgage Amounts for Purchases.

(2) Eligible Nonprofit and State and Local Government Agency Borrower

Mortgagees must calculate the maximum mortgage amount in accordance with the requirements of Section 203(k) Maximum Mortgage Amounts for Purchases.

Where the eligible nonprofit or state or local government agency Borrower purchases the HUD REO Property at a discount, Mortgagees must calculate the discounted purchase price in accordance with the requirements for calculating the discounted purchase price for GNND transactions. The discounted purchase price must be used when determining the Adjusted As-Is Value.

(3) GNND and $100 Down

The maximum mortgage amount that FHA will insure on a GNND 203(k) purchase is the lesser of:
- the Adjusted As-is Value, plus:

- o Financeable Repair and Improvement Costs, for Standard 203(k) or Limited 203(k);
- o Financeable Mortgage Fees, for Standard 203(k) or Limited 203(k);
- o Financeable Contingency Reserves for Standard 203(k) or Limited 203(k);
- o other purchaser-paid closing costs, including prepaid items; and
- o Financeable Mortgage Payment Reserves, for Standard 203(k) only;
- o minus $100; or
- 110 percent of the After Improved Value (100 percent for condominiums), minus $100; or
- the Nationwide Mortgage Limits.

vii. Additional Section 203(b) With Repair Escrow Requirements

(A) FHAC Insuring Application

The Mortgagee must check "Yes" in the Escrow Data field. The Mortgagee must enter the amount of the escrow, including the contingency, in the HUD REO Repair Amount field.

(B) Required Documentation

Effective for case numbers assigned on or after October 31, 2016, the Mortgagee must comply with the Repair Completion Escrow Requirement.

viii. Additional GNND Requirements for FHAC Insuring Application

(A) Repair Escrow

If insured under Section 203(b) with Repair Escrow, the Mortgagee must check "Yes" in the Escrow Data field. The Mortgagee must enter the amount of the escrow, including the contingency, in the HUD REO Repair Amount field.

(B) Required Documentation

The Mortgagee must comply with the Repair Completion Escrow Requirement.

(C) Sales Price

Mortgagees must enter the discounted purchase price.

(D) Secondary Financing

Mortgagees must complete information regarding secondary financing by entering:
- "Yes" in the Secondary Financing field;
- the amount of the discount by which the sales price was reduced in the Amount field;

- "Federal Government" in the Source of Funds field; and
- "HUD GNND" in the Source Name field.

(E) $100 Down

In the $100 REO Down Payment Program field, Mortgagees must enter "Yes."

ix. Additional $100 Down Requirements for FHAC Insuring Application

In the $100 REO Down Payment Program field, Mortgagees must enter "Yes."

9. 203(k) Consultant Requirements

a. Overview

A Federal Housing Administration (FHA)-approved 203(k) Consultant is required for all Standard 203(k) Mortgages and may be used for Limited 203(k) Mortgages. Any Consultant who performs work on a 203(k) must be listed on the FHA 203(k) Consultant Roster. The Consultant inspects the Property and prepares the architectural exhibits, the Work Write-Up and Cost Estimate.

For information on how to become an approved 203(k) Consultant, refer to Doing Business with FHA.

b. Consultant Duties

The Consultant must perform the following duties in accordance with the requirements set forth below.

i. Feasibility Study

If requested by the Borrower or Mortgagee to determine if a project is financially feasible, the Consultant must prepare a Feasibility Study.

ii. Consultant Inspection

The Consultant must inspect the Property to ensure:
- there are no rodents, dry rot, termites and other infestation on the Property;
- there are no defects that will affect the health and safety of the occupants;
- there exists adequate structural, heating, plumbing, electrical and roofing systems; and
- there are upgrades to the Structure's thermal protection (when necessary).

The Consultant must prepare a report on the current condition of the Property that categorically examines the Structure utilizing the 35 point checklist. The report must address any deficiencies that exist and certify the condition of all major systems: electrical, plumbing, heating, roofing and structural.

The Consultant must determine the repairs/improvements that are required to meet the U.S. Department of Housing and Urban Development (HUD)'s Minimum Property Requirements (MPR), Minimum Property Standards (MPS) and local requirements.

iii. Architectural Exhibits

The Consultant is responsible for identifying all required architectural exhibits. The Consultant must prepare the exhibits, or, if not qualified to prepare all of the necessary exhibits, must obtain the exhibits from a qualified subcontractor.

iv. Work Write-Up and Cost Estimate

The Consultant must prepare an unbiased Work Write-Up and Cost Estimate without the use of the contractor's estimate. The Work Write-Up and Cost Estimate must be detailed as to work being performed per the project proposal, including the necessary reports described in the Architectural Exhibit Review section.

v. Draw Request Inspection

The Consultant must inspect the work for completion and quality of workmanship at each draw request.

vi. Change Order

At the Borrower's or Mortgagee's request, the Consultant must review the proposed changes to the Work Write-Up and prepare a change order.

vii. Work Stoppages or Deviations from the Approved Write-Up

The Consultant must inform the Mortgagee of the progress of the rehabilitation and of any problems that arise, including:
- work stoppages of more than 30 consecutive Days or work not progressing reasonably during the rehabilitation period;
- significant deviations from the Work Write-Up without the Consultant's approval;
- any issues that could affect adherence to the program requirements or property eligibility; or
- any issues that could affect the health and safety of the occupants or the security of the Structure.

c. Consultant Fee Schedule

Below are the maximum fees that may be charged by the Consultant.

i. Feasibility Study

If requested by the Borrower or Mortgagee to determine if a 203(k) Mortgage is feasible, the Consultant may charge an additional fee of $100 for the preparation of a Feasibility Study.

ii. Work Write-up

The Consultant may charge the fees listed below for the preparation of the Work Write-Up and review of architectural exhibits:
- $400 for repairs less than $7,500
- $500 for repairs between $7,501 and $15,000
- $600 for repairs between $15,001 and $30,000
- $700 for repairs between $30,001 and $50,000

- $800 for repairs between $50,001 and $75,000
- $900 for repairs between $75,001 and $100,000
- $1,000 for repairs over $100,000

The Consultant may charge an additional $25 per additional Dwelling Unit.

iii. Draw Inspection Fee

For each draw request, the Consultant may charge an inspection fee that is reasonable and customary for work performed in the area where the Property is located, provided the fee does not exceed a maximum of $350.

iv. Change Order Fee

The Consultant may charge $100 per change order request.

v. Re-inspection Fee

The Consultant may charge a $50 fee when re-inspection of a Work Item is requested by the Borrower or Mortgagee.

vi. Mileage Fee

The Consultant may charge a mileage fee at the current Internal Revenue Service (IRS) mileage rate when the Consultant's place of business is more than 15 miles from the Property.

d. Improvements Standards

i. General Improvement Standards

The Consultant must ensure that the Property will comply with HUD's MPR or HUD's MPS after the improvements have been completed.

ii. Improvement Standards for Storm Shelters

When a storm shelter is part of the rehabilitation, the Consultant must ensure that its construction is consistent with guidelines issued by the Federal Emergency Management Agency (FEMA).

iii. Foundation Standards

(A) Existing Structure Moved to a New Foundation

Prior to placement of the existing Structure on the new foundation, the Consultant must obtain from the Borrower a report from a licensed structural engineer stating that the foundation is structurally sound and capable of supporting the Structure.

After placement of the existing Structure on the new foundation, the Consultant must obtain from the Borrower a report from a licensed structural engineer stating that the Structure has been properly placed and secured to the new foundation.

(B) Structure is Reconstructed on the Existing Foundation

Prior to reconstruction of the Structure, the Consultant must obtain from the Borrower a report from a licensed structural engineer stating that the foundation is structurally sound and capable of supporting the Proposed Construction of the Structure.

(C) Existing Structure will be Elevated

Prior to elevation of the existing Structure, the Consultant must obtain from the Borrower a report from a licensed structural engineer stating that the foundation is structurally sound and capable of supporting the Structure.

After elevation of the existing Structure, the Consultant must obtain from the Borrower a report from a licensed structural engineer stating that the Structure has been properly placed and secured to the new foundation.

e.   Consultant 35 Point Checklist

The Consultant must inspect the Property and address the following 35 points, if applicable, in the Work Write-Up and Cost Estimate:

1. **Masonry**. Describe masonry work to be performed, such as: point brickwork; stucco; construction of brick walls; construction/repair of brick, masonry or stone chimney; etc. Most estimates must be based on square footage projections.

2. **Siding**. Describe siding work to be performed, such as: replacement of defective siding, fascia and soffits; installation of new vinyl siding with aluminum window trim; etc. Most estimates must be based on square footage, lineal footage and length projections.

3. **Gutters and Downspouts**. Describe gutter and downspout work to be performed, such as: replacement of bad or missing gutters and downspouts; cleaning and opening downspouts; installation of splash block; etc. Most estimates must be based on lineal footage projections.

4. **Roof**. Describe roof work to be performed, such as: installation of a new built-up roof, with new metal gravel stops; installation of 240 Sealtab asphalt shingles on all roofs with a 3:12 pitch or greater; etc. Roofs that already have two layers of shingles should not be roofed again. Remove the existing shingles, then roof with new shingles. Most estimates must be based on square footage projections.

5. **Shutters**. Describe shutter work to be performed, such as: installation of shutters at windows; etc. Most estimates must be based on pair pricing.

6. **Exteriors**. Describe exterior work to be performed, such as: removal of defective, buckled wood members; providing a structurally sound porch floor, properly finished; replacement of existing porch with masonry steps and stoops; providing ornamental iron or wood railing or parts; etc. Most estimates must be based on lineal or square footage projections.

7. **Walks**. Describe walk work to be performed, such as: installation of new concrete walks; installation of concrete steps at (____); etc. Most estimates must be based on square and lineal footage projections.

8. **Driveways**. Describe driveway work to be performed, such as: remove old driveway and apron; install blacktop asphalt drive (minimum two feet) over existing drive and apron; install new concrete driveway (minimum four feet) and apron with wire mesh; etc. Most estimates must be based on square and lineal footage projections.

9. **Painting (Exterior)**. Describe exterior painting work to be performed, such as: scrape, sand smooth and paint a minimum of two coats of good quality paint on all exterior woodwork and metal; etc. Most estimates must be based on square and lineal footage projections. If the Property was built before 1978, a U.S. Environmental Protection Agency (EPA) or state-certified lead-safe renovation contractor must be used for the painting work; machine sanding and use of propane or gasoline torches (open-flame methods) are not permitted, and just washing and repainting without thorough removal or covering with siding does not constitute adequate treatment.

   Required Work Items: All defective (cracking, scaling, chipping, peeling, loose, or flaking paint and paint that is to be disturbed by this Painting (Exterior) point or other points in the Work Write-Up must be scraped, primed and double coated. Because of the concern for lead paint ingestion, all peeling paint conditions must include scraping, priming and double coating of surface areas. If the Property was built before 1978, paint mitigation must be in compliance with EPA's Renovation, Repair, and Painting Rule and HUD's lead-based paint regulations regarding paint mitigation at 24 CFR 200.810(c). Some states may require more specific treatment.

10. **Caulking**. Describe caulking to be performed, such as: caulk all windows and door frames; etc. Most estimates must be based on lineal footage or lump sum projections.

    Required Work Item: Caulk all openings, cracks or joints in the building envelope to reduce air infiltration.

11. **Fencing**. Describe fencing work to be performed, such as: installation of new fencing; resetting existing fencing; etc. Most estimates must be based on lineal footage projections.

12. **Grading**. Describe grading work to be performed, such as: removal of debris from yards; application of finish earth; grade and seed; etc. Most estimates must be based on square yard and lump sum projections.

13. **Windows**. Describe window work to be performed, such as: installation of new metal replacement windows; replacement of rotted or defective sash; replacement of rotted sills at exterior; replacement of basement windows; replacement of cracked/broken glass; replacement of missing glazing putty; repair or replacement of screens; etc. If a particular manufactured window is used, then the Work Write-Up should specify to justify the cost of the windows. Most estimates must be based on per window projections.

14. **Weather-stripping**. Describe weather-stripping to be performed, such as: installation of new weather-stripping at all exterior doors; weather-strip all windows; install metal interlocking thresholds at exterior doors; etc. Most estimates must be based on per unit and linear footage projections.

    Required Work Item: Weather-strip all doors and windows in living areas to reduce infiltration of air when existing weather-stripping is inadequate or nonexistent.

15. **Doors (Exterior)**. Describe door work to be performed, such as: install new 1 3/4" exterior solid core wood door(s); install 1 3/4" metal insulated door; install three new door butts; install new exterior door trim; install new lockset with deadbolt; etc. Most estimates must be based on per unit and linear footage projections. Address weather-stripping and caulking of all replacement doors and trim.

16. **Doors (Interior)**. Describe interior door work to be performed, such as: replacement of defective doors; installation of new doors with locksets; installation of locksets where missing or malfunctioning; readjusting all doors for proper closing; installation of bedroom closet doors; installation of bi-fold doors at (_____); installation of door trim at (_____); etc. Most estimates must be based on per unit projections.

17. **Partitions** (Do not include drywall costs). Describe partitioning work to be performed, such as: framing of new walls and partitions; framing for new closet; etc. Most estimates must be based on lineal or square footage projections.

18. **Plaster/Drywall**. Describe plaster and drywall work to be performed, such as: patch all defective plaster/drywall; finish smooth with existing wall/ceiling finish; install drywall at (_____); etc. Most estimates must be based on lump sum and square footage projections.

19. **Decorating**. Describe painting work to be performed, such as: paint interior walls; remove all existing wallpaper at (_____); wallpaper walls at (_____); treat defective (cracking, scaling, chipping, peeling, loose, or flaking) paint and paint that is to be disturbed by this Decorating point or other points in the Work Write-Up, and refinish surfaces at (_____); etc. Most estimates must be based on square and lineal footage projections.

    Required Work Items: All defective (cracking, scaling, chipping, peeling, loose, or flaking) paint and paint to be disturbed by this Decorating point or other points in the Work Write-Up must be scraped, primed and double coated. Because of the concern for lead paint ingestion, all peeling paint conditions must include scraping, priming and double coating of surface areas. If the Property was built before 1978, paint mitigation must be in compliance with EPA's Renovation, Repair, and Painting Rule and HUD's lead-based paint regulations regarding paint mitigation at 24 CFR 200.810(c). Some states may require more specific treatment.

20. **Wood Trim**. Describe wood trim work to be performed, such as: replace all cracked, broken, mismatched trim, jambs, etc.; remove all unused hinges, curtain rod hangers, nails, screws, etc.; replace all wood trim at interior door units, base, shoe & other trim; replace defective wall paneling at (____); etc. Most estimates must be based on square and lineal footage, per unit, and lump sum projections.

21. **Stairs**. Describe stair work to be performed, such as: replace bad basement treads and risers; replace main stairs, treads and risers; replace broken and/or missing baluster; provide handrails; install new stairs at (____); etc. Most estimates must be based on lump sum and lineal footage projections.

22. **Closets**. Describe closet work to be performed, such as: install new shelves, clothing rods; etc. Most estimates must be based on lineal footage projections.

23. **Wood Floors**. Describe wood floor work to be performed, such as: replace all defective flooring, holes in floors, etc., with wood flooring to match existing floors; sand, fill and refinish wood floors; install new hardwood floors at (____); etc. Most estimates must be based on square footage projections.

24. **Finish Floors**. Describe finish floor work to be performed, such as: install vinyl tile or sheet goods with 1/4" underlayment at (____); install carpet and pad at (____); etc. Specify nonstandard type flooring to justify the cost estimate. Most estimates must be based on square yard projections.

25. **Ceramic Tile**. Describe ceramic tile work to be performed, such as: install ceramic tile wainscot in bathtub area for shower height; install ceramic tile floor at (____); install Marlite wainscot in bathtub area for shower height; replace defective tile in bath; replace defective tile in kitchen; etc. Most estimates must be based on square footage or lump sum projections.

26. **Bath Accessories**. Describe bath accessory work to be performed, such as: replace medicine cabinet in bath; install towel bar(s); install soap dish; install grab bar in tub/shower; etc. Most estimates must be based on per unit projections.

27. **Plumbing**. Describe plumbing work to be performed, such as: install new hot and cold water piping; install 30 gallon (minimum) glass-lined gas hot water heater (52 gallon if electric); install new kitchen stainless steel sink; install three-piece bathroom with shower over tub; install laundry tray with faucet; replace washers at faucets; replace defective sewer lines; connect to public sewer line; replace defective faucet at (____); etc. Most estimates must be based on per unit, lump sum and lineal footage projections.

Required Work Item: When feasible, connect to public sewer system where available.

28. **Electrical**. Describe electrical work to be performed, such as: install 100 amp service; replace frayed exterior wire from service to main and into exterior panel box; install new ceiling light wall switches; install new lighting fixtures at (____); install new exterior lighting; replace wall receptacles; install three-way switch; install smoke detectors; install exterior wall exhaust fan(s); etc. Most estimates must be based on per unit and lump sum projections.

    Required Work Items: The amp service must be upgraded to the greater of 100 amp or local code. Each sleeping area must be provided with a minimum of one approved, listed and labeled smoke detector installed adjacent to the sleeping area. Smoke detectors may be battery powered when installed in existing or rehabilitated Structures. However, where new construction is being added to an existing building, the smoke detector must receive its primary power from the building wiring, in conformance to local codes and ordinances.

29. **Heating**. Describe heating and air conditioning work to be performed, such as: install new forced warm air heater; install new hot water boiler; install automatic flow control valve; install temp control valve at boiler; install heat supply outlet in each room; install high performance items such as geothermal heating and cooling, wind energy systems or photovoltaic systems; etc. Most estimates must be based on per unit and lump sum projections.

    Required Work Items: If a new heating/cooling system is proposed, the Consultant must ensure that the contractor properly sizes the system. New heating systems, burners and air conditioning systems must be no greater than 15 percent oversized, except to satisfy the manufacturer's next closest nominal size.

30. **Insulation**. Describe insulation work to be performed, such as: install insulation in crawl space, (R-____); install insulation batts in attic, (R-____); install insulation batts in exterior walls, (R-____); etc. Most estimates must be based on square footage projections.

    Required improvements:
    - Insulate all openings in exterior walls where the cavity has been exposed as a result of the rehabilitation.
    - Insulate ceiling areas where necessary.
    - Replacement heating, ventilating, and air conditioning systems supply and return pipes and ducts must be insulated whenever they run through unconditioned spaces.

31. **Cabinetry**. Describe cabinetry work to be performed, such as: install new base cabinets at (____); install new kitchen countertop; install new vanity at (____); replace vanity countertop at (____); etc. It may be necessary to provide cabinet

elevations to show proper placement of cabinets. Most estimates must be based on lump sum and linear footage projections.

32. **Appliances**. Describe new appliances to be installed, such as: install new range at (____); install new refrigerator at (____); install new dishwasher at (____); etc. Most estimates will involve per unit projections.

    Required Work Item: Appliances must be new to be included in the Mortgage. The Borrower may provide used appliances; however, the cost cannot be included in the Mortgage.

33. **Basements**. Describe basement work to be performed, such as: install minimum three feet thick concrete floor; cement parge basement walls; provide dry basement; install new sump pump; replace termite (or other wood-boring insect) damaged joists; etc. Most estimates must be based on lump sum, per unit, and square footage projections.

34. **Cleanup**. Describe cleanup work to be performed, such as: remove debris from property exterior; remove debris from property interior; broom clean all floors, clean all windows; clean all plumbing fixtures and appliances; rental for dumpster; etc. Most estimates must be based on lump sum projections.

35. **Miscellaneous**. Describe any other work to be performed, such as: demolition of existing house or garage; repair of detached outbuildings; move existing house onto mortgaged lot; installation of new foundation; landscaping; repair of swimming pools; etc.

f. Architectural Exhibit Review

The Consultant must prepare or obtain and review all applicable architectural exhibits. Architectural exhibits may include, but are not limited to, the following:
- well certification;
- septic certification;
- termite report (including all outbuildings);
- proposed plot plans for new additions;
- foundation certification by a licensed structural engineer if:
  - the existing Structure will be moved to a new foundation;
  - the Structure is being reconstructed on the existing foundation; or
  - the existing Structure will be elevated.
- cabinetry plans and elevations;
- New Construction exhibits to obtain a building permit for an addition;
- grading and drainage plans; or
- engineering and soil/geotechnical reports.

g. Preparing the Work Write-Up and Cost Estimate

The Consultant must prepare a Work Write-Up that identifies each Work Item. The Work Write-Up must be prepared in a categorical manner that addresses each of the 35 point checklist items. The Consultant must indicate which Work Items require permits.

The Consultant must also prepare a Cost Estimate for each Work Item in the Work Write-Up. The Cost Estimate must separately identify labor costs and itemize the cost of materials per Work Item. Work Item refers to a specific repair or improvement that will be performed. The Consultant must use Cost Estimates that are reasonable for the area in which the Property is located. Lump sum costs are permitted only in line items where a lump sum estimate is reasonable and customary.

i. Conformance with Minimum Property Requirements or Minimum Property Standards

The Work Write-Up must specifically identify whether the Work Item is required to meet MPS or MPR, will involve structural changes, or is a Borrower-elective.

ii. Health and Safety

The Consultant must ensure that all health and safety concerns and any appraiser requirements are addressed in the Work Write-Up before the addition of any other Work Items.

h. Feasibility Study

If requested by the Borrower or Mortgagee, the Consultant must perform a Feasibility Study that consists of a preliminary inspection of the Property and an estimate of the materials and cost for the work that will be necessary to comply with HUD requirements.

i. Draw Request Inspection

The Consultant must perform draw request inspections when requested by the Mortgagee. The Consultant must ensure that all building permits are onsite for the work that was performed. The Consultant must ensure that the work:
- has been completed satisfactorily; and
- conforms to all local codes and ordinances.

j. Change Order

When requested by the Mortgagee or the Borrower, the Consultant must review the proposed changes or additions to the Work Write-Up. The Consultant must evaluate any costs and adjust other Work Items, if necessary, to complete the change order. The Consultant must provide all costs for labor and materials as a result of the change order on form HUD-92577, *Request for Acceptance of Changes in Approved Drawings and Specifications*. The proposed work per the change order is not permissible to proceed until approved by the Mortgagee.

k. Additional Required Documentation

The Consultant must provide the Mortgagee with the following documentation.

i. 203(k) Consultant's Certification

All Consultants are required to sign the following certification after preparing/reviewing the Work Write-Up and Cost Estimate, stating:

> *"I hereby certify that I have carefully inspected this property for compliance with the general acceptability requirements (including health and safety) in HUD's Minimum Property Requirements or Minimum Property Standards. I have required as necessary and reviewed the architectural exhibits, including any applicable engineering and termite reports, and the estimated rehabilitation cost and they are acceptable for the rehabilitation of this property. I have no personal interest, present or prospective, in the property, applicant, or proceeds of the mortgage. I also certify that I have no identity-of-interest or conflict-of-interest with the borrower, seller, mortgagee, real estate agent appraiser, plan reviewer, contractor, or subcontractor or any party with a financial interest in the transaction. To the best of my knowledge, I have reported all items requiring correction and the rehabilitation proposal now meets all HUD requirements for 203(k) Rehabilitation Mortgage Insurance."*
>
> *Warning: HUD will prosecute false claims and statements. Conviction may result in criminal and/or civil penalties. (18 U.S.C 1001, 1010, 1012; 31 U.S.C 3729, 3802).*

_____

Consultant's Signature   *Date*

ii. Consultant/Borrower Agreement

The Consultant and Borrower must sign a written agreement that fully explains the services to be performed and the fees to be charged for each service. The written agreement must disclose to the Borrower that any inspection performed by the Consultant is not a "Home Inspection" as detailed in the disclosure form HUD-92564-CN, *For Your Protection: Get a Home Inspection.*

iii. Inspections and Draw Requests

(A) Draw Request Form

At each draw inspection, the Consultant must complete form HUD-9746-A, *Draw Request Section 203(k),* to indicate completion of the repairs in compliance with the Work Write-Up and architectural exhibits. The Consultant must ensure all repairs meet all local codes and ordinances, including any required permits and inspections. The Consultant must ensure that both the Borrower and the contractor sign the form to certify that the work has been completed in a workmanlike manner before authorizing payments.

Handbook 4000.1   483
Effective Date: 09/14/2015 | Last Revised: 07/10/2019
*Refer to the online version of SF Handbook 4000.1 for specific sections' effective dates

Generally, a release of funds may not be requested for materials that have been paid for but not yet installed.

(B) Exception

The Consultant may request a release of funds for:
- materials costs for items, prepaid by the Borrower in cash or by the contractor, where a contract is established with the supplier and an order is placed with the manufacturer for delivery at a later date; or
- up to 50 percent of materials costs for items, not yet paid for by the Borrower or contractor, where a contract is established with the supplier and an order is placed with the manufacturer for delivery at a later date.

To request release of funds for these items, the Consultant must provide the Mortgagee with a copy of the contract and order with the draw request.

iv. Change Order Requests

The Consultant must complete a change order request on form HUD-92577, *Request for Acceptance of Changes in Approved Drawings and Specifications,* for contingency items and other changes that may increase or decrease the cost of rehabilitation or the value of the Property.

Work must be 100 percent complete on each change order item before the Consultant may authorize release of funds for the work noted on the change order. The Consultant must ensure that all repairs meet all local codes and ordinances, including any required permits and inspections.

B. TITLE II INSURED HOUSING PROGRAMS REVERSE MORTGAGES

> ### RESERVED FOR FUTURE USE
>
> This section is reserved for future use, and until such time, FHA-approved Mortgagees must continue to comply with all applicable law and existing Handbooks, Mortgagee Letters, Notices and outstanding guidance applicable to a Mortgagee's participation in FHA programs.

C. CONDOMINIUM PROJECT APPROVAL

> ### RESERVED FOR FUTURE USE
>
> This section is reserved for future use, and until such time, FHA-approved Mortgagees must continue to comply with all applicable law and existing Handbooks, Mortgagee Letters, Notices and outstanding guidance applicable to Condominium Projects in FHA programs.

D. APPRAISER AND PROPERTY REQUIREMENTS FOR TITLE II FORWARD AND REVERSE MORTGAGES

The appraisal process provides the Mortgagee with necessary information to determine if a property meets the minimum requirements and eligibility standards for a Federal Housing Administration (FHA)-insured Mortgage and will serve as adequate security for a specific FHA-insured Mortgage. Mortgagees bear primary responsibility for determining eligibility and the sufficiency of collateral; however, the Appraiser provides preliminary verification that the Property Acceptability Criteria have been met and an appraised value for the property.

Property refers to the real estate entity that will serve as adequate security for a specific FHA-insured Mortgage.

The requirements in this section of the *FHA Single Family Housing Policy Handbook (SF Handbook)* contain the Property Acceptability Criteria for FHA mortgage insurance, which include Minimum Property Requirements (MPR) and Minimum Property Standards (MPS), and include by reference, associated rules and regulations. The criteria apply to residential Properties containing one- to four-family housing units, individual condominium units, and Manufactured Housing units, and related property improvements and the sites on which they are located, as well as the immediate environment for the dwelling, including streets and other services or facilities associated with the site. Manufactured Housing Properties have additional requirements contained in the Property Acceptability Criteria for Manufactured Housing for Title II Insured Mortgages section. This section also provides requirements for Appraisers in establishing a credible appraised value for a Property that is to serve as security for an FHA-insured Mortgage.

II. ORIGINATION THROUGH POST-CLOSING/ENDORSEMENT
D. Appraiser and Property Requirements for Title II Forward and Reverse Mortgages
1. Commencement of the Appraisal

1. Commencement of the Appraisal

a. Information Required before Commencement of Appraisal

The effective date of the appraisal cannot be before the FHA case number assignment date unless the Mortgagee certifies that the appraisal was ordered for conventional lending or government-guaranteed loan purposes and was performed pursuant to FHA guidelines.

The appraisal must be in full compliance with the Uniform Standards of Professional Appraisal Practice (USPAP), which requires that this be classified as a new assignment. The intended use of the appraisal must indicate that it is solely to assist FHA in assessing the risk of the Property securing the FHA-insured Mortgage. Additionally, FHA and the Mortgagee must be indicated as the intended users of the appraisal report.

If the Appraiser determines that the scope of work is met with regard to MPR, MPS, and USPAP compliance, and further determines that a re-inspection of the Property is not necessary, the effective date of the appraisal may be the date of the original inspection. However, if an FHA-compliant inspection is required, the date of the inspection will become the effective date of the new appraisal.

The Appraiser must obtain all of the following from the Mortgagee before beginning an appraisal:
- a complete copy of the executed sales contract for the subject, if a purchase transaction;
- the land lease, if applicable;
- surveys or legal descriptions, if available;
- any other legal documents contained in the loan file; and
- a point of contact and contact information for the Mortgagee so that the Appraiser can communicate any noncompliance issues.

b. Additional Information Required Before Commencement of an Appraisal on New Construction

The Appraiser must obtain, from the Mortgagee, a fully executed form HUD-92541, *Builder's Certification of Plans, Specifications, and Site*, dated no more than 30 Days prior to the date of the appraisal order and documents related to New Construction, including plans, specifications, and any exhibits provided that will assist the Appraiser in determining what is to be built, or, if now Under Construction, what will be built when finished.

2. General Appraiser Requirements

The Appraiser must follow FHA guidance and comply with the Uniform Standards of Professional Appraisal Practice (USPAP) when completing appraisals of Property used as security for FHA-insured Mortgages. The Appraiser must observe, analyze, and report that the Property meets HUD's MPR and MPS.

Minimum Property Requirements refer to general requirements that all homes insured by FHA be safe, sound, and secure.

Minimum Property Standards refer to regulatory requirements relating to the safety, soundness and security of New Construction.

Every Property must be safe, sound, and secure so that the Mortgagee can determine eligibility. The Appraiser must note every instance where the Property is not safe, sound, and secure and does not comply with HUD's MPR and MPS.

When performing an appraisal, the Appraiser must review and analyze the following:
- the land lease, if applicable;
- surveys or legal descriptions, if available; and
- any other legal documents contained in the loan file,

and report the results of that analysis in the appraisal report.

Sales Transaction or New Construction

When performing an appraisal for a sales transaction or on New Construction, the Appraiser must also review and analyze the following:
- the complete copy of the executed sales contract for the subject; and
- documents related to New Construction, including plans, specifications, and any exhibits provided that will assist the Appraiser in determining what is to be built, or, if now Under Construction, what will be built when finished;

and report the results of that analysis in the appraisal report.

If the seller is not the owner of record, the Appraiser must include an explanation in the appraisal report.

3. Acceptable Appraisal Reporting Forms and Protocols

FHA only accepts appraisals in the Mortgage Information Standards Maintenance Organization (MISMO) 2.6 with embedded PDF format, as created directly by the appraiser (first generation). FHA does not accept private or proprietary data formats or appraisal reports that have been manipulated or "translated" by anyone or any process.

The Appraiser must complete the Fannie Mae Form 1004 MC/Freddie Mac Form 71, *Market Conditions Addendum to the Appraisal Report,* for every appraisal. Other forms to be used in the completion of an FHA appraisal are as follows:

Property/Assignment Type	Acceptable Reporting Form
Single Family, Detached, Attached or Semi-Detached Residential Property	Fannie Mae Form 1004/Freddie Mac Form 70, *Uniform Residential Appraisal Report (URAR)*; Mortgage Industry Standards Maintenance Organization (MISMO) 2.6 Government-Sponsored Enterprise (GSE) format

Property/Assignment Type	Acceptable Reporting Form
Single Unit Condominium	Fannie Mae Form 1073/Freddie Mac Form 465, *Individual Condominium Unit Appraisal Report;* MISMO 2.6 GSE format
Manufactured (HUD Code) Housing	Fannie Mae Form 1004C/Freddie Mac Form 70B, *Manufactured Home Appraisal Report;* MISMO 2.6 Errata 1 format
Small Residential Income Properties (Two to Four Units)	Fannie Mae Form 1025/Freddie Mac Form 72, *Small Residential Income Property Appraisal Report;* MISMO 2.6 Errata 1 format
Update of Appraisal (All Property Types)	Summary Appraisal Update Report Section of Fannie Mae Form 1004D/Freddie Mac Form 442, *Appraisal Update and/or Completion Report;* MISMO 2.6 Errata 1 format
Compliance or Final Inspection for New Construction or Manufactured Housing	Form HUD-92051, *Compliance Inspection Report,* in Portable Document Format (PDF)
Compliance or Final Inspection for Existing Property	Certification of Completion Section of Fannie Mae Form 1004D/Freddie Mac Form 442, *Appraisal Update and/or Completion Report;* MISMO 2.6 Errata 1 format

Instructions for reporting the results of the appraisal, including data and file format and delivery, are found in the FHA Single Family Housing Appraisal Report and Data Delivery Guide.

a. Additional Required Documentation for Appraisals of New Construction [Text was deleted in this section.]

When New Construction is less than 90% complete at the time of the appraisal, the Appraiser must document the floor plan, plot plan, and exhibits necessary to determine the size and level of finish.

When New Construction is 90 percent or more complete, the Appraiser must document a list of components to be installed or completed after the date of appraisal.

b. Application of Minimum Property Requirements and Minimum Property Standards by Construction Status

i. Existing Construction

(A) Definition

Existing Construction refers to a Property that has been 100 percent complete for over one year or has been completed for less than one year and was previously occupied.

(B) Standard

For Existing Construction, the Appraiser must notify the Mortgagee of the deficiencies when the Property does not comply with HUD's MPR.

ii. New Construction

(A) Definition

New Construction refers to Proposed Construction, Properties Under Construction, and Properties Existing Less than One Year as defined below:

- Proposed Construction refers to a Property where no concrete or permanent material has been placed. Digging of footing is not considered permanent.
- Under Construction refers to the period from the first placement of permanent material to 100 percent completion with no Certificate of Occupancy (CO) or equivalent.
- Existing Less than One Year refers to a Property that is 100 percent complete and has been completed less than one year from the date of the issuance of the CO or equivalent. The Property must have never been occupied.

(B) Standard

For New Construction, the Appraiser must notify the Mortgagee of the deficiencies when the Property does not comply with HUD's MPR and MPS, including 24 CFR §§ 200.926a-200.926e.

iii. Determination of Defective Conditions

(A) Definition

Defective Conditions refer to defective construction, evidence of continuing settlement, excessive dampness, leakage, decay, termites, environmental hazards or other conditions affecting the health and safety of occupants, collateral security or structural soundness of the dwelling.

(B) Standard

The Appraiser must identify readily observable defective conditions.

Defective Conditions Requiring Repair

The Appraiser must identify defective conditions that are curable and will make the Property comply with HUD's MPR, and provide an estimated cost to cure.

iv. Inspection by a Qualified Individual or Entity

If the Appraiser cannot determine that a Property meets HUD's MPR or MPS, an inspection by a qualified individual or Entity may be required.

Conditions that require an inspection by qualified individuals or Entities include:
- standing water against the foundation and/or excessively damp basements;
- hazardous materials on the site or within the improvements;
- faulty or defective mechanical systems (electrical, plumbing or heating/cooling);
- evidence of possible structural failure (e.g., settlement or bulging foundation wall, unsupported floor joists, cracked masonry walls or foundation);
- evidence of possible pest infestation;
- leaking or worn-out roofs; or
- any other condition that in the professional judgment of the Appraiser warrants inspection.

Appraisers may not recommend inspections only as a means of limiting liability. The reason or indication of a particular problem must be given when requiring an inspection.

Required Analysis and Reporting

The Appraiser must observe, analyze and report defective conditions and must also provide photographic documentation of those conditions in the appraisal report.

If inspection is required, the Appraiser must cite the reason for requiring an inspection.

c. Minimum Property Requirements and Minimum Property Standards

MPR and MPS form the basis for identifying the deficiencies of the Property that the Appraiser must note within the appraisal report.

i. Legal Requirements

(A) Real Estate Entity

The Appraiser must contact the Mortgagee if the subject Property is not a single, marketable real estate entity, and/or does not consist of a primary plot with a secondary plot contributing to the use and marketability of the Property as a single marketable real estate entity.

(B) Property Rights

(1) Definition

Fee Simple refers to an absolute ownership unencumbered by any other interest or estate.

Handbook 4000.1
Effective Date: 09/14/2015 | Last Revised: 07/10/2019
*Refer to the online version of SF Handbook 4000.1 for specific sections' effective dates

490

Leasehold refers to the right to hold or use Property for a fixed period of time at a given price, without transfer of ownership, on the basis of a lease contract.

(2) Standard

An Appraiser must contact the Mortgagee if the property rights to be appraised are not on real estate held in Fee Simple or Leasehold that comply with HUD's requirements below.

(C) Planned Unit Development

(1) Definition

A Planned Unit Development (PUD) refers to a residential development that contains, within the overall boundary of the subdivision, common areas and facilities owned by a Homeowners' Association (HOA), to which all homeowners must belong and to which they must pay lien-supported assessments. A unit in a PUD consists of the fee title to the real estate represented by the land and the improvements thereon plus the benefits arising from ownership of an interest in the HOA.

(2) Standard

An Appraiser must contact the Mortgagee if the Property is located in a PUD that does not meet this definition.

(D) Leasehold Interests

(1) Definition

Leasehold Interests refer to real estate where the residential improvements are located on land that is subject to long-term lease from the underlying fee owner, creating a divided estate in the Property.

(2) Standard

(a) Forward Mortgage Requirements

A Mortgage secured by real estate under Leasehold requires a renewable lease with a term of not less than 99 years, or a lease that will extend not less than 10 years beyond the maturity date of the Mortgage.

(b) Reverse Mortgage (HECM) Requirements

A reverse mortgage, or Home Equity Conversion Mortgage (HECM), secured by real estate under Leasehold requires a renewable lease for not less than 99 years, or a lease having a remaining period of not less than 50 years beyond the date of the 100th birthday of the youngest mortgagor. Sub-Leasehold Estates are not eligible for FHA mortgage insurance.

(3) Required Analysis and Reporting

An Appraiser must contact the Mortgagee if the Leasehold Interest does not meet this requirement.

ii. Legal and Land Use Considerations

(A) Party or Lot Line Wall

(1) Standard

A building constructed on or next to a property line must be separated from the adjoining building by a wall extending the full height of the building from the foundation to the ridge of the roof.

(2) Required Analysis and Reporting

The Appraiser must note if the party or lot line wall does not extend to the roof or beyond.

(B) Non-Residential Use of Property

(1) Standard

The non-residential portion of the total floor area may not exceed 49 percent.

Any non-residential use of the Property must be subordinate to its residential use, character and appearance. Non-residential use may not impair the residential character or marketability of the Property. The non-residential use of the Property must be legally permitted and conform to current zoning requirements.

(2) Required Analysis and Reporting

The Appraiser must calculate the non-residential portion of any residential Property. Storage areas or similar spaces that are integral parts of the non-residential portion must be included in the calculation of the non-residential area.

The Appraiser must comment on any non-residential use within the Property and state the percentage of the total floor area that is utilized as non-residential. The Appraiser must report whether the non-residential usage is legal and in compliance with current zoning requirements.

The Appraiser must contact the Mortgagee if the non-residential portion of the Property exceeds 49 percent.

(C) Zoning

(1) Standard

FHA requires the Property to comply with all applicable zoning ordinances.

(2) Required Analysis and Reporting

The Appraiser must determine if current use complies with zoning ordinances.

If the existing Property does not comply with all of the current zoning ordinances but is accepted by the local zoning authority, the Appraiser must report the Property as "Legal Non-Conforming" and provide a brief explanation. The Appraiser must analyze and report any adverse effect that the non-conforming use has on the Property's value and marketability, and state whether the Property may be legally rebuilt if destroyed.

(D) Encroachments

(1) Definition

An Encroachment refers to an interference with or intrusion onto another's property.

(2) Standard

The Appraiser must report the presence of any Encroachments so that the Mortgagee can determine eligibility.

(3) Required Analysis and Reporting

The Appraiser must identify any Encroachments of the subject's dwelling, garage, or other improvement onto an adjacent Property, right-of-way, utility Easement, or building restriction line. The Appraiser must also identify any Encroachments of a neighboring dwelling, garage, other physical Structure or improvements onto the subject Property.

The Appraiser must notify the Mortgagee if, upon observation, it appears that an Encroachment affects the subject Property.

(E) Easements and Deed Restrictions

(1) Definition

An Easement refers to an interest in land owned by another person, consisting of the right to use or control the land, or an area above or below it, for a specific limited purpose.

A Deed Restriction refers to a private agreement that restricts the use of real estate in some way, and is listed in the deed.

(2) Standard

The Appraiser must note the presence of any Easements and Deed Restrictions to assist the Mortgagee in determining eligibility.

(3) Required Analysis and Reporting

The Appraiser must analyze and report the effect that Easements and other legal restrictions, such as Deed Restrictions, may have on the use, value and marketability of the Property. The Appraiser must review recorded subdivision plats when available through the normal course of business.

iii. Externalities

(A) Definition

Externalities refer to off-site conditions that affect a Property's value. Externalities include heavy traffic, airport noise and hazards, special airport hazards, proximity to high pressure gas lines, Overhead Electric Power Transmission Lines and Local Distribution Lines, smoke, fumes, and other offensive or noxious odors, and stationary storage tanks.

(B) Standard

The Appraiser must report the presence of Externalities so that the Mortgagee can determine eligibility.

(C) Required Analysis and Reporting

The Appraiser must consider how Externalities affect the marketability and value of the Property, report the issue and the market's reaction, and address any positive or negative effects on the value of the subject Property within the approaches to value.

(1) Heavy Traffic

The Appraiser must analyze and report if close proximity to heavily traveled roadways or railways has an effect on the marketability and value of a site because of excess noise and safety issues.

(2) Airport Noise and Hazards

The Appraiser must identify if the Property is affected by noise and hazards of low flying aircraft because it is near an airport. The Appraiser must review airport contour maps and analyze accordingly. The Appraiser must determine and report the marketability of the Property based on this analysis.

(3) Special Airport Hazards

The Appraiser must identify if the Property is located within a Runway Clear Zone (also known as a Runway Protection Zone) at a civil airport or Clear Zone military airfield and consider the effect of the airport hazards on the marketability when valuing the subject Property.

For Properties located in an Accident Potential Zone 1 (APZ 1) at military airfields, the Appraiser must require compliance with the Department of Defense (DoD) Guidelines and a buyer's acknowledgement.

(a) Existing Dwelling

The Appraiser must condition the appraisal on the Borrower's acknowledgment of the hazard.

(b) Proposed Construction, Under Construction, and Existing Less than One Year

The Appraiser must note that the Property is ineligible for FHA insurance and notify the Mortgagee.

(4) Proximity to High Pressure Gas Lines

The Appraiser must identify if the dwelling or related property improvement is near high-pressure gas or liquid petroleum pipelines or other volatile and explosive products, both aboveground and subsurface. The Appraiser must determine and report the marketability of the Property based on this analysis.

The Appraiser must notify the Mortgagee of the deficiency of MPR or MPS if the Property is not located more than 10 feet from the nearest boundary of the pipeline Easement.

(5) Overhead Electric Power Transmission and Local Distribution Lines

(a) Definitions

Overhead Electric Power Transmission Lines refer to electric lines that supply power from power generation stations to Local Distribution Lines.

Local Distribution Lines refer to electric lines that commonly supply power to residential housing developments, similar facilities and individual Properties.

(b) Required Analysis and Reporting

The Appraiser must notify the Mortgagee of the deficiency of MPR or MPS if the Overhead Electric Power Transmission Lines or the Local Distribution

Lines pass directly over any dwelling, Structure or related property improvement, including pools, spas, or water features.

The Appraiser must notify the Mortgagee of the deficiency of MPR or MPS if the dwelling or related property improvements are located within an Easement or if they appear to be located within an unsafe distance of any power line or tower.

The Appraiser must note and comment on the effect on marketability resulting from the proximity to such site hazards and nuisances. The Appraiser must also determine if the guidelines for Encroachments apply.

(6) Smoke, Fumes and Offensive or Noxious Odors

The Appraiser must notify the Mortgagee if excessive smoke, chemical fumes, noxious odors, stagnant ponds or marshes, poor surface drainage or excessive dampness threaten the health and safety of the occupants or the marketability of the Property.

The Appraiser must consider the effect of the condition in the valuation of the Property if the conditions exist but do not threaten the occupants or marketability.

(7) Stationary Storage Tanks [Text was deleted in this section.]

If the subject property line is located within 300 feet of an aboveground, stationary storage tank with a capacity of 1,000 gallons or more of flammable or explosive material, then the Property is ineligible for FHA insurance, and the Appraiser must notify the Mortgagee of the deficiency of MPR or MPS.

iv. Site Conditions

(A) Access to Property

(1) Definition

Adequate Vehicular Access to Property refers to an all-weather road surface over which emergency and typical passenger vehicles can pass at all times.

(2) Required Analysis and Reporting

The Appraiser must notify the Mortgagee of the deficiency of MPR or MPS if the Property does not have safe pedestrian access and Adequate Vehicular Access from a public street or private street that is protected by a permanent recorded Easement, ownership interest, or is owned and maintained by an HOA. Shared driveways that are not part of an HOA must also meet these requirements.

The Appraiser must note whether there is safe pedestrian access and Adequate Vehicular Access to the site and analyze any effect on value or marketability.

The Appraiser must report evidence of a permanent Easement.

The Appraiser must ask if a maintenance agreement exists and comment on the condition of the private road or lane.

(B) Onsite Hazards and Nuisances

(1) Definition

Onsite Hazards and Nuisances refer to conditions that may endanger the health and safety of the occupants or the structural integrity or marketability of the Property.

(2) Standard

The Appraiser must report the presence of all Onsite Hazards and Nuisances so that the Mortgagee can determine eligibility and any corrective work that may be necessary to mitigate potential adverse effects from the special conditions.

(3) Required Analysis and Reporting

The Appraiser must note and comment on all Onsite Hazards and Nuisances affecting the Property. The Appraiser must also provide photographs of potential problems or issues to assist the Mortgagee in understanding the problem.

Special site conditions include rock formations, unstable soils or slopes, high ground water levels, springs, and other conditions that may have a negative effect on the value.

New and Proposed Construction

The Appraiser must report any special conditions that may exist or arise during construction and necessitate precautionary or hazard mitigation measures.

(C) Topography

The Appraiser must notify the Mortgagee of the deficiency of MPR or MPS if the surface and subsurface water is not diverted from the dwelling to ensure positive drainage away from the foundation.

The Appraiser must make the appraisal subject to an inspection by a qualified individual or Entity if the purchase contract or any other documentation indicates, or if the Appraiser observes dampness because of a foundation issue.

The Appraiser must report to the Mortgagee any danger due to topographic conditions (e.g., earth and mudslides from adjoining properties, falling rocks and avalanches) to the subject Property or the adjoining land.

(D) Grading and Drainage

The Appraiser must check for readily observable evidence of grading and drainage problems. Proper drainage control measures may include gutters and downspouts or appropriate grading or landscaping to divert the flow of water away from the foundation.

The Appraiser must make the appraisal subject to repair if the grading does not provide positive drainage away from the improvements. The Appraiser must note any readily observable evidence of standing water adjacent to the foundation that indicates improper drainage. The Appraiser must report this in the "Site" section of the report, if the standing water is problematic.

(E) Suitability of Soil

The Appraiser must consider the readily observable soil and subsoil conditions of the site, including the type and permeability of the soil, the depth of the water table, surface drainage conditions, compaction, rock formations and other physical features that affect the value of the site, or its suitability for development or support of the existing improvements.

The Appraiser should also consider events and published reports regarding the instability of the soil and surface support of the land as related to the subject and proximate properties.

The Appraiser must analyze and report how this would affect the Property.

(F) Land Subsidence and Sinkholes

(1) Definition

Land Subsidence refers to the lowering of the land-surface elevation from changes that take place underground, including damage caused by sinkholes.

(2) Standard

Danger of Land Subsidence may be encountered where buildings are constructed on uncontrolled fill or unsuitable soil containing foreign matter such as a high percentage of organic material, areas of mining activity or extraction of subsurface minerals, or where the subsoil or subsurface is unstable and subject to slippage or expansion. Typical signs include fissures or cracks in the terrain, damaged foundations, sinkholes or settlement problems.

(3) Required Analysis and Reporting

The Appraiser must notify the Mortgagee of the deficiency of MPR or MPS if there is probable or imminent danger of Land Subsidence so that the Mortgagee can determine eligibility or the need to require the purchase of subsidence insurance.

The Appraiser must analyze and report any readily observable conditions of the surface of the land that indicate potential problems from subsidence or the potential for lack of support for the surface of the land or building foundations.

In mining areas, the Appraiser must analyze and report the depth or extent of mining operations and the site of operating or abandoned shafts or tunnels to determine if the danger is imminent, probable or negligible.

(G) Oil or Gas Wells

(1) Operating or Proposed

The Appraiser must examine the site for the existence of any readily observable evidence of an oil or gas well and report the distance from the dwelling.

The Appraiser must notify the Mortgagee of the deficiency of MPR or MPS if the dwelling is located within 75 feet of an operating or proposed well. The distance is measured from the dwelling to the site boundary, not to the actual well site.

(2) Abandoned

If the Appraiser notes an abandoned gas or oil well on the subject site or an adjacent Property, the Appraiser must stop work and notify the Mortgagee.

The Appraiser may resume work when the Mortgagee provides a letter from local jurisdiction or the appropriate state agency, stating that the subject well was permanently abandoned in a safe manner.

The Appraiser may only complete the appraisal on a Property located near a gas well that emits hydrogen sulfide if the minimum clearance has been established by a petroleum engineer. The Appraiser must assess any impact that the location of the well has on the value and marketability of the Property.

Hydrogen Sulfide

Hydrogen sulfide gas emitted from petroleum product wells is toxic and extremely hazardous. Minimum clearance from sour gas wells may be established only after a petroleum engineer has assessed the risk and state authorities have concurred on clearance recommendations for petroleum industry regulation and for public health and safety.

The Appraiser may only complete an appraisal on a Property if the Mortgagee has required an inspection by a qualified person and provided evidence that the minimum clearance has been established.

(H) Slush Pits

(1) Definition

A Slush Pit refers to a basin in which drilling "mud" is mixed and circulated during drilling to lubricate and cool the drill bit and to flush away rock cuttings.

(2) Required Analysis and Reporting

If the Property has a Slush Pit, the Appraiser must make the appraisal subject to the removal of all unstable and toxic materials and the site made safe.

(I) Property Eligibility in Special Flood Hazard Areas

The Appraiser must review the Federal Emergency Management Agency (FEMA) Flood Insurance Rate Map (FIRM) and make appropriate notations on the applicable appraisal reporting form. If the Property appears to be located within a Special Flood Hazard Area (SFHA), the Appraiser must attach a copy of the flood map panel to the appraisal report.

The Appraiser must enter the FEMA zone designation on the reporting form, and identify the map panel number and map date. If the Property is not shown on any map, the Appraiser must enter "not mapped." The Appraiser must quantify the effect on value, if any, for Properties situated within a designated SFHA.

(J) Coastal Barrier Resources System

The Appraiser must stop work and notify the Mortgagee of the deficiency of MPR or MPS if the Property is located within a Coastal Barrier Resources System (CBRS) designated area.

The Appraiser must review the FEMA FIRM to determine if a Property is located within a CBRS. The FIRM will identify CBRS boundaries through patterns of backward-slanting diagonal lines, both solid and broken. If it appears that the Property is located in a CBRS, the Appraiser must review CBRS location maps to confirm.

(K) Lava Zones

When a Property is located in Hawaii, the Appraiser must review the U.S. Geological Survey (USGS) Lava Flow Hazard Zone maps. The Appraiser must notify the Mortgagee of the deficiency of MPR or MPS if the Property is located in Zones 1 or 2.

Handbook 4000.1
Effective Date: 09/14/2015 | Last Revised: 07/10/2019
*Refer to the online version of SF Handbook 4000.1 for specific sections' effective dates

500

The Appraiser must report in the "Comments" section that the Property is in the Lava Flow Hazard Zone and provide the Zone Number.

(L) Mineral, Oil, and Gas Reservations or Leases

The Appraiser must analyze and report the degree to which the residential benefits may be impaired or the Property damaged by the exercise of the rights set forth in oil, gas, and mineral reservations or leases.

The Appraiser should consider the following:
- the infringement on the property rights of the fee owner caused by the rights granted by the reservation or lease; and
- the hazards, nuisances, or damages that may arise or accrue to the subject Property from exercise of reservation or lease privileges on neighboring properties.

(M) Soil Contamination

(1) Definition

Soil Contamination refers to the presence of manmade chemicals or other alterations to the natural soil environment.

(2) Standard

Conditions that indicate Soil Contamination include the existence of underground storage tanks used for heating oil, pools of liquid, pits, ponds, lagoons, stressed vegetation, stained soils or pavement, drums or odors.

(3) Required Analysis and Reporting

The Appraiser must check readily observable evidence of Soil Contamination and hazardous substances in the soil. The Appraiser must report the proximity to dumps, landfills, industrial sites or other sites that could contain hazardous wastes that may have a negative influence on the marketability and/or value of the subject Property.

(N) Residential Underground Storage Tanks

The Appraiser must note any readily observable surface evidence of residential underground storage tanks, such as fill pipes, pumps, ventilation caps, etc. If there is readily observable evidence of leakage or onsite contamination, the Appraiser must make a requirement for further inspection.

v. New Construction Site Analysis

The Appraiser must obtain a fully executed form HUD-92541, *Builder's Certification of Plans, Specifications, and Site*, signed and dated no more than 30 Days prior to the date the appraisal was ordered, before performing the appraisal on Proposed Construction, Properties Under Construction or Properties Existing Less than One Year.

The Appraiser must review the form and analyze and report any discrepancies between the information provided by the builder and the Appraiser's observations.

vi. Excess and Surplus Land

(A) Definition

Excess Land refers to land that is not needed to serve or support the existing improvement. The highest and best use of the Excess Land may or may not be the same as the highest and best use of the improved parcel. Excess Land may have the potential to be sold separately.

Surplus Land refers to land that is not currently needed to support the existing improvement but cannot be separated from the Property and sold off. Surplus Land does not have an independent highest and best use and may or may not contribute to the value of the improved parcels.

(B) Required Analysis and Reporting

The Appraiser must include the highest and best use analysis in the appraisal report to support the Appraiser's conclusion of the existence of Excess Land. The Appraiser must include Surplus Land in the valuation.

If the subject of an appraisal contains two or more legally conforming platted lots under one legal description and ownership, and the second vacant lot is capable of being divided and/or developed as a separate parcel where such a division will not result in a non-conformity in zoning regulations for the remaining improved lot, the second vacant lot is Excess Land. The value of the second lot must be excluded from the final value conclusion of the appraisal and the Appraiser must provide a value of only the principal site and improvements under a hypothetical condition.

vii. Characteristics of Property Improvements

(A) Requirements for Living Unit

The Appraiser must notify the Mortgagee of the deficiency of MPR or MPS if each living unit does not contain any one of the following:
- a continuing and sufficient supply of safe and potable water under adequate pressure and of appropriate quality for all household uses;

- sanitary facilities and a safe method of sewage disposal. Every living unit must have at least one bathroom, which must include, at a minimum, a water closet, lavatory, and a bathtub or shower;
- adequate space for healthful and comfortable living conditions;
- heating adequate for healthful and comfortable living conditions;
- domestic hot water; or
- electricity adequate for lighting, cooking and for mechanical equipment used in the living unit.

FHA does not have a minimum size requirement for one- to four-family dwellings and condominium units. For Manufactured Housing requirements, see the Manufactured Housing section.

(B) Access to Living Unit

The Appraiser must notify the Mortgagee of the deficiency of MPR or MPS if access to the living unit is not provided without passing through any other living unit or access to the rear yard is not provided without passing through any other living unit. For attached dwellings, the access may be by means of alley, Easement, common area or passage through the dwelling.

The Appraiser must report when the Property has security bars on bedroom windows or doors.

(C) Non-Standard House Styles

(1) Definition

Non-Standard House Style refers to unique Properties in the market area, including log houses, earth sheltered housing, dome houses, houses with lower than normal ceiling heights, and other houses that in the Appraiser's professional opinion, are unique.

(2) Required Analysis and Reporting

The Appraiser must provide a comment that the non-standard house style appears structurally sound and readily marketable and must apply appropriate techniques for analysis and evaluation. In order for such a Property to be fully marketable, the Appraiser must demonstrate that it is located in an area of other similar types of construction and blend in with the landscape.

The Appraiser may require additional education, experience, or assistance for these types of Properties.

(D) Modular Housing

(1) Definition

Modular Housing refers to Structures constructed according to state and local codes off-site in a factory, transported to a building lot, and assembled by a contractor into a finished house. Although quality can vary, all of the materials – from framing, roofing and plumbing to cabinetry, interior finish and electrical – are identical to what is found in comparable quality conventional "stick-built" housing.

(2) Required Analysis and Reporting

The Appraiser must treat Modular Housing the same as stick-built housing, including reporting the appraisal on the same form. The Appraiser must select and analyze appropriate comparable sales, which may include conventionally built housing, Modular Housing or Manufactured Housing.

(E) Identifying an Accessory Dwelling Unit

(1) Definition

An Accessory Dwelling Unit (ADU) refers to a habitable living unit added to, created within, or detached from a primary one-unit Single Family dwelling, which together constitute a single interest in real estate. It is a separate additional living unit, including kitchen, sleeping, and bathroom facilities.

(2) Required Analysis and Reporting

As part of the highest and best use analysis, the Appraiser must make the determination to classify the Property as a Single Family dwelling with an ADU, or a two-family dwelling. The conclusion of the highest and best use analysis will then determine the classification of the Property and the analysis and reporting required.

An ADU is usually subordinate in size, location and appearance to the primary Dwelling Unit and may or may not have separately metered utilities or separate means of ingress or egress. The Appraiser must not include the living area of the ADU in the calculation of the Gross Living Area (GLA) of the primary dwelling.

The Appraiser must notify the Mortgagee of the deficiency in MPR or MPS if more than one ADU is located on the subject Property.

(F) Additional Manufactured Home on Property

The Appraiser may consider a Manufactured Home to be an ADU if it meets the highest and best use and FHA requirements.

The Appraiser may value a Manufactured Home on the Property that physically or legally may not be used as a dwelling and does not pose any health and safety issues by its continued presence as a storage unit.

(G) Leased Equipment, Components, and Mechanical Systems

The Appraiser must not include the value of leased mechanical systems and components in the Market Value of the subject Property. This includes furnaces, water heaters, fuel or propane storage tanks, solar or wind systems (including power purchase agreements), and other mechanical systems and components that are not owned by the property owner. The Appraiser must identify such systems in the appraisal report.

d. Gross Living Area

i. Definition

Gross Living Area (GLA) refers to the total area of finished, above-grade residential space calculated by measuring the outside perimeter of the Structure. It includes only finished, habitable, above-grade living space.

ii. Required Analysis and Reporting

The Appraiser must:
- identify non-contiguous living area and analyze its effect on functional utility;
- ensure that finished basements and unfinished attic areas are not included in the total GLA; and
- use the same measurement techniques for the subject and comparable sales, and report the building dimensions in a consistent manner.

When any part of a finished level is below grade, the Appraiser must report all of that level as below-grade finished area, and report that space on a different line in the appraisal report, unless the market considers it to be Partially Below-Grade Habitable Space.

In the case of non-standard Properties and floor plans, the Appraiser must observe, analyze, and report the market expectations and reactions to the unique Property.

iii. Additions and Converted Space

The Appraiser must treat room additions and garage conversions as part of the GLA of the dwelling, provided that the addition or conversion space:
- is accessible from the interior of the main dwelling in a functional manner;
- has a permanent and sufficient heat source; and
- was built in keeping with the design, appeal, and quality of construction of the main dwelling.

Handbook 4000.1
Effective Date: 09/14/2015 | Last Revised: 07/10/2019
*Refer to the online version of SF Handbook 4000.1 for specific sections' effective dates

505

Room additions and garage conversions that do not meet the criteria listed above are to be addressed as a separate line item in the sales grid, not in the GLA. The Appraiser must address the impact of inferior quality garage conversions and room additions on marketability as well as Contributory Value, if any.

The Appraiser must analyze and report differences in functional utility when selecting comparable properties of similar total GLA that do not include converted living space. If the Appraiser chooses to include converted living spaces as GLA, the Appraiser must include an explanation detailing the composition of the GLA reported for the comparable sales, functional utility of the subject and comparable properties, and market reaction.

Alternatively, the Appraiser may consider and analyze converted living spaces on a separate line within the sales comparison grid including the functional utility line in order to demonstrate market reaction.

The Appraiser must not add an ADU or secondary living area to the GLA.

iv. Partially Below-Grade Habitable Space

(A) Definition

Partially Below-Grade Habitable Space refers to living area constructed partially below grade, but has the full utility of GLA.

(B) Required Analysis and Reporting

The Appraiser must report the design and measurements of the subject, the market acceptance or preference, how the levels and areas of the dwelling are being calculated and compared, and the effect that this has on the analysis.

Regardless of the description of the rooms, bedrooms or baths as above grade or below grade, the Appraiser must analyze all components of the subject Property in the valuation process.

v. Bedrooms

The Appraiser must not identify a room as a bedroom that cannot accommodate ingress or egress in the event of an emergency, regardless of location above or below grade.

e. Appliances

i. Definition

Appliances refer to refrigerators, ranges/ovens, dishwashers, disposals, microwaves, and washers/dryers.

ii. Standard

Appliances that are to remain and that contribute to the market value opinion must be operational.

iii. Required Analysis and Reporting

The Appraiser must note all appliances that remain and contribute to the Market Value.

f. Swimming Pools

The Appraiser must report readily observable defects in a non-covered pool that would render the pool inoperable or unusable. If the pool water contains algae and is aesthetically unappealing, but the Appraiser has no evidence that the pool is otherwise contaminated, no cleaning is required. Swimming pools must be operational to provide full Contributory Value.

The Appraiser must condition the appraisal report for pools with unstable sides or structural issues to be repaired or permanently filled in accordance with local guidelines, and the surrounding land re-graded if necessary.

If the swimming pool has been winterized, or the Appraiser cannot determine if the pool is in working order, the Appraiser must complete the appraisal with the extraordinary assumption that the pool and its equipment can be restored to full operating condition at normal costs.

g. Utilities – Mechanical Components

The Appraiser must notify the Mortgagee if mechanical systems do not appear:
- to have reasonable future utility, durability, and economy;
- to be safe to operate;
- to be protected from destructive elements; or
- to have adequate capacity.

The Appraiser must observe the physical condition of the plumbing, heating and electrical systems. The Appraiser must operate the applicable systems and observe their performance. If the systems appear to be damaged or do not appear to function properly, the Appraiser must condition the appraisal for repair or further inspection.

If the Property is vacant, the Appraiser must note in the report whether the utilities were on or off at the time of the appraisal.

If the utilities are off at the time of the inspection, the Appraiser must ask to have them turned on and complete all requirements under Mechanical Components. However, if it is not feasible to have the utilities turned on, then the appraisal must be completed without the utilities turned on or the mechanical systems functioning.

Handbook 4000.1
Effective Date: 09/14/2015 | Last Revised: 07/10/2019
*Refer to the online version of SF Handbook 4000.1 for specific sections' effective dates

507

If the utilities are not on at the time of observation and the systems could not be operated, the Appraiser must:

1. render the appraisal as subject to re-observation;
2. condition the appraisal upon further observation to determine if the systems are in proper working order once the utilities are restored; and
3. complete the appraisal under the extraordinary assumption that utilities and mechanical systems, and appliances are in working order.

The Appraiser must note that the re-observation may result in additional repair requirements once all the utilities are on and fully functional.

If systems could not be operated due to weather conditions, the Appraiser must clearly note this in the report. The Appraiser should not operate the systems if doing so may damage equipment or when outside temperatures will not allow the system to operate.

Electrical, plumbing, or heating/cooling certifications may be required when the Appraiser cannot determine if one or all of these systems are working properly.

i. Heating and Cooling Systems

The Appraiser must examine the heating system to determine if it is adequate for healthful and comfortable living conditions, regardless of design, fuel or heat source.

The Appraiser must notify the Mortgagee of the deficiency of MPR or MPS if the permanently installed heating system does not:

- automatically heat the living areas of the house to a minimum of 50 degrees Fahrenheit in all GLAs, as well as in non-GLAs containing building or system components subject to failure or damage due to freezing;
- provide healthful and comfortable heat or is not safe to operate;
- rely upon a fuel source that is readily obtainable within the subject's geographic area;
- have market acceptance within the subject's marketplace; and
- operate without human intervention for extended periods of time.

Central air conditioning is not required but, if installed, must be operational. If the air conditioning system is not operational, the Appraiser must indicate the level of deferred maintenance, analyze and report the effect on marketability, and include the cost to cure.

ii. Electrical System

The Appraiser must notify the Mortgagee of the deficiency of MPR or MPS if the electrical system is not adequate to support the typical functions performed in the dwelling without disruption, including appliances adequate for the type and size of the dwelling.

The Appraiser must examine the electrical system to ensure that there is no visible frayed wiring or exposed wires in the dwelling, including garage and basement areas, and report if the amperage and panel size appears inadequate for the Property. The Appraiser must operate a sample of switches, lighting fixtures, and receptacles inside the house and garage, and on the exterior walls, and report any deficiencies. The Appraiser is not required to insert any tool, probe or testing device inside the electrical panel or to dismantle any electrical device or control.

iii. Plumbing System

The Appraiser must notify the Mortgagee of the deficiency of MPR or MPS if the plumbing system does not function to supply water pressure, flow and waste removal.

The Appraiser must flush the toilets and operate a sample of faucets to observe water pressure and flow, to determine that the plumbing system is intact, that it does not emit foul odors, that faucets function appropriately, that both cold and hot water run, and that there are no readily observable evidence of leaks or structural damage under fixtures.

The Appraiser must examine the water heater to ensure that it has a temperature and pressure-relief valve with piping to safely divert escaping steam or hot water.

If the Property has a septic system, the Appraiser must examine it for any signs of failure or surface evidence of malfunction. If there are readily observable deficiencies, the Appraiser must require repair or further inspection.

h. Roof Covering

The Appraiser must notify the Mortgagee of the deficiency of MPR or MPS if the roof covering does not prevent entrance of moisture or provide reasonable future utility, durability and economy of maintenance and does not have a remaining physical life of at least two years.

The Appraiser must observe the roof to determine whether there are deficiencies that present a health and safety hazard or do not allow for reasonable future utility. The Appraiser must identify the roofing material type and the condition observed in the "Improvements" section of the report.

The Appraiser must report if the roof has less than two years of remaining life, and make the appraisal subject to inspection by a professional roofer.

When the Appraiser is unable to view the roof, the Appraiser must explain why the roof is unobservable and report the results of the assessment of the underside of the roof, the attic, and the ceilings.

i. Structural Conditions

The Appraiser must report on structural conditions so that the Mortgagee can determine if the foundation and Structure of the Property will be serviceable for the life of the Mortgage.

The Appraiser must perform a visual observation of the foundation and Structure of the improvements and report those results. If the Appraiser notes any structural issues, the Appraiser must address the nature of the deficiency in the appraisal where physical deficiencies or adverse conditions are reported and require inspection.

j. Defective Paint

If the dwelling or related improvements were built after 1978, the Appraiser must report all defective paint surfaces on the exterior and require repair of any defective paint that exposes the subsurface to the elements.

If the dwelling or related improvements were built on or before December 31, 1978, refer to the section on Lead-Based Paint.

k. Attic Observation Requirements

The Appraiser must observe the interiors of attic spaces.

The Appraiser is not required to disturb insulation, move personal items, furniture, equipment or debris that obstructs access or visibility. If unable to view the area safely in their entirety, the Appraiser must contact the Mortgagee and reschedule a time when a complete visual observation can be performed, or complete the appraisal subject to inspection by a qualified third party. In cases where access through a scuttle is limited and the Appraiser cannot fully enter the attic, the insertion of at least the head and shoulders of the Appraiser will suffice.

If there is evidence of a deficient condition (such as a water-stained ceiling, insufficient ventilation, or smell of mold), the Appraiser must report this condition, and render the appraisal subject to inspection and repairs if necessary.

If there is no access or scuttle, the Appraiser must report the lack of accessibility to the area in the appraisal report. There is no requirement to cut open walls, ceilings or floors.

An observation performed in accordance with these guidelines is visual and is not technically exhaustive.

l. Foundation

The Appraiser must examine the foundation for readily observable evidence of safety or structural deficiencies that may require repair. If a deficiency is noted, the Appraiser must describe the nature of the deficiency and report necessary repairs, alterations or required inspections in the appraisal where physical deficiencies or adverse conditions are reported.

For Manufactured Housing, the appraisal must be conditioned upon the certification of an engineer or architect that the foundation is in compliance with the Permanent Foundations Guide for Manufactured Housing (PFGMH).

i. Basement

The Appraiser must notify the Mortgagee of the deficiency of MPR or MPS if the basement is not free of dampness, wetness, or obvious structural problems that might affect the health and safety of occupants or the soundness of the Structure.

ii. Sump Pumps

The Appraiser must notify the Mortgagee of the deficiency of MPR or MPS if the sump pump is not properly functioning at the time of appraisal. A sump pump may be hard-wired by an acceptable wiring method or may have a factory electrical cord that is to be connected to a receptacle suitable for such use.

m. Crawl Space Observation Requirements

The Appraiser must visually observe areas of the crawl space and notify the Mortgagee of the deficiency of MPR and MPS when the crawl space does not satisfy any of the following criteria:

- The floor joists must be sufficiently above ground level to provide access for maintaining and repairing ductwork and plumbing.
- If the crawl space contains any system components, the minimum required vertical clearance is 18 inches between grade and the bottom of the floor joists.
- The crawl space must be properly vented unless the area is mechanically conditioned.
- The crawl space must be free of trash, debris, and vermin.
- The crawl space must not be excessively damp and must not have any water pooling. If moisture problems are evident, a vapor barrier and/or prevention of water infiltration must be required.

The Appraiser must report any evidence that may indicate issues with structural support, dampness, damage, or vermin that may affect the safety, soundness and security of the Property.

In cases where access through a scuttle is limited, and the Appraiser cannot fully enter the crawl space, the insertion of at least the head and shoulders of the Appraiser will suffice. If there is no access to the crawl space but there is evidence of a deficient condition (such as water-stained subflooring or smell of mold), the Appraiser must report this condition and the Mortgagee must have a qualified third party perform an inspection.

If there is no access, the Appraiser must report the lack of accessibility to the area in the appraisal report. There is no requirement to cut open walls, ceilings or floors.

Not all houses (especially historic houses) with a vacant area beneath the flooring are considered to have a crawl space; it may be an intentional void, with no mechanical systems and no intention or reason for access.

n. Environmental and Safety Hazards

The Appraiser must report known environmental and safety hazards and adverse conditions that may affect the health and safety of the occupants, the Property's ability to serve as collateral, and the structural soundness of the improvements.

Environmental and safety hazards may include defective lead-based paint, mold, toxic chemicals, radioactive materials, other pollution, hazardous activities, and potential damage to the Structure from soil or other differential ground movements, subsidence, flood, and other hazards.

i. Lead-Based Paint

(A) Improvements Built on or Before 1978

The Appraiser must note the condition and location of all defective paint and require repair in compliance with 24 CFR § 200.810(c) and any applicable EPA requirements. The Appraiser must observe all interior and exterior surfaces, including common areas, stairs, deck, porch, railings, windows and doors, for defective paint (cracking, scaling, chipping, peeling, or loose). Exterior surfaces include those surfaces on fences, detached garages, storage sheds, and other outbuildings and appurtenant Structures.

(B) Condominium Units Built on or Before 1978

The Appraiser must observe the interior of the unit, common unit and exterior surfaces and appurtenant Structures of the specific unit being appraised; and address the overall condition, maintenance and appearance of the Condominium Project. The Appraiser must note the condition and location of all defective paint in the unit, common area and exterior, and require repair in compliance with 24 CFR § 200.810(c) and any applicable EPA requirements.

ii. Methamphetamine Contaminated Property

If the Mortgagee notifies the Appraiser or the Appraiser has evidence that a Property is contaminated by the presence of methamphetamine (meth), either by its manufacture or by consumption, the Appraiser must render the appraisal subject to the Property being certified safe for habitation.

If the effective date of the appraisal is prior to certification that the Property (site and dwelling) is safe for habitation, the Appraiser will complete the appraisal subject to certification that the Property is safe for habitation.

If the effective date of the appraisal is after certification that the Property (site and dwelling) is safe for habitation, and the Mortgagee has provided a copy of the certification by the certified hygienist, the Appraiser must include a copy of the certification in the appraisal report.

The Appraiser must analyze and report any long-term stigma caused by the Property's contamination by meth and the impact on value or marketability.

iii. Wood Destroying Insects/Organisms/Termites

The Appraiser must observe the foundation and perimeter of the buildings for evidence of wood destroying pests. The Appraiser's observation is not required to be at the same level as a qualified pest control specialist.

If there is evidence or notification of infestation, including a prior treatment, the Appraiser must mark the evidence of infestation box in the "Improvements" section of the appraisal and make the appraisal subject to inspection by a qualified pest control specialist.

o. Repair Requirements

When examination of New or Existing Construction reveals non-compliance with MPR and MPS, the Appraiser must report the repairs necessary to make the Property comply, provide an estimated cost to cure, provide descriptive photographs, and condition the appraisal for the required repairs.

If compliance can only be effected by major repairs or alterations, the Appraiser must report all readily observable property deficiencies, as well as any adverse conditions discovered performing the research involved in completion of the appraisal, within the reporting form.

Regardless of the Appraiser's suggested repairs, the Mortgagee will determine which repairs are required.

i. Limited Required Repairs

The Appraiser must limit required repairs to those repairs necessary to:
- maintain the safety, security and soundness of the Property;
- preserve the continued marketability of the Property; and
- protect the health and safety of the occupants.

ii. As-Is Condition and Cosmetic Repairs

The Appraiser may complete an as-is appraisal for existing Properties when minor property deficiencies, which generally result from deferred maintenance and normal wear and tear, do not affect the health and safety of the occupants or the security and soundness of the Property. Cosmetic or minor repairs are not required, but the Appraiser must report and consider them in the overall condition when rating and valuing the Property. Cosmetic repairs include missing handrails that do not pose a threat to safety, holes in window screens, cracked window glass, defective interior paint surfaces in housing constructed after 1978, minor plumbing leaks that do not cause damage (such as a dripping faucet), and other inoperable or damaged components that in the Appraiser's professional judgment do not pose a health and safety issue to the occupants of the house.

If an element is functioning well but has not reached the end of its useful life, the Appraiser should not recommend replacement because of age.

iii. Defective Conditions Requiring Repair

The nature and degree of any noted deficiency will determine whether the Appraiser must address the deficiency in the narrative comments area of the report under "condition of the property" or "physical deficiencies" affecting livability or structural soundness.

iv. Conditions Requiring Inspection by a Qualified Individual or Entity

The Appraiser must notify the Mortgagee and make the appraisal subject to an inspection by a qualified individual or Entity when the observation reveals evidence of a potential safety, soundness, or security issue beyond the Appraiser's ability to assess. The Appraiser must report and describe the indication of a particular problem when requiring an inspection of any mechanical system, structural system, or other component requiring a repair.

p. Utility Services

i. Definition

Utility Services refer to those services consumed by the public such as individual electric, water, natural gas, sewage, and telephone.

ii. Required Analysis and Reporting

The Appraiser must notify the Mortgagee of the deficiency of MPR or MPS if the subject Property is an attached, detached, or manufactured Single Family dwelling and the utilities are not independent for each living unit. This does not apply to ADUs.

The Appraiser must also notify the Mortgagee of the deficiency of MPR or MPS if utilities are not located on Easements that have been permanently dedicated to the local government or appropriate public utility body.

(A) Multiple Living Units Under Single Ownership

The Appraiser should not note a deficiency of MPR or MPS if the Property contains multiple living units under a single Mortgage or ownership (two- to four-family Properties) that utilize common services, such as water, sewer, gas and electricity and is served by one meter in jurisdictions that allow single meter rental properties, unless separate utility service shut-offs are not provided for each.

The Appraiser must notify the Mortgagee of the deficiency of MPR or MPS if other facilities are not independent for each living unit, except common services such as laundry, storage space or heating, which may be provided in two- to four-living unit buildings under a single Mortgage.

(B) Living Units Under Separate Ownership

The Appraiser should not note the deficiency of MPR or MPS if the Property contains living units under separate ownership and part of a larger planned community, that utilize common utility services provided from the main to the building line when protected by an Easement or covenant and maintenance agreement, unless individual utilities serving a living unit pass over, under, or through another living unit without provision for repair and maintenance of utilities without trespass on adjoining properties, or legal provision for permanent right of access for maintenance and repair of utilities.

If a single drain line in the building serves more than one unit, and the building drain clean-outs are not accessible from the exterior, the Appraiser must note the deficiency of MPR or MPS to the Mortgagee.

iii. Public Water Supply Systems

(A) Definition

A Public Water Supply System refers to a system that is owned by a governmental authority or by a utility company that is controlled by a governmental authority.

(B) Standard

When a public water supply system is present, the water quality is considered to be safe and potable and to meet the requirements of the health authority with jurisdiction unless:
- the Appraiser indicates deficiencies with the water or notifies the Mortgagee that the water is unsafe; or
- the health authority with jurisdiction issues a public notice indicating the water is unsafe.

(C) Required Analysis and Reporting

The Appraiser must:
- report any readily observable or known deficiencies with the water;
- notify the Mortgagee when water is determined to be unsafe, report, and provide a cost to cure; and
- address any impact on value and marketability, and make the appropriate adjustments.

iv. Community Water Systems

(A) Definition

A Community Water System refers to a central system that is owned, operated and maintained by a private corporation or a nonprofit property owners' association.

(B) Required Analysis and Reporting

If the Property is on a Community Water System, the Appraiser must note the name of the water company on the appraisal report.

v. Individual Water Supply Systems

(A) Definition

An Individual Water Supply System refers to a potable water source providing water to an individual Property.

(B) Standard [Text was deleted in this section.]

When an Individual Water Supply System is present, water quality must meet the requirements of the health authority with jurisdiction. If there are no local (or state) water quality standards, then water must be potable, which may be demonstrated by compliance with the current EPA Manual of Individual and Non-Public Water Supply Systems.

(C) Required Analysis and Reporting

The Appraiser must report on the availability of connection to a public and/or Community Water System and any jurisdictional conditions requiring connection.

When the Appraiser obtains evidence that any of the water quality requirements are not met, the Appraiser must notify the Mortgagee and provide an estimated cost to cure.

The Appraiser must note the deficiency of MPR or MPS if the subject Property contains a well located within the foundation walls of an existing dwelling and there is no evidence that the local jurisdiction recognizes and permits such a location, that it is common for the market area, and does not adversely affect marketability unless the well is located within the foundation walls of a New Construction dwelling in an arctic or sub-arctic region.

The Appraiser must report when water to a Property is supplied by dug wells, cisterns or holding tanks used in conjunction with water purchased and hauled to the site. The Appraiser must report whether such systems are readily accepted by local market participants and that the water supply system may violate MPR or MPS.

The Appraiser must note the deficiency of MPR or MPS if the subject Property has a water source that includes a mechanical chlorinator or is served by springs, lakes, rivers, sand-point or artesian wells.

A pressure tank with a minimum capacity of 42 gallons must be provided. However, pre-pressured tanks and other pressurizing devices are acceptable if delivery between pump cycles equal or exceed that of a 42-gallon tank. Tanks must be equipped with a clean-out plug at the lowest point and a suitable pressure relief valve.

The Appraiser must note any readily observable deficiencies regarding the well and require test or inspection if any of the following apply:
- the water supply relies upon a water purification system due to the presence of contaminates;
- corrosion of pipes (plumbing);
- areas of intensive agricultural uses within one quarter mile;
- coal mining or gas drilling operations within one quarter mile;
- a dump, junkyard, landfill, factory, gas station, or dry cleaning operation within one quarter mile; or
- an unusually objectionable taste, smell, or appearance of well water.

The Appraiser must also be familiar with the minimum distance requirements between private wells and sources of pollution and, if discernible, comment on them. The Appraiser is not required to sketch or note distances between the well, property lines, septic tanks, drain fields, or building Structures but may provide estimated distances where they are comfortable doing so. When available, the Appraiser should obtain from the homeowner or Mortgagee a copy of a survey or other documents attesting to the separation distances between the well and septic system or other sources of pollution.

vi. Shared Wells

(A) Definition

A Shared Well refers to a well that services two to four homes where there is a binding Shared Well Agreement between the property owners that meets FHA requirements.

(B) Required Analysis and Reporting

If the Property has a Shared Well, the Appraiser must report it and note any readily observable deficiencies. The Appraiser must also obtain a Shared Well Agreement and include it in the appraisal report so that the Mortgagee may review the agreement to determine eligibility. The Appraiser must also require an inspection and water testing under the same circumstances as an individual well.

vii. Individual Residential Water Purification Systems

(A) Definition

An Individual Residential Water Purification System refers to equipment, either point-of-entry or point-of-use, installed on Properties that otherwise do not have access to a continuous supply of safe and potable water.

Handbook 4000.1
Effective Date: 09/14/2015 | Last Revised: 07/10/2019
*Refer to the online version of SF Handbook 4000.1 for specific sections' effective dates

517

(B) Required Analysis and Reporting

If a Property is served by an individual residential water purification system, the Appraiser must indicate which type of system is installed on the Property, either point-of-entry or point-of-use.

The Appraiser must report on the conditions requiring connection of the individual residential water purification system.

q. Onsite Sewage Disposal Systems

i. Definition

An Onsite Sewage Disposal System refers to wastewater systems designed to treat and dispose of effluent on the same Property that produces the wastewater.

ii. Required Analysis and Reporting

The Appraiser must note the deficiency of MPR or MPS and notify the Mortgagee if the Property is not served by an off-site sewer system and any living unit is not provided with an Onsite Sewage Disposal System adequate to dispose of all domestic wastes in a manner that will not create a nuisance, or in any way endanger the public health.

The Appraiser must visually inspect the Onsite Sewage Disposal System and its surrounding area. The Appraiser must require an inspection to ensure that the system is in proper working order if there are readily observable signs of system failure. The Appraiser must report on the availability of public sewer to the site.

The Appraiser must note the deficiency of MPR or MPS and notify the Mortgagee if the Appraiser has evidence that the Onsite Sewage Disposal System is not sufficient.

4. Valuation and Reporting Protocols

a. Photograph, Exhibits and Map Requirements

The Appraiser must include a legible street map showing the location of the subject and each of the comparable properties, including sales, rentals, listings, and other data points utilized. If substantial distance exists between the subject and comparable properties, additional legible maps must be included.

The Appraiser must include a building sketch showing the GLA, all exterior dimensions of the house, patios, porches, decks, garages, breezeways, and any other attachments or out buildings contributing value. The sketch must show "covered" or "uncovered" to indicate a roof or no roof (such as over a patio). The Appraiser must show the calculations used to arrive at the estimated GLA. The Appraiser must provide an interior sketch or floor plan for Properties exhibiting functional obsolescence attributable to the floor plan design.

The Appraiser must provide photographs as required in the table below and any additional exterior and interior photographs, reports, studies, analysis, or copies of prior listings in support of the Appraiser's observation and analysis.

FHA Minimum Photograph Requirements	
Photograph Exhibit	**Minimum Photograph Requirement**
Subject Property Exterior	• Front and rear at opposite angles to show all sides of the dwelling • Improvements with Contributory Value not captured in the front or rear photograph • Street scene photograph to include a portion of the subject site • For New Construction, include photographs that depict the subject's grade and drainage • For Proposed Construction, a photograph that shows the grade of the vacant lot
Subject Property Interior	• Kitchen, main living area, bathrooms, bedrooms • Any other rooms representing overall condition • Basement, attic, and crawl space • Recent updates, such as restoration, remodeling and renovation • For two- to four-unit Properties, also include photographs of hallways, foyers, laundry rooms and other common areas
Comparable Sales, Listings, Pending Sales, Rentals, etc.	• Front view of each comparable utilized • Photographs taken at an angle to depict both the front and the side when possible • Multiple Listing Service (MLS) photographs are acceptable to exhibit comparable condition at the time of sale. However, Appraisers must include their own photographs as well, to document compliance
View	• Photographs of any negative or positive view influences that substantially affect value or marketability
Subject Property Deficiencies	• Photographs of the deficiency or condition requiring inspection or repair
Condominium Projects	• Additional photographs of the common areas and shared amenities of the Condominium Project

b. Intended Use and Intended Users of Appraisal

The intended use of the appraisal is solely to assist FHA in assessing the risk of the Property securing the FHA-insured Mortgage (24 CFR § 200.145(b)).

FHA and the Mortgagee are the intended users of the appraisal report.

The FHA Appraiser does not guarantee that the Property is free from defects. The appraisal establishes the value of the Property for mortgage insurance purposes only.

c. Development of the Market Value

i. Value Required

(A) Definition of Market Value

Market Value refers to the most probable price which a Property should bring in a competitive and open market under all conditions requisite to a fair sale, the buyer and seller, each acting prudently, knowledgeably and assuming the price is not affected by undue stimulus. Implicit in this definition is the consummation of a sale as of a specified date and the passing of title from seller to buyer under conditions whereby: (1) buyer and seller are typically motivated; (2) both parties are well informed or well advised, and each acting in what they consider their own best interest; (3) a reasonable time is allowed for exposure in the open market; (4) payment is made in terms of cash in U. S. dollars or in terms of financial arrangements comparable thereto; and (5) the price represents the normal consideration for the Property sold unaffected by special or creative financing or Sales Concessions granted by anyone associated with the sale.

Adjustments to the comparables must be made for special or creative financing or Sales Concessions. No adjustments are necessary for those costs, which are normally paid by sellers as a result of tradition or law in a market area; these costs are readily identifiable since the seller pays these costs in virtually all sales transactions. Special or creative financing adjustments can be made to the comparable Property by comparisons to financing terms offered by a third-party institutional lender that is not already involved in the Property or transaction. Any adjustment should not be calculated on a mechanical dollar for dollar cost of the financing or concession but the dollar amount of any adjustment should approximate the market's reaction to the financing or concessions based on the Appraiser's judgment.

(B) Standard

The Appraiser must determine the Market Value of the subject Property.

(C) Required Analysis and Reporting

The Appraiser must analyze all data researched and collected prior to reporting the value. The Appraiser must include all components of the real estate in the analysis. The Appraiser must not include the value of Personal Property in the appraisal.

ii. Appraisal Conditions

(A) Definition

Appraisal Conditions refer to anything the Appraiser requires to occur or be known before the value of conclusion can be considered valid.

(B) Standard

Conclusions about the observed conditions of the Property provide the rationale for the opinion of Market Value.

The completed appraisal form, together with the required exhibits, constitutes the reporting instrument for FHA-insured Mortgages. Conditions of the Property, mortgage type and the market will determine if the appraisal is to be performed as-is, or if the value opinion needs to be conditioned upon an extraordinary assumption(s), a hypothetical condition(s), subject to an additional inspection, or completion of construction, repairs or alterations.

(C) Required Analysis and Reporting

The Appraiser must state in the appraisal report whether repairs, alterations or inspections are necessary to eliminate conditions threatening the continued use, security, and marketability of the Property.

The following table illustrates property conditions under which an Appraisal Condition must be made.

Report Conclusion	Appraisal Condition
1. There is/are no repair(s), alteration(s) or inspection condition(s) noted by the Appraiser. 2. Establishing the As-Is Value for a 203(k). 3. The Property is being recommended for rejection. 4. Intended use is for Pre-Foreclosure Sale (PFS) in accordance with 24 CFR § 203.370 or Claims Without Conveyance of Title (CWCOT) @ 24 CFR § 203.368. 5. Intended use is for Real Estate Owned (REO) in accordance with 24 CFR § 291.100.	"As-is"
1. Proposed Construction where construction has not started. 2. Under Construction but not yet complete (less than 90%). 3. Certain Section 203(k) Rehabilitation Mortgages depending on scope of work.	"Subject to completion per plans and specifications"

1. Repair or Alteration Condition(s) noted by the Appraiser to:
  • protect the health and safety of the occupants;
  • protect the security of the Property;
  • correct physical deficiencies or conditions affecting structural integrity.
2. Certain Section 203(k) Rehabilitation Mortgages depending on scope of work.
3. Under Construction, more than 90% complete with only minor finish work remaining (buyer preference items e.g., floor coverings, appliances, fixtures, landscaping, etc.). This eliminates the need for plans and specifications.
	"Subject to the following repairs or alterations"

Report Conclusion	Appraisal Condition
Required inspection(s) to meet HUD's Minimum Property Requirements and Minimum Property Standards.as noted by the Appraiser.	"Subject to the following required inspection"

iii. Valuation Development

(A) Standard

There are three valuation approaches as applied to one-to four-residential unit Properties:
- sales comparison approach;
- cost approach; and
- income approach to value.

(B) Required Analysis and Reporting

The Appraiser must obtain credible and verifiable data to support the application of the three approaches to value.

The Appraiser must perform a thorough analysis of the characteristics of the market, including the supply of properties that would compete with the subject and the corresponding demand.

The Appraiser must perform a highest and best use of the Property, using all four tests and report the results of that analysis.

(C) FHA Data Requirements for the Subject and Comparable Properties

The Appraiser must verify the characteristics of the transaction (such as sale price, date, seller concessions, conditions of sale) and the characteristics of the comparable property at the time of sale through reliable data sources.

The Appraiser must verify transactional data via public records and the parties to the transaction: agents, buyers, sellers, Mortgagees, or other parties with relevant information. If the sale cannot be verified by a party to the transaction, the Appraiser may rely on public records or another verifiable impartial source.

MLS records and property site visits alone are not acceptable verification sources.

(D) Effective Age and Remaining Economic Life

(1) Standard

The effective age reflects the condition of a Property relative to similar competitive properties. The effective age may be greater than, less than, or equal to the actual age. Any significant difference between the actual and effective ages requires an explanation.

(2) Required Analysis and Reporting

The Appraiser must state the remaining economic life as a single number or as a range for all property types, including condominiums. The Appraiser must provide an explanation if the remaining economic life is less than 30 years.

The Appraiser must apply the appropriate technique to estimate the economic life of the subject and not just report a number without analysis.

(E) Approaches to Value

The Appraiser must consider and attempt all approaches to value and must develop and reconcile each approach that is relevant.

(1) Cost Approach to Value

The Appraiser may use any of the credible and recognized methods to complete the cost approach (unit in place, segregated costs, price per unit, detailed builder's cost method, or any other credible source that can be duplicated by the reader).

If the Appraiser uses cost estimates provided by the contractor or builder of the Property, the cost estimates must be reasonable and independently verified.

(a) Land Valuation

(i) Standard

If the cost approach is applicable, the Appraiser must estimate the site value. Acceptable methodology used to estimate land value include sales comparison, allocation, and extraction.

(ii) Required Analysis and Reporting

The Appraiser must include a summary of the supporting documentation and analysis in the appraisal. The Appraiser must maintain comparable land sales data and analysis or other supporting information in the Appraiser's file and include it by reference in the appraisal. For Properties with Excess Land, the Appraiser must include all comparable land sale data and analysis in the report.

(b) Estimate of Cost New for Housing

(i) Standard

The Appraiser may use either the replacement cost or the reproduction cost.

(ii) Required Analysis and Reporting

The Appraiser must state the method used and the source of the data.

The Appraiser must use the current version of a published cost data source recognized by the industry. The Appraiser must report the quality rating selected and utilized, as well as identify the source of the data, and its publication and/or effective date. The Appraiser is expected to be aware of local cost data from builders, contractors, building supply firms, and other building industry participants as a check against the published cost data.

The Appraiser must also provide a supporting explanation when applying adjustments to the published cost data, such as adjustments for:
- transportation and labor in remote areas;
- entrepreneurial profit; or
- fees and charges unique to the area.

Instructions for the cost approach as applied to Manufactured Homes are addressed in the FHA Single Family Housing Appraisal Report and Data Delivery Guide - Manufactured Home Appraisal Report.

(2) Income Approach to Value for Residential Properties

(a) Standard

The Appraiser should apply the income approach to a Single Family residential Property when there is evidence of recently rented and then sold data pairs.

The Appraiser must verify if the subject or the comparable rentals and sales are subject to rent control restrictions. If comparable sales do not have rent control restrictions similar to those of the subject, an appropriate adjustment should be applied.

(b) Required Analysis and Reporting

The Appraiser must analyze rental data and provide support for the estimated market rents and adjustments applied to the comparable rentals in the reconciliation of this approach.

The Appraiser must derive the Gross Rent Multiplier (GRM) factor from market data and support it prior to applying it to the market rent for the subject.

(3) Sales Comparison Approach

(a) Standard

The sales comparison approach is required for all appraisals.

(b) Required Analysis and Reporting

The Appraiser must present the data, points of comparison, and analysis; provide support for the Appraiser's choice of comparable properties, and the adjustments for dissimilarities to the subject; and include sufficient description and explanation to support the facts, analyses and the Appraiser's conclusion.

If the data from the market area is insufficient to support some of these requirements, the Appraiser must provide the best information available and include an explanation of the issue, the data available, the conclusions reached and the steps taken by the Appraiser to attempt to meet the guidelines.

(c) Comparable Sale Selection

(i) Characteristics of the Property

Comparable sale selection must be based on properties having the same or similar locational characteristics, physical characteristics and the priority the market assigns to each factor, including:
- site;
- site view;
- location;
- design;
- appeal;
- style;
- age;
- size;
- utility;
- quality;
- condition; and
- any other factor that in the Appraiser's professional judgment is recognized as relevant in the subject market.

(ii) Characteristics of the Transaction

Definition

An Arm's Length Transaction refers to a transaction between unrelated parties and meets the requirements of Market Value.

Standard

The Appraiser must utilize Arm's Length Transactions for comparable properties except when there is evidence that REO sales or short sale/Pre-Foreclosure Sale (PFS) transactions are so prevalent that normal Arm's Length Transactions are not present or supported by the market trend.

A transaction involving a foreclosure transfer to a mortgagee is not evidence of the Market Value, and is not a valid type of comparable sale for an FHA-insured Mortgage.

The common types of property transfers listed below require investigation and analysis to ensure that they meet the definition of an Arm's Length Transaction:

- REO sale – transfer from mortgagee to new owner;
- short sale/PFS;
- estate sale;
- court ordered sale;
- relocation sale; and
- flip transactions.

Required Analysis and Reporting

The Appraiser must include as many comparable properties as are necessary to support the Appraiser's analysis and conclusion. At a minimum, the Appraiser must include the most recent and relevant sales, preferably within the last six months. The Appraiser must include at least three sales that settled no longer than 12 months prior to the effective date of the appraisal. The Appraiser must provide additional support by including more sales, offerings, offerings now under contract, or relevant sales that settled more than 12 months prior to the effective date of the appraisal.

The Appraiser must analyze the whole market, including when there are a number of sales that may or may not be classified as arm's length sales or may not be classified as directly similar to the Property.

(d) Adjusting Comparable Properties

(i) Standard

Calculation of the Contributory Value includes methods based on the:
- direct sales comparison approach;
- cost approach; and
- income approach.

(ii) Required Analysis and Reporting

The Appraiser must apply all appropriate techniques and methods, conduct an analysis, and report the results. The Appraiser must include the reasoning that supports the analyses, opinions, and conclusions in the report.

(e) Comparable Selection in Diverse Real Estate Markets

(i) Standard

Comparable sales should be selected based on similar locational and physical characteristics, not sales price.

Subdivisions, Condominiums or Planned Unit Development Projects

Arm's length resale activity from within the established subdivision, condominium or PUD project is often the best indicator of value.

(ii) Required Analysis and Reporting

The Appraiser must include an analysis of the comparable properties that includes an explanation. The analysis must reflect typical Borrower expectations and behavior.

Subdivisions, Condominiums or Planned Unit Development Projects

If the Appraiser uses sales of comparable properties that are located outside of the subject's subdivision or project, the analysis must reflect typical Borrower expectations and behavior.

For Properties in new subdivisions, or units in new (or recently converted) Condominium Projects, the Appraiser must include, for comparison, properties in the subject market area as well as properties within the subject subdivision or project. Whenever possible, the Appraiser must select at least one sale from a competing subdivision or project and one sale from within the subject subdivision or project so that this market acceptance may be directly compared. If the new project is mature enough to have experienced arm's length resales, the Appraiser must also analyze and report those properties.

(f) Comparable Sale Selection in Rural and Slow Growth Markets

If insufficient comparable sales have occurred within the previous six months, the Appraiser must include at least three sales that occurred less than 12 months prior to the date of appraisal.

Where there is a scarcity of recent comparable sales data, the Appraiser may include sales older than 12 months as additional sales in markets. The Appraiser must report the most recent and relevant sales, and include a thorough explanation of the market conditions, the levels of supply and demand, and a reason for the lack of recent sales data.

(g) Sales Concessions

(i) Definition

Sales Concessions refer to non-realty items, upgraded features in newly constructed houses, or special financing incentives.

(ii) Standard

Adjustments are not calculated on a dollar for dollar cost of the financing or Sales Concession. However, the dollar amount of any adjustment should approximate the market's reaction to the Sales Concessions based on the Appraiser's analysis of observable and supportable market trends and expectations. The adjustment should reflect the difference between the sales price with the Sales Concessions, and what the Property would have sold for without the concessions under typical market conditions.

(iii) Required Analysis and Reporting

The Appraiser must verify all comparable sales transactions for Sales Concessions and report those findings in the appraisal. The Appraiser must clearly state how and to what extent the sale was verified. If the sale cannot be verified with someone who has first-hand knowledge of the transaction (buyers, sellers, real estate agents involved in the transaction, or one of their representatives), the Appraiser must report the lack of verification.

The Appraiser must make market-based adjustments to the comparable sales for any sales or financing concessions that may have affected the sales price. The Sales Concessions of the comparable properties are adjusted to typical market expectations, not to the specific terms or conditions of the sale of the subject. The Appraiser must include an explanation of the effect of the Sales Concessions on the sale price of the comparable.

(h) Bracketing

(i) Definition

Bracketing refers to selecting comparable properties with features that are superior to and inferior to the subject features.

(ii) Standard

Comparable properties must be selected based on the principle of substitution, and the analysis will reveal the relevance of that data. Comparable properties should not be chosen only because their prices bracket a desired or estimated value.

(iii) Required Analysis and Reporting

In analyzing the comparable pool to determine the best comparable sales to display and compare in the adjustment grid, the Appraiser must use Bracketing techniques when possible and appropriate.

(i) Market Condition (Time) Adjustments

(i) Definition

Market Condition Adjustments refer to adjustments made to reflect value changes in the market between the date of the contract for the comparable sale and the effective date of the appraisal.

(ii) Standard

Within the sales adjustment grid, the potentially comparable properties may be adjusted if they were contracted for sale during a market period different from that of the date of valuation. If a market-to-market (time) adjustment is warranted, it must be applied to the date of contract rather than the date of closing or deed recordation.

(iii) Required Analysis and Reporting

The Appraiser must provide a summary comment and support for all conclusions relating to the trend of the current market.

(F) FHA Appraisal Requirements in Changing Markets

(1) Standard

An analysis of market trends for at least the past 12 to 24 months preceding the effective date of the appraisal is necessary in order to establish a benchmark for reporting present market conditions.

The final conclusion must be based on the reconciliation of all data.

(a) Increasing Markets

In an increasing market, positive Market Condition Adjustments should be applied if there is sufficient proof of the trend from a credible source based on a thorough analysis of specific market trends and as evidenced by a sale and resale comparison.

(b) Declining Markets

Although there is no standard industry definition, for purposes of performing appraisals of Properties that are to be collateral for FHA-insured Mortgages, a Declining Market refers to any neighborhood, market area or region that demonstrates a decline in prices or deterioration in other market conditions as evidenced by an oversupply of existing inventory and extended marketing times. Generally, a trend in the housing market is identifiable when it extends for a period of at least six months or two quarters prior to the effective date of the appraisal.

In a Declining Market, negative Market Condition Adjustments should be applied if there is sufficient proof of the trend from a credible source based on a thorough analysis of specific market trends and as evidenced by a sale and resale comparison.

(2) Required Analysis and Reporting

The Appraiser must accurately report market conditions and determine when housing trends are increasing, stable or declining. The Appraiser must provide a summary comment as to the continuance of the current trend or if the trend appears to be changing, and provide support for all conclusions. If the Appraiser bases the adjustment on a published source, the Appraiser must include a copy of which must be included in the addendum.

The Appraiser must include an absorption rate analysis, and at least two comparable sales that closed within 90 Days prior to the effective date of the appraisal. If the Appraiser cannot comply with this requirement due to the lack of market data, a detailed explanation is required.

The Appraiser must include a minimum of two active listings or pending sales on the appraisal grid (in addition to at least three recently settled sales).

For active listings or pending sales, the Appraiser must:
- ensure they are market tested and have reasonable market exposure to avoid the use of overpriced properties as comparable properties;
- use the actual contract purchase price, or, when not available, adjust comparable properties to reflect listing to sale price ratios;
- include the original list price, any revised list prices, and calculate the total Days on Market (DOM). The Appraiser must provide an explanation for the DOM that does not approximate periods reported in the "Neighborhood" section of the appraisal reporting form;
- reconcile the Adjusted Values of active listings or pending sales with the Adjusted Values of the settled sales provided; and
- if the Adjusted Values of the settled comparable properties are higher than the Adjusted Values of the active listings or pending sales, determine if a Market Condition Adjustment is appropriate.

(G) Final Reconciliation and Conclusion

(1) Definition

Final Reconciliation refers to the process by which an Appraiser evaluates and selects from among alternative conclusions to reach a final value estimate, and reports the results of the analysis.

(2) Standard

After the approaches to value are completed, the Appraiser must check the data, calculations and conclusions. The Appraiser must reconcile each approach to value, and must reconcile all approaches into a final estimate of value for the Property.

(3) Required Analysis and Reporting

If the appraisal has no conditions, the Appraiser must render an as-is value opinion.

If the Appraiser must conclude the report under a hypothetical condition or extraordinary assumption, the Appraiser must report the issues and requirements as one of the following:
- "subject to completion per plans and specifications on the basis of a hypothetical condition that the improvements have been completed;"
- "subject to the following repairs or alterations (list them) on the basis of a hypothetical condition that the repairs or alterations have been completed;" or

II. ORIGINATION THROUGH POST-CLOSING/ENDORSEMENT
D. Appraiser and Property Requirements for Title II Forward and Reverse Mortgages
5. Property Acceptability Criteria for Manufactured Housing for Title II Insured Mortgages

- "subject to a required inspection based on the extraordinary assumption that the condition or deficiency does not require alteration or repair."

(H) Signature

(1) Standard

The FHA Roster Appraiser must sign the certification of the appraisal and perform all parts of the analysis and reconciliation. Appraiser trainees or licensees may not sign the appraisal report.

A trainee or licensee may assist in any part of the appraisal, but the opinions and analysis must be performed by the FHA Roster Appraiser. A trainee or licensee may accompany the FHA Roster Appraiser on the observations but may not perform the observations in place of the FHA Roster Appraiser.

The FHA Roster Appraiser must select the comparable properties and perform all critical analyses contained in the appraisal report as well as the Market Conditions Addendum to the appraisal form. The FHA Roster Appraiser must also inspect the subject Property and at least the exterior of the comparable properties.

(2) Required Analysis and Reporting

If another appraiser or trainee appraiser provided assistance or participated in the preparation of the appraisal, the FHA Roster Appraiser must disclose the name of the appraiser or trainee appraiser in the report and their role in developing the appraisal.

5. Property Acceptability Criteria for Manufactured Housing for Title II Insured Mortgages

a. Definitions

Manufactured Housing refers to Structures that are transportable in one or more sections. They are designed to be used as a dwelling when connected to the required utilities, which include the plumbing, heating, air-conditioning and electrical systems contained therein. Manufactured Housing is designed and constructed to the federal Manufactured Home Construction and Safety Standards (MHCSS) as evidenced by an affixed HUD Certification Label. Manufactured Housing may also be referred to as mobile housing, sectionals, multi-sectionals, double-wide, triple-wide or single-wide.

A Manufactured Home refers to a single dwelling unit of Manufactured Housing.

b. Standard

The Appraiser must notify the Mortgagee and report a deficiency of MPR or MPS if a Manufactured Home does not comply with the following:

II. ORIGINATION THROUGH POST-CLOSING/ENDORSEMENT
D. Appraiser and Property Requirements for Title II Forward and Reverse Mortgages
5. Property Acceptability Criteria for Manufactured Housing for Title II Insured Mortgages

- have a floor area of not less than 400 square feet;
- was constructed on or after June 15, 1976, in conformance with the federal MHCSS, as evidenced by an affixed HUD Certification Label in accordance with 24 CFR § 3280.11 (Manufactured Homes produced prior to that date are ineligible for insured financing);
- The Manufactured Home and site exists together as a real estate Entity in accordance with state law (but need not be treated as real estate for taxation purposes);
- was moved from the factory or dealer directly to the site;
- was designed to be used as a dwelling with a permanent foundation built to comply with the PFGMH;
- The finished grade elevation beneath the Manufactured Home or, if a basement is used, the grade beneath the basement floor is at or above the 100-year return frequency flood elevation;
- The Structure is designed for occupancy as a Principal Residence by a single family; or
- The lease meets the requirements of Valuation of Leasehold Interests.

c. **Foundation Systems**

i. **New Construction for Manufactured Housing**

(A) Definition

New Construction for Manufactured Housing refers to a Manufactured Home that has been permanently erected on a site for less than one year prior to the case number assignment date.

(B) Standard

The space beneath the house must be enclosed by a continuous foundation type construction designed to resist all forces to which it is subject without transmitting forces to the building superstructure. The enclosure must be adequately secured to the perimeter of the house and be constructed of materials that conform, accordingly, to HUD MPS (such as concrete, masonry or treated wood) and the PFGMH for foundations.

(C) Required Analysis and Reporting

If the Manufactured Home foundation does not meet the requirements for New Construction, the Appraiser must notify the Mortgagee and report the deficiency of the MPR or MPS.

II. ORIGINATION THROUGH POST-CLOSING/ENDORSEMENT
D. Appraiser and Property Requirements for Title II Forward and Reverse Mortgages
5. Property Acceptability Criteria for Manufactured Housing for Title II Insured Mortgages

ii. Existing Construction for Manufactured Housing

(A) Definition

Existing Construction for Manufactured Housing refers to a Manufactured Home that has been permanently installed on a site for one year or more prior to the case number assignment date.

(B) Standard

If the perimeter enclosure is non-load-bearing skirting comprised of lightweight material, the entire surface area of the skirting must be permanently attached to backing made of concrete, masonry, treated wood or a product with similar strength and durability.

Skirting

Skirting refers to a non-structural enclosure of a foundation crawl space. Typically, but not always, it is a lightweight material such as vinyl or metal attached to the side of the Structure, extending to the ground (generally, not installed below frost depth).

(C) Required Analysis and Reporting

If the Manufactured Home foundation does not meet the requirements for Existing Construction, the Appraiser must notify the Mortgagee and report the deficiency in the MPR or MPS.

d. Running Gear

i. Definition

Running Gear refers to a mechanical system designed to allow the Manufactured Housing unit to be towed over public roads.

ii. Standard

The towing hitch and Running Gear must be removed.

iii. Required Analysis and Reporting

The Appraiser must notify the Mortgagee and report deficiency of MPR or MPS if the Running Gear or towing hitch are still attached to the Manufactured Housing unit.

II. ORIGINATION THROUGH POST-CLOSING/ENDORSEMENT
D. Appraiser and Property Requirements for Title II Forward and Reverse Mortgages
5. Property Acceptability Criteria for Manufactured Housing for Title II Insured Mortgages

e. Perimeter Enclosure

i. Standard

The space beneath Manufactured Homes must be properly enclosed. The perimeter enclosure must be a continuous wall that is adequately secured to the perimeter of the unit and allows for proper ventilation of the crawl space.

ii. Required Analysis and Reporting

The Appraiser must notify the Mortgagee and report a deficiency of MPR or MPS if the Manufactured Housing unit is not properly enclosed. The Appraiser must call for repairs or further inspection, if warranted.

f. HUD Certification Label

i. Definition

HUD Certification Label, also known as a HUD seal or HUD tag, refers to a two inch by four inch aluminum plate permanently attached to Manufactured Housing.

ii. Standard

Manufactured Homes must have an affixed HUD Certification Label located at one end of each section of the house, approximately one foot up from the floor and one foot in from the road side, or as near that location on a permanent part of the exterior of the house as practicable. Etched on the HUD Certification Label is the certification label number, also referred to as the HUD label number. Label numbers are not required to be sequential on a multi-section house.

iii. Required Analysis and Reporting

The Appraiser must report the HUD label number for all sections, or report that the HUD Certification Label is missing or that the Appraiser was unable to locate it.

g. Data Plate

i. Definition

Data Plate refers to a paper document located on the interior of the Property that contains specific information about the unit and its manufacturer.

ii. Standard

Manufactured Homes have a Data Plate affixed in a permanent manner, typically adjacent to the electric service panel, the utility room or within a cabinet in the kitchen.

Handbook 4000.1
Effective Date: 09/14/2015 | Last Revised: 07/10/2019
*Refer to the online version of SF Handbook 4000.1 for specific sections' effective dates

535

II.   ORIGINATION THROUGH POST-CLOSING/ENDORSEMENT
D.   Appraiser and Property Requirements for Title II Forward and Reverse Mortgages
5.   Property Acceptability Criteria for Manufactured Housing for Title II Insured Mortgages

iii. Required Analysis and Reporting

The Appraiser must report the information on the Data Plate within the appraisal, including the manufacturer name, serial number, model and date of manufacture, as well as wind, roof load and thermal zone maps.

If the Data Plate is missing or the Appraiser is unable to locate it, the Appraiser must report this in the appraisal and is not required to secure the Data Plate information from another source.

h. Flood Zone

The Appraiser must stop work and contact the Mortgagee if the Appraiser determines that a Manufactured Home is located in FEMA Flood Zones A or V. The Appraiser may continue to work on the assignment if the Mortgagee provides a Letter of Map Amendment (LOMA) or Letter of Map Revision (LOMR) or flood elevation certification. If the Appraiser is provided with a LOMA or LOMR that removes the Property from the flood zone, the Appraiser does not need to indicate that the Property is in a flood zone. If provided with an elevation certificate, the Appraiser must indicate the Property is in a flood hazard area on the appraisal report.

i. Additions to Manufactured Housing

If the Appraiser observes additions or structural changes to the original Manufacture Home, the Appraiser must condition the appraisal upon inspection by the state or local jurisdiction administrative agency that inspects Manufactured Housing for compliance, or a licensed structural engineer may report on the structural integrity of the manufactured dwelling and the addition if the state does not employ inspectors.

j. Measurement Protocols

The Appraiser must calculate GLA based on the overall length, including living areas and other projections that are at least seven feet in height. The Appraiser must not include bay windows, roof overhangs, drawbars, couplings or hitches in the length and width measurements.

k. Sales Comparison Approach for Manufactured Housing

The Appraiser must include a sufficient number of sales to produce a credible value. The Appraiser must include at least two Manufactured Homes in the comparable sales grid.

l. Estimate of Cost New for Manufactured Housing [Text was deleted in this section.]

The Appraiser must apply the cost approach for New Construction Manufactured Housing.

6. Condominium Projects

a. Definition

A Condominium Project refers to a multi-unit Property in which persons hold title to individual units and an undivided interest in common elements. Common elements (areas) include underlying land and buildings, driveways, parking areas, elevators, outside hallways, recreation and landscaped areas, and other elements described in the condominium declaration. Common areas are typically managed by a condominium association.

b. Standard

A Condominium Project must be on the list of FHA-approved condominiums unless it meets the definition for a Site Condominium.

c. Required Analysis and Reporting

The Appraiser must check if the Condominium Project is on the list of FHA-approved condominiums.

d. Site Condominium

i. Definition

A Site Condominium refers to a project of Single Family, totally detached dwellings encumbered by a declaration of condominium covenants or a condominium form of ownership. They have no shared garages or any other attached buildings. Project approval is required for Site Condominiums that do not meet this definition.

ii. Required Analysis and Reporting

The Appraiser must report the appraisal on Fannie Mae Form 1073/Freddie Mac Form 465, *Individual Condominium Unit Appraisal Report*.

e. Manufactured Housing Condominium Projects

i. Standard

Individual Manufactured Housing units in Condominium Projects are eligible for FHA insurance, on both HECM and forward Mortgages.

ii. Required Analysis and Reporting

The Appraiser must report the appraisal on Fannie Mae Form 1004C/Freddie Mac Form 70-B, *Manufactured Home Appraisal Report*.

In addition to the requirements for analysis and reporting of the Manufactured Home, the Appraiser must inspect the Condominium Project and provide the project information

II. ORIGINATION THROUGH POST-CLOSING/ENDORSEMENT
D. Appraiser and Property Requirements for Title II Forward and Reverse Mortgages
7. Valuation of Leasehold Interests [Text was deleted in this section.]

data as an addendum to the appraisal report. Required data includes all data elements as found in the Project Information Section of Fannie Mae Form 1073/Freddie Mac Form 465.

7. Valuation of Leasehold Interests [Text was deleted in this section.]

a. Definition

Leasehold Interests refer to real estate where the residential improvements are located on land that is subject to long-term lease from the underlying fee owner, creating a divided estate in the Property.

Ground Rent refers to the rent paid for the right to use and occupy the land. Improvements made by the ground lessee typically revert to the ground lessor at the end of the lease term.

b. Standard

Eligible Leasehold terms must meet the requirements included in Leasehold Interests.

c. Required Analysis and Reporting

The Appraiser must obtain a copy of the lease from the Mortgagee. The Appraiser must analyze and report the terms of the ground lease, including the amount of the Ground Rent, the term of the lease, if the lease is renewable, if the lessee has the right of redemption (the right to obtain a Fee Simple title by paying the value of the Leased Fee to the lessor, thereby cancelling the Ground Rent), and if the Ground Rent can increase or decrease over the life of the lease term.

The Appraiser must estimate and report the value of the Leasehold Interest using the calculation in the box below. The Appraiser must provide support for the capitalization rate selected.

Calculation of the Leasehold Interest
Formulas:
Value of Leased Fee = Ground Rent / Capitalization Rate
Value of Leasehold = Value of Fee Simple - Value of Leased Fee

In valuing the Leasehold Interest, the Appraiser must apply the appropriate techniques to each of the approaches to value included in the analysis.

- In the cost approach, the value of the land reported must be its Leasehold Interest.
- In the GRM income approach, the sales used to derive the GRM factor must be based on properties under similar Ground Rent terms (or be adjusted to similar Ground Rent terms).
- In the sales comparison analysis, the comparable sales must be adjusted for their lack of similarity to the subject in the "Ownership Rights" section of the sales adjustment grid.

II. ORIGINATION THROUGH POST-CLOSING/ENDORSEMENT
D. Appraiser and Property Requirements for Title II Forward and Reverse Mortgages
8. Additional Appraisal Requirements for 223(e) Mortgages

8. Additional Appraisal Requirements for 223(e) Mortgages

Section 223(e) is a mortgage insurance program for Properties located in older, declining urban areas. The program allows for the acquisition, repair, and/or renovation or construction of a residential Property.

The Appraiser must provide a remaining physical life in addition to the remaining economic life if the Mortgagee orders an appraisal for a Property to be insured under the 223(e) program.

9. Unimproved Property Appraisal

a. Definition

Unimproved Property Appraisal refers to the valuation of an interest in land without human made Structures.

b. Standard

An Unimproved Property Appraisal may be warranted when:
- the Property does not include building improvements;
- the prior improvements on the Property were demolished;
- the improvements are in such deteriorated condition as to provide no Contributory Value to the Property; or
- condemnation proceedings by the local authority have acquired the improvements in part or in their entirety.

c. Required Analysis and Reporting

The Appraiser must provide a written narrative format or a commercially available reporting form. The appraisal report must include, at minimum, the following:
- property address;
- legal description;
- owner of record;
- occupancy;
- assessment and tax information;
- property rights appraised;
- site size;
- zoning;
- highest and best use;
- shape;
- topography;
- drainage;
- availability of utilities;
- if it is located within a FEMA-designated SFHA;
- a sales grid, including:
  - detailed information on at least three comparable sales;

- o a quantitative comparison of those property attributes to the subject; and
- o a comparison of the number of comparable unimproved properties sold with the number of offered and listed for sale to determine supply and demand, absorption rate, and other market data required so that the report is not misleading;
- certification and limiting conditions as included in the *URAR*, Fannie Mae Form 1004/Freddie Mac Form 70; and
- any other forms and documentation necessary to comply with USPAP Standard 2.

When completing the sales grid, the Appraiser must compare and appropriately adjust the sales of comparable unimproved building lots or sites for differences in location, size, zoning, utility connection or availability of utility connection, site improvement and any other pertinent factors. The Appraiser must then reconcile the adjusted sales into a value conclusion.

The Appraiser must calculate and extract any costs to be incurred from razing the existing improvements and cleaning up the site from the value of the supporting land to arrive at a final conclusion of value of the site as if vacant and ready to be put to its highest and best use.

10. Update of Appraisal

Appraisers may perform an update of a previously completed appraisal using the Fannie Mae Form 1004D/Freddie Mac Form 442/March 2005 when requested by the Mortgagee.

The Appraiser must adhere to the Scope of Work and Appraiser's Certification listed on the form, which includes an exterior inspection of the subject Property from, at least, the street; and research, analyze and verify current market data to determine whether the Property has or has not declined in value since the effective date of the appraisal report being updated.

If the Appraiser concurs with the original appraisal report and determines that the value has not declined, the Appraiser must indicate this on the form, provide any necessary comments, and provide a photo of the front of the subject Property taken from the public street. If the Appraiser does not concur with the original data report or the Property Value has declined, the Appraiser must indicate this on the form and a photo is not required.

11. Market Conditions Addendum, Fannie Mae Form 1004MC/Freddie Mac Form 71, Instructions Applicable to FHA Appraisals

a. Standard

The Appraiser must complete the Fannie Mae Form 1004MC/Freddie Mac Form 71, *Market Conditions Addendum to the Appraisal Report*, for all appraisal assignments. The analysis and valuation of FHA-insured Properties must properly analyze and address market trends in the subject's market. Whether these trends are positive, neutral or negative, proper data collection and reporting are imperative components of a complete market conditions analysis; this is most important where markets are demonstrating negative trends.

II. ORIGINATION THROUGH POST-CLOSING/ENDORSEMENT
D. Appraiser and Property Requirements for Title II Forward and Reverse Mortgages
12. Programs and Products - Required Analysis and Reporting

b. Required Analysis and Reporting

The Appraiser must analyze the broad market area first (neighborhood analysis), then analyze the specific market (direct sales comparison), and then report how the subject relates to its market area.

The Appraiser must provide support for conclusions regarding housing trends and overall market conditions as reported in the "Neighborhood" section of the appraisal report form. The Appraiser's analysis and conclusions must be based on the information reported on this form. The Appraiser's study of the market affecting the subject Property must include sufficient data for a statistical analysis to be relevant.

The Appraiser must fill in all the information to the extent it is available and reliable and must provide analysis as indicated. If any required data is unavailable or is considered unreliable, the Appraiser must provide an explanation. It is recognized that not all data sources will be able to provide data for the shaded areas on the form; if it is available, however, the Appraiser must include the data in the analysis.

If data sources provide the required information as an average instead of the median, the Appraiser must report the available figure and identify it as an average. The Appraiser must explain any anomalies in the data, such as seasonal markets, New Construction, foreclosures, etc.

12. Programs and Products

a. Section 248 Indian Land Program

i. Property Rights to be Appraised

The Appraiser must identify the interest to be appraised based on the type of ownership.

(A) Fee Simple Unrestricted

Fee Simple Unrestricted ownership refers to ownership in Real Property that may be bought, sold and transferred between Native American and non-Native American purchasers without review by the tribe or the Bureau of Indian Affairs (BIA).

(B) Tribal Trust Lands, Restricted Trust Land

(1) Standard

The FHA Section 248 program insures Mortgages on houses that are located on Indian tribal trust land or Restricted Trust Lands. For these Properties, leased ownership of the underlying land remains with the tribe and will be subject to a long-term, 50-year ground lease (or a 25-year lease with a 25-year renewable term).

(2) Required Analysis and Reporting

The Appraiser must determine the value for the Leasehold Estate using the analysis and reporting guidance on Leasehold in this *SF Handbook*.

ii. Access to Property

Tribally owned and maintained streets and utilities are considered publicly owned. The Appraiser must report Easements and maintenance agreements for non-public, common ownership interests that affect the access and utility of the Property.

iii. Approaches to Value

The Appraiser must be familiar with the applicable ownership and use restrictions and develop a credible value for the Property. The supply of comparable sales and rental transactions varies by site and by tribe. Until sufficient sales exist on a reservation or within the specific Indian area to provide a reasonable sales comparison approach for determining the value of tribal trust Leaseholds or allotted land sales, the Appraiser must rely on other value indicators. The appraisal process must be documented more thoroughly than a typical market appraisal. USPAP Standards #1 and #2 are effective in allowing the Appraiser to "correctly employ those recognized methods and techniques that are necessary to produce a credible appraisal." In addition, "in reporting the results of a Real Property appraisal an appraiser must communicate each analysis, opinion and conclusion in a manner that is not misleading." An appraisal on trust land may rely more on the cost approach or data developed from other tribes. HUD will accept the report if the Appraiser has documented the research, information developed and conclusions clearly for the intended users to understand.

iv. Cost Approach to Value

The cost approach is often the primary indication of value based on the unique nature of land rights in the reservation. The value of the site as vacant will depend on the property rights held by an individual. If the Appraiser's analysis indicates that the value of the site may be zero or a small Leasehold value, the Appraiser must enter this information in the "Cost Approach" section of the form and enter the statement "subject is on Tribal Trust Land with annual rent not capitalized" in the "Comments" section. If a market exists and an interest in the land was purchased, the value is estimated via traditional cost approach methods described in this *SF Handbook*.

(A) Cost Approach for New Construction

The following are instructions specific to New Construction on tribal lands.

In addition to including the cost of water, septic, and any other onsite costs in the cost approach, for lands within the reservation the Appraiser may provide an allowance for off-site development costs. The lesser of actual pro-rated costs or up to 15 percent of the cost of the construction of the subject house may be added for off-site

• infrastructure associated with development of the subject lot. This policy applies principally to New Construction where such charges are assessed by tribally approved entities, such as housing entities or housing authorities, or agreements with other federal or local government bodies for providing power, utilities, sewer, water or road construction. The costs to bring utilities, including public water, sewer, electricity and telephone, to sites represent significant development costs. The traditional tract development of residential houses may not be a part of the local culture. Therefore, the utility costs to hook up to any form of a public system in a more rural area can exceed local standards.

In remote areas, the construction costs in construction cost manuals may have to be adjusted for transportation, labor or other costs not included in the basic estimate. Architect fees are not typically reflected in the base building costs. Due to special circumstances, the normal allocation for this fee may not automatically reflect the above actual cost. The Appraiser must provide a supporting explanation for the adjustments to the construction costs.

(B) Cost Approach for Existing Construction

Where market sales are limited, FHA requires the cost approach to be completed on all tribal trust appraisals, including a credible estimate of depreciation. In addition to developing the cost approach described in this *SF Handbook* the Appraiser must report the following:

1. the name of the cost service;
2. the source and date, if electronic version. Upload as an exhibit into the report when available;
3. the page numbers of cost tables or factors, if paper version. The reviewer or reader must be able to replicate;
4. all current multipliers applicable to locale and time as updated and published by the cost service used; and
5. depreciation due to normal aging, which may be derived from the tables in the cost service book.

A computer-generated cost analysis is acceptable in place of the above as long as the printout contains sufficient information to verify that all significant property features have been properly addressed in the cost analysis.

v. Sales Comparison Approach to Value

The Appraiser must follow the sales comparison approach instructions outlined in this *SF Handbook*. In addition to the typical data sources the Appraiser must obtain sales information from the local tribal or BIA realty office if available. The Appraiser may consider sales from other reservations within the region if appropriate.

The order of selection preferences for sales depends upon the type of interest in the land being appraised:

- tribal trust Leasehold sales (market sales between tribal members);
- sales of allotted land trust between tribal members;
- Fee Simple within the reservation (residual value of the improvements by adjusting out the land contribution); or
- Fee Simple proximate to the reservation.

The Appraiser must report the property rights in the "Ownership" line of the grid and apply an appropriate adjustment (if any). In addition, the Appraiser must explain the differences in ownership rights of the comparable properties as compared to the subject, and the basis for any adjustment.

vi. Income Approach to Value

If the Appraiser determines that this approach can be credibly completed, refer to the Income Approach section in this *SF Handbook*. If the Property includes a rental unit(s), the Appraiser must provide an estimate of monthly rent for each unit and note if the rent is limited to the tribal sub-market.

vii. Final Reconciliation of Value

The Appraiser must follow the final reconciliation of value instructions outlined in this *SF Handbook*. Where market information is limited and the support for the sales comparison analysis is weaker, the Appraiser may need to place greater consideration on the cost approach.

b. Section 247 Hawaiian Home Lands Program

Due to the nature of the title and property rights, the Appraiser must develop the cost for both Existing and Proposed Construction. When appropriate, the Appraiser must attempt to apply the income and sales comparison approaches.

The Appraiser must include the following language in the Appraiser report: "*The value defined for this appraisal is not 'Market Value' as defined in the standard documents of form appraisal reports. This appraisal has been completed for FHA mortgage insurance purposes, per HUD instructions for Department of Hawaiian Home Lands (DHHL) properties.*"

The Appraiser must develop a cost approach from a published cost service in addition to developing the cost approach described in this SF Handbook. The Appraiser's report must include:
- photocopies of all pages used to derive the cost figures, except as noted below;
- application of all current multipliers necessary and published by the cost service;
- no marketing expense to the cost analysis of a DHHL property appraisal because these Properties are not freely marketable;
- entrepreneurial venture may only be included if reasonable profit and overhead are not already included in all costs;

II. ORIGINATION THROUGH POST-CLOSING/ENDORSEMENT
D. Appraiser and Property Requirements for Title II Forward and Reverse Mortgages
12. Programs and Products - Standard 203(k) and Limited 203(k) Rehabilitation Mortgages

- depreciation due to normal aging, which may be derived from the tables in the cost service book. Depreciation from incurable external or functional obsolescence should be based on verifiable market extractions, by paired-sales analysis and capitalized rent loss.

The Appraiser must include a computer-generated cost analysis as long as the printout conforms to the format of the cost service form and contains sufficient information to verify that all significant property features have been properly addressed in the cost analysis. Accordingly, the Appraiser will not be required to supplement a computer-generated cost analysis with photocopies from the cost service book.

c. Standard 203(k) and Limited 203(k) Rehabilitation Mortgages

The Appraiser may be asked to perform two separate types of valuation by the Mortgagee for Standard 203(k) and Limited 203(k) Rehabilitation Mortgages. The Mortgagee may order both reports from the same Appraiser or select two different Appraisers for the two valuation assignments.

If a Mortgagee requires both an as-is and an after-improved value of the Property, the case will require two separate appraisal assignments and reports:
- an analysis to provide the as-is value; and
- a separate analysis performed under the hypothetical condition that the repairs have been completed.

i. Appraisal of the Property "As Is"

(A) Standard

Assignment conditions for this appraisal are the same as in all FHA appraisal assignments, except that the value of the Property is to be estimated "as is" even though the Property may not meet the Property Acceptability Criteria required for FHA-insured Properties.

(B) Required Analysis and Reporting

The Appraiser must provide an analysis and report of the value of the subject Property "as is." If the Appraiser observes property conditions that do not meet the Property Acceptability Criteria, the Appraiser must report those items or conditions and note that the Property, in its "as is" condition, does not meet the Property Acceptability Criteria for an FHA-insured Mortgage. This appraisal must not be rendered "subject to repairs."

Handbook 4000.1
Effective Date: 09/14/2015 | Last Revised: 07/10/2019
*Refer to the online version of SF Handbook 4000.1 for specific sections' effective dates

545

ii. After Improved Value of the Property

(A) Definition

After Improved Value refers to the value as determined by the Appraiser based on a hypothetical condition that the repairs or alterations have been completed.

(B) Standard

The Appraiser must provide an "After Improved Value." The Appraiser must make the appraisal "subject to the following repairs or alterations on the basis of a hypothetical condition that the repairs or alterations have been completed."

(C) Required Analysis and Reporting

The Appraiser must review the 203(k) Consultant's Work Write-Up or the contractor's proposal and Cost Estimates. The Appraiser must notify the Mortgagee of any health and safety issues in the Property that are not addressed in the Work Write-Up or proposal. When the Consultant or contractor has modified the Work Write-Up or proposal, the Appraiser must complete the appraisal based on the final Work Write-Up or the contractor's final proposal and Cost Estimates.

The Appraiser must include the Work Write-Up or proposal as an exhibit to the appraisal report.

d. Special Energy-Related Building Components

i. Special Energy Components

(A) Definition

A Special Energy System refers to any addition, alteration, or improvement to an existing or new Structure that is designed to utilize wind, geothermal or solar energy to produce energy to support the habitability of the Structure.

(B) Standard

Active, passive and photovoltaic solar energy systems are permitted in this program. Solar collectors must be located where they will be free from natural or man-made obstructions to the sun. Special Energy Systems not part of the real estate must not be included in the appraised value.

(C) Required Analysis and Reporting

The Appraiser must analyze and report the local market acceptance of special energy-related building components and equipment, including solar energy components, high-energy efficiency housing features and components, geothermal systems, and wind powered components.

ii. Other Energy Related Building Components

(A) Definition

Other Energy Related Building Components refer to components in the Property designed to reduce energy requirements.

(B) Required Analysis and Reporting

The Appraiser must note which features are installed in a house and calculate how each component affects the value of the Property.

iii. Measurement and Reporting of Contribution to Value

(A) Definition

Contributory Value refers to the change in the value of a Property as a whole, whether positive or negative, resulting from the addition or deletion of a property component.

(B) Standard

Measurement of the Contributory Value of the component is accomplished by the application of techniques based on one or more of the recognized three approaches to value: cost approach, income approach, and sales comparison approach. Each of these recognized methods and techniques requires the Appraiser to collect, verify, and analyze all information necessary for credible assignment results.

(C) Required Analysis and Reporting

The Appraiser must apply all appropriate methods and techniques necessary for credible assignment results.

(D) Sales Comparison Based Extraction Method

If there is sufficient data based on direct sales comparison to produce credible results, the Appraiser must calculate the adjustment and explain the methodology and analysis supporting the method and results in the appraisal report. The Appraiser must apply the extracted adjustment to the comparable sales and include the reasoning that supports the analyses, opinions, and conclusions in the report.

If there is insufficient data to perform a matched pairs analysis the Appraiser must analyze and report one of the approaches below to calculate an appropriate adjustment.

(E) Cost Approach Based Method

The Appraiser must include the details of the item(s) being valued and measure the Contributory Value of the component(s) to the whole by calculating the cost of the item less accrued depreciation. The Appraiser must include consideration of physical depreciation, functional obsolescence (including superadequacies) and external obsolescence in the estimate of accrued depreciation and apply the resulting calculation of the Contributory Value to the comparable sales.

(F) Income Approach Based Methods

(1) Gross Rent Multiplier Method

If the Property is located in a market where the Appraiser can calculate a GRM, and rental data for properties with similar special energy components is available, the Appraiser must extract an adjustment relevant to the rental value of the feature from the analysis of those similar rentals and apply the appropriate GRM factor to calculate an adjustment for the comparable sales.

(2) Net Income/Savings Capitalization Method

The Appraiser may use an income approach solution based on capitalization of savings attendant to the alternative energy source. The Appraiser may estimate the present value of the future benefit using the discounted cash flow technique or commercially available tools; however, the Appraiser must be competent to use them and provide an explanation of the analysis.

(G) Reconciliation of the Approaches

The Appraiser may elect to utilize some of the tools and training available from professional organizations and energy-related firms. The Appraiser must provide a credible analysis and reconciliation explaining the methodology and support for the adjustment.

As related to special building components, the Appraiser must provide an analysis of the information and conclusions supporting the application of adjustments.

The Appraiser must reconcile all the methods utilized and resolve to a final opinion of the adjustment, analyzing both the quantity and quality of available data.

iv. Property Assessed Clean Energy

(A) Definition

Property Assessed Clean Energy (PACE) refers to programs that may provide an alternative means of financing energy and other PACE-allowed improvements for residential Properties using financing provided by private enterprises in conjunction with state and local governments. Generally, the repayment of the PACE obligation is collected in the same manner as a special assessment tax is collected by the local government, rather than paid directly by the Borrower to the party providing the PACE financing.

Generally, the PACE obligation is also secured in the same manner as a special assessment tax against the Property. In the event of a sale, including a foreclosure sale, of the Property with outstanding PACE financing, the obligation will continue with the Property causing the new homeowner to be responsible for the payments on the outstanding PACE amount. In cases of foreclosure, priority collection of delinquent payments for the PACE assessment may be waived or relinquished.

(B) Required Analysis and Reporting

The Appraiser must review the sales contract and property tax records for the Property to determine the amount of any outstanding PACE obligation:

- if the Mortgagee notifies the Appraiser that the subject Property is subject to a PACE obligation;
- when the Appraiser observes that the property taxes for the subject Property are higher than average for the neighborhood and type of dwelling; or
- when the Appraiser observes energy-related building components or equipment or is aware of other PACE-allowed improvements during the inspection process.

The Appraiser must report the outstanding amount of the PACE obligation for the subject Property.

Where energy and other PACE-allowed improvements have been made to the Property through a PACE program, the Appraiser must analyze and report the impact on the value of the Property from the PACE-related improvements subject to the PACE assessments being extinguished.

e. HUD Real Estate Owned Properties

i. Definition

A HUD REO Property, also known as a HUD home or a HUD-owned home, refers to a one- to four-unit residential Property acquired by HUD as a result of a foreclosure on an FHA-insured Mortgage or other means of acquisition, whereby the Secretary of HUD becomes the property owner and offers it for sale to recover the mortgage insurance claim that HUD paid to the Mortgagee.

ii. Standard

An appraisal may be ordered on a HUD REO Property as one of one or more evaluation tools to establish list price or subsequent price adjustments.

(A) Assignment Type

Under "Assignment Type" in the "Subject" section of the appraisal reporting form, the Appraiser must mark the box labeled "other" and indicate that the Property is a HUD REO Property.

(B) Intended Use of Appraisal

The intended use of the appraisal for a HUD REO Property is as one of one or more evaluation tools to establish list price or subsequent price adjustments.

(C) Intended User

The intended user of an appraisal of a HUD REO Property is HUD/FHA or its contractors.

iii. Required Analysis and Reporting

(A) Appraiser's Inspection

The Appraiser must inspect the interior and exterior of the Property. The Appraiser must describe any differences found between the information contained in the Property Condition Report (PCR) and the Appraiser's observations. The Appraiser must support this description with photographs when warranted.

(B) Utilities - Mechanical Components

If the utilities are off at the time of inspection, the Appraiser must ask to have them turned on and complete all requirements under Mechanical Components. However, if it is not feasible to have the utilities turned on, then the appraisal must be completed without the utilities turned on or the mechanical systems functioning.

(C) Sales Comparison Approach, Use of Real Estate Owned Sales as Comparable Sales

When considering sales to be utilized as comparables, the Appraiser must note the conditions of the sale and the motivation of the sellers and purchasers.

In some markets, non-arm's length sales constitute the majority of recent transactions of similar properties and thus are significant in the analysis of the subject. This assignment is to estimate Market Value, so REO sales, short sales and other non-arm's length transactions must not automatically be chosen as comparables. If there is compelling evidence in the market to warrant their use, the Appraiser must provide additional explanation and support in the "Analysis" section of the sales comparison approach.

Transfers to a Mortgagee or Entity that owns the Mortgage by deed of trust, through foreclosure sale or sheriff's sale, are not acceptable as comparable sales.

Appraisers must exercise due diligence and care in the research and validation of REO sales to ensure similarity to the subject, especially in physical condition.

(D) Appraisal Conditions

The Appraiser must provide an analysis and report of the value of the subject Property "as is." The appraisal report must include the applicable property specific appraisal reporting form, all required exhibits, and a copy of the PCR.

For Manufactured Housing, the Appraiser must **not** require a certification that the foundation complies with the PFGMH.

(E) Extraordinary Conditions

The as-is value can be impacted by extraordinary conditions. If the Property has an illegal use or an extraordinary condition, the Appraiser must estimate the cost to bring the Property into compliance with zoning or typical marketability. The Appraiser must report whether any grandfathered use is allowed. The Appraiser may contact the Asset Management (AM) contractor for guidance and clarification when appraising a HUD home that is impacted by extraordinary circumstances.

(F) Statement of Insurability

The Appraiser must include a Statement of Insurability in the "Comments" section of the appraisal report.

(1) Insurable

The Appraiser must state that the Property is insurable if, at the time of the appraisal, the Property meets MPR and MPS without needing repairs.

(2) Insurable With Repair Escrow

If the Property requires no more than $10,000 in repair, the Appraiser must state that the Property is insurable with a repair escrow.

(3) Uninsurable

If the cost of repairs is greater than $10,000, the Appraiser must state that the Property is uninsurable.

(G) Submitting the Appraisal

The submission of the appraisal report and data is uploaded in HUD's P260 web-based internet portal or subsequent system.

The Appraiser must obtain a completed copy of the PCR from the contractor and submit the PCR with the appraisal report.

(H) Claims Without Conveyance of Title Properties

(1) Assignment Type

Under "Assignment Type" in the "Subject" section of the appraisal reporting form, the Appraiser must mark the box labeled "other" and indicate that the Property is a HUD Claims Without Conveyance of Title (CWCOT) Property.

(2) Intended Use of Appraisal

The intended use of the appraisal is to develop the as-is Market Value, which is a Mortgagee's tool for calculating the Commissioner's Adjusted Fair Market Value (CAFMV) (24 CFR § 203.368).

(3) Intended User

FHA is the intended user of a CWCOT appraisal.

(4) Appraiser's Inspection

The Appraiser must inspect the interior and exterior of the Property. If the Appraiser cannot enter the Property, the Appraiser may perform the valuation based on an exterior-only inspection on the Fannie Mae Form 2055/Freddie Mac Form 2055, *Exterior-Only Inspection Residential Appraisal Report*, dated March 2005, or the Fannie Mae Form 1075/Freddie Mac Form 466, *Exterior-Only Inspection Individual Condominium Unit Appraisal Report*, for a condominium Property. The Appraiser must indicate that the Property could not be entered and identify the sources of the factual property data employed by the Appraiser in determining the value.

(5) Appraisal Conditions

CWCOT Properties are to be appraised "as is," in the condition as it exists on the effective date of the appraisal. The value to be determined is Market Value. The Appraiser must provide an analysis and report of the value of the subject Property "as is."

Under "Reconciliation" in the "This appraisal is made" segment, the Appraiser must mark the box labeled "as is."

(I) Pre-Foreclosure Sale Program

(1) Assignment Type

Under "Assignment Type" in the "Subject" section of the appraisal reporting form, the Appraiser must mark the box labeled "other" and indicate that the Property is a HUD Pre-Foreclosure Sale (PFS) Property.

(2) Intended Use of Appraisal

The intended use of the appraisal is to develop the as-is Market Value, which is a Mortgagee's tool for determining the list price of a HUD PFS Property (24 CFR § 203.370).

(3) Intended User

FHA is the intended user of a PFS appraisal.

(4) Sales Comparison Approach

Sales selection requirements for PFS are the same as the sales comparison approach in the REO section of this *SF Handbook*.

(5) Appraisal Conditions

PFS Properties are to be appraised "as is," in the condition as it exists on the effective date of the appraisal. The value to be determined is Market Value. The Appraiser must provide an analysis and report of the value of the subject Property "as is."

Under "Reconciliation" in the "This appraisal is made" segment, the Appraiser must mark the box labeled "as is."

iv. Appraisals for HUD Real Estate Owned Properties Purchased With a New FHA-insured Mortgage

A new appraisal must be prepared for all transactions involving the purchase of a HUD REO Property with a new FHA-insured Mortgage. The appraisal must be prepared in accordance with the requirements of HUD Real Estate Owned Properties except as noted.

(A) Property Meets HUD's MPR

If the appraisal reveals that the Property meets HUD's MPR, the Appraiser must complete the appraisal report "as is."

(B) Property Requires Repairs

If the appraisal reveals that the Property requires repairs in order to meet HUD's MPR, the Appraiser must provide an estimate of the cost to cure and complete the report "Subject to the following repairs or alterations on the basis of the hypothetical condition that the repairs or alterations have been completed."

13. Mixed Use One- to Four-Unit Single Family Properties

a. Definition

Mixed Use refers to a Property suitable for a combination of uses including any of the following: commercial, residential, retail, office or parking space.

b. Required Analysis and Reporting

The Appraiser must include all components of the real estate in the analysis. The Appraiser must not include business valuation or the value of Personal Property or business fixtures in the appraisal.

The Appraiser must provide measurements and calculations of the building area on the building sketch to show what portion of the Property is allocated to residential use, and what portion is allocated to non-residential use.

The Appraiser must provide a statement as to whether the commercial use will or will not affect the health and safety of the occupants of the residential Property.

E. TITLE I INSURED PROGRAMS

> ### RESERVED FOR FUTURE USE
>
> This section is reserved for future use, and until such time, FHA-approved Mortgagees and Title I Lenders must continue to comply with all applicable law and existing Handbooks, Mortgagee Letters, Notices and outstanding guidance applicable to a Title I Lender's participation in FHA programs.

F. APPRAISER AND PROPERTY REQUIREMENTS FOR TITLE I

> ### RESERVED FOR FUTURE USE
>
> This section is reserved for future use, and until such time, FHA-approved Mortgagees and Title I Lenders must continue to comply with all applicable law and existing Handbooks, Mortgagee Letters, Notices and outstanding guidance applicable to a Title I Lender's participation in FHA programs.

III.   SERVICING AND LOSS MITIGATION

A. TITLE II INSURED HOUSING PROGRAMS FORWARD MORTGAGES

This section provides the standards and procedures applicable to the servicing of all Single Family (one to four units) Mortgages insured under Title II of the National Housing Act, except for Home Equity Conversion Mortgages (HECM). The Mortgagee must fully comply with all of the following standards and procedures when servicing a Mortgage insured by the Federal Housing Administration (FHA).

1. Servicing of FHA-Insured Mortgages

Only FHA-approved Mortgagees may service FHA-insured Mortgages. Mortgagees may service Mortgages they hold or that are held by other FHA-approved Mortgagees.

a. Servicing in Compliance with Law

i.   Definition

The Mortgage Holder is the Entity who holds title to the FHA-insured Mortgage and has the right to enforce the mortgage agreement.

The Mortgage Servicer is the Entity responsible for performing servicing actions on FHA-insured Mortgages on its behalf or on behalf of or at the direction of another FHA-approved Mortgagee.

ii. Standard

Holders must ensure all FHA-insured Mortgages are serviced by a Servicer in accordance with FHA requirements and all applicable laws.

Servicers must service all FHA-insured Mortgages in accordance with FHA requirements and all applicable laws.

(A) Laws Applicable to Mortgage Servicing Generally

Mortgagees must comply with all laws, rules, and requirements applicable to mortgage servicing, including full compliance with the applicable requirements under the purview of the Consumer Financial Protection Bureau (CFPB), including the Real Estate Settlement Procedure Act (RESPA) and the Truth in Lending Act (TILA).

FHA requirements that are more stringent or restrictive than those provided for in applicable law are set forth in this *SF Handbook* and the Mortgagee must comply with these requirements.

(B) Contract Terms

Where mortgage contract terms are more stringent or restrictive than those provided for in applicable law, the Mortgagee must comply with the mortgage contract terms.

(C) Nondiscrimination Policy

Mortgagees must comply with all antidiscrimination laws, rules, and requirements applicable to servicing performing FHA-insured Mortgages and FHA-insured Mortgages in Default, including full compliance with the applicable requirements of:
- Title VIII of the Civil Rights Act of 1968 (Fair Housing Act);
- the Fair Credit Reporting Act, Public Law 91-508; and
- the Equal Credit Opportunity Act (ECOA), Public Law 94-239 and 12 CFR Part 202.

The Mortgagee must make all determinations with respect to the adequacy of the Borrower's income in a uniform manner without regard to race, color, religion, sex, national origin, familial status, handicap, marital status, actual or perceived sexual orientation, gender identity, source of income of the Borrower, or location of the Property.

b. Responsibility for Servicing Actions

Holders are responsible for all servicing actions, including the acts of its Servicers.

Servicers are responsible for their actions in servicing FHA-insured Mortgages, including actions taken on behalf or at the direction of the Holder.

The costs associated with subservicing may not be imposed on the Borrower or passed along to HUD in a claim for mortgage insurance benefits.

i. Responsibility during Transfers of Servicing Rights

(A) Definitions

The Transferor Servicing Mortgagee is the Mortgagee that transfers servicing responsibilities.

The Transferee Servicing Mortgagee is the Mortgagee to which the servicing responsibilities have been transferred.

The Transfer Date is the date on which the Borrower's Mortgage Payment is first due to the Transferee Servicing Mortgagee.

(B) Standard

The Transferor Servicing Mortgagee remains responsible for the servicing of an FHA-insured Mortgage until the Transfer Date. The Transferor Servicing Mortgagee must verify that the change of legal rights to service has been reported accurately.

On the Transfer Date, the Transferee Servicing Mortgagee assumes responsibility for:

- all servicing actions, including ensuring resolution of any servicing errors that were, and remain, the responsibility of the Transferor Servicing Mortgagee;
- obtaining the complete mortgage file, including origination and servicing records; and
- ensuring that the original Mortgage, mortgage Note, or deed of trust is preserved.

(C) Required Documentation

The Transferor Servicing Mortgagee must report the Transfer Date and update the mortgage record in FHA Connection (FHAC) within 15 Days of the Transfer Date.

ii. Responsibility for Servicing when the Mortgage is Sold

(A) Definition

A Mortgage Sale is a transaction in which a holder sells the Mortgage to another FHA-approved Mortgagee.

(B) Standard

The Selling Mortgagee relinquishes all rights and obligations under the contract for mortgage insurance on the effective date of the sale. The Selling Mortgagee remains responsible for Mortgage Insurance Premiums (MIP) until notice of the sale is received by HUD via FHAC.

The Purchasing Mortgagee is the Mortgagee that purchases the Mortgage and thereby succeeds to all rights and obligations of the Selling Mortgagee under the contract for mortgage insurance. As of the effective date of the sale, the Purchasing Mortgagee becomes responsible for outstanding MIP obligations, regardless of the date of accrual, and must confirm that the details of the mortgage sale have been reported accurately.

(C) Required Documentation

The Selling Mortgagee must report the effective date of the sale of the Mortgage as the "Transfer Date" and update the mortgage record in FHAC within 15 Days of the date of the sale.

iii. Registration with Mortgage Electronic Registration System, Inc.

(A) Definition

The Mortgage Electronic Registration System (MERS) is an electronic tracking system identified as nominee for a holder of a Mortgage.

(B) Standard

Mortgagees may voluntarily register FHA-insured Mortgages with MERS. The holder remains responsible for all servicing actions.

c. Providing Information to HUD

The Mortgagee must respond to verbal or written requests for individual account information, including all servicing information and related data and the entire mortgage origination file, from HUD staff or from a HUD-approved counseling agency acting with the consent of the Borrower.

When HUD staff request information, the Mortgagee must make available legible documents and in the format (electronic or hard copy) requested within 24 hours of the request, or as otherwise permitted by HUD.

d. Communication with Borrowers and Authorized Third Parties

i. Definition

Authorized Third Parties are parties who are not Borrowers on the Mortgage but who are authorized to communicate with Mortgagees regarding a Mortgage.

ii. Standard

The Mortgagee must provide mortgage information and arrange for individual consultation, upon request by the Borrowers.

The Mortgagee must comply with all laws, rules, and requirements applicable to third-party access to mortgage information.

iii. Required Documentation

If communicating with an Authorized Third Party, the Mortgagee must include documentation of the authorization in the servicing binder:
- a copy of a signed authorization from the Borrower;
- a copy of a Power of Attorney (POA), order of guardianship, or other documentation authorizing that third party to act on behalf of the Borrower; or
- other documentation showing legal authorization to access the Borrower's records.

e. Payment Administration

i. Receipt of Payments

The Mortgagee must either use a Trust Clearing Account or special custodial account to hold all payments on the insured Mortgage.

The Mortgagee's Trust Clearing Account may be used for collections received on all types of Mortgages. If a Trust Clearing Account is not used, the Mortgagee must immediately transfer payments into a special custodial account.

ii. Application of Payments

Mortgagees using special custodial accounts must withdraw an amount equal to the principal, interest, and service charges within 30 Days after deposit and post to the Borrower's records accordingly.

The Mortgagee must apply Borrower payments in the following order:
- to mortgage insurance premiums (MIPs) due, if any;
- to charges for ground rents, taxes, special assessments, including any assessments related to a Property Assessed Clean Energy (PACE) obligation, flood insurance premiums, if required, and fire and other hazard insurance premiums;
- to interest on the Mortgage;
- to amortization of the principal of the Mortgage; and
- to Late Charges, provided, however, that any amounts owed for Late Charges must be handled consistent with TILA regulations.

The Mortgagee may only apply funds for payments of optional insurance coverage premiums after the application of funds to all other elements of the monthly Mortgage Payment.

iii. Return of Partial Payments for Less than the Amount Due

(A) Definition

A Partial Payment is a payment of any amount less than the full amount due under the Mortgage at the time the payment is tendered, including Late Charges and amounts advanced by the Mortgagee on behalf of the Borrower.

(B) Standard

For performing Mortgages, the Mortgagee may return any Partial Payment to the Borrower with a letter of explanation.

(C) Required Documentation

The Mortgagee must note in its servicing file any Partial Payments received and, if applicable, documentation on the date the payment was returned with a letter of explanation.

iv. Application of Partial Prepayments

(A) Definition

A Partial Prepayment is a payment of part of the principal amount before the date on which the principal is due.

An Advance Full Monthly Payment is the payment of an amount larger than the full monthly payment, equaling an additional full monthly payment.

(B) Standard

The Mortgagee must apply Partial Prepayments as requested by the Borrower as either:
- advance full monthly payments; or
- additional payments toward reducing principal and future monthly payments.

In the event that the Borrower does not specify how the Partial Prepayment should be applied, the Mortgagee should communicate with the Borrower to determine the method of application or apply the payment in a manner previously communicated to the Borrower.

If the Borrower elects to have Partial Prepayments equal to a full monthly payment applied as an advance full monthly payment, the Mortgagee must allow the Borrower to skip an equal number of installments in the future without creating a mortgage Default or incurring a Late Charge.

v. Prepayment

(A) Definitions

A Partial Prepayment is a payment of part of the principal amount before the date on which the principal is due.

A Payoff or Prepayment in Full is the payment in whole of the principal amount of the mortgage Note in advance of expiration of the term of the mortgage Note.

The Installment Due Date is the first Day of the month, as provided for in the security instrument.

(B) Standard

The Mortgagee must accept a prepayment of a Mortgage in whole or in part on any Installment Due Date without penalty to the Borrower.

(C) Prepayment Procedures

(1) Mortgages Closed On or After January 21, 2015

The Mortgagee must accept a prepayment on a Mortgage closed on or after January 21, 2015, at any time and in any amount. The Mortgagee must calculate the interest as of the date the prepayment is received, not as of the next Installment Due Date.

(2) Mortgages Closed Before January 21, 2015

(a) Mortgages Insured On or After August 2, 1985

The Mortgagee must accept a prepayment on a Mortgage insured on or after August 2, 1985 and closed before January 21, 2015, if the Borrower prepays the Mortgage in full on the first Day of any month in the term of the Mortgage.

If prepayment is offered on a day other than the Installment Due Date, the Mortgagee may:
- refuse to accept the prepayment until the first Day of the next month; or
- accept the prepayment and require the payment of interest to the first Day of the next month. For Prepayment in Full, this option may only be used if the Mortgagee has provided the Payoff Disclosure to the Borrower.

(b) Mortgages Insured Prior to August 2, 1985

(i) Definitions

Notice of Intent to Prepay refers to the advance notice that Borrowers on Mortgages insured before August 2, 1985 must provide in order to prepay their FHA-insured Mortgages in full without penalty.

The 30-Day Advance Prepayment Notice Period refers to the time requirement for the Borrower to provide advance notice to the Mortgagee for prepayment of an FHA-insured Mortgage insured prior to August 2, 1985.

(ii) Standard

The Mortgagee must accept prepayment on a Mortgage insured prior to August 2, 1985, if the Borrower:

- submits to the Mortgagee a Notice of Intent to Prepay at least 30 Days prior to the prepayment; and
- prepays the Mortgage in full on the first Day of any month in the term of the Mortgage.

If a prepayment is offered on a day other than the Installment Due Date, the Mortgagee may:

- refuse to accept the prepayment until the first Day of the month following the expiration of the 30-Day Advance Prepayment Notice Period; or
- accept prepayment and require the payment of interest to the first Day of the month following the expiration of the 30-Day Advance Prepayment Notice Period. For Prepayment in Full, this option may only be used if the Mortgagee has provided the Payoff Disclosure to the Borrower.

(iii) Borrower's Notice of Intent to Prepay

For Mortgages insured prior to August 2, 1985, the Borrower must send and the Mortgagee must receive the Borrower's Notice of Intent to Prepay at least 30 Days prior to prepayment.

If the Borrower submits a prepayment without previously sending a Borrower's Notice of Intent to Prepay, the Mortgagee may consider receipt of the prepayment as the Borrower's Notice of Intent to Prepay. The Mortgagee may choose to:

- provide a Payoff Disclosure, enabling the Mortgagee to:
  - defer acceptance of prepayment until the first Day of the month following the date prepayment is tendered; or
  - accept the prepayment and require the payment of interest to the first Day of the month following the date prepayment is tendered; or
- accept the prepayment on the date tendered, which limits the Mortgagee's collection of interest to that prepayment date.

(iv) Effective Dates for Notice of Intent to Prepay

The effective date of the Notice of Intent to Prepay is the date that the Notice was received by the Mortgagee, unless the Borrower can produce documentation showing that the Notice was received earlier. The 30-Day Advance Prepayment Notice Period required for Mortgages insured prior to August 2, 1985, begins on this date of receipt.

(c) Installment Due Date Falls on a Non-Business Day

When the Installment Due Date falls on a non-business day, the Mortgagee must consider a Borrower's Notice of Intent to Prepay or the receipt of the prepayment amount for a Mortgage closed before January 21, 2015 timely if received on the next business day.

(3) Payoff Disclosure Requirements

When notified of the Borrower's intent to prepay, the Mortgagee must send the Payoff Disclosure and copy of the payoff statement directly to the Borrower, even if the Mortgagee is dealing with an Authorized Third Party.

The Mortgagee will forfeit any interest collected after the date of prepayment if these disclosure requirements are not met.

(D) Trustee's Fee for Satisfactions

If specifically provided for in the security instrument, the Mortgagee may charge the Borrower the amount of the trustee's fee, plus any reasonable and customary fee for payment, or for the execution of a satisfaction, release or trustee's deed when the debt is paid in full.

(E) Recording Fees for Satisfactions

The Mortgagee may charge the Borrower a reasonable and customary fee for recording satisfactions in states where recordation is not the responsibility of the Mortgagee.

f. Servicing Fees and Charges

i. Definition

Allowable Fees and Charges are those costs associated with the servicing of the Mortgage that are permitted to be charged to the Borrower.

Prohibited Fees and Charges are those costs associated with the servicing of the Mortgage that may not be charged to the Borrower.

ii. Standard

(A) Reasonable and Customary Fees and Charges

The Mortgagee may collect certain reasonable and customary fees and charges from the Borrower after the Mortgage is insured and as authorized by HUD below. All fees must be:
- reasonable and customary for the local jurisdiction;

- based on actual cost of the work performed or actual out-of-pocket expenses and not a percentage of either the face amount or the unpaid principal balance of the Mortgage; and
- within the maximum amount allowed by HUD.

(B) Requests for Approval for Other Fees or Charges

The Mortgagee may request approval from the National Servicing Center (NSC) for any fee, charge, or unusual service not specifically mentioned in this *SF Handbook*. The Homeownership Center (HOC) will determine the maximum amount of any fee based on what is reasonable and customary in the area.

(C) Prohibited Fees and Charges

The Mortgagee must not charge the Borrower for the following services:
- costs of telephone calls, telegrams, personal visits with the Borrower, certified mail, or other activities that are normally considered a part of a prudent Mortgagee's servicing activity;
- Mortgagee's use of an independent contractor such as a tax service to furnish tax data and information necessary to pay property taxes or make the payments on behalf of the Mortgagee;
- preparing and providing evidence of Payoff, Reconveyance, or termination of the Mortgage;
- providing information essential to the Payoff;
- recording the Payoff of the Mortgage in states where recordation is the responsibility of the Mortgagee; or
- fees for services performed by attorneys or trustees who are salaried members of the Mortgagee's staff.

iii. Required Documentation

The Mortgagee must include in the servicing file:
- documentation of the amount of any fees and charges paid or payable by the Borrower; and
- documentation supporting the actual cost of any work performed or out-of-pocket expenses.

g. Escrow

i. Definition

An Escrow Account is a set of funds collected by the Mortgagee for payment of taxes, insurance, and other items required by the mortgage Note.

ii. Escrowing of Funds

(A) Standard

The Mortgagee must segregate escrow funds, including those funds escrowed at closing, and deposit the funds in a special custodial account characterized by the following:

- with a financial institution whose accounts are insured by the Federal Deposit Insurance Corporation (FDIC) or the National Credit Union Administration (NCUA);
- that does not limit the Mortgagee's access to funds, require an advance notice of withdrawal, or require the payment of a withdrawal penalty;
- that clearly identifies the type of funds being held in that account; and
- the Mortgagee may maintain a "cushion" that may not be increased beyond what is acceptable under RESPA regulations.

Mortgagees utilizing a Trust Clearing Account must withdraw the portion that is to be applied to escrows within 48 hours of the deposit and must transfer the portion to the escrow account for the Borrower's Mortgage.

Mortgagees are not prohibited from holding escrow funds for all types of Mortgages in a single bank account; however, the Mortgagee must not commingle escrow funds, even temporarily, with funds used for the Mortgagee's general operating purposes.

(B) Interest on Escrows

HUD regulations neither forbid nor require that escrow accounts earn interest.

However, if escrow funds are invested, the Mortgagee must pass on to the Borrower the net income derived from the investment in accordance with the following:

- The Mortgagee must make investments and payments in compliance with state and federal agency requirements governing the handling and payment of interest earned on a Borrower's escrow account.
- The Mortgagee may only deduct the actual cost of administering the interest-bearing account before passing on to the Borrower the net earnings from the investment of their funds.
- The Mortgagee may not charge the Borrower expenses for maintaining the interest-bearing escrow account in an amount exceeding the gross interest earned from investing the funds in that account.

(C) Items to be Escrowed

The Mortgagee must require that the total Borrower Mortgage Payment includes escrow funds to provide for payment of property charges in accordance with 24 CFR § 203.23, the security instrument, and applicable law. Items to be escrowed include:

- real estate taxes;

- special assessments, including any assessments related to a PACE obligation;
- hazard insurance required by the Mortgagee;
- flood insurance as applicable;
- FHA MIP;
- Ground Rent, if any;
- other items which can attain priority over the Security Instrument as a lien or encumbrance on the Property, other than condominium or Homeowners' Association (HOA) fees.

(D) Required Documentation

The Mortgagee must retain documentation of its holding of all escrow funds on deposit.

iii. Escrow Analysis

The Mortgagee must perform analysis, at least annually, of the escrow account to provide for adequate collections to pay escrow bills when due without creating excessive surpluses. The Mortgagee must begin these analyses no later than the end of the second year of the life of the Mortgage.

The Mortgagee must retain any escrow surplus discovered when performing the annual escrow account analysis for a Delinquent Mortgage pursuant to the terms of the mortgage documents and federal law and regulation, including RESPA.

iv. Processing Payments from Escrow Accounts

When making payments from escrow accounts, Mortgagees must:
- send payment directly to the billing agency or the taxing authority, or as otherwise directed by state or local law;
- request a bill from the billing agency if a bill has not been received within a reasonable amount of time before the payment due date;
- contact the Borrower, if necessary, to obtain the bill or the information needed to pay such bills if a bill is not received within a reasonable amount of time before the known payment due date; and
- make Disbursements as bills become payable, even if making the payment requires advancing corporate funds when the escrow deposits are inadequate to meet these obligations.

The Mortgagee may contract with a tax service organization to manage the payment of taxes.

(A) Timeliness of Payments from Escrow Accounts

(1) Standard

The Mortgagee must ensure that all Disbursements are made as bills become payable.

If the Mortgagee fails to timely disburse escrow proceeds, the Mortgagee is prohibited from passing on to the Borrower any penalties resulting from the late payments unless:

- the late payment was the result of the Borrower's error or omission; and
- the Mortgagee attempted to obtain the billing information from the Borrower, billing agency, or the taxing authority in sufficient time to enable it to timely make the Disbursement.

(2) Required Documentation

The Mortgagee must document in its servicing file its efforts to obtain the billing information from the Borrower, billing agency, or the taxing authority.

(B) Payment of Insurance Premiums

(1) Long-term Policies

(a) Definition

Long-term Policies are those insurance policies with terms of greater than one year.

(b) Standard

The Mortgagee may not reject a long-term policy if the carrier and amount are otherwise acceptable to the Mortgagee.

(c) Collecting Funds for Renewal Premiums

The Mortgagee may collect funds for renewal premiums on long-term policies in the following ways:

- For renewal with the same policy term: The Mortgagee may immediately begin collecting a monthly amount calculated to make funds available 30 Days before the policy expires; or
- For renewal with a one-year term: The Mortgagee may defer collection of monthly escrows until 13 months before the expiration date of the policy then begin monthly collection of 1/12th of the renewal premium for a policy providing similar coverage.

The Mortgagee may require a Borrower wishing to renew for a longer term to make a lump sum deposit to escrow for the additional amount required to pay the renewal premium with the Mortgagee 30 Days before the expiration date of the present policy. If the additional deposit is not made, the Mortgagee may renew the policy for one year and continue to escrow as for a one-year policy.

(2) Optional Policies

(a) Standard

The Mortgagee may advance corporate funds when the escrow deposits are inadequate to meet obligations for payment of premiums for optional insurance coverage, but the Mortgagee must not charge against the escrow account any funds for these advances.

(i) Personal Property and Personal Liability Insurance

The Mortgagee must only escrow for the payment of Personal Property and personal liability insurance coverage premiums if:
- the Borrower has obtained Personal Property and personal liability insurance coverage not directly related to the mortgaged Property; and
- the premiums are combined with dwelling insurance in one insurance premium payment.

(ii) Life Insurance and Disability Insurance

Mortgagees may not deposit premiums for life or disability insurance coverage in the same bank accounts as other escrow payments.

The Mortgagee must maintain separate records for these life or disability insurance coverage payments.

HUD does not require Mortgagees to itemize the Borrower's monthly contribution for life or disability coverage on payment coupons.

(b) Required Documentation

The Mortgagee must note on the initial and annual escrow statements any Borrower's discretionary payment made as part of a monthly Mortgage Payment for optional policies.

(3) Insurance Protecting Only the Mortgagee

The Mortgagee must not charge the Borrower any part of the cost of insurance coverage that does not benefit the Borrower.

v. Use of Escrow Funds

The Mortgagee must only use escrow funds for the purpose for which they were collected.

The Mortgagee must never deduct amounts from a Borrower's escrow account to pay the following:
- penalties for late payments not directly resulting from the Borrower's error or omission;
- attorney's fees incurred in foreclosure actions that are not completed;
- inspection fees; and
- mortgage Delinquencies or refunds of overpaid subsidy.

h. Insurance Coverage Administration

i. Hazard Insurance

If the Mortgagee requires the Borrower to purchase hazard insurance, the Mortgagee must:
- be named as a "Loss Payee" on the hazard insurance policy; and
- escrow sufficient funds for the payment of renewal premium.

(A) Payment of Renewal Premium

When the Mortgagee has required the Borrower to purchase hazard insurance, the Mortgagee must pay renewal premiums through one of the following methods:
- remit the renewal premium when it is due; or
- advance escrow funds until there are sufficient funds for the payment of the renewal premium, if the Borrower is required to pay the premiums and fails to do so.

The Mortgagee must not insist on more coverage than is necessary to protect its investment. The Mortgagee must escrow renewal premiums for the entire amount if the Borrower chooses to insure the Property for more than the minimum amount.

(B) Fee for Change in Hazard Insurance Policy

The Mortgagee may assess a reasonable and customary fee, up to the amount listed in Appendix 3.0, for processing the Borrower's request to change hazard insurance coverage when the existing policy has not yet expired.

ii. Flood Insurance

For Properties located within a Special Flood Hazard Area (SFHA), the Mortgagee must ensure that insurance is in force for the life of the Mortgage or so long as such coverage remains available, unless the area in which the Property is located is no longer designated as an SFHA. If, due to rezoning, a Property securing an FHA-insured Mortgage becomes located in an SFHA, the Mortgagee must enforce HUD's flood insurance requirements on coverage amounts and maintenance.

iii. Hazard or Flood Insurance Proceeds

(A) Insurance Claims

The Mortgagee must take necessary steps to ensure that hazard or flood insurance claims are filed and settled as expeditiously as possible.

(B) Loss Settlement Amounts for Borrower Expenses and Personal Property

The Mortgagee must promptly release to the Borrower all insurance settlement proceeds received for coverage of a Borrower's Personal Property, temporary housing, and other transition expenses. The Mortgagee may not withhold Disbursement of such proceeds to cover an existing arrearage without the written consent of the Borrower.

(C) Insurance Proceeds for Home Damage

(1) Definition

A Viable Repair Plan is a plan for repairs of a mortgaged Property within the amounts available through insurance proceeds and borrower funds.

(2) Standard

The Mortgagee must expedite the release of insurance proceeds for needed home repairs after approving a Viable Repair Plan.

(D) Application of Insurance Proceeds to Unpaid Principal Balance

The Mortgagee may only apply insurance proceeds payable for home damages to arrearages and/or reduction of the unpaid principal balance if:
- the amount of the proceeds exceeds the costs to repair the damages to the home; or
- the insurance proceeds are insufficient to repair the home damages based on a certified repair estimate, and the Borrower is unable to demonstrate that they have additional funds from other sources to complete the repairs.

iv. Optional Policies

(A) Personal Property and Personal Liability Insurance

The Mortgagee may allow the Borrower to add Personal Property and personal liability insurance premiums to their monthly payments.

(B) Life or Disability or Optional Coverage Income Policies

The Mortgagee must clearly separate the collection of unpaid optional coverage premiums from the collection of any unpaid Mortgage Payment. If the payment does not include all or a part of an optional coverage premium, the Mortgagee may not treat the failure to pay as a failure to pay a part of the Mortgage Payment.

i. Mortgage Insurance Premium Remittance

i. Definition

Annual or Periodic MIPs are those MIPs that are remitted to HUD each month.

ii. Standard

The Mortgagee must remit one-twelfth of the annual MIPs each month to HUD, regardless of whether it was received from the Borrower. The Mortgagee can access the Advance Premium Notice and case-level billing information in FHAC to determine monthly collections of MIPs after the first premium year.

The Mortgagee must remit MIPs in accordance with the original amortization schedule. MIPs accrue from the beginning of amortization, without regard to what time frame exists between endorsement and the beginning of amortization and without regard to any Partial Prepayments, Delinquent payments, agreements to postpone payments, or agreements to recast the Mortgage.

For refinances, the Mortgagee must remit MIPs on the Mortgage being paid off through the month in which that Mortgage is paid in full.

iii. Mortgage Insurance Premium Reports

(A) Use of FHAC

The Mortgagee can access the Advance Premium Notice and case-level billing information in FHAC to determine monthly collections of MIPs after endorsement.

(B) Reports after Transfer or Sale

If, 90 Days after acquisition, a transferred or sold Mortgage has not appeared on HUD's monthly MIP report to the Transferee Servicing Mortgagee or Purchasing Mortgagee, that Mortgagee must ensure that the Servicer/Holder Transfer function is completed in FHAC.

j. Post-Endorsement Mortgage Amendments

i. Definition

A Post-Endorsement Mortgage Amendment is a change to the mortgage instruments, the nature of the obligation, or the security after the Mortgage has been insured.

ii. Modifying a Performing Mortgage

(A) Modification without HUD Approval

The Mortgagee may modify a performing Mortgage without HUD approval when:
- the modification is only for a reduction of the interest rate;
- the mortgage term is decreased and the Mortgage Payment will be increased $100 or less per month; or
- the mortgage term is decreased and the Mortgage is more than three years old.

(B) Modification Requiring HUD Approval

The Mortgagee must request and receive approval from the NSC prior to modifying a performing Mortgage when the mortgage term is decreased and:
- the Mortgage Payment will increase over $100 per month; or
- the Mortgage is three years old or less.

The Mortgagee may modify the Mortgage to decrease the mortgage term by increasing the monthly payment so long as all of the following conditions are met:
- The Mortgagee has received HUD approval.
- The Mortgage is current and the Borrower's payment history is satisfactory to the Mortgagee.
- The Mortgagee has determined that the higher monthly payment is within the Borrowers' ability to pay under the underwriting standards in Origination through Post-Closing/Endorsement.
- The modification agreement contains a clause permitting reversion to original mortgage terms if reversion can salvage a Delinquent account and prevent foreclosure.
- The modification agreement contains a certification by the Borrowers stating that they are aware of the positive and negative aspects of the modification and that they have voluntarily agreed to the increased payments.

(C) Principal Amount of Modified Performing Mortgage

The new principal amount of the modified Mortgage is the total unpaid amount due and payable under the original Mortgage. The Mortgagee may not include the following in the new principal amount:
- any revision of periodic MIP payments; and

- any legal or administrative costs attributable to the modification (these costs may be collected separately from the Borrower).

(D) Recordation of Lien

The Mortgagee must perform the legal steps required to accomplish the modification and must ensure that the Mortgage remains a valid first lien against the Property.

(E) Fee for Modification of Performing Mortgage

The Mortgagee may charge the Borrower a reasonable and customary fee for processing and recording a modification of a performing Mortgage when not modified under HUD's Loss Mitigation Program.

(F) Required Documentation

(1) Servicing File

For all modifications, the Mortgagee must retain the following in their servicing files:
- a mortgage modification document, in the form of:
  o an amended original Note, with all changes initialed by all parties; or
  o a modification agreement executed by all parties;
- documentation evidencing that criteria for modifying the Mortgage with or without HUD approval, as appropriate, were met;
- documentation showing calculations of the modified principal amount and the new monthly payment amount; and
- proof that any unpaid escrow added to the new principal amount was credited to the Borrower's escrow account.

(2) Reporting to HUD

The Mortgagee must report mortgage characteristics for all modifications through FHAC.

iii. Partial Release of Security

(A) Partial Releases from Condemnation Not Requiring HUD Approval

(1) Standard

The Mortgagee may execute a partial release of security without HUD approval if the partial release results from condemnation and all of the following conditions are met:
- the portion of the Property being conveyed does not exceed 10 percent of the area of the mortgaged Property;
- there is no damage to existing Structures or other improvements;

- there is no unrepaired damage to sewer, water, or paving;
- the Mortgagee has applied all of the payment received as compensation for the taking of the Property to reduce the unpaid principal balance of the Mortgage; and
- the government action requiring conveyance occurs after insurance of the Mortgage.

(2) Required Documentation

(a) Claim Review File

If the Mortgagee files a claim for mortgage insurance benefits, the Mortgagee must submit a certification that the requirements for partial releases of security as a result of condemnation have been met and retain a copy of the certification in the Claim Review File.

(b) Reporting to HUD

The Mortgagee must notify the Appropriate HOC of the release by letter within 30 Days of the Mortgagee's signing of the release.

(B) Partial Releases Requiring HUD Approval

(1) Request Process

The Mortgagee must obtain HUD approval for any partial releases other than Partial Releases from Condemnation Not Requiring HUD Approval. The Mortgagee must send the following to the Jurisdictional HOC for the Property:

- a written request containing the following information:
  - whether or not the Mortgage is in good standing;
  - the amount of the outstanding principal balance;
  - the due date of the last unpaid installment;
  - if the Mortgage is Delinquent, the number of Delinquent payments;
  - a list of unpaid special assessments, if any, and the total amount payable;
  - a complete legal description of the Property to be released;
  - the Borrower's reasons for requesting that the Mortgagee make the release, including how the land to be released will be used;
  - the monetary consideration, if any, to be received by the Borrower;
  - the amount of a prepayment, if any, to the mortgage principal;
  - any restrictions to be imposed on the land to be released;
  - a survey or sketch of the Property showing:
    - the dimensions of the portion to be released;
    - the location of existing and proposed improvements; and
    - the relation of the Property to surrounding properties;

o plans and specifications, including Cost Estimates of any alterations proposed for the remaining Property after the release; and
o the case number of the mortgaged Property; and
- a valid FHA appraisal that reflects:
o the value before the partial release of security; and
o the value of the remaining Property after the partial release of security.

(2) HUD Review

HUD will process the request for the partial release of security and notify the Mortgagee of the approval or rejection in writing.

(3) Required Documentation

The Mortgagee must retain a copy of HUD's approval or rejection in the servicing file.

(C) Fees for Partial Release of Security

The Mortgagee may charge to the Borrower reasonable and customary costs, up to the amounts listed in Appendix 3.0, involved in processing of the following modifications of the mortgaged Property:
- partial releases
- condemnation
- order of taking
- subordination or consent to Easement
- lot line dispute/adjustment
- subdivision consent
- consent to change in covenants and restrictions

iv. Change of Location of Dwelling or Improvements

(A) Relocation Requiring HUD Approval

(1) Request to HUD

Except in the emergency situations described in Emergency Relocation Not Requiring HUD Approval, the Mortgagee must obtain HUD approval prior to relocation. The Mortgagee must submit to the NSC via Extensions and Variances Automated Requests System (EVARS):
- the Mortgagee's request for a change in improvement location; and
- supporting documentation, including architectural exhibits, a copy of the permit, and a description of materials.

HUD will analyze the request and notify the Mortgagee of the approval or denial of the request.

Handbook 4000.1   576
Effective Date: 03/14/2016 | Last Revised: 07/10/2019
*Refer to the online version of SF Handbook 4000.1 for specific sections' effective dates

(2) Relocation Requirements

The Mortgagee must ensure that relocations are performed as follows:
- the Mortgagee obtains a good and valid first lien on the new lot;
- the lien of the insured Mortgage has been extended to cover the new lot and the old lot has or has not been released from the lien, as appropriate;
- all damages to the Structure before, during, or after the relocation are repaired without cost to HUD; and
- the new lot is in an area known to be reasonably free from natural hazards or, if in an SFHA, the community participates in the National Flood Insurance Program (NFIP) and the Property will be insured against floods.

(3) Required Documentation

The Mortgagee must retain a copy of HUD's approval or denial in the servicing file.

After the move has been completed and the appropriate substitute documents have been recorded, the Mortgagee must forward to HUD any documentation regarding the changes in the nature of the lien and retain copies in the servicing file.

(B) Emergency Relocation Not Requiring HUD Approval

(1) Permanent Relocation

(a) Standard

The Mortgagee may consent to the relocation of existing improvements in emergency situations, where immediate action must be taken to preserve the safety of the occupants and/or the undamaged condition of the existing improvements, without HUD approval.

(b) Notification to HUD of Completed Permanent Relocation

The Mortgagee must notify the NSC via EVARS within 30 Days of the completed permanent relocation and submit a supplementary case binder containing supporting documentation for the change in improvement location.

The Mortgagee must include the following in its notification of the completion of the permanent relocation:
- the FHA case number of the mortgaged Property;
- the address and legal description of the lot of the improvement's previous location and the address and legal description of the new permanent location;
- a statement that HUD regulatory requirements have been met;
- a statement that the original Note is in full force and effect; and

- the outstanding balance of the insured Mortgage, and, if Delinquent, the number of payments, the dollar amount of the delinquency, and an explanation of how the delinquency is expected to be cured.

(c) Required Documentation

The Mortgagee must retain in the servicing file a copy of its notification of the completion of the permanent relocation.

(2) Temporary Relocation

(a) Standard

When a temporary move becomes necessary, the Mortgagee may consult the NSC via EVARS before the move, for written assurance that the mortgage insurance will not be affected adversely during the move.

All damages to the Structure before, during, or after the relocation have been or will be repaired without cost to HUD.

(b) Notification to HUD of Completed Temporary Relocation

Within 30 Days of the completion of the temporary relocation, the Mortgagee must submit written notification to the NSC via EVARS, advising that the temporary relocation has been completed. This notification must include the following:
- the FHA case number of the mortgaged Property;
- the address and legal description of the lot of the improvement's previous location and the address and legal description of the new temporary lot; and
- a statement that:
  - o the move to the temporary lot has been accomplished; and
  - o any damage caused by the temporary move has been or will be repaired at no cost to HUD.

(c) Required Documentation

The Mortgagee must retain in the servicing file a copy of the notification to HUD of completed temporary relocation.

k. Mortgage Insurance Premium Cancellation and Termination

i. Definition

MIP Cancellation is the ending of MIP payments on an FHA-insured Mortgage closed on or after January 1, 2001, and assigned a case number before June 3, 2013.

ii. Standard

The policies in this section apply only to FHA-insured Mortgages that:
- closed on or after January 1, 2001; and
- have a case number assignment before June 3, 2013.

HUD automatically cancels FHA MIPs under the conditions set forth below. The Loan-to-Value (LTV) ratio is based on the principal balance excluding Upfront MIP (UFMIP). The FHA contract of insurance remains in force for the Mortgage's full term, unless otherwise terminated.

HUD will not consider new appraised values in calculating if the Borrower has reached the required LTV ratio necessary for annual MIP cancellation.

HUD bases the cancellation of the annual MIP on the initial amortization schedule. In cases where Mortgage Payments have been accelerated or modified, HUD may base cancellation on the actual amortization of the Mortgage as provided to HUD by the servicing Mortgagee.

(A) Mortgage Term of More Than 15 Years

For Mortgages with terms more than 15 years, HUD automatically cancels the annual MIP when the LTV ratio reaches 78 percent of the lesser of the initial sales price or appraised value at origination, provided the Borrower has paid the annual MIP for at least five years.

(B) Mortgage Term 15 Years or Less and LTV Ratio of Greater than 90 Percent with Case Numbers Assigned on and after July 14, 2008, and Before June 3, 2013

HUD automatically cancels the annual MIP when the LTV ratio reaches 78 percent of the lesser of the initial sales price or appraised value at origination regardless of the length of time the Borrower has paid the annual MIP for Mortgages that:
- have terms 15 years or less;
- have a case number assigned on and after July 14, 2008, and before June 3, 2013; and
- have LTV ratios greater than 90 percent.

(C) Mortgage Term 15 Years or Less and LTV Ratio of 90 Percent and Greater, Closed on or after January 1, 2001, and with Case Numbers Assigned before July 14, 2008

HUD automatically cancels the annual MIP when the LTV ratio reaches 78 percent of the lesser of the initial sales price or appraised value regardless of the length of time the Borrower has paid the annual MIP for Mortgages that:
- have terms 15 years or less;

- closed on or after January 1, 2001, but have their case number assigned before July 14, 2008; and
- have LTV ratios 90 percent or greater.

(D) Mortgage Term 15 Years or Less and LTV Ratio Greater than 78 percent but Equal or Less Than 90 Percent

HUD automatically cancels the annual MIP when the LTV ratio reaches 78 percent of the lesser of the initial sales price or appraised value at origination regardless of the length of time the Borrower has paid the annual MIP for Mortgages that:
- have terms 15 years or less;
- have case numbers assigned on or after April 18, 2011; and
- have LTV ratios of greater than 78 percent but equal to or less than 90 percent.

HUD does not charge annual MIP for Mortgages that:
- have terms 15 years or less; have a case assigned on or after April 18, 2011, but before June 3, 2013; and have LTV ratios of 78 percent or less;
- have terms 15 years or less; have a case number assigned on or after July 14, 2008 but before April 18, 2011; and have LTV ratios of 90 percent or less; or
- have terms 15 years or less; closed on or after January 1, 2001 and have a case number assigned before July 14, 2008; and have LTV ratios of less than 90 percent.

(E) Borrower-Initiated Cancellation of MIP

A Borrower who meets the following requirements may request cancellation of the collection of annual MIPs through their Mortgagee when:
- the Borrower has reached the 78 percent threshold in advance of the scheduled amortization due to prepayments, but not sooner than five years from the Closing Date except for 15-year term Mortgages; and
- the Borrower has not been more than 30 Days Delinquent on the Mortgage during the previous 12 months.

(F) Processing MIP Cancellation

The Mortgagee must process the MIP cancellation using the Monthly MIP cancellation function in FHAC.

iii. Termination of MIP on Mortgages with Case Numbers Assigned on or after June 3, 2013

For Mortgages with FHA case numbers assigned on or after June 3, 2013, HUD automatically terminates FHA MIP as stated in Appendix 1.0 - Mortgage Insurance Premiums.

iv. Distributive Shares

(A) Definition

A Distributive Share is a share of any excess earnings from the Mutual Mortgage Insurance Fund (MMIF) that may be distributed to a Borrower after mortgage insurance termination.

(B) Payment of Distributive Shares

At HUD's discretion, HUD may pay Distributive Shares when mortgage insurance is terminated. Upon termination of the FHA mortgage insurance of a Mortgage, HUD will determine if Distributive Shares are available.

HUD is not liable for unpaid Distributive Shares that remain unclaimed six years from the date notification was first sent to the Borrower's last known address.

l. Mortgage Insurance Termination

i. Definition

A Mortgage Insurance Termination is the ending of FHA Single Family mortgage insurance at which time the Mortgagee's obligation to remit MIP to HUD ends. Upon termination, the Borrower and Mortgagee will enjoy only those rights, if any, to which they would be entitled under the National Housing Act if the insurance contract terminated as a result of the insured Mortgage being paid in full.

ii. Standard

(A) Termination of Mortgage Insurance

HUD terminates the FHA insurance contract as follows:
- automatically when the Mortgage reaches maturity; or
- when the Mortgagee reports a termination code, such as:
  - prepayment (Borrower paid the Mortgage in full before the maturity date);
  - use of Home Disposition Option or non-conveyance foreclosure (the Property was acquired by a Mortgagee or third party at a foreclosure sale or was redeemed after foreclosure and no insurance claim or Claims Without Conveyance of Title (CWCOT) will be submitted to HUD);
  - conveyance for insurance benefits; or
  - voluntary termination (both the Mortgagee and Borrower agreed to voluntarily terminate FHA insurance).

The Mortgagee must report termination of a case to HUD via FHAC, Business to Government (B2G), or the Electronic Data Interchange (EDI) within 15 Days of the actual event.

(B) Voluntary Termination of Mortgage Insurance

(1) Definition

A Voluntary Termination of Mortgage Insurance is a mutual agreement between the Borrower and the Mortgagee to terminate FHA mortgage insurance.

(2) Standard

The Borrower and the Mortgagee may agree to voluntarily terminate FHA mortgage insurance at any time.

(a) Borrower's Consent to Voluntary Termination

The Mortgagee must obtain a signed Borrower's Consent to Voluntary Termination of FHA Mortgage Insurance from each Borrower on the Mortgage.

(b) Request for Voluntary Termination

To request voluntary termination, the Mortgagee must:
- submit the request for voluntary termination of mortgage insurance via FHAC within 15 Days of receiving the executed Borrower's Consent form; and
- certify in FHAC that all Borrowers on the Mortgage have signed the consent form.

(C) Effective Date of Termination

(1) Standard

The effective date of termination of the contract of insurance is the last Day of the month in which one of the following occur:
- the date a voluntary termination request is received by the Commissioner;
- the date the Mortgage was prepaid; or
- where the Mortgagee notifies the Commissioner that a claim will not be filed, the date foreclosure proceedings were initiated or the Property was acquired by another party, including the Mortgagee.

(2) Required Documentation

The Mortgagee must note in the servicing file and report in FHAC, B2G, or EDI the date on which the voluntary termination request is received by the Commissioner; the date notice is received by the Commissioner that the Mortgage was prepaid; or the date notice is received by the Commissioner that a claim will not be filed, or that the Property will not be conveyed. For FHA-to-FHA refinances, the Mortgagee processing the new refinance must report the projected and actual Closing Date.

(D) MIP Due Until Effective Date of Termination

The Mortgagee is obligated to pay MIP due until the effective date of termination.

(E) Escrow Balance Returned to Borrower

If no claim for insurance benefits will be filed, the Mortgagee must timely release the funds held in escrow in accordance with federal regulations, including RESPA, after the termination of the FHA-insured Mortgage.

m. Disclosures

i. Statement of Escrow Account

At the Borrower's request, the Mortgagee must promptly furnish a statement of the escrow account in a clear and understandable form, with sufficient information to permit the Borrower to reconcile the account.

ii. Payoff Disclosure

(A) Definition

A Payoff Disclosure is a disclosure accompanying the payoff statement and, for Mortgages closed before January 21, 2015, describing the procedures for prepayment of a Mortgage.

(B) Standard

When notified of the Borrower's intent to prepay a Mortgage, the Mortgagee must send to the Borrower directly the Payoff Disclosure and copy of the payoff statement.

(C) Required Documentation

The Mortgagee must retain a copy of the Payoff Disclosure in the servicing file.

iii. Annual Prepayment Disclosure Statements

(A) Definition

An Annual Prepayment Disclosure Statement is a statement of the amount outstanding on the Mortgage and, for Mortgages closed before January 21, 2015, the requirements that the Borrower must fulfill upon prepayment to prevent accrual of interest after the date of prepayment.

(B) Standard

The Mortgagee must provide the Borrower with a written <u>Annual Prepayment Disclosure Statement</u> on an annual basis.

(C) Required Documentation

The Mortgagee must retain a copy of the Annual Prepayment Disclosure Statement in the servicing file.

iv. Statement for Income Tax Purposes

(A) Definition

The Statement for Income Tax Purposes is an Internal Revenue Service (IRS) Form 1098, *Mortgage Interest Statement,* or equivalent that provides documentation of taxes and interest paid by the Borrower during the preceding calendar year.

(B) Standard

The Mortgagee must provide the Borrower with a Statement for Income Tax Purposes by January 30 of each year.

(C) Required Documentation

The Mortgagee must retain a copy of each annual Statement for Income Tax Purposes in the servicing file.

n. Record Retention – Servicing File

i. Definition

The Servicing File is the Mortgagee's record of all servicing activity on an FHA-insured Mortgage.

ii. Standard

Mortgagees must retain all servicing files for a minimum of seven years after the transfer or sale of the Mortgage or termination of mortgage insurance. The Mortgagee must maintain accurate records for each Mortgage serviced. In addition to the specific documentation requirements stated in this *SF Handbook*, these records must include the following information:

- mortgage origination and endorsement documentation, including copies of the following documents, if applicable: the Conditional Commitment for insurance, the Firm Commitment, form HUD-92900-LT, *FHA Loan Underwriting and Transmittal Summary*, and the Mortgage Insurance Certificate (MIC);
- MIP payments made;

- documentation related to any recovery of hazard insurance proceeds; and
- the FHA-insured Mortgages in the Mortgagee's portfolio and information on which Mortgages have been acquired, sold, paid in full, and voluntarily terminated.

The Mortgagee must also retain, in electronic and hard copy, the Mortgage, mortgage Note, deed of trust, or a lost note affidavit acceptable under state law, with the electronic copy marked "copy."

For cases for which a claim is filed, the Mortgagee must retain documentation in compliance with the Claim Review File section for at least seven years after the final claim or latest supplemental claim settlement date.

iii. Record Reconciliations

HUD may require Mortgagees to provide information evidencing reconciliation of Mortgagee records with HUD. This information may include identification, by Mortgage, of the following:

- amount of MIP due and paid to HUD by time period for each insured Mortgage;
- date insurance was terminated or servicing transferred, if applicable; and
- date servicing was acquired, for Mortgages acquired after September 1, 1982.

All Mortgagees must ensure that HUD's records accurately reflect the status of the Mortgage and both the correct holder and servicer of record.

iv. Electronic Storage

Where retention of a hard copy or original document is not required, Mortgagees may use electronic storage methods for all servicing-related documents required in accordance with HUD regulations, handbooks, Mortgagee Letters, and notices.

Regardless, the Mortgagee must be able to make available to HUD in the format (electronic or hard copy) requested legible documents within 24 hours of a request or as otherwise prescribed by HUD.

2. Default Servicing

a. Mortgages in Delinquency or Default

i. Definitions

A mortgage account is Delinquent any time a payment is due and not paid.

If the Borrower fails to make any payment or perform any other obligation under the Mortgage, and such failure continues for a period of 30 Days, the Mortgage is considered in Default.

The Date of Default is 30 Days after:

- the first uncorrected failure to perform any obligation under the Mortgage; or
- the first failure to make a monthly payment which subsequent payments by the Borrower are insufficient to cover when applied to the overdue monthly payment in the order in which they become due.

ii. Standard

The Mortgagee must ensure all FHA-insured Mortgages in Delinquency or Default are serviced in accordance with FHA requirements and all applicable laws.

For the purpose of determining the date of Default and timelines related to Default, HUD considers all months to have 30 Days.

b. HUD Default Servicing Contact

The National Servicing Center (NSC) in Oklahoma City, Oklahoma, manages HUD's Loss Mitigation Program. HUD NSC staff is available to provide customer service to Mortgagees, Servicers, counselors, other authorized representatives, and Borrowers on loss mitigation issues.

c. Reporting to Consumer Reporting Agencies and the IRS

The Mortgagee is responsible for:

- complying with applicable law and federal regulations relating to reporting to consumer reporting agencies; and
- ensuring that all reported information is accurate.

The Mortgagee is also responsible for any required IRS reporting regarding acquisition of secured Property or cancellation of mortgage debt, in accordance with the Internal Revenue Code (IRC).

d. Late Charges

i. Definition

Late Charges are charges assessed if a Mortgage Payment is received more than 15 Days after the due date.

ii. Standard

The Mortgagee may consider a Borrower's payment late if the payment is received by the Mortgagee more than 15 Days after the due date. The Mortgagee may assess a late charge on the 17th Day of the month.

For Mortgages assigned a case number on or after March 14, 2016, the Mortgagee may assess a Late Charge, not to exceed 4 percent of the overdue payment of Principal and Interest (P&I) and in accordance with applicable law.

For Mortgages assigned a case number before March 14, 2016, the Mortgagee may assess a Late Charge calculated based on overdue PITI if permitted under the terms of the mortgage Note and under applicable law.

(A) Notifying the Borrower of the Late Charge

Before collecting the Late Charge or returning a Mortgage Payment to the Borrower for failing to pay the Late Charge, the Mortgagee must provide the Borrower with an advance written notice of the charge.

The Mortgagee must include in the advance notice the following information:
- the due date of the payment;
- the amount of the regular monthly payment;
- the date on which the Late Charge will be imposed; and
- the amount of the Late Charge (or the full amount now due which consists of the regular monthly payment plus the Late Charge amount).

(B) Application of Subsequent Payment to Unpaid Late Charges

After advance notice has been sent to the Borrower, the Mortgagee may:
- treat any subsequent payment that does not include the Late Charge in accordance with HUD's Partial Payment section; and
- deduct amounts due for Late Charges owed for a previous installment.

(C) Default/Foreclosure Due to Unpaid Late Charges

A Mortgage may be technically in Default by its terms if a Late Charge is not paid within 30 Days after it becomes due. However, the Mortgagee may not initiate foreclosure action when the only delinquency is due to:
- unpaid Late Charges that are due on the account; and/or
- unpaid monthly payments that remain unpaid because the Mortgagee did not comply with HUD's Partial Payments for Mortgages in Default section.

iii. Required Documentation

The Mortgagee must ensure that its servicing file reflects any Late Charges assessed and includes any advance written notice of such charges sent to the Borrower.

e. Partial Payments for Mortgages in Default

i. Acceptance of Partial Payments

Unless subject to the exceptions in the <u>Return of Partial Payments for Mortgage in Default</u> section, the Mortgagee must accept any Partial Payment and either:

- apply the payment to the Borrower's account; or
- identify the payment with the Borrower's account and hold the payment in a suspense account. When a full monthly installment due under the Mortgage is accumulated, the Mortgagee must apply that amount to the Borrower's account.

ii. Application of Partial Payments Totaling a Full Monthly Payment

(A) Standard

When Partial Payments held for disposition total a full monthly payment, the Mortgagee must apply these payments to the Borrower's account, after deduction of amounts due to the Mortgagee for Late Charges and refunds of Mortgagee advances.

This application of Partial Payments as a full monthly installment advances the date of the oldest unpaid installment, but not the date on which the account first became Delinquent.

(B) Required Documentation

When applying the Partial Payment totaling a full monthly payment, the Mortgagee must:

- report the appropriate <u>Status Code</u> in the Single Family Default Monitoring System (SFDMS); and
- advance the Oldest Unpaid Installment (OUI) date one month.

iii. Return of Partial Payments for Mortgage in Default

(A) Standard

If the Mortgage is in Default, the Mortgagee may return the Partial Payment to the Borrower with a letter of explanation only under the following circumstances:

- when the payment represents less than half of the full amount then due;
- when the payment is less than the amount agreed to in an oral or written Forbearance Plan;
- when the payment is less than the amount stated in an approved Trial Payment Plan (TPP) Agreement, whether or not an executed Agreement is received by the Mortgagee;
- when the Property is occupied by a rent-paying tenant and the rents are not being applied to the Mortgage Payments;
- when foreclosure has been started; or

- when it is 14 Days or more after the Mortgagee has mailed the Borrower a statement of the full amount due, including Late Charges, which advises that it intends to refuse to accept future Partial Payments (see Application of Subsequent Payment to Unpaid Late Charges), and either of the following conditions have occurred:
  - four or more full monthly installments are due but unpaid; or
  - a delinquency of any amount, including Late Charges, has continued for at least six months since the account first became Delinquent.

(B) Required Documentation

The Mortgagee must ensure that its servicing file reflects any Partial Payments returned to the Borrower and includes any letters of explanation for the returned payments.

f. Lien Status

The Mortgagee must preserve the first lien status of the FHA-insured Mortgage. HUD will not pay a claim on a Mortgage that lacks first priority position.

g. Imminent Default

i. Definition

A Borrower facing Imminent Default is defined as a Borrower who is current or less than 30 Days past due on their Mortgage Payment and is experiencing a significant, documented reduction in income or some other hardship that will prevent them from making the next required Mortgage Payment during the month that it is due.

ii. Standard

The Mortgagee must obtain documentation necessary to verify that the Borrower is experiencing a significant reduction in income or some other hardship that will prevent them from making the next required Mortgage Payment during the month that it is due.

iii. Required Documentation

The Mortgagee must include in its servicing file documentation of the basis for the determination that the Borrower's financial condition will result in a Default.

iv. Loss Mitigation Options that are Applicable for Borrowers Facing Imminent Default

Upon reviewing the financials of the Borrower facing Imminent Default, the following Options are to be applied through the normal waterfall process to determine eligibility:

- Forbearance Agreement;
- FHA-Home Affordable Modification Program (FHA-HAMP);

- Pre-Foreclosure Sale (PFS) Program; and
- Deed-in-Lieu (DIL) of Foreclosure.

h. Early Default Intervention

The Mortgagee must determine the Borrower's ability to make monthly Mortgage Payments and take loss mitigation action or commence foreclosure, if loss mitigation is not feasible, within six months of the date of Default, or within such additional time approved by the NSC via EVARS.

The Mortgagee must notify each Borrower, co-signer, and any other party requiring notice by state law that the Mortgage is in Default.

i. Delinquent Mortgage Identification

The Mortgagee must identify Delinquent Mortgages and their payment status and provide such information to appropriate servicing and collection staff on a daily basis.

ii. SFDMS Default Reporting

(A) Definition

Single Family Default Monitoring System (SFDMS) is HUD's system for tracking Mortgagee data on Delinquent Mortgages until a delinquency is resolved through reinstatement or termination.

(B) Standard

The Mortgagee must report in SFDMS the Delinquency/Default Status Codes that accurately reflect the stage of delinquency or Mortgagee action.

(1) Types of Mortgages to Report

Each month, the Mortgagee must report Delinquent servicing activities for all Mortgages that are 30, 60, and 90 Days or more Delinquent as of the last Day of the month.

The Mortgagee must report the statuses of three classes of Mortgages each month:
- New Delinquencies: The Mortgagee must report Delinquent accounts when one full installment is due and unpaid (30 Days Delinquent - Status Code 42) and must continue reporting the applicable Status Code until the delinquency is resolved.
- Open Delinquencies: The Mortgagee must continue to report a Status Code 42 until a servicing action has been initiated/approved and/or completed which would warrant a Status Code change.

- Delinquencies Resolved During the Cycle Month: The Mortgagee must report the appropriate Status Code to reflect that the delinquency has been addressed.

(2) Time Frame for Reporting

For every case for which reporting is required, the Mortgagee must submit delinquency data documenting the status as of the end of the month. The Mortgagee must submit this data by the fifth business day of the following month. Mortgagees may submit additional delinquency data throughout the month.

(C) SFDMS Codes

(1) Delinquency/Default Status Codes

The Mortgagee must report the correct Delinquency/Default Status (DDS) Code reflecting the status of the Mortgage.

The Mortgagee must include applicable status dates when reporting DDS Codes. SFDMS permits the submission of delinquency data throughout the month.

(2) Delinquency/Default Reason Codes

The Mortgagee must ascertain and report the specific reason for the Delinquency/Default using the Delinquency/Default Reason (DDR) Codes.

(D) Error Reports and Correction

The Mortgagee may receive Error Reports from two systems:
- EDI, which provides the All Transaction Sets 824 (TS824) Report (see the Electronic Data Interchange Implementation Guide for additional information); or
- FHAC.

The Mortgagee is responsible for retrieving Error Reports from these systems and submitting necessary corrections by the fifth business day. HUD will not provide additional time to enter corrections.

(E) Correction of a Previously Reported Status Code

When a Mortgagee discovers that a previous Status Code was reported in error, the Mortgagee must:
- report a Status Code 25, *Cancel*, to advise HUD that the last Status Code reported was in error and should be preserved as a historical record without having an effect on the default sequence; and
- report the correct Status Code.

iii. Collection Communication Timeline

(A) Definition

The Collection Communication Timeline sets forth the servicing actions that Mortgagees must take when contacting a Borrower with a Delinquent Mortgage.

(B) Standard

The Mortgagee must perform in a timely manner the servicing actions set forth in the following Collection Communication Timeline.

Day	Mortgagee Action
1	Payment due date; no action required until the Mortgage becomes Delinquent.
10	The Mortgagee must begin attempts at telephone contact with Borrowers at risk of Early Payment Default or Re-Default in accordance with the Specialized Collection Techniques for Early Payment Default section.
17	The Mortgagee must begin attempts to make telephone contact with the Borrower with a Delinquent Mortgage in accordance with the Telephone Contact Efforts section.
20	The Mortgagee must begin mail or electronic communication collection attempts.
30	The Mortgagee must report the delinquency to HUD via SFDMS.
32	The Mortgagee must send the following: • Notice of Homeownership Counseling Availability; • Servicemembers Civil Relief Act (SCRA) Disclosure (form HUD-92070); • Delinquency Notice Cover Letter; and • "Save your Home – Tips to Avoid Foreclosure" pamphlet (form HUD-2008-5-FHA).
45	The Mortgagee should begin analysis to identify appropriate Loss Mitigation Options, if any. If unable to reach the Borrower(s), the Mortgagee must perform an Occupancy Inspection.
61	The Mortgagee must attempt a face-to-face interview with the Borrower no later than this date, unless exempt under 24 CFR 203.604.
90	The Mortgagee must report the appropriate Default Reason Code for the Default in SFDMS. The Mortgagee must have evaluated all Loss Mitigation Options to determine whether any are appropriate. The Mortgagee must reevaluate for Loss Mitigation each month thereafter.

(C) Required Documentation

The Mortgagee must document in their servicing file all communication efforts to reach the Borrower early in their delinquency.

iv. Specialized Collection Techniques for Early Payment Defaults and Re-Defaults

(A) Definitions

Early Payment Defaults refer to all Mortgages that become 60 Days Delinquent within the first six payments.

A Re-Default is a mortgage Default occurring within six months after reinstatement or the successful use of a permanent Home Retention Option.

(B) Standard

For Borrowers at risk of Early Payment Default or Re-Default, the Mortgagee must:
- commence telephone contact by the 10th Day after the first missed payment to remind Borrowers of Mortgage Payment time frames;
- make a minimum of two calls per week after the 10th Day of delinquency, until:
  - contact is established;
  - the Mortgagee determines that the phone contact information is inaccurate, or no longer in service; or
  - until the Mortgagee determines through an Occupancy Inspection that the Property is vacant or abandoned; and
- make reasonable efforts to obtain an alternate phone number and/or follow up with the Borrower using other methods of communication until contact is established.

(C) Required Documentation

The Mortgagee must document in their servicing file all specialized collection efforts to reach the Borrowers at risk of Early Payment Default or Re-Default.

v. Telephone Contact Efforts

(A) Standard

The Mortgagee must attempt to contact the Borrower via telephone beginning on the 17-20th Day of delinquency, calling a minimum of two times per week until:
- contact is established; or
- the Mortgagee has determined through an Occupancy Inspection that the mortgaged Property is vacant or abandoned.

The Mortgagee is expected to:

- vary the times and days of the week of call attempts to maximize the likelihood of making contact with the Borrower; and
- have policies in place to reduce the call abandon rate and minimize the call wait time.

Promptly after establishing live contact, the Mortgagee must determine whether the Borrower is occupying the Property, ascertain the reason for the delinquency, and inform the Borrower about the availability of Loss Mitigation Options.

Mortgagees are encouraged to have written policies in place for their customer service, loss mitigation, foreclosure prevention, and collections departments for handling inbound and outbound collection calls in accordance with the requirements of this section. Mortgagees should also include in their Quality Control (QC) Plans their methodologies for assessing their compliance with these policies.

(B) Required Documentation

The Mortgagee must document in their servicing file all communication efforts to reach a Borrower with a Delinquent Mortgage by telephone.

vi. Collection Letters and Electronic Communications

(A) Standard

(1) Letters and Automatic Notices

The Mortgagee must begin mail or electronic communication collection attempts between the 20-25th Day of delinquency.

(2) Electronic Methods of Communication

The Mortgagee must communicate through one of the following methods of communication, if it elects to communicate electronically with Borrowers:
- email;
- secure web portals (such as online account management tools accessible by Borrowers); and
- other reliable communication methods through which the Mortgagee has been able to effectively communicate with Borrowers in the past.

The Mortgagee must ensure that their electronic signature technology complies with all requirements of the Electronic Signatures in Global and National Commerce (E-SIGN) Act, 15 U.S.C. 7001 *et seq.* The Mortgagee must include within the electronic communication the Mortgagee's email address, telephone number, and/or website address.

Mortgagees are encouraged to have policies in place to reduce the Mortgagee's time to respond to Borrowers' electronic communications. Mortgagees are encouraged to have written policies in place for their customer service, loss mitigation, foreclosure prevention, and collections departments for handling inbound electronic communications in accordance with the requirements of this section and to include in their QC Plans their methodologies for assessing their compliance with these policies.

(3) Selecting Best Method of Communication

The Mortgagee must use the method or methods of communication most likely to receive a response from each Borrower and take into account the Borrower's expressed preference for using certain methods of communication.

The Mortgagee must effectively communicate with persons with hearing, visual, and other communications-related disabilities and persons with limited English proficiency.

(B) Required Documentation

The Mortgagee must document in their servicing file all mail and electronic communication attempts to reach a Borrower with a Delinquent Mortgage.

vii. Reporting the Delinquency to HUD

The Mortgagee must report accounts in Default in HUD's SFDMS using the appropriate Default Status Code and Default Reason Code, if the reason for Default is known, and must continue reporting the applicable Status Code until the delinquency is resolved.

viii. Assigned Loss Mitigation Personnel

The Mortgagee must designate personnel to respond to the Borrower's inquiries and to assist them with Loss Mitigation Options no later than the 45th Day of delinquency.

The Mortgagee must provide the contact information of their loss mitigation or customer assistance hotline, offering direct phone access to assigned loss mitigation personnel, in the Delinquency Notice Cover Letter.

ix. Required Notices to Borrower by 45th Day of Delinquency

(A) Standard

Beginning on the 32nd Day, but no later than the 45th Day from the date payment was due, the Mortgagee must send a:
- Notice of Homeownership Counseling Availability; and
- Servicemembers Civil Relief Act (SCRA) Disclosure (form HUD-92070).

(1) Notice of Homeownership Counseling Availability

The Mortgagee must provide a Borrower with a Delinquent Mortgage with a notice describing the availability of housing counseling offered by HUD-approved housing counseling agencies and by the Mortgagee. The Mortgagee may use the model Notification to Homeowners of Availability of Housing Counseling Services or create their own, so long as the Notification:

- informs the Borrower with a Delinquent Mortgage of the availability of housing counseling services provided by HUD-approved housing counseling agencies;
- is provided in accessible formats or languages when such Borrower communications have been requested by persons with disabilities and persons with limited English proficiency;
- provides instructions for locating a HUD-approved housing counseling agency in the Borrower's area and includes the HUD toll-free telephone number (800) 569-4287, through which Borrowers can obtain a list of housing counseling agencies;
- provides instructions for persons with hearing or speech impairments to access HUD's toll-free number via Text Telephone (TTY) by calling the Federal Information Relay Service at (800) 877-8339;
- provides instructions for using the HOPE NOW toll-free telephone number (888) 995-HOPE (4673); and
- describes housing counseling and the potential benefits of engaging in housing counseling.

If using the model Notification, the Mortgagee must not alter this Notification or use the HUD seal on any other document.

(2) Servicemembers Civil Relief Act Disclosure

The Mortgagee must send the form for the required notice of servicemember rights (form HUD-92070) to all Borrowers in Default on a residential Mortgage and must include the toll-free Military OneSource number to call if servicemembers or their dependents require further assistance.

(B) Required Documentation

The Mortgagee must document in their servicing file the dates on which it sent the Notice of Homeownership Counseling Availability and the SCRA disclosure. The Mortgagee must be able to provide to HUD, upon request, the language in its Notice of Homeownership Counseling Availability.

x. Required Notices to Borrower by 60th Day of Delinquency

(A) Standard

Beginning on the 32nd Day but no later than the 60th Day from the date payment was due, the Mortgagee must send the:

- Delinquency Notice Cover Letter; and
- "Save your Home – Tips to Avoid Foreclosure" pamphlet (form HUD-2008-5-FHA).

(1) Delinquency Notice Cover Letter

The Mortgagee must send the "Save Your Home: Tips to Avoid Foreclosure" brochure with a cover letter that includes:

- highly visible information about any availability of language access services offered by the Mortgagee for Borrowers with limited English proficiency (this information must be provided, at a minimum, in Spanish and must include an advisement to seek translation or other language assistance);
- the following information related to the Mortgage:
  - number of late payments;
  - total amount of any Late Charges incurred;
  - the month of each late payment; and
  - the original due date of each late payment;
- the Mortgagee's mailing address and toll-free telephone numbers for Borrowers needing to contact the Mortgagee's assigned loss mitigation and/or customer assistance personnel;
- a request for current Borrower financial information necessary for Loss Mitigation analysis;
- toll-free telephone numbers for Borrowers needing to contact the Mortgagee's loss mitigation and/or customer assistance personnel; and
- the toll-free telephone number for Borrowers seeking information on HUD-approved housing counseling agencies, (800) 569-4287, along with the toll-free Federal Information Relay Service number of (800) 877-8339 for Borrowers who may need a Telecommunication Device for the Deaf (TDD) to call the housing counseling line.

(2) "Save Your Home: Tips to Avoid Foreclosure" Brochure

The brochure (form HUD-2008-5-FHA) is available in English, Spanish, Chinese, and Vietnamese. Mortgagees may either obtain the brochure by accessing HUD's Direct Distribution Center or reproduce electronic versions of the brochure at their own expense.

The Mortgagee may not change the contents of the brochure in any way.

(3) Resending Notices

The Mortgagee must resend the cover letter and accompanying "Save your Home: Tips to Avoid Foreclosure" brochure (form HUD-2008-5-FHA) any time the Mortgage becomes 45 Days Delinquent unless the beginning of the new delinquency occurs less than six months after a prior notice and pamphlet was mailed.

(4) Exception for Borrowers in Bankruptcy

(a) Standard

The Mortgagee is not required to send the cover letter and "Save Your Home: Tips to Avoid Foreclosure" brochure if the Borrower has filed bankruptcy before becoming 45 Days Delinquent, and, in the opinion of the Mortgagee's legal counsel, providing the cover letter and brochure would be a violation of the automatic stay.

The Mortgagee must send the cover letter and "Save Your Home: Tips to Avoid Foreclosure" once the automatic stay is lifted.

(b) Required Documentation

The Mortgagee must document this bankruptcy-related exception in the servicing file.

(B) Required Documentation

The Mortgagee must document in their servicing file the dates on which it sent the Delinquency Notice Cover Letter and "Save Your Home: Tips to Avoid Foreclosure" brochure.

xi. Occupancy Inspection

(A) Definitions

An Occupancy Inspection is a visual inspection of a mortgaged Property by the Mortgagee to determine if the mortgaged Property has become vacant or abandoned and to confirm the identity of any occupants.

An Occupancy Follow-Up is an attempt to communicate with the Borrower via letter, telephone, or other method of communication, other than on-site inspection, to determine occupancy when the Mortgage remains in Default after the initial inspection and the Mortgagee has not determined the Borrower's occupancy status.

(B) Standard

If the Mortgagee is unable to reach the Borrower(s) by the 45th Day of delinquency, the Mortgagee must perform a visual inspection of the mortgaged Property to determine occupancy status.

(1) Initial Occupancy Inspection

The Mortgagee must perform the initial Occupancy Inspection no later than the 60th Day of delinquency when:
- the Mortgage is in Default;
- a payment has not been received within 45 Days of the due date; and
- efforts to reach the Borrower or occupant have been unsuccessful.

(2) Follow-Ups and Continued Inspections

If the Mortgagee is unable to determine the Borrower's occupancy status through the initial Occupancy Inspection, the Mortgagee must perform Occupancy Follow-Ups and, if necessary, Occupancy Inspections every 25-35 Days from the last inspection until the occupancy status is determined.

(3) Occupancy Inspections during Bankruptcy

When payments are not submitted as scheduled by a Borrower in bankruptcy, the Mortgagee must contact either the bankruptcy trustee or the Borrower's bankruptcy attorney for information concerning the status of the Borrower, to determine if an Occupancy Inspection is needed.

The Mortgagee must continue to perform exterior-only visual inspections until the Default is cured, the Property is disposed of, or the bankruptcy court has granted approval for the Mortgagee to contact the Borrower or to take any required Property P&P actions.

If the Mortgagee determines that the Property is vacant or abandoned during the period in which the Mortgagee is prohibited from contacting the Borrower, the Mortgagee must note:
- the date it made its determination in the servicing file; and
- that contact with the attorney or trustee has been made.

(4) Determination that the Property is Vacant or Abandoned

If the Mortgagee determines through an Occupancy Inspection that the Property is vacant or abandoned, the Mortgagee must:
- send a letter, via certified mail or other method providing delivery confirmation, to Borrowers at the property address informing them of the Mortgagee's determination that the Property is vacant or abandoned. This letter must include the Mortgagee's contact information;

- commence <u>Vacant Property Inspections;</u> and
- take appropriate <u>Property Preservation and Protection</u> actions to secure and maintain the Property.

(C) Required Documentation

The Mortgagee must retain in the servicing file:
- the dates and methods of Occupancy Follow-Ups and vacancy letters;
- evidence of payment to the inspector;
- copies of all completed inspection reports; and
- any accompanying follow-up documentation for Occupancy Inspections.

For all inspections, Mortgagees must also retain in its inspection report the general condition of the Property and any actions taken to protect and preserve the Property, and must include on each inspection report the following items, where applicable:
- date of the inspection
- identity of the individual inspector and the inspection company
- Is the Property occupied?
- Is the house locked?
- Is the grass mowed and/or are shrubs trimmed?
- Is there any apparent damage?
- Is any exterior glass broken?
- Are there any apparent roof leaks?
- Does the house contain Personal Property and/or debris?
- Are any doors or windows boarded?
- Is the house winterized?
- Are there any repairs necessary to adequately preserve and protect the Property?

xii. Face-to-Face Interviews

(A) Standard

The Mortgagee must have a face-to-face interview with the Borrower or make a reasonable effort to arrange a face-to-face interview no later than the 61st Day of delinquency, unless exempt.

(1) Face-to Face Meetings Not Required

The Mortgagee is not required to conduct a face-to-face interview if:
- the Borrower does not live in the mortgaged Property;
- the holding Mortgagee, servicing Mortgagee, or branch office of either is not located within 200 miles of the mortgaged Property (unless the Mortgage is insured under <u>Section 248</u>);

- the Borrower has clearly indicated that they will not cooperate with a face-to-face interview; or
- the Borrower's payment is current due to an agreed-upon repayment plan or Forbearance Plan.

(2) Reasonable Effort in Arranging a Face-to-Face Interview

The Mortgagee must send to the Borrower via Certificate of Mailing or Certified Mail a letter providing information on:
- the availability of face-to-face interviews; and
- how to schedule the interview.

The Mortgagee must also attempt to contact the Borrower at the mortgaged Property to provide information on the availability of face-to face interviews. The Mortgagee may use a third-party vendor to establish this contact with the Borrower and to schedule the Borrower's face-to-face interview with a Mortgagee representative.

(3) Mortgagee Representative Authority

The Mortgagee must ensure that the employee representing the Mortgagee at face-to-face interviews has the authority to propose and accept reasonable repayment plans. Where a Mortgagee's representative exceeds their authority by agreeing to a repayment plan at the time of the face-to-face interview, the Mortgagee must still accept the repayment plan agreed to by its representative, without regard as to whether the representative overstepped their authority.

(B) Required Documentation

The Mortgagee must document in its servicing file:
- the reason the face-to-face meeting is not required, if applicable;
- the dates and methods of its attempts at arranging a face-to-face interview; and
- the date of its face-to-face interview with the Borrower.

xiii. Reporting the Reason for the Default to HUD

(A) Standard

The Mortgagee must ensure that FHA's SFDMS reflects the appropriate Default Reason Code for the Default by the 90th Day of delinquency.

(B) Unable to Contact Borrower

If the Mortgagee reports DDR Code 31, *Unable to Contact Borrower*, in SFDMS, the Mortgagee must document its efforts to contact the Borrower in the servicing file and continue to try to determine the reason for the delinquency Default.

xiv.   Vacant Property Inspections

(A) Definition

A Vacant Property Inspection is an inspection by the Mortgagee of a Property that is not occupied.

(B) Standard

The Mortgagee must take reasonable actions to protect the value of the security, including performing the following required inspections for vacant or abandoned Properties.

The Mortgagee is liable for any damage resulting from the Mortgagee's failure to preserve and protect the Property unless the Mortgagee can prove that the damage occurred prior to the date the Property became vacant.

(1) First-Time Vacant Property Inspection

(a) Definition

A First-Time Vacant (FTV) Property Inspection is the first inspection performed by the Mortgagee to ascertain the condition of a vacant or abandoned Property.

(b) Standard

The Mortgagee must perform the FTV Property Inspection on the date it takes possession of a vacant or abandoned Property.

The Mortgagee must:
- secure the Property, if possible;
- pressure-test all water supply and upload photographs of the results of the test into P260;
- address all imminent and urgent safety hazards and determine what repairs are required to prevent damage to the property; and
- photograph the primary exterior facades and interior areas of the primary and secondary Structures, including any damage found.

(c) Required Documentation

The Mortgagee must document the overall condition and any damage to the grounds and Structures in the inspection report.

The Mortgagee must advise HUD when the mortgaged Property becomes vacant by reporting in SFDMS:
- the Occupancy Status Code; and

- the date when the Mortgagee determined that the mortgaged Property became vacant.

(2) Vacant Property Inspection

(a) Standard

(i) Vacant Property Inspection Cycle

The Mortgagee must perform Vacant Property Inspections every 25-35 Days after the FTV Property Inspection until the mortgage Default is cured or until conveyance of the property to HUD. In areas of high vandalism or where local ordinances require more frequent Vacant Property Inspections, Mortgagees may perform Vacant Property Inspections more frequently than HUD's 25-35 Day requirement and request reimbursement for these inspection costs.

At each inspection, the Mortgagee must:
- photograph the overall condition of the interior and exterior of the primary and all secondary Structures;
- monitor the security and maintenance of the Property;
- assess and manage damage that requires repair, replacement, or removal; and
- address all emergency repairs.

(ii) Required Documentation

The Mortgagee must document all Property P&P activities performed on vacant Properties.

(3) Required Documentation

The Mortgagee must retain in the servicing file:
- evidence of payment to the inspector;
- copies of all completed inspection reports and photographs of the Property; and
- any police reports and/or letters from a local law enforcement agency evidencing the need for additional protective measures.

i. Loss Mitigation Review Process

i. Servicemember Status

The Mortgagee must offer eligible servicemember Borrowers mortgage protections under the SCRA and Servicing FHA-Insured Mortgages for Servicemember-Borrowers.

ii. Complete Loss Mitigation Requests

(A) Definition

A Complete Loss Mitigation Request is a request for loss mitigation assistance that contains all information the Mortgagee requires from the Borrower in order to evaluate Loss Mitigation Options.

(B) Standard

The Mortgagee must timely evaluate and respond to Complete Loss Mitigation Requests. For loss mitigation requests received after the initiation of foreclosure, the Mortgagee must evaluate and respond to Complete Loss Mitigation Requests according to the time frame requirements in Loss Mitigation during the Foreclosure Process.

When a Mortgagee receives incomplete loss mitigation requests, the Mortgagee must notify the Borrower in writing:
- which documents are needed for review; and
- when the documents should be sent back to the Mortgagee.

This notice must include the required statement that the Borrower should consider contacting Mortgagees of any other Mortgages secured by the same Property to discuss available Loss Mitigation Options.

(C) Required Documentation

The Mortgagee must note in its servicing file:
- the dates it received a Complete Loss Mitigation Request;
- the dates it sent any notices to the Borrower requesting additional documentation, if applicable; and
- what documentation was requested, if applicable.

iii. Evaluation of the Borrower's Financial Condition

(A) Borrower's Financial Information

(1) Standard

The Mortgagee must obtain detailed financial information from the Borrower in order to evaluate them for Loss Mitigation Options. The Mortgagee may accept financial information during a telephone interview subject to confirmation with appropriate supporting documentation.

The Mortgagee must review and validate the Borrower's financial information and qualifying status to determine there is no deliberate manufacturing or misrepresentation of the Borrower's financial information or other qualifying status. Deliberate manufacturing or misrepresentation of financial information or qualifying status by the Borrower will disqualify the Borrower from participation.

(a) Living Expenses

The Mortgagee must confirm all Borrowers' monthly living expenses with appropriate supporting documentation when the existing total Mortgage Payment (i.e., PITI) is equal to or less than 31 percent of the Borrowers' current monthly gross income. The Mortgagee must ensure that all expenses on the Borrower's credit report are included in the Mortgagee's calculation of living expenses, along with any other expenses, which can be supported by bills and receipts or by allowances for the five necessary expenses (food, housekeeping supplies, apparel and services, personal care products and services, and miscellaneous) established as national standards for food, clothing, and other items as part of the IRS Collection Financial Standards.

Refer to IRS National Standards: Food, Clothing and Other Items for more information.

(b) Borrower Income

For purposes of a loss mitigation analysis, Borrower income must include:
- the income of each Borrower who is occupying or not occupying the Property; and
- the income of each owner-occupant non-Borrower who will be added as a Borrower and assume personal liability for repayment of the Mortgage in accordance with the agreed upon loss mitigation terms.

(c) Hardship

Hardship for purposes of FHA's Loss Mitigation Options is demonstrated by providing evidence of an increase in living expenses or a loss of income. FHA-approved Mortgagees have the delegated authority to request the documentation they deem necessary from Borrowers to substantiate a hardship.

(2) Required Documentation

The Mortgagee must retain documentation of financial information in the Claim Review File.

Supporting documentation for hardship can be in the form of bank statements, medical bills, home repair bills, and other similar documentation.

(B) Analysis of Borrower's Financial Information for Surplus Income

(1) Definition

Surplus Income Percentage is a percentage calculated in the Mortgagee's financial analysis to determine which Loss Mitigation Options are appropriate based on the Borrower's income.

(2) Standard

The Mortgagee must analyze the Borrower's current and future ability to meet the monthly Mortgage Payment by estimating the Borrower's assets and surplus income as follows:

- Step 1: Estimate the Borrower's normal monthly living expenses (e.g., food, utilities, etc.), debt service on the Mortgage, and other obligations, including Homeowners' Association (HOA)/Condominium Fees, based on current information, and projected for:
  - o a period of three months; or
  - o if review is for Special Forbearance (SFB) - Unemployment Option, for the length of the SFB - Unemployment Agreement.
- Step 2: Estimate the Borrower's anticipated monthly net income for the same period listed above, making necessary adjustments for income fluctuations.
- Step 3: Subtract expenses from income to determine the amount of surplus income available each month.
- Step 4: Divide surplus income by monthly net income to determine the Surplus Income Percentage.

The Mortgagee must ensure that the selected workout strategy reflects the Borrower's ability to pay. The Mortgagee must require Borrowers who want to retain the Property and who have sufficient surplus income and/or other assets to reinstate the Mortgage through a repayment strategy.

iv. Continuous Income for Loss Mitigation Evaluations

(A) Definition

Continuous Income is income received by the Borrower that is reasonably likely to continue from the date of the Mortgagee's loss mitigation evaluation through at least the next 12 months.

(B) Standard

Continuous Income includes the following:
- Employment Income (e.g., wages, salary, or self-employment earnings);
- Social Security;

- disability;
- veterans' benefits;
- Child Support;
- survivor benefits;
- Pensions; and
- other documented income that is reasonably likely to continue from the date of the Mortgagee's loss mitigation evaluation through at least the next 12 months.

In determining the amount of Continuous Income available to a Borrower, the Mortgagee must review the Borrower's documented sources of income and expenses and calculate the Borrower's surplus/deficit income or gross income necessary for applicable Loss Mitigation Options.

v. 90-Day Review Requirement

(A) Definition

The 90-Day Review is a Mortgagee's required evaluation, occurring before four monthly installments are due and unpaid, of a Defaulted Mortgage for appropriate Loss Mitigation Options.

(B) Standard

To comply with this loss mitigation review requirement, the Mortgagee must:
- contact the Borrower to gather information about their circumstances, intentions, and financial condition; and
- attempt to complete its evaluation of the Mortgage for all appropriate Loss Mitigation Options.

After its review of a Borrower's loss mitigation request, the Mortgagee must send a written Notice to Borrower after Loss Mitigation Review.

(C) Required Documentation

The Mortgagee must document in the Claim Review File its aggressive efforts to reach each Borrower in Default well in advance of the 90-Day Review deadline.

vi. Monthly Review

(A) Standard

The Mortgagee must evaluate on a monthly basis all Loss Mitigation Options available for Borrowers in Default as long as the Mortgage remains Delinquent.

(B) Required Documentation

The Mortgagee's servicing records must include monthly notations, documenting the Mortgagee's analysis and determination with respect to the appropriateness of each Loss Mitigation Option. If the Borrower indicates that there has been no change in their circumstances, the Mortgagee may note this in its records.

As long as the Borrower is performing on an approved Loss Mitigation Option, including Trial Payment Plans, the Mortgagee has met the monthly review requirement and must note this in the Claim Review File.

vii. Loss Mitigation Reporting

The Mortgagee must report in SFDMS the <u>Delinquency Workouts Status Codes</u> that accurately reflect the stage of loss mitigation review.

If the Mortgagee has determined that the Borrower is ineligible for Loss Mitigation and the Mortgagee will be initiating foreclosure, the Mortgagee must report in SFDMS the appropriate Ineligible for Loss Mitigation Code.

viii. Notice to Borrower after Loss Mitigation Review

The Mortgagee must send a written notice to the Borrower after an evaluation of the Borrower for Loss Mitigation Option eligibility, which indicates:
- the Mortgagee's determination as to whether or not the Borrower qualifies for a Loss Mitigation Option;
- the actual reason or reasons they have been denied for any HUD Loss Mitigation Option;
- the process for appeals or escalation of cases;
- the process and time frame for submission of additional information that may impact the Mortgagee's evaluation;
- the Mortgagee's points of contact; and
- the possibility of the Borrower's Mortgage being included in a Single Family Loan Sale *or* being foreclosed upon if loss mitigation is not viable, unsuccessful, denied, or unable to be considered (due to the Borrower's failure to fully respond to the Mortgagee's request for additional information).

ix. Loss Mitigation Agreements

(A) Standard

The Mortgagee must ensure that Loss Mitigation Option Agreements are executed by all parties necessary to ensure:
- that HUD's first lien position is preserved; and
- that the Agreement is enforceable under state and local law.

(B) Mortgagee Signature

Where a Mortgagee signature is needed on a Loss Mitigation Option Agreement, the servicing Mortgagee with this delegated authority may provide this signature.

(C) Authorized Third Parties

When a Loss Mitigation Option Agreement is to be signed by an Authorized Third Party with authority to act on behalf of the Borrower, the Mortgagee must ensure that the Claim Review File includes a copy of that party's authorization.

(D) Electronic Signatures

The use of electronic signatures is voluntary. HUD will accept an electronic signature conducted in accordance with the Policy on Use of Electronic Signatures on HUD Loss Mitigation documents requiring signatures, unless otherwise prohibited by law.

(E) No Waiver of Rights

The Mortgagee must not include any language in any loss mitigation documents that requires Borrowers to waive their rights under state or federal law or under the mortgage contract as a condition for consideration, approval, or implementation of a Loss Mitigation Option.

x.   Loss Mitigation during Bankruptcy Proceedings

(A) Standard

The Mortgagee must comply with and seek relief, if appropriate, from the automatic stay. The Mortgagee may review Borrowers with active Chapter 7 or Chapter 13 bankruptcy cases for Loss Mitigation Options to the extent that such loss mitigation does not violate federal bankruptcy laws or orders of the bankruptcy court or bankruptcy trustee.

(1) Eligibility for Loss Mitigation

The Mortgagee may consider for Loss Mitigation Options those Borrowers who have received a Chapter 7 bankruptcy discharge and did not reaffirm the FHA-insured mortgage debt under applicable law.

(2) Bankruptcy Proceedings for which Borrower has an Attorney

The Mortgagee must, upon receipt of notice of a bankruptcy filing:
- send information to the Borrower's attorney indicating that loss mitigation may be available; and
- provide instructions sufficient to facilitate workout discussions including:
  - requirements for additional financial information documentation;

o applicable time frames; and

o Mortgagee contact information.

(3) Bankruptcy Proceedings for which Borrower does not have an Attorney (Bankruptcy Pro Se)

Where the Borrower filed the bankruptcy pro se, the Mortgagee must send to the Borrower information relating to the availability of Loss Mitigation Options, with a copy to the bankruptcy trustee. The Mortgagee must ensure that this communication does not infer that it is in any way an attempt to collect a debt.

(B) Required Documentation

The Mortgagee must retain in its Claim Review File documentation supporting its efforts to comply with or seek relief from automatic stays and documentation supporting any delays in meeting required HUD timelines.

(C) Reporting Bankruptcy

The Mortgagee must report in SFDMS the Account in Bankruptcy Codes reflecting the status of the bankruptcy proceedings.

xi. Escalated Cases

(A) Definition

Escalated Cases are written Borrower inquiries and complaints requiring additional Mortgagee review because they include allegations of:
- improper analysis of Borrower information or denials of Loss Mitigation Options;
- foreclosures initiated or continued in violation of HUD's policy; or
- other violation of HUD Collections and Loss Mitigation policies.

(B) Standard

The Mortgagee must escalate cases to its designated escalation team at the written request of:
- HUD staff; or
- the Borrower or Borrower's Authorized Third Party representative.

(C) Escalation Processes

The Mortgagee must escalate and respond to cases in accordance with their written internal policies.

The Mortgagee must ensure that, at a minimum, the policies include the following:

- designate which staff members will be responsible for resolving escalated cases. These staff members must:
  - o   not be the same staff members responsible for the first evaluation of the loss mitigation application; and
  - o   have access to the Borrowers' servicing files;
- provide for timely responses to escalated cases as follows:
  - o   within seven Days of categorizing a Borrower's inquiry or complaint as an escalated case, the Mortgagee should notify the Borrower in writing that their inquiry and/or complaint has been escalated and that a resolution to their case will be provided no later than 30 Days from the date of escalation; and
  - o   if the Mortgagee is unable to resolve an escalated case within 30 Days, the Mortgagee must send the Borrower written updates on the status of their case every 15 Days until the case is resolved;
- provide Borrowers with the direct contact information of the department and/or staff member responsible for resolving its escalated cases;
- include methodologies for assessing a Servicer's compliance with its escalation policies. These methodologies must be included in a Mortgagee's QC Plan; and
- detail the Mortgagee's process for resolving escalated cases and managing foreclosure activity when a foreclosure sale has been scheduled.

j.   HUD's Loss Mitigation Program

i.   Definitions

A Loss Mitigation Option is one of the following strategies under FHA's Loss Mitigation Program requirements intended to minimize economic impact to the MMIF and to avoid foreclosure, if possible:
- SFB-Unemployment
- FHA-HAMP Loan Modifications, Partial Claims, and Combination Loan Modification/Partial Claims
- PFS
- DIL of Foreclosure

ii.   Standard

Mortgagees are required to evaluate all Defaulted Mortgages for Loss Mitigation Options.

In implementing HUD's Loss Mitigation Program, the Mortgagee must:
- consider all reasonable means to address delinquency at the earliest possible time;
- adhere to the requirements for communication with Borrowers in Default as set out in the Collection Communication Timeline;
- utilize HUD's Loss Mitigation Options to avoid foreclosure, when feasible;
- initiate foreclosure within six months of Default; and

- re-evaluate each Delinquent Mortgage monthly for loss mitigation eligibility until reinstatement or completion of a Home Disposition Option, foreclosure, or Single Family Loan Sale (SFLS).

(A) Mortgage Status

The Mortgagee must review for Loss Mitigation Options those Borrowers who are in Default or in Imminent Default.

When reviewing Borrowers for Loss Mitigation Options, a streamlined or refinanced Mortgage on the same Property and by the same Borrowers is not considered a new Mortgage for seasoning requirements.

The Mortgagee may offer eligible Borrowers Loss Mitigation Options in accordance with program-specific procedures for:

- Section 203(q) Mortgages, Mortgages on Property in Allegany Reservation of Seneca Indians;
- Section 248 Mortgages on Indian Land insured pursuant to Section 248 of the National Housing Act; and
- Section 247 Mortgages, Mortgages on Hawaiian Home Lands insured pursuant to Section 247 of the National Housing Act.

(B) Owner Occupancy

(1) Definitions

An Owner-Occupant Borrower is a Borrower residing in the Property secured by the FHA-insured Mortgage as a Principal Residence.

A Non-Occupant Borrower is a Borrower on a Mortgage securing a Property that is not occupied by any Borrower.

(2) Standard for Non-Occupant Borrowers

The Mortgagee may consider Non-Occupant Borrowers for:

- Home Disposition Options when the subject Property was not purchased as a rental investment or used as a rental for more than 18 months; or
- Informal or Formal Forbearances.

(3) Required Documentation

The Mortgagee must document in the Claim Review File the justification for approval of any Non-Occupant Borrowers for Loss Mitigation Options and, if applicable, retain a copy of the Request for Variance received from the NSC via EVARS.

(4) Exceptions to Owner Occupancy Requirements

(a) Borrowers with Multiple FHA-Insured Mortgages

(i) Standard

The Mortgagee may consider Loss Mitigation Options other than the Deed-in-Lieu (DIL) Option for those Borrowers who meet the eligibility requirements for policy exceptions listed in the Exceptions to the FHA Policy Limiting the Number of Mortgages per Borrower section.

(ii) Required Documentation

The Mortgagee must document in the Claim Review File the justification for any exceptions for Borrowers with multiple FHA-insured Mortgages.

(b) Non-Borrowers who Acquired Title through an Exempted Transfer

The Mortgagee may consider for Home Retention Options a non-borrower who acquires title to a Property securing an FHA-insured Mortgage if the mortgage is not due and payable pursuant to the Garn-St. Germain Depository Institutions Act, and that the non-borrower:

- will occupy the home as a Principal Residence;
- submits to a credit review;
- meets financial criteria for loss mitigation assistance; and
- is willing to assume personal liability for repayment of the Mortgage in accordance with the agreed loss mitigation terms.

(c) Non-Borrowers who Acquired Title not through an Exempted Transfer

The Mortgagee may consider for loss mitigation a non-borrower who is not covered by an exempted transfer under the Garn-St. Germain Depository Institutions Act and who acquired title but does not hold sole title to the Property as follows:

- the non-borrower will be added as a Borrower; and
- the non-borrower will be considered for loss mitigation with the cooperation and approval of the existing Borrowers.

(d) Co-Insured Mortgages

The Mortgagee must not offer any Loss Mitigation Option other than the Informal or Formal Forbearance or SFB-Unemployment Options on co-insured Mortgages until the 60th payment has been received.

(e) Vacant or Abandoned Properties

(i) Standard

The Mortgagee may consider Non-Occupant Borrowers for Home Disposition Options only when the Properties have been recently vacated by circumstances related to the Default.

(ii) Required Documentation

The Mortgagee must document these circumstances relating to the vacancy in the Claim Review File.

(C) Eligibility to Participate in HUD Programs

(1) Standard

The Mortgagee must verify that the Borrowers are eligible to participate in HUD's Loss Mitigation Program. As a part of determining eligibility, the Mortgagee must utilize the appropriate system to determine if the Borrower is excluded from HUD's Loss Mitigation Program.

To be eligible to participate in HUD's Loss Mitigation Program, the Borrower:
- may not own other real estate subject to FHA insurance, except within the stated exceptions;
- has not been the Borrower, except through inheritance or as a co-signer only, on prior loans on which an FHA claim has been paid within the past three years; and
- for purposes of FHA-HAMP:
  o may not be debarred, suspended or subject to a HUD Limited Denial of Participation (LDP) as determined in accordance with Excluded Parties requirements; and
  o may not have unresolved delinquent Federal Debt as determined in accordance with Borrower Ineligibility Due to Delinquent Federal Non-Tax Debt requirements. The Delinquent FHA-insured Mortgage associated with the Loss Mitigation does not constitute a disqualifying delinquent Federal Debt.

The Credit Alert Verification Reporting System (CAIVRS) must be used when determining the Borrower's eligibility for the following Loss Mitigation Options:
- SFB
- PFS Program
- DIL of Foreclosure

(2) Required Documentation

The Mortgagee must retain in its Claim Review File documentation evidencing that the Borrower is eligible to participate in an FHA transaction.

iii. HUD's Loss Mitigation Option Priority Waterfall

The Mortgagee must evaluate Owner-Occupant Borrowers utilizing the process in the Loss Mitigation Home Retention Option Priority Waterfall below to determine which, if any, Home Retention Options are appropriate in accordance with HUD guidance.

The Mortgagee must not condition the use of a Loss Mitigation Option on the receipt of a Borrower's cash contribution or Borrower's payment of <u>fees or charges</u>.

Loss Mitigation Home Retention Waterfall Options			
Step	**Decision Point**	**Yes**	**No**
1	Household or Borrower(s) has experienced a verified loss of income or increase in living expenses?	Step 2	**Informal or Formal Forbearance/repayment plan workout tools**
2	One or more Borrowers receive Continuous Income in the form of Employment Income (e.g., wages, salary, or self-employment earnings), Social Security, disability, veterans' benefits, Child Support, survivor benefits, and/or Pensions?	Step 3	**Special Forbearance**
3	Front-end ratio is at or less than 31%?	Step 4	**FHA-HAMP** (Step 5)
4	85% of surplus income is sufficient to cure arrears within 6 months?	Formal Forbearance/repayment plan for no more than 6 months.	**FHA-HAMP** (Step 5)

Step 5	**FHA-HAMP Loan Modification**[2] *(Requires Successful Completion of Trial Payment Plan)*

The use of an FHA-HAMP Option is to both alleviate the Borrower's burden of immediate repayment of arrears and to adjust monthly payments to a level sustainable by the household's current income. The FHA-HAMP Option may *or* may not include a Partial Claim.

Partial Claim: The total amount available is the lesser of: (1) the unpaid principal balance as of the date of Default associated with the initial Partial Claim, if applicable, multiplied by 30%, less any previous Partial Claim(s) paid on this Mortgage; (2) if there are no previous Partial Claim(s), the unpaid principal balance as of the date of the current Default multiplied by 30%; or (3) the total amount required to meet the target payment. The Partial Claim amount may include: arrearages; legal fees and foreclosure costs related to a canceled foreclosure action; and principal deferment (per below calculation). No portion of the Partial Claim may be used to bring the modified PITI monthly payment below the target payment.

Loan Modification:
1. Calculate the target monthly payment:
    A. Calculate 31% of gross income
    B. Calculate 80% of current Mortgage Payment
    C. Calculate 25% of gross income
    D. Take the greater of B and C
    E. Take the lesser of A and D
2. Calculate PITI monthly payment on the total outstanding debt to be resolved at the market interest rate[3] and 360 months' term.
3. If the result of Step 2 is at or below the result from Step 1E, then the Borrower is eligible for an FHA-HAMP Standalone Loan Modification only at the market interest rate; otherwise, go to Step 4.
4. Calculate amount required to meet target payment.
    A. Reduce loan balance used in Step 2 until calculated Mortgage Payment reaches target amount from Step 1 or else the maximum allowable principal deferment is reached per amount available as calculated above per instructions in the "Partial Claim" section.
    B. If the final Mortgage Payment is greater than 40% of current income, and the unemployment status is verifiable, then the Borrower is eligible for a reduced payment option under the Special Forbearance.
    C. If there is no verifiable unemployment status and the Borrower has already been reviewed for retention options under the waterfall but does not qualify for any (i.e., the Borrower does not have sufficient surplus income or other assets that could repay the indebtedness), then the Borrower is eligible for FHA's non-retention options.

---

[2] An FHA-HAMP Standalone Loan Modification is required if a Mortgage Payment at or below the target payment can be achieved by re-amortizing the Mortgage/outstanding debt for 360 months at the Market Rate. An FHA-HAMP Standalone Partial Claim is required if the

iv. Required Documentation

The Mortgagee must document its implementation of HUD's Loss Mitigation Program by:

- reporting loss mitigation actions through SFDMS;
- documenting in the Claim Review File all loss mitigation actions, including all efforts to contact the Borrowers; and
- retaining all documentation used to analyze and make loss mitigation determinations and to confirm compliance with loss mitigation requirements.

k. Home Retention Options

i. Definition

Home Retention Options are the Loss Mitigation Options of Informal and Formal Forbearances, SFB-Unemployment and FHA-HAMP.

ii. Forbearance Plans

(A) Definitions

Forbearance Plans refer to arrangements between a Mortgagee and Borrower that may allow for a period of reduced or suspended payments and may provide specific terms for repayment.

Informal Forbearance Plans refer to oral agreements allowing for reduced or suspended payments for a period of three months or less and may provide specific terms for repayment.

Formal Forbearance Plans are written agreements executed by one or more of the Borrowers, allowing for reduced or suspended payments for a period greater than three months, but not more than six months, unless otherwise authorized by HUD, and such plans may include specific terms for repayment.

(B) Standard

The Mortgagee must first evaluate the Borrower for both Informal and Formal Forbearance Plans.

Borrower's (i) current interest rate is at or below Market Rate; (ii) the Borrower's current Mortgage Payment with re-analyzed escrow is at or below the target payment; and (iii) the Borrower is not eligible for an FHA-HAMP Standalone Loan Modification.

[3] Pursuant to HUD Handbook 4000.1, "Market Rate" is defined as a rate that is no more than 25 basis points greater than the most recent Freddie Mac Weekly Primary Mortgage Market Survey (PMMS) Rate for 30-year fixed-rate conforming mortgages (U.S. average), rounded to the nearest one-eighth of one percent (0.125%), as of the date a Trial Payment Plan is offered to a Borrower. The Weekly PMMS results are published on the Freddie Mac website at http://www.freddiemac.com/pmms/.

Handbook 4000.1
Effective Date: 03/14/2016 | Last Revised: 07/10/2019
*Refer to the online version of SF Handbook 4000.1 for specific sections' effective dates

617

The Mortgagee must offer Informal Forbearance Plans to a Borrower with a Delinquent Mortgage who does not have losses of income or increases in living expenses that can be verified.

The Mortgagee must offer a Formal Forbearance Plan when:
- the Borrower does not have a loss of income or increase in living expenses that can be verified;
- the Mortgagee determines that 85 percent of the Borrower's surplus income is sufficient to bring the Mortgage current within six months; or
- if the Mortgagee determines that the Borrower is otherwise ineligible for other Home Retention Options but has sufficient surplus income or other assets that could repay the indebtedness.

In order to proceed with a Formal Forbearance Plan the Mortgagee must receive a signed Formal Forbearance Plan from the Borrower, after which an authorized Mortgagee representative must execute the Formal Forbearance Plan and file it in the Claim Review File.

Informal and Formal Forbearances are not eligible for loss mitigation incentive payments.

(C) Forbearance Reporting

The Mortgagee must report the appropriate Delinquency/Default Status (DDS) Code reflecting the use of Informal and Formal Forbearance.

For Formal Forbearance Plans that would run past the deadline to initiate foreclosure, the Mortgagee must request an extension of time in EVARS, including in the request a statement that the Borrower qualified for the Formal Forbearance Plan under HUD's Loss Mitigation Home Retention Option Priority guidance.

iii. HUD Postponement of Principal Payments for Servicemembers

(A) Standard

The Mortgagee may, by written agreement with the Borrower, postpone for the period of military service and three months thereafter any part of the monthly Mortgage that represents amortization of principal.

The Mortgagee must include in the agreement a provision for the resumption of monthly payments after such period, in amounts which will completely amortize the mortgage debt within the maturity, as provided in the original Mortgage.

(B) Required Documentation

The Mortgagee must retain in the servicing file a copy of the written agreement postponing principal payments.

iv. Special Forbearance – Unemployment

(A) Definition

The SFB-Unemployment Option is a Home Retention Option available when one or more of the Borrowers has become unemployed and this loss of employment has negatively affected the Borrower's ability to continue to make their monthly Mortgage Payment.

(B) Eligibility

(1) Defaulted Mortgage Status

The Mortgage must meet the following conditions at the time the SFB-Unemployment Agreement is executed:

- be at least three months past due (61 Days Delinquent), but not more than 12 months due and unpaid; and
- not be in foreclosure, or foreclosure action has been suspended or canceled, when the SFB-Unemployment Agreement is executed.

(2) Borrower Qualifications

(a) Standard

The Mortgagee must ensure that the Borrower meets all of the following eligibility requirements for an SFB-Unemployment Option:

- The Borrower has recently experienced a verified loss of income or increase in living expenses due to loss of employment.
- The Borrower must be an Owner-Occupant Borrower and will occupy the Property as a Principal Residence during the term of the SFB-Unemployment Agreement, unless an exception is granted.
- One or more Borrowers is not currently receiving Continuous Income or, alternatively, an analysis of the financial information under FHA-HAMP resulted in a Mortgage Payment greater than 40 percent of current gross monthly income and one of the Borrowers has a verifiable unemployment status.
- A Borrower has a verified unemployment status and:
  - o no Borrower is currently receiving Continuous Income; or
  - o an analysis of Borrower financial information under the Home Retention Priority Waterfall indicates that the SFB-Unemployment Option is the best or only option available for the Borrower.

(b) Exception to Owner-Occupant Requirement for Sale or Assumption

The Mortgagee may offer an SFB-Unemployment Option to an unemployed Borrower when the Mortgagee has knowledge that the mortgaged Property is for sale or an assumption of the Property is in process.

(c) Required Documentation

The Mortgagee must obtain from the Borrower such supporting documentation of the Borrower's unemployment as:
- Third Party Documentation including receipts of unemployment benefits; or
- an affidavit signed by the Borrower, stating the date that the Borrower became unemployed and stating that the Borrower is actively seeking, and is available, for employment.

The Mortgagee must retain this documentation in the Claim Review File.

(3) Property Condition

The Mortgagee must conduct any review it deems necessary, including a property inspection, when the Mortgagee has reason to believe that the physical conditions of the Property adversely impact the Borrower's use or ability to support the debt as follows:
- financial information provided by the Borrower shows large expenses for property maintenance;
- the Mortgagee receives notice from local government or other third parties regarding property condition; or
- the Property may be affected by a disaster event in the area.

If significant maintenance costs contributed to the Default or are affecting the Borrower's ability to make payments under the Mortgage or SFB-Unemployment Agreement, the Mortgagee may provide in the SFB-Unemployment Agreement a period of mortgage forbearance during which repairs specified in the agreement will be completed at the Borrower's expense.

(C) Review under the Loss Mitigation Home Retention Priority Waterfall

The Mortgagee must assess the Borrower's financial ability to repay their mortgage delinquency and must determine if the loss of employment is the major cause which has resulted in mortgage Default.

The Mortgagee must use the five-step process of the Loss Mitigation Home Retention Option Priority Waterfall to:
- determine that it is a Borrower of record who has experienced the loss of employment;
- determine the loss of employment has had a direct impact on the Borrower's ability to make the monthly Mortgage Payment; and
- enable the Mortgagee to determine a reasonable monthly Mortgage Payment while the Borrower is performing on the SFB-Unemployment Option, even if the Borrower has a negative surplus amount.

Once the Mortgagee's review of the Borrower's financials has been completed and it has been determined that the SFB-Unemployment is the most appropriate Option, the Mortgagee will develop the SFB-Unemployment Agreement.

(D) Special Forbearance – Unemployment Agreement

(1) Definition

The Special Forbearance-Unemployment Agreement is a written agreement between a Mortgagee and the Borrowers, one or more of whom has become unemployed, allowing for reduced and/or suspended Mortgage Payments.

(2) Standard

The Mortgagee must prepare a Special Forbearance-Unemployment Agreement that provides for the following:
- identifies the specific months for which the account is Delinquent and notes the total arrearage that accrued prior to the beginning of the Agreement;
- suspends and/or reduces the current monthly Mortgage Payment;
- ensures that the forbearance payment installments required under the terms of the Agreement are based on the Borrower's ability to pay;
- disallows late fees to be assessed while the Borrower is performing under the terms of the Special Forbearance-Unemployment Agreement;
- indicates that if the Borrower's financial circumstances change, the Mortgagee may adjust the monthly payment based on an evaluation of the Borrower's new financial information;
- disallows the accrued arrearage to exceed the equivalent of 12 months Delinquent Principal, Interest, Taxes, and Insurance (PITI) (the 12 months of PITI for Adjustable Rate Mortgages (ARM), Graduated Payment Mortgages (GPM), and Growing Equity Mortgages (GEM) will be calculated by multiplying 12 times the monthly payments due on the date of Default);
- specifies the date that the Special Forbearance-Unemployment Agreement will expire if it is not earlier revised or terminated because of a change in the Borrower's financial circumstances; and
- permits the Borrower to pre-pay the mortgage delinquency at any time.

The SFB-Unemployment Agreement will not include terms for reinstatement because the Mortgagee must re-evaluate the Borrower for more permanent Loss Mitigation Options to cure a Default once the Borrower is gainfully employed and/or the SFB-Unemployment Agreement expires.

(3) Required Documentation

The Mortgagee must retain in the Claim Review File:

- evidence that the Mortgagee analyzed the Borrower's financial condition;
- evidence that the SFB-Unemployment Agreement is supported by the financial analysis; and
- a copy of the SFB-Unemployment Agreement, executed by at least one Borrower and by an authorized agent of the Mortgagee.

(4) Effective Date

The Executed SFB-Unemployment Agreement date is the date the Mortgagee executes the SFB-Unemployment Agreement.

The SFB-Unemployment Agreement is considered "executed" when:
- at least one of the Borrowers has signed and dated the Agreement;
- the Agreement has been returned to the Mortgagee; and
- the authorized Mortgagee representative has signed and dated the Agreement as well.

(5) Cancellation or Suspension of Foreclosure

(a) Standard

Upon execution of an SFB-Unemployment Agreement, if foreclosure has already been initiated, the Mortgagee must cancel or temporarily suspend foreclosure action, where such suspension is permissible under state law.

(b) Required Documentation

The Mortgagee must include in the Claim Review File documentation showing that the Borrower provided new information that made them eligible for an SFB-Unemployment Option after foreclosure was initiated.

(6) Review of SFB-Unemployment Agreements

(a) Standard

The Mortgagee must review the Borrower's continued eligibility for SFB-Unemployment on a monthly basis and must adjust the terms of the Agreement if there is a change in financial circumstances.

(b) Required Documentation

The Mortgagee must clearly document in the Claim Review File the Borrower's compliance with the terms of the Agreement and any adjustment of terms due to changes in financial circumstances.

(7) Re-Evaluation of the SFB-Unemployment Agreement

The Mortgagee must review the Borrower's continued eligibility for SFB-Unemployment or, alternatively, eligibility for other Loss Mitigation Options if the Borrower presents evidence that their financial circumstances have changed. The Mortgagee must ensure that the re-evaluated SFB-Unemployment Agreement will not allow for the Mortgage to become more than 12 months of PITI Delinquent.

(E) Payment Application

The Mortgagee may reduce, suspend, or both, the required monthly Mortgage Payment for the time period of the SFB-Unemployment Agreement.

The Mortgagee must place payments submitted by the Borrower during the SFB-Unemployment period in a suspense or memo fund account which is to be identified as belonging to the Borrower. When the suspense funds total a full monthly payment, the Mortgagee must apply the payment to the Borrower's account.

If the Borrower does not complete the SFB-Unemployment Agreement, all funds held in suspense will be applied to the Borrower's account.

(F) Foreclosure-Related Fees and Costs

The Mortgagee may address foreclosure-related fees and costs due to a foreclosure cancellation/suspension through the qualification of a permanent Loss Mitigation Option or at the expiration of the SFB-Unemployment Agreement.

The Mortgagee must not require the Borrower to pay more than the foreclosure-related fees and costs HUD has identified as customary and reasonable. See Appendix 4.0 – HUD Schedule of Standard Attorney Fees.

(G) Expiration of SFB-Unemployment Agreement

(1) Re-evaluation of Borrower

During the month in which the SFB-Unemployment Agreement is to expire, the Mortgagee must evaluate the Borrower to determine if the Borrower qualifies for:
- an additional period of forbearance beyond the initial expiration, but not allowing for more than 12 months of Delinquent PITI, due to continued unemployment; or
- a permanent Loss Mitigation Option.

(2) Notification to Borrower

The Mortgagee must notify the Borrower, in writing, the results of the review, including the following information:

Handbook 4000.1
Effective Date: 03/14/2016 | Last Revised: 07/10/2019
*Refer to the online version of SF Handbook 4000.1 for specific sections' effective dates

623

- whether or not they qualify for a Loss Mitigation Option;
- the reason for denial; and
- allowing the Borrower a minimum of seven Days to submit additional information that may impact the Mortgagee's evaluation.

(H) Option Failure

An SFB-Unemployment Option is considered failed if the Borrower:
- abandons the Property;
- informs the Mortgagee that the terms of the SFB-Unemployment Agreement will not be fulfilled; or
- fails to perform under the terms of the SFB-Unemployment Agreement for 60 Days, without any advisement to the Mortgagee of any problems that prevented the Borrower from complying with the Agreement's terms.

If the SFB-Unemployment Option fails, the Mortgagee must initiate foreclosure or complete another Loss Mitigation Option. HUD provides an automatic 90-Day extension during which the Mortgagee must take one of these actions.

(I) Special Forbearance Incentive

The Mortgagee may claim an incentive for each SFB-Unemployment Agreement. Mortgagees with "A" Tier Ranking System (TRS) II scores will be eligible for an incentive of $200 per SFB-Unemployment claim. The Mortgagee may not file more than one SFB-Unemployment incentive claim per Default due to the Borrower's unemployment.

(J) Reporting of SFB-Unemployment

The Mortgagee must report in SFDMS the use of an SFB-Unemployment.

v. FHA-HAMP

(A) Definition

The FHA-HAMP Option is a Loss Mitigation Option using a Loan Modification and/or Partial Claim to allow the Mortgage to be reinstated, by establishing an affordable monthly payment, and providing for principal deferment as needed.

A Partial Claim is FHA's reimbursement of a Mortgagee advancement of funds on behalf of the Borrower in an amount necessary to assist in reinstating the Delinquent Mortgage under the FHA-HAMP Option.

(B) Eligibility

(1) Mortgage Status

(a) Defaulted Mortgage

The Mortgagee must ensure that the Mortgage meets the following eligibility criteria for an FHA-HAMP:

- the Mortgage is in Default or Imminent Default;
- at least 12 months have elapsed since the date of the first payment on the original Mortgage, as evidenced on HUD's Neighborhood Watch system;
- a minimum of four Mortgage Payments have been paid by the Borrower on the current Mortgage;
- Default is due to a verified loss of income or increase in living expenses;
- the Mortgage must not be in foreclosure at the time the FHA-HAMP documents are executed; and
- three or more full monthly payments are due and unpaid (i.e., 61 Days or more past due) when the FHA-HAMP documents are executed.

(b) Mortgage in Imminent Default

To modify a Mortgage facing Imminent Default under FHA-HAMP, the Mortgagee must ensure that the following conditions are met:

- at least 12 months elapsed since the Closing Date of the original Mortgage, as evidenced on HUD's Neighborhood Watch system;
- a minimum of four Mortgage Payments have been paid by the Borrower on the current Mortgage;
- Imminent Default due to a verified loss of income or other hardship as explained in the definition of Imminent Default;
- the Mortgagee obtains documentation evidencing the cause of the Imminent Default; and
- three or more full monthly payments are due and unpaid (i.e., 61 Days or more past due) when the FHA-HAMP documents are executed.

(c) FHA Streamline Refinance Mortgage

If the Mortgage is an FHA Streamline Refinance, the Mortgagee may use previous payment history on the prior FHA-insured Mortgage to determine if the Borrower has met the minimum requirement for four Mortgage Payments. A Streamline Refinance or change in FHA case numbers will not reset the 30 percent maximum Partial Claim statutory limit.

Handbook 4000.1
Effective Date: 03/14/2016 | Last Revised: 07/10/2019
*Refer to the online version of SF Handbook 4000.1 for specific sections' effective dates

625

(2) Borrower Qualifications

The Mortgagee must ensure that the Borrower meets the following eligibility criteria for the FHA-HAMP Option:

- The Borrower has recently experienced a verified loss of income or increase in living expenses and all Borrowers on the Note have signed and submitted hardship affidavits attesting to and describing the hardship.
- One or more Borrowers receives Continuous Income.
- The Mortgagee's calculations show that the resulting monthly Mortgage Payment not exceeding 40 percent of the Borrower's gross monthly income can be offered, provided that either:
  - o the Borrower(s) front-end ratio is **greater than** 31 percent; or
  - o 85 percent of the Borrower's surplus income is insufficient to cure arrears within six months.
- The Borrower has successfully completed a TPP based on the FHA-HAMP monthly Mortgage Payment amount.
- The Borrower has not executed an FHA-HAMP agreement in the past 24 months.

The Mortgagee must ensure that the Borrower is an Owner-Occupant Borrower who is occupying the Property as a Principal Residence. FHA-HAMP may not be used as a means to reinstate a Mortgage prior to sale or assumption.

(3) Property Condition

The Mortgagee must conduct any review it deems necessary, including a property inspection, when the Mortgagee has reason to believe that the physical conditions of the Property adversely impact the Borrower's use or ability to support the debt as follows:

- financial information provided by the Borrower shows large expenses for property maintenance;
- the Mortgagee receives notice from local government or other third parties regarding property condition; or
- the Property may be affected by a disaster event in the area.

(C) Review under the Loss Mitigation Home Retention Priority Waterfall

The Mortgagee must use the five-step process of the Loss Mitigation Home Retention Option Priority Waterfall to:

- project the Borrower's surplus monthly net income for a minimum of three months;
- determine if the Borrower is eligible for an Informal Forbearance, a Formal Forbearance, and/or SFB-Unemployment before considering the FHA-HAMP Option; and

- determine whether FHA-HAMP is appropriate for a Borrower whose surplus income is negative, but the resulting FHA-HAMP Mortgage Payment is 40 percent or less of the Borrower's gross monthly income.

(D) FHA-HAMP Options

The Mortgagee must complete a retroactive escrow analysis of the Mortgage.

The Borrower must not receive any cash from the FHA-HAMP Option. The modified payment must be 40 percent or less of the Borrower's gross monthly income.

The Mortgagee must use the calculations in HUD's Loss Mitigation Option Priority Waterfall to determine which, if any, FHA-HAMP Option is most appropriate. See FHA-HAMP Loan Modification Provisions for interest rate and principal balance requirements for FHA-HAMP Loan Modifications.

(1) FHA-HAMP Standalone Loan Modification

The Mortgagee may offer an FHA-HAMP Standalone Loan Modification if:
- the Mortgagee can achieve an affordable Mortgage Payment at or below the targeted payment without the use of an FHA-HAMP Partial Claim; and
- the Borrower meets all requirements of the FHA-HAMP Option.

If Partial Claim funds are exhausted, the Mortgagee may offer an FHA-HAMP Standalone Loan Modification up to a final Mortgage Payment not exceeding 40 percent of gross monthly income, provided that all other program requirements have been met.

(2) FHA-HAMP Standalone Partial Claim

The Mortgagee must offer an FHA-HAMP Standalone Partial Claim as an appropriate Loss Mitigation Option for Owner-Occupant Borrowers if all the following criteria are met:
- The Borrower's current interest rate is at or below the Market Rate.
- The Borrower's current Mortgage Payment with re-analyzed escrow is at or below the targeted monthly payment.
- A Mortgage Payment at or below the targeted monthly payment cannot be achieved by re-amortizing the Mortgage/outstanding debt for 360 months at the Market Rate.
- The FHA-HAMP Partial Claim will not exceed the 30 percent maximum statutory limit for all Partial Claims combined.
- The Borrower meets all requirements of the FHA-HAMP Option.
- Three or more full monthly payments are due and unpaid (i.e., 61 Days or more past due) when the Partial Claim promissory Note is executed.

(a) Statutory Maximum for Partial Claims

The maximum cumulative value of all Partial Claims paid with respect to a Mortgage must not exceed 30 percent of the Mortgage's unpaid principal balance. This maximum cumulative value must be established as of the date of Default at the time of payment of the initial Partial Claim on such Mortgage, and will remain constant for the life of the Mortgage.

(b) Interest on Partial Claims

No interest will accrue on the Partial Claim.

(c) Payment of Partial Claim

HUD will not require payment on the Partial Claim until the maturity of the FHA-HAMP Mortgage, the sale of the Property, or the Payoff or non-FHA refinancing of the Mortgage.

(3) Combination of FHA-HAMP Loan Modification and the FHA-HAMP Partial Claim

The Mortgagee may offer FHA-HAMP Loan Modification and FHA-HAMP Partial Claim together for Mortgages in Default or in Imminent Default.

The Mortgagee may utilize an FHA-HAMP Combination Loan Modification Partial Claim when establishing an affordable monthly payment that requires a Partial Claim in an amount needed to cover:
- arrearages
- legal fees and foreclosure costs
- principal deferment

If the amount of arrearages, legal fees and foreclosure costs, and principal deferment exceed the statutory maximum for the Partial Claim, the Mortgagee may still utilize this combination of an FHA-HAMP Combination Loan Modification and Partial Claim for an eligible Borrower, so long as the modified payment is 40 percent or less of the Borrower's gross monthly income.

(E) Capitalization of Delinquency in FHA-HAMP Loan Modification

The Mortgagee may only include the following in the FHA-HAMP Loan Modification:
- arrearages for unpaid accrued interest (outstanding arrearages capitalized into the FHA-HAMP Loan Modification are not subject to statutory limits on Partial Claims);
- Mortgagee advances for escrowed items; and
- related legal fees and foreclosure and bankruptcy costs for work actually performed for the current Default episode as of the date of the foreclosure

cancellation and not higher than the foreclosure-related fees and costs HUD has identified as customary and reasonable.

The Mortgagee must not capitalize:
- late fees; and
- costs to complete needed repairs as part of the FHA-HAMP agreement.

(F) FHA-HAMP Loan Modification Provisions

(1) Standard

The Mortgagee must ensure that the FHA-HAMP Loan Modification fully reinstates the Mortgage and complies with the interest rate and modified principal balance provisions below. The Mortgagee must complete an escrow analysis of the Mortgage. The Mortgagee must not provide the Borrower with any cash from the FHA-HAMP Loan Modification.

(2) Interest Rate

The Mortgagee must ensure that any modified loan, including ARM, GPM or GEM is a fixed rate Mortgage.

At the Mortgagee's discretion, the Mortgagee may reduce Note interest rates below Market Rate; however, discount fees associated with rate reductions are not reimbursable. When increasing Note interest rates, the Mortgagee must calculate the maximum interest allowable as the Market Rate.

(a) Market Rate

Market Rate is a rate that is no more than 25 bps greater than the most recent Freddie Mac Weekly Primary Mortgage Market Survey (PMMS) Rate for 30-year fixed rate conforming Mortgages (U.S. average), rounded to the nearest one-eighth of 1 percent (0.125 percent), as of the date a TPP is offered to a Borrower.

(b) Market Rate Resources

The Weekly Primary Mortgage Market Survey results are published on the Freddie Mac website.

(3) Modified Loan Term

The Mortgagee must re-amortize the total unpaid amount due over 360 months from the due date of the first installment required under the modified FHA-insured Mortgage.

(G) FHA Mortgage Insurance Coverage and MIP

When the FHA-HAMP Loan Modification has been processed in accordance with HUD requirements, HUD will extend FHA mortgage insurance coverage to the new principal balance and modified maturity date. FHA insurance will remain in force until the Mortgage has been paid in full or otherwise terminated. The amount of MIP will continue to be based on the scheduled unpaid principal balance of the original Mortgage, without taking into consideration delinquencies or prepayments.

(H) FHA-HAMP Trial Payment Plans

The Mortgagee must ensure that the Borrower successfully completes a TPP prior to executing any FHA-HAMP Option.

(1) Definition

A Trial Payment Plan (TPP) is a payment plan for a minimum period of three months, during which the Borrower must make the agreed-upon consecutive monthly payments prior to final execution of the FHA-HAMP agreement.

(2) Standard

The Mortgagee must ensure that the Borrower successfully completes a TPP before executing permanent FHA-HAMP agreements, for a minimum of three months.

(3) Entering into the Trial Payment Plan Agreement

(a) Definition

A Trial Payment Plan (TPP) Agreement is a written document codifying the TPP terms, which must be agreed upon by all Borrowers.

(b) Standard

(i) Trial Payment Plan Starts 12 Months after Closing Date

Where a Borrower is eligible for an FHA-HAMP Option, the Mortgagee must ensure that the Borrower's TPP begins only after 12 months have elapsed since the Closing Date of the FHA-insured Mortgage.

(ii) Trial Payment Plan Terms

The Mortgagee must ensure that the following apply to interest rates and monthly payments under the TPP Agreement:
- The interest rate for the TPP and the permanent FHA-HAMP Loan Modification must not be greater than Market Rate.

- The permanent Market Rate is established when the TPP is offered to the Borrower.
- The established monthly permanent FHA-HAMP Loan Modification Payment must be the same or less than the established monthly trial payment.
- Agreement documents stipulate that after successfully completing the TPP, the Borrower must continue making payments in accordance with the terms of his or her signed TPP Agreement until his or her permanent FHA-HAMP Mortgage has been ratified by all parties.

(iii) Start of Trial Payments

The Mortgagee must send the proposed TPP Agreement to the Borrower at least 15 Days before the date the first trial payment is due with notification of an established deadline date for Borrower acceptance or rejection of the Trial Payment Plan Terms. The acceptance/rejection deadline date must be on or before the first trial payment due date.

(iv) Trial Payment Plan Signatures

All parties on the original Note and Mortgage and all parties that will be subject to the modified Mortgage and/or Partial Claim must execute the TPP Agreement unless:
- a Borrower or co-Borrower is deceased;
- a Borrower and co-Borrower are divorced; or
- a Borrower or co-Borrower on the original Note and Mortgage has been released from liability in connection with an assumption performed in accordance with HUD's requirements.

On a case-by-case basis, the Mortgagee may provide an exception to the above TPP signature requirements when a Borrower is unable to sign a TPP Agreement due to physical disability, mental condition, or military deployment.

In order to proceed with a TPP the Mortgagee must receive a signed TPP from the Borrower, after which an authorized Mortgagee representative must execute the TPP and file it in the Claim Review File.

(c) Required Documentation

The Mortgagee must retain the following in the Claim Review File:
- a copy of the signed TPP Agreement; and
- documentation evidencing the Mortgagee's review and approval of the TPP Agreement (per the requirements in this section), if the TPP

Agreement was not signed by all parties on the original Note and FHA-insured Mortgage.

(4) Trial Payment Plan – Application of Payments

For FHA-HAMP Mortgages, the Mortgagee must treat a trial payment in an amount less than a full monthly payment under the existing Mortgage as a Partial Payment and place them in the Borrower's suspense account. These Partial Payments are to then be applied in accordance with HUD's Partial Payments for Mortgages in Default guidance and any applicable federal regulations.

For unapplied funds remaining at the end of the trial payment period that do not total a full PITI Mortgage Payment, the Mortgagee may apply the Borrower's funds towards:
- any calculated escrow shortage;
- the unpaid principal balance when calculating the FHA-HAMP Mortgage's monthly Mortgage amount; or
- the FHA-HAMP Partial Claim amount.

(5) End of Trial Payment Plan Period

(a) Standard

The Mortgagee must offer the Borrower a permanent FHA-HAMP Option after the Borrower's successful completion of a TPP.

The Mortgagee must:
- prepare the permanent FHA-HAMP Modification Agreement early enough to allow sufficient processing time for the modification to be effective no later than the first day of the second month following the final Trial Payment Plan month;
- provide the Borrower with the permanent FHA-HAMP documents to be executed by required parties at least 30 Days before the effective date of the modification with notification of the date by which signed documents must be returned;
- sign the FHA-HAMP Modification Agreement and provide a fully ratified copy to the Borrower no later than 15 Days following receipt of the Borrower-signed documents; and
- update its servicing system and files to reflect the FHA-HAMP transaction.

(b) Trial Payment Plan Failure

The Borrower has failed the TPP when one of the following occurs:
- the Borrower does not return the executed TPP Agreement within the month the first trial payment is due;

- the Borrower vacates or abandons the Property; or
- the Borrower does not make a scheduled TPP payment by the last Day of the month the payment was due.

(c) Review for Other Loss Mitigation Options after Trial Payment Plan Failure

(i) Standard

The Mortgagee must re-evaluate the Borrower's eligibility for other appropriate Loss Mitigation Options if a Borrower fails to successfully complete a TPP associated with an FHA-HAMP Option, as follows:

- if the Borrower provides documentation demonstrating their financial circumstances have changed since the Mortgagee's previous loss mitigation evaluation, the Mortgagee must verify the change in financial circumstances and re-evaluate the Borrower for Loss Mitigation Options; or
- if the Borrower does not provide documentation demonstrating their financial circumstances have changed since the Mortgagee's previous loss mitigation evaluation, the Mortgagee must evaluate the Borrower for Home Disposition Options prior to initiating foreclosure.

(ii) Required Documentation

The Mortgagee must include documentation supporting any changes in the Borrower's financial circumstances or employment status in the Mortgagee's Claim Review File.

(6) Funds Remaining at the End of Trial Payment Period

(a) Successful Completion of Trial Payment Plan

For unapplied funds remaining at the end of the trial payment period that do not total a full PITI payment, the Mortgagee must apply these funds to any calculated escrow shortage or to reduce any amounts that would otherwise be capitalized onto the principal balance.

(b) Trial Payment Plan Failure

If the Borrower does not complete the TPP, the Mortgagee must apply all funds held in suspense to the Borrower's account in the established order of priority.

(7) Trial Payment Plans during Foreclosure

The Mortgagee must suspend and/or terminate foreclosure action, depending on state law requirement, during the TPP. In the event the Borrower fails to make a payment required under a TPP, the Mortgagee must review the Borrower for other appropriate Loss Mitigation Options before commencing or continuing a foreclosure.

HUD provides an automatic 90-Day extension for the Mortgagee to commence or recommence foreclosure or initiate another Loss Mitigation Option, should a TPP fail.

(8) Reporting of Trial Payment Plans

The Mortgagee must report the use of an FHA-HAMP Option in SFDMS.

(I) FHA-HAMP Loan Modification Documents

The Mortgagee must ensure that the Mortgage is not in foreclosure at the time the FHA-HAMP Loan Modification documents are executed. The Mortgagee must remove the Mortgage from foreclosure prior to executing the FHA-HAMP documents. See Loss Mitigation during the Foreclosure Process.

FHA does not provide a model for FHA-HAMP Loan Modification documents, but the Mortgagee must ensure the FHA-insured Mortgage remains in a first lien position and is legally enforceable.

(J) FHA-HAMP Partial Claim Documentation and Delivery Requirements

(1) FHA-HAMP Partial Claim Promissory Note and Subordinate Mortgage

(a) Standard

The Mortgagee must prepare the Partial Claim promissory Note and subordinate Mortgage as follows:
- the promissory Note must be executed with the name of the Secretary;
- the subordinate Mortgage must be prepared and recorded; and
- the Partial Claim promissory Note and subordinate Mortgage/deed of trust must include:
  - the full FHA Case Number;
  - the provisions of HUD's model Partial Claim Promissory Note and Partial Claim Subordinate Mortgage or a substantially similar document; and
  - any amendments as required by state or federal law or regulations.

The Mortgagee must provide the Borrower with a Partial Claim promissory Note and subordinate Mortgage to be signed by the Borrower and recorded by the Mortgagee.

(b) Required Documentation

The Mortgagee must retain in its Claim Review File:
- a copy of the executed Partial Claim promissory Note and subordinate Mortgage;
- evidence that the Mortgage was timely submitted for recording; and
- the date the Mortgagee received the executed Partial Claim documents from the Borrower and the date the subordinate Mortgage was sent to be recorded.

(2) Recordation of FHA-HAMP Partial Claim Documents

The Mortgagee must submit executed Partial Claim security instruments for recordation within five business days from the date of receipt from the Borrower or, where HUD execution is required, receipt from HUD. The Mortgagee must submit the security instruments for recordation before filing the FHA-HAMP incentive claim with HUD.

The Mortgagee must ensure that the recordation of the Partial Claim security instruments does not jeopardize the first lien status of the FHA-insured Mortgage; there is no lien priority requirement for the filing of a Partial Claim.

(3) Legal Fees and Foreclosure Costs for Partial Claims

The Mortgagee may include actual foreclosure fees and costs incurred as of the date of the foreclosure cancellation in the Partial Claim.

HUD will not reimburse attorney's fees in excess of the amounts reflected in the HUD Schedule of Standard Attorney Fees.

The Mortgagee must not include in subsequent disposition claims foreclosure fees and costs that were included and paid in the Partial Claim.

(4) Execution of Partial Claim Documents after Trial Payment Plan

The Mortgagee must ensure that the Borrower has successfully completed a TPP before executing the Partial Claim promissory Note and subordinate Mortgage.

(5) Reconciliation of Partial Claim Proceeds to Promissory Note Amounts

If the Mortgagee miscalculates the Partial Claim amount, resulting in an overpayment to the Mortgagee, the Mortgagee must remit the overpaid amount immediately to HUD's Servicing Contractor.

In the event the Mortgagee claimed less than the actual Partial Claim promissory Note amount, the Mortgagee must absorb the cost of the miscalculation.

The Mortgagee must include their review process for ensuring the accurate calculation of Partial Claims in their required QC Plan.

(6) Delivery of Partial Claim Documents

(a) Standard

The Mortgagee must deliver to HUD's Servicing Contractor:
- no later than 60 Days from the execution date, the original Partial Claim promissory Note;
- no later than six months from the execution date, the recorded subordinate Mortgage; and
- with each delivery of Partial Claim documents, the Mortgagee must include a cover letter with the FHA case number for the documents that are being delivered.

(b) Partial Claim Discrepancies

When HUD has received Partial Claim documents that do not fully support the amount claimed by the Mortgagee, HUD will consider the documents incomplete. The Mortgagee must timely correct the deficiencies to satisfy the six-month deadline for the Mortgage to provide complete and accurate Partial Claim documents.

The Mortgagee may use the monthly Missing Documents Report to determine if any Partial Claim documents are missing and outside of the delivery times.

HUD's Servicing Contractor may follow up with the Mortgagee if there are any discrepancies between the Mortgagee's cover letter and the documents received.

(7) Requests for Extensions of Time for Delivery of Partial Claim Documents

(a) Standard

Mortgagees must periodically check on the status of all unreturned recorded Partial Claim Mortgages by, for example, using the Missing Documents Report.

The Mortgagee may request an extension by submitting the request to the NSC for HUD approval via EVARS when:
- Partial Claim document delivery has been delayed due to events beyond the Mortgagee's control; or

- circumstances have occurred preventing the Mortgagee from timely delivery.

The Mortgagee must request the extension in EVARS by:
- checking Box 7, "Unable to submit recorded partial claim Mortgage within 6 months of execution;"
- entering the number of Days needed to meet HUD's delivery requirements;
- indicating the reason for the delay in "Basis for Extension Request;" and
- detailing any attempts to follow up on documents, including specific dates where possible.

HUD will not approve extensions pertaining to Partial Claim promissory Notes.

(b) Required Documentation

The Mortgagee must retain in the Claim Review File documentation of any extensions received from HUD.

(8) Failure to Timely Provide Partial Claim Note and Subordinate Mortgage

When the Mortgagee fails to provide HUD with the Partial Claim promissory Note and subordinate Mortgage within the required time frames, HUD may require reimbursement of the full amount of the Partial Claim.

When directed by HUD, the Mortgagee must reimburse:
- the full claim amount (insurance benefits consisting of the arrearage, principal deferment, if necessary, and any HUD-allowed costs paid in the Mortgagee's claim for mortgage insurance benefits); and
- the incentive fee.

Upon reimbursement of the full amount of the Partial Claim, HUD will endorse any Partial Claim documents in its possession over to the Mortgagee and return them. The Mortgagee must properly record such documents within 30 business days of receipt from HUD.

The Mortgagee must not reverse the application of the Partial Claim funds. The Mortgagee may only pursue repayment of the Partial Claim funds from the Borrower under the original terms of the Partial Claim promissory Note and subordinate Mortgage.

HUD will not accept any documentation regarding the Partial Claim and HUD will not refund any funds to the Mortgagee after the Mortgagee has repaid the Partial Claim in accordance with this section.

(9) Servicing of FHA-HAMP Partial Claims

The Mortgagee remains responsible for servicing the FHA-HAMP Partial Claim until the debt and security instruments are legally recorded in the appropriate jurisdiction and delivered to HUD.

Mortgagees must notify HUD when the first Mortgage is being paid in full or refinanced in order for HUD to provide a payoff figure on a Partial Claim. HUD's Servicing Contractor must be contacted to request a payoff quote on the outstanding Partial Claim.

(K) Lien Status

The Mortgagee must ensure first lien status of the modified Mortgage and must comply with any applicable state or federal laws and regulations in recording the subordinate FHA-HAMP documents.

(1) Subordination Request

If title to the Property is encumbered with an FHA Title I Mortgage and the Mortgagee servicing the Title II Mortgage has determined that a Subordination Agreement is necessary to ensure HUD's first lien status, the Mortgagee may forward a subordination request to:

U.S. Department of Housing and Urban Development
Home Improvement Branch
451 7th Street, SW, Room 9272
Washington, DC 20410

For Partial Claims or Secretary-held Mortgages, the Mortgagee must contact HUD's Loan Servicing Contractor.

(2) Subordination Notification

If title to the Property is encumbered with an FHA Title I Mortgage which has been assigned to the Secretary and the Mortgagee servicing the Title II Mortgage has determined that a Subordination Agreement is not required to ensure HUD's first lien status, the servicing Mortgagee of the Title II Mortgage may send a written notification to:

U.S. Department of Housing and Urban Development
Albany Financial Operations Center
52 Corporate Circle
Albany, NY 12203

(L) Option Failure

(1) Option Failure as New Default

If the Mortgage becomes Delinquent following use of the FHA-HAMP Option, the Mortgagee must treat this as a new Default and service the Defaulted Mortgage accordingly.

(2) Delivery of FHA-HAMP Documents to HUD

If the Mortgage is foreclosed following use of the FHA-HAMP Option, the Mortgagee must upload the FHA-HAMP Loan Modification into P260 when a conveyance claim is filed.

(M) FHA-HAMP Incentive

The Mortgagee may claim an incentive for use of the FHA-HAMP Option if:
- the permanent FHA-HAMP documents are executed within 60 Days of the Borrower's successful completion of their TPP;
- the Mortgagee reports to HUD the characteristics of the FHA-HAMP Loan Modification; and
- three or more full monthly payments are due and unpaid (i.e., 61 Days or more past due) when the FHA-HAMP documents are executed.

(N) No Charge to Borrower for FHA-HAMP Loan Modification

The Mortgagee may not charge the Borrower a fee for processing and recording an FHA-HAMP modification of a Mortgage that is in Default or Imminent Default.

(O) Reporting of FHA-HAMP Loan Modification Terms

The Mortgagee must report in SFDMS the use of FHA-HAMP.

When an FHA-HAMP Loan Modification is used, the Mortgagee must report the characteristics of the modified Mortgage, whether or not the Mortgagee is eligible for an incentive for that modification, through FHAC or EDI.

(P) Non-Incentivized Loan Modification

The Mortgagee may modify Mortgages in Imminent Default. HUD does not offer incentives for these types of Loan Modifications unless performed under FHA-HAMP requirements. See Modifying a Performing Mortgage.

(Q) Reporting of Non-Incentivized Loan Modification Terms

The Mortgagee must report in SFDMS the use of a Loan Modification.

If the Mortgage is in Default, the Mortgagee must report the characteristics of all modified Mortgages through <u>FHAC</u> or EDI. For non-incentivized modifications of performing Mortgages, the Mortgagee must report the characteristics of the Loan Modification in <u>FHAC</u>.

l. Home Disposition Options

i. Definition

Home Disposition Options are the Loss Mitigation Options of PFS and DIL.

ii. Pre-Foreclosure Sales

(A) Definitions

A Pre-Foreclosure Sale (PFS), also known as a Short Sale, refers to the sale of real estate that generates proceeds that are less than the amount owed on the Property and the lien holders agree to release their liens and forgive the deficiency balance on the real estate. There are three types of PFS transactions:
- Streamlined PFS;
- Streamlined PFS for Servicemembers with Permanent Change of Station (PCS) Orders; and
- Standard PFS.

(B) Eligibility

(1) Defaulted Mortgage Status

The Mortgagee may consider the PFS Option for Borrowers who are in Default or who are current but facing Imminent Default. The Borrower need not be in Default for Mortgagee approval of the PFS option; however, on the date the PFS closing occurs, the Mortgagee must ensure that the Mortgage is in Default status (minimum 31 Days Delinquent).

(2) Borrower Eligibility

(a) Streamlined PFS

(i) Definition

A Streamlined PFS is a PFS Option available for Owner-Occupant and Non-Occupant Borrowers and does not require verification of hardship.

(ii) Streamlined PFS Standards

The Mortgagee must ensure that Non-Occupant Borrowers meet the following requirements:

- Borrower(s) are 90 Days or more Delinquent on their FHA-insured Mortgage as of the date of the Mortgagee's review; and
- each Borrower has a credit score of 620 or below.

The Mortgagee must ensure that Owner-Occupant Borrowers meet the following requirements:

- Borrower(s) are 90 Days or more Delinquent on their FHA-insured Mortgage as of the date of the Mortgagee's review;
- each Borrower has a credit score of 620 or below; and
- Borrowers must have been reviewed for Loss Mitigation Home Retention Options as follows:
  - the Borrower has failed a TPP within the last six months;
  - the Borrower has failed on an FHA-HAMP Option within the last two years;
  - the Borrower has been deemed ineligible for a Loss Mitigation Home Retention Option;
  - the Borrower received an SFB - Unemployment but did not otherwise qualify for a permanent Loss Mitigation Home Retention Option by the end of the Special Forbearance period; or
  - the Borrower has been deemed eligible for and offered a Loss Mitigation Home Retention Option. However, all Borrower(s) must have a credit score below 580 and must provide written documentation stating that they choose not to accept the Loss Mitigation Home Retention Option.

(iii) Eligible Properties

The Mortgagee may offer the Streamlined PFS process for all Properties securing FHA-insured Mortgages, provided that all Borrowers meet all program requirements. Such Properties may be vacant but cannot be condemned.

(b) Streamlined PFS for Servicemembers with PCS Orders

(i) Definition

A Streamlined PFS for Servicemembers with PCS Orders is a Streamlined PFS that may be offered to servicemembers who must relocate to a new duty station at least 50 miles away from their existing residence, without the Mortgagee verifying hardship.

(ii) Streamlined PFS for Servicemembers with PCS Orders Standards

The Mortgagee must ensure that servicemembers meet the following requirements for a Streamlined PFS for Servicemembers with PCS Orders:

- The servicemember has PCS Orders to relocate to a duty station at least 50 miles away from their existing residence and provides the Mortgagee with a copy of such orders.
- The servicemember submits an affidavit certifying that:
  o the Property securing the FHA-insured Mortgage is or was their Principal Residence when the PCS orders were issued; and
  o new permanent housing has been or will be obtained as a result of the orders.

(iii) Eligible Properties

The Mortgagee may offer the Streamlined PFS process for all Properties securing FHA-insured Mortgages, provided that all Borrowers meet all program requirements. Such Properties may be vacant, but cannot be condemned.

(c) Standard PFS

(i) Definition

A Standard PFS Option is a PFS Option available for Owner-Occupant Borrowers who are experiencing a hardship affecting their ability to sustain their Mortgage, as determined by the Deficit Income Test (DIT) and:
- are in Default; or
- are current or less than 30 Days past due but facing Imminent Default due to a hardship as described in the Eligible Borrowers section.

(ii) Standard PFS Standards

The Mortgagee must first assess whether the Borrower meets the requirements of a Streamlined PFS Option, prior to reviewing the Borrower for a Standard PFS.

(iii) Eligible Properties

The Mortgagee may offer the Standard PFS process for all owner-occupied Properties securing FHA-insured Mortgages, provided that all Borrowers meet all program requirements.

(iv) Eligible Borrowers

The Mortgagee may consider for Standard PFS transactions those Borrowers in Default or in Imminent Default due to one or more of the following hardships:

- a loss of or reduction in income that was supporting the Mortgage;
- a change in household financial circumstances;
- death of a co-Borrower;
- long-term/permanent illness or disability of a Borrower or dependent Family Member;
- divorce or legal separation of a Borrower; or
- distant employment transfer or relocation greater than 50 miles one-way from the Borrower's current Principal Residence to be closer to employment.

(v) Required Imminent Default Documentation

When approving a Borrower for a Standard PFS based on the Borrower's Imminent Default for one of the reasons listed in the Eligible Borrowers section above, the Mortgagee's Claim Review File must include the following:

- evidence of the Borrower's Imminent Default hardship(s); and
- evidence that the DIT results in a negative value.

(vi) Required Financial Documentation for Standard PFS

Prior to approving a Borrower for a Standard PFS, the Mortgagee must obtain the following documentation of the Borrower's finances:

- for DIT, at least one of the following:
  - o at least two of the Borrower's most recent pay stubs or, if self-employed, the most recent quarterly or year-to-date profit and loss statement, compiled by a Certified Public Accountant (CPA);
  - o the Borrower's Social Security Income (SSI) statements and/or disability payment statements, if applicable; or
  - o the Borrower's most recent Form W-2, Form 1099, or federal tax return; and
- for Cash Reserve contribution calculations, all of the following:
  - o the three most recent monthly bank statement(s);
  - o the three most recent months of brokerage statement(s); and
  - o the most recent federal tax return at the time the Borrower requests an approval for a Standard PFS.

(vii) Deficit Income Test for Standard PFS

Definition

The Deficit Income Test (DIT) is a financial analysis test used for Standard PFS transactions to determine if a Borrower can sustain their Mortgage.

Verification of Income and Expenses

For Standard PFS transactions, to determine a Borrower's income and expenses for the DIT, the Mortgagee must:

- verify the Borrower's monthly net income by obtaining one of the following:
  o at least two of the Borrower's most recent pay stubs or, if self-employed, the most recent quarterly or year-to-date profit and loss statement, compiled by a CPA;
  o the Borrower's SSI statements and/or disability payment statements, if applicable; or
  o the Borrower's most recent Form W-2, Form 1099, or federal tax return; and
- verify the Borrower's monthly expenses by ensuring that all expenses on the Borrower's credit report are factored into the DIT along with any other expenses that are supported by bills, payment receipts, and/or the standard payment amounts under an IRS Index (such as the IRS Collection Financial Standards). For large past-due balances or for accounts included in bankruptcy proceedings, the Mortgagee should refer to the minimum monthly payment required prior to the delinquency when using the DIT.

DIT Calculation

In performing the DIT, the Mortgagee subtracts the Borrower's total monthly expenses from the total monthly net income.

DIT Results

A DIT yielding a negative amount indicates that the Borrower's expenses exceed their income each month and thus a PFS may be an appropriate Loss Mitigation Option for the Borrower.

The Mortgagee must review a Borrower with a positive DIT amount for Loss Mitigation Home Retention Options, unless that Borrower was previously denied for those options or if that Borrower qualifies for a Streamlined Option.

(viii) Exceptions for Non-Owner Occupants in Standard PFS Transactions

HUD authorizes Mortgagees to grant exceptions to Non-Occupant Borrowers when the following can be demonstrated:

- need to vacate: the non-occupancy was related to the cause of Default; and

- not purchased/used as rental: the subject Property was not purchased as a rental or used as a rental for more than 18 months prior to the Borrower's acceptance into the PFS Program.

(d) Corporations or Partnerships Requesting PFS Option

The Mortgagee must submit a variance request to use the PFS Option to the NSC via EVARS when the Property is owned by a corporation or partnership.

(3) Property Condition

(a) Surchargeable Damage

(i) Definition

Surchargeable Damage is damage to a Property caused by fire, flood, earthquake, tornado, boiler explosion (for condominiums only) or Mortgagee Neglect.

(ii) Standard

The Mortgagee is responsible for the cost of Surchargeable Damage.

(iii) PFS Request for Damaged Property

The Mortgagee must request NSC approval via EVARS before approving the use of the PFS Option for a Property with Surchargeable Damage as follows:

- The Mortgagee must first obtain the Government's Estimate of the Cost to Repair the Surchargeable Damage by contacting HUD's Mortgagee Compliance Manager (MCM).
- Upon receipt of the Government's Estimate of the Cost to Repair, the Mortgagee must submit form HUD-90041, *Request for Variance: Pre-foreclosure Sale Procedure*, via EVARS to obtain NSC approval prior to entering into a PFS Agreement with the Borrower. The Mortgagee must note on the variance request the specific reason for the request and attach any supporting documents needed for the NSC's review.

(iv) "As-Is" Subject to Surchargeable Damage

If the Property is being sold "As Is" subject to the Surchargeable Damage, the Mortgagee must deduct the Government's Repair Cost Estimate of the damage from its PFS Claim.

(v) "As Repaired" Subject to Surchargeable Damage

If the Property is being sold "As Repaired" and funds for surchargeable repairs will be escrowed or provided as a credit to the Borrower at closing, the Mortgagee must not include in its Net Sale Proceeds calculation the amount of the repair escrow or repair credit.

(b) Damage other than Surchargeable Damage

If the damage is not considered Surchargeable Damage, the Mortgagee is not required to obtain NSC approval prior to approving the PFS Agreement.

(c) Hazard Insurance Claim

Where applicable, the Mortgagee must work with the Borrower to file a hazard insurance claim and either:
- use the proceeds to repair the Property; or
- adjust the PFS Claim by the amount of the insurance settlement (Non-Surchargeable Damage) or the Government's Repair Cost Estimate.

(d) Disclosure of Damage after PFS Approval

In the event the Mortgagee becomes aware that the Property has sustained significant damage after a Borrower has received the Approval to Participate in the PFS Program, the Mortgagee must re-evaluate the Property to determine if it continues to qualify for the PFS Program or terminate participation if the extent of the damage changes the Property's Fair Market Value (FMV).

(4) Condition of Title

The Mortgagee must ensure that all FHA-insured mortgaged Properties sold under the PFS Program have marketable title.

Before approving a Borrower for participation in the PFS program, the Mortgagee must obtain a title search or preliminary report and determine whether the title is impaired by:
- unresolvable title problems;
- liens that cannot be discharged as permitted by HUD; or
- a PACE obligation.

(C) PFS Outreach Requirements

(1) Form HUD-90035

When a Borrower has expressed an interest in participating in the PFS program or has been identified by the Mortgagee as a qualified candidate for the PFS Program, the Mortgagee must mail form HUD-90035, *Information Sheet: Pre-*

foreclosure Sale Procedure, adding its toll-free or collect telephone number to the form.

(2) Disclosure Requirements for PFS Transactions

Before approving the Borrower for the PFS Option, the Mortgagee must notify the Borrower in writing of the following:

- The Mortgage must be in Default on the date the PFS transaction closes, pursuant to section 204(a)(1)(D) of the National Housing Act, 12 U.S.C. 1710.
- PFS transactions are reported to consumer reporting agencies and will likely affect the Borrower's ability to obtain another Mortgage and other types of credit.
- If the Borrower is a servicemember, it is recommended that the Borrower obtain guidance from their employer regarding the PFS's impact on their security clearance and employment.

Where the Property is encumbered with a PACE obligation, the property sales contract must indicate whether the obligation will remain with the Property or be satisfied by the seller at, or prior to closing. Where the obligation will remain, all terms and conditions of the PACE obligation must be fully disclosed to the buyer in accordance with applicable law (state and local) and made part of the sales contract.

(D) Owner-Occupant Borrower Compensation

(1) Compensation Amount

HUD offers Owner-Occupant Borrowers who act in good faith and successfully sell their Properties using the PFS Option a compensation of up to $3,000 as follows:

- The Owner-Occupant Borrower who is required to make a Cash Reserve contribution may only receive the amount necessary to satisfy those costs, up to the $3,000 consideration limit.
- The Owner-Occupant Borrower who is not required to make a minimum Cash Reserve contribution may receive any remaining amount for transition or relocation assistance only.

(2) Use of Compensation

The Owner-Occupant Borrower may:

- apply the entire amount of the $3,000 compensation or a portion of it to resolve liens, including a PACE obligation; and/or
- offset the sales transaction costs not paid by HUD (including a home warranty plan fee, costs of optional repairs, and the buyer's closing expenses).

The Mortgagee must instruct the Closing Agent to:

- pay the HUD relocation or transition assistance from Net Sale Proceeds; and
- itemize on the Closing Disclosure or similar legal document any relocation or transition assistance received by HUD or from other entities.

(3) Required Documentation

The Mortgagee must ensure that the Closing Disclosure or similar legal document accurately reflects the use of any Borrower compensation amount.

(E) Cash Reserve Contributions for Standard PFS Transactions

(1) Definition

Cash Reserves include all non-retirement liquid assets available for withdrawal or liquidation from all financial institutions. Such accounts include, but are not limited to, the following:

- brokerage, mutual funds, checking, savings, money market or certificate of deposits, other depository accounts, and stocks;
- other equity instruments such as marketable debt of federal, state, or local governments, Government-Sponsored Enterprises (GSE), corporations and other businesses; and
- other securities and commodities (including futures, traded on an exchange or marketplace generally available to the public) for which values can be readily verified using Schedules B (Interest & Dividends), D (Capital Gains & Losses) and E (Supplemental Income & Loss) of the Borrower's most recent federal tax return.

(2) Standard

Before approving a Borrower to participate in a Standard PFS transaction, the Mortgagee must:

- calculate the total Cash Reserves using the highest ending balance of each Cash Reserve asset; and
- disclose to the Borrower the amount of the Borrower's Cash Reserve contribution to be applied towards the Standard PFS transaction.

HUD does not require Cash Reserve contributions for Streamlined PFS transactions.

(3) Cash Reserve Contribution Threshold

The Cash Reserve contribution threshold is $5,000.

(4) Cash Reserves Greater than the Threshold

The Mortgagee must require the Borrower with Cash Reserves greater than the contribution threshold to contribute 20 percent of the total amount exceeding the contribution threshold towards the mortgage debt.

The Mortgagee must not require the Borrower to contribute more than the difference between the unpaid principal balance and the appraised value of the Property.

(5) Cash Reserves At or Below the Threshold Amount

If the Cash Reserve calculation returns an amount at or below the contribution threshold amount, or a negative amount, the Mortgagee is not required to obtain a contribution from the Borrower in connection with the PFS transaction.

(F) PFS Program Participation Requirements

(1) Approval to Participate

(a) Definition

A PFS Approval to Participate is an agreement signed by the Borrower to confirm their willingness to comply with the PFS Program requirements.

(b) Standard

After determining that a Borrower and Property meet the PFS eligibility requirements, the Mortgagee must notify the Borrower by sending:
- an Approval to Participate in the PFS Program (form HUD-90045, *Approval to Participate*), including the date by which the Borrower's Sales Contract must be executed under Pre-Foreclosure Sale Marketing Period guidance; and
- a Pre-Foreclosure Sale Addendum.

The Mortgagee must send these documents to the Borrower via methods providing confirmation or a timestamp of delivery.

The Mortgagee must receive the signed Approval to Participate within 10 Days of the date on the Approval to Participate.

(2) Use of Real Estate Broker

(a) Borrower Retention of Real Estate Broker

The Borrower is responsible for retaining the services of a real estate broker/agent within seven Days of the date of the Approval to Participate.

(b) Required Listing Disclosure

The Mortgagee must ensure that the established Listing Agreement between the seller and the agent/broker includes the following cancellation clause: "Seller may cancel this Agreement prior to the ending date of the listing period without advance notice to the Broker, and without payment of a commission or any other consideration if the Property is conveyed to the mortgage insurer or the mortgage holder. The sale completion is subject to approval by the mortgagee."

(c) Real Estate Broker Duties

The real estate broker/agent must market the Property within the pre-established time frame stated in the Approval to Participate and list the Property in accordance with the property valuation requirements.

(d) Real Estate Broker Conflicts of Interest

The real estate broker/agent selected must have no conflict of interest with the Borrower, the Mortgagee, the Appraiser or the buyer associated with the PFS transaction. The broker/agent must not claim a sales commission on a PFS of a broker's/agent's own Property or that of a spouse, sibling, parent, or child.

Any conflict of interest, appearance of a conflict, or self-dealing by any of the parties to the transaction is strictly prohibited.

(3) Arm's Length PFS Transaction

(a) Definition

An Arm's Length PFS Transaction is between two unrelated parties that is characterized by a selling price and other conditions that would prevail in an open market environment and without hidden terms or special understandings existing between any of the parties (e.g., buyer, seller, Appraiser, sales agent, Closing Agent, and Mortgagee).

(b) Standard

The Mortgagee must ensure that the following arms-length requirements apply to parties involved in PFS transactions:
- Any PFS proposed by the Borrower or their agent and approved by the Mortgagee must be an Arm's Length Transaction between the Borrower and prospective buyer, subject to the exceptions in the Permitted Non-Arms-Length Transaction section.
- Except for real estate agents and brokers representing a party to the PFS, no party that is a signatory on the sales contract, including addenda, can serve in more than one capacity.

- The broker hired to sell the Property must not share a business interest with the Mortgagee. If the Mortgagee knows that a shared interest exists between Appraiser and sales agent, the Mortgagee must note this in the Claim Review File.
- All doubts will be resolved in a manner to avoid a conflict of interest, the appearance of conflict, or self-dealing by any of the parties.

(c) Permitted Non-Arms-Length Transactions

HUD permits non-Arm's Length PFS Transactions, to the extent necessary to comply with state law, where state law prohibits placement of an Arm's Length Transaction requirement on property sales.

If clauses (a) and (c) of the PFS Addendum are impermissible under state law, the Mortgagee may strike these clauses from the PFS Addendum prior to execution, provided that the transaction complies with all PFS program requirements.

(d) Relocation Service Contribution

The Mortgagee may permit a Relocation Service affiliated with the Borrower's employer to contribute a fixed sum towards the proceeds of the PFS transaction without altering the arms-length nature of the sale, so long as the result is an outright sale of the Property and cancellation of the FHA mortgage insurance.

(4) Mortgagee Monitoring of PFS Transaction

The Mortgagee must monitor the PFS transaction in its entirety to ensure the Borrower's compliance with the terms in the Approval to Participate and with all PFS Program requirements.

The Mortgagee must terminate a Borrower's participation in the PFS Program in the event of noncompliance.

(5) Property Maintenance

The Mortgagee must inspect Properties during the PFS period if:
- the Property is vacant;
- the Mortgagee has reason to suspect that the Property has become vacant; or
- the Borrower or Authorized Third Party has not maintained contact with the Mortgagee.

(G) Property List Price and Valuation

(1) List Price

The Mortgagee must ensure that the Borrower lists the Property for sale at no less than the "As Is" value as determined by an appraisal completed in accordance with the requirements in the Appraiser and Property Requirements for Title II Forward and Reverse Mortgages section of this *SF Handbook*.

(2) Appraisals

(a) Standard

The Mortgagee must obtain a standard electronically-formatted appraisal performed by an FHA Roster Appraiser pursuant to the following requirements:

- The appraisal must contain an "As-Is" FMV for the subject Property.
- A copy of the appraisal must be provided to the homeowner, sales agent, or HUD, upon request.

(b) Appraisal Validity Period

The as-is appraisal used for a PFS transaction is valid for 120 Days. If a Mortgagee determines that a subsequent as-is appraisal is required, the Mortgagee may obtain a new as-is appraisal, even if the Property was appraised by an FHA Roster Appraiser within the preceding 120 Days.

(c) Required Analysis and Reporting of a PACE Obligation

The Appraiser must review the sales contract and property tax records for the Property to determine the amount outstanding and the terms of the PACE obligation:

- if the Mortgagee notifies the Appraiser that the subject Property will remain subject to a PACE obligation;
- when the Appraiser observes that the property taxes for the subject Property are higher than average for the neighborhood and type of dwelling; or
- when the Appraiser observes energy-related building components or equipment or is aware of other PACE-allowed improvements during the inspection process.

The Appraiser must report the outstanding amount of the PACE obligation for the subject Property and provide a brief explanation of the terms.

Where energy and other PACE-allowed improvements have been made to the Property through a PACE program, and the PACE obligation will remain outstanding, the Appraiser must analyze and report the impact on value of the

Handbook 4000.1   652

Effective Date: 03/14/2016 | Last Revised: 07/10/2019
*Refer to the online version of SF Handbook 4000.1 for specific sections' effective dates

Property, whether positive or negative, of the PACE-related improvements and any additional obligation (i.e., the PACE special assessment).

(3) Request for Variance for Property Valuation

(a) Standard

A Mortgagee must submit a request for a variance through EVARS to approve a PFS transaction if one of the following conditions exists:
- the current appraised value of the Property is less than the unpaid principal balance by an amount of $75,000 or greater;
- the appraised value is less than 50 percent of the unpaid principal balance; or
- the appraisal is deemed unacceptable because the as-is value cannot be affirmed using a Broker's Price Opinion (BPO) or Automated Valuation Model (AVM) within 10 percent of the value.

(b) Variance Request

The Mortgagee must note on the variance request the specific reason for the request and attach any supporting documents needed for HUD review. The Mortgagee must obtain approval before authorizing the marketing of the Property.

(4) Broker's Price Opinions and Automated Valuation Models

(a) Standard

When the appraisal has been deemed unacceptable, the Mortgagee must obtain a BPO or AVM that is within 10 percent of the value of the Property as determined by the as-is appraisal performed by an FHA Roster Appraiser. An acceptable BPO or AVM is one that is utilized by the Mortgagee in its existing standard business processes.

(b) Required Documentation

The Mortgagee must retain in the Claim Review File a copy of the BPO or AVM supporting the Property Value.

(H) Pre-Foreclosure Sale Marketing Period

(1) Maximum Marketing Period

The Borrower has four months from the date of the Borrower's Approval to Participate to acquire a Contract of Sale.

(2) Minimum Marketing Period

The Mortgagee must ensure that PFS Properties are listed in the Multiple Listing Service for a minimum of 15 Days before offers are evaluated. After this initial listing period, the broker/agent may evaluate offers as they are received.

This 15-Day minimum marketing period must occur during the Marketing Period following the date of the Borrower's Approval to Participate.

(3) Extension to PFS Marketing Period

HUD provides an automatic two-month extension to the deadline to initiate foreclosure for completion of a PFS transaction under the following conditions:
- the Mortgagee has an "A" TRS II/Tier 1 score under HUD's TRS II; or
- there is a signed Contract of Sale, but settlement has not occurred by the end of the fourth month following the date of the Borrower's Approval to Participate in the PFS Program.

(4) Monthly Review of Marketing Status

On a monthly basis, Mortgagees must review the Property's marketing status with the Borrower and/or real estate broker/agent.

(5) Previously Initiated Foreclosures

The Mortgagee must not cancel a foreclosure to initiate a PFS marketing period for a Property of a Borrower meeting the PFS eligibility requirements. The Mortgagee may only cancel a scheduled foreclosure sale if the Mortgagee has received an acceptable Contract of Sale that meets the PFS requirements.

(I) Evaluation of Offers

(1) Standard

The Mortgagee must receive from the listing real estate agent/broker an offer that:
- yields the highest net return to HUD; and
- meets HUD's requirements for bids.

The listing agent/broker must ensure that:
- all offers submitted to the Mortgagee for approval are signed by both the seller and the buyer prior to submission; and
- the PFS Addendum is signed by all of the applicable parties (except for the Closing Agent).

(2) Back-up Offers

Once an offer has been submitted to the Mortgagee for approval, the listing agent/broker must retain any offer that the seller elects to hold for "back-up" until a determination has been made on the previously submitted offer.

(3) Required Documentation

The listing agent/broker must retain all offers received, including offers not submitted for approval, in accordance with state law.

(J) Contract Approval by Mortgagee

(1) Standard

In reviewing the Contract of Sale, the Mortgagee must:
- ensure that the PFS sale is an outright sale of the Property and not a sale by assumption;
- review the sales documentation to determine that there are:
  o no hidden terms or special agreements existing between any of the parties involved in the PFS transaction; and
  o no contingencies that might delay or jeopardize a timely settlement; and
- determine that the Property was marketed pursuant to HUD requirements and that the minimum required Tiered Net Sale Proceeds have been met.

The following anti-fraud measures apply to PFS transactions:
- A Mortgagee must not approve a Borrower for a PFS if the Mortgagee knows or has reason to know of a Borrower's fraud or misrepresentation of information.
- All parties involved in a PFS transaction must sign and date a PFS Addendum as a contingency for a PFS transaction to close.

(2) Sales Contract Review Period

After receiving an executed Contract of Sale from the Borrower, the Mortgagee must send to the Borrower form HUD-90051, *Sales Contract Review*, no later than five business days from the Mortgagee's receipt of an executed Contract for Sale.

(3) Net Sale Proceeds

(a) Definition

Net Sale Proceeds are the proceeds of a PFS sale, calculated by subtracting reasonable and customary closing and settlement costs from the property sales price.

(b) Standard

Regardless of the Property's sale price, a Mortgagee may only approve a PFS Contract for Sale if the Tiered Net Sale Proceeds are at or above HUD's minimum allowable thresholds. HUD's requirements for minimum Tiered Net Sale Proceeds, as based on the length of time a Property has been competitively marketed for sale under an Approval to Participate, are as follows:

- First 30 Days of marketing: The Mortgagee may only approve offers that will result in minimum Net Sale Proceeds of 88 percent of the "as-is" appraised FMV.
- Next 30 Days of marketing: The Mortgagee may only approve offers that will result in minimum Net Sale Proceeds of 86 percent of the "as-is" appraised FMV.
- For the remaining duration of the PFS marketing period: The Mortgagee may only approve offers that will result in minimum Net Sale Proceeds of 84 percent of the "as-is" appraised FMV.

The Mortgagee has the discretion to deny or delay sales where an offer may meet or exceed the 84 percent, if it is presumed that continued marketing would likely produce a higher sale amount.

The Mortgagee is liable for any FHA Insurance Claim Overpayment on a PFS transaction that closes with less than the required Tiered Net Sale Proceeds, unless a variance has been granted by HUD.

(c) Settlement Costs

(i) Allowable Settlement Costs

The Mortgagee may include the following settlement costs in its Net Sale Proceeds calculation:

- sales commission consistent with the prevailing rate but, not to exceed 6 percent;
- real estate taxes prorated to the date of closing;
- local/state transfer tax stamps and other closing costs customarily paid by the seller, including the seller's costs for a Title Search and Owner's Title Insurance;
- compensation payable to the Owner-Occupant Borrower of $3,000, if not required to pay a cash contribution;
- upon extinguishing the Owner-Occupant Borrower's compensation of $3,000, HUD will allow an additional $1,500 of Net Sale Proceeds to be used to resolve junior liens, for a total of $4,500;
- for Non-Occupant Borrowers, HUD will allow $1,500 of Net Sale Proceeds to be used to resolve junior liens;

- the entire outstanding Partial Claim amount must be paid when calculating the Net Sale Proceeds. The seller, buyer, or other Interested Party may contribute the difference if the amount of Net Sale Proceeds falls below the allowable threshold; and
- up to 1 percent of the buyer's first mortgage amount if the sale includes FHA financing.

(ii) Unacceptable Settlement Costs

The Mortgagee must not include the following costs in the Net Sale Proceeds calculation:
- repair reimbursements or allowances;
- home warranty fees;
- discount points or mortgage fees for non FHA-financing;
- Mortgagee's Title Insurance fee; and
- third-party fees incurred by the Mortgagee or Borrower to negotiate a PFS.

(d) Third-Party Fees

With the exception of reasonable and customary real estate commissions, the Mortgagee must ensure that third-party fees incurred by the Mortgagee or Borrower to negotiate a PFS are not included on the Closing Disclosure or similar legal documents unless explicitly permitted by state law.

The Mortgagee, its agents, or any outsourcing firm it employs must not charge any fee to the Borrower for participation in the PFS Program.

(e) Partial Claim

The Mortgagee must ensure that all outstanding Partial Claims are paid in full.

The Mortgagee must deduct any outstanding balance on a Partial Claim Note from the Net Sale Proceeds. The Mortgagee must send proceeds from the PFS sufficient to satisfy the Partial Claim directly to HUD's Loan Servicing Contractor.

If, after satisfying the Partial Claim, the Net Sale Proceeds fail to meet the applicable Tiered Net Sale Proceeds requirement, the Mortgagee must request and obtain approval from HUD via EVARS before closing.

(4) Title I Liens

If the Mortgagee discovers that a Borrower has a HUD Title I Mortgage secured by the Property, the Mortgagee must contact the Title I subordinate lien holder to advise of the Borrower's participation in a PFS. HUD may require the Mortgagee to negotiate the release of the lien in order to proceed with a PFS.

If the Title I Mortgage has been assigned to HUD, the Mortgagee must contact HUD's Financial Operations Center for guidance:

U.S. Department of Housing and Urban Development
Financial Operations Center
52 Corporate Circle
Albany, New York 12203.
1-800-669-5152/ fax (518) 862-2806

(5) Section 235 Recapture

The Mortgagee must first determine if the Mortgage is subject to recapture as referenced in Section 235 Mortgages. If a recapture amount is owed to HUD, the Mortgagee must contact HUD's Servicing Contractor prior to approving the PFS.

(K) Closing and Post-Closing Responsibilities

Prior to closing, the Mortgagee must provide the Closing Agent with:
- form HUD-90052, *Closing Worksheet*, which lists all amounts payable from Net Sale Proceeds; and
- the PFS Addendum that was signed by:
  o   buyers;
  o   buyers' agent;
  o   sellers;
  o   sellers' agent (listing agent);
  o   escrow closing agent; and
  o   transaction facilitators/negotiators, if applicable.

The Mortgagee will receive from the Closing Agent a calculation of the actual Net Sale Proceeds and a copy of the Closing Disclosure or similar legal document.

(1) Mortgagee Review of Final Terms of PFS Transaction

The Mortgagee must ensure that:
- the final terms of the PFS transaction are consistent with the purchase contract;
- only allowable settlement costs have been deducted from the seller's proceeds;
- the Net Sale Proceeds will be equal to or greater than the allowable thresholds;
- form HUD-90052 is included in the Claim Review File; and
- they report the PFS Sale to consumer reporting agencies.

(2) Closing Agent Responsibilities after Final Approval

Once the Mortgagee gives final approval for the PFS and the settlement occurs, the Closing Agent must:

- pay the expenses out of the Net Sale Proceeds and forward the Net Sale Proceeds to the Mortgagee;
- forward a copy of the Closing Disclosure or similar legal document to the Mortgagee to be included in the Claim Review File no later than three business days after the PFS transaction closes; and
- sign the PFS Addendum on or before the date the PFS transaction closes, unless explicitly prohibited by state statute.

(3) Satisfaction of Mortgage Debt

Upon receipt of the portion of the Net Sale Proceeds designated for mortgage satisfaction, the Mortgagee must satisfy the Mortgage debt and may file a claim for mortgage insurance benefits.

(4) Discharge of Junior Liens

The Mortgagee must provide for the discharge of junior liens as follows:

- If the Borrower has the financial ability, the Borrower must be required to satisfy or obtain release of liens.
- If the Owner-Occupant Borrower receives compensation ($3,000), this compensation may be applied towards discharging liens.
- If no other sources are available, both the Owner-Occupant Borrower and the Non-Occupant Borrower may obligate up to an additional $1,500 from sale proceeds towards discharging liens or encumbrances.

(L) Early Termination of PFS Program Participation

(1) Standard

(a) Borrower-Initiated Termination

The Mortgagee must permit a Borrower to voluntarily terminate participation in the PFS Program at any time.

(b) Mortgagee-Initiated Termination

The Mortgagee may terminate a Borrower's PFS Program participation at its discretion for any of the following reasons:

- discovery of unresolvable title problems;
- determination that the Borrower is not acting in good faith to market the Property;
- significant change in property condition or value; or

- re-evaluation based on new financial information provided by the Borrower that indicates that the case does not qualify for the PFS Option.

(c) Notification of PFS Program Participation Termination

The Mortgagee must forward to the Borrower a date-stamped written explanation for terminating their program participation. This letter is to include the "end-of-participation" date for the Borrower.

(2) Required Documentation

The Mortgagee must retain a copy of the Notification of PFS Program Participation Termination in the servicing file.

(M) Failure to Complete a PFS Transaction

At the expiration of the PFS marketing period, should the Borrower be unable to complete a PFS transaction, the Mortgagee must re-evaluate available Loss Mitigation Options as follows:

- determining eligibility for one of the Loss Mitigation Home Retention Options, if the Borrower's financial condition has improved to the point that reinstatement is a viable option; and
- trying to obtain a DIL of Foreclosure, if reinstatement is not feasible.

Within 90 Days after the expiration of the PFS marketing period, the Mortgagee must consider and approve the Borrower for an alternate Loss Mitigation Option or complete the first legal action to initiate foreclosure.

Should additional time be needed to complete a DIL or to initiate foreclosure, Mortgagees must submit a request for an extension of time to the NSC via EVARS.

(N) Extensions of Foreclosure Time Frame for PFS

(1) Standard

After PFS early termination or option failure, HUD provides an automatic 90-Day extension to the deadline to complete a Loss Mitigation Option or to perform the first legal action initiating foreclosure. The automatic 90-Day extension begins the Day after the PFS Approval to Participate expires or is terminated.

If the Mortgagee has not yet received the Net Sale Proceeds from the Closing Agent and the automatic 90-Day extension is nearing expiration, the Mortgagee must submit a request for extension to the NSC via EVARS.

(2) Required Documentation

The Mortgagee must note the use of any extensions, whether automatic or requested, on form HUD-27011.

(O) Deficiency Judgments

If a foreclosure occurs after the Borrower unsuccessfully participated in the PFS process in good faith, neither the Mortgagee nor HUD will pursue the Borrower for a deficiency Judgment.

(P) PFS Incentive

The Mortgagee may claim an incentive for each completed PFS transaction that complies with all HUD PFS requirements.

(Q) Mortgage Insurance Termination

The Mortgagee must not submit a mortgage insurance termination on PFS transactions. HUD can only pay FHA mortgage insurance benefits when the status of the mortgage insurance is "active."

(R) Reporting of PFS

The Mortgagee must report in SFDMS the appropriate Claim Termination of Insurance Code to indicate when the PFS has been held.

iii. Deed-in-Lieu of Foreclosure

(A) Definition

A Deed-in-Lieu (DIL) of Foreclosure is a Loss Mitigation Home Disposition Option in which a Borrower voluntarily offers the deed as collateral Property to HUD in exchange for a release from all obligations under the Mortgage. There are three types of DIL transactions:
- Streamlined DIL;
- Streamlined DIL for Servicemembers with PCS Orders; and
- Standard DIL.

(B) Eligibility

(1) Mortgage Status

The Mortgagee must ensure that the Mortgage meets the following eligibility requirements for the DIL Option:
- the Mortgage is in Default and the cause of Default must be incurable; or

- the Borrower is at risk of Imminent Default and the Borrower provides to the Mortgagee documentation that supports their Imminent Default.

(2) Borrower Eligibility

HUD expects Borrowers to first attempt to market the Property under the PFS Program prior to use of the DIL Option.

(a) Streamlined DIL

(i) Definition

A Streamlined Deed-in-Lieu (DIL) is a DIL transaction for Owner-Occupant Borrowers and Non-Occupant Borrowers and does not require verification of hardship.

(ii) Streamlined DIL Standards

The Mortgagee must ensure that the Borrowers:
- meet the requirements for Streamlined PFS transactions; and
- have attempted to complete a PFS transaction.

(iii) Eligible Properties

The Mortgagee may offer the Streamlined DIL process for all Properties securing FHA-insured Mortgages, provided that all Borrowers meet all program requirements. Such Properties may be vacant, but cannot be condemned.

(b) Streamlined DIL for Servicemembers with PCS Orders

(i) Definition

A Streamlined DIL for Servicemembers with PCS Orders Option is a Streamlined DIL that may be offered to servicemembers who must relocate to a new duty station at least 50 miles away from their existing residence, without the Mortgagee verifying hardship.

(ii) Streamlined DIL for Servicemembers with PCS Orders Standards

The Mortgagee must ensure that servicemembers meet the requirements for a Streamlined PFS for Servicemembers with PCS Orders and have attempted to complete a PFS Option.

(iii) Eligible Properties

The Mortgagee may offer the Streamlined DIL process for all Properties securing FHA-insured Mortgages, provided that all Borrowers meet all program requirements. Such Properties may be vacant, but cannot be condemned.

(c) Standard DIL

(i) Definition

A Standard DIL is a DIL available for Owner-Occupant Borrowers who experienced a verifiable hardship that has affected their ability to sustain their Mortgage but who do not meet the requirements of a Streamlined DIL Option.

(ii) Standard DIL Standard

Borrowers applying for the Standard DIL Option must provide verification of hardship and must submit a Complete Loss Mitigation Request for review. The Mortgagee must evaluate the Borrower's financial information to determine whether the Borrower's financial circumstances have changed to make them eligible for other Loss Mitigation Options.

(d) DIL Exceptions for Borrowers with More than One FHA-Insured Mortgage

The Mortgagee must submit a request for NSC approval via EVARS for approval to offer a DIL Option to a Borrower who owns more than one FHA-insured Property.

(e) Exceptions for Non-Occupant Borrowers in Standard DIL Transactions

HUD authorizes Mortgagees to offer Standard DIL to Non-Occupant Borrowers when the following can be demonstrated:
* Need to vacate: the non-occupancy was related to the cause of Default; or
* Not purchased/used as rental: the subject Property was not purchased as a rental or used as a rental for more than 18 months prior to the offering of the DIL Option.

The Mortgagee must submit a variance request to use the DIL Option to the NSC via EVARS when the Property is owned by a corporation or partnership.

(3) Condition of Title

The Borrower or Mortgagee must be able to convey a clear and marketable title to the Secretary. The Mortgagee must obtain a title search or preliminary report and determine whether the title is impaired by:

- unresolvable title problems;
- liens that cannot be discharged as permitted by HUD; or
- a PACE obligation.

(4) Deficiency Judgment

HUD will not accept a DIL when it has elected to pursue a deficiency Judgment against the Borrower.

(C) Disclosure Requirements for DIL

Before approving a Borrower for a DIL, the Mortgagee must notify the Borrower in writing of the following:

- The Mortgage must be in Default on the date the DIL special warranty deed is executed, pursuant to Section 204 of the National Housing Act (12 U.S.C. 1710).
- DIL transactions are generally reported to consumer reporting agencies, and will likely affect the Borrower's ability to obtain another Mortgage and other types of credit.
- If the Borrower is a servicemember, it is recommended that the Borrower obtain guidance from their employer regarding the DIL's impact on their security clearance and employment.

(D) Cash Reserve Contributions for Standard DIL Transactions

(1) Standard

Prior to approving a Borrower to participate in a Standard DIL transaction, the Mortgagee must calculate and disclose to the Borrower the amount of the Borrower's Cash Reserve contribution to be applied towards the Standard DIL transaction. HUD does not require Cash Reserve contributions for Streamlined DIL transactions.

The Mortgagee must calculate the total Cash Reserves using the highest ending balance of each cash reserve asset.

(2) Cash Reserve Contribution Threshold

The Cash Reserve contribution threshold is $5,000.

(3) Cash Reserves Greater than the Threshold

The Mortgagee must require the Borrower with Cash Reserves greater than the contribution threshold to contribute 20 percent of the total amount exceeding the contribution threshold towards the mortgage debt.

The Mortgagee must not require the Borrower to contribute more than the difference between the unpaid principal balance and the appraised value of the Property. If the appraisal used for the PFS program is no longer valid, the Mortgagee may use the most recently obtained appraisal for the purpose of calculating the Cash Reserve contribution.

(4) Cash Reserves At or Below the Threshold Amount

If the Cash Reserve calculation returns an amount at or below the contribution threshold amount, or a negative amount, the Mortgagee is not required to obtain a contribution from the Borrower in connection with the DIL transaction.

(E) DIL Borrower Consideration

(1) Consideration Amount

HUD offers Owner-Occupant Borrowers a consideration of up to $2,000 upon vacating the Property and satisfaction of the requirements of the DIL Agreement. HUD will not pay this consideration if the Property is occupied at conveyance.

(2) Use of Consideration Amount

The Owner-Occupant Borrower may apply the entire amount of the consideration or a portion of it to resolve liens, including PACE obligation liens.

The Owner-Occupant Borrower who is required to make a Cash Reserve contribution may only receive the amount necessary to satisfy liens, up to the consideration limit.

(F) DIL Agreement

(1) Standard

The Borrower and the Mortgagee must execute a DIL Agreement in writing. HUD does not require a specific format for documenting a DIL Agreement. The Mortgagee must ensure that the DIL documentation is in compliance with all applicable laws and regulations.

(2) DIL Agreement Terms

The Mortgagee must ensure that the DIL Agreement contains the following:
- certification that the Borrower does not own other Property subject to a Mortgage insured by or held by HUD;
- the Transfer Date;
- notification of possible income tax consequences;
- acknowledgement that Borrowers who comply with all requirements of the Agreement will not be pursued for deficiency Judgments;

- a statement describing the physical condition in which the Property will be conveyed;
- agreement with the Borrower to convey the Property vacant and free of Personal Property, unless HUD has approved an Occupied Conveyance;
- itemization of keys, built-in-fixtures, and equipment to be delivered by the Mortgagee on or before the Transfer Date;
- evidence that utilities, assessments, and HOA dues are paid in full by the Transfer Date, unless otherwise agreed to by all parties; and
- the amount of consideration payable to and/or on behalf of the Borrower will not exceed $2,000.

(3) Required Documentation

The Mortgagee must retain a copy of the executed DIL Agreement in the Claim Review File.

(G) DIL Conveyance to HUD

(1) Mortgage in Default

The Mortgagee must ensure that the Mortgage is in Default when the DIL is recorded and the Property conveyed to HUD.

(2) Discharge of Liens

The Mortgagee must provide for the discharge of liens as follows:
- The Mortgagee must complete a title search and must ensure that the secure release of liens and/or endorsements to the title policy are obtained.
- HUD will not accept titles subject to most liens, including IRS and HOA liens. HUD will allow liens securing repayment of Section 235 assistance payments, Partial Claim advances, and Title I liens.
- HUD will allow a notice of lien recorded in the land records securing repayment of a PACE obligation that may only become subject to an enforceable claim (i.e., a lien) for delinquent regularly scheduled PACE special assessment payments and otherwise complies with the eligibility and acceptability criteria for Properties encumbered with a PACE obligation provided in Section II.A.1.b.iv(A)(6) of the prior *SF Handbook* published in December 2016.
- If the Owner-Occupant Borrower receives consideration, this consideration may be applied towards discharging liens.

(3) Special Warranty Deed

The Borrower and the Mortgagee must convey the Property through a special warranty deed and, when possible, the Borrower must convey title directly to

HUD. The Mortgagee must cancel and surrender to the Borrower the original credit instrument, indicating that the Mortgage has been satisfied.

If it is necessary to convey title to the Mortgagee, and then to HUD, the Mortgagee must document the reason in the Claim Review File.

(4) Conveyance Time Frame

The Mortgagee must record the special warranty deed and deliver the original, recorded deed to HUD's MCM within 45 Days of the date the clear and marketable title was conveyed to the Secretary.

(5) Occupied Properties

The Mortgagee must ensure that the Property is vacant at the time of conveyance.

HUD will not accept a DIL if the collateral Property is occupied at the time of conveyance to HUD, unless authorized for Occupied Conveyance.

(6) Option Not to Convey

The Mortgagee may elect not to convey title to HUD and to terminate the contract of mortgage insurance. If this occurs, the Mortgagee must use form HUD-27050-A in FHAC to notify HUD.

(H) DIL Compensation

The Mortgagee may submit a claim for an incentive for each completed DIL transaction that complies with all HUD DIL requirements.

(I) Extensions for Foreclosure Time Frames

The Mortgagee must complete the DIL or initiate foreclosure within six months of the date of Default as follows, unless the Mortgagee qualified for an automatic 90-Day extension by first attempting a Loss Mitigation Option or has received an extension approved by the NSC via EVARS:

- If the DIL follows a failed SFB-Unemployment Agreement or PFS, the DIL must be completed or foreclosure initiated within 90 Days of the failure.
- If the DIL follows any other Loss Mitigation Option, it must be completed or foreclosure initiated within six months of the date of Default.

(J) Reporting to Consumer Reporting Agencies and the IRS

The Mortgagee must not report DIL transactions to consumer reporting agencies as foreclosures.

(K) Reporting of DIL

The Mortgagee must report in SFDMS the appropriate Claim Termination of Insurance Code to indicate when the DIL was completed.

m. Loss Mitigation Incentives

The Mortgagee may submit a claim for an incentive for the successful completion of the approved Loss Mitigation Actions listed below.

Loss Mitigation Action	Compensation
SFB-Unemployment	$100 ($200 for Mortgagees with an "A" TRS II/ Tier 1 Score).
FHA-HAMP	$500 for an FHA-HAMP Partial Claim. $750 for an FHA-HAMP Loan Modification, plus up to $250 for reimbursement of title search, endorsement to the title policy, and/or recording fees actually incurred.
PFS	$1,000
DIL	$250

Mortgagees receiving "Pay for Success" payments from the U.S. Department of Treasury are still eligible to receive Loss Mitigation incentives from FHA.

n. Non-Monetary Default

By executing the deed of trust and Note for an FHA-insured Mortgage, the Borrower agrees to submit the monthly Mortgage Payment by the first of each month and to adhere to the uniform covenants listed in the deed of trust and Note. The following provides guidance associated with the Borrower's failure to adhere to these covenants.

i. Definition

Non-Monetary Default is a Default where the Borrower fails to perform obligations, other than making monthly payments, contained in the mortgage security instrument for a period of 30 Days.

ii. Mortgagee Cure

When the Non-Monetary Default may be cured or otherwise resolved by Mortgagee action without resorting to foreclosure action, the Mortgagee must advance and charge to the Borrower all amounts due for servicing activities, as defined in the mortgage agreement, if:
- the Borrower fails to make required payments or charges;
- the Borrower fails to perform any other covenants and agreements contained in the security instrument; or
- there is a legal proceeding that may affect the Mortgagee's rights in the Property.

iii. Hazard Insurance

If the Borrower fails to maintain hazard insurance coverage when it is stated as an obligation in the Mortgage, the Mortgagee may advance funds or force-place insurance as follows.

(A) Mortgagee Advances

The Mortgagee may advance the funds to pay the renewal premiums. The Mortgagee must renew the same type of policy and the same coverage carried previously by the Borrower.

(B) Force-Placed Insurance

If Borrowers fail to renew hazard insurance coverage when required, the Mortgagee may force-place hazard and/or flood insurance where consistent with federal regulations. While the Mortgagee may, at its discretion, obtain more coverage than is necessary to protect the Mortgagee's interest, HUD limits its reimbursement of these premiums.

iv. Taxes, Assessments and Government or Municipal Charges

The Mortgagee may advance funds and charge the Borrower when the Borrower fails to pay taxes, assessments, water rates, and other governmental or municipal charges, fines, or impositions not included in the Borrower's monthly Mortgage Payment.

v. Homeowners' Association Fees

If the Borrower fails to pay Condominium/HOA Fees, the Mortgagee must take any action necessary to protect the first lien position of the FHA-insured Mortgage against foreclosure actions brought by a condominium/HOA or any other junior lien holder.

vi. Code Violations

If the Borrower fails to address a code violation notice from the municipality where the Property is located, the Mortgagee must perform activities necessary to preserve and protect the Property, as authorized under the security instruments. See Mortgagee Property Preservation and Protection.

vii. Demolition Orders

The Mortgagee must forward copies of all notices pertaining to demolition orders and hearings to HUD's MCM immediately upon discovery.

The MCM will advise the Mortgagee as to whether to proceed with the demolition or to postpone the demolition until after conveyance to HUD.

viii.   Due-on-Sale Clause

The Mortgagee must review the Mortgage's legal documents to determine any covenant restrictions pertaining to assumption. See Change of Borrowers (Assumptions) for more information.

o. Distressed Asset Stabilization Program

RESERVED FOR FUTURE USE
This section is reserved for future use, and until such time, FHA-approved Mortgagees and any other interested participants must continue to comply with all applicable law and existing Handbooks, Mortgagee Letters, Notices and outstanding guidance applicable to their participation in FHA programs.

p. Claims Without Conveyance of Title

i.   Definitions

A Claims Without Conveyance of Title (CWCOT) is a procedure under which the Mortgagee attempts to secure a third party purchaser for the mortgaged Property so that conveyance to HUD is not required in exchange for mortgage insurance benefits.

A Competitive Sale is a CWCOT-related sale where a Mortgagee elects to use an independent third-party provider to conduct the foreclosure sale or in connection with any Post-Foreclosure Sales Efforts and where the Property is marketed for a minimum of 15 Days.

A Non-Competitive Sale is a CWCOT-related sale where a Mortgagee elects not to use an independent third-party provider to conduct the foreclosure sale or in connection with any Post-Foreclosure Sales Efforts and/or the Property is not marketed for a minimum of 15 Days.

ii. Qualification Criteria for Use of Commissioner's Adjusted Fair Market Value

(A) Definition

The Commissioner's Adjusted Fair Market Value (CAFMV) is the estimate of the FMV of the mortgaged Property, less adjustments, which may include without limitation, HUD's estimate of holding costs and resale costs that would be incurred if title to the mortgaged Property were conveyed to HUD.

(B) Standard

Unless otherwise required by statute or jurisdiction, the Mortgagee must use the CAFMV for all foreclosure sales and Post-Foreclosure Sales Efforts for Mortgages in Default when all of the following criteria are met:

- the FHA mortgage insurance is still active for the FHA case number;
- the FHA-insured Mortgage is not subject to indemnification;
- the Mortgagee has worked with the Borrower to exhaust all Home Retention Options and has determined that the Borrower's case does not meet the criteria for a Home Disposition Option, or the Mortgagee has been unable to locate the Borrower, and the Property is vacant or has been abandoned by the Borrower;
- the Property has no Surchargeable Damage; and
- the Mortgagee's projected conveyance claim amount would be equal to or greater than the CAFMV.

(C) Small Servicer Exemption

(1) Definition

Small Servicers are those Servicers defined in 12 CFR 1026.41(e)(4)(ii).

(2) Standard

HUD permits but does not require the use of CAFMV by small servicers.

iii. Property Valuation and CAFMV

(A) Required Appraisal

Unless otherwise directed by HUD, Mortgagees must first obtain and review for accuracy an "as-is" FHA appraisal, which includes both an interior and exterior evaluation of the Property.

If the Property is occupied and an interior appraisal cannot be obtained, an "exterior-only" appraisal may be used.

(1) Appraisal Validity

The appraisal must be valid on the date of the foreclosure sale. Appraisals are valid for 120 Days.

(2) Extension to Appraisal Validity Period

HUD provides an automatic 30-Day extension from the appraisal expiration date for delays due to bankruptcy, court delays or delays outside of the Mortgagee's control.

(3) Required Analysis and Reporting of a PACE Obligation

The Appraiser must review property tax records for the Property to determine the amount outstanding and the terms of the PACE obligation:

- if the Mortgagee notifies the Appraiser that the subject Property will remain subject to a PACE obligation;
- when the Appraiser observes that the property taxes for the subject Property are higher than average for the neighborhood and type of dwelling; or
- when the Appraiser observes energy-related building components or equipment or is aware of other PACE-allowed improvements during the inspection process.

The Appraiser must report the outstanding amount of the PACE obligation for the subject Property and provide a brief explanation of the terms.

Where energy and other PACE-allowed improvements have been made to the Property through a PACE program, the Appraiser must analyze and report the impact on value of the Property, whether positive or negative, of the PACE-related improvements and any additional obligation (i.e., the PACE special assessment).

(4) Required Documentation

If the Property is to be conveyed to HUD, the Mortgagee must upload into P260 a copy of the appraisal used to determine CAFMV.

(B) Determining the CAFMV

After determining the Property's appraised value, the Mortgagee's authorized employees must access the CAFMV link in FHAC to determine a Property's CAFMV.

The CAFMV remains valid and in effect for 120 Days from the date of the appraisal.

(C) Damage to the Property after Appraisal

The Mortgagee must immediately notify the NSC via cwcot@hud.gov if it becomes aware of any damage to the Property after the appraisal. The NSC will provide the Mortgagee with additional instructions should damage occur.

(D) Updated Appraisals due to Postponed Foreclosure Sales

If the foreclosure sale does not take place within 120 Days from the date of the appraisal, and within such additional time provided under Extension to Appraisal Validity Period, the Mortgagee must request an updated appraisal and obtain an updated CAFMV.

iv. Independent Third-Party Providers

(A) Definition

An Independent Third-Party Provider is a party that conducts the foreclosure sale or additional Post-Foreclosure Sales Efforts under CWCOT procedures.

(B) Standard

Mortgagees may utilize an Independent Third-Party Provider to conduct the foreclosure sale and market a Property (securing an FHA-insured Mortgage) prior to such sale, where permitted by jurisdiction.

The Mortgagee must ensure that the Independent Third-Party Provider is not one of the following:
- an Affiliate or subsidiary of the Mortgagee;
- any Entity over which the Mortgagee has significant influence; or
- any Entity with which the Mortgagee has a conflict of interest in fact or appearance.

For successful third-party sales, HUD will reimburse Mortgagees for Independent Third-Party Provider service fees incurred up to an amount that does not exceed 5 percent of the Property's net sales price. Revenue sharing agreements of the reimbursed fee between the Mortgagee and the Independent Third-Party Provider are not permitted.

v. CWCOT Bidding Procedures

The Mortgagee must bid the CAFMV at the foreclosure sale.

Either the Mortgagee or a third party will be the successful bidder at the foreclosure sale. Notwithstanding the foreclosure sale, the Borrower or a third party may exercise a legal right and redeem the Property.

vi. Reporting CWCOT

If a third party purchased the Property at foreclosure through CWCOT procedures, the Mortgagee must report in SFDMS the appropriate Claim Termination of Insurance Code.

q. Reinstatement

i. Standard

The Mortgagee must allow reinstatement of the Mortgage if the Borrower offers, in a lump sum payment, all amounts to bring the account current, including costs incurred by the Mortgagee in instituting foreclosure, except under any of the following circumstances:

- within the two years immediately preceding the initiation of the current foreclosure action, the Mortgagee has accepted reinstatement in a previous foreclosure action;
- reinstatement will preclude foreclosure following a subsequent Default; or
- reinstatement will adversely affect the priority of the mortgage lien.

ii. Incurred Costs

(A) Property Inspections/Preservation

When a Mortgage in Default is reinstated, the Mortgagee may charge the Borrower the costs of property inspections and/or preservation, so long as the costs are:
- reasonable and customary for those services, as established in the Mortgagee Property Preservation and Protection Action section; and
- consistent with HUD requirements, state law, and security instruments.

(B) Inspection Cost Collected from Borrower

The Mortgagee may collect the cost of the inspections from the Borrower only when:
- the Mortgage was reinstated or paid in full;
- the Mortgagee has performed and properly documented the inspections pursuant to HUD requirements; and
- the cost of each inspection was reasonable and within the cost limitation established by HUD.

The Mortgagee must not collect inspection costs from the Borrower's escrow account or charge for an Occupancy Inspection performed after successful contact with the Borrower or occupant.

(C) Attorney's and Trustees' Fees

If the Mortgagee cancels a foreclosure action for a Loss Mitigation Option, a reinstatement, or a payment in full, the Mortgagee may charge the Borrower for attorney's fees as follows:
- The attorney's fees to be paid by the Borrower must be commensurate with the work actually performed to that point.
- The amount charged may not be in excess of the fee that HUD has established as reasonable and customary for claim purposes.

iii. Reinstatement during CWCOT

If the Mortgagee is using CWCOT procedures and the Borrower reinstates the Mortgage after foreclosure has been instituted, the Mortgagee must:
- cancel the appraisal if the appraisal has not yet been completed; or
- request that the Borrower reimburses the Mortgagee for the cost of the appraisal as part of foreclosure-related expenses, if the appraisal cost was validly incurred.

iv. Reporting Reinstatements

When a Delinquent Mortgage is reinstated, the Mortgagee must report the appropriate Account Reinstated Code in SFDMS to indicate whether:
- use of repayment plans or HUD's Loss Mitigation Options assisted in the reinstatement;
- reinstatement was due to a sale of the Property using a mortgage assumption; or
- the Borrower was able to reinstate the Mortgage on their own.

r. Foreclosure

When a Borrower with a Mortgage in Default cannot or will not resume and complete their Mortgage Payments, the Mortgagee must take steps to acquire the Property or see that it is acquired by a third party. Before starting foreclosure, the Mortgagee must review its servicing record to be certain that servicing has been performed in accordance with HUD guidance. When foreclosure is appropriate, Mortgagees must initiate and complete foreclosure in a timely manner.

i. Mortgagee Action Before Initiation of Foreclosure

The Mortgagee must exercise reasonable diligence in collecting past due Mortgage Payments by:
- utilizing Early Delinquency Servicing Workout tools;
- determining eligibility of HUD's Loss Mitigation Program when appropriate;
- performing the first legal action to initiate foreclosure, to acquire title and possession of the Property, when necessary;
- ensuring that the Mortgage has been accurately reported to consumer reporting agencies in accordance with applicable federal law; and
- ensuring that any former Borrower, co-Borrower and/or co-signer personally liable for payment of the mortgage debt has been notified, as appropriate.

(A) Assignments for Special Mortgages

The Mortgagee must not foreclose on Mortgages insured pursuant to Sections 203(q), 247, and 248 of the National Housing Act. The Mortgagee must comply with HUD's collection communication requirements and may then assign the Mortgage to HUD as follows:
- Section 203(q) Mortgages: may assign the Mortgage to HUD, after the Mortgage has been in Default for 90 Days.
- Section 247 Mortgages: may assign the Mortgage to HUD, after the Mortgage has been in Default for 180 Days.
- Section 248 Mortgages: may assign the Mortgage to HUD, after the Mortgage has been in Default for 90 Days.

(B) Time Frame for Utilization of Loss Mitigation or Initiation of Foreclosure

The Mortgagee must utilize a Loss Mitigation Option or initiate foreclosure within six months of the date of Default. FHA considers the Mortgagee to have satisfied this requirement if, within the six-month time frame, the Mortgagee takes one or a combination of the following actions:

- enter into an SFB-Unemployment Agreement;
- complete a refinance of an insured cooperative housing Mortgage;
- complete an assumption;
- execute a Trial Payment Plan Agreement for an FHA-HAMP Option;
- execute a PFS Approval to Participate;
- execute a DIL agreement; or
- initiate the first legal action to begin foreclosure.

(C) When to Initiate Foreclosure

After at least three consecutive full monthly Mortgage Payments are due but unpaid, a Mortgagee may initiate a foreclosure for monetary Default if one of the following conditions is met:

- The Mortgagee has completed its review of the Borrower's loss mitigation request, determined that the Borrower does not qualify for a Loss Mitigation Option, properly notified the Borrower of this decision, and rejected any available appeal by the Borrower.
- The Borrower has failed to perform under an agreement on a Loss Mitigation Option, and the Mortgagee has determined that the Borrower is ineligible for other Loss Mitigation Options.
- The Mortgagee has been unable to make a determination of the Borrower's eligibility for any Loss Mitigation Option due to the Borrower not responding to the Mortgagee's efforts to contact the Borrower.

(D) Exceptions to Foreclosure Initiation Time Frame

(1) Standard

A Mortgagee may initiate foreclosure on a Delinquent Mortgage if one of the following conditions is met:

- The Mortgagee has determined that the mortgaged Property has been abandoned, or has been vacant for more than 60 Days.
- The Borrower, after being clearly advised of the Options available for relief, including the PFS and DIL Options, has clearly stated to the Mortgagee, in writing, that they have no intention of fulfilling their obligation under the Mortgage.
- The mortgaged Property is not the Borrower's Principal Residence and it is occupied by tenants who are paying rent, but the Rental Income is not being applied to the mortgage debt.
- The Property is owned by a corporation or partnership.

(a) Vacant or Abandoned Properties

If the Mortgage is in Default, the Mortgagee must commence foreclosure:
- no later than six months after the date of Default; or
- no later than 120 Days after the latter of the date that:
  - the Property becomes vacant; or
  - the Property is discovered or should have been discovered vacant or abandoned; or
  - for Properties that have 2, 3, or 4 units, all units are discovered or should have been discovered vacant or abandoned.

(b) Prohibition of Foreclosure due to State Legislation

In some states, the Mortgagee must delay, cancel, and/or reschedule a foreclosure action to comply with state law requirements. HUD provides an automatic 90-Day extension after the expiration of the time during which foreclosure is prohibited to commence foreclosure where:
- the foreclosure sale would have been conducted in the required time frame but was canceled to comply with state law; and
- the initial legal action to commence foreclosure was timely.

(c) Prohibition of Foreclosure due to Federal Law or Regulations

Where a federal regulation requires a delay in the initiation of foreclosure, the Mortgagee must initiate foreclosure no later than 90 Days after the expiration of the time during which foreclosure is prohibited. The status of the Defaulted Mortgage should be reported in SFDMS using the established Delinquency/Default Reason (DDR) Code for federally mandated delay.

(d) Prohibition of Foreclosure due to Bankruptcy

If federal bankruptcy does not permit commencement of foreclosure within the standard six-month time frame, or requires foreclosure to be discontinued, the Mortgagee must commence or, if applicable, recommence foreclosure within 90 Days after the applicable release of stay or bankruptcy discharge date.

(e) Prohibition of Foreclosure due to Servicemembers Civil Relief Act

Mortgagees are allowed an automatic 90-Day extension from the date the applicable SCRA foreclosure moratorium expires.

(f) Moratorium on Foreclosure due to Disaster

Mortgages secured by Properties in Presidentially-Declared Major Disaster Areas (PDMDA) are subject to a 90-Day moratorium on foreclosures following the disaster. See Presidentially-Declared Major Disaster Areas.

HUD provides the Mortgagee an automatic 90-Day extension from the date of the moratorium expiration date to commence or recommence foreclosure action or evaluate the Borrower under HUD's Loss Mitigation Program.

(2) Automatic Extensions for Foreclosure Initiation Time Frame for Loss Mitigation Option

HUD provides automatic 90-Day extensions to the deadline to complete a Loss Mitigation Option or to perform the first legal action initiating foreclosure, provided the Mortgagee has:

- evaluated and approved the Borrower for a Loss Mitigation Home Retention Option prior to the expiration of the initial six-month period to initiate foreclosure, or issued an Approval to Participate in the PFS Program resulting in early termination or option failure;
- reported the Loss Mitigation Option via SFDMS; and
- from the date the Borrower defaulted under a Loss Mitigation Option or a TPP Agreement failed, initiated foreclosure action after review of the Borrowers for other Loss Mitigation Options.

Mortgagees may use these automatic extensions as outlined in Automatic Extensions to HUD's Initiation of Foreclosure Timeline.

HUD does not provide automatic extensions for completion of a DIL; the Mortgagee must submit any request for extension of time for completion of a DIL to the NSC for HUD approval via EVARS. HUD does not provide automatic extensions for attempting a repayment plan, Formal Forbearance, Informal Forbearance, Delinquent refinance, or assumption.

(3) Loss Mitigation Denial

The Consumer Financial Protection Bureau (CFPB) Loss Mitigation regulations are at RESPA (Regulation X) at 12 CFR 1024.41.

HUD provides an automatic 90-Day extension to the initiation of foreclosure timeline in any case in which the Mortgagee needs additional time to comply with the appeals process required by the CFPB. The 90-Day extension begins on the date the Mortgagee denies loss mitigation and sends the Borrower the notice required under CFPB regulations.

(4) Requests for Other or Additional Extensions to the Time Requirement to Utilize Loss Mitigation Option

For additional time extensions, and for extensions of time for any other reason not listed above, the Mortgagee must request the extension via EVARS prior to the expiration of the existing time frame and provide:

- the dates that required notices were sent to the Borrower;

Handbook 4000.1

678

Effective Date: 03/14/2016 | Last Revised: 07/10/2019
*Refer to the online version of SF Handbook 4000.1 for specific sections' effective dates

- the date that the Mortgagee received the Complete Loss Mitigation Request;
- the date that the Mortgagee approved or denied the Borrower for Loss Mitigation Options; and
- a clear explanation of the Mortgagee's need for an extension to this deadline.

(5) Required Documentation

The Mortgagee must retain documentation of form HUD-50012, *Mortgagee's Request for Extensions of Time*, in the Claim Review File and must ensure that all extensions of time to initiate foreclosure are reflected in its claim submission.

For all extensions of time requests, the Mortgagee must:
- note the reason for the extension and relevant dates that necessitated the extension and retain documentation supporting the reason and dates in the Claim Review File;
- report the applicable status codes in SFDMS; and
- report on form HUD-27011, Part A:
  o the dates relating to the extension;
  o in Block 19, the Expiration Date of the 90-day extension being used;
  o in the "Mortgagee's Comments" section, the extension being used and the reason(s) for the extension; and
  o in the "Mortgagee's Comments" section, the statement, "I certify that the use of this extension is for the reason(s) stated above."

(E) Curtailment of Claims

Mortgagees are responsible for self-curtailment of interest and property expenses on Single Family claims when Reasonable Diligence Time Frames or reporting requirements are not met. Property expenses do not include real estate taxes and hazard insurance premiums.

(F) Management Review

The Mortgagee must review its records before initiation of foreclosure in making a decision to foreclose as follows:
- The Mortgagee must develop a form or checklist to document that they have reviewed the Mortgage for foreclosure. A supervisor higher than the person submitting the Mortgage for foreclosure must sign or electronically acknowledge that they have reviewed and approve the document evidencing the decision to foreclose.
- The Servicer must have the mortgage holder's approval of its decision to foreclose or have the delegated authority to make such decisions.
- The Mortgagee is expected to continue to service the Mortgage throughout foreclosure proceedings and to work with the Borrower to avoid foreclosure

pursuant to the Loss Mitigation During the Foreclosure Process section requirements and program requirements related to changes in the Borrower's financial circumstances.

(G) Manufactured Housing Review

Due to the title evidence requirements for Manufactured Housing, the Mortgagee must:
- review each Property at the time of foreclosure referral to determine if the collateral for the FHA-insured Mortgage is a Manufactured Home; and
- ensure that all the Title Evidence for Manufactured Housing requirements are met before conveying a Manufactured Home to HUD.

(H) PACE Obligation Review

The Mortgagee must:
- review each Property at the time of foreclosure referral to determine if the Property is encumbered with a PACE obligation;
- confirm that any identified PACE obligation may only become subject to an enforceable claim (i.e., a lien) for delinquent regularly scheduled PACE special assessment payments and otherwise complies with the eligibility and acceptability criteria for Properties with a PACE obligation provided in Section II.A.1.b.iv(A)(6) of the prior *SF Handbook* published in December 2016; and
- contact the HUD National Servicing Center for guidance if a noncompliant PACE obligation is identified.

ii. Conduct of Foreclosure Proceedings

When foreclosure is necessary, the Mortgagee must give timely notice to HUD via SFDMS and exercise reasonable diligence in processing and completing foreclosure proceedings to acquire good marketable title and possession of the Property. HUD expects Mortgagees to comply with all federal, state and local laws when prosecuting a foreclosure and pursuing a possessory action.

(A) Initiating Foreclosure

(1) First Legal Action to Initiate Foreclosure

The Mortgagee must perform the first legal action to initiate foreclosure for each state as provided in Appendix 5.0 – First Legal Actions to Initiate Foreclosure and Reasonable Diligence Time Frames.

(2) Notice to HUD of Foreclosure Initiation

The Mortgagee must give notice to HUD within 30 Days of initiating foreclosure by reporting the foreclosure status in the monthly SFDMS report.

The Mortgagee must report the foreclosure status for the current cycle or following cycle in which the first required public legal action is taken to initiate foreclosure.

(3) Notice to HOA or Condominium Associations

The Mortgagee must name and properly serve HOA and condominium associations reflected in the Mortgage or origination documents, recorded covenants/declarations, initial foreclosure referral and/or title search review, or made known to the Mortgagee during the foreclosure proceedings.

(B) SCRA Protection during Foreclosure

The Mortgagee must obtain court permission before foreclosing on a Mortgage falling under provisions of the SCRA. A foreclosure sale or Manufactured Housing repossession during the period of military service and subsequent periods specified within the SCRA is invalid unless it is:

- made pursuant to a court order granted before such sale with a return made and approved by the court; or
- held pursuant to a written agreement, entered into after the commencement of Active Duty, between the parties involved.

(C) Loss Mitigation During the Foreclosure Process

The Mortgagee may evaluate the Borrower for a Loss Mitigation Option during the foreclosure process where:

- the Borrower submits their initial Complete Loss Mitigation Request; or
- the Mortgagee has determined that the Borrower was ineligible for loss mitigation based on a Complete Loss Mitigation Request; and a change in circumstances has occurred so that a Borrower may be eligible for a subsequent loss mitigation review.

(1) Requests Received during Foreclosure

The following describes Mortgagee action regarding foreclosure proceedings and loss mitigation requests, depending on when the request is received by the Mortgagee.

(a) 45 or More Days to Scheduled Foreclosure Sale Date

(i) Response

When the loss mitigation request is received 45 Days or more prior to the scheduled foreclosure sale date, the Mortgagee must notify the Borrower in writing within five business days of receiving the request that:

- the Borrower's request has been received; and
- the request is complete or incomplete.

(ii) Review

Within 30 Days of receiving a Complete Loss Mitigation Request, the Mortgagee must review a Borrower's request for eligibility for all Loss Mitigation Options.

(iii) Foreclosure Action

A Mortgagee must not move forward with a scheduled foreclosure sale during its loss mitigation review.

(b) More than 37 Days but Less than 45 Days to Scheduled Foreclosure Sale Date

(i) Review

Within 30 Days of receiving a Complete Loss Mitigation Request, the Mortgagee must review a Borrower's request for eligibility for Loss Mitigation Options when received more than 37 Days but less than 45 Days to the scheduled foreclosure sale date.

If an incomplete request is received and is not completed despite the Mortgagee's repeated requests to the Borrower for information, the Mortgagee may, at its discretion, evaluate an incomplete loss mitigation request and offer a proprietary, non-incentivized Loss Mitigation Option.

(ii) Foreclosure Action

The Mortgagee must not move forward with a scheduled foreclosure sale during its loss mitigation review.

(c) 37 or Fewer Days Prior to the Scheduled Foreclosure Sale Date

(i) Review

A Mortgagee must use its best efforts to complete a thorough and accurate review when the Borrower's request is received 37 Days or fewer prior to the scheduled foreclosure sale date.

(ii) Foreclosure Action

HUD does not require the Mortgagee to suspend the foreclosure sale. The Mortgagee may proceed with a foreclosure sale if the Mortgagee:
- determines after its review of available information that a Borrower is ineligible for loss mitigation; or

- using its best efforts, is still unable to complete a thorough and accurate review of a Borrower's request by the scheduled foreclosure sale date.

(2) Terminating Foreclosure Proceedings for Loss Mitigation

When a Borrower requests loss mitigation assistance after the Mortgagee has initiated foreclosure, the Mortgagee must suspend and/or terminate the foreclosure proceedings, depending on the state law requirement, after all of the following have occurred:

- verifying that a Borrower's financial situation qualifies them for a Loss Mitigation Option;
- allowing the Borrower at least 14 Days to consider the Mortgagee's offer of loss mitigation assistance, if the request for loss mitigation was received more than 37 Days prior to the scheduled foreclosure sale date; and
- receiving an executed Loss Mitigation Option Agreement from the Borrower, indicating that the Borrower understands and agrees to the Loss Mitigation Option terms; receiving a signed sales contract under an approved PFS program participation; or receiving a DIL agreement executed by the Borrower.

(3) Communication Between Departments

The Mortgagee must ensure that strong communication lines are established between their Loss Mitigation and Foreclosure departments to facilitate the coordination of loss mitigation efforts and the sharing of documentation and information relating to a Borrower's delinquency. Both departments must be aware when a Borrower's file is under review for HUD's Loss Mitigation Program.

(D) Borrower Sale of the Property before Foreclosure Sale

HUD encourages the Mortgagee, when possible, to provide the Borrower with an opportunity to sell the Property and to provide a reasonable time to complete the sale. The Mortgagee should not initiate foreclosure if it appears that a sale is probable and should accept payments tendered while the Property is for sale and before foreclosure is started.

(E) Reasonable Diligence in Completing Foreclosure

(1) Definition

The Reasonable Diligence Time Frame is the period of time beginning with the first legal action required by the jurisdiction to commence foreclosure and ending with the later date of acquiring good marketable title to, and possession of, the Property.

(2) Standard

The Mortgagee must exercise reasonable diligence in processing foreclosures and in acquiring title to and possession of Properties, in accordance with HUD's Reasonable Diligence Time Frames.

When circumstances beyond the Mortgagee's control occur, the Mortgagee may treat delays in completing the foreclosure process as exceptions to the Reasonable Diligence Time Frames and may exclude such delays when calculating the time to complete a foreclosure if an extension has been granted by HUD.

(a) Delay Due to Use of Loss Mitigation Home Retention Option

When determining compliance with the Reasonable Diligence Time Frame, the Mortgagee may exclude the time that the Borrower was performing under an SFB-Unemployment Agreement or TPP.

(b) Delay Due to Foreclosure Mediation

Where mediation is required after the initiation of foreclosure but before the foreclosure sale, the Mortgagee may exclude the time required to complete the mediation when determining compliance with the Reasonable Diligence Time Frame.

(c) Delay Due to Active Duty Military Service

If a Borrower is on Active Duty military service and the Mortgage was obtained prior to entry into Active Duty military service, the Mortgagee may exclude the period during which the Borrower is on Active Duty military service when computing the Reasonable Diligence Time Frame.

(d) Delay Due to Bankruptcy

When a Borrower files bankruptcy after foreclosure proceedings have been initiated, an automatic extension for foreclosure and acquisition of the Property will be allowed as long as:
- the Mortgagee ensures that all necessary bankruptcy-related legal actions are handled in a timely and effective matter;
- the case is promptly referred to a bankruptcy attorney after the bankruptcy is filed; and
- the Mortgagee monitors the action to ensure that the case is timely resolved through dismissal, termination of the automatic stay, or trustee abandonment of all interest in the secured Property.

HUD will reimburse legal expenses related to resolving bankruptcies in accordance with Attorney's Fees.

The time frame for completing the bankruptcy action will vary based on the chapter under which the bankruptcy is filed.

(i) Chapter 7 Bankruptcy

HUD allows the Mortgagee an additional 90 Days from the date of the release of stay of the Chapter 7 bankruptcy to recommence the foreclosure.

(ii) Chapter 11, 12 or 13 Bankruptcy

When the Mortgagee cannot proceed with foreclosure action because of a Chapter 13 (or Chapter 11 or 12) bankruptcy, the Mortgagee must closely monitor the payments required by the bankruptcy court. If the Borrower becomes 60 Days delinquent in payments required under a Chapter 13 (or Chapter 11 or 12) plan, the Mortgagee must ensure that prompt legal action is taken to resolve the matter.

Any delay the Mortgagee encounters must be fully documented and must be beyond the Mortgagee's control.

(e) Delay in Acquiring Possession

When a separate legal action is necessary to gain possession following foreclosure, an automatic extension of the Reasonable Diligence Time Frame will be allowed for the actual time necessary to complete the possessory action.

HUD provides this automatic extension if the Mortgagee takes the first legal action to initiate the eviction or possessory action within 30 Days of:
- the completion of foreclosure proceedings; or
- the expiration of federal or local restrictions on eviction.

The additional time needed under applicable federal, state, or local laws to obtain possession of a Property is taken into consideration when evaluating a Mortgagee's compliance with HUD's Reasonable Diligence Time Frame. Upon the expiration period associated with the applicable occupancy rights, Mortgagees are expected to proceed promptly with possessory actions.

(3) Required Documentation

The Mortgagee must document in its Claim Review File any delay in completing foreclosure and all activities performed by the Mortgagee to mitigate and abide by these time frames. The Mortgagee must maintain a comprehensive audit trail and chronology to support any delay in compliance with the Reasonable Diligence Time Frames.

Where the Mortgagee has submitted a request for an extension of time to the NSC via EVARS, the Mortgagee must maintain a copy of the NSC's written response in the Claim Review File.

For automatic extensions, the Mortgagee must reflect these extensions in form HUD-27011 and retain in the Claim Review File documentation supporting those extensions.

(F) HUD Schedule of Attorney Fees

(1) Definition

The HUD Schedule of Attorney Fees (Schedule) states the maximum fee amount that may be reimbursed in an FHA insurance claim for a foreclosure attorney, bankruptcy clearance, possessory action, and completion of a DIL.

(2) Standard

The HUD Schedule of Attorney Fees reflects the customary legal services pertinent to mortgage Defaults. Each fee on the Schedule is the total maximum amount, instead of an hourly rate, reimbursable in a claim for mortgage insurance benefits.

The HUD Schedule of Attorney Fees does not reflect additional expenses incurred due to foreclosure and/or mediation because of the wide differences in costs and lengths of time of foreclosure completion, depending on the jurisdiction in which the foreclosure actions are occurring. For any additional expenses incurred due to required legal actions, such as mediation or probate proceedings, the Mortgagee may claim these amounts by submitting a documented cost breakdown and retaining in the Claim Review File a written justification for those costs.

(G) CWCOT Bidding at the Foreclosure Sale

(1) Mortgagee as Successful Bidder

(a) Amount Equal to the CAFMV

If the Mortgagee is the successful bidder for an amount equal to the CAFMV, the Mortgagee may elect to either:
- retain title to the Property and file a claim for insurance benefits under CWCOT; or
- convey the title to the Property to HUD and its claim for insurance benefits as a conveyance claim.

(b) Amount Greater than CAFMV

Where the Mortgagee is the successful bidder for an amount greater than the CAFMV, unless the sheriff or other appropriate local authority has mandated the subject bid as the minimum bid that could be set for the Property, the Mortgagee is deemed to have elected to retain title of the Property and therefore must not convey title to the Property to HUD.

(2) Third Party as Successful Bidder

(a) Amount Equal to or Greater than CAFMV

Where a third party is the successful bidder at the foreclosure sale for an amount equal to or greater than the CAFMV, the Mortgagee must submit its claim for insurance benefits under CWCOT.

(b) Amount Less than CAFMV

Where a third party is the successful bidder at the foreclosure sale for an amount less than the CAFMV, the Mortgagee may not file a claim for any insurance benefits.

(3) Borrower or Third Party Redemption

Where the Borrower or a third party redeems the Property and acquires title for an amount not less than the CAFMV, the Mortgagee must submit its claim for insurance benefits under CWCOT.

(H) CWCOT Post-Foreclosure Sales Efforts

If the Property does not sell to a third party at the foreclosure sale, the Mortgagee may pursue additional sales efforts and may utilize independent third-party providers to conduct such sales prior to making a final decision to convey a Property to HUD

The Mortgagee must still comply with HUD's conveyance time frames, unless a sales contract has been ratified. Where a sales contract has been ratified, HUD provides Mortgagees with an automatic 30-Day extension from the deadline for conveyance.

(I) Electronic Record Retention of Foreclosure-Related Documents

The Mortgagee must retain documents relating to loss mitigation review in electronic format, in addition to requirements for retaining hard copies or originals of foreclosure-related documents, for foreclosures occurring on or after October 1, 2014. These documents include, but are not limited to:
- evidence of the Servicer's foreclosure committee recommendation;
- the Mortgagee's Referral Notice to a foreclosure attorney, if applicable; and

- a copy of the document evidencing the first legal action necessary to initiate foreclosure and all supporting documentation.

(J) Foreclosure Reporting

The Mortgagee must report in SFDMS the Account in Foreclosure Codes that accurately reflect the current stage of foreclosure.

s. Acquiring Possession

On the date the deed is filed for recording, the Mortgagee must certify that the Property is vacant and free of Personal Property, unless HUD has agreed to accept title with the Property occupied. This, and the procedures described below, applies whether title is acquired by foreclosure or by DIL of Foreclosure.

i. Applicable Law Protecting Tenants

When determining compliance with the reasonable diligence requirement, the Mortgagee may exclude the time required to comply with federal, state, and local laws extending the time required to complete possessory actions.

ii. Identification of Property Occupants

Before completion of foreclosure the Mortgagee must:
- confirm the identity of all occupants;
- determine each occupant's possible rights for continued occupancy under HUD's Occupied Conveyance procedures; and
- follow HUD's Occupied Conveyance procedures by sending occupants the Notice to Occupant of Pending Acquisition (NOPA) 60 to 90 Days before the Mortgagee expects to acquire title.

iii. Notice to Occupant of Pending Acquisition

(A) Definition

The Notice to Occupant of Pending Acquisition (NOPA) is a notice to the Borrower and heads of household that the Mortgagee will be acquiring title to the Property and then conveying Property to HUD.

(B) Standard

At least 60 Days but not more than 90 Days before the Mortgagee reasonably expects to acquire title, the Mortgagee must notify the Borrower and each head of household occupying a unit of the Property of the possibility that the Mortgagee will convey the Property to HUD following foreclosure.

The NOPA must:

- provide a summary of the conditions under which continued occupancy is permissible;
- advise the Borrower:
  - that potential acquisition of the Property by HUD is pending (see the NOPA Letter);
  - that HUD requires Properties be vacant at the time of conveyance to HUD, unless the Borrower or other occupant can meet the regulatory conditions for continued occupancy, the habitability criteria, and the eligibility criteria (see form HUD-9539, *Request for Occupied Conveyance*);
  - of the process for requesting to remain in the Property (see Continued Occupancy and/or Temporary Nature of Continued Occupancy); and
  - that the Property must otherwise be vacated before the scheduled time of acquisition; and
- be sent via certified mail or with a signature confirmation service to ensure receipt of the notice by occupants.

(C) Required Documentation

The Mortgagee must provide to HUD's MCM by uploading into P260:
- an electronic copy of each NOPA; and
- all documentation and information obtained regarding existing leases and tenancies.

iv. Occupied Conveyance Requests to HUD

(A) Definition

An Occupied Conveyance is the conveyance to HUD of a Property that is not vacant.

(B) Standard

HUD will notify the Mortgagee if it has received an occupant's request to remain in the Property. If the Mortgagee has not received such notification from HUD within 45 Days after sending the notices, the Mortgagee must convey the Property vacant, unless otherwise directed by the MCM.

(C) Approved Occupied Conveyance Requests

If HUD grants Occupied Conveyance, the Mortgagee must convey the Property occupied under HUD's Occupied Conveyance regulations and procedures provided by the MCM per 24 CFR § 203.670.

(D) Denied Occupied Conveyance Requests

If HUD denies Occupied Conveyance, the Mortgagee must determine if there is occupancy protection under federal, state, or local law that would require the

Mortgagee to delay possessory action. If the Mortgagee determines that such laws are applicable, the Mortgagee must:

- follow those requirements before evicting the occupant; and
- attempt to obtain documentation of existing leases and tenancies for the Claim Review File as evidence of the applicability of the occupancy protection laws and the additional time needed to comply with them.

v.   Rents under Bona Fide Leases

The Mortgagee must attempt to:

- collect rents payable under bona fide leases and tenancies providing post-foreclosure occupancy rights; and
- in the event of default, take possessory action pursuant to the rental contract terms and applicable law.

The Mortgagee must reflect any rents it received during the term of the bona fide lease or tenancy on its claim for mortgage insurance benefits.

vi.   Preservation and Protection Costs due to Extended Lease or Tenancy

The Mortgagee may request reimbursement of additional routine P&P costs, including lawn maintenance and inspections that are incurred as a result of an extended lease or tenancy under applicable law.

vii. Cash for Keys Consideration

(A) Definition

Cash for Keys is a monetary consideration offered as an alternative to legal eviction to property occupants after foreclosure.

(B) Standard

If property occupants fail to vacate the Property after receiving the first Notice to Quit, the Mortgagee may offer up to $3,000 per dwelling in exchange for the occupants vacating the property within 30 Days of the Cash for Keys Relocation Offer. Before releasing the funds, the Mortgagee must inspect the Property to ensure that:

- the Property is in Broom-swept Condition; and
- all built-in appliances and fixtures remain in the Property.

(C) Required Documentation

The Mortgagee must document in its Claim Review File the date and amount of the Relocation Offer, the date of the actual vacancy, and the date the occupant received the funds.

viii. Evictions and Eviction Personnel

(A) Standard

The Mortgagee must ensure that evictions are conducted in accordance with state and local law and:
- with no more than four people for a townhouse or condominium; and
- with no more than six people for a Single Family detached dwelling.

(B) Required Documentation

The Mortgagee must include in the Claim Review File:
- photographs showing that all Personal Property and debris have been removed from the Property as part of the eviction;
- the number of people required and present to complete the eviction;
- whether the eviction was canceled or re-scheduled; and
- documentation supporting eviction costs, including those costs due to state or local law requirements for eviction time frame, removal, or storage.

t. Conveyance of Acquired Properties

i. Conveyance Time Frame

The Mortgagee must acquire clear, marketable title and transfer the Property to HUD within 30 Days of the latter of:
- recordation of the foreclosure deed;
- recordation date of a DIL of Foreclosure;
- acquisition of the Property;
- expiration of the redemption period; or
- HUD-approved time extensions.

In cases where the Mortgagee arranges for a direct conveyance of the Property to the Secretary, the Mortgagee must convey the Property to HUD within 30 Days of the end of the Reasonable Diligence Time Frame.

ii. Condition of Properties

(A) Acceptable Conveyance Condition

Acceptable Conveyance Condition refers to how at the time of conveyance to HUD, the Mortgagee must ensure that the Property meets all of the following conditions:
- The Property is undamaged by fire, flood, earthquake, hurricane, tornado, boiler explosion (if a condominium) or Mortgagee Neglect.
- The Property is secured and, if applicable, winterized.
- All insured damages including theft and vandalism, if any, are repaired per the scope of work indicated on the insurance documents.

- Interior and exterior debris is removed, with the Property's interior maintained in Broom-swept Condition, the lawn is maintained, and all vehicles and any other personal property are removed in accordance with state and local requirements.
- The Mortgagee has good and marketable title.

Broom-swept Condition is the condition of a Property that is, at a minimum, reasonably free of dust and dirt and free of hazardous materials or conditions, personal belongings, and interior and exterior debris.

(B) HUD Contact

(1) Mortgagee Compliance Manager

HUD's MCM is the single point of contact to administer Mortgagee compliance functions and property preservation activities.

(2) P260

P260 is HUD's web-based internet portal, which allows Mortgagees to submit requests, notifications, and documents and obtain approvals for pre- and post-conveyance activities.

(C) Mortgagee Property Preservation and Protection Action

(1) Definition

Property Preservation and Protection (P&P) actions are maintenance, security, and repair work required by HUD in order to ensure that the Property meets HUD's conveyance condition standards.

Mortgagee Neglect is the Mortgagee's failure to take action to preserve and protect the Property from the time it is determined (or should have been determined) to be vacant or abandoned, until the time it is conveyed to HUD.

(2) Standard

The Mortgagee must preserve and protect Properties that are the security for FHA-insured Mortgages that are in Default or presently in foreclosure. The Mortgagee is responsible for the management, scheduling, and execution of all activities and actions taken to preserve, secure, maintain and protect the Property, regardless of the amount that HUD may reimburse. The Mortgagees may use any qualified individual or business to perform P&P services on Properties that were secured by FHA-insured Mortgages; however, the Mortgagee remains fully responsible to HUD for its actions and the actions of its agents, individuals and firms that performed such services.

The Mortgagee remains responsible for property damage or destruction to vacant or abandoned Property resulting from Mortgagee Neglect. Such neglect includes, but is not limited to:

- failure to adequately and accurately verify the occupancy status of a Property;
- failure to complete timely and accurate property inspections;
- failure to promptly and appropriately secure and to continue to preserve and protect all vacant Properties according to HUD standards; and
- failure to promptly notify the Mortgagee Compliance Manager (MCM) of receipt of code violations and demolition notices and/or take appropriate action.

To ensure that the Mortgagee is not held liable for damage to the Property by waste committed by the Borrower, their heirs, successors, or assigns, the Mortgagee must document and photograph any damage resulting from the Borrower that is identified during the First-Time Vacant (FTV) securing of the Property.

(3) Required Documentation

The Mortgagee must:

- take before and after photographs and upload them into P260 for each claimed Property P&P expense;
- document and photograph any damage resulting from the Borrower that is identified using the FTV inspection; and
- retain in the Claim Review File:
  - all copies of paid invoices or receipts or other documentation supporting all property preservation expenses claimed by the Mortgagee; and
  - a chronology of the Mortgagee's Property P&P actions.

If documentation is incomplete, inadequate, or not provided, HUD will not accept a Mortgagee's certification of property condition and may:

- re-convey the Property to the Mortgagee; or
- seek reimbursement from the Mortgagee for HUD's estimate of the cost of the repairs required to repair and restore the Property to conveyance condition.

HUD will require repayment of all or part of any claim reimbursement if it is determined that expenses claimed and paid were unnecessary or excessive, or that services claimed were not performed or were performed improperly or incompletely.

Handbook 4000.1
Effective Date: 03/14/2016 | Last Revised: 07/10/2019
*Refer to the online version of SF Handbook 4000.1 for specific sections' effective dates

693

(4) Property Preservation Allowances

(a) Definition

The Maximum Property Preservation Allowance is a pre-approved reimbursement for the aggregate of all property preservation expenses that do not exceed the line item allowable amounts listed in HUD's Property Preservation Allowances and Schedules.

(b) Standard

The Maximum Property Preservation Allowance is $5,000 per Property.

(c) Requests for Exceeding Property Preservation Allowances

(i) Request

The Mortgagee must request over-allowable approval from the MCM via P260 when:

- the aggregate of all Property P&P expenses exceed the Maximum Property Preservation Allowance;
- a Property P&P cost will exceed the maximum line item allowance listed in the Property Preservation Allowances and Schedules; or
- there is no specific line item allowable stated in the schedule for the expense.

When the Mortgagee submits an over-allowable request to exceed the Maximum Property Preservation Allowance, the Mortgagee must demonstrate their incurred P&P costs are at or near the Maximum Property Preservation Allowance.

(ii) Required Documentation

The Mortgagee must upload all supporting documentation into P260, including a detailed description of what actions will be or were taken, an itemized list of the repairs and materials that will be or were used, relevant room dimensions, receipts, and photographs, and a chronological listing of all Property P&P expenses incurred before submittal of the over-allowable expense request.

The following chart details requirements for over-allowable requests.

If Claimed Property Preservation Expenses are:	And the Cost of a Single Line Item Expense is:	Need Over-allowable Approval?
$5,000 or less	Greater than Appendix A	Yes
$5,000 or less	Less than Appendix A	No
Greater than $5,000	Greater than Appendix A	Yes
Greater than $5,000	Less than Appendix A	Yes

(d) Appeals of Over-Allowable Request Decisions

The Mortgagee may appeal an initial over-allowable decision via P260, for review by the MCM.

The Mortgagee may submit an additional appeal to the MCM via P260, who will review the appeal and, at its discretion, approve or deny the appeal or determine if further review by HUD is needed. HUD's or the MCM's decision on the second appeal is final and no further appeals will be accepted.

(5) Property P&P Requirements of Authorities Having Jurisdiction

(a) Definition

An Authority Having Jurisdiction (AHJ) refers to a state or local government, HOA, or other organization responsible for enforcing the requirements of a property-related code or standard including state law and local ordinance.

(b) Standard

Mortgagees are not exempt by HUD policy from adhering to state and local laws relating to the P&P of Properties securing FHA-insured Mortgages.

The Mortgagee must review the AHJ requirements, including those relating to occupancy of the Structures, to determine applicability for repair or remediation prior to conveyance of the Property to HUD.

Where state or local law inhibits the Mortgagee performing HUD's required Property (P&P) actions, such as connecting or disconnecting utilities, the Mortgagee must send the MCM notice of the restriction on the Property P&P action and a proposal on how the Mortgagee will otherwise protect the Property from damage.

Where the AHJ requires additional or more extensive P&P actions than required by HUD for conveyance, the Mortgagee may submit an over-allowable request via P260. The Mortgagee must upload with its request all documentation supporting the proposed additional work requirements and expenses necessary for compliance.

(c) Required Documentation

Where state or local law inhibits the Mortgagee performing HUD's required Property (P&P) actions, the Mortgagee must note the restriction in the Claim Review File and include a copy of the notice to the MCM, the MCM's approval or denial of the Mortgagee's proposal, and the applicable state, local, or AHJ requirement.

(6) Photograph Requirements

(a) Standard

The Mortgagee must use digital photography to document:
- the condition of the Property at the FTV Property Inspection and any damage identified; and
- the before and after conditions of the Property when performing Property P&P actions.

The Mortgagee must ensure a date stamp is printed within each photograph and labeled accordingly with a description of the contents of the photograph.

(b) Required Documentation

The Mortgagee must take and upload before and after photographs into P260 for each claimed Property P&P expense.

(7) Securing and Maintaining the Property

(a) Standard

The Mortgagee must secure the Property to prevent unauthorized entry and protect against weather-related damage, and must visibly display 24-hour emergency telephone contact information in a weather-tight location on a window or door or as otherwise required by an AHJ.

(i) Locksets

Where the Property has been conveyed to the Mortgagee after the foreclosure sale, the Mortgagee must:
- ensure that the lockset on the main entranceway remains secured; and

- re-key or replace all locksets on all secondary external entranceways and secure interior doorways, including attached garages and basements.

When rekeying, the Mortgagee must re-set all locksets at the Property to a random identical key code and document the key code in in the "Mortgagee's comments" of Part A of form HUD-27011. If locksets cannot be replaced or re-keyed or are antique or architectural locksets, the Mortgagee may utilize alternative methods to secure the door and prevent damage to the hardware or door.

(ii) Exterior Doors

The Mortgagee must secure all exterior doors. For exterior sliding glass doors, the Mortgagee must latch these doors and install or provide slider locks, anti-lift blocks, security bars, or another secondary security mechanism.

The Mortgagee must not brace, nail shut, or otherwise block or damage the door. If no other locking mechanism exists, the Mortgagee must board/secure access doors, pet doors, and other panels providing access to basements and crawl spaces, where permitted by state or local law.

(iii) Garage/Overhead Doors

The Mortgagee must secure the garage or overhead doors by:
- using existing locksets at garage/overhead doors if they can be re-keyed to the random identical key code for the Property;
- securing the garage/overhead doors with a padlock and hasp if no other locking mechanism exists;
- repairing or replacing inoperable garage doors; and
- disconnecting automatic garage door openers, if present, and leaving any remote keys or transmitters securely in the Property.

(iv) Outbuildings

The Mortgagee must secure sheds and outbuildings by:
- reusing and re-keying existing locksets at sheds and outbuildings to the dwelling key code, if possible;
- securing shed and outbuilding doors with a padlock and hasp if no other locking mechanism exists; and
- boarding/securing the outbuildings, if no doors or other securing mechanism exists. The Mortgagee may convey with boarded/secured outbuildings and sheds without prior approval.

(v) Windows and Glazing

The Mortgagee must secure all windows by:
- employing or installing locking mechanisms on all windows;
- removing all broken glass debris from the interior and exterior of the Property; and
- replacing broken or cracked window glazing. Where the AHJ requires replacement of dual-pane, tempered, thermal-sealed or other specialized glazing in kind, the Mortgagee must obtain prior over-allowable approval from the MCM.

The Mortgagee must not brace, nail shut, or otherwise block or damage the windows.

(vi) Boarding/Securing of Property Openings

Re-Securing due to Vandalism or Unauthorized Property Access

The Mortgagee must re-secure and re-glaze windows, doors, and other access openings when the Property has been vandalized or accessed without authorization.

Boarding/Securing Required by the AHJ

The Mortgagee may secure windows, doors, and other access openings by boarding/securing if required by an AHJ and may convey with such boarding/securing in place.

Boarding/Securing where Unable to Secure by Other Methods

The Mortgagee may request approval from the MCM to board/secure openings that cannot be protected by any other method or where an imminent safety hazard exists, and to convey with boarding in place.

All boarding/securing materials that are leased or rented for the Mortgagee's convenience must be removed prior to conveyance of the Property to HUD.

(b) Roof Assembly Repair

The Mortgagee must ensure that all roof assemblies, including those securing attached garages, porches and patios, detached garages and any secondary structures associated with the origination collateral, and related weatherproofing are free of active leaks or other sources of water intrusion.

When a roof assembly leak is discovered, the Mortgagee must immediately repair the roofing system and mitigate further damage. The Mortgagee may provide such temporary repairs as tarping or patching until the permanent repair or replacement can be installed. The Mortgagee must ensure that permanent repairs or replacements, with materials matching or similar in color and material type, have been completed prior to conveyance to HUD. The Mortgagee is not required to obtain prior HUD approval for temporary repairs for which costs do not exceed the temporary roof repair line item allowable amount.

(c) Pools, Hot Tubs and Spas

(i) In-Ground Pools, Hot Tubs and Spas

Mortgagees must secure all in-ground swimming pools, hot tubs, and spas as required by local laws, codes and ordinances. The Mortgagee must:
- secure the pool, hot tub, and/or spa with a removable safety cover anchored to the pool deck or, if a cover cannot be anchored to the pool deck, board or otherwise secure the pool, hot tub, and/or spa; and
- secure and repair any fences around the pool, hot tub, and/or spa to restrict access.

The Mortgagee must not drain operational in-ground pools. If the pool is empty, it is not necessary to re-fill the pool. The Mortgagee must drain hot tubs or spas located indoors or outdoors.

The Mortgagee must perform monthly maintenance and chemical treatments for operational pools. Where the Mortgagee must repair or drain the pool to mitigate damage or safety hazards, the Mortgagee must submit an over-allowable request.

(ii) Above-Ground Pools

Mortgagees must secure all above-ground swimming pools as required by local laws, codes and ordinances. In addition to local requirements, the Mortgagee must:
- drain the pool;
- secure the pool with a removable cover; and
- secure and repair any fences around the pool in order to restrict access.

Where the above-ground pool is in poor condition or cannot be secured, the Mortgagee must:
- remove the above-ground pool and any built-up decking; and
- remediate any resulting depression in the ground that may constitute a hazard.

(iii) Ponds or Gardens

The Mortgagee must drain, if feasible, or cover any small backyard ponds, water gardens, or other water features.

(d) Drainage Systems and Basements

The Mortgagee must re-attach, replace, repair and clear of debris existing roof drainage and foundation drainage systems. If no drainage system exists at the time of the FTV Property Inspection, the Mortgagee is not required to provide or install new systems.

The Mortgagee must ensure that downspouts provide positive drainage away from the structure and that gutters are cleared and do not prevent drainage.

If the FTV Property Inspection reveals basement flooding, the Mortgagee must drain or pump the basement, identify the water sources, and make other such repairs to prevent equipment damage, mold and organic growth, and structural and material damage.

(e) Mold, Fungus, Discoloration and Related Moisture Damage and Organic Growth

(i) Standard

When mold or related moisture damage is found in the Property during the FTV Property Inspection, the Mortgagee must mitigate the source of the moisture to prevent further damage. HUD will not reimburse costs related to mold or organic growth abatement if it determines that such mold or organic growth is due to Mortgagee Neglect. The Mortgagee must thoroughly document the condition and scope of the moisture damage at the FTV Property Inspection.

(ii) Over-Allowable Request

The Mortgagee must submit an over-allowable request to the MCM for approval in the following circumstances:
- initial efforts to eliminate the mold or organic growth and to remove moisture are ineffective and additional treatments are needed to remove moisture and prevent mold and moisture damage; or
- the mold or organic growth poses a potential health and safety hazard.

Where the mold or organic growth poses a potential health or safety hazard, the Mortgagee must provide with its request:

- a written report and/or any lab reports or other testing data supporting the health or safety hazard determination;
- photographs of the discoloration;
- dimensions of the affected areas;
- a description of the initial mitigation efforts, including the basis for the selection of the method used;
- the proposed scope of work for the abatement; and
- at least two bids from licensed or certified mold remediation or hazardous materials contractors.

(f) Debris Removal, Cleaning, and Minor Repair

The Mortgagee must ensure that all interior and exterior debris is removed from the Property, including attics, basements, barns, storage spaces, and outbuildings, and that the Property is in Broom-swept Condition. The Mortgagee may request reimbursement for the storage or disposition of any Personal Property removed from the Property when such storage and disposition is required by the AHJ.

(i) Equipment, Fixtures, and Appliances

The Mortgagee must ensure that all equipment, fixtures, and appliances present at the FTV Property Inspection and associated with origination collateral remain in the Property, unless approved by HUD for disposal.

The Mortgagee must empty and wipe clean the interior of all refrigerators and freezers. The Mortgagee must secure exterior clothes dryer vents and similar openings to prevent entry of pests. The Mortgagee must ensure that bathtubs, sinks and toilets are cleaned and emptied.

(ii) Graffiti

The Mortgagee must remove or cover with similar or matching color all exterior and interior graffiti on all structures and fencing.

(iii) Exterior Debris

The Mortgagee must ensure that the Property is free of external debris by removing all vehicles, boats, trailers, any unsafe or hazardous structures, and other Personal Property, as allowed and in accordance with state and local law requirements.

The Mortgagee may allow to remain in place affixed Personal Property in sound and usable condition that may add value to the Property, such as fountains, children's play structures, sheds, ramadas, pergolas, or gazebos.

(iv) Fences

The Mortgagee must ensure that fences and gates present at the FTV Property Inspection are maintained in secure and upright condition, with no missing panels or sections.

(v) Pests

The Mortgagee must ensure that the Property is free of animals, vermin, and insect infestation and that any dead animals, vermin, and insects are removed from the Property.

When the Mortgagee determines the Property is infested with pests and that the infestation and removal may constitute a health or safety hazard, the Mortgagee may obtain professional pest control services; otherwise, the Mortgagee may employ over-the-counter pest control products.

When evidence of live wood boring insects is discovered, the Mortgagee must request an over-allowable for an inspection by a professional pest control service, and provide the report and treatment recommendations for over-allowable consideration to abate.

(vi) Floors and Walkways

The Mortgagee must ensure that interior walking surfaces are safe or otherwise patched, replaced, or repaired to be free of hazards as follows:
- any floor finishes, including carpeting, sheet vinyl, wood, laminate, ceramic or vinyl tiles, and all tack strips and fittings that are damaged, loose, or otherwise hazardous, must be removed. The Mortgagee is not required to replace these finishes once removed; and
- holes or openings in interior walking surfaces must be patched, replaced, or repaired. Weak or spongy flooring must be inspected and, if needed, repaired to address hazardous conditions with an approved over-allowable.

The Mortgagee must repair damaged or missing handrails or stair treads on elevated exterior porches, patios, decks, and balconies where the distance from the finished floor to the ground surface is greater than 18 inches. If repair is not feasible, the Mortgagee must provide temporary rails, fencing, or other means to prevent or mitigate falls.

(vii) Regulated Hazardous Materials

The Mortgagee must handle and dispose of hazardous materials regulated by federal, state, or local law in accordance with those laws.

Where removal of hazardous materials exceeds HUD's reimbursable amounts for debris removal, the Mortgagee must submit an over-allowable request prior to incurring those costs. The Mortgagee must include with the request:

- the relevant code or regulation describing the specific handling or disposal requirements;
- if testing is required to confirm the presence of hazardous materials, detailed reports or test results, with information on the location of the materials, the scope of the work, and recommended methods for removal, abatement or remediation of the materials; and
- at least two bids from licensed or certified hazardous materials contractors.

(8) Yard Maintenance and Snow Removal

(a) Definitions

Grass Cuts are the Property P&P actions of mowing, weeding, edge trimming, sweeping of all paved areas, and removing all lawn clippings, related cuttings, and debris.

(b) Standard

The Mortgagee is responsible for maintaining lawn and yard areas and trees, shrubs, and vines in compliance with AHJ requirements by performing Grass Cuts.

The Mortgagee must ensure that yards are maintained as follows:
- Grass must be cut to a maximum of two inches in height.
- Grass and weeds must be cut to the edge of the property line, and trimmed around foundations, bushes, trees, and planting beds.
- Grass, trees, tree limbs, shrubs, and other vegetation that are obstructing the public right of way must be trimmed or removed.
- Desert, xeriscape, or rock scape landscaping maintenance must be maintained through removal or spraying of weeds, grass trimming or cutting, and the removal of related cuttings and incidental debris.
- Dead trees or tree limbs that pose a safety hazard or may potentially damage the Property must be removed or trimmed.

(c) Grass Cuts

(i) Standard

The Mortgagee must complete initial and ongoing Grass Cuts and desert landscaping according to the timelines set in the Grass Cut Schedule.

Should a Property require earlier or more frequent Grass Cuts or desert landscaping maintenance due to specific micro-climate conditions or other property requirements, the Mortgagee must perform such cuts or landscaping.

If additional or more frequent Grass Cuts are required as a result of code violations or neighbor complaints, the Mortgagee must submit to the MCM a request to exceed the allowable amount and documentation supporting the amended timeline.

(ii) Required Documentation

Should a Property require earlier or more frequent Grass Cuts or desert landscaping maintenance due to specific micro-climate conditions or other property requirements, or if additional or more frequent Grass Cuts are required as a result of code violations or neighbor complaints, the Mortgagee must include in the Claim Review File documentation supporting the Mortgagee's amended timeline.

(d) Shrubs

The Mortgagee must trim shrubs and remove cuttings once in a growing season, between April 1 and October 31.

(e) Snow Removal

The Mortgagee must ensure that the Property is safe and accessible throughout the winter season by:
- removing snow from the entire entryway, public and other front yard walkways, porch and driveway following a minimum three-inch accumulation; and
- complying with local codes and ordinances governing the removal of snow and ice.

(f) HOA Yard Maintenance

If an HOA or condominium association provides for the yard maintenance and snow removal actions, the Mortgagee must not order duplicate yard maintenance and snow removal actions.

(9) Winterization Requirements

(a) Time Frame for Winterization

The Mortgagee must winterize the Property once, according to the Winterization Schedule. All Properties located in the State of Alaska must be continuously winterized at all times.

Where earlier or extended winterization is required due to specific micro-climate conditions or other property requirements, the Mortgagee must perform such winterization and include in the Claim Review File documentation supporting the Mortgagee's amended winterization timeline.

Where the initial winterization is no longer effective, the Mortgagee must re-winterize the Property and include in the Claim Review File documentation demonstrating the need to re-winterize.

(b) Utilities

(i) Standard

The Mortgagee must turn all utilities off unless:
- prohibited by state or local law;
- required to remain on per HOA or condominium association requirements;
- the Property is an attached unit or a dwelling with shared systems such as a row house or townhouse;
- required to remain on to protect the Property;
- required to operate equipment such as sump pumps, swimming pools, wells, dehumidifiers, or other equipment or systems required to remain in operation; or
- where the Mortgagee determines that utility disconnection fees and charges make it cost-effective to maintain utility service rather than disconnect the service.

The Mortgagee must ensure that active piping and exposed electrical wiring is capped, valved, or otherwise terminated.

If utilities remain on, the Mortgagee must note in the Claim Review File the reasons for maintaining utility service and, if applicable, include a copy of the state or local requirement for maintaining utility service.

(ii) Condominiums and Attached Dwellings

The Mortgagee may permit utilities to remain on in Properties where the utilities are shared with other units or attached dwellings.

(iii)Sump Pumps

The Mortgagee must ensure that all installed or required sump pumps are in-place, operational, and working at all times, where state or local law permits electricity to remain on. The Mortgagee must repair or replace any non-functioning or missing equipment.

(iv) Utility Accounts

The Mortgagee must retain all utility accounts in its name until conveyance of the Property to HUD.

In states where utilities should remain on, if there is any reason to believe that a Borrower may abandon a Property, the Mortgagee must contact the utility company to request notification of non-payment of utilities so that utilities can be transferred to the Mortgagee's name if the Borrower vacates the Property.

(v) Propane and Oil Systems

In those jurisdictions requiring heat to remain on, the Mortgagee must put a "KEEP FULL" contract on with a local supplier when the Property has a propane or oil heating system. Otherwise, the Mortgagee must ensure that active piping is capped, valved, or otherwise terminated and all fuel tanks are emptied.

(vi) Domestic Water

The Mortgagee must not cut water lines or remove water meters, unless required by the AHJ.

(vii)   Wells

If the water supply is a private well, the Mortgagee must:
- turn off the well at the breaker panel;
- secure the breaker;
- disconnect and cap, valve, or otherwise terminate the water supply line between the Property and pressure tank;
- install a hose bib on the pressure tank side of the breaker, tagging the hose bib "For Water Testing;"
- drain all pressure tanks;
- drain pump housing if the pump is surface-mounted;
- disconnect the check valve and drain all pump, suction, and discharge pipes, if the pump is submersible; and
- winterize all fixtures.

(viii)   Water, Plumbing, and Heating Systems

The Mortgagee must:
- shut off or disconnect the domestic water supply at the curb; for private wells the Mortgagee shall turn off the well at the breaker panel and disconnect the water supply line between the Property and pressure tank;

- drain all plumbing and heating systems; and
- ensure that all toilets are cleaned and emptied.

Where a toilet or other plumbing fixture has been compromised by an unauthorized entry or wastewater backflow, the Mortgagee must complete re-winterization and cleaning.

(c) Winterization of Swimming Pools

During the winterization period, the Mortgagee must drain all lines and filters and secure and maintain operational swimming pools to prevent damage.

(d) Additional Winterization Requirements for Properties located in Alaska

In addition to the winterization requirements described above, the Mortgagee must ensure that for all properties located in the State of Alaska:
- the heat remains on, with the thermostat set at 55 degrees Fahrenheit; and
- all utilities remain connected and in working order, where permitted by state or local law.

(e) Responsibility for Damage Due to Freezing

The Mortgagee is responsible for any damage to plumbing and heating systems, sump pumps, and wells caused by untimely, inadequate, or improper maintenance or winterization.

HUD will consider any damage caused by freezing and not documented at the FTV Property Inspection to be the responsibility of the Mortgagee and not reimbursable by HUD.

(10) Demolition

If the Mortgagee proposes to demolish or remove a primary dwelling structure, a significant section of the structure or a secondary structure that is associated with the origination collateral, the Mortgagee must request approval from the MCM to demolish and convey as a vacant lot. The Mortgagee is not required to request HUD approval to demolish damaged or unusable sheds and outbuildings that were not included in the property value at origination. For requests to demolish a primary dwelling structure, the Mortgagee must submit to the MCM:
- a BPO analysis estimating the value of the Property as-is and as a vacant lot;
- proposed demolition costs; and
- a detailed chronology of the servicing and Property P&P activities related to the Property, including all efforts to address any damages or violations.

Where a local jurisdiction mandates demolition of a Property after foreclosure, the Mortgagee must provide the following to the MCM immediately upon discovery of the demolition order:

- copies of all notices pertaining to demolition orders and hearings; and
- inspection reports and photographic documentation establishing the condition of the Property when the Mortgagee first entered or took possession of the Property.

The MCM will advise the Mortgagee as to whether to proceed with the demolition or to postpone the demolition until after conveyance to HUD.

(a) Requests Less than Five Business Days before Conveyance

The MCM will reject any requests received less than five business days before the end of the time frame to convey to HUD, unless the Mortgagee can demonstrate that it had received the demolition notification with insufficient time to make a request by the five business day deadline.

(b) Cost of Demolition

The cost of demolition is not included in the maximum cost limit per Property.

(c) Damage due to Mortgagee Neglect

If HUD determines that the damage to the Property is due to Mortgagee Neglect, the Mortgagee is responsible for the cost to demolish the Property. The MCM will determine the acceptance of the vacant lot.

(D) Conveyance of Damaged Properties

(1) Conveyance without Prior HUD Approval

The Mortgagee may convey Properties without prior written approval when:

- the Property is in conveyance condition, with no Surchargeable Damage; and
- the aggregate of all allowable Property P&P expenses does not exceed the Maximum Property Preservation Allowance and claimed P&P costs do not exceed the line item Property Preservation Allowances.

(2) Conveyance Requiring HUD Approval

(a) Request to HUD

The Mortgagee must request and obtain approval from the MCM before conveyance under any of the following circumstances:

- conveyance of a Property damaged while under the control of the Mortgagee or as a result of Mortgagee Neglect;

- conveyance of a Property with unrepaired insurable damage and insurance repair proceeds;
- conveyance of a Property as-is with unfinished renovations, violations, liens, or other outstanding state law and local code compliance issues; and
- demolition and/or conveyance of a vacant lot.

(b) Required Documentation for Request

In its request to convey the damaged Property, the Mortgagee must include the following documentation:
- the date of vacancy;
- evidence validating the property condition at vacancy;
- supporting documentation including inspection reports, photographs, repair bids, and receipts;
- a chronology of actions performed by the Mortgagee to preserve and protect the Property;
- for damaged Properties with approval to convey with insurance proceeds, all related damage reimbursement funding, including insurance deductibles, recoverables, and depreciation; and
- for Properties with unfinished renovations, violations, liens, or other outstanding state and local law compliance issues:
  - the BPO showing the value of the Property as-is and the value with repairs completed;
  - copies of violations, liens, or relevant state or local law;
  - hazard insurance claim information;
  - a detailed description of the reason(s) that the Mortgagee cannot feasibly repair or secure the Property, proposed actions or actions taken, and a detailed repair estimate of the damages; and
  - a detailed estimate of cost to repair the Property.

If no documentation or inadequate documentation is received from the Mortgagee, HUD will attribute all damage to the Mortgagee.

(3) Mortgagee Failure to Obtain Required HUD Approval

If the Mortgagee fails to obtain HUD approval when required, prior to conveying a damaged Property, HUD may:
- reconvey the Property;
- require a reduction to the claim for insurance benefits:
  - the hazard insurance recovery or HUD's estimate of the cost of repairing damage; or
  - the cost to repair and restore the Property to required conveyance condition; or
- take other such action as permitted by regulation.

Handbook 4000.1
Effective Date: 03/14/2016 | Last Revised: 07/10/2019
*Refer to the online version of SF Handbook 4000.1 for specific sections' effective dates

709

(4) Appeal of Surchargeable Damage Decision

The Mortgagee may appeal a surchargeable request decision via P260. The Mortgagee may submit an additional appeal to HUD via P260. The second appeal decision is final and no further appeals will be accepted.

(E) Hazard Insurance Recovery

The Mortgagee must take all appropriate action to recoup all available hazard insurance proceeds, including recoverable depreciation.

(1) Extension of Time to Convey Title to HUD

Where conveyance of title to HUD jeopardizes the Mortgagee's ability to receive hazard insurance proceeds, the Mortgagee must request an extension of time from the MCM, providing a specific reason why the extension is warranted.

(2) Reimbursement for Recoverable Depreciation

The Mortgagee must seek reimbursement for any recoverable depreciation after repairs have been completed; all damages must be repaired prior to conveyance.

(3) Recovery for Vandalism or Theft

(a) Standard

If there is evidence of vandalism or theft resulting in damage or missing built-in appliances, equipment, or fixtures, the Mortgagee must file a claim to obtain all available insurance proceeds for damages to the Property.

Unless the Mortgagee obtains HUD approval to convey with unrepaired insurable damage and insurance repair proceeds, the Mortgagee must use these insurance proceeds funds or corporate funds to fully repair or replace the structures, appliances, equipment, or fixtures damaged.

(b) Required Documentation

The Mortgagee must document in the Claim Review File all relevant claim correspondence with the insurance company.

(F) Requests for Pre-Conveyance Inspection

(1) Definition

A Pre-Conveyance Inspection is an inspection performed by HUD, at the Mortgagee's request, before conveyance to determine if a Property meets HUD's conveyance standards.

(2) Standard

The Mortgagee may request a Pre-Conveyance Inspection of a Property that has sustained damage due to Borrower neglect or Surchargeable Damage, and not Mortgagee Neglect.

(3) Submission of Pre-Conveyance Inspection Request

The Mortgagee may submit a request for a Pre-Conveyance Inspection to the MCM before the deed to HUD is recorded or sent for recording and before the submittal of a claim.

(4) HUD Review of Request

The MCM will review the request to determine whether a Pre-Conveyance Inspection is needed and may consider the following criteria in its decision:
- The Property has completed over-allowable repairs exceeding $10,000.
- The Property is affected by re-occurring vandalism and the Mortgagee is requesting approval to convey the Property as-is to HUD.
- The Property has code violations and the Mortgagee is requesting approval to convey the Property as-is to HUD.
- The Property is located in a PDMDA and has completed repairs exceeding $10,000.
- The Property has an insurable claim with completed repairs exceeding $5,000.
- The Property has unrepaired Borrower neglect damage affecting mechanical, electrical, plumbing, or structural system integrity.
- The Property has uninsurable and unfinished renovations and the Mortgagee is requesting approval to convey the Property as-is to HUD.

(5) Pre-Conveyance Inspection

If the request for the Pre-Conveyance Inspection is approved, the MCM will order the Pre-Conveyance Inspection from HUD's Field Service Manager (FSM), who will contact the Mortgagee to coordinate the inspection. Upon completion of the inspection, the FSM will provide an inspection report indicating:
- whether the Property is in conveyance condition; or
- which further actions the Mortgagee must take to place the Property into Acceptable Conveyance Condition.

The Mortgagee must ensure that all required actions identified on the Pre-Conveyance Inspection report are completed before conveyance to HUD.

iii. Condition of Title

The Mortgagee must convey good and marketable title to the Secretary.

HUD regulations list certain specific and common exceptions to title to which HUD will not object. HUD may waive additional objections, based on local practice and the general marketability of title clouded by those objections, or if the Mortgagee is willing to accept a reduced claim for mortgage insurance benefits.

(A) Liens

HUD will not accept title subject to liens, other than the following.

(1) IRS Liens

HUD will not object to title where there is a lien in favor of the IRS, regardless of its position, if the following conditions are met:
- The IRS has been notified of the foreclosure.
- The IRS lien was established after the date of the mortgage lien.
- The Mortgagee bid at least the full amount of the indebtedness plus the cost of foreclosure.

(2) Section 235 Liens

HUD will accept title subject to a junior lien securing the repayment of Section 235 assistance payments.

(3) PACE Obligation

HUD will allow a notice of lien recorded in the land records securing repayment of a PACE obligation that may only become subject to an enforceable claim (i.e., a lien) for delinquent regularly scheduled PACE special assessment payments and otherwise complies with the eligibility and acceptability criteria for Properties encumbered with a PACE obligation provided in Section II.A.1.b.iv(A)(6) of the prior *SF Handbook* published in December 2016.

(B) Payment of Taxes

(1) Taxes at Conveyance

(a) Standard

Prior to the conveyance of a Property to HUD, the Mortgagee must satisfy all taxes and special assessment, including any PACE assessments:
- That are due and payable prior to or on the date of conveyance; or
- due and payable within 30 Days after the date of conveyance.

(b) Required Documentation

The Mortgagee must:

- certify that all available tax and assessment bills due at conveyance and within 30 Days of conveyance are paid as of the date of conveyance;
- document such payment and identify the most recent period for which taxes were paid in Item 32, "Schedule of Tax Information," of form HUD-27011, Part A; and
- upload to P260 documentation, such as a paid receipt or a copy of the Mortgagee's tax payment history screen, validating that such payment was made.

The Mortgagee must also retain invoices, paid bill receipts, or other proof of payment in the Claim Review File.

(2) Tax Penalties

When late fees and/or interest penalties are incurred a result of the Mortgagee's failure to pay taxes prior to conveyance, HUD will not reimburse the Mortgagee for late fees and/or interest penalties paid by the Mortgagee, and the Mortgagee must reimburse HUD for any late fees and/or interest penalties paid by HUD.

(3) Mortgagee Failure to Pay Taxes, Late Fees, and/or Interest Penalties

Where taxes, late fees and/or interest penalties are owed to the taxing authority when a Property is conveyed to HUD, HUD may elect to:
- Reconvey the Property back to the Mortgagee; or
- refuse to accept the conveyance.

(C) Payment of HOA/Condominium Fees

(1) Definitions

A Homeowners' Association (HOA)/Condominium Assessment is a periodic payment required of property owners by an HOA or condominium association.

HOA/Condominium Fees include HOA/Condominium Assessments plus interest, Late Charges, collection/attorney fees, and other penalties.

(2) Standard

Prior to the conveyance of a Property to HUD, the Mortgagee must pay HOA/Condominium Fees that are due and that become due within 30 Days of the date of conveyance. While the payment of Condominium and HOA Fees is the Borrower's responsibility, Mortgagees must ensure that Properties conveyed to HUD have clear title.

The Mortgagee must take the following actions:

- provide notice of foreclosure proceedings to HOAs/condominium management companies;
- unless prohibited by state law, ensure that outstanding HOA/Condominium Fees are included as part of the foreclosure proceedings in the event that the HOA/condominium management company does not pursue these amounts in foreclosure;
- negotiate the amount required to obtain a release of outstanding HOA/Condominium Fees;
- obtain a release of outstanding HOA/Condominium Fees;
- ensure that the HOA/condominium lien, if any, is removed from the title to the Property prior to conveying the Property to HUD; and
- pay the HOA/Condominium Assessment required under applicable law before conveyance to HUD, where HOA/Condominium Fees do not survive foreclosure or result in a lien on the Property.

(3) Required Documentation

The Mortgagee must document the payment of all final bills and pre- and post-foreclosure liens for HOA/Condominium Fees in the "Mortgagee's Comments" section of form HUD-27011, Part A.

Within 15 Days of conveyance, the Mortgagee must upload to P260 the paid HOA/condominium invoice and any other documentation necessary to verify that the Mortgagee made such payments prior to conveyance, and, if applicable, document any common area requirements associated with gaining access to the Property.

(4) Lack of Information on HOA or Condominium Association Assessments and Fees

(a) Standard

On a case-by-case-basis, at its sole discretion, HUD may accept conveyances where the Mortgagee has requested and has been unable to obtain sufficient information on HOA/Condominium Fees to resolve them prior to conveyance.

(b) Required Documentation

The Mortgagee must request a variance through HUD's MCM by submitting:
- a certification stating that the Mortgagee has exhausted all methods of obtaining and paying the outstanding HOA/Condominium Assessments; and
- documentation evidencing its attempts to obtain and pay these assessments and fees as follows:
  - at least three phone calls;

○ certified mail notices to HOA/condominium contacts from the Mortgagee's attorneys; and

○ documentation validating the pursuit of available legal remedies and evidencing the resolution or final decisions resulting from arbitration or court proceedings.

(D) Payment of Water and Sewer Bills and Other Assessments

(1) Standard

The Mortgagee must retain utility accounts including electricity, gas, home heating oil, water, and sewer in its name until conveyance of the Property to HUD.

Prior to the conveyance of a Property to HUD, Mortgagees must research, obtain, and pay all available utility bills that may become a lien attached to a Property after foreclosure as follows:

- In states where utilities are not required to remain on to protect the Property, Mortgagees must obtain and pay a final bill up to the date of conveyance.
- In states where utilities are required to remain on, Mortgagees must pay:
  ○ all available bills that are due prior to conveyance; and
  ○ within 60 Days after the date of conveyance, the final bill calculated to the Day on which utilities are transferred to HUD.

(2) Required Documentation

For Properties in states where utilities are not required to remain on to protect the Property, no later than 60 Days after conveyance, the Mortgagee must upload to P260 the paid invoice and any other documentation necessary to verify that the Mortgagee made such payments.

For Properties in states where utilities are required to remain on, the Mortgagee must upload to P260 the paid invoices and any other documentation necessary to verify that the Mortgagee made the payment for the final bill.

(3) Failure to Pay Utility Bills

If the Mortgagee fails to pay utility bills, HUD, at its sole discretion, may:

- issue a Notice of Non-Compliance and demand payment from the Mortgagee in an amount sufficient to satisfy any liens or encumbrances, including penalties and interest, which prevent or delay a sale; or
- Reconvey the Property to the Mortgagee.

iv. Notice of Property Transfer

The Mortgagee must notify the Commissioner on the date the deed to the Secretary is filed for recording, by:
- filing form HUD-27011 in FHAC; and
- submitting a copy to HUD's MCM.

v. Submission of Title Evidence for Conveyance to HUD

(A) Submission of Title Evidence to the MCM

(1) Standard

The Mortgagee must submit to HUD's MCM via P260 the following documentation reflecting ownership vested in the name of the Secretary no more than 45 Days after the date the deed is filed for record:
- original title evidence;
- a copy of form HUD-27011, Part A;
- a copy of the mortgage instrument, containing a complete legal description of the Property; and
- a copy of the recorded deed.

(2) Extension to the Deadline to Submit Title Evidence

To request an extension to the deadline to submit title evidence, the Mortgagee must:
- submit a request for an extension via P260 before the expiration of the 45-Day time frame; and
- provide documentation supporting the reason for the request.

(B) Title Evidence

The Mortgagee must provide one of the following types of title evidence of recorded title to the Secretary. The Mortgagee may also submit similar evidence of title that conforms to the standards of a supervising branch of the federal, state, or territory government.

(1) Fee or Owner's Title Policy

The Mortgagee may submit:
- a fee or owner's policy of title insurance, in the name of the Secretary and inuring to the benefit of the Secretary's successors in office;
- a guaranty or guarantee of title; or
- a certificate of title, issued by a title company, duly authorized by law and qualified by experience to issue such instruments.

(2) Mortgagee Policy of Title Insurance

The Mortgagee may submit a Mortgagee's policy of title insurance supplemented by an Abstract and an Attorney's Certificate of Title covering the period after the Closing Date. The Mortgagee must ensure that, under the terms of the policy, the liability of the title company will continue in favor of the Secretary after title is conveyed to them.

(3) Abstract and Legal Opinion

The Mortgagee may submit:
- an abstract of title, prepared by an abstract company or individual engaged in the business of preparing abstracts of title; and
- a legal opinion as to the quality of the title. The Mortgagee must ensure that this legal opinion is prepared and signed by an attorney experienced in examination of titles.

(4) A Torrens or Similar Title Certificate

The Mortgagee may submit a Torrens or similar title certificate.

(C) Title Evidence for Manufactured Housing

(1) Standard

In title evidence for Manufactured Housing, the Mortgagee must include evidence that:
- the Manufactured Home is attached to the land; and
- the Manufactured Home is classified and taxed as real estate.

The Mortgagee must ensure that all state or local requirements for proper purging of the title have been met.

(2) Required Documentation

The Mortgagee must:
- upload the title evidence into P260 on or before the filing date of form HUD-27011, Part A; and
- certify in the "Mortgagee's Comments" section of form HUD-27011, Part A that the required additional title work has been completed and uploaded.

(D) HUD Review of Title Evidence

The MCM will review the title evidence and notify the Mortgagee of its approval or rejection of the title evidence or if additional information is needed.

If the Mortgagee does not receive a response from the MCM regarding its title evidence submission within five business days and title evidence is later rejected, the Mortgagee may request that the Government Technical Representative (GTR) grant an extension of time.

(E) HUD Requests for Additional Title Information

If HUD requests additional title information, the Mortgagee must provide this information within 10 Days of the request to avoid rejection of the title evidence.

If title evidence is later approved after the submission of additional information, HUD will provide the Mortgagee with a title approval letter showing the "Date Title Received" as the date the Mortgagee resubmitted the complete title evidence.

(F) Return of the Original Title Evidence to the Mortgagee

If there is a title defect in the initial title package, the Mortgagee may request the return of the original title package from the MCM so that the title company may reissue a corrected policy.

vi. Responsibility for Property at Conveyance

The Mortgagee is responsible for the Property until all HUD regulatory requirements leading to conveyance have been complied with, including:
- filing for record the deed to the Secretary of HUD; and
- filing form HUD-27011 in FHAC for claim processing and payment.

The Mortgagee remains responsible for the Property and any loss or damage thereto should the claim be suspended due to the need for review or correction of a hard edit error, notwithstanding the filing of the deed to the Secretary.

(A) Damage at Inspection at or after Conveyance

HUD will presume that any damage discovered during HUD's first inspection of the Property after conveyance occurred while the Mortgagee had possession, unless the Mortgagee is able to provide evidence to the contrary.

(B) Expenses Incurred at or after Conveyance

Without the express written approval of the MCM, the Mortgagee must not incur expenses for P&P of the Property or for eviction of the occupant on or after the date the deed is filed for record.

HUD will not reimburse P&P or property-related expenses incurred after the deed has been recorded in HUD's name, other than payment of certain utility bills or HOA payments.

(C) Cancellation of Hazard Insurance

The Mortgagee must request the hazard insurance be canceled as of the date the deed is filed for record. The Mortgagee may calculate the amount of the return premium due on a short-rate basis.

vii. Extension of Time for Conveyance

(A) Standard

To request an extension to the deadline to convey the Property to HUD, the Mortgagee must:

- submit a request for an extension via P260 before the expiration of the time frame; and
- provide documentation supporting the reason for the request.

(B) Required Documentation

The Mortgagee must maintain a copy of the written response from the HUD representative in the Mortgagee's Claim Review File.

(C) Appeal of Extension Decision

The Mortgagee may appeal a decision on a request for an extension via P260 for review by the MCM. The Mortgagee may submit an additional appeal via P260 for review by HUD. HUD's decision is final and no further appeals will be accepted.

viii. HUD Acceptance of Conveyance

HUD considers a Property conveyed by the Mortgagee to HUD when:

- the Mortgagee has deeded the Property to HUD; and
- HUD accepts conveyance of the Property, as evidenced by the payment of Part A of the claim from HUD to the Mortgagee. For suspended claims, the Mortgagee remains responsible for the Property, and any loss or damage thereto, notwithstanding the filing of the deed to the Secretary for record, and such responsibility is retained by the Mortgagee until HUD regulations have been fully complied with.

ix. Reconveyance

(A) Definition

A Reconveyance is a conveyance of a Property from HUD back to the Mortgagee due to the Mortgagee's failure to comply with HUD's conveyance requirements.

(B) Standard

If a Mortgagee fails to fully comply with the terms of the insurance contract, including HUD's conveyance requirements, HUD may:
- Reconvey title to the Mortgagee; and
  - o cancel the Mortgagee's claim for insurance benefits; and
  - o request reimbursement for expenses incurred for acquisition, holding and Reconveyance, less any income received from the Property, from the date the deed to HUD was filed for record to the date of Reconveyance; or
- enter into a Reconveyance Bypass Agreement with the Mortgagee.

The Mortgagee may reapply for insurance benefits.

u. Deficiency Judgments

Where the mortgaged Property is sold at the foreclosure sale for less than the unpaid balance of the debt, HUD may seek a deficiency Judgment, unless prohibited by the terms of the Mortgage.

i. HUD-required Deficiency Judgments

(A) Mortgages Insured On or After March 28, 1988

For Mortgages insured pursuant to Firm Commitments issued on or after March 28, 1988, or pursuant to direct endorsement processing when the Mortgagee's underwriter signed the credit worksheet on or after March 28, 1988, HUD may require the Mortgagee to pursue a deficiency Judgment. Where HUD requires the Mortgagee to pursue a deficiency Judgment, HUD will provide the Mortgagee with instructions and with its estimate of the FMV of the Property, less adjustments. Upon receipt of such notification, the Mortgagee must:
- tender a bid at the foreclosure sale in that amount; and
- attempt, in accordance with state law, to obtain a deficiency Judgment.

(B) Mortgages Insured Before March 28, 1988

For Mortgages insured pursuant to Firm Commitments issued before March 28, 1988, or pursuant to direct endorsement processing when the Mortgagee's underwriter signed the credit worksheet before March 28, 1988, HUD may request the Mortgagee to pursue a deficiency Judgment.

ii. Procedures for Claims Without Conveyance of Title

Unless specifically requested by FHA, the Mortgagee is not required by FHA to pursue any deficiency Judgments in connection with CWCOT procedures.

iii. Assignment of Judgments

(A) When Filing a Claim for Insurance Benefits

The Mortgagee must assign deficiency Judgments to HUD and transmit the Judgment to the NSC no later than 30 Days after the Judgment was obtained, if the Mortgagee filed a claim for mortgage insurance benefits.

(B) When Not Filing a Claim for Insurance Benefits

The Mortgagee may engage in Judgment collection activities if a claim for FHA insurance benefits is not filed.

3. Programs and Products

a. Adjustable Rate Mortgages

See Section 251 Adjustable Rate Mortgages (ARM) for information on originating ARMs.

i. Definitions

The Change Date is the effective date of an adjustment to the interest rate, as shown in Paragraph 4(A) of the model Adjustable Rate Note form.

The Initial Index Figure is the most recent figure available before the Closing Date of the Mortgage.

The Current Index Figure is:
- the most recent index figure available 30 Days before the date of each interest rate adjustment, for Mortgages closed before January 10, 2015; and
- the most recent figure available 45 Days before the date of each interest rate adjustment, for Mortgages closed on or after January 10, 2015.

ii. Adjusting the Interest Rate on an ARM

To set the new interest rate on an ARM annually, the Mortgagee must review the mortgage documents containing interest rate provisions, and:
- determine the change between the Initial Index Figure and the Current Index Figure; or
- add a specified margin to the Current Index Figure.

Once the new adjusted interest rate is calculated, the Mortgagee must provide notice of the change to the Borrower.

(A) Determining the Current Index Figure on an ARM

The table below describes the Current Index Figure to use based upon the particular day of the week on which the 30th Day falls.

When the 30th Day falls on a ...	AND the 30th Day prior to a Change Date...	Then use the index figure issued on...
Monday that is a business day	and the issue date of an H.15 release both occur on the same day (that is, they both occur on a Monday)	that Monday.
Monday that is a federal holiday	falls on a Monday that is a federal holiday	the prior week.
day of the week other than Monday	n/a	the Monday of that week (or issued on Tuesday, if Monday is a federal holiday).

(B) Determining the Calculated Interest Rate on an ARM

The calculated interest rate is the current index plus the margin (the number of Basis Points (bps) identified as "margin" in Paragraph 4(C) of the model Adjustable Rate Note), rounded to the nearest 1/8th of one percentage point (0.125 percent).

(C) Determining the New Adjusted Interest Rate on an ARM

To determine the new adjusted interest rate, the Mortgagee must compare the calculated interest rate to the existing interest rate in effect for the preceding 12 months.

(1) Calculated Rate is Equal to Existing Rate

If the calculated interest rate is equal to the existing interest rate, then the new adjusted rate will be the same as the existing interest rate.

(2) Calculated Rate is Less than Existing Rate

If the calculated interest rate is less than the existing interest rate, then the new adjusted rate will be:
- the calculated interest rate for 1-, 3-, and 5-year ARMs if the calculated interest rate is less than one percentage point higher or lower than the existing interest rate; or
- the calculated interest rate for 5-, 7-, and 10-year ARMs if the calculated interest rate is less than two percentage points higher or lower than the existing interest rate.

(3) Calculated Rate is More than Existing Rate

If the calculated interest rate is more than the existing interest rate, then the new adjusted rate will be:

- limited to one percentage point higher or lower than the existing interest rate for 1-, 3-, and 5-year ARMs, if the new calculated interest rate is more than one percentage point (100 bps) higher or lower than the existing interest rate. (Note: index changes in excess of one percentage point may not be carried over for inclusion in an adjustment in a subsequent year); or
- the calculated interest rate for 5-, 7- and 10-year ARMs, if the calculated interest rate is more than two percentage points (200 bps) higher or lower than the existing interest rate. (Note: index changes in excess of two percentage points may not be carried over for inclusion in an adjustment in a subsequent year).

(D) Interest Rate Adjustments over the Term of the ARM

The Mortgagee must not adjust the interest rate over the entire term of the Mortgage resulting in a change in either direction of more than:

- five percentage points (500 bps) from the initial contract interest rate for 1-, 3-, and 5-year ARMs; or
- six percentage points (600 bps) for 5-, 7-, and 10-year ARMs.

(E) Effective Date of the ARM Interest Rate Adjustment

The adjusted interest rate is effective on the Change Date and remains in effect until the next Change Date.

During the term of the Mortgage, the Change Date must fall on the same date of each succeeding year.

iii. Computing the Monthly Installment Payment after an ARM Adjustment

The Mortgagee must determine a new monthly payment each time there is an interest rate adjustment. The Mortgagee must calculate the portion of the monthly payment attributable to P&I by:

- determining the amount necessary to fully amortize the unpaid principal balance for the remaining term of the Mortgage;
- crediting all eligible prepayments; and
- not debiting any delinquency.

To calculate the monthly installment, the Mortgagee must use the scheduled principal balance that would be due on the Change Date, but reduced by the amount of any prepayments made to the principal.

All ARM adjustments affect interest rates only; negative amortization is not permitted.

iv. ARM Adjustment Notices

(A) Standard

At least annually and before any adjustment to a Borrower's monthly payment may occur, the Mortgagee must provide written notification regarding the adjustment.

(1) Time Frame

(a) For Mortgages Closed Before January 10, 2015

If the notice follows an adjustment in the monthly payment, the Mortgagee must provide the Borrower notice:

- at least 25 Days before any adjustment; or
- at least 30 Days before the adjustment if the mortgage agreement contains a provision stating that 30-Day requirement.

(b) For Mortgages Closed On or After January 10, 2015

The Mortgagee must provide notice in compliance with the time frames set out in TILA.

(2) Required ARM Notice Content

The content of the Adjustment Notice must advise the Borrower of:

- the new mortgage interest rate;
- the amount of the new monthly payment;
- the current index interest rate value; and
- how the payment adjustment was calculated.

(3) Sending the ARM Adjustment Notice

The Mortgagee must send the Adjustment Notice to the Borrower:

- by Certified Mail, return receipt requested; or
- by first-class mail to all property owners identified on its records.

(B) Required Documentation

The Mortgagee must retain the following in the servicing file:

- evidence that timely notice was sent to the Borrower; and
- annual adjustment computations for the mortgage term.

(C) Failure to Provide the ARM Adjustment Notice

If the Mortgagee fails to provide notice to the Borrower for more than one year, then the Mortgagee must determine an adjusted interest rate for each omitted year, in order to determine the adjusted interest rates for subsequent years, and perform the following:

(1) Interest Rate Increase

If the Mortgagee's calculations result in an increase of the interest rate, the Mortgagee has forfeited their right to collect the increased amount and the Borrowers are relieved from the obligation to pay the increased payment amount.

(2) Interest Rate Decrease

If the Mortgagee's calculations result in a decrease of the interest rate, the Mortgagee must refund the excess, plus interest from the date of the excess payment to the date of repayment at a rate equal to the sum of the margin and index in effect on the Change Date.

The Mortgagee must first apply any refund to any existing delinquency, and if excess funds remain, the Mortgagee must, at the Borrower's request:
- provide the Borrower with a cash refund; or
- apply the remaining excess to the unpaid principal balance of the Mortgage.

(D) Errors in the ARM Adjustment Notice

HUD requires that errors be corrected if:
- the Mortgagee miscalculates the interest rate and/or the monthly payment; and
- the errors are reflected in the notice.

v. Commencement of Monthly Payment after ARM Adjustment

After the Mortgagee gives the Borrower proper notice of the adjustment, the Borrower will begin paying the new monthly payment 30 Days after the Change Date.

vi. Assumptions of ARMs

In addition to sending the applicable Notice to Homeowner, Release of Personal Liability in Assumptions, the Mortgagee must attach a copy of the original ARM Disclosure Statement that established the index, margin, and the Change Date.

b. Assumptions

i. Assumability of FHA-Insured Mortgages

All FHA-insured Mortgages are assumable. The Mortgagee must not impose, agree to, or enforce legal restrictions on conveyances or assumptions after closing except when:
- specifically permitted by HUD regulations; or
- the restriction had been specified in a junior lien granted to the Mortgagee after settlement.

The Mortgagee must review the mortgage documents to determine what restrictions have been placed on the Mortgage.

ii. Notice to Homeowner

The Mortgagee must send the applicable Notice to Homeowner: Release of Personal Liability to:
- all applicants for FHA-insured Mortgages, before settlement; and
- sellers or buyers who request information on HUD's creditworthiness review criteria or procedures for assumptions or releases from personal liability.

iii. Fees for Assumptions

(A) Allowable Charges Separate from Assumption Processing Fees

The Mortgagee may charge the assuming Borrower reasonable and customary fees not to exceed the actual costs for third party expenses incurred in connection with assumption processing:
- non-refundable fees for credit reports and verifications of employment; and
- up to $45.00 for fees for the preparation and execution of release of liability forms (form HUD-92210.1, *Approval of Purchaser and Release of Seller*), where a Borrower requests an executed release of liability form as evidence that the Borrower was released during a previous creditworthiness review.

(B) Refund of Assumption Processing Fees

In the event a Mortgage is not assumed, Mortgagees must refund one-half of its processing fees if the assumptor's credit is approved, but assumption does not occur for reasons beyond the control of the assumptor.

(C) Change of Hazard Insurance

The Mortgagee may not assess a fee for processing the assumptor's request to change hazard insurance coverage when the existing policy has not yet expired.

(D) Section 143 of the Internal Revenue Code of 1986

The Mortgagee must not charge the Borrower any additional fees for ensuring that assumptions of mortgage revenue bond Mortgages comply with requirements of the Internal Revenue Code (IRC).

iv. Notification to HUD of Changes

The Mortgagee must notify HUD via FHA Connection (FHAC) of assumptions:
- within 15 Days of any change of Borrower; or
- within 15 Days of the date the Mortgagee receives actual or constructive knowledge of the transfer of ownership.

v. Payment of Partial Claim Due to Assumption

When the Borrower no longer owns the Property, the Partial Claim becomes due and payable.

At the time of the assumption, the Mortgagee must acquire an official Partial Claim payoff letter from HUD's Servicing Contractor.

vi. Exercise of Due-on-Sale Clause

When a prohibited sale or transfer of the Property occurs, the Mortgagee must enforce the due-on-sale clause by:
- requesting approval from the National Servicing Center (NSC) via fax to accelerate the Mortgage, provided that acceleration is permitted by law; and
- accelerating the Mortgage if approval is granted.

vii. Acceleration of the Mortgage

(A) Requests for Acceleration

The Mortgagee may request approval from the NSC to accelerate Mortgages for assumptions made:
- without credit approval; or
- where HUD assumption requirements are not met and the Borrower cannot or will not comply with HUD's requirements at the time the assumption is discovered.

(B) Acceleration not Permitted

The Mortgagee may not accelerate for the assumptions when:
- acceleration for assumption without credit approval is prohibited by state law;
- the seller retains an ownership interest in the Property; or
- the transfer is by devise or descent.

viii.   Communication with Borrowers Regarding Assumptions

Upon any inquiry by a seller regarding HUD's assumption requirements or upon learning that an assumption has occurred, the Mortgagee must:

- attempt to obtain the forwarding address of the selling Borrower;
- advise the selling Borrower to update the mailing address as needed; and
- advise the selling Borrower that any existing PACE obligation that will remain with the Property must be fully disclosed to the buyer in accordance with applicable law (state and local) and made part of the sales contract.

ix. Reporting of Defaults on Assumed Mortgages to Consumer Reporting Agencies

If an assumed Mortgage goes into Default, the Mortgagee must not report these Defaults to consumer reporting agencies for former Borrowers, whether those Borrowers remain legally liable for the mortgage debt or have been released from liability. The Mortgagee should notify any Borrowers that remain liable for the mortgage debt that the assumed Mortgage is in Default.

c. Presidentially-Declared Major Disaster Areas

i. Disaster Declarations

Under the Robert T. Stafford Disaster Relief and Emergency Assistance Act, the President has authority to declare a major disaster for any area which has been affected by damage of sufficient severity and magnitude to warrant major disaster assistance. Disaster Declarations and information regarding available federal assistance for each disaster incident are posted on the Federal Emergency Management Agency's (FEMA) website.

Whenever the President declares a major disaster, the Mortgagee must implement the procedures set forth in this section for each designated area that is eligible for federal disaster assistance.

ii. Moratorium on Foreclosures

(A) Standard

FHA-insured Mortgages secured by Properties located in Presidentially-Declared Major Disaster Areas (PDMDA) will be subject to a moratorium on foreclosures following the Disaster Declaration. The foreclosure moratorium is:
- effective for a 90-Day period beginning on the date of the Disaster Declaration for that area (HUD may communicate further specific guidance for extension of moratorium periods for individual disasters);
- applicable to the initiation of foreclosures and foreclosures already in process; and
- considered an additional period of time approved by HUD for the Mortgagee to take loss mitigation action or commence foreclosure.

The Mortgagee may submit a request for an extension to HUD's foreclosure-related deadlines via HUD's Extensions and Variances Automated Requests System (EVARS) when prohibited from performing a required activity due to the foreclosure moratorium.

(B) Required Documentation

The Mortgagee must retain in its Claim Review File any approved extensions from HUD related to a foreclosure moratorium.

(C) Hazard or Flood Insurance Settlement

The Mortgagee must take no action to initiate or complete foreclosure proceedings, after expiration of a disaster-related foreclosure moratorium, if such action will jeopardize the full recovery of a hazard or flood insurance settlement.

iii. Monitoring of Repairs to Substantially Damaged Homes

(A) Definition

A building is considered to be "Substantially Damaged," as defined in the National Flood Insurance Program (NFIP) regulations, when "damage of any origin is sustained by a structure whereby the cost of restoring the structure to its before damaged condition would equal or exceed 50 percent of the market value of the structure before the damage occurred."

(B) Standard

The Mortgagee must take appropriate actions to ensure that repairs to Substantially Damaged Properties comply with the federal building elevation standards, including those established by FEMA. The Mortgagee must ensure compliance with any higher applicable building elevation standard adopted by the state or local government.

iv. Loss Mitigation for Borrowers in PDMDAs

Should Presidentially-Declared Major Disasters adversely impact a Borrower's ability to make on-time Mortgage Payments, the Mortgagee must provide the Borrower with forbearance and HUD loss mitigation assistance, where appropriate, as provided in applicable FHA policy guidance.

(A) Loss Mitigation Owner-Occupant Requirement

The Mortgagees must not deny a Borrower any Loss Mitigation Option solely for failure to occupy a mortgaged Property if the following conditions are met:
- the mortgaged Property is located within a PDMDA;
- the dwelling was the Principal Residence of a Borrower immediately prior to the disaster event;
- a Borrower intends to re-occupy the mortgaged Property upon restoration of the home to habitable condition; and
- the total accumulated mortgage arrearages have not exceeded the equivalent of 12 months Principal, Interest, Taxes, and Insurance (PITI).

(B) Forbearance Options for Disaster-Affected Borrowers

Before considering an affected Borrower for a permanent solution utilizing one of FHA's Loss Mitigation Home Retention Options, the Mortgagee must first evaluate the Borrower for a forbearance, which allows for one or more periods of reduced or suspended payments without specific terms of repayment.

The Mortgagee may offer forbearance relief to a Borrower with a mortgaged Property or place of employment located within a PDMDA as follows.

(1) Informal Forbearance for Borrowers in PDMDAs

The Mortgagee may consider Borrowers in PDMDAs for an Informal Forbearance and may offer additional Informal Forbearance periods if the foreclosure moratorium is extended.

(2) Formal Forbearance for Borrowers in PDMDAs

The Mortgagee may consider Formal Forbearances for Borrowers in PDMDAs while they are pursuing home repairs and/or resolving verifiable financial difficulties related to the disaster, provided that:
- the forbearance period does not exceed the estimated time needed to complete home repairs as supported by a contract or repair estimate; and
- the total accumulated mortgage arrearages during the forbearance period does not exceed the equivalent of 12 months PITI.

(C) Loan Modification without a Financial Evaluation

For Borrowers who receive Informal or Formal Forbearances based solely on location of their mortgaged Property or place of employment within a PDMDA, the Mortgagee must offer Rate and Term modifications at the conclusion of the forbearance period based on the following criteria.

(1) Eligibility for Loan Modification without Financial Evaluation

The Mortgagee must ensure that Borrowers and their FHA-insured Mortgages meet the following eligibility requirements for a Loan Modification without a financial evaluation:
- The Mortgage was current or less than 30 Days past due as of the date of the applicable Disaster Declaration.
- The Mortgagee obtains a Verification of Employment (VOE) confirming that the Borrower's employment status is the same as prior to the disaster.
- Home damages have been repaired.
- The dwelling is owner-occupied.

(2) Terms of the Loan Modification

The Mortgagee must modify the Mortgage as follows:
- The total monthly Mortgage Payment, or PITI, on the modified Mortgage must be less than or equal to the existing payment on the FHA-insured Mortgage.
- The Borrower must successfully complete a three-month Trial Payment Plan (TPP).
- The Mortgagee must capitalize into a modified mortgage balance:
  - the accumulated arrearages for unpaid accrued interest; and

- eligible unreimbursed Mortgagee advances and related fees and costs chargeable to the Mortgage.
- The Mortgagee waives late fees if the Borrower satisfies all conditions of the TPP.
- The Mortgagee extends the term of the Mortgage to 360 months from the modification effective date.
- The Mortgagee sets the interest rate at the Market Rate as defined by HUD.

(D) Required Financial Evaluation for other Loss Mitigation Home Retention Options

Following evaluation for and completion of approved forbearances, the Mortgagee must evaluate eligible Borrowers for other Loss Mitigation Home Retention Options.

(1) Borrower Eligibility

The Mortgagee must evaluate for other Loss Mitigation Home Retention Options for those Borrowers who meet one of the following criteria:
- Borrowers who are not eligible for the "Loan Modification without a Financial Evaluation" Option;
- Borrowers eligible for "Loan Modification without a Financial Evaluation" who are experiencing a continuation of lower income or higher living expenses following the disaster; and
- Borrowers eligible for "Loan Modification without a Financial Evaluation" who do not successfully complete the required TPP.

Borrowers who do not currently have an increase in living expenses but are Delinquent due to a forbearance received following a Disaster Declaration are deemed to satisfy the eligibility conditions for FHA Loss Mitigation Home Retention Options.

(2) Use of Loan Modification Option

The Mortgagee must ensure that the Borrower repairs home damages and occupies the dwelling as an owner-occupant before completing the Loan Modification.

(E) Home Disposition Options

Being located in a disaster area does not automatically preclude the mortgage Property from the availability of Home Disposition Options.

(F) Suspension of Reporting to Consumer Reporting Agencies

The Mortgagee must suspend reporting of delinquencies to consumer reporting agencies for a Borrower who is granted disaster-related Mortgage Payment relief and is otherwise performing as agreed, unless such reporting is required for a Loan Modification.

(G) Waiver of Late Charges

The Mortgagee must waive Late Charges as long as the Borrower is on a Forbearance Plan or paying as agreed on a Loss Mitigation Option.

d. Hawaiian Home Land Mortgages (Section 247 Mortgages)

i. Reporting of Delinquent Mortgages

(A) Standard

The Mortgagee must report in SFDMS the Delinquency/Default Status Codes that accurately reflect the stage of delinquency or mortgagee action.

In addition, the Mortgagee must notify the State of Hawaii Department of Hawaiian Home Lands (DHHL) each month of:
- which Section 247 insured Mortgages on Leaseholds of Hawaiian Home Lands are 30 or more Days Delinquent on the last Day of the month, and
- the status of Mortgages that were reported as Delinquent the previous month.

(B) Contact Information for Submission of Reports

The Mortgagee may use form HUD-92068-A, *Monthly Delinquent Loan Report*, completed in FHAC, to meet its DHHL reporting requirements. The Mortgagee must submit the information by the fifth business day following the close of each month to:

Department of Hawaiian Home Lands
Loan Services Branch
P.O. Box 1879
Honolulu, Hawaii 96805
Attn: FHA Insured Section 247

(C) HUD's Loss Mitigation Program

The Mortgagee may offer the following Loss Mitigation Options to eligible Borrowers with Section 247 Mortgages:
- SFB-Unemployment; and
- FHA-HAMP Loan Modifications.

If the resultant front-end ratio of the modified Mortgage is greater than 40 percent, the Borrower is not eligible for loss mitigation.

Due to Hawaii state law prohibitions on the placement of junior liens on Properties secured by Section 247 Mortgages, the Mortgagee must not use Partial Claims with Section 247 Mortgages.

ii. Assignment of Section 247 Assignments

(A) Standard

The Mortgagee may assign the Delinquent insured Mortgage and Note to HUD if all of the following conditions are met:

- the Mortgage has been in Default for 180 Days or more;
- when the Mortgage is 90 Days Delinquent, the Mortgagee has notified DHHL of the Default in writing;
- the Mortgagee has attempted a face-to-face interview with the Borrower at least 30 Days before the application for assignment is submitted, unless exempt; and
- the Mortgagee has evaluated the Borrower for loss mitigation in accordance with HUD guidance.

The Mortgagee must not foreclose on or approve a PFS or DIL transaction on Section 247 Mortgages; the only disposition option available to the Mortgagee is assignment.

(B) Endorsement on Original Note

To assign the Note to HUD, an authorized agent of the Mortgagee must sign the following endorsement on the original Note: "All right, title and interest of the undersigned to the within credit instrument is hereby assigned to the Secretary of Housing and Urban Development of Washington, D.C., their successors and assigns."

(C) Lost Note Affidavit

If the original Note cannot be located, the Mortgagee must submit the Lost Note Affidavit.

iii. Submission of Title Evidence Package and Servicing Records for Assignment

(A) Standard

At the time of the filing of its claim for insurance benefits, the Mortgagee must submit the title evidence and servicing records package to HUD at:

Associate Regional Counsel - Hawaii
Office General Counsel
U.S. Department of HUD
611 W. Sixth Street, 13th Floor
Los Angeles, CA 90017

The Mortgagee must include with its title evidence package:
- a transmittal letter; and
- servicing records.

(1) Transmittal Letter

The Mortgagee must include with its assignment package a transmittal letter indicating the name and telephone number of the person HUD is to contact for more information about the submission.

(2) Title Evidence Package

The Mortgagee must ensure that the Title Evidence Package contains all of the documents listed in the checklist below:
- Title Evidence Package Checklist;
- original Note endorsed to HUD in the format required by form HUD-27011, Part A;
- original Mortgage with evidence of recordation by DHHL;
- recorded Consent to Mortgage signed by DHHL;
- recorded intervening assignments of Mortgage, if any;
- recorded Assignment of Mortgage (AOM) to HUD with required warranty;
- copy of Borrower's Homestead Lease and recorded Lease Assignments and Amendments, if any; and
- recorded Mortgage Insurance Program Rider to the Homestead Lease.

(3) Servicing Records

The Mortgagee must submit to HUD the following servicing records:
- copies of form HUD-27011;
- copy of Title Submission Certification;
- proof of request to endorse fire policy;
- mortgage history commencing from date of first payment;
- copy of signed Management Review Checklist, plus all supporting servicing records;
- initial DHHL notification letter; and
- evidence of loss mitigation efforts.

(B) Field Office Counsel Review

After review of the title documents, Honolulu Field Office Counsel will either:
- issue a title approval letter to the submitting Mortgagee and forward the assignment package to the NSC for servicing review and final approval; or
- if the title documents contain deficiencies, issue a title deficiency letter providing the Mortgagee 30 Days to cure such deficiencies.

iv. Reconveyance to Mortgagee

If the claim has been paid and HUD does not accept assignment of the Mortgage and Note, HUD will:
- reassign the Mortgage to the Mortgagee, and
- request repayment of the claim amount.

If the claim has not yet been paid, HUD will return the submitted documents to the Mortgagee.

e.   Insured Mortgages on Indian Land (Section 248 Mortgages)

Face-to-Face Interviews

The Mortgagee must have a face-to-face interview with the Borrower or make a reasonable effort to arrange a face-to-face interview no later than the 61st Day of delinquency, unless exempt under the <u>Face-to-Face Meetings Not Required</u> section.

i.   Face-to Face Meetings Not Required

The Mortgagee is not required to conduct a face-to-face interview if:
- the Borrower does not live in the mortgaged Property;
- the Borrower has clearly indicated that they will not cooperate with a face-to-face interview; or
- the Borrower's payment is current due to an agreed-upon repayment plan or Forbearance Plan.

ii.   Reasonable Effort in Arranging a Face-to-Face Interview

(A) Standard

In addition to the <u>reasonable effort standards</u> for all FHA-insured Mortgagees, the Mortgagee must make at least one telephone call to the Borrower to arrange a face-to-face interview.

(B) Required Documentation

The Mortgagee must document in its servicing file all attempts in contacting the Borrower to arrange a face-to-face interview.

iii.   Information Provided to the Borrower

(A) Standard

The Mortgagee must inform the Borrower of the following:
- that HUD will make information regarding the status and payment history of the Borrower's Mortgage available to local credit bureaus and prospective creditors;
- other available mortgage assistance, if any; and
- the names and contact information of HUD officials to whom further communications may be addressed.

(B) Required Documentation

The Mortgagee must note in its servicing file when and how the Borrower was informed of the information above.

f. Section 222 Mortgages

Authority for Mortgages insured under Section 222 of the National Housing Act was repealed on July 30, 2008. The following policies apply for existing Section 222 Mortgages, for which Mortgage Insurance Premiums (MIP) are paid by the servicemember-Borrower's branch of the military service until the servicemember's eligibility is terminated.

i. Requirements for Section 222 Mortgages

(A) Military Branch Responsibility

The military branch is responsible for payment of MIP on a Section 222 Mortgage when the Borrower is:

- a certified servicemember at the time of application; and
- the owner of the Property at the time of FHA endorsement.

(B) Establishing Eligibility

The servicemember-Borrower must submit the original and two copies of a written certification of a servicemember's eligibility, issued by the servicemember's commanding or personnel officer, with their application for mortgage insurance under Section 222. The respective service branch determines benefits eligibility.

ii. Transfers to Section 222

If the original Mortgage is insured under another section of the National Housing Act, the servicemember may request to transfer the insured Mortgage to Section 222.

(A) Transfer Requests

A servicemember requesting transfer of an insured Mortgage to Section 222 must provide the Mortgagee with the original and two copies of a written certification of a servicemember's eligibility, issued by the servicemember's commanding or personnel officer.

(B) Forwarding Documents

If in agreement with the transfer, the Mortgagee must forward these copies with a letter requesting transfer of the Mortgage to the following address:

U.S. Department of Housing and Urban Development
Insurance Operations Division
Attention: Systems Management Branch
Washington, DC 20410

The Mortgagee must pay MIP until notified by the FHA Comptroller that the request to transfer has been completed.

iii. Sale of a Property Covered by a Section 222 Mortgage

When a servicemember-Borrower sells the mortgaged Property, the Mortgagee must complete a Mortgage Record Change in FHAC.

(A) Sale of Mortgaged Property to Another Eligible Servicemember

If a mortgaged Property is sold to another eligible servicemember who assumes the Section 222 Mortgage, the Mortgagee must request from the assumptor written certification from their service branch of their eligibility for a Section 222 Mortgage.

If the Mortgagee fails to provide this certification to HUD when requesting insurance, HUD will hold the Mortgagee, and not the service branch, responsible for payment of MIP. The Mortgagee should continue to collect premiums from the servicemember-Borrower and pay the premiums to FHA.

(B) Collection of MIP from Servicemember Assumptor

When a mortgaged Property is sold to another eligible servicemember who will assume the Section 222 Mortgage, the Mortgagee must continue to collect premiums from the assumptor until advised by FHA that the service branch will be responsible for future premiums.

If the Mortgagee has been paying the MIP as a result of prior termination of the service branch's responsibility for payment of premiums, the Mortgagee must continue to collect premiums from the servicemember-Borrower and pay the premiums to FHA.

iv. MIP Payments upon Notice of Termination

Under Section 222, HUD does not require the Mortgagee to collect MIP from the Borrower or to remit premiums to FHA until advised by FHA that the service branch will no longer pay the premiums.

When FHA is notified that the mortgaged Property has been sold or that the servicemember has been discharged, retired, or has died, FHA will:
- request confirmation from the service branch of the termination of MIP; and
- notify the Mortgagee to begin collecting MIP from the servicemember-Borrower.

v. Continued Payment of MIP by Service Branch When Servicemember Dies on Active Duty

The service branch is responsible for determining continued eligibility of servicemember-Borrowers. If a servicemember-Borrower dies while on Active Duty and is survived by a spouse, the service branch will be responsible for the following:
- continuing to pay MIP on the Mortgage until two years after the servicemember's death or until the spouse disposes of the Property, whichever occurs first;

- notifying FHA when eligibility terminates; and
- paying MIP until confirmation of the termination is received by the FHA Comptroller. FHA will notify the Mortgagee of its responsibility for payment of the MIP.

vi. Loss Mitigation for Section 222 Mortgages

The Mortgagee must evaluate all applicable Loss Mitigation Options for Section 222 Mortgages.

g. Good Neighbor Next Door

i.   Owner-Occupancy Term

The Good Neighbor Next Door (GNND) participant must live in the Property as their sole residence for an owner-occupancy term of 36 months, beginning on one of the following dates:

- 30 Days after closing if the home requires no more than $10,000 in repairs before occupancy;
- 90 Days after closing if the home requires more than $10,000, but not more than $20,000 in repairs; or
- 180 Days after closing if the home requires more than $20,000 in repairs prior to occupancy.

(A) Annual Certification

(1) Standard

GNND participants must certify on form HUD-9549-D, *Good Neighbor Next Door Sales Program*, every year of the owner-occupancy term that they are living in the Property.

HUD's Loan Servicing Contractor will mail form HUD-9549-D to the GNND participant. The GNND must sign, date, and return the form according to the instructions in the letter.

(2) Failure to Return Certification

If the GNND participant fails to complete and return the annual certification, HUD will take action to determine whether the GNND participant still meets program requirements. These actions include, but are not limited to:

- referral to an investigator, who may perform an on-site visit to verify the occupancy of the Property; and
- referral to HUD's Office of Inspector General (OIG) for further investigation and possible prosecution.

(B) Term Interruption Requests

When the GNND participant requires an interruption to the owner-occupancy term, the Borrower may request approval for a term interruption from HUD.

The GNND participant must submit a written and signed request at least 30 Days before the anticipated interruption to HUD's Servicing Contractor. The request must include the following information:

- the reason(s) why the interruption is necessary;
- the dates of the intended interruption; and
- a certification that:

- o the GNND participant is not abandoning the home as their permanent residence; and
- o the GNND participant will resume occupancy of the home upon the conclusion of the interruption and complete the remainder of the 36-month owner-occupancy term.

(C) Active Duty Military Service

Eligible GNND program participants who are also military service members protected by the SCRA are not required to submit their written request to HUD 30 Days in advance of an anticipated interruption, but must submit their written request as soon as practicable upon learning of a potential interruption.

HUD may grant exceptions to the occupancy requirement for participants who are called to Active Duty service. These participants must notify the NSC when Active Duty military service would require temporary relocation outside of the commuting area of the Property purchased under the GNND program.

(D) Failure to Complete Owner-Occupancy Term

If the GNND participant sells their home or stops living in the home as their sole residence prior to the expiration of the owner-occupancy term, they will owe HUD the amount due on the second Mortgage as of the date the Property is either sold or vacated.

ii. Second Mortgage and Note Servicing

HUD's Servicing Contractor is responsible for the servicing of GNND second Mortgages.

GNND Participants must submit requests for subordinations, pay-off amounts, mortgage releases, or other servicing information to HUD's Servicing Contractor.

(A) Subordinations

To request subordination of a GNND Mortgage, the GNND participant, or the Closing Agent responsible for closing the new Mortgage must:
- contact HUD's Loan Servicing Contractor to receive a Subordination Information Sheet; and
- submit the required documentation, as listed in the Subordination Information Sheet, to HUD's Loan Servicing Contractor.

(B) Payoffs

To pay off a GNND Mortgage before the expiration of the owner-occupancy term, the GNND participant must mail or fax to HUD's Loan Servicing Contractor a request for a Payoff, including the following information:

- GNND participant's name;
- full property address;
- estimated date of Payoff;
- name, address, telephone number, and return fax number of the Entity requesting the Payoff; and
- signed permission of the GNND participant to collect this information.

(C) Releases

At the end of the required owner-occupancy term, HUD will release the GNND second Mortgage as long as all of the following conditions are met:
- The GNND participant has completed and returned the required annual certifications.
- The GNND participant is not currently under investigation by OIG.
- The GNND participant is in compliance with all GNND regulations.

HUD's Loan Servicing Contractor will prepare this release and file the mortgage satisfaction with the GNND participant's local county recorder's office.

Handbook 4000.1
Effective Date: 03/14/2016 | Last Revised: 07/10/2019
*Refer to the online version of SF Handbook 4000.1 for specific sections' effective dates

743

h. HOPE for Homeowners

The Housing and Economic Recovery Act of 2008 amends the National Housing Act to authorize the temporary Homeownership and Opportunity for People Everywhere (HOPE) for Homeowners Program (also referred to as the H4H Program). Under the program, a Borrower facing difficulty paying their Mortgage will be eligible to refinance into an affordable FHA-insured Mortgage. The H4H Program was effective for endorsements on or after October 1, 2008, through September 30, 2011.

i. HUD Contact

Mortgagees should contact HUD's Servicing Contractor for questions related to servicing or satisfaction of H4H Exit Premium Mortgages (EPM).

ii. Annual Premium

The Mortgagee must collect the annual premium at 0.75 percent of the Base Loan Amount. The Mortgagee must follow standard FHA guidelines for the cancellation of the annual premium.

iii. Voluntary Termination of Mortgage Insurance

The Borrower and Mortgagee may mutually request termination of mortgage insurance. The Borrower will not receive a refund of any UFMIP received by HUD and will remain obligated for the exit premium and appreciation Mortgages.

iv. Sale and Payoff

Upon sale or other disposition of the Property securing an H4H Mortgage, the Borrower must satisfy HUD's equity interest, if not already satisfied through refinance. HUD is entitled to its respective percentage of the initial equity amount as stated in the EPM, even if there are no net proceeds or if net proceeds are negative.

Upon receipt of a payoff request, HUD's Servicing Contractor will calculate the payoff amount for its equity interest and issue a payoff demand to the Closing Agent.

v. Refinancing

HUD will permit the refinancing of an H4H Mortgage subject to the requirements established in this section. In the event of any refinance of the H4H Mortgage, the Borrower must pay to HUD its full equity interest as stated in the EPM.

HUD will permit the refinancing into another conventional loan product no earlier than 12 months from the date of closing on the H4H Mortgage. The Borrower may refinance if:

- the refinance results in a 30-year amortizing fixed rate Mortgage with a Principal and Interest (P&I) payment that is lower than the P&I payment due on the existing H4H Mortgage;
- the proceeds from the refinance are sufficient to pay off the percent of initial equity due to HUD; and
- the cash received by or on behalf of the Borrower is limited to the Borrower's applicable percentage of initial equity created by the H4H Mortgage, as stated in the EPM, any earned equity the Borrower has accrued, and any appreciation.

vi. Default and Loss Mitigation

The Mortgagee may utilize HUD's Loss Mitigation Program for H4H Mortgages, subject to the following special considerations.

(A) FHA-HAMP Loan Modifications

HUD will subordinate the EPM to the modification of an H4H Mortgage completed in accordance with HUD's Loss Mitigation Program.

(B) FHA-HAMP Partial Claim

For a Partial Claim Note, HUD does not require subordination of the EPM.

(C) Pre-Foreclosure Sale

The Mortgagee must include the total dollar amount of the EPM in the total debt calculation for the negative equity ratio calculations.

(D) Deed-in-Lieu

HUD will accept a DIL subject to the EPM lien.

vii. Exit Premium

(A) Definition

Initial equity is the lesser of:
- the appraised value at the time of the H4H loan origination less the original principal balance on the H4H Mortgage; or
- the outstanding amount due under all existing mortgages less the original principal balance on the H4H Mortgage.

(B) Standard

In the event of refinance, sale, or other disposition, HUD is entitled to receive the following percentage of initial equity:

Year	% of equity to be paid to FHA
During Year 1	100% of equity
During Year 2	90% of equity
During Year 3	80% of equity
During Year 4	70% of equity
During Year 5	60% of equity
After Year 5	50% of equity

i. Nehemiah Housing Opportunity Grants Program

Title VI of the Housing and Community Development Act of 1987 established the Nehemiah Housing Opportunity Grants Program (NHOP), which authorized HUD to make grants to nonprofit organizations enabling them to provide Mortgages to families purchasing homes constructed or substantially rehabilitated in accordance with a HUD-approved program. The program was funded by Congress in 1989, 1990, and 1991. It is no longer an active program as grant funds were exhausted in April 1991. HUD's Servicing Contractor handles the satisfaction of liens still outstanding from this program.

j. Servicing FHA-Insured Mortgages for Servicemember-Borrowers

i. Servicemembers Civil Relief Act

The Servicemembers Civil Relief Act of 2003 (SCRA) as amended by Public Law 108-189, effective December 19, 2003, provides legal protections and debt relief for persons in Active Duty military service. The following protections apply to the servicing of FHA-insured Mortgages:

- mortgage relief;
- termination of leases;
- protection from eviction;
- 6 percent cap on interest rates;
- stays of proceedings; and
- reopening Default Judgments.

(A) Relief Provisions for the Military

SCRA provides legal protections and debt relief for persons in Active Duty military service the criteria for which are established in 50 U.S.C. App. § 3911. Dependents of servicemembers are entitled to protection in limited situations. "Dependents" is also defined in 50 U.S.C. App. § 3911.

(B) Obligations and/or Liabilities Prior to Entering into Active Military Service

(1) Interest Rate Cap

(a) Standard

Obligations or liabilities incurred by a servicemember and/or servicemember's spouse jointly before entering into active military service must not bear interest at a rate in excess of 6 percent per year during the period of military service and one year thereafter (unless superseded by updates to the SCRA Act), in the case of an obligation or liability consisting of a Mortgage, trust deed, or other security in the nature of a Mortgage.

(b) Required Documentation

The Mortgagee must apply the interest rate cap if it receives from the servicemember the documents listed below no later than 180 Days after the date of the servicemember's termination or release from military service:

- a written notice;
- a copy of military orders calling the servicemember to military service; and
- orders further extending military service, if any.

(c) Mortgagee Implementation

The Mortgagee must limit interest to 6 percent per year effective the date on which the servicemember is called to military service. Only a court may grant exceptions if the ability of the servicemember to pay interest upon the obligation or liability at a rate in excess of 6 percent per year is not materially affected by being in military service.

(2) Reduction of Monthly Payments

When interest must be reduced to 6 percent on an FHA-insured Mortgage due to SCRA, the Mortgagee may calculate interest due for the period of Active Duty on a per diem basis or permit the lower interest rate for the entire first and last months of service.

(a) Mortgagee is Notified of SCRA Applicability

Where the servicemember notifies the Mortgagee of their eligibility for SCRA protection, the Mortgagee must:
- advise the servicemember or representative of the adjusted amount due;
- provide adjusted coupons or billings; and
- ensure reduced payments are not returned as insufficient.

(b) Mortgagee is Not Notified of SCRA Applicability

Where the servicemember does not notify the Mortgagee of their eligibility for SCRA protection and submits a reduced payment, the Mortgagee must:
- attempt to contact the Borrower or representative to determine whether the Borrower is on Active Duty; and
- return insufficient payment if appropriate explanation is not provided and otherwise in compliance with HUD guidance.

(C) Verification of Military Service

The Mortgagee may request a statement of military service from the U.S. Department of Defense's Servicemembers Civil Relief Act (SCRA) website.

ii. Postponement of Foreclosure

(A) Reasonable Diligence Time Frame Calculation

When calculating deadlines to commence foreclosure or acquire Property by other means, the Mortgagee may exclude the period of time when the Borrower is in Active Duty military service. HUD does not consider postponement or delay in initiating a foreclosure while the Borrower is Active Duty military service a failure to exercise reasonable diligence.

The Mortgagee may voluntarily withhold foreclosure with or without applying Partial Payments that advance the date of Default.

(B) Required Documentation

The Mortgagee must document any delays associated with compliance with the SCRA in the Claim Review File.

k. Section 235 Mortgages

Effective May 4, 2015, HUD removed the regulations for its Section 235 Program, which authorized HUD to provide mortgage subsidy payments to Mortgagees to assist lower-income families who were unable to meet the credit requirements generally applicable to FHA mortgage insurance programs. Authority to insure new Mortgages under Section 235 expired October 1, 1989. To the extent that any Section 235 mortgages remain in existence, or second mortgages for the recapture of subsidy payment pursuant to HUD's regulations governing the Section 235 Program, the removal of these regulations does not affect the requirements for transactions entered into when Section 235 Program regulations were in effect. A Borrower with an existing Section 235 Mortgage may still refinance the Mortgage.

Section 235 Mortgages have additional servicing requirements due to the Assistance Payment Contract. The Mortgagee must continue servicing Section 235 Mortgages in accordance with published guidance, preserved here verbatim. Mortgagees should direct questions regarding Section 235 Mortgage servicing to the NSC.

i. Section 235 Mortgages

Formerly HUD Handbook 4330.1, REV-5, Chapter 10

10-1 GENERAL (24 CFR 235). Under the Section 235 program, HUD assists mortgagors in making their monthly mortgage payments by paying directly to the mortgagee a portion of the mortgagor's monthly payment as long as the mortgagor remains eligible for subsidy under this program.

Servicing of Section 235 mortgages is generally the same as that described in the previous chapters of this handbook for mortgages insured under other HUD programs, except this program has added requirements due to the assistance payments contract (Subpart C of 24 CFR 235).

A. Mortgages Subject To Recapture (24 CFR, Part 235, Subpart C). Pursuant to a firm commitment issued on or after May 27, 1981, all or part of the assistance payments is subject to recapture under certain circumstances. (Recaptures and mortgagees' responsibilities with respect to recaptures are discussed in detail in Chapter 11).

B. Reactivation Of Section 235. The Appropriations Act of 1984 reactivated the Section 235 program in accordance with Section 226 of the Housing and Urban Rural Recovery Act (HURRA) of 1983. The provisions of the reactivated program (which is known as Section 235 Revised/Recapture/10), are discussed in Paragraph 10-36.

10-2 CONTRACT FOR MONTHLY ASSISTANCE PAYMENTS (24 CFR 235). The terms and conditions of the assistance payment contract are contained in Subpart C of Part 235 of the HUD regulations. The issuance of the Mortgage Insurance Certificate (MIC), Form HUD-59100, to the HUD-approved mortgagee incorporates these provisions by reference to the contract between HUD and the mortgagee.

A. What Constitutes Execution Of The Contract (24 CFR 235.310). Issuance of form HUD-59100 constitutes execution of the contract for assistance payments with respect to that particular mortgage. The date of endorsement of the MIC does not affect the term of the contract.

B. Date Contract Term Begins. The term of the contract begins on either the date of disbursement of the mortgage proceeds or the date the mortgagor occupies the property, whichever occurs later.

NOTE: "Date of disbursement" in this instance means the date the funds escrowed to assure completion (in accordance with Form HUD-92300, Mortgagee's Assurance of Completion), have been disbursed.

C. Date Contract Term Ends (24 CFR 235.345). The term of the contract ends on the first day of the month following the occurrence of one of the events listed under Paragraph 10-19.

D. Definitions (24 CFR 235.5). Listed below are definitions of some of the terms used in this chapter as they pertain to the Section 235 program.

1. "Family" or "Household" (24 CFR 235.5). These terms mean:

   a. a pregnant woman, or two or more persons related by blood, marriage, or operation of law, who occupy the same unit;
   b. a handicapped person who has a physical or mental impairment which is expected to be of a continued duration and which impedes his/her ability to live independently unless suitable housing is available; or
   c. a single person, 62 years of age or older.

2. "Adjusted Annual Income" (24 CFR 235.5). This term means the annual family income remaining after making certain exclusions from gross annual income as shown in 24 CFR 235. 5(a)(1), (2) and (3).

3. "Gross Annual Income" (24 CFR 235.5). This term means the total income (i.e., before any adjustments, tax deductions or any other deductions), received by all members of the mortgagor's household for those items listed in Paragraph 10-9.

4. "Minor" (24 CFR 235.3). This term means a person under the age of 21 but shall not include a mortgagor or the spouse of a mortgagor.

5. "Cooperative Member" (24 CFR 235. 325). This term means a person who is a member of a cooperative association which operates a housing project financed with a mortgage insured under Sections 213 or 221 of the National Housing Act and meets the conditions set forth under 24 CFR 235.325 and 235 330.

6. "Active Contract". This term means a Section 235 assistance payment contract that is not currently suspended or terminated.

7. "Recertification of Family Income and Composition". This term means the process for determining whether a mortgagor's household;

    a. continues to qualify for the Section 235 assistance now being received; and/or
    b. is eligible for more or less assistance than is currently being received.

10-3 CONTRACT FOR MONTHLY ASSISTANCE PAYMENTS UNDER THE HOUSING AND URBAN RURAL RECOVERY ACT OF 1983. The Section 235 Revised/Recapture/10 Program provides for the following:

A. an assistance payments contract executed by the mortgagee and HUD which includes the "Notice To Buyer", signed by the mortgagors; and

B. the mortgagee must submit to the local HUD Field Office having jurisdiction over the mortgage the completed and executed contract along with the closing package at the time of insurance endorsement. (HUD will execute the contract and return it to the mortgagee with the Mortgage Insurance Certificate.)

10-4 CONTINUING ELIGIBILITY FOR ASSISTANCE. Once the assistance payments contract has been executed and the mortgage insured, many of the initial eligibility requirements (such as owning other property, family size, etc.,) no longer restrict the mortgagor's continuing eligibility for assistance.

A. Requirements To Continue Receiving Assistance. In order to continue receiving assistance payments, the mortgagor must meet all four of the following conditions:

    1. Owner-occupancy Continues. Must be a mortgagor (as described in 24 CFR 235.315) or a cooperative member (as described in 24 CFR 235.325) and live in the mortgaged property;

        a. Co-mortgagors. Where there are co-mortgagors, this requirement will be satisfied as long as one co-mortgagor lives in the mortgaged property.

        b. Absentee Occupant. If a mortgagor is away from the mortgaged property for a period up to one year this requirement will be satisfied if the absence is due to circumstances beyond his/her control and the mortgagor has taken no action which would indicate this property is no longer his/her primary residence. Each case must be decided on its own merit as to whether the circumstances meet the occupancy requirement. If additional guidance is needed, the HUD Field Office having jurisdiction over the mortgaged property should be contacted. Examples of an "absentee occupant" may include, but not necessarily be limited to, a member of the armed forces, and/or a hospitalized mortgagor.

        NOTE: Assistance payments must be suspended where the mortgagor:

        (1) actually collects rent for the mortgaged property;

Handbook 4000.1
Effective Date: 03/14/2016 | Last Revised: 07/10/2019
*Refer to the online version of SF Handbook 4000.1 for specific sections' effective dates

753

> (2) vacates the mortgaged property for any reason other than for a temporary absence;
>
> (3) offers the property for rent or sale;
>
> (4) fails to make the mortgage payments after vacating the property;
>
> (5) rents another property which the mortgagor is occupying for any reason other than for a temporary absence (as described in (1) - (4) above) from his mortgaged property;
>
> (6) purchases and occupies another property (mortgagor or co-mortgagor)

c. Appointed Trustee/Guardian. In the event of the death of the mortgagor and a trustee/ guardian was appointed as the only survivors were minors, this requirement may be satisfied if the appointed trustee/guardian lives in the mortgaged property with the surviving minors.

2. Contract Remains Active. Must be under an assistance payments contract that has not been suspended or terminated;

3. Meets Income Requirements. Mortgagor has insufficient income to make the full monthly mortgage payment with 20 or 28 percent of income depending on the firm commitment date of the mortgage; and

   NOTE: The 20 percent calculation applies to mortgages insured pursuant to a firm commitment issued on or before October 26, 1984. The 28 percent calculation applies to mortgages insured pursuant to a firm commitment issued on or after October 27, 1984.

4. Recertifies As Required. Recertifies as to occupancy, employment, family composition, and income at least annually and at such other times as required by HUD regulations 24 CFR 235.350.

B. Basis Of Assistance Calculation. If the four conditions cited in Paragraph A above are met, only the amount of assistance remains to be calculated. This calculation is based on periodic recertifications of income, family composition, occupancy and employment as discussed in Paragraph 10-5.

C. Disclosure And Verification Of Social Security Number (SSN). The disclosure and verification of the SSN is an explicit condition of continued eligibility for Section 235 assistance. All mortgagors (and members of their households six years of age and older) are required to disclose and verify complete and accurate SSNs in connection with any recertification.

D. Verification Of The SSN Is A One-time Requirement. If a mortgagor provides the mortgagee with documentation to verify the SSN at the time of an annual recertification (October 1990), it is not necessary to provide the documentation to verify the SSN for any subsequent recertifications. However, disclosure of the SSN must be provided at the time of each recertification. Mortgagees must advise mortgagors of the requirements in writing.

E.   Documentation Requirements.

1.   Documentation is required for each SSN disclosed. To document the SSN, all individuals should furnish a copy of a valid Social Security Card (SSC) issued by the Social Security Administration of the Department of Health and Human Services. (The SSN has nine digits separated by hyphens as follows: 000-00-0000).

2.   In those cases where the individual is unable to provide a copy of a valid SSC, mortgagees may accept copies of any two of the following documents which would contain the SSN and the individual's identity:

   a.   A drivers license.
   b.   An identification card issued by a Federal, state or local agency.
   c.   An identification card issued by an employer or trade union.
   d.   Earnings statements or payroll stubs.
   e.   Bank statements or personal checks.
   f.   Internal Revenue Service (IRS) Form 1099.
   g.   Unemployment benefit letter.
   h.   Retirement benefit letter.
   i.   Life insurance policies.
   j.   Court records: such as marriage and divorce judgments or bankruptcy records.
   k.   Other documents that the mortgagee determines adequate evidence of a valid SSN.

F.   Individuals who have applied for legalization under the Immigration Reform and Control Act of 1986 (IRCA) are an exception to the documentation requirements stated above.

1.   These individuals have a SSN to disclose but will not have the copy of the SSC as documentation. Acceptable documentation from those individuals is a letter from the Immigration and Naturalization Service (INS) assigning them the SSN.

2.   IRCA applicants generally applied for a SSC at the time they applied for amnesty. The Social Security Administration assigned these individuals a SSN and issued a SSC. However, this card was forwarded to INS and was placed in the applicant's file. INS sends a letter to IRCA applicants informing them that a SSN has been assigned and they may use it until they are granted temporary lawful resident status.

G.   Unacceptable Documentation. Mortgagees may not accept documents that:

1.   Are produced or completed by individuals, such as business cards, self completed wallet identification cards, or other store purchased cards. (People often purchase a plastic or metal SSC from companies or mail order firms.)

2.   Have little or no importance, such as club membership or library cards.

3.   Mortgagees have the discretion to include similar documents in this category.

H. Invalid Or False Documents. A mortgagee may reject documents that are invalid or false. To be considered invalid or false, the document must fall under one of the following categories:

1. Invalid Social Security Numbers - Some individuals use invalid numbers taken from sample cards put in new wallets or from similar advertising.

2. False Documents - False Identification documents can be either counterfeit, altered, or impostors:

    a. Counterfeit - A forgery of a genuine document or a copy of a document which may appear authentic but is not legally issued.

    b. Altered - A genuine document that has had some identification changed to match the bearer. Most often the name, photograph, address or age and physical description are changed on altered documents.

    c. Imposter - A genuine document obtained under false pretenses, or a blank genuine document stolen from the issuing agency.

I. Procedures For Rejecting SSNs Or Documentation. When a mortgagee suspects that it has been given an invalid or false document to evidence the SSN, it should notify the homeowner and require an explanation or additional proof of the SSN. If the additional documentation is questionable, the mortgagee may require the SSC be provided, or a duplicate card obtained if the original is not available. If the additional documentation does not satisfy the mortgagee that it is valid or genuine, the following actions must be taken:

1. The assistance payments contract must be suspended effective the 1st day of the first month after receipt of the additional documentation.

2. The assistance payments contract cannot be reinstated until the validity of the SSN can be verified. The mortgagee must advise the homeowner in writing of the action.

3. If the validity of the SSN is verified, the assistance payments contract is to be reinstated effective the 1st day of the month following receipt of the documentation.

J. Certifications.

1. If individuals disclose their SSN, but are unable to meet the verification requirement, a written certification must be executed by the individual to this effect. The certification should state the individual's name, SSN, and that he/she is unable to submit the documentation. The certification must be signed, and dated by each individual who does not have the documentation. If the individual is under 18 years of age, the certification must be executed by his/her parent or guardian.

2. The individual then has 60 days from the date of certification to obtain necessary documentation to verify the SSN disclosed. If an individual is at least 62 years of age, the mortgagee may at its discretion, extend the period up to an additional 60 days (or 120) days after certification).

3. The mortgagee may refer the homeowner to the local Social Security Office so that he/she may complete and submit Form SS-5, "Application for Social Security Card," to request a duplicate Social Security Card.

4. If any individual has not been assigned a SSN, a certification executed by that individual is required. The certification should state the individual's name, and that he/she has not been assigned a SSN. The individual should then date and sign the certification. If the individual is under 18 years of age, the certification must be executed by/his parent or guardian. This certification is required annually. No further action is needed. A mortgagee cannot require an individual to apply for a SSN.

K. Criminal Violations.

1. Since the SSN was considered an administrative tool for many years, it was not considered necessary to have a penalty provision covering the fraudulent application for or use of a SSN. However, as time passed and the SSN came into broader use, the need to protect it became more apparent. Penalty provisions were added to the Social Security Act and are contained in 42 U. S. C. 408(f), (g) or (h). Violations of these statutes include:

   a. Providing false information to obtain a SSN.
   b. Using a SSN based on false information to get a federally financed benefit.
   c. Using someone else's SSN.
   d. Misusing a SSN for any reason.
   e. Making, possessing, buying, or selling counterfeit Social Security cards.

2. If documentation obtained indicates that the homeowner knowingly intended to deceive the mortgagee, referral of the information should be forwarded to the Office of Inspector General for the Department of Health and Human Services (DHHS) may be contacted by toll free hotline: 1-800-368-5779 or by contacting a Regional Inspector General for investigation.

10-5 RECERTIFICATION OF INCOME, FAMILY COMPOSITION, OCCUPANCY AND EMPLOYMENT.

A. Recertification Requirements. In an effort to fully apprise mortgagors of their responsibility and the importance of reporting all required information timely, mortgagees must notify mortgagors of the requirement not only at the time of the annual recertification but also at an additionally specified time within 30 days after the end of each calendar year. It is suggested that this be accomplished at the same time the mortgagor is provided a statement of the interest paid and the taxes disbursed from the escrow account during the preceding year.

1. Requirement For All Mortgages (24 CFR 235. 350 and 235. 355). Mortgagees must secure recertifications of gross income, family composition, occupancy, and employment at least annually and as otherwise required by HUD regulations to ensure that the amount of assistance paid on behalf of the mortgagor is that which is authorized by statute.

2. Disclosure and Verification of Social Security Numbers (24 CFR 235.350(d)). Mortgagor must meet the disclosure and verification requirements for Social Security Numbers in connection with any recertification.

3. Requirement For Mortgages Insured On Or After January 5, 1976. The annual recertification must contain a statement of the total gross income (i.e., before adjustments and/or deductions) reported for all adult family members living in the household as shown on their last federal income tax returns.

   NOTE: If the "total" gross income reported on their last federal income tax returns is "individually or collectively" more than 25 percent above the income reported on the recertification, the mortgagee must require a written explanation of the difference in income from the mortgagor.

B. Recertification Form To Be Used. The only acceptable form on which mortgagors and their families may recertify is the Form HUD-93101, Recertification of Family Income and Composition, Section 235(b). The recertification must include the following:

   1. the signature of at least one mortgagor;
   2. the date of the signatures;
   3. current income, total income for last 12 months and expected income for next 12 months of all family members;
   4. names and addresses of sources of income for verification purposes; and
   5. Social Security Numbers of all family members 6 years of age and older.

10-6 WHEN RECERTIFICATIONS ARE REQUIRED (24 CFR 235.350).

A. Annual Recertifications.

   1. Date Recertification Must Be Performed. Except where the mortgagor has been recertified within 90 days prior to the anniversary (or arbitrary anniversary) date, the mortgagee must recertify the mortgagor at least annually on either:

      a. the anniversary date of the first mortgage payment due under the mortgage; or
      b. an arbitrary anniversary date established by the mortgagee for its entire portfolio of Section 235 mortgages.

   2. Events Which Permit Recertification Anniversary Dates To Be Changed. Once established, annual and arbitrary anniversary dates are to remain constant except when:

a. the mortgage is recast;

b. the mortgage is transferred to a new mortgagee or servicer; and/or

c. prior written approval has been obtained from the local HUD Field Office where the mortgagee is located with a copy of such approval must be maintained in each individual case file. A copy must also be provided as an attachment to the Form HUD-93102 assistance payment request form notifying HUD Headquarters Office of Finance and Accounting's Subsidy Accounting Branch.

NOTE: When any of the above events occur, the mortgagee or servicer automatically has the option of:

(1) using the anniversary date of the first mortgage payment due under the mortgage;

(2) using the same arbitrary anniversary date (assuming an arbitrary date was being used) as the transferring mortgagee or servicer; or

(3) selecting a different arbitrary anniversary date.

B. Intermittent Recertifications.

1. For Mortgages Insured Before January 5, 1976. Recertifications must be done within 30 days of the effective date of any "addition to" the adult family's "source of income". An "additional" source of income" may be due to, but not necessarily limited to, the following:

a. a family member (other than a mortgagor) may have reached the age of 21. If this family member was a wage earner, this would require that his/her wages now be taken into consideration when computing assistance payments;

b. an adult who did not work previously may have obtained employment;

c. an adult who had a job may have elected to get an additional part-time job; and/or

d. a family wage earner may have gotten married.

e. an adult wage earner joins the family through marriage.

NOTE: Unless the increase was due to a change in source, the mortgagor needs only to recertify at the next anniversary—at which time the increase must be reported to the mortgagee.

2. For Mortgages Insured On Or After January 5, 1976. Recertification is required within 30 days of the date when the total gross income increases by $50 or more per month, regardless of whether the source changes.

It is the mortgagor's responsibility for providing this information to the mortgagee.

Mortgagors must be made aware that their failure to advise the mortgagee of an increase in income within the 30-day time frame could result in that mortgagor being required to repay a significant amount of overpaid assistance (24 CFR 235. 350(c)).

C. Recertifications. At The Direction Of The Secretary Of HUD. The Secretary of HUD, and/or his designee, may require recertification any time there is reason to believe recertification is warranted (24 CFR 235.350(a)(3)).

D. Optional Recertifications. At The Request Of The Mortgagor (24 CFR 235.355). The mortgagor has the option of requesting that the mortgagee accept a recertification any time there is a reduction (of any amount) in the adult family income.

Should the change not be made within the 30-day time frame due to the mortgagor's failure to notify the mortgagee, any increase in assistance resulting from income decrease will be made effective the first day of the month following the date the recertification is received by the mortgagee and not retroactively. (24 CFR 235.360).

1. Acceptable Reasons For Performing Optional Recertifications. The mortgagor may request an optional recertification due to, but not necessarily limited to, any of the following reasons:

   a. an adult wage earner's death;
   b. an adult wage earner moving out of the property;
   c. an adult wage earner becoming unemployed; and/or
   d. an adult wage earner's loss and/or reduction of overtime or salary.

   NOTE: If the mortgagor is already receiving the maximum assistance allowed based on income (i.e., maximum allowed under Formula Two), the recertification requesting that assistance be increased need not be processed. However, the mortgagor must be advised, in writing, of the reason for the mortgagee's inability to increase the assistance payment.

2. Time Frame For Making The Request.

   a. In the case of self-employed adult family members, the reduction must have continued for at least 90 days prior to the mortgagor's request for recertification. The best information available must be used to ensure that the reduced income has been in effect for 90 days. Assistance must not be based on the unsupported word of the mortgagor.

   b. For mortgagors NOT self-employed, the reduction or loss of income must reduce the family income to less than the income that was used in computing the most recent assistance.

3. Time Frame for Mortgagee To Process Optional Recertification. The mortgagee must request on HUD Form 93101-A to make any assistance increase effective the first day of the month following the month the mortgagor's recertification is received.

10-7 ANNUAL RECERTIFICATION OF MORTGAGORS.

A. Time Frame For Requesting Recertifications. Unless the assistance payments contract has been suspended or terminated, annual recertifications must be secured by the mortgagee:

1. no earlier than 60 days before and no later than 30 days after the mortgage (or arbitrary) anniversary date; and
2. the HUD-93101-A must be received by HUD Headquarters Office of Finance and Accounting's (OFA's) Subsidy Accounting Branch no later than 45 days after the mortgage anniversary (or arbitrary anniversary) date.

NOTE: The Subsidy Accounting Branch (SAB) will identify as suspended the subsidy payments on cases when required annual recertifications are not received by the 45th day after the anniversary date. SAB will notify mortgagees by letter that an account has been identified as suspended.

When subsidy is identified as suspended by SAB due to untimely recertification, it will not be paid retroactively unless the HUD-93114 request for reinstatement and the HUD-93101-A are accompanied by a statement from the mortgagee. The statement must include the reason for mortgagee's failure to adhere to recertification requirements.

Assistance payments identified as suspended by SAB shall not be retroactively reinstated because a mortgagor failed to properly respond to a timely request from the mortgagee for recertification.

For examples of the effective dates of payment changes resultant from recertifications, see Paragraph 10-15C.

B. "Reasonable Effort" Action Required Of Mortgagee. A reasonable effort must be made by the mortgagee to comply with the time frames shown in Paragraph 10-7A. In order for the mortgagee's actions to meet the "reasonable effort" requirement, the mortgagee's actions must include, but not necessarily be limited to, the following:

1. sending a written notice to the mortgagor, early enough to result in obtaining recertification no earlier than 60 days before and no later than 30 days after the mortgage anniversary (or arbitrary anniversary) date, which:

   a. advises the mortgagor of the annual recertification requirement;
   b. transmits a Form HUD-93101 that must be filled out and returned to the mortgagee;
   c. advises the mortgagor that failure to return the completed HUD-93101 within the required time frame will result in suspension of subsidy payments;
   d. advises the mortgagor that assistance payments will not be made retroactively and that the mortgagor will be responsible for making the full mortgage payment during the period of suspension;
   e. advises the mortgagor that the reinstatement of suspended subsidy payments will not be effective until the first payment month which occurs after 30 days from the date of the mortgagee's receipt of HUD-93101 from the mortgagor; and

     f.   provides a telephone number and contact name to be used by the mortgagor to obtain responses to recertification questions.

   2. providing special help (whether requested or not) to mortgagors who are unable to recertify due to lack of education, language barrier, physical or emotional impairments.

     NOTE: Mortgagees are expected to assist mortgagors in completing forms and/or advising relatives or community assistance agencies when mortgagors need assistance in filling out forms.

10-8 MORTGAGOR FAILS TO RECERTIFY WITHIN TIME FRAME (24 CFR 235.375(b)(4)). If the mortgagor fails to respond to the mortgagee's request for recertification within the required time frame, the mortgagee is required to request via Form HUD-93114 that the HUD Headquarters OFA's Subsidy Accounting Branch suspend assistance payments effective the first month after the date that the recertification was required.

NOTE: The Subsidy Accounting Branch will identify the case as suspended and will not pay assistance payments when a recertification is due and neither a HUD-93101-A nor a HUD-93114 is received from the mortgagee by the 45th day after the anniversary date.

   A. Mortgagor Recertifies After Suspension. If the recertification is received by the mortgagee after assistance payments have been suspended, the mortgagee must submit Form HUD-93114, together with HUD-93101-A, requesting that the assistance payments be reinstated as an adjustment transaction Code 2 on the next regular month's billing Forms HUD-93102 and HUD-300.

     NOTE: The billing forms and all adjustment transaction documents (i.e., Forms HUD-93114, HUD-93101-A, HUD-93102 and HUD-300) should be submitted as one package to the Subsidy Accounting Branch for processing. The reason for the adjustment in Column 3 on Form HUD-300 should be noted as "Late mortgagor recertification".

     The reinstatement will be effective on the first payment month which occurs after the date of the mortgagee's receipt of Form HUD-93101 from the mortgagor.

     NOTE: No assistance will be paid for the period during which a recertification should have been received (i.e., 30 days after it was requested) and the date it was actually received.

   B. Contract Suspended Due To Mortgagee's Failure To Meet "Reasonable Effort" Requirement. In situations where HUD determines that the action taken by the mortgagee when contacting the mortgagor with regard to the recertification fails to meet the "reasonable effort" requirement (as stated in Paragraph 10-7B) and the assistance was subsequently suspended, the mortgagee must go back to that mortgagor and allow that mortgagor to recertify as long as he/she recertifies within 30 days of this second written request. The mortgagee must:

Handbook 4000.1   762
Effective Date: 03/14/2016 | Last Revised: 07/10/2019
*Refer to the online version of SF Handbook 4000.1 for specific sections' effective dates

1. secure recertification and complete verification;

   NOTE: If more than one recertification was missed, for each missed recertification the mortgagee must reconstruct family income as accurately as possible for each anniversary date.

2. make any resulting change in assistance effective retroactive to the period for each recertification in question; and

3. if the recertification results in overpaid assistance, careful consideration must be given in order to choose a method which will allow for the recovery of overpaid assistance that may have accumulated without creating an undue hardship on the mortgagor.

   However, the mortgagee must immediately refund the total overpaid assistance amount to HUD. The overpaid amount should be included as an adjustment transaction on the next regular month's billing which should be accompanied by applicable Forms HUD-93114 (requesting reinstatement) and HUD-93101-A (recertifying income). The periods of overpayment (i.e., month and year) must be included in Column 3 of Form HUD-300. The reason for adjustment should be noted as "Late Recertification Request".

   NOTE: When assistance has been suspended and a request for reinstatement is retroactive, the current monthly billing amount should be treated as a Code 1 transaction on Form HUD-300. The retroactive billing amount should be treated as a Code 2 adjustment transaction on Form HUD-300.

   Both the reason for adjustment (i.e., late mortgagor recertification, recertification request; suspended in error, etc.) and the beginning and ending effective period (month and year) must be included in Column 3 of Form HUD-300. Failure to provide this information or failure to attach the required Forms HUD 93101-A and HUD-93114, as appropriate, will result in non-payment of the adjustment amount.

   Disallowed adjustment amounts due to lack of documentation must be included on the next regular month's billing. The HUD Headquarters OFA's Subsidy Accounting Branch will process only one Form HUD-93102 for each billing period.

10-9 DETERMINING INCOME.

A. Gross Annual Income (24 CFR 235.5(d)). Assistance is based on gross income which is made up of the total income (prior to any adjustments, taxes or other deductions) received by all members of the mortgagor's household.

   NOTE: Members of the mortgagor's "family or household" are considered to be all persons living in the mortgaged property who are related to the mortgagor by blood, marriage or operation of law.

1. Income Sources Included. For the purposes of annual or other required recertifications which project income, the following sources must be included:

   a. wages, child support, alimony, and rental income;
   b. Social Security or welfare benefits;
   c. retirement benefits, military and veterans' usability benefits;
   d. unemployment benefits;
   e. interest and dividend payments;
   f. lottery winnings paid over extended periods; and
   g. insurance benefits paid on a fixed schedule.

2. Income Sources Excluded. Income from the following sources must NOT be included:

   a. lump sum insurance benefits;
   b. lump sum winnings from a lottery;
   c. hospital or other medical insurance benefits;
   d. bonuses and/or overtime (if they DO NOT represent a pattern of annual payments over a period of time);
   e. food stamps;
   f. scholarships; or
   g. any unusual income such as payments made to Vietnam Veterans from the Agent Orange Settlement Fund.

      NOTE: The Agent Orange Compensation Exclusion Act (Public Law 101-201) requires that none of the payments made to Vietnam Veterans from the Agent Orange Settlement Fund be considered income for the purpose of determining eligibility for or the amount of benefits under any Federal or federally assisted program. This requirement must be adhered to when processing Section 235 Annual or other required Recertifications of Family Income and Composition.

   h. any temporary income such as income of a wage earner from temporary employment that has been discontinued at the time recertification is taking place.

B. Income Requiring Special Consideration. The mortgagee is to use the mortgagor's verified current income or the mortgagor's stated "expected income", WHICHEVER IS HIGHER.

   "Expected income" is different from income received over the past 12 months (or year-to-date income) in that if there has been a recent increase in the mortgagor's (and/or family member's) hourly wage or salary, that new hourly rate or salary would serve as the basis for projecting the "expected income" for the next 12-month period.

1. Overtime Pay. Overtime pay must be included in the total income if the employer verifies that overtime is currently being paid on a regular basis regardless of whether the employee states (or fails to state) at the time of verification that the overtime is expected to continue in the future. If there is a continuing record of overtime work,

the only time the overtime income is to be excluded is when the employer verifies that overtime will be discontinued.

2. Self-Employment. Include in gross income all income listed on Internal Revenue Service's (IRS) Form 1040. When calculating the income of self-employed mortgagors, the deductions set out in Schedule C, Profit (or Loss) from Business or Profession, must be recalculated for HUD purposes. Salary or wage distributions for the mortgagor or co-mortgagor, depletion or depreciation) are not deducted from the gross business income for HUD purposes.

   NOTE: For example, Schedule C is not the only form where self-employment income is claimed, farmers may have a Schedule F instead of a Schedule C. All sources of self-employment income must be included.

   a. Recalculate Business Income On IRS Form 1040. Mortgagees must recalculate the business income (Item 12 on IRS' Form 1040). If the recalculated income shows a loss, that loss cannot be used to offset other forms of income reported on Items 7 through 22 on IRS Form 1040.

   b. Item 12 on the mortgagor's IRS Form 1040 may reflect a negative amount in some cases. However, when the mortgagee recalculates the Schedule C as prescribed in Paragraph 2a above, it could result in a positive amount to be included in income. Elimination of the deductions for depletion and depreciation may, from HUD's perspective, result in a business profit.

3. Special-Purpose Payments. These are payments made to the mortgagor's household that would be discontinued if not spent for a specific purpose. Payments which are intended to defray specific expenses of an unusual nature and which are expended solely for those expenses should not be considered as income. Examples include, but are not necessarily limited to, the following:

   a. Medical Expenses. Funds provided by a charitable organization to defray medical expenses, to the extent to which they are actually spent to meet those expenses.

   b. Foster Children. Payments for the care of foster children who are not otherwise related to the mortgagor's household by blood, marriage, or operation of law.

NOTE: Foster children are not considered members of the family. Therefore, no $300 adjustments to income are to be made because of their presence.

   c. VA Educational Benefits and/or Scholarships. VA educational benefits and/or the proceeds of scholarships are not considered income to the extent the benefits or proceeds are actually used for educational expenses (i.e., tuition, books, lab fees, etc.). Any excess income after deducting actual educational expenses must be included as income.

NOTE: Costs of transportation to and from school or for cost of housing for living away from home to attend school are not considered educational expenses.

d. Payments In Kind. Items such as food stamps, meals, clothing, or transportation provided by the employer is not considered as income if used for that expressed purpose. However, cash reimbursement for any of these items is considered as income to the extent it continues when not spent to defray a specific expense.

e. Insurance Benefits.

(1) Health/Accident/Disability Insurance.

(a) Premiums Paid By Mortgagor. Benefits received from policies where the mortgagor is both the insured and the beneficiary are not to be considered income if the mortgagor paid the premiums.

(b) Premiums Not Paid By Mortgagor. If these premiums were paid by someone outside the mortgagor's household (such as an employer), the benefits would be considered as income.

(2) Other Types of Insurance. The benefits of other type insurance policies would be considered as income if the benefits are paid in two or more installments unless they meet the test of special purpose payments as described in Paragraph 10-9B3 above.

Regardless of the type or reason for payment, insurance benefits paid in a lump sum are not to be considered income. However, if the mortgagor chose to invest any or all of the money from this lump sum payment, all interest (or other gain) from this investment would be considered as income.

f. Earnings of Minors. Income of all family members within the mortgagor's household must be included in the family's total gross income which is used as a base for computing the assistance.

All income of all members of the family is included in gross family income. In arriving at the family's adjusted income, five percent of this total is subtracted before subtracting the earnings of minors. Note that only the earnings of minors are subtracted. Income of minors from sources other than earnings is not subtracted.

For example, income to a minor from a trust or an insurance policy is not earnings and is not subtracted. It is thus immaterial whether income other than earnings is paid to a minor or to an adult family member for the benefit of the minor. In neither case would it be deducted in arriving at adjusted income.

g. Military Pay and Allowances. All cash payments to a member of the armed forces are considered as income, regardless of the reason for the payment, unless the payment is made only once and for a special purpose, such as a lump sum re-enlistment bonus.

Many military personnel may exercise a degree of choice in some areas of compensation. For example, they may choose between eating in a government cafeteria without charge or receiving an allowance for rations in cash and paying for any meals consumed in the cafeteria. If the allowance is received in cash, it is income. Otherwise, it is not.

h. Reimbursement for Expenses. If the family member's employment requires spending considerable time away from home on a regular basis and the employer provides reimbursement for the unusual living expenses incurred as a result, the reimbursement is not normally considered to be income.

Exceptions to this rule:

(1) If the reimbursement is paid for periods other than when the employee is actually away from home, the entire reimbursement is considered as income regardless of whether the employee accounts to the employer for actual expenses and the reimbursement is fixed on a daily basis (or some other standard) and is inadequate to cover all normal living expenses; and

(2) if the employee accounts to the employer for expenses, and the expenses equal or exceed the reimbursement, the reimbursement is not considered income. However, if the reimbursement exceeds the expenses, the excess reimbursement is considered income.

NOTE: Where expenses exceed the reimbursement, the amount not covered by the reimbursement cannot be deducted from the family's gross annual income.

10-10 VERIFYING INCOME. To calculate assistance payments, the mortgagor's verified current income, or the reported expected income, WHICHEVER IS HIGHER, must be used. The mortgagor's option to recertify is his/her only protection when there is a loss of income. When mortgagees fail to use the highest income reported, overpaid assistance results.

A. Third-party Verification Required. Third-party verification of the mortgagor's statements, similar to that required when a mortgage is originated, is required at the time of each recertification.

EXCEPTION: Third-party verifications are not required for self-employed persons.

B. Verification Not Available. Where third-party verification cannot be obtained and/or the mortgagor's statements cannot be reconciled with the verification, the local HUD Field Office having jurisdiction over the mortgaged property should be contacted for assistance in establishing the income.

C. Unacceptable Forms Of Verification. Examples of unacceptable forms of verification include, but are not necessarily limited to, the following:

1. Federal income tax returns or Forms W-2's (withholding tax forms), except for self-employed persons and where HUD has reviewed the case and has established that this would be the best information available;

2. where verifications have passed through the hands of the mortgagor and/or the person whose income is being verified; and/or

3. checks and/or pay stubs which show only the net amount of the check.

D. Acceptable Forms Of Verification. The most difficult part of income verification is determining that all sources of earned income have been reported by all members of the mortgagor's household.

1. Listed below, ranked in the order of preference, are acceptable forms of verification for earned income.

   a. Pay Stubs and Checks. If these show gross income as well as net, these documents are considered to be the most reliable source of accurate information concerning recent income.

      (1) Documentation for Preceding Six months Is To Be Requested. The most recent information available is to be used for recertifications. Salary information requested should include at least any pay stubs and/or copies of check(s) received by any household member just prior to the mortgagee's request as well as any checks or income received within at least the last six-month period.

      (2) Each Source of Income Must be Documented. Care should be taken to assure that the mortgagor provides information with respect to each source of income. If a source is missing, one of the other forms of verification should be used with respect to that source.

   b. HUD Form 92004-G Request for Verification of Employment. This form of verification is acceptable (or similar forms designed by the mortgagee to elicit the same information) only if it is delivered directly to and from the employer without passing through the hands of the mortgagor and/or the employee whose salary is being verified.

      NOTE: If the HUD form is used, it should be modified to add, in the remarks section, a request for information about anticipated wage increases.

   c. Telephone Verification. While some employers may be reluctant to provide income information by telephone, they will usually verify that the mortgagor is or is not employed with that company. In using the telephone:

(1) Contact Designated Personnel. It should be established by the mortgagee that the person spoken to is either:

    (a) the mortgagor's supervisor; or

    (b) an employee of that company who has been authorized by that company to give out employment verifications.

(2) Maintain Mortgagor's Privacy. The detailed reason for the call (i.e., to determine if the employee remains eligible for Sections 235 subsidy) should not be disclosed to any parties other than those described in the preceding paragraph.

(3) Document Telephone Call. Each telephone call should be fully documented as follows:

    (a) the date;
    (b) the time;
    (c) the parties of the conversation; and
    (d) the information provided by the employer.

d. Use of Standard Benefit Scales. Some localities have established that a family with a given composition receiving public assistance or unemployment compensation as its sole source of income must receive assistance in a set amount.

NOTE: Where this is the case, the income taken from the current schedule of benefits established by that source may be accepted as the family's income without individual verification of the benefits.

e. Use of Public Housing Authority's Standard Minimum Income Scales. Some Public Housing Authorities have established schedules of minimum incomes for various occupations in their areas, especially those with fluctuating, seasonal, and irregular patterns. These schedules are based on experience indicating that workers in each of the covered occupations can be expected to earn at least a minimum each year under normal working conditions.

(1) Income Reported At Or Above Minimum Scale. If the mortgagor has stated an income at or above the minimum found in these tables, the mortgagor's statement may be accepted without further verification.

(2) Income Reported At Less Than Minimum Scale. Where the mortgagor can provide convincing evidence that a lower income is accurate, the lower figure may be used.

2. Income from Self-Employment. As noted in Paragraph 10-9 with respect to self-employment, the income of self-employed persons must often be adjusted to avoid reducing it for non-cash expenditures such as depletion and depreciation. Supporting

documentation (such as statements showing deposits consistent with claimed income) should be obtained from self-employed mortgagors.

a. Audited Profit and Loss Statements. A copy of the latest audited Profit and Loss Statement may be requested from the mortgagor.

NOTE: Due to the expense involved, mortgagors are not to be required to obtain an audited Profit and Loss Statement for the sole purpose of the mortgagee using it for income verification to determine Section 235 subsidy. However, should a recent audited Profit and Loss Statement exist for other purposes, the mortgagee may require that a copy be provided for income verification.

b. Unaudited Profit and Loss Statements. These are acceptable only if prepared by someone other than the mortgagor. Even then, they are of questionable validity as they are based solely on information provided to the preparer by the mortgagor. Any apparent discrepancy should be followed up thoroughly.

c. Financial Statements. A financial statement is a picture of the financial condition of the business at a specific time. It must be noted that a financial statement does not provide information about the income of the mortgagor, but only serves as a basis for determining that the business can afford to pay the mortgagor what is claimed as earned income.

NOTE: When the self-employed mortgagor is a principal owner of a corporation, that person's income is generally a combination of salary and dividends on investment in the corporation.

In these situations, the corporation's undistributed earnings should also be considered as income of the mortgagor to the extent of that person's ownership.

3. Unearned Income. Income from sources other than employment or self-employment must also be verified, and there are probably as many ways to do this as there are different sources of income. It is left to mortgagees to determine the best source of information in each case.

E. Verification Not Required. Certain types of income need not be verified.

1. Minors. Incomes of minors (persons living in the household who are under the age of 21) need not be verified. Only the income of "adult" members of the family need be verified. "Adult" for this purpose is any mortgagor and spouse of any mortgagor (regardless of age) and any other person related to any mortgagor by blood, marriage, or operation of law who occupies the mortgaged property and is 21 years old or older.

2. Latest Verification Performed Within Last Six Months. On mortgages insured prior to January 5, 1976, income which has been verified within the six months preceding the mortgagee's receipt of the signed Form HUD-93101 need not be verified if:

a. the family members report no change in employers; and

b. the income reported is either the same as that verified earlier or reflects a change which was expected and/or verified as a part of the previous verification.

3. Disqualifying Income. If either the current or expected income as reported by the mortgagor is adequate to enable the mortgagor to make the full monthly payment with 20 or 28 percent of income (depending on when the mortgage was insured), no further verification is necessary before suspending the assistance payments contract.

10-11 FAMILY COMPOSITION. Family composition need not be verified, but, all changes in the status of adult and family members must be questioned.

A. Separations. Where a mortgagor has left the property due to a separation, the remaining mortgagor may certify as to the composition of the remaining portion of the household.

B. Death. Normally, if there is no owner-mortgagor occupying the property, assistance cannot be paid. In the event of the death of one or more mortgagors, there could be a question as to both the title to the property and the mortgage obligation. The status may be even more uncertain if the only survivors are minor children.

1. Obtaining Clear Title/Disposing of Property. Where the only survivors are minor children, it may be necessary to initiate court proceedings in order to have a guardian appointed for the purpose of clearing and/or disposing of the title of the property.

2. Commencement of Assistance Payments. In the event of a death or separation leaving no owner-mortgagor, the mortgagee may begin billing for assistance immediately as though there had been an assumption at the time of the death or separation, provided the mortgagee can identify an individual who meets all of the following conditions:

   a. is a member of the surviving family (even though he/or she may not have qualified as a "family" member for assistance purposes earlier);

   b. will probably become the holder of title (either in his/her own name or in trust for one or more of the survivors);

   c. will assume the mortgage obligation in the same capacity;

   d. will occupy the mortgaged property with the survivors; and

   e. will qualify for assistance within the limits prescribed for initial eligibility (see Paragraph 10-22).

3. Establishing Eligibility. It must be recognized that to determine who will most likely inherit or be appointed as a guardian or trustee on behalf of the survivors before the estate is settled can only be based on assumptions. Once the mortgagee can reasonably determine who that individual will be and whether the conditions in Paragraph 10-11B2 have been met, eligibility must be established.

   NOTE: Establishing eligibility need not be delayed until the disposition of title has been completed and the mortgage obligation is formally assumed by the new mortgagor.

Should it become evident that those assumptions are incorrect, the assistance payments contract must be suspended effective with the date of death or separation and any assistance paid in the interim must be refunded to HUD.

10-12 COMPUTING ASSISTANCE (24 CFR 235.335). The maximum monthly assistance that can be paid by HUD is the lesser amount computed under two formulas, commonly referred to as "Formula One" and "Formula Two". Instructions for these computations are given on Form HUD-93101-A under Section A and B.

   A. Formula One. The "Formula One" assistance payment is the difference between the full monthly mortgage payment (i.e., principal, interest, and all escrowed items) due under the mortgage and either 20 or 28 percent of the mortgagor's adjusted monthly income. (See Section A and B of the Form 93101-A to determine how the assistance payment is computed.)

NOTE: The 20 percent calculation applies to mortgages pursuant to a firm commitment issued on or before October 26, 1984. The 28 percent calculation applies to mortgages insured pursuant to a firm commitment issued on or after October 27, 1984.

The "Formula One" payment must be recomputed whenever there is a change in the total payment or when there is a change in the income or family composition reflected in a recertification.

   B. Formula Two. The "Formula Two" assistance payment is the difference between the actual monthly payment to principal, interest, and the mortgage insurance premium (MIP) under the mortgage and the monthly payment to principal and interest (without the MIP) that the mortgagor would have to pay if the mortgage bore interest at some lower rate. Those lower rates vary, depending on when the mortgage was insured, as indicated below:

Date of Closing Note Rate	Note Rate	Interest Rate to Compute Second Element of Formula Two	P&I Factor per $1,000 Term
8/9/68-1/4/76	No difference	1.00%	$3.22
1/5/76-3/6/78	No difference	5.00%	$5.37
3/7/78-3/8/81	No difference	4.00%	$4.78
3/9/81 and later	13.50% or lower	4.00%	$4.78
	13.75-14.00%	4.75%	$5.22
	14.25-14.50%	5. 50%	$5.68
	15.00%	6.00%	$6.00
	15.50%	6.75%	$6.49
	16.00%	7.25%	$6.83
	16.50%	8.0%	$7.34
	17.50%	8.00%	$7.34

10-13 INTERIM ASSISTANCE PAYMENTS. When it is impossible to complete the verification of all or part of the family's income at the time of the effective date of a change in the assistance payment, the assistance payment should be temporarily adjusted, if appropriate, based upon information provided by the mortgagor on Form HUD-93101 until all income can be verified or until the local HUD Field Office makes a decision as to the amount of assistance to be paid based on available documentation.

A. Basis For Computing Interim Assistance Payments. Interim changes in assistance payments should be based on the highest family income figure which can be developed from any source (or sources) until the mortgagor's family income can be verified or a decision is made by the local HUD Field Office.

B. Affect On Payments. Interim changes in assistance payments should:

1. not result in overpayment of subsidy unless the mortgagor understates income;
2. result in the Formula One assistance (after verification) being equal to or greater than the interim adjustment; and
3. not affect Formula Two calculations as the Formula Two are not income related.

C. HUD Assistance Requested. Whenever acceptable verifications cannot be obtained, the local HUD Field Office should be asked to make a decision as to the total family income to be used to determine the amount of assistance to be paid on behalf of the mortgagor.

D. Documentation Needed. Requests to local HUD Field Offices for assistance in determining correct assistance should include:

1. Form HUD-93101, Recertification of Family Income and Composition, Section 235(b);
2. all income verifications received to date that pertain to this recertification, including summaries of any received verbally;
3. copies of any correspondence related to the recertification or verification of income.
4. a summary of any attempted verifications or reconciliation of differences may not have been made clear by the basic documentation; explain the problem encountered; and
5. the names, addresses and telephone numbers of any income source identified by or for any family member.

10-14 FIRST MONTHLY ASSISTANCE PAYMENT. Where mortgage closings do not take place on the first day of a month, the first assistance payment on a new mortgage will normally be smaller or larger than subsequent assistance payments (depending on how interest for the first partial month is collected from the mortgagor).

If the interest is collected at closing or as a separate payment of interest only on the first of the month following closing, the initial assistance payment will be smaller. If the interest is collected as a part of the first full monthly installment, both that payment and the assistance payment will be larger.

In calculating this first assistance payment, the mortgagee's basic calculations are the same. Both "Formula One" and "Formula Two" assistance payments are to be calculated, but the mortgagor's income and the full monthly payment used in "Formula One" and the monthly payments to principal, interest and MIP on the actual mortgage and to principal and interest on a mortgage at the appropriate interest rate used in "Formula Two" must be adjusted to reflect the number of days for which interest was actually collected.

10-15 ASSISTANCE PAYMENTS ADJUSTMENTS (24 CFR 235.360). Most adjustments take place as a result of changes in income or family composition reflected in a recertification or due to an increase in the full monthly payment required by the mortgage.

    A. Adjustments. Assistance payment adjustments will be made either retroactively or prospectively as described below.

        1. Retroactively. Assistance payments may be adjusted retroactively (i.e., adjusted back to the date the change should have taken effect). Payments may be adjusted retroactively under the following circumstances:

            a. to correct errors or to include previously unreported income (i.e., $50.00 increases);
            b. to reinstate a suspended assistance payments contract when:

                (1) there is an assumption and the assumptor is found eligible for assistance; or
                (2) a foreclosure action is withdrawn;

            c. when an "interim" assistance payment was put into effect in accordance with Paragraph 10-13; and
            d. when directed to do so by HUD.

        2. Prospectively. Most assistance payments will be adjusted prospectively (i.e., adjustments made effective within 30 days after the processing of recent or anticipated changes when reported by the mortgagor as required). These changes may be due to, but not necessarily limited to, the following:

            a. changes in income or family composition reflected in a recertification; or
            b. an increase in the full monthly payment required under the mortgage.

    B. Computation Changes. "Formula Two" assistance payments change every twelve months (on the anniversary of the beginning of amortization) at the time MIP changes for the coming year.

        NOTE: This adjustment must be made even when the mortgagee has established an arbitrary anniversary date for the purpose of processing recertifications.

    C. Effective Dates Of Changes (24 CFR 235. 360). The effective date of payment change recorded in Block 19 on Form HUD-93101-A must be in accordance with the following schedule:

Handbook 4000.1   774
Effective Date: 03/14/2016 | Last Revised: 07/10/2019
*Refer to the online version of SF Handbook 4000.1 for specific sections' effective dates

Action Requiring Change	Effective Date
Annual recertification if mortgagor's share of payment increases	First day of first or second moth after receipt of Form HUD 93101 at the mortgagee's discretion
Annual recertification if mortgagor's share of payment decreases	THE first day of the first month after receipt of Form HUD-93101
Reported increase in income	THE first day of the first month after the effective date of income increase
Reported decrease in income	The first day of the first month after receipt of Form HUD-93101
Change in total monthly payment required under the mortgage	The date of the monthly payment amount change
Change in "Formula Two" assistance due to an MIP change	The anniversary date of the beginning of amortization

10-16 ADVISING MORTGAGORS OF CHANGES. The mortgagee must notify the mortgagor of changes in assistance payments no less than 10 days before the due date of the first payment affected by the change.

A. Required Advance Notice Not Given. Any time there is an increase in the mortgagor's share of the payment and the required 10-day advance notice cannot be given to the mortgagor, the mortgagee must arrange a schedule that is acceptable to both parties (must be one that is realistic and does not put an undue hardship on the mortgagor) for collecting any additional amounts that may become due before the 10-day advance notice period can be given.

NOTE: Payment schedule arrangements made between the mortgagor and the mortgagee should not result in overpaid assistance. The amount of assistance requested from HUD on Form HUD-93102 should be reduced effective on the effective date of payment change in accordance with the schedule provided in Paragraph 10-15C, regardless of when the mortgagee collects the higher mortgagor's share of the monthly payment amount.

B. Written Notice To Mortgagor. The notice to the mortgagor should include, but not necessarily be limited to, the following information:

1. the total monthly mortgage payment, excluding items not required by the mortgage (such as premiums for life and/or disability insurance);
2. HUD's share of the mortgage payment and whether it was computed under "Formula One" or "Formula Two";
3. the mortgagor's share of that payment;
4. any additional amounts that must be paid by the mortgagor in connection with the mortgage payment which was excluded in Item 1 above (such as premiums for life and/or disability insurance);

5. the monthly gross income used to calculate the assistance payment for the purpose of providing a bench mark to help the mortgagor know when to report increases of $50 or more per month;

6. the due date of the first payment due from the mortgagor which reflects the increase.

10-17 RETENTION OF DOCUMENTATION (24 CFR 235.365). Form HUD-93114 and all other pertinent records must be in the mortgagor's case file for the life of the insured mortgage plus three years. In the event the mortgage is transferred to another mortgagee or servicer, and/or assigned to HUD, this documentation must remain a part of the mortgagor's case file and must be conveyed to the new mortgagee, servicer, and/or HUD which shall retain the entire case file for the life of the mortgage plus [seven] years.

10-18 SUSPENSION OF ASSISTANCE PAYMENTS (24 CFR 235. 375).

A. Events Which Require Suspension. Events listed below (and are also given under Item 15 of Form HUD-93114 require the suspension of assistance payments. Effective dates are also given as to when each is to be suspended.

1. When the mortgagor or cooperative member ceases to meet the occupancy criteria for continued assistance;

    Effective Date: the first day of the month following the date the mortgagor or cooperative member ceased to meet the criteria;

2. The mortgagee determines that the mortgagor or cooperative member ceases to qualify for assistance payments because of income increases enabling the mortgagor or cooperative member to pay the full monthly payments using 20 or 28 percent (whichever applies) of the family income.

    Effective Date: the date that the mortgagor received the increase in family income which enabled payment of the full monthly mortgage payment with 20 or 28 percent of the adjusted gross family income;

3. The required recertification of occupancy, employment, income and family composition cannot be obtained from the mortgagor.

    Effective Date: For annual recertifications, the assistance payment contract must be suspended if the recertification Form HUD-93101 has not been received 30 days after the anniversary date, or the disclosure and verification of the Social Security numbers are not provided. For other required recertifications, the contract is suspended as of the first day of the month following expiration of the 30-day period given the mortgagor for recertification.

    NOTE: Assistance payments are not to be suspended when a mortgagor requests recertification due to a reduction in income (i.e., optional recertification), and then fails to recertify.

4. Mortgage obligation or cooperative membership is assumed by a party before eligibility has been established.

    Effective Date: The first day of the month following the date on which the seller fails to meet the occupancy criteria as set out in paragraph, or the assumptor assumes the mortgage or cooperative membership, whichever is earlier.

5. Foreclosure is initiated.

    Effective date: The first day of the month following the date the first legal action required by state law is taken by the mortgagee's attorney to foreclose on the mortgage.

B. Suspension Notification Required. A notice shall be sent to the mortgagor advising of the suspension when:

1. the suspension of assistance payments is the result of a mortgagor being able to make the full monthly payment using the appropriate 20 or 28 percent of family income;
2. the mortgagor fails to submit a required recertification; or
3. the mortgagor fails to meet the disclosure and verification requirements for Social Security numbers in connection with a recertification.

C. Content Of Suspension Notice. The notice to the mortgagor must include the following:

1. thc date of the suspension;
2. the reason for suspension (as stated in Paragraph 10-18A);
3. the mortgagor's total required monthly mortgage payment;
4. a statement advising that for a period of 3 years immediately following the suspension, assistance payments may be reinstated at any time within that 3-year period if:

    a. circumstances occur which would eliminate the reason for the suspension; and
    b. provided that another event (listed in Paragraph 10-18A) has not taken place which would in itself require that the assistance payment contract continue to be suspended.

D. Reinstatement Effective Dates. A suspended assistance payment contract shall be reinstatement as follows:

1. Suspension Due To Mortgagor's Non-occupancy Status. Assistance payments may be reinstated effective with the first monthly billing after the mortgagee receives Form HUD-93101 notification that the mortgagor meets the occupancy requirement.

2. Suspension Due to Over-Income Mortgagor. Assistance payments may be reinstated effective the first day of the month after the mortgagee receives Form HUD-93101 notification that the mortgagor is no longer "over income" and meets all other continued eligibility criteria.

NOTE: Reinstatement may be as a result of a reduction in the mortgagor's family income and/or due to an increase in the total monthly mortgage payment (such as an increase in amount being escrowed).

3. Suspension Due To Mortgagor's Failure to Recertify. Assistance payments may be reinstated effective the first day of the month after the mortgagee receives the required Form HUD-93101.

4. Suspension Due To Mortgagor's Failure to Disclose and Verify Social Security Numbers (24 CFR 235.375(b)(4)). Assistance payments may be reinstated effective the first day of the month after the mortgagee receives the social security number information.

5. Suspension Due To Initiation of Foreclosure. Upon the withdrawal of foreclosure action, assistance payments may be reinstated retroactively to the date of suspension provided that, during the period the assistance payments were suspended, the mortgagor continued to meet all other criteria for receiving assistance payments.

    a. Negotiation of Reinstatement Terms. The terms of reinstatement of the mortgage (i.e., whether the delinquency is to be paid in a lump sum, or additional sums are to be paid each month until the mortgage is current etc. ,) may be negotiated between the mortgagee and the mortgagor. However, the terms agreed upon must be realistic and may not affect the monthly mortgage payment on which the Formula One assistance payment is based.

    b. Reimbursement of Foreclosure Costs. Mortgagee retains the right to be reimbursed by the mortgagor for any costs incurred with respect to the withdrawn foreclosure action. However, these costs must be kept separate and apart from any Section 235 assistance. These costs may not be added to the monthly mortgage payment used to calculate the assistance payments and may not be billed to HUD as a separate item.

10-19 TERMINATION OF ASSISTANCE PAYMENT CONTRACT (24 CFR 235.375).

A. Events Which Require Termination. Events are listed below (and also given under Item 16 of HUD-93114) which require the termination of the assistance payment contract:

1. when the contract of mortgage insurance is terminated;

    EXCEPTION: The assistance payment contract is not terminated because HUD accepts an assignment of the mortgage.

2. the mortgage is assumed by a mortgagor or cooperative member who is not eligible for assistance; or

3. the assistance payment contract has been properly suspended for three consecutive years without the subsidy being reinstated within that three-year period of suspension; or

4. when the assistance payment contract for Section 246 10-year mortgages terminate unless extended by the Secretary.

B. Termination Effective Dates. Assistance payment contracts terminated for the events cited in the preceding paragraph shall be made effective the first day of the month following the date of the event which requires the termination of the contract.

C. Contracts Terminated In Error. Where the assistance payment contract is terminated in error, the mortgagee shall reinstate the contract immediately upon discovering the error. Form HUD-93114 must be submitted with the box checked under Item 17(1). (Item 17(1) denotes "Terminated in Error" as the reason for the reinstatement.) Documentation of the error is to be retained in the mortgagor's case file for the life of the mortgage.

NOTE: Once a Section 235 assistance payment contract has been properly terminated it may not be reinstated.

10-20 ESCROW ACCOUNTS. Basically escrow accounts for Section 235 mortgages are serviced the same as escrow accounts for other insured mortgages (i.e., in accordance with procedures discussed in Chapter 2). However, certain differences will be encountered. Mortgagees must determine which escrow items and/or what portion of the premium for an acceptable escrow item may be included in the total monthly mortgage payment prior to computing the amount of subsidy the mortgagor is entitled to under the Section 235 program. Guidance for making this determination is as follows:

A. Escrow Items Which May Be Included In Assistance Computations. Only certain items required under the mortgage may be included in the assistance computations. The escrow items that are acceptable, and the guidelines for determining the acceptable portion of the premium for that escrow item (if the entire amount cannot be included) are listed below:

1. Hazard Insurance. Only the cost of either the standard fire and extended coverage or basic homeowner's policy may be included in the assistance calculations. If a basic homeowner's policy is used, the mortgagee must be sure that any premiums for other items, such as cars, boats or other properties are not included in the assistance calculations. If the cost of the basic homeowner's policy appears excessive, the mortgagee must contact the agent and establish the cost of a standard fire and extended coverage policy and use the lesser of the two.

   NOTE: Do not include disability or life insurance premiums.

2. Flood Insurance. The entire premium may be included in the computation if the insurance is required by HUD or the mortgagee.

3. Taxes. The entire amount for taxes and special assessments which are levied by a government body may be included in the assistance calculations. Caution, specified assessments may be payable over several tax years. Only the prorated portion due for a specific tax year may be included.

NOTE: Do not include ground rents, assessments by mortgagors' associations, and special assessments levied by persons or private organizations.

B. Additional Disclosures Required Prior To Closing. Prior to closing, mortgagees must make mortgagors aware of the following:

1. the availability of any tax exemption (i.e., available to the mortgagor at the time of closing) for which the mortgagor may qualify;
2. that the responsibility for applying for the exemption is that of the mortgagor;
3. that their assistance payments will be computed based on the assumption that the mortgagor will be receiving the tax exemption for which they qualify;

C. Adjustment Of "Excessive" Surpluses And Shortages. Where an escrow analysis reveals an "excessive" surplus or an "excessive" shortage, a retroactive analysis must be performed.

NOTE: Definition of "Excessive" Surpluses and Shortages. An "excessive" surplus or shortage is defined as any amount that is greater or less than requirements by more than 15 percent of the actual disbursements from the account during the most recent full year. Before applying the 15 percent rule, the mortgagee may add one-sixth to the actual disbursements if it has chosen to maintain the surplus permitted in Chapter 2 of this Handbook.

D. When Retroactive Adjustments Are Required. Retroactive adjustments must be made at the following times:

1. When The First Analysis Is Performed After Settlement. If a shortage or surplus is discovered at this time, the shortage or surplus was probably caused by an incorrect amount being collected at settlement to establish the escrow account.

    NOTE: If the cause is due to an improper amount being collected at settlement, HUD would not be billed for any portion of the shortage or refunded any portion of the surplus.

2. When The Escrow Analysis Reveals an "excessive" surplus or shortage Allowed (as stated in the "NOTE" under Paragraph 10-20C).

3. When The Mortgage Is Being Assumed Or Paid In Full. Any necessary adjustment revealed by the required escrow analysis must be made prior to completion of either of these transactions. However, if this is not possible and/or the mortgagee later discovers an adjustment should have been made for underpaid assistance, make the appropriate refund to the mortgagor and bill HUD for the underpayment amount using an adjustment transaction Code 2 on the next regular month's billing Forms HUD-93102 and HUD-300. The specific reason for adjustment must be provided in Column 3.

For example, underestimated tax escrow. The beginning and ending effective periods of the adjustment (month and year) must be included in the reason for adjustment in Column 3 on Form HUD-300. A copy of the escrow analysis clearly depicting the cause of escrow shortage and the period must accompany Forms HUD-93102 and HUD-300.

4. When The First Escrow Analysis Of A Suspended Or Terminated Contract Is Performed.

5. When A Prospective Adjustment Would Reduce Assistance To Zero. (A retroactive adjustment is required to confirm the proper suspension of the assistance payments contract.)

E. Prospective Adjustments. Except as cited above, the mortgagee may exercise its option to make prospective adjustments.

F. Adjustment Procedure. Regardless of whether the adjustment is to be prospective or retroactive, the procedure is the same:

1. Adjust the "Formula One" Assistance Payment.

   a. Determine the exact amount needed in order to make proper disbursements as they become due;
   b. Determine if there were any reported changes (i.e., valid recertifications submitted to the mortgagee) in the mortgagor's household income during the period for which escrow is being collected;
   c. Recalculate the "Formula One" assistance payment for any period where the income differed;

2. Verify Accuracy of the "Formula Two" Assistance Payment. If there was an anniversary of amortization during the period, the "Formula Two" payment should have been adjusted at that time because of the change in MIP. If no adjustment was made, the "Formula Two" payment must be recomputed for the period after that anniversary.

   NOTE: A common error to look for when verifying Formula Two computations is the use of the wrong column in the Section 235 Factor Table Amortization Year - Formula Two when determining the anniversary factor. The first column on each page of this Factor Table is the factor for the first year (the origination factor) -- not the factor for the first recertification.

   For example, to compute the Formula Two assistance for the first annual recertification of a mortgage, the factor shown in the 2nd column would be the correct factor to use.

3. Compare the Two Results. For each period where the mortgagor's household income differed, the smaller of the recomputed "Formula One" assistance payment and the

correct "Formula Two" assistance payment is the amount that HUD should have been billed. Total the correct payments for the entire disbursement period for which money was being collected and compare these payment amounts with the amounts actually billed. The difference is the overpayment or underpayment of assistance.

10-21 BILLING FOR ASSISTANCE/HANDLING CHARGES. In order to receive Section 235 Original, Revised, Revised with Recapture or Revised, Recapture/10 Program assistance payments and handling charges, mortgagees must submit billings to HUD on a monthly basis using an original and one copy of Form HUD-93102, Mortgagee's Certification and Application for Assistance or Interest Reduction Payments. Both the original and the copy of the Form-HUD-93102 must contain original signatures of an authorized mortgagee official.

NOTE: Only one Form HUD-93102 per mortgage will be accepted for processing each month regardless of the mortgagee's servicing organization or billing procedures. Form HUD-93102 will be returned unprocessed if it is not accompanied by Form HUD-300 detailing as required all billing amounts included in Blocks 1, 2, 3 or 5 on Form HUD-93102.

A. Time Frame For Submitting Form HUD-93102. The Form HUD-93102 must be submitted to HUD (at the exact address shown on the back of the Form) no earlier than the 5th and no later than the 20th of each month in accordance with the instructions printed on the back of this Form.

NOTE: Adjustment amounts determined necessary subsequent to submission of a Form HUD-93102 for a given month must be included on the next regular month's billing on the Form HUD-93102 line(s) provided for billing adjustment amounts. Duplicate Forms HUD-93102 submitted in the same month will be returned to the mortgagee unprocessed.

B. Submission/Completion Of HUD-93102.

1. A Single Form HUD-93102 For The Total of All Section 235 Program Assistance Payment Requests. One billing must be submitted on Form HUD-93102 which includes billing amounts for all Section 235 assistance payments due for either the Original program in Block 1, the Revised program in Block 2, the Revised with Recapture program in Block 3, or the Revised Recapture/10 program in Block 5. The billing must be submitted with an original and one copy of Form HUD-93102. Both the original and the copy must contain original signatures of an authorized mortgagee official. Failure to submit the original and a copy will cause payment processing delays.

NOTE: Mortgagees are no longer required to submit two separate Forms HUD-93102 for Section 235 assistance payments.

The current Form HUD-93102, dated March 1988 must be used. Expired Forms HUD-93102 will be returned unprocessed.

If a billing is resubmitted for any reason, it must be clearly marked "Resubmission" on its face.

Payments will be made to the servicer identified in HUD's records regardless of any directions to the contrary that may be inserted on the billing form. HUD will only send payments to the servicer of record. Form HUD-92080, Mortgage Record Change must be submitted in accordance with Chapter 6 to report a change of servicers.

2. Adjustments To The Regular Monthly Billing Amounts. The adjustment Line 2 in each Block 1, 2, 3 or 5 on Form HUD-93102 must be used to request retroactive payment of assistance for prior months.

   Line 1 in Blocks 1, 2, 3 or 5 should include the total amount of assistance for the current billing period only.

   Any billing amounts included on an adjustment Line 2 on Form HUD-93102 must be reflected as adjustment transactions using transaction Code 2 listed on Form HUD-300 should balance with the sum of the adjustment amounts on Lines 2 in Blocks 1, 2, 3 or 5 on Forms HUD-93102. Failure to verify that the adjustment amounts and the regular billing amounts on Form HUD-93102 balance with transaction code 1, regular billing and transaction Code 2, adjustment billing amounts on Form HUD-300 will cause payment processing delays.

3. Prior month billing amounts, adjustment transaction Codes 2. Prior month billing amounts must reflect the beginning and ending effective period (month and year) and an explanation of adjustment code in Column 3 as defined below. Any adjustment must also be supported by documentation requirements as defined below.

Reason for Adjustment	Adjustment Code	Documentation Required
Reinstatement of after suspension or termination in error	1	HUD-93114
Reinstatement after borrower's failure to recertify timely	2*	HUD-93114, HUD-93101-A
Handling charges returned due to mortgagee' failure to meet contractual obligations	3	None
Suspension	4	HUD-93114
Termination	5	HUD-93114
Escrow Shortage	6	Escrow Analysis
Escrow Surplus	7	Escrow Analysis
Income Increase	8	HUD-93101-A, HUD-93101
Increase Decrease	9	HUD 93101-A, HUD-93101

NOTE: If more than one explanation of adjustment code applies to a single transaction, all applicable codes should be recorded in Column 3 on Form HUD-300 and all applicable documentation should be submitted.

Failure to identify the period of billing, the explanation of adjustment code or the documentation required, as defined above will cause non-payment of assistance for the affected cases. The mortgagee will have to re-bill non-paid cases on the next monthly billing. Payment may not be requested on a second bill for the same month.

Adjustment Code 2 must not be used in connection with the 7% interest penalty assessed due to fraud, misrepresentation and/or failure to meet contractual obligations. The 7% penalty must be submitted to HUD in accordance with Paragraph 10-29A.

C. Submission/Completion Of Form HUD-300. A Form HUD-300, Monthly Summary of Assistance Payments Due Under Sections 235(b), 235(j), or 235(i), or of Interest Reduction Payments Due Under Section 236, must accompany the completed Form HUD-93102.

1. Mortgagees using facsimile versions of Form HUD-300 must include on the modified version, all data required on the actual Form HUD-300.

2. Any transaction Code 1, current month's regular billing amount which is more or less than the amount billed in the prior month must be supported by appropriate documentation as follows:

Reason for Change	Documentation Required
Case reinstated	Form HUD-93114 and unless suspended in error, Forms HUD-93101-A and HUD-93101
Income increase or decrease	Form HUD-93101-A
Monthly mortgage payment amount changed due to escrow shortage or surplus	A copy of the escrow analysis clearly depicting what caused the required decrease or increase in escrow (e.g., taxes underestimated by $20 per month)

D. Review For Billing Accuracy. HUD will review billings for propriety, legality and correctness. When a billing is received that is not signed by an authorized mortgagee official, not accompanied by a Form HUD-300, and/or requests amounts which cannot be reconciled to FHA/HUD case detail provided on Form HUD-300, it will be returned to the mortgagee unpaid. No payment will be made until the mortgagee has submitted a corrected billing for that month.

When the amount billed for a case is more or less than the amount billed in the prior month, no payment will be made for the case unless the billing is accompanied by the required Form HUD-93101-A, escrow analysis, or HUD mortgage recapture approval letter, whichever is applicable.

When a mortgagee determines than an income increase is not retroactive, as reflected by the "effective date of payment change" entered in Block C (7) on Form HUD-93101-A (i.e., the mortgagor's income increase was not received prior to the date that the mortgagee received the mortgagor's recertification), a copy of HUD-93101 must be attached to the Form HUD-93101-A for accounting office verification of the overpaid subsidy determination.

When the effective date of payment change reflects that an income decrease is retroactive, Form HUD-93101 must be attached to Form HUD-93101-A for verification of the underpayment determination (also see Paragraph 10-31).

No payment will be made on cases when non-retroactive subsidy decrease, or retroactive subsidy increase amounts as described above are not documented for verification by attachment of both Forms HUD-93101-A and HUD-93101 to the billing Form HUD-93102.

Subsidy increases due to escrow shortage will not be paid for any case unless:

1. the billing is accompanied by an escrow analysis; and
2. for each escrow item disbursed which was included in the subsidy amount calculation, copies of the canceled checks and invoices for accounting office verification of the shortage computation are attached.

E. Mortgagee Liability (24 CFR 235. 361(b)). Mortgagees are responsible for the accuracy of the billings and shall be held liable for fraud or false certification made on these billings (see Paragraph 10-28B). All billings must be signed by an authorized mortgagee official. Improper billings may result in the imposition of substantial financial penalties as the Program Fraud Civil Remedies Act applies to assistance payments.

NOTE: Mortgagee signing officials should give special attention to the meaning of the certification signed by authorized mortgagee officials on Form HUD-93102. The signing official is certifying, subject to the Program Fraud Civil Remedies Act, that:

1. the assistance payment amount requested for each case included in the bill has been correctly calculated both for the amounts and the periods claimed due in accordance with the provisions of this Handbook;
2. the bill does not include any amounts on behalf of mortgagors who have not complied with recertification requirements within the time limits specified in this Handbook, or in the manner set forth in 24 CFR 235. 350;
3. the bill does not include amounts on behalf of mortgagors not eligible for assistance in accordance with provisions set forth in 24 CFR 235 and as set forth in this Handbook;

4. no amount in the billing has been previously claimed in an outstanding bill, determined by HUD as not payable in a previous bill (i.e., determined not payable after a HUD review of required billing support documents) or paid in a previous bill;

5. supporting details, records and worksheets, together with a copy of the applicable billing are being held in the mortgagee's file; and

6. all aforementioned documents will be furnished or made available upon request of an authorized official of HUD or of the Comptroller General of the United States. A determination made upon review that certification to the above was false may result in the imposition of substantial financial penalties.

F. Receipt Of HUD's Payment. When a billing is submitted to HUD in accordance with outstanding instructions and within the time frame shown in Paragraph 10-21, payment should reach the mortgagee on or about the first day of the following month.

G. Monthly Billing. HUD will process payment for only one monthly billing form. Duplicate requests will be returned to the mortgagee unprocessed.

1. Monthly billings must be submitted on the current Form HUD-93102, dated March 1988 which may be obtained from the Government Printing Office. Obsolete Forms HUD-93102 will be returned unprocessed.

2. Recertifications of income which accompany the billing must be submitted on the current Form 93101-A, dated March 1990

3. Monthly billings should include:

    a. the assistance amount due for the current billing period on Line 1 of the appropriate Block 1, 2, 3 or 5; plus

    b. the assistance amount for any prior months the mortgagor was entitled to assistance but for which the assistance amount was not paid on a previously submitted Form HUD-93102 or included on an outstanding Form HUD-93102 on Line 2 of the appropriate Block 1, 2, 3 or 5; minus

    c. adjustments for overpaid amounts due HUD which is also on Line 2 of the appropriate Block 1, 2, 3 or 5;

    d. the net total of Line 1 and Line 2 on Line 3 of the appropriate Blocks 1, 2, 3 or 5; and

    e. the summary total from Line 3 of Blocks 1, 2 and 3 in Block 4.

    NOTE: Overpaid subsidy identified in response to HUD conducted mortgagee reviews requiring retroactive assistance payments reviews to be performed by mortgagees should not be included on the regular monthly billing. The required review must be completed within the time frame specified by HUD's (or its agent's) mortgagee review report. Overpayment must be submitted on a separate billing clearly denoted in large print at the top of the billing as a "Retroactive Review Billing".

    This billing must be accompanied by:

> (1) a check made payable to HUD for the total overpayment amount; and
> (2) a mortgagee review findings report which lists in columns, the following information:
>
>> (a) the name of each overpaid mortgagor:
>> (b) the FHA case number;
>> (c) the month and year of the beginning and ending period of overpaid subsidy (i.e., 3/86-5/88);
>> (d) the overpayment amount;
>> (e) an explanation of:
>>
>>> i.   the cause of overpayment (using explanations of adjustment codes from Paragraph 10-21);
>>> ii.   the date of the event which resulted in the overpayment; and
>>> iii.   the effective period of the adjustment.
>>
>> (f) the mortgagee's calculation of the overpayment amount; and
>> (g) attachments Forms HUD-93101-A, HUD-93101, HUD-93114 (one HUD-93114 to suspend the assistance payments and one to reinstate the assistance payments for retroactive suspensions resulting in overpayments) and/or escrow analyses as applicable to the explanation given for overpayment.
>>
>> Copies of the check and Forms HUD-93102 and HUD-300 must also be sent to the appropriate HUD local Office that conducted the review.

H.   Rounding Off Billing Amounts. At the option of the mortgagee, assistance may be billed in either of the following ways:

1.   using the exact amount to which the mortgagor is entitled; or
2.   using the amount arrived at after rounding off the exact amount to the nearest dollar (i.e., $.01-$.49 round down to zero; $0.50-$.99 round up to $1.00).

Regardless of which method is used when billing HUD, mortgagees must be consistent and must use the same method (i.e., rounding off or using the exact amount) must be used for all amounts billed and used when crediting the individual mortgagor's account.

I.   Billing Of Handling Charges. The mortgagee is entitled to a $3.00 handling fee per month, per active Section 235 mortgage account.

10-22 ASSUMPTIONS. Assistance may be continued on behalf of an assumptor if that assumptor meets all qualifying requirements as of the day the mortgage assumption actually takes place (i.e., the day the mortgage is executed by the assumptor at closing).

A. Assistance Eligibility. The information on Form HUD-93100-4 must reflect that, on the day of closing, the assumptor's status qualified him/her for assistance based on the eligibility criteria for new mortgagors.

NOTE: The assumptor's household is not required (as the original mortgagor was) to have five or more members if the property has four or more bedrooms.

B. Additional Underwriting Requirements For Section 235 Assumptions. Assumptions of Section 235 mortgages are treated the same as those insured under any other section of the Act except for the following additional underwriting requirements:

1. where subsidy eligibility must be determined, the assistance application (Form HUD 93100-4) is to be reviewed before the credit application and, if assistance is to be authorized, the amount of assistance is to be used as income in the credit evaluation; and
2. if the firm commitment to insure the original mortgage or direct endorsement underwriter's credit approval was issued on or after May 27, 1981, the assumptor must sign, at closing, a note agreeing to pay any recapture of assistance that may be due HUD in order to satisfy this lien on the property (24 CFR 235.12). (See Chapter 11).

C. Mortgagee Responsibility. In addition to enforcing the [HUD's creditworthiness requirements], when the mortgagee becomes aware there has been or will be an assumption, the following action must be taken:

1. make the assumptor aware that he/she may be eligible for assistance;
2. prepare the necessary documents to determine eligibility for assistance (if assumptor wishes to be considered for assistance);
3. where the assumptor appears to be eligible for assistance, processing must be delayed until the local HUD Office has determined whether assistance can be approved in order that any assistance may be considered in the credit analysis;
4. make the assumptor aware of his/her recapture responsibilities (as listed below) if the firm commitment (or direct endorsement credit approval) was issued on or after May 27, 1981:

   a. there is an existing lien against the property in favor of HUD which shall remain there until satisfied;
   b. the recapture will become due immediately due if he/she does not:

      (1) qualify for assistance;
      (2) agree to accept the assistance for which he/she qualifies;
      (3) agree to execute a new note at closing;

   c. the recapture becomes due once the assumptor acquires title to the property. He/she will be held liable for the full amount required to satisfy HUD's lien on the property;

5. where appropriate, take the necessary action to obtain and prepare the required documentation and collect the amount due HUD to satisfy the recapture lien in accordance with Chapter 11; and

6. suspend the assistance payments contract if the mortgage is assumed before HUD approves the assumptor for assistance.

D. HUD Responsibility. In addition to enforcing [HUD's creditworthiness requirements], when HUD becomes aware that there has been or will be an assumption, it will:

1. determine the assumptor's eligibility for assistance;

2. if eligible, determine the initial amount of assistance for which the assumptor qualifies;

3. where appropriate, determine whether the assumptor's credit qualifies (if the case is not being processed by a direct endorsement mortgagee);

4. where appropriate, take the necessary action to:

   a. obtain and prepare the required documentation to determine the recapture amount due in order to satisfy the Section 235 lien;

   b. collect and deposit the amount due HUD;

   c. prepare the satisfaction of the recapture lien in accordance with instructions provided in Chapter 11;

   d. obtain the signatures of an authorized HUD official and get the satisfaction notarized; and

   e. forward the executed and notarized satisfaction to the mortgagee in accordance with instructions outlined in Chapter 11.

E. Cut-off/Start-up Dates For Assistance. Assistance should be cut off and started as follows:

1. When assumptors are approved before acquiring title:

   a. subsidy will cease on behalf of the seller effective the first day of the month after he/she moves out of the property;

   b. subsidy will begin on behalf of the approved assumptor effective the first day of the following month (i.e., the month after the seller moved out) PROVIDED the assumptor has moved into the property and has acquired title to the property by the effective date.

   NOTE: For this purpose, the acquisition date may be considered as the date the deed was recorded unless the mortgagor can demonstrate an earlier date.

   c. if the assumptor does not acquire title and occupy the property within 90 calendar days after the seller moves out, the assistance payments must be suspended.

   NOTE: Suspension will continue until the first day of the month after the assumptor has moved into the property and has acquired title to the property.

2. When assumptors are approved after acquisition of title:

    a. subsidy will cease on behalf of the seller effective with the first day of the month after occupancy ends;

    b. subsidy will begin on behalf of the assumptor effective (depending on the length of delay between the assumption and application for assistance) as follows:

        (1) Delay of 90 Days or Less. If no more than 90 days elapse between title acquisition and application for assistance, payments shall be made retroactive to the first day of the month following title acquisition or occupancy of the property, whichever is later.

        (2) Delays of More Than 90 Days. If more than 90 days elapse between title acquisition and application for assistance, payments shall be made effective from the first day of the month following application, PROVIDED the assumptor has title and occupies the property when the application is submitted and through the time that the application for assistance is approved.

10-23 DELINQUENCIES AND DEFAULTS. Mortgagees are expected to treat Section 235 mortgages in the same manner as other insured mortgages when they become delinquent. The mortgagor remains eligible for assistance until the mortgagee takes the first legal action required to initiate foreclosure or until some other event requires suspension or termination of the assistance payments contract.

    A. Partial Payments. Assistance payments for periods when the mortgagor fails to make his/her share of the mortgage payment are not to be considered partial payments of the mortgagor's share of the full monthly mortgage amount. HUD assistance payments must be accepted regardless of the amount or the length of the delinquency. Before foreclosure may be started, all partial payments of the mortgagor's share must be applied toward the unpaid monthly installments, beginning with the earliest unpaid installment.

        1. All assistance payments earned up to the time of the action to foreclose the mortgage must be billed for and applied to complete the monthly installments in the order in which they become due, e.g., to MIP, escrow, interest, and principal, beginning with the earliest unpaid installment. All unearned assistance payments should be applied as a reduction towards the amount billed HUD monthly on Form HUD-93102.

        2. Reinstatement of the account by the mortgagor may not be delayed pending receipt of earned but unpaid assistance payments, and those payments must be billed for promptly when the mortgagee decides to accept reinstatement from the mortgagor.

        NOTE: The rules governing return of partial payments in Paragraph 7-9 apply only to the mortgagor's share of the payment, not to the portion that is paid by HUD.

    B. Forbearance. Assistance payments are not affected by forbearance agreements. They are treated as partial payments as described in the preceding paragraph. During these periods, however, the mortgagor must maintain eligibility for assistance (i.e., by continuing to occupy the property, providing required recertifications, etc.) and the mortgagee must continue to make adjustments to the amount of assistance for which the mortgagor is entitled as though the mortgagor were making his/her portion of the monthly payments as required.

C. Special Forbearance. Assistance payments are not affected by special forbearance agreements. The special forbearance agreement:

1. shall be prepared in accordance with instructions outlined in Paragraph 8-4; and
2. shall include an additional provision recognizing that the assistance payments will continue to be adjusted as required under the Section 235 program;

D. Recasting. When a Section 235 mortgage is recast, the monthly payment due under the mortgage as recast becomes the base for calculating both "Formula One" and "Formula Two" assistance payments. The new principal amount after recasting is considered the original mortgage amount for amortization purposes and the new maturity date governs.

NOTE: MIP is not affected by recasting. Regardless of the new unpaid principal balance, the MIP continues to be calculated on the original scheduled unpaid balances.

10-24 ASSIGNMENT TO HUD. Assistance payments are not affected by an assignment of the mortgage to HUD. The assistance payment contract shall remain in effect up to the date the assignment is filed for record.

NOTE: The last assistance payments for which the mortgage should bill HUD are those for the month immediately preceding the month in which the mortgage is assigned.

10-25 PREPAYMENTS. Section 235 prepayments shall be as follows:

A. Partial. If partial prepayments have been applied to reduce future monthly payments (see Paragraph 5-3A2), both "Formula One" and "Formula Two" must be recalculated based on the revised payments.

B. In Full. The last assistance payment payable will be for the month the mortgage was paid in full presuming the mortgagor was in occupancy and was the legal owner on the first day of the month.

10-26 TRANSFER OF SERVICING. A transfer of servicing has the following affect on a Section 235 mortgage:

A. Assistance Eligibility. A mortgagor's eligibility for assistance will not be affected;

B. Recertifications. Annual recertification may be affected if:

1. the mortgagees involved in the transfer use different anniversary dates for recertification; and
2. the transfer would result in a lapse of more than 15 months between recertifications.

C. Additional Recertification Required. Where the situation described in Paragraph 10-26B occurs, the new mortgagee or servicer must require recertification twice in the first year after acquisition—one on the anniversary date used previously by the former mortgagee or servicer and the second one on the anniversary date that is being used by the new mortgagee or servicer.

D. Additional Notice To Mortgagor. Within 10 days of the transfer, the new mortgagee or servicer must:

1. advise the mortgagor of the transfer of the mortgage; and
2. provide the mortgagor with the new recertification schedule.

NOTE: The above disclosures may be included with the notice of servicing transfer required by Paragraph 6-11B or sent as a separate notice. However, if the above disclosure is sent as a part of the normal notice required by Paragraph 6-11B when a mortgage is transferred, the notice must be received by the mortgagor at least 10 days before the due date of the first payment to the new mortgagee or servicer.

E. Seller's/Purchaser's Servicing Responsibility. When an insured mortgage is sold, the purchasing mortgagee succeeds to all rights and becomes bound by all of the obligations of the selling mortgagee under the contract of mortgage insurance. Purchasing mortgagees should be aware that they will be held fully responsible to HUD financially for errors or omissions on the part of the selling mortgagee (or its agents), discovered after the transfer is reported, even though those errors or omissions may have taken place before it was reported to HUD.

10-27 POSSIBLE VIOLATIONS OF LAW OR REGULATIONS. Mortgagees are not expected to seek out evidence of wrongdoing on the part of mortgagors. Neither are they expected to extensively investigate allegations of wrongdoing brought to their attention. However, if a matter can be reasonably explained and/or resolved without extensive investigation, those facts should be used in computing assistance.

A. Mortgagee Responsibility.

1. General. The mortgagee's actions taken independently of instructions from HUD must always be exercised with due care, using the best information available including recent information reflected in the mortgagor's recertification, with its supporting verifying data.

2. Report Clues/Evidence of Mortgagor's Possible Wrongdoing. Possible clues and/or evidence of possible wrongdoing on the part of the mortgagor are to be forwarded to the local HUD Office for whatever action it deems appropriate. Until notified by the local HUD Office as to the action that will be taken (if any), the mortgagee should make the appropriate adjustments in assistance payments as instructed in Paragraph 10-27A1. Such clues and/or evidence may include, but are not limited to, the following:

a. a verification of income showing a date of employment or an increase in income much earlier than the date(s) certified to by the mortgagor which cannot be reconciled;

b. an application for another type of loan which shows a new spouse with income and/or other additional sources of income not shown in the recertification;

c. a disclosure, during negotiation of a repayment plan to cure a default, that the mortgagor or other family members have income not reported in the recertification;

d. a name change of the person or a different person signs the recertification for which no reason is known;

e. the receipt of allegations from either identified or anonymous sources containing enough specific information that would lead a person to believe that the recertification might contain false information; and

3. **Information Not to be Reported.** The mortgagee is charged with acting on its own initiative, basing its actions on the best information available (as outlined in Paragraph 10-27A1), and for documenting its files as to why a particular action was taken.

The following are the examples of cases where the mortgagee shall take appropriate action including completion of all required retroactive recertifications and therefore, need not refer the case to HUD include, but not limited to, the following:

a. where the mortgage was insured before January 5, 1976, and the mortgagor did not report an increase in income caused by a change in the source of income of any adult family member until the first normal recertification following the increase; and

NOTE: Reason for Not Reporting to HUD—A $50 increase (or more) per month on these mortgages does not require an additional recertification. The assistance payments are adjusted at the time of the annual recertification effective as of the date the income increase occurred.

b. where the mortgage was insured on or after January 5, 1976, and the mortgagor failed to notify the mortgagee of changes in total family income as noted in (a) above or the mortgagor did not report a $50 increase (or more) per month in adult family income until the annual recertification and overpaid assistance resulted.

NOTE: Reason for Not Reporting to HUD—While the mortgagor is obligated to report a $50 increase (or more) per month in adult family income when they are received, it was reported at the time of the annual recertification. Once the mortgagee learns that such an increase did go into effect and went unreported by the mortgagor, the mortgagee is to take the necessary steps to determine when the $50 (or more) income increased per month. Assistance must then be recomputed and the overpaid assistance refunded to HUD.

B. HUD Field Office Responsibility. The HUD Field Office Manager will review any information sent in with respect to possible wrongdoing on the part of a mortgagor and will determine whether further investigation is warranted.

1. Where An Investigation Is Warranted. Where it is warranted, the Field Office Manager will take the necessary steps to refer a case to the appropriate HUD office for investigation.

2. Where An Investigation Is Not Warranted. Where administrative action is appropriate and former investigation is not warranted, the Field Office Manager will notify the mortgagee, in writing, of its decision. Written instructions will also be provided to the mortgagee as to how it should proceed with the adjustment of the assistance payments.

C. Office Of The HUD Inspector General. The actual conduct of investigations into possible fraud or referral of information to other agencies for further investigation and decisions relating to prosecution is the responsibility of the Inspector General. Mortgagees will not normally be advised of the progress of investigations and should make no assumptions as to their possible outcome and its impact on assistance payments.

10-28 CAUSES OF OVERPAID ASSISTANCE. Overpaid assistance exists anytime assistance is billed and paid for any amounts greater than those for which a mortgagee/mortgagor is entitled. Listed below are the most common situations which result in overpaid assistance:

A. Mortgagee's Failure To Meet Contractual Obligations. This occurs when the mortgagee fails to meet its obligations under the assistance payments contract as follows:

1. requesting a handling charge on cases when recertifications have not been requested timely;
2. failing to act in a timely manner when:

    a. requesting a required recertification at the proper time;
    b. recalculating assistance payments;
    c. submitting Form HUD-93101-A and HUD-93114, as applicable;
    d. adjusting subsidy payments when a recertification Form HUD-93101 is received containing information which requires suspension or adjustment of assistance payments billed;
    e. retroactively calculating adjustments in assistance payments from the date of income increases and crediting overpaid assistance amounts to HUD when annual or interim recertifications reflect income increases;
    f. timely requesting HUD to suspend assistance payments when mortgagors fail to respond to recertification requests within the specified time frame;
    g. requesting reinstatements to be non-retroactive when suspensions were due to mortgagors failure to timely respond to certification requests; and/or
    h. verifying recertified income in the manner set forth in Paragraph 10-10.

B. Mortgagee Fraud Or Misrepresentation. This occurs when:

1. mortgagees falsify certifications on monthly billing Form HUD-93102 submitted to HUD for assistance payments (see Paragraph 10-21E); or
2. any other fraud and/or misrepresentation in the Section 235 program.

C. Mortgagor Errors Or Omissions. The most common mortgagor errors are failures (for whatever reason) to:

1. report increases of adult family income of $50 or more per month when the mortgage was insured on or after January 5, 1976;
2. advise the mortgagee when the property is sold;
3. advise the mortgagee when he/she no longer meets occupancy or some other basic eligibility requirement; and/or
4. include an income source on a required recertification.

D. Mortgagor Fraud Or Misrepresentation. When a mortgagor fails to include income amounts or sources, and/or misrepresents occupancy or other eligibility data, on a recertification in an attempt to receive assistance for which he/she is not eligible.

10-29 REPAYMENT OF OVERPAID ASSISTANCE (24 CFR 235.361).

A. Overpayments Caused By The Mortgagee. The mortgagee must refund to HUD all overpaid assistance and all handling charges for each month during which there was an overpayment, plus interest computed at the rate of seven percent per annum on the entire amount from the date of the first overpayment when an overpayment results from the following circumstances:

1. fraud or misrepresentation on the part of the mortgagee; and/or
2. the mortgagee's failure to meet a contractual obligation, as described in Paragraph 10-28.

The total overpayment amount must be credited on the next month's billing on Form HUD-93102 and should include return of handling charges paid for each period of overpayment for each case. Form HUD-300, Column 3, must reflect an explanation of the overpayment cause and the affected beginning and ending period (month and year).

The 7% interest amount must be sent in a separate check made payable to HUD with an itemized listing of the 7% calculation and total interest due for each overpaid case. The check with the itemized listing should accompany the Form HUD-93102 billing.

B. Overpayment Caused By Error. When an overpayment is caused by an error on the part of the mortgagee or the mortgagor only the overpaid assistance need be refunded. The mortgagee shall refund the overpaid assistance by:

1. reimbursing HUD the total overpaid amount on the next month's billing (on Form HUD-93102); and

2. collecting the overpaid assistance from the mortgagor in a lump sum or in installments while exercising due caution not to cause a default by the manner of collection selected (24 CFR 235.361(c)).

3. Only as a last resort should the mortgagee apply a mortgage payment or payments to the recovery of the overpaid amount.

   NOTE: If the error which created the overpaid assistance was caused by the mortgagee then the mortgagee must repay HUD, however, HUD does not require the mortgagee to collect repayment from the mortgagor.

C. Mortgagor No Longer Obligated Under The Mortgage.

1. On cases where the mortgagor is no longer obligated under the mortgage, the mortgagee must send the mortgagor's last known address to the HUD Office having jurisdiction over the mortgage.

2. The Claims Collection Officer in the HUD Field Office is responsible for the collection activities.

10-30 CAUSES OF UNDERPAYMENTS. Listed below are circumstances which may result in underpayments and are the only causes for which a mortgagee may bill for underpaid assistance:

A. math errors;

B. using a wrong factor in calculating the "Formula Two" assistance payment;

C. underestimating escrow requirements; and/or

D. the mortgagee's failure to initiate an optional recertification after notification from a mortgagor of a reduction of income.

   NOTE: Failure of a mortgagor to request an optional recertification at the time of a reduction in the income of an adult family member is not a justification to bill for an underpayment at a later date.

10-31 COLLECTING UNDERPAID ASSISTANCE. The total underpayment amount may be added to the next month's billing (on Form HUD-93102). Retroactive billings for underpaid subsidy must be accompanied by Forms HUD-93101-A and 93101, Form HUD-93114 requesting reinstatement of a suspension in error, or an escrow analysis with support documents as defined in Paragraph 10-21D.

NOTE: Underpayment requests will not be paid when the required documentation does not accompany Form HUD-93102, or the explanation of adjustment is not provided on Form HUD-300 with documentation required as defined in Paragraph 10-21B3.

10-32 RECORDS MAINTENANCE (24 CFR 235.365 and 235.830). HUD Field Offices will periodically review mortgagee records to establish that assistance is being billed properly. These reviews will normally cover recertifications, verifications, billings, suspensions, terminations, documentation, and escrow analysis. In addition to the records maintenance required on other types of mortgages, mortgagees must have complete records to support the amounts billed each month on each mortgage from the time of origination through termination of assistance payments (also see Paragraph 10-17), including recapture of assistance where applicable (see Chapter 11). These records must be adequate to support every dollar of assistance billed. Where records do not exist to substantiate the amount of assistance billed, assistance will be considered overpaid and must be refunded unless the mortgagee can reconstruct adequate records to support the payments. For each case, the records must include:

A. all initial applications (Forms HUD-93100-4) and required recertifications (Form HUD-93101 and 93101-A), with supporting verifications and other related documentation;

B. all optional recertifications that resulted in changes in assistance, with supporting verifications and other related documentation;

C. for each suspension, reinstatement, or termination:

1. a Form HUD-93114;
2. all individual escrow analyses related to overpaid or underpaid assistance; and
3. individual ledgers (or other records) showing application of assistance to the account;

D. all monthly billings (Forms HUD-93102) for assistance payments with supporting documentation for all adjustments for overpaid or underpaid assistance;

E. for each monthly billing (Form HUD-93102), a case-by-case summary showing, for each case included in the billing, the following data elements:

1. the date of endorsement for insurance;
2. the original mortgage amount;
3. the certified adjusted annual income used that month;
4. the total mortgage payment that month;
5. the "Formula One" calculation;
6. the "Formula Two" calculation;
7. the amount of assistance due;
8. the explanation of adjustment code as provided in Chapter 10-21B3;
9. the beginning and ending effective dates (month and year) of adjustment transactions Code 2;
10. the handling charge; and
11. the total bill.

10-33 RESPONSIBILITY FOR TRANSFERRING RECORDS. Mortgagees acquiring mortgages from other mortgagees and/or changing servicers are fully responsible for records that should have been maintained by the selling/transferring mortgagee or servicer.

NOTE: If it is determined after a change of servicers that assistance has been overpaid, the servicer at the time of the discovery will be responsible for refunding the overpayment.

10-34 REPORTING TO HUD. For monitoring purposes, the following Section 235 reports are to be submitted to HUD Headquarters.

NOTE: These reports should not be submitted to Field Offices unless specifically requested.

A. Reports On Recertifications. A Form HUD-93101-A must be submitted on each case recertified. The appropriate address is printed on the form.

B. Ad Hoc Reporting. As needed, HUD will request information on the cumulative assistance paid on an account to date (i.e., from origination through termination of the assistance contract) to determine the amount of recapture due HUD in order to satisfy the recapture lien. Records must be maintained in such a manner as to enable the mortgagee to provide this information. Such information must be made available to HUD upon request.

10-35 INFORMATION TO MORTGAGORS (24 CFR 203.508(c) and 235.1001). Within 30 days after the end of each calendar year, the mortgagee must provide the mortgagor with a statement advising the following:

A. the total amount of assistance applied to the mortgagor's account during the preceding year;

B. the taxes and interest paid on the mortgagor's behalf during the year; and

C. a notice as to the probable deductibility of interest payments using substantially the language shown below:

"If you itemize deductions on your income tax returns, please read this notice. Under Section 1. 163-1(d) of Federal Income Tax Regulations, you, as the mortgagor, may deduct for Federal income tax purposes, only that part, if any, of mortgage interest payments made during the year which exceeded the amount of assistance payments made by HUD during the year. You are urged to contact your tax advisor or State and local tax offices for guidance regarding the deductibility of payments on your State or local income tax returns."

10-36 REVISED/RECAPTURE/10 PROGRAM (24 CFR 235.12). The Appropriations Act of 1984 reactivated the Section 235 Program as revised by the Housing and Urban Rural Recovery Act of 1983. Mortgages insured under Section 235 beginning in early 1985 are identified with case number suffixes (the last three numbers) 246, 346, and 546. The assistance payments contract on these mortgages is limited by the Housing and Urban Rural Recovery Act of 1983 to 10 years after mortgage origination. When the 10 year period ends, the mortgagee must terminate the assistance payment contract, if there is not a request by the Department to continue such assistance. The assistance paid during the contract period is subject to recapture by HUD under certain circumstances. Procedures and requirements of these mortgages are the same as for other Section 235 mortgage except as indicated below:

A. Documentation At Origination. Assistance payments on these mortgages are disbursed and monitored using an automated system. In order to set up a new case in the automated system, the HUD Field Office must have:

1. the completed Mortgage Insurance Certificate indicating the FHA/HUD case number;
2. the separate assistance payments contract which has been executed by both HUD and the mortgagee and the "Acknowledgement of Mortgagors", signed by the mortgagors;
3. the mortgage interest rate;
4. the due date of the first principal and interest payment;
5. the mortgagee and/or servicer's complete name, address and mortgagee number assigned by HUD;

B. "Formula One" Assistance. Under this program, the "Formula One" assistance payment is the difference between the full monthly mortgage payment and 28 percent of the mortgagor's adjusted monthly family income (as opposed to 20 percent under earlier versions of the program). The actual assistance paid is still the lesser of the "Formula One" and "Formula Two" payments.

C. Recapture Of Assistance (24 CFR 235.12). In addition to the limited term of assistance, these mortgages are distinguished by a provision for recapture of assistance when the property is sold. (See Chapter 11 for detailed recapture procedures.)

D. Mortgage Assumptions. Mortgages insured under this program are assumable under the same conditions as are any other insured mortgages. However, mortgagors will not be eligible for assistance after the tenth anniversary of the first payment due under the original mortgage. Assumptors and potential assumptors should be advised of these limitations and how these limitations shall affect them.

NOTE: Allowable fees for assumptions of Section 235 mortgages are found in Chapter 4, Paragraph 4-4A3.

10-37 ALIEN MORTGAGORS. To be eligible for assistance, a mortgagor must be a citizen of the United States or an alien admitted for permanent residence.

A. Citizenship/Permanent Alien Status Proof Required. Evidence of this eligibility must be submitted to the mortgagee whenever:

1. there is a new application for assistance;
2. an existing cooperative membership is purchased;
3. an assisted mortgage is assumed;
4. an assisted mortgage is assigned to HUD; or
5. an assisted mortgage that has been in default is reinstated under 24 CFR 203.608.

B. Forms Of Acceptable Proof. When any of the events in the preceding paragraph occur, the mortgagee must ask the mortgagor to provide proof of eligibility based on citizenship. Acceptable proof may include:

1. a Birth Certificate;
2. a United States Passport
3. an Alien Registration Card (i.e., "Green Card"); or
4. a Naturalization Certificate.

C. Mortgagee Certification. The mortgagee must then certify that acceptable proof as stated in the preceding paragraph has been submitted by all persons from whom it is required. NOTE: If the mortgagee cannot make this certification, the assistance payments contract must be suspended and the mortgagor notified of the consequences.

D. Fraudulent Or Invalid Documentation (24 CFR 235.361(b)). If the documentation should prove to be fraudulent, invalid or inadequate, the mortgagor will be required to repay all assistance payments to HUD. In addition, the mortgagee may be required to refund overpaid assistance payments, plus handling charges and interest.

E. When Assistance May Be Reinstated. Assistance payments may be resumed at HUD's discretion if all aliens not able to establish eligibility have moved from the property or have established eligibility.

ii. Recapture of Section 235 Assistance Payments

Formerly HUD Handbook 4330.1, REV-5, Chapter 11

11-1 GENERAL. The Housing and Community Development Acts of 1980 and 1981 changed Section 235 of the National Housing Act to allow the Secretary of the Department of Housing and Urban Development (HUD) to require recapture of all, or a portion of, the assistance payments made on behalf of mortgagors under Section 235(i) who obtain FHA-insured mortgages.

11-2 MORTGAGES AFFECTED BY RECAPTURE PROVISION (24 CFR 235.12(a)).
Section 235 mortgages are subject to a recapture where a firm commitment (or, under the Direct Endorsement Program, where the underwriter's approval of the Mortgage Credit Analysis Worksheet) was dated on or after May 27, 1981.

A. If the Firm Commitment date is on or before May 26, 1981, the first mortgage is not under the Section 235 Recapture Program, even though the settlement date occurred after May 26, 1981. The suffix of the FHA case number of mortgages insured under the first and second Section 235 Assistance Program allocations ends in the number five (5).

B. If the Firm Commitment date is on or after May 27, 1981, the first mortgage is under the Section 235 Recapture Program, even though the suffix of the FHA case number may end in the number five (5). The suffix for mortgages insured under the Section 235 Recapture Program ends in the numbers fifty-six (56) and sixty-six (66).

C. If the Firm Commitment date is on or after October 22, 1984, the first mortgage is under the Section 235 Revised/Recapture/10 Program. The suffix of the FHA case number for mortgages insured under the Section 235 Revised/Recapture/10 Program ends in the number forty-six (46). (Refer to paragraph 10-36).

11-3 METHOD OF SECURING REPAYMENT (24 CFR 235.12(d)). The mortgagor is required to execute, at the time of closing of the first mortgage, a second note and mortgage or deed of trust (referred to as the security instrument or the HUD lien), with addendum, in favor of the Secretary to secure repayment of the assistance. The property is pledged as security for the second mortgage (i.e., the recapture lien).

11-4 MORTGAGEE'S RESPONSIBILITY PRIOR TO INSURANCE ENDORSEMENT. Upon making application with the mortgagee for assistance under the Section 235 program, the mortgagee shall make the mortgagor aware of the recapture provision by providing a copy of the "Notice To Buyer"

A. Contents Of "Notice To Buyer". This notice describes:

   1. the provisions of the law which requires the repayment of all, or a portion of, the assistance payments which are paid on the mortgagor's behalf (and any subsequent assumptor of the mortgage) prior to the release of the second mortgage on the property;
   2. the events which will "trigger" the recapture;
   3. the formula used by HUD to determine the amount of recapture due to satisfy the second mortgage;
   4. the importance of retaining all paid receipts and/or
   5. bills relating to improvements made to a property; and
   6. the financial responsibility that is acquired by an assumptor if the mortgage is assumed.

B. Mortgagor's Written Acknowledgement Required. At closing, the mortgagor must acknowledge that he/she has been made aware of the recapture provision by signing and dating an original and two copies of the "Notice To Buyer".

C. Position Of Lien. It is the mortgagee's responsibility to assure that the recapture lien, drawn in favor of the Secretary, is properly recorded in the appropriate position. The recapture lien may not be junior to any lien other than an FHA-insured first lien, unless:

   1. there is a second lien held by a state or local government agency required by law to hold a second lien (such as a lien to secure repayment of funds advanced under a housing assistance program to make the initial cash investment or to assist in making mortgage payments); or
   2. HUD has determined that it would be in the Secretary's best interest to accept a junior lien position.

D. Preparation Of Closing Documents. Upon approval of Form HUD-93100-4 on Section 235 cases subject to the recapture provision, the HUD Field Office will add the following paragraph as a condition to its firm commitment:

"Second mortgage with addendum, and note in the format prescribed by HUD to be executed and recorded for the maximum amount of assistance as established by Formula II which could be paid over the term of the mortgage. $_____ (Amount to be entered on second note and mortgage (or deed of trust)".

1. Security Instruments. Upon issuance of a firm commitment, the HUD Field Office having jurisdiction over the mortgage will instruct the mortgagee to modify the HUD-approved mortgage or deed of trust document for insured mortgages in that particular State to include the information for the Section 235 recapture mortgage or deed of trust, as follows:

   a. under the document caption, insert the words "with Addendum, for Repayment of Section 235 Assistance";
   b. enter the words "the Secretary of Housing and Urban Development" as the mortgagee and delete any reference to a corporation;
   c. delete any reference to monthly installments;
   d. enter a statement that the principal sum of the mortgage will not exceed the amount computed under the note. The following language is acceptable:

      ". . . but not to exceed an amount computed under the terms of a note executed by the mortgagor on _____; with interest, if any, according to the terms of the note.";

   e. delete the two paragraphs relating to the payment of escrow items; and

   f. an addendum should also be added to provide for the special repayment provisions required by Section 235.

      NOTE: The Note must be reproduced locally. HUD Field Office Counsel shall review model security instruments to be used to determine that they comply with local law and meet HUD requirements.

2. Information to be Inserted. The mortgagee completes these documents by inserting the following information:

   a. appropriate dates;
   b. names;
   c. property description;
   d. interest rate (which will be the same as the rate on the first mortgage); and
   e. the maximum amount of assistance that may be paid over the full term of the mortgage.

      NOTE: The maximum amount will be the "Formula II" assistance payment shown on the Application for Assistance, Form HUD-93100-4, Line G-7.

E. Title Insurance. The title insurance does not need to recognize the junior recapture lien.

F. Hazard Insurance. The Secretary does not need to be named as a payee in the hazard insurance policy.

11-5 REQUIREMENTS AT CLOSING. The originating mortgagee is responsible for the following at the time of closing:

A. Execution Of Lien Documents (24 CFR 235.12(d)). The documents creating the lien in favor of the Secretary shall be executed at the same time as those creating the first lien.

B. Identifying Costs. Costs associated with the transaction may be paid by either the buyer or the seller, subject to the usual underwriting restrictions on such costs. Costs associated with both mortgages may be shown on the same HUD-1, Settlement Statement, as long as the HUD-1 clearly reflects what the costs were for and which costs were paid by the seller and which were paid by the purchaser.

11-6 RECORDING THE LIENS. The documents creating the second lien should be delivered for recording at the same time as those creating the first lien. It is the mortgagee's responsibility to assure that the liens are recorded in the proper order.

NOTE: Should the recapture lien be inadvertently recorded in first-lien position, HUD will agree to subordinate its lien to correct this error as the mortgagee's lien will not be insurable if it is not in first-lien position.

11-7 INSURANCE ENDORSEMENT. The mortgagee's lien is submitted for mortgage insurance endorsement in the normal manner, accompanied by the following documents: the executed, original "Notice to Buyer"; a copy of the Note in favor of the Secretary; and copies of the executed security instruments with evidence that the originals have been delivered for recording (unless the original, recorded documents have been returned before the case is submitted for insurance endorsement).

NOTE: The application for FHA insurance will not be processed unless it is accompanied by the Notice to Buyer.

A. Where it is not customary for recorders to provide receipts for documents accepted for recording, the mortgagee's certification will be accepted as adequate evidence that the original documents have been delivered for recording.

B. When the original documents have been recorded and returned, they are to be forwarded immediately to the appropriate HUD Field Office with the original note in favor of the Secretary. They will be retained by that HUD Field Office until the lien is satisfied.

11-8 GENERAL SERVICING. Servicing of the mortgage is governed by the procedures outlined in Chapter 10 until one of the events described in Paragraph 11-9 occurs which will "trigger" the recapture provision.

NOTE: Should the mortgagee find at any time that a case is not under the Recapture Program, but that a second mortgage (or deed of trust) with addendum and a note was executed by the mortgagor and recorded by the mortgagee, the mortgagee must contact the HUD Field Office, single Family Loan Management Branch. The insurance binder must be reviewed by HUD and a justification prepared for satisfying the HUD lien without calculating a recapture amount.

11-9 EVENTS TRIGGERING RECAPTURE PROVISION (24 CFR 235.12(a)). The recapture provision is "triggered" when any one of the following events occurs:

A. a property is sold to a party not eligible for assistance;

B. the mortgage is assumed by a party eligible for assistance but does not agree to accept assistance and/or assume liability for repayment of assistance paid on behalf of the seller (and previous mortgagors);

C. a property is rented (or, in the case of properties with more than one unit, the owner's unit is rented) for more than one year; or

D. the mortgagor (or the mortgagor's agent) requests that the Secretary's lien be released.

11-10 FORMULA FOR CALCULATING RECAPTURE (24 CFR 235.12(b) and (c)). When the recapture provision is "triggered", the amount of recapture shall be determined by HUD to be THE LESSER OF:

A. the total amount of assistance paid on behalf of the mortgagor (and any previous mortgagors); or

B. 50 percent of the net appreciation (as determined by HUD) of a property.

NOTE: Net appreciation is any increase in the value of a property over the original purchase price, minus reasonable costs of sale, costs of refinancing the first mortgage or cost of the appraisal when paying off the HUD lien, and minus the reasonable costs of improvements made to a property.

11-11 MORTGAGEE'S ROLE IN RECAPTURE PROCESS. Whenever one of the events described in Paragraph 11-9 occurs, the mortgagee is charged with the responsibility for the following:

A. Advising both the HUD Field Office having jurisdiction over the mortgage and the HUD Headquarters Office of Finance and Accounting, Subsidy Accounting Branch that an event has occurred which "triggers" the recapture provision. This notification shall include as much information as the mortgagee has available (i.e., FHA case number, the date of a prepayment associated with a sale; the name and address of the assumptor, if the assumptor is not living at the property address; the date the mortgage was assumed and the fact that the assumptor elected not to receive or did not qualify for assistance, etc.).

B. Providing both the local HUD Field Office and the HUD Headquarters Office of Finance and Accounting, Subsidy Accounting Branch, a statement in writing, signed by an officer of the company, of the total amount of assistance paid on behalf of the original mortgagor and all assumptors, if any, less handling charges and the total of any assistance payments which may have been inadvertently applied to the mortgagor's account.

C. Providing copies of original documents (i.e., signed settlement statements, sales contracts, etc., which are contained in the mortgagee's case file) that the mortgagor cannot provide, but are needed by HUD to determine the amount of recapture due to satisfy the HUD lien.

D. Serving as the "go-between" where necessary and advising the mortgagor of the documentation required to calculate the recapture amount due HUD.

NOTE: THE MORTGAGEE MUST NOT CALCULATE THE RECAPTURE AMOUNT.

NOTE: If the mortgagee receives the recapture amount due either directly from the mortgagor or as a disbursement from closing, the mortgagee shall promptly forward these funds directly to the local HUD Office.

THE MORTGAGEE MUST NOT ASSUME ANY DUTIES CONCERNING THE CALCULATION OF THE RECAPTURE AMOUNT.

E. Verifying and certifying that all appropriate recertifications (from the time of inception through the time of termination of the assistance payments contract) have been correctly processed and billed.

At the request of a Field Office, the mortgagee shall submit recertifications for review by that Field Office before the recapture process begins.

F. Repaying any overpaid assistance (that may have been discovered as a result of Paragraph 11-11E) as described in Chapter 10.

NOTE: Any amounts of overpaid assistance paid to HUD because of this requirement are to be so indicated and subtracted from the amount reported in compliance with Paragraph 11-11B.

Any overpaid assistance should be handled as a separate transaction from the recapture amount when processing a recapture case for satisfaction of HUD's lien.

NOTE: If a check for an overpaid assistance amount is received or if the overpaid assistance is included in the same check as the recapture amount, the check must be forwarded to HUD Headquarters, Office of Finance and Accounting and a copy should be sent to the HUD Field Office having jurisdiction over the mortgage immediately along with the back-up documentation for the overpaid assistance amount.

G. Terminating the assistance payment contract in accordance with Chapter 10, Paragraph 10-19.

NOTE: If the mortgagor is refinancing the first mortgage, the mortgagee is charged with the responsibility for items B, D, E, F, and G.

11-12 HUD'S ROLE IN THE RECAPTURE PROCESS. When the local HUD Field Office is advised by a mortgagee, an attorney, a title company or other settlement party, of a pending or accomplished event which triggers recapture (as listed in Paragraph 11-9), the HUD Field Office may request the following items in order to compute the recapture amount due to satisfy the HUD lien:

A. a copy of the recorded second mortgage (or deed of trust) with addendum and executed note (should the HUD Field Office not have the original documents in its files);

B. a copy of the executed sales contract and HUD-1 settlement statement (signed by the settlement attorney) where the original mortgagor purchased the property;

C. a copy of the executed sales contract and HUD-1 settlement statement (signed by the settlement attorney) of any assumptor who purchased the property prior to the last mortgagor;

D. a copy of the executed sales contract and HUD-1 settlement statement (signed by the settlement attorney) when the last mortgagor (i.e., the last one receiving assistance) sold the property;

E. copies of paid receipts and/or bills marked "paid in full" for any improvements made to a property (by the original mortgagor and/or any assumptor);

F. a letter from the mortgagee, signed by an officer of the company, stating the total amount of assistance paid on behalf of the original mortgagor and all assumptors (if any).

G. an appraisal report on the property and a statement of the cost of the appraisal, if needed; and

H. a statement of the costs of refinancing the first mortgage, when needed.

11-13 DETERMINING THE RECAPTURE AMOUNT. To determine the recapture amount for a Section 235 recapture case, the documentation requested in Paragraph 11-12 must be reviewed. A formula is used to calculate the recapture amount. The cost of sale (or the cost of refinancing the first mortgage) and the cost of improvements to a property are subtracted from the appreciation of the property to arrive at net appreciation. See Paragraph 11-10.

11-14 REASONABLE COSTS OF SALE. Since the title of the property changes when the property is sold, the costs of sale must clearly indicate which costs were paid by the seller and which were paid by the purchaser and are subject to the usual underwriting restrictions on such costs. Costs of sale shall also conform to what is considered by the local HUD Field Office to be reasonable and customary for that area of the country. Otherwise, the excess will be disallowed. Costs of sale must be clearly identified on a HUD-1, Settlement Statement, signed by the appropriate person. If there is no HUD-1, the costs of sale must be itemized and supported by receipts.

A. Costs Allowed. Costs of sale items which HUD will allow to be claimed against the net appreciation of a property if the costs are paid by the original mortgagor and/or subsequent assumptors of the mortgage are:

1. broker's commission;
2. discount points (not origination fee);
3. property survey;
4. appraisal fee;
5. State and local taxes (charged in connection with the transaction, such as transfer taxes (not property taxes or amounts escrowed for the future payment of taxes);
6. attorney fees;
7. fees for the preparation and recording of documents;
8. notary fees;
9. costs of advertising the property for sale (but not if these costs are paid by the broker and included in the commission);
10. title search, but not if included in attorney's fee;
11. title insurance;
12. pest control inspection;
13. pumping out septic tank as a condition of sale (where required by State law);
14. buyer's protection plans providing the buyer with a warranty as to the condition of the property and covering repair or replacement of certain elements of the property for a limited time; and/or
15. any other costs resulting from a State and/or local requirement.

B. Costs Not Allowed.

1. buydown fee (If there are no discount points allowed (see A.2. above), the buydown fee can be claimed against the appreciation of the property);
2. tax funding service fee; and
3. VA funding fee.

11-15 REASONABLE COST OF REFINANCING THE FIRST MORTGAGE. Since the title to a property does not change when the first mortgage is refinanced, the costs of refinancing do not include all of the costs allowed for costs of sale when a property is sold. Refinancing costs must be clearly identified on a HUD-1, Settlement Statement, signed by the appropriate person. If there isn't a HUD-1, the cost of refinancing should be itemized and supported by receipts.

A. Costs Allowed. If there are any prior assumptors of a mortgage that is being refinanced, the costs of assuming the mortgage (for each transaction) can be claimed against the appreciation of a property if the charges are documented. Costs of refinancing the first mortgage which HUD will allow to be claimed against the appreciation of a property (if the costs are paid by the last eligible mortgagor) are:

1. appraisal fee;

  2. one discount point (not origination fee);
  3. property survey;
  4. pest control inspection;
  5. title search;
  6. lender's title insurance; and
  7. fees for the preparation and recording of documents.

B. Costs Not Allowed.

  1. Buydown fee (if there are no discount points, one point of the buydown fee can be claimed against the appreciation of the property);
  2. tax funding service fee;
  3. VA funding fee; and
  4. mortgagor's title insurance (title of property).

11-16 REASONABLE COSTS OF IMPROVEMENTS.

A. To qualify As An Improvement. Improvements must be over and above deferred or routine maintenance to be allowed as claims against the appreciation of a property. They must be:

  1. acceptable to HUD;
  2. improvements that were not present or a part of a property at the time the mortgage was originated, unless it is an upgrade (see Paragraph 11-16B9 below);
  3. considered to be permanent improvements in that they will remain with a property when it is sold as they cannot be removed from the property without causing damage to existing structures and/or the property; and

  4. improvements for which the mortgagor can substantiate the cost with documented proof that such improvements were done to the mortgaged property site and for which the mortgagor has receipts marked "paid-in-full" as required in Paragraph 11-12E.

B. Allowable Improvements. Acceptable types of improvements which HUD will allow to be claimed against the appreciation of a property when computing the recapture amount include, but are not necessarily limited to, the following:

  1. room additions and other permanent additions, such as, but not necessarily limited to, porches, patios, decks, garages and carports;
  2. permanent landscaping and/or other site improvements that tend to increase the value of a property, such as fences, trees, shrubbery, lawns (if no lawn was provided initially) retaining walls, etc.;
  3. built-in bookshelves, cabinets, etc.,
  4. appliance additions (stoves, refrigerators, built-in dishwashers, built-in microwave ovens, clothes washers and dryers, and attic and ceiling fans) which are conveyed to buyer by seller;

NOTE: If items in #4 above are replacement items, they are not allowed against the appreciation of a property.

If the mortgagor bought original appliances after purchase of a new property, original costs of appliances can be claimed against the appreciation of a property. (In some sections of the country, appliances are not furnished by the builder, unless requested by the mortgagor.)

Portable appliances are not allowed against the appreciation of a property.

The Field Office Evaluation staff shall be notified on a case-by-case basis to determine whether washers and dryers or other such permanent fixtures that are considered to be regional appreciation value assets can be claimed against the appreciation of a property.

5. finishing or refinishing of basements or other rooms when the area was unfinished at the time of origination or the refinishing substantially alters the nature of the area and enhances the value of a property;
6. the addition of storm windows and/or doors or replacing regular windows with replacement windows (for the purpose of saving energy);
7. installation of permanent heating or cooling systems where none existed, the addition of a solar heating system or replacing a conventional heating system with a solar heating system;
8. carpeting areas where floors were previously without finished coverings (such as, a room addition, or a basement area);
9. upgrading: appliances, cabinets, carpeting, electrical and plumbing fixtures, etc.

NOTE: If the mortgagor upgraded an item that the builder was to install at the time the structure was erected, the cost of the improvement is the difference in price for upgrading. If such items are replaced, the replacements cannot be claimed against the appreciation of a property.

10. television dish. (If the dish is listed in the sales contract and/or appraisal report and cannot be removed from the property without damaging the landscape, it can be claimed against the appreciation of the property.)
11. sheds and outbuildings. (If structures enhance a property and cannot be removed without damaging the landscape, they can be claimed against the appreciation of a property.)
12. building permits and inspection fees for property additions;
13. swimming pools are allowed as improvements on a case-by-case basis if:

    a. the swimming pool is below ground and enhances the value of a property (per appraisal) and/or is taxed by the municipality, its cost can be claimed against the appreciation of a property;
    b. the swimming pool is above ground, it may or may not be allowed against the appreciation of a property depending on the area of the country it is located. If the

pool is not taxed by the municipality or is not given a value in the appraisal of the property, its cost cannot be claimed against the appreciation of a property;

    c. a swimming pool or other such fixture, i.e., outdoor hot tub, is affixed to a property and cannot be moved without damaging the fixture or the landscape, is taxed by the local municipality and/or enhances the value of the property (per appraisal), its cost can be claimed against the appreciation of a property;

14. special assessments, such as water and sewer lines connecting a property to the water and sewer lines of a municipality, the paving of streets, sidewalks and alleys, wiring for electricity and telephones and piping for gas must be handled on a case-by-case basis; and

15. land issues (those considered to be improvements must be handled on a case-by-case basis).

NOTE: The HUD Field Office must be contacted for guidance in handling special assessments and land issues as improvements and their costs as claims against the appreciation of a property.

C. Miscellaneous Improvements Of Less Than $100 Per Project. Miscellaneous improvements which are less than $100 per project are to be considered incidentals and are not to be allowed as a claim against the appreciation of a property. Included in this category are such items as molding, weatherstripping, sod, grass seed, fertilizer, etc.

D. Group Improvements As Projects. When a major improvement which involve the purchase/rental of numerous items of equipment and/or materials is claimed, it must be grouped together as one project. However, each item purchased for that project must reflect its own separate cost.

E. "Sweat Equity". Where the work is performed by the mortgagor (i.e., "sweat equity"), no monetary value will be given for the "sweat equity" with respect to being used as a claim against the appreciation of a property. However, the cost of building permits, inspections, renting items of equipment and purchasing the supplies and materials necessary to accomplish the work can be allowed.

F. Rental Equipment. Costs of renting equipment for the specific use in completing an acceptable improvement (as described in Paragraph 11-16B) may be used as claims against the appreciation of a property.

1. Rental equipment which may qualify as claims against the appreciation of a property includes, but is not necessarily limited to, backhoes, bulldozers, cement mixers, jackhammers, electric or airdriven nail/brad/staple guns, posthole augers, fencewire stretchers, etc., which were rented for the sole use in completing a specific home improvement listed in Paragraph 11-16B.

2. Equipment which does not qualify as a claim against the appreciation of the property includes miscellaneous tools and equipment purchased for use in completing an improvement as described in Paragraph 11-16D and will also be used for performing

Handbook 4000.1   810
Effective Date: 03/14/2016 | Last Revised: 07/10/2019
*Refer to the online version of SF Handbook 4000.1 for specific sections' effective dates

other tasks and/or home improvements. Such items may include, but are not necessarily limited to, shovels, picks, ladders, carpenter levels, saws, drills, hammers, utility knives, screwdrivers, wire cutters, wrenches, caulking guns, cement trowels, etc.

G. Where The Cost Of An Improvement Is Paid Using A Monthly Installment Payment Plan. Where an improvement is paid for on a monthly installment plan (whether paid to the company providing the service, a bank, a credit card company, etc.) only the initial cost of the improvement (excluding any interest, finance charges or late charges) may be used as a claim against the appreciation of a property.

H. Receipts/Documentation Of Improvements. In order to support the cost of an improvement, the mortgagor must present receipts or invoices on company letterhead marked "paid-in-full" for each allowable home improvement. Receipts which are written on paper without a business letterhead, or without specific (or legible) entries as to what service was provided, who provided the service, the date the service was provided, and/or what type of material was purchased, and where appropriate, at what property address the service was performed, etc., may be subject to further scrutiny and/or rejection by the HUD Field Office.

I. Replacements. Items such as roof replacements, heating system replacements (except solar heating systems), and exterior and interior painting are home maintenance. They must not be claimed against the appreciation of a property as improvements.

J. Items Not Allowed As Improvements.

  1. Draperies, curtain rods, window shades and blinds are never allowed as improvements unless they are approved by Headquarters.

  2. Plumbing fixtures (such as faucets and water purifiers) and light fixtures cannot be claimed against the appreciation of a property unless they are installed as part of a major improvement or they are approved by Headquarters.

  3. Intercommunications systems must not be claimed against the appreciation of a property.

11-17 FRAUD AND ABUSE. Careful scrutiny is to be given where substantial improvements have been made over a short period of time, shortly after purchase of a property, and/or over an extended period, which exceed $10,000 while assistance was still being paid.

NOTE: Occurrences such as these, will lead to the HUD Field Office questioning the mortgagor's need for assistance and/or the possibility of fraud in the original application process.

11-18 CALCULATING THE RECAPTURE AMOUNT.

A. Calculating The Recapture Amount. The HUD Field Office shall calculate the amount of recapture due in order to satisfy the lien using the formula shown in Paragraph 11-10 and on the Recapture of Assistance Payments Worksheet. Only the HUD Field Office shall calculate the amount of assistance to be recaptured.

B. Selling Price. If the HUD Field Office feels that the reported selling price is substantially below the property value or discovers that the property is being sold for less than the amount for which it was purchased, the HUD Field Office has the option of requesting that the mortgagee obtain an appraisal of the property.

NOTE: If the appraised value is five (5) percent or more above the sales contract price, the recapture will be based on the appraised value rather than the selling price shown on the sales contract.

11-19 DISPOSITION OF THE RECAPTURE CHECK. The HUD Field Office has the responsibility of collecting the recapture amount from the mortgagor or the mortgagor's representative. Should the recapture amount be collected by the mortgagee, the check must be forwarded to the appropriate HUD Field Office and the Office shall forward it to a lockbox in Atlanta, Georgia.

11-20 RELEASING THE RECAPTURE LIEN. Upon receiving the full recapture amount required to satisfy the second mortgage, or second deed of trust, the HUD Field Office will prepare, execute, record and forward the recorded Satisfaction of Lien to the mortgagee or the agent representing the mortgagor. The mortgagee or mortgagor's agent will then be responsible for forwarding the document to the mortgagor.

11-21 SATISFYING THE LIEN BEFORE OBTAINING RECAPTURE AMOUNT. If the settlement on a property is imminent, the second mortgage or second deed of trust has not been satisfied, and there is a request to satisfy the lien before closing, the mortgagor must be informed that since there is not enough time to do the recapture formula to determine the recapture amount, the full amount of assistance paid on the mortgagor's behalf must be submitted to HUD so that the HUD lien can be satisfied before settlement of the mortgage. When the recapture calculation has been completed, if there is an overpayment, the overpayment shall be refunded to the mortgagor.

11-22 ASSIGNMENT TO HUD. In those cases where the HUD Field Office has decided to accept an assignment of the first mortgage, the recapture lien shall remain in place. The mortgagee must advise both the HUD Field Office and the HUD Headquarters Office of Finance and Accounting, GPA - Subsidized Housing Programs Division, Attention: Accounts Payable Section (the mailing address on Form HUD-93102) in writing, signed by an officer of the company, of the total amount of assistance paid through the date of assignment.

11-23 FORECLOSURES - HUD-ACQUIRED PROPERTIES. For those properties conveyed to HUD as a result of foreclosure, the mortgagee must advise the HUD Field Office, in writing, signed by an officer of the company, of the total amount of assistance paid over the term of the mortgage. It will not be necessary for HUD to prepare a satisfaction of lien for the HUD lien. A foreclosure that is properly processed by the mortgagee's foreclosing attorney will wipe out all existing liens on the property, including HUD's lien. However, if the HUD lien exists after foreclosure of the first mortgage, the HUD Field Office must satisfy the lien at the request of the foreclosing attorney.

11-24 DEED-IN-LIEU OF FORECLOSURE. For the mortgage that is conveyed to HUD as a result of a deed-in-lieu of foreclosure, the recapture lien shall remain in place. The mortgagee must advise the HUD Field Office, in writing, signed by an officer of the company, of the total amount of assistance paid over the term of the mortgage.

NOTE: Once the property is in HUD's Property Disposition inventory, the HUD Field Office will prepare and record a satisfaction of the recapture lien in order to provide a clear title when the property is sold by HUD.

11-25 RELOCATION OF MORTGAGOR BY EMPLOYER.

A. Termination Of Assistance. If an employer requires a Section 235 mortgagor to relocate, and the employer assumes the responsibility of selling the mortgagor's property, the mortgagee must terminate the assistance at the appropriate time. (Chapter 10, Paragraph 10-19.) The mortgagee must furnish the HUD Field Office with a statement of the total amount of assistance paid on behalf of the original mortgagor and any assumptors of the mortgage.

B. Value Of Property. The mortgagee must provide the HUD Field Office with an appraisal to determine the fair market value of a property or the HUD Field Office must request an appraisal of the property.

11-26 DISLOCATION OF MORTGAGOR (EMINENT DOMAIN).

A. Relocate To Another Property. If a State or local government dislocates a Section 235 mortgagor because it needs the property for public use, the mortgagor may relocate to another property under the same mortgage. The FHA case number must remain the same for the purpose of paying assistance on the mortgagor's behalf.

   1. The State or local government must NOT pay the first mortgage in full.

   2. The mortgagee must agree to transfer the first and second mortgages or first and second deeds of trust to a new property.

   3. The mortgagee must amend the first and second mortgages or deeds of trust security instruments to read the legal description of the new property.

   4. The new property must be equal in value to the old property.

   5. The mortgagee must transfer the Section 235 assistance with the first mortgage or deed of trust to the new property.

   6. The amended mortgages or deeds of trust must be executed, dated, and recorded to reflect the transfer of these documents to the new property.

7. The mortgagee must send the recorded, amended second mortgage or deed of trust to the HUD Field Office where it will be filed with the original security instruments.

B. Unable To Transfer Mortgages. If the mortgagor is unable to get the first and second mortgages or first and second deeds of trust on a property transferred to another property of equal value, the State or local government must purchase the property from the mortgagor. The mortgagee must contact the HUD Field Office of the pending sale of the property. The HUD Field Office must take the appropriate steps to satisfy the HUD lien on the property.

11-27 SUBORDINATION OF THE HUD LIEN. If subordination of the HUD lien on a property is in the best interest of the Secretary, the HUD Field Office may approve subordination of a recapture lien in the case of refinancing a first mortgage or securing a Title I loan for improving the property. The mortgagee must contact the HUD Field Office for details on subordinating the HUD lien.

11-28 SUMMARY. The appropriate HUD Field Office should be notified if any one of the following events occurs:

A. The first mortgage on a property has been paid in full through sale of the property.

B. The first mortgage has been assumed by a mortgagor not eligible for assistance or the new mortgagor does not want to participate in the Section 235 Assistance Program.

C. The first mortgage has been refinanced.

D. The first mortgage has been assigned to HUD.

E. The property has been rented for more than a year. (If more than one unit, the owner's unit is rented.)

F. The assistance has been terminated after a 36-month suspension.

G. The mortgagor has been relocated or dislocated from a property under circumstances beyond his/her control.

H. The mortgagor has requested that the HUD lien be subordinated to a lessor position when the first mortgage is refinanced

Explanations of A through H above.

In A., above, the mortgagor must be notified that the Recapture Provision becomes effective.

In B., above, the mortgagor must be notified that the Recapture Provision becomes effective.

In C. above, the mortgagee refinancing the first mortgage should notify the HUD Field Office if it (the mortgagee) wants the HUD lien satisfied due to the fact that the HUD lien moves into first-lien position when the original first mortgage is paid-in-full.

In D. above, if the first mortgage is assigned to HUD, the mortgagee must submit a statement of the full amount of assistance paid by HUD on behalf of the original mortgagor and all assumptors of the mortgage to the HUD Field Office. In E. above, the HUD Field Office must calculate the recapture amount and maintain a file on the case. In F. above, the HUD Field Office must request a decision from the mortgagor as to whether he/she wants the HUD lien satisfied after termination of the assistance.

In G., above, there are specific procedures to follow for processing the relocation case. For the dislocation case, there are special conditions that must be considered to retain the original first mortgage and Section 235 assistance by transferring both to another property of equal value. In H., above, there are special conditions under which a Section 235 Recapture mortgage can be subordinated.

iii. Maintenance of Escrow Accounts - Analysis

Formerly HUD Handbook 4330.1, REV -5, Section 2-7E

2-7 MAINTENANCE OF ESCROW ACCOUNTS - ANALYSIS (24 CFR 203.550(b)).

E. Mortgages Insured Under Section 235. [HUD's escrow requirements apply] equally to mortgages insured under Section 235. With these mortgages, the logical time for escrow analysis is on or just after the anniversary date of the first payment due under the mortgage since it is then that the MIP changes and annual recertification is required. Both of these events may affect the amount of assistance to which the mortgagor is entitled and delays in analysis could result in a need for significant retroactive adjustments.

Both Formulas I and II must be recomputed as of the anniversary date regardless of changes in escrow requirements. Mortgagees may, however, elect to analyze Section 235 escrow accounts at any time, provided assistance is recomputed at the time of annual recertification to reflect any changes in the mortgagor's income or family composition, as well as the annual change in MIP. (See Chapter 10 for detailed instructions.)

iv. Statement For Income Tax Purposes

Formerly HUD Handbook 4330.1, REV-5, Section 2-10B

2-10 PROVIDING LOAN INFORMATION (24 CFR 203.508).

B. Statement For Income Tax Purposes (24 CFR 203.508(c)). By January 30 of each year, the mortgagee must furnish the mortgagor with a statement of taxes and interest paid during the preceding calendar year (24 CFR 203.508(c)). HUD takes no position on the income tax impact of these amounts.

If the mortgage is insured under Section 235, the statement must also include an accounting of the total amount of assistance paid by HUD and applied to the account during the preceding year (24 CFR 235. 1001). This Section 235 Statement may be a part of the escrow accounting or may be in a separate statement accompanying the Income Tax Statement (See Paragraph 10-35B). The mortgagee may either:

1. report the excess of interest payments over assistance payments during the year, or

2. report both the total interest and assistance payments during the year.

NOTE: This Income Tax Statement must include or be accompanied by a statement which includes substantially the following language:

"If you itemize deductions on your income tax returns, please read this notice. Under Section 1. 163-1(d) of Federal Income Tax Regulations, you, as the mortgagor, may deduct for Federal income tax purposes only that part, if any, of mortgage interest payments made during the year that exceeded the amount of assistance payments made by HUD during the year. You are urged to contact your tax advisor or State and local tax offices for guidance regarding the deductibility of payments on your State or local income tax returns."

v. Late Charges

Formerly HUD Handbook 4330.1, REV-5, Section 4-2D

4-2 LATE CHARGES (24 CFR 203.25).

D. Computing Late Charges.

NOTE: When the mortgage is insured under Section 235, OR the mortgage is subject to a buy-down, only the mortgagor's portion of the monthly payment is used when computing a late charge.

vi. Assumptions

Formerly HUD Handbook 4330.1, REV-5, Section 4-4

4-4 ASSUMPTIONS.

A. Maximum Allowable Fees. Fees for processing assumptions must be based on the mortgagee's actual costs and cannot exceed the maximum amount authorized in this Handbook. (See Chapter 6 for requirements concerning assumptions.) The maximum amounts allowed by HUD for processing various types of assumption are as follows:

1. Section 235 Assumptions.

   a. Assumption Without A Release of Liability and Where Assistance Is Requested But Disapproved. Where no credit checks are required and the mortgagor applies for assistance but is not considered eligible for Section 235 subsidy the maximum fee that may be charged is $140.00.

b. Assumption Without A Release of Liability and Where Assistance Is Requested and Approved. Where a credit check is not required and the Section 235 subsidy will be terminated, the maximum fee that may be charged is $185.00.

c. Assumption With A Release of Liability and Where Assistance Is Not Requested or Approved. Where a credit check is required and the Section 235 subsidy will be terminated, the maximum fee that may be charged is $500.00.

d. Assumption With A Release of Liability and Assistance Is To Continue. Where a credit check is required and the Section 235 subsidy will continue on behalf of the assumptor, the maximum fee that may be charged is $500.00.

vii. Escrow Balance Returned to Mortgagor

Formerly HUD Handbook 4330.1, REV-5, Section 5-2

5-2 PREPAYMENT IN FULL (24 CFR 203.558).

G. Escrow Balance Returned to Mortgagor. When the mortgage insurance is terminated without payment of a claim for insurance benefits (i.e., payment in full) the remaining funds held in escrow for the payment of taxes and hazard insurance shall be * released to the mortgagor promptly (i.e., no later than 30 calendar days after the payoff). *

EXCEPTION: An analysis must be performed in accordance with Paragraph 10-20D3 on all Section 235 prepayments in full prior to refunding any escrow money to the mortgagors.

H. Section 235 Mortgages. In addition to the other requirements cited under Paragraph 5-2, for all Section 235 mortgages that are prepaid in full, the following requirements apply:

1. mortgagees must perform an analysis in accordance with Paragraph 10-20D3 prior to refunding any escrow money to the mortgagor as stated in the "Exception" cited in the preceding paragraph; and

2. mortgagees must determine in accordance with the instructions outlined in Chapter 11 if the mortgage is insured pursuant to a firm commitment issued after May 27, 1981 as to whether;

a. the prepayment has triggered the recapture provision in connection with HUD's Section 235 mortgage on the property; and
b. the appropriate action has been taken as required by Chapter 11.

viii. Partial Payments

Formerly HUD Handbook 4330.1, REV-5, Section 7-9

7-9 PARTIAL PAYMENTS (24 CFR 203.556). …When the mortgage is insured under Section 235, the "full amount due under the mortgage" is considered to be the full amount due from the mortgagor only.

ix. SCRA Interest Rate Cap

Formerly Mortgagee Letter 2006-28 Mortgage and Foreclosure Rights of Servicemembers under the Servicemembers Civil Relief Act (SCRA)

A few Section 235 mortgages still have assistance payments from HUD applied to them on behalf of lower-income mortgagors. Assistance for these mortgages may be affected by the six percent interest rate limitation. On all accounts receiving assistance when the note rate of interest exceeds six percent, the amount of assistance must be reanalyzed, and the subsidy amount must be recalculated using the full mortgage payment at a six percent rate when determining the amount of assistance. For some accounts, the interest rate deduction will cause the suspension of assistance for the period of active duty. Whenever an interest rate reduction is made with retroactive effect and the Section 235 assistance is reduced, any over-billed subsidy must be returned to HUD as a refund or adjustment to the subsequent Section 235 monthly billing. When active duty terminates and the note rate resumes, the assistance must be recalculated and restored in accordance with the usual procedures. Any income recertification requests received from mortgagors in accordance with 24 CFR § 235.355 must be processed expeditiously. Please also reference ML 91-20, *Effect of the Soldiers' and Sailors' Civil Relief Act of 1940* on *FHA Insured Mortgages* for additional guidance in calculating Formula 2 subsidy.

B. TITLE II INSURED HOUSING PROGRAMS REVERSE MORTGAGES

RESERVED FOR FUTURE USE
This section is reserved for future use, and until such time, FHA-approved Mortgagees must continue to comply with all applicable law and existing Handbooks, Mortgagee Letters, Notices and outstanding guidance applicable to a Mortgagee's participation in FHA programs.

C. TITLE I INSURED PROGRAMS

RESERVED FOR FUTURE USE
This section is reserved for future use, and until such time, FHA-approved Lenders must continue to comply with all applicable law and existing Handbooks, Mortgagee Letters, Notices and outstanding guidance applicable to a Title I Lender's participation in FHA programs.

IV.   CLAIMS AND DISPOSITION

A. TITLE II CLAIMS

This section provides the standards and procedures applicable to the submission of claims for all Single Family (one to four units) Mortgages insured under Title II of the National Housing Act, except for Home Equity Conversion Mortgages (HECM). The Mortgagee must fully comply with all of the following standards and procedures when submitting a claim for Federal Housing Administration (FHA) mortgage insurance benefits.

1. Claim Submission Process

a. Preparation and Submission of Claims

i.   Who Can Submit Claims

The holding Mortgagee or the servicing Mortgagee must submit the claim. While authorized parties may prepare or submit the claim on behalf of the Mortgagee, HUD will only pay the claim as stated in Disbursement of Claim.

ii. Liability for Claims Filed

Mortgagees are liable for the contents of any claims filed. By submitting a claim, whether electronically or by paper, the Mortgagee certifies that the statements and information contained in the claim are true and correct.

HUD will prosecute false claims and statements and Mortgagees may be subject to criminal and/or civil penalties or other action.

iii. FHA Case Number

The Mortgagee must ensure that the FHA case number is on all Parts of form HUD-27011, *Single Family Application for Insurance Benefits*, and on the cover page of any claims correspondence and documents sent to the Mortgagee Compliance Manager (MCM) and HUD.

iv. Insured Mortgages

The Mortgagee may only submit a claim for a Mortgage that is insured by FHA.

v. Borrower's Social Security Number

(A) Mortgages for which an Application for a Firm Commitment was Signed On or After August 14, 1986

The Mortgagee must include at least one of the Borrowers' Social Security Numbers (SSN) in Item 33 of Part A on all claim forms for Mortgages for which an application for a Firm Commitment was signed on or after August 14, 1986.

If additional space is needed, the Mortgagee may enter the co-Borrowers' SSNs in the "Mortgagee's comments" section.

(B) Mortgages for which an Application for a Firm Commitment was Signed Before August 14, 1986

(1) Standard

Where the application for a Firm Commitment was signed before August 14, 1986, the Mortgagee may submit a claim form without a Borrower's SSN if:

- the Mortgagee has made the annual requests for the Borrower's SSN, as required by the Internal Revenue Service (IRS), but the Borrower has failed to provide the requested SSN;
- the Mortgagee has made an exhaustive search of all available records and cannot find the Borrower's SSN; or
- the Borrower is deceased or cannot be located to provide the missing SSN.

(2) Required Documentation

To submit the claim form without the Borrower's SSN, the Mortgagee must:

- attach to the claim a signed certification or include in the "Mortgagee's comments" section the following language: "I certify that no social security number is available for FHA Case Number ___, upon which this claim is based. I further certify that I or representatives of my company have searched for all available records and made all annual requests for the Borrower's social security number that are required by the IRS;" and
- detail in the "Mortgagee's comments" section the Mortgagee's efforts in attempting to obtain the Borrower's SSN.

vi. Form HUD-27011, Single Family Application for Insurance Benefits

The Mortgagee must use form HUD-27011 to submit a claim for insurance benefits. Form HUD-27011 consists of the following five parts. See the *Claim Filing Technical Guide* for detailed information on completing this form.

(A) Part A – Initial Application

The Mortgagee must submit initial case data through Part A for each claim. Part A includes information relating to the Mortgage, Property, property condition, Mortgagee, payment history, and the foreclosure or, if appropriate, the conveyance, assignment, Claims without Conveyance of Title (CWCOT), or Pre-Foreclosure Sale (PFS).

(B) Part B – Fiscal Data

The Mortgagee must submit fiscal data related to allowable expenses and accrued interest through Part B for each claim. Part B provides all summary information relating to receipts and disbursements incurred by the Mortgagee that affect the amount of insurance claim.

For all claims other than conveyance claims, the Mortgagee must submit Part B simultaneously with Part A.

(C) Part C – Support Document

Part C contains itemized information relating to disbursements for the Property Preservation and Protection (P&P). Where applicable, the Mortgagee must prepare this document prior to completion of Part B.

(D) Part D – Support Document (Continuation 1)

Part D contains itemized information relating to such items as taxes, hazard insurance premiums, Mortgage Insurance Premiums (MIP), foreclosure costs, acquisition fees and costs, bankruptcy fees and costs, and other miscellaneous costs. Where applicable, the Mortgagee must prepare this document prior to completion of Part B.

(E) Part E – Support Document (Continuation 2)

Part E contains itemized information relating to closing costs found on the Closing Disclosure and amounts due from and to the buyer at closing. The Mortgagee must prepare Part E in order to claim allowable associated appraisal, administrative, and other closing costs for all claim types.

Where applicable, the Mortgagee must prepare this document prior to completion of Part B.

vii. Methods of Submission of Claims

Mortgagees must use one of the following methods to file claims.

(A) Electronic Data Interchange

(1) Definition

The Electronic Data Interchange (EDI) is an online system for Mortgagees to electronically file claims.

(2) Standard

The Mortgagee may submit claims via EDI for all claims other than Loss Mitigation Home Retention incentive claims and supplemental claims.

(3) EDI Technical Guidance

The Mortgagee may find information on using EDI in HUD's EDI Implementation Guide.

(4) Application Advice and Error Correction

The Mortgagee may identify errors in their submissions by reviewing Transaction Set (TS) 824. The Mortgagee must take necessary corrective action, including correction or submission of documentation, within 60 Days of the generation of TS 824 to avoid deletion of its EDI claim.

(B) FHA Connection

(1) Definition

FHA Connection (FHAC) is an online system for Mortgagees to access and communicate to HUD origination, servicing, and mortgagee approval and recertification information.

(2) Standard

The Mortgagee may submit claims via FHAC for conveyances, Loss Mitigation Home Retention Option incentives, CWCOT, and PFS claims.

The Mortgagee may not use FHAC for filing Single Family Loan Sale (SFLS) claims, Property located on Indian Land claims, Hawaiian Home Land claims, and supplemental claims.

The Mortgagee must enter and submit claims individually; the submitted claims will be batched and loaded nightly into the HUD Claims system for processing the next business day.

(3) FHAC Technical Guidance

The Mortgagee may find information on using FHAC in HUD's FHA Connection Guide.

(4) Transmission Confirmation

The Mortgagee must include a copy of the Single Family Insurance System (SFIS) Claims Input Result screen in the Claim Review File. This screen appears when the claim has been successfully transmitted and will show the claim detail and receipt date.

(5) Error Correction

The Mortgagee must review its claim status via FHAC to determine whether a claim has been suspended and in need of correction or documentation. The Mortgagee must take necessary corrective action, including correction or submission of documentation, within 60 Days of the suspension to avoid deletion of its claim submission.

(6) Mortgagee Contact Information

The Mortgagee must include a staff member contact name and phone number in all claims submitted via FHAC. Alternatively, the Mortgagee may enter the name of a department or functional area that can be contacted regarding FHAC submissions.

(C) Paper Submission Process

(1) Definition

A Paper Claim is a hard copy of form HUD-27011 or equivalent that is mailed to HUD for processing of a claim for mortgage insurance benefits.

(2) Standard

The Mortgagee may submit paper claims for all claims other than Loss Mitigation Home Retention incentive claims and SFLS claims, where disallowed by the Participating Servicer Agreement (PSA). The Mortgagee must submit supplemental claims in accordance with HUD guidance pertaining to Claim Type 05 submissions.

The Mortgagee may use a computer-generated form to submit a paper claim only if it is substantially identical to the form HUD-27011 in size and format.

(3) HUD Processing Fee

HUD will assess a $100 processing fee for each Part A and B of form HUD-27011 filed as a paper claim, with the exception of:
- supplemental claims;
- claims for Mortgages insured under Section 247 (Hawaiian Home Lands) or Section 248 (Insured Mortgages on Indian Land); and
- reacquisition packages.

(4) Certification of Claim Accuracy

The Mortgagee must ensure that the paper claim form is signed by an authorized Mortgagee official (authorized agent). By signing the form HUD-27011, the authorized Mortgagee official is certifying that all information and statements contained in the claim are true and correct.

HUD will return the claim submission to the Mortgagee if it is not signed or if it contains a stamped, illegible, or duplicated signature.

(5) Electronic Signatures

The use of electronic signatures is voluntary. HUD will accept an electronic signature conducted in accordance with the Policy on Use of Electronic Signatures on claim documents requiring signatures, unless otherwise prohibited by law.

(6) Submission of the Initial Paper Claim

The Mortgagee must send via mail or courier the original form HUD-27011 Parts A, B, C, D, and/or E with required attachments to:

U.S. Department of Housing and Urban Development
Single Family Claims Branch
Review and Compliance Section
Attn: Claim Reviewer
Room 6251
451 7th Street, SW
Washington, DC 20410

The Mortgagee may request information regarding its HUD-designated Claim Reviewer by emailing fha_sfclaims@hud.gov.

(7) Pre-Screening

(a) Definition

Pre-Screening of Claims is the process by which HUD reviews paper claim packages before processing to determine whether any data is missing, incomplete, or inaccurate.

(b) Standard

If any discrepancies or deficiencies are found, HUD ceases its review of the claim and will return the unprocessed claim to the Mortgagee.

HUD considers the official receipt date of the paper claim to be the date that HUD receives a claim that passes pre-screening.

b. Claim Status

Beginning at least two business days after transmission to HUD's Claims system, the Mortgagee may view claim status on FHAC as follows:
- for paid claims, an Advice of Payment letter or Payment Advice will be available;
- for suspended claims, a list of suspended edit codes, with explanations will be available; and
- for deleted claims, a message noting that the claim has been deleted.

Additionally, for claims submitted via EDI, the Mortgagee may review the following Transaction Sets (TS) to determine claim status:
- TS 820 to identify paid claims, and
- TS 824 to identify suspended claims.

c. Claim Review File

i. Standard

For each claim filed, the Mortgagee must maintain evidence of compliance with HUD's servicing requirements. In addition to retaining the documentation required in the servicing file, the Mortgagee must include the following documentation in its Claim Review File:
- Default servicing documentation, including:
  - communication with Borrowers and with HUD;
  - required notices;
  - evidence of evaluation under HUD's Loss Mitigation Program, including 90-Day Reviews;
  - documentation evidencing the Mortgagee's compliance with HUD's reasonable diligence requirements;
  - documentation justifying any delays in meeting HUD time frames;

- o if applicable, documentation relating to compliance with federal or state prohibitions or delays;
- o a copy of the summary of all Single Family Default Monitoring System (SFDMS) status codes reported, available via either the FHAC or through Neighborhood Watch web applications; and
- o a print-out of the FHAC screen showing the check mark at the top of the page confirming that the reporting of Status Code 68 was successful (including the date of submission legibly shown), or a copy of the TS 824 confirming that the Status Code 68 transaction was timely submitted to HUD without a fatal error; and

- claims and/or conveyance documentation, including:
  - o a copy of the first public legal action to initiate foreclosure with the date the action was taken;
  - o a copy of the foreclosure deed recorded by the local recording authority with the date of recordation;
  - o a copy of the first public legal action to initiate eviction, if applicable;
  - o all documentation pertaining to bankruptcy, if applicable;
  - o a copy of the deed or assignment with the date of recordation, along with a copy of the transmittal letter, if the deed or assignment was sent to a recording authority;
  - o a copy of the Mortgage Insurance Certificate (MIC);
  - o a copy of the mortgage Note and modification, if applicable;
  - o the title approval letter, if applicable;
  - o the title submission certification, for assignments only;
  - o evidence showing that the certificate of title to the Manufactured Home is properly retired;
  - o invoices and receipts or other documentation of payment made supporting all disbursements for which reimbursement is claimed. Where the Mortgagee made such disbursements in bulk, the documentation must reflect the specific disbursements made for each mortgage;
  - o all loan servicing and transaction records (e.g., escrow history, payment history, transaction codes, collection notes, etc.) dated on or after the last complete installment date, as reported in Item 8 of Part A, form HUD-27011;
  - o all property inspection reports (e.g., initial, occupied, and vacant);
  - o any photographs needed to support P&P expenses and evictions;
  - o written responses from HUD's MCM regarding approval of extensions or expenses;
  - o documentation to support any extensions in Items 19, 20, and 21 of Part A, form HUD-27011, if applicable;
  - o a copy of the buydown and rental agreements;
  - o Advice of Payment letters or claims billing statements, if applicable;
  - o a copy of the hazard insurance policy and flood insurance policy, if applicable;
  - o documentation supporting the refund or estimated refund of hazard insurance premiums, if applicable;
  - o a copy of any appraisals;

○ a copy of the calculation of the Commissioner's Adjusted Fair Market Value (CAFMV);
○ a copy of the wire or canceled check for CWCOT and PFS claims;
○ a copy of the Closing Disclosure, if applicable;
○ for claims involving Reconveyance and reacquisition, evidence that the title or property issue requiring Reconveyance has been corrected; and
○ all parts of the claim form, schedules, attachments, and any other supporting documents.

ii. Record Retention Period

The Mortgagee must retain this documentation for at least seven years after the final claim or latest supplemental claim settlement date:

- The final settlement date is the date of the last acknowledgement or payment received by the Mortgagee in response to the submission of a claim. In certain cases, the acknowledgement may be in the form of a bill.
- The supplemental settlement date is the date of the final payment or acknowledgement of such supplemental claim. In certain cases, the acknowledgement may be in the form of a bill.

iii. Electronic Storage

The Mortgagee may use electronic storage methods for all other required servicing and claim-related documents where retention of a hard copy or original document is not required.

iv. HUD Requests for Information

The Mortgagee must make available to HUD hard or electronic copies of identified claim files within 24 hours of a request, or as otherwise requested by HUD. HUD may charge a fee for the review of a Claim Review File that is not provided to HUD when requested.

v. Missing Claim Files

If the Mortgagee is unable to produce the Claim Review File at HUD's request during the record retention period, HUD may consider all amounts for expenses and interest to have been paid in error.

2. Claim Types

Mortgagees may submit the following claim types for Single Family forward Mortgages.

a. Claim Type 01 - Conveyances

The Mortgagee may submit a claim after conveyance of a Property to HUD through foreclosure or by Deed-in-Lieu (DIL) of Foreclosure under Claim Type 01.

i. Computation of Interest

(A) Calculating Debenture Interest

(1) Debenture Interest Rates

(a) Mortgages Endorsed for FHA Insurance after January 23, 2004

For Mortgages that were endorsed after January 23, 2004, and are not Direct Endorsements, the Mortgagee must calculate debenture interest as the monthly average yield for the month in which the Default on the Mortgage occurred, on United States Treasury Securities adjusted to a constant maturity of 10 years.

(b) Mortgages Endorsed for FHA Insurance On or Before January 23, 2004

For Mortgages that were insured on or before January 23, 2004 and were not Direct Endorsements, the Mortgagee must calculate the debenture interest rate as the higher of the rates in effect on:
- the date the Mortgage was endorsed for insurance; or
- the date of Firm Commitment.

(c) Direct Endorsements and Coinsurance Programs

(i) Mortgages Endorsed for FHA Insurance After January 23, 2004

For applications involving Mortgages originated under the Single Family Direct Endorsement Program and endorsed for FHA insurance after January 23, 2004, the Mortgagee must calculate the debenture interest rate as the monthly average yield for the month in which the Default on the Mortgage occurred, on United States Treasury Securities adjusted to a constant maturity of 10 years.

(ii) Mortgages Insured On or Before January 23, 2004

For Direct Endorsement Mortgages insured on or prior to January 23, 2004, the Mortgagee must calculate debenture interest as the rate in effect on the date the Mortgage was endorsed for insurance.

(2) Time Frames for Debenture Interest

(a) Interest up to Date of Claim Settlement

(i) Definition

The Date of Initial Claim Settlement is the date that HUD approves the settlement of Part A of form HUD-27011 for payment.

The Date of Final Claim Settlement is the date that HUD approves the settlement of Part B of form HUD-27011 for payment.

(ii) Standard

Part A

Provided that the Mortgagee has met all time requirements, HUD will pay debenture interest on the unpaid principal balance from the date of Default to the date of initial claim settlement.

Part B

HUD will compute interest on expenditures from the date of the submission of Part B to the date of the final claim settlement.

(b) Interest up to Disbursement Date

(i) Definition

The Disbursement Date, as applicable to claims, is the date the Mortgagee paid for an expense.

(ii) Standard

For each Disbursement itemized on Parts C, D and E, the Mortgagee must compute the debenture interest from the latter of the Disbursement Date or date of Default, to the earliest of the following dates:
- Part A's date of interest curtailment;
- the date Part B is prepared; or
- Part B's date of interest curtailment.

*(iii)*Required Documentation

The Mortgagee must enter in Item 204 (Part C) and Item 304 (Part D) the date to which interest is calculated for expenditures claimed on form HUD-27011, Part B. This will be the same date as entered in Item 104, Part B, provided no time requirement or approved extension has been missed.

(B) Calculating Interest for an Expenditure using Daily Interest Rate Factors

(1) Definition

The Daily Interest Rate Factor is the annual interest rate expressed as a decimal, divided by 365 (or 366 in leap years), and rounded to the fourth place to the right of the decimal, for the purpose of calculating interest on claimed expenditures.

(2) Standard

The Mortgagee must calculate the amount of interest to be claimed for an expenditure as follows:
- identify the effective debenture interest rate based on the endorsement date of the mortgage for mortgages endorsed before January 23, 2004, or the date of Default for mortgages endorsed on or after January 23, 2004;
- find the Daily Interest Rate Factor (see Appendix 8.c Daily Interest Rate Factor in the *Claim Filing Technical Guide*) corresponding to the effective debenture interest rate;
- multiply the Daily Interest Rate Factor by the amount paid; then
- multiply this result by the number of Days (see Appendix 8.b Julian Calendar in the *Claim Filing Technical Guide*) from the date paid (or Default date, if later) for each line Item to the earlier of:
  - the date in Item 104 (submission date for Part B); or
  - the date of the earliest time requirement missed (Items 204 and 304).

(3) Interest for Expenditures Before the Date of Default

(a) Standard

If the Mortgagee makes an expenditure or advance before the date of Default, the Mortgagee may only calculate debenture interest from the date of Default.

HUD will not pay debenture interest on expenses prior to the date of Default.

(b) Required Documentation

When filing the claim, the Mortgagee must:
- enter the date of Default in the "Date Paid" column of Parts C, D, and E; and
- place the actual date paid in parentheses, following the description of the expenditure or advance.

(C) Calculating Interest for Default after SFB-Unemployment or Special Forbearance

(1) Standard

(a) Time Frame for Mortgage Note Interest

When the Mortgagee files a claim for insurance benefits after a Default under a Special Forbearance (SFB) - Unemployment Agreement or Special Forbearance agreement, HUD will pay mortgage note interest for the period beginning on the due date of the last completely paid installment, up to the earliest of the following dates:

- date of initiation of foreclosure proceedings;
- date of acquisition of title and possession by DIL of Foreclosure;
- date the Property was acquired by the Commissioner under a direct conveyance from the Borrower; or
- 90 Days after the date of the Default of the SFB-Unemployment Agreement or Special Forbearance Agreement; or such other date as HUD may approve in writing prior to expiration of this 90-Day period.

(b) Calculating Mortgage Note Interest using Daily Interest Rate Factors

To obtain the amount of accrued mortgage interest due, the Mortgagee must:

- multiply the Daily Interest Rate Factor (see Appendix 8.c Daily Interest Rate Factor in the *Claim Filing Technical Guide*) by the amount of the unpaid principal balance; and
- multiply the result by the number of days from the due date of the last completely paid installment to the date selected above as the "ending date."

(c) Time Frame for Debenture Interest

When the Mortgagee files a claim for insurance benefits after a Default under an SFB-Unemployment Agreement or SFB Agreement, HUD will pay debenture interest for the period beginning on the earliest of the following dates:

- the date of initiation of foreclosure proceedings;
- the date of acquisition of title and possession by DIL of Foreclosure;
- the date the Property was acquired by the Commissioner under a direct conveyance from the Borrowers; or
- 90 Days after the date of the Default of the SFB-Unemployment Agreement or SFB Agreement, or other such date as HUD may approve in writing prior to expiration of this 90-Day period.

This debenture interest period ends on the date of the initial claim payment or the date of interest curtailment.

(d) Calculating Debenture Interest

HUD will compute the debenture interest at the time of payment of Part B, using the rate in effect at the time of the mortgage Default. Where "Mortgage Note Interest" is claimed on Part B because of an SFB-Unemployment Agreement or SFB Agreement, HUD will subtract from the claim any debenture interest already paid for the same period.

(2) Interest on Claim Form

The Mortgagee must reflect the use of an SFB-Unemployment Agreement or SFB Agreement by entering the following in Item 121:
- From: Enter the date of the last completely paid installment after all funds received under the Agreement are applied according to the terms of the Mortgage (Item 8, part A). If no Mortgage Payments were made, enter a date 30 Days before the due date of the first scheduled payment (Item 7, Part A).
- To: Enter the earliest of the following dates:
  - the date of initiation of foreclosure proceedings;
  - the date of acquisition of title and possession by DIL of Foreclosure;
  - the date the Property was acquired by the Commissioner under a direct conveyance from the Borrower; or
  - 90 Days, or such other time as approved by the MCM, following the date of the Borrower's SFB-Unemployment Agreement or SFB Agreement failure.
- Rate: Enter the mortgage interest rate as it appears on the mortgage Note.
- Column C: Enter the amount of mortgage interest due.

(3) Required Documentation

The Mortgagee must send to HUD with Part B of form HUD-27011 a copy of the:
- Executed SFB-Unemployment Agreement or SFB Agreement; and
- the payment history.

The Mortgagee must retain copies of these documents in the Claim Review File.

(D) Curtailment of Interest

(1) Definition

Curtailment of Interest is the cutoff of the accrued interest calculation as of the date on which the Mortgagee fails to take a required action.

The Date of Interest Curtailment is the date that the Mortgagee first failed to take a required action.

(2) Standard

The Mortgagee must self-curtail interest on Single Family claims when it fails to meet HUD's foreclosure, reasonable diligence, or reporting time frame requirements as of the date on which the required action should have been taken.

If more than one time requirement is missed and there are no applicable extensions, the Mortgagee must calculate the interest to the earliest missed time requirement.

(a) Failure to Timely Initiate Foreclosure

The Mortgagee must curtail interest if it fails to meet the time requirement, including applicable extensions, to initiate foreclosure, regardless of whether later payments advanced the date of Default.

(b) Failure to Give HUD Notice of Foreclosure

The Mortgagee must curtail interest if it fails to meet the time requirement to give notice to HUD of the foreclosure via SFDMS. Until the Mortgagee properly reports the foreclosure initiation, the Mortgagee must reduce its claim by an amount equivalent to 30 Days of interest for each SFDMS reporting cycle missed.

(c) Failure to Meet Reasonable Diligence Time Frames

The Mortgagee must curtail interest if it fails to meet HUD's Reasonable Diligence Time Frames, including applicable extensions, in:
- completing foreclosure;
- acquiring good marketable title to and possession of the Property; and
- if applicable, starting eviction or possessory action.

(d) Failure to Meet Time Frame to Convey to HUD

The Mortgagee must curtail interest if it fails to meet HUD's time frame in conveying the Property to HUD.

(3) Required Documentation

The Mortgagee must indicate the interest curtailment date on form HUD-27011, as follows:
- In Part A, the Mortgagee must enter the curtailment date in Item 31, ensuring that this date is before the date in Item 9. The Mortgagee must indicate in the "Mortgagee's comments" section the reason for the curtailment.

- When a curtailment date is entered in Item 204 Part C and 304 Part D, the Mortgagee must indicate in the "Mortgagee's comments" section of Part B the reason for the curtailment.

The Mortgagee must retain copies of any approved extensions received from HUD in the Claim Review File.

(4) Remittance of Claim Payments for Failure to Self-Curtail

If a Mortgagee determines during its Quality Control (QC) review that it failed to self-curtail when submitting the claim, the Mortgagee must remit claim-related payments to HUD through the Claim Remittance feature in FHAC. For more information on remitting payments, see the Quick Start: Single Family Servicing Claims Processing guide.

ii. Computation of Claim Amount

The Mortgagee may claim up to 100 percent of the unpaid principal balance, plus allowable costs and debenture interest.

(A) Damage to Conveyed Properties

(1) Definition

Surchargeable Damage is damage to a Property caused by fire, flood, earthquake, tornado, boiler explosion (for condominiums only) or Mortgagee Neglect.

Mortgagee Neglect is the Mortgagee's failure to take action to preserve and protect the Property from the time it is determined (or should have been determined) to be vacant or abandoned, until the time it is conveyed to HUD.

Non-Surchargeable Damage is damage to a Property that is not Surchargeable Damage.

(2) Standard

(a) HUD-Required Repairs of Damage to the Property

In cases of Surchargeable Damage, HUD may require the Mortgagee to repair a Property before conveyance, and the Mortgagee may not request reimbursement for such repairs.

In cases of Non-Surchargeable Damage that occurred during the time of the Mortgagee's possession, HUD may require the Mortgagee to repair such damage before conveyance, and HUD will reimburse the Mortgagee for reasonable payments not in excess of the Secretary's estimate of the cost of repair, less any insurance recovery.

(b) Conveyance of Property with Surchargeable Damage

Where HUD has authorized the Mortgagee to convey a damaged Property unrepaired, HUD will deduct from the mortgage insurance benefits the greater of:
- any insurance recovery received by the Mortgagee; or
- HUD's estimate of the cost to repair the Property.

(c) Estimating the Recovery Amount

If the Mortgagee has not received the hazard insurance proceeds by the time of the Part A claim submission, the Mortgagee may estimate the recovery.

(d) Adjustment of Recovery Amount

If the actual recovery amount is less than the amount estimated, the Mortgagee may request reimbursement of the difference between the amount of proceeds expected and the proceeds received if both are greater than HUD's estimate of damage.

The Mortgagee is not entitled to a reimbursement if it would reduce the deduction in insurance benefits to less than HUD's estimate of damage.

(e) Mortgagee Certification for Properties Damaged by Fire

(i) Definition

The Mortgagee Certification for Properties Damaged by Fire is a certification prepared by the Mortgagee in order to convey to HUD certain eligible Properties damaged by fire.

(ii) Standard

When the Mortgagee meets all regulatory requirements for conveying a Property damaged by fire that was not covered by fire insurance at the time of the damage, or the amount of insurance coverage was inadequate to fully repair the damage, the Mortgagee must include a Mortgagee Certification at the time that a claim is filed to limit the deduction from insurance benefits to the amount of insurance recovery received by the Mortgagee, if any.

The Mortgagee Certification must include the following statements:
- at the time the Mortgage was insured, the Property was covered by fire insurance in an amount at least equal to the lesser of 100 percent of the insurable value of the improvements, or the principal balance of the Mortgage;

- the insurer later canceled this coverage or refused to renew it for reasons other than nonpayment of premium;
- the Mortgagee made diligent efforts within 30 Days of any cancellation or non-renewal of hazard insurance, and at least annually thereafter, to secure other coverage or coverage under a Fair Access to Insurance Requirements (FAIR) Plan, in an amount at least equal to the lesser of 100 percent of the insurable value of the improvements, or the principal balance of the Mortgage, or if coverage to such an extent was unavailable at a reasonable rate (as defined in 24 CFR § 230.379(a)(4)(i)), the greatest extent of coverage that was available at a reasonable rate;
- the extent of coverage obtained by the Mortgagee was the greatest available at a reasonable rate, or if the Mortgagee was unable to obtain insurance, none was available at a reasonable rate; and
- the Mortgagee performed all required Property P&P actions.

(iii) Required Documentation

The Mortgagee must upload into P260 a copy of the Mortgagee Certification and must retain a copy in the Claim Review File.

(f) Conveyance Without Approval of Property with Unrepaired Surchargeable Damage

If a Mortgagee conveys a damaged Property to HUD without prior notice or approval, the MCM will notify the Mortgagee in writing of its Finding. Depending on the extent of the damage and the MCM's Finding, HUD may reconvey the Property and require reimbursement for all expenses incurred in connection with such acquisition and Reconveyance, or deduct from the mortgage insurance benefits the greater of HUD's estimate of the cost of repair or any insurance recovery.

(3) Required Documentation

The Mortgagee must document all Surchargeable Damage and Non-Surchargeable Damage to the Property on the claim form as follows:
- for Surchargeable Damage, mark "Yes" in Item 24, complete Items 26 and 27, and identify the damage in the "Mortgagee's comments" section;
- for Non-Surchargeable Damage, mark "No" in Item 24, identifying the damage in the "Mortgagee's comments" section; and
- include amounts of hazard insurance recovery received in Line 118 or, if adjusting the amount based on a Part A estimate, in Line 119.

(4) Failure to Indicate Damage on the Claim Form

If the Property is conveyed damaged but is not identified as damaged on form HUD-27011, HUD will make no further reimbursement until the MCM has evaluated the Mortgagee's responsibility for the damage.

(B) Funds Held by the Mortgagee

(1) Standard

HUD deducts from the mortgage insurance benefits those funds that are retained by the Mortgagee.

(2) Required Documentation

The Mortgagee must report these held funds as follows:
- Unapplied Section 235 Assistance Payments - Item 123, Part B, Column A.
- Funds Held Pursuant to a Buydown Agreement - Item 109, Part B, Column A.
- Rental Income - Item 115, Part B, Column A.
- Hazard Insurance Recovery - Item 118, Part B, Column A, if not reported on Part A.
- Hazard Insurance Recovery - Item 27, Part A, and Item 119, Part B, column A if the entry in Part A is an estimate.
- All other funds - Identify the nature and the amount of the funds and enter in Item 109, Part B, Column A.

(C) Escrow Funds

(1) Funds Remaining In Escrow Account

(a) Standard

The Mortgagee must report on the claim form those funds remaining in the escrow account on the date the deed is filed for record.

(b) Required Documentation

The Mortgagee must enter amounts for funds remaining in the escrow account in Item 109, Part B as follows:
- The Mortgagee must include in Item 109 any funds received on the Mortgage that have not been applied to reduce the indebtedness, such as Partial Payments, hazard insurance refunds, estimated hazard insurance refunds, buydown funds, and funds held in escrow for on-site repairs.

- For payment of expenses for which funds are escrowed, the Mortgagee must charge those payments to the escrow account until the escrow account balance equals zero.
- The Mortgagee must not enter a negative balance in Item 109 and must not enter amounts for escrow advances in Items 305 or 311.

The Mortgagee must include in the "Mortgagee's comments" section an explanation of the funds included in Item 109.

(2) Mortgagee Advances for Escrow Expenditures

(a) Standard

The Mortgagee may claim reimbursement advances for escrow expenditures. There must be no remaining funds in the escrow account.

The Mortgagee must calculate interest on advances from the Disbursement Date to the earliest of the following dates:
- the earliest missed time frame; or
- the date the claim is prepared.

(b) Required Documentation

The Mortgagee must enter any advances for escrow expenditures in Items 305 or 311, as appropriate. The Mortgagee must not charge these advances to Item 109.

When the first occurrence of an expense results in a negative balance to escrow, the Mortgagee must enter this amount in Item 305 or 311, whichever is appropriate.

(D) Property Preservation and Protection Costs

(1) Standard

HUD will reimburse Mortgagees up to the Maximum Property Preservation Allowance, or as permitted by HUD as approved over-allowables, for Property P&P actions so long as:
- the actions are performed before the date of conveyance, even if the Mortgagee renders payment after conveyance; and
- the actions are performed in accordance with HUD guidance.

See Appendix 6.0 – Maximum Property Preservation Allowances (applies to Servicing only) for Maximum Property Preservation Allowances per specific action and per Property.

The Mortgagee may not request reimbursement for any costs related to obtaining bids for P&P actions.

(a) Photographs

The Mortgagee may request a <u>flat fee reimbursement</u> for photographs, regardless of the number of pictures required.

(b) Inspections

The Mortgagee may request reimbursement for costs for:
- up to 13 inspections per calendar year per Property, with one inspection performed for each 25-35-Day cycle in accordance with HUD guidance and with additional protective measures supported by <u>documentation</u>;
- Pre-Conveyance Inspections that do not coincide with the regular inspection schedule; and
- additional inspections as otherwise required by HUD.

(c) Debris Removal

(i) Standard

HUD will reimburse the Mortgagee for debris removal amounts up to the maximum amount in the <u>P&P Cost schedule</u> and up to amounts authorized by the MCM.

(ii) Required Documentation

The Mortgagee must retain in the Claim Review File:
- before and after photographs reflecting the debris removal and including the date and property address; and
- salvage and dumping fee receipts or other documentation stating the date, property address, number of cubic yards dumped, and number and type of appliances disposed of.

(2) Required Documentation

The Mortgagee must retain in the Claim Review File documentation supporting all property preservation expenses claimed by the Mortgagee.

Where the Mortgagee was instructed by HUD to perform a specific service after the date of conveyance, the Mortgagee must include in the "Mortgagee's comments" section of form HUD-27011 notation of the request and a list of expenses associated with completing the request.

(3) HUD Review of P&P Expenses

HUD's MCM will evaluate all claimed costs for P&P. HUD will require the Mortgagee to repay these costs if HUD determines that:
- amounts paid for reimbursement were unnecessary, excessive, or unsupported; or
- services claimed were not performed or were not performed in accordance with HUD guidance.

(E) Homeowners' Association/Condominium Assessments and Fees

(1) Standard

The Mortgagee may claim reimbursement for:
- Homeowners' Association (HOA)/Condominium Fees due within 30 Days after the date of conveyance to HUD and paid by the Mortgagee before conveyance;
- penalties, interest, and/or late fees incurred by the former Borrower and paid by the Mortgagee; and
- the fees and assessments amounts listed below.

(a) Where HOA/Condominium Fees Survived Foreclosure

(i) Fees Not Included in Foreclosure

Where HOA/Condominium Fees were not included in the foreclosure proceedings and these fees survive foreclosure, the Mortgagee may claim reimbursement for the negotiated amount required to obtain a release of outstanding HOA/Condominium Fees.

HUD will only reimburse the Mortgagee for payment of assessments that were incurred from the foreclosure sale date to the date of conveyance.

(ii) Fees Were Included in Foreclosure and Property is in State where HOA/Condominium Liens Can Take Priority

When the Property is located in a State in which HOA/condominium liens can take priority over HUD's first lien and these fees were included in the foreclosure and survived foreclosure, the Mortgagee may claim reimbursement for the negotiated amount required to obtain a release of outstanding HOA/Condominium Fees.

HUD will only reimburse Mortgagees for HOA Fees up to the total value of the periodic HOA/Condominium Assessments due and paid from the date the Borrower defaulted on their HOA/Condominium Assessment to the date of conveyance.

(b) Where there is an HOA/Condominium Lien that Survives Foreclosure

When the Property is not located in a State in which HOA/Condominium Fees can take priority over HUD's first lien, the fees were included in the foreclosure, and there is a lien on the Property that survives foreclosure, the Mortgagee may claim reimbursement for the negotiated amount required to obtain a release of outstanding HOA/Condominium Fees.

HUD will only reimburse Mortgagees for HOA Fees up to the state law mandated amount.

(c) Where HOA/Condominium Fees Do Not Survive Foreclosure or Create a Lien

Where HOA/Condominium Fees will not survive foreclosure or create a lien surviving foreclosure, the Mortgagee may claim reimbursement for the HOA/Condominium Assessment amounts required under applicable law.

(2) Required Documentation

After resolving HOA/Condominium Fee amounts, the Mortgagee must perform the following in P260:

- no later than 15 Days after conveyance, upload into P260 the paid HOA/condominium invoice and any documentation necessary to verify that the Mortgagee made such payments prior to conveyance; and
- document in P260 any common area requirements associated with gaining access to the Property.

The Mortgagee must also reflect the amounts on form HUD-27011 as follows:

- enter HOA/condominium amounts in Item 111 of Part B and Item 305 on Part D; and
- document the payment of all final bills and liens for HOA/Condominium Fees in the "Mortgagee's comments" section of Part C.

(F) Hazard Insurance Premiums

HUD will reimburse the Mortgagee for hazard insurance premiums sufficient to protect the Mortgagee's interest up until the date the deed to the Secretary is filed for record, so long as the hazard insurance premiums were paid in accordance with HUD guidance.

(1) Calculating the Hazard Insurance Premium Refund

If the amount of the actual premium refund is not known at the time Part B of form HUD-27011 is prepared, the Mortgagee must calculate an estimate on a "short rate" basis as follows:

- determine the number of Days the policy was in effect, from the effective date of the policy to the earlier of the cancellation date or the date the deed to the Secretary was filed for record (see Appendix 8.b Julian Date Calendar of the *Claim Filing Technical Guide*);
- use the Short Rate Method Table in Appendix 8.a of the *Claim Filing Technical Guide* to determine the percentage of the premium utilized, and subtract this figure from 100 to determine the percentage of premium remaining; and
- multiply the percentage of premium remaining by the total premium to determine the estimated amount of the premium refund.

(a) Actual Hazard Insurance Premium Refund More than Estimated Refund

If the actual premium return is $10 or more than the Mortgagee's estimated amount, the Mortgagee must file a supplemental remittance.

(b) Actual Hazard Insurance Premium Less than Estimated Refund

If the actual premium return is less than the Mortgagee's estimated refund, the Mortgagee may request a refund by:
- filing a supplemental claim form; and
- providing a copy of the insurance carrier's statement of the return premium.

(2) Required Documentation

The Mortgagee must include the refund amount or estimated refund amount in Item 109, Part B of form HUD-27011, and include in the "Mortgagee's comments" section the amount and whether this amount is actual or estimated.

(3) Claims without Estimated Hazard Insurance Premium Refunds or Where No Refund was Received

The Mortgagee may submit a Part B claim without an estimated hazard insurance premium refund, provided the Mortgagee includes documentation to HUD demonstrating:
- that the insurer remitted the refund to the Borrower; or
- that the insurer has a policy of not remitting funds to the Mortgagee in that jurisdiction.

If the Mortgagee submits a Part B claim with an estimated hazard insurance premium refund, but the refund was not received, the Mortgagee may submit a supplemental claim for reimbursement of the estimated hazard insurance premium refund entered on line 109 of the Part B claim, provided the Mortgagee includes documentation to HUD demonstrating:

- that the insurer remitted the refund to the Borrower; or
- that the insurer has a policy of not remitting funds to the Mortgagee in that jurisdiction.

(G) Utility Bills

The Mortgagee may request reimbursement for final utility bills by itemizing them in Item 305 of Part D of form HUD-27011.

(H) Eviction and Other Possessory Action Costs

(1) Definition

Eviction and Other Possessory Action Costs are those costs associated with gaining possession of an occupied Property.

(2) Standard

The Mortgagee may request full reimbursement of eviction and other possessory action costs that are:
- required by state and local law in jurisdictions where the Mortgagee is required to bring a separate possessory action in addition to foreclosure; and
- reasonable and customary for that jurisdiction and actually necessary to accomplish the eviction or other possessory action.

Where debris removal is required by state and local law as part of the eviction or possessory action, the Mortgagee may claim these costs as eviction costs.

HUD will not reimburse the Mortgagee for the following fees and costs:
- fees and costs in excess of reasonable and customary fees and costs and lacking documentation supporting the amount claimed;
- fees and costs unnecessary for the protection, acquisition, or conveyance of the Property, such as courier services, document retrieval, express mail, or property inspection by attorneys;
- Mortgagee's overhead items such as postage, telephone, duplication, or collection services; or
- compensation paid to an attorney or trustee who is a salaried employee of the Mortgagee.

(3) Required Documentation

The Mortgagee may include costs for evictions and possessory actions in Line 111 of form HUD-27011.

The Mortgagee must include in the Claim Review File documentation supporting any claimed costs associated with compliance with state and local law.

(I) Tax Bills

(1) Standard

The Mortgagee may request reimbursement for all tax bills paid.

The Mortgagee may not request reimbursement for late fees and/or interest penalties charged by the taxing jurisdiction for late payment of taxes.

(2) Required Documentation

The Mortgagee must:
- upload into P260 any documentation (such as a paid receipt, a copy of the Mortgagee's tax payment history screen, or other documentation showing the amount paid, the purpose of the payment, and the date the payment was made by the Mortgagee) that is necessary to validate that such payment was made;
- certify in the claim form that all tax bills due within 30 Days of conveyance are paid as of the date of conveyance;
- document payment of tax bills in Item 32, "Schedule of Tax Information," of Part A of form HUD-27011; and
- retain invoices, paid bill receipts, and other documentation necessary to validate that such payment was made in the Claim Review File.

(J) Deed-in-Lieu Borrower Consideration

To claim the DIL Borrower Consideration after successful use of DIL in accordance with HUD policies, the Mortgagee must enter it in Item 305 as an Acquisition Cost.

(K) Attorney's Fees

(1) Standard

(a) Up to Maximum Fee in HUD Schedule

The Mortgagee may claim reimbursement for up to the amounts shown on the HUD Schedule of Standard Attorney Fees for fees reasonably relating to the amount of work performed for the current Default.

The Mortgagee may claim no more than 75 percent of the maximum attorney fee for incurred fees associated with a routine foreclosure that was not completed because any of the following occurred after the Mortgagee initiated foreclosure:
- the Borrower filed for a bankruptcy petition;
- the Borrower executed a DIL of Foreclosure; or
- the Borrower successfully completed a PFS.

HUD will reimburse allowable attorney fees in accordance with HUD guidance pertaining to the <u>reimbursement of foreclosure costs</u>.

(b) For Amounts Exceeding the Maximum Fee and Not Provided for in HUD Schedule

For additional expenses incurred due to required legal actions such as mediation or probate proceedings, the Mortgagee may claim reimbursement for these costs by:

- providing a documented cost breakdown and written justification with the claim submission and retaining a copy in the Claim Review File; and
- filing a supplemental claim for amounts above the maximum fee.

(c) Fees Relating to Bankruptcy

The Mortgagee may claim reimbursement for attorney's fees as follows:

- up to the fee set in the HUD Schedule for costs actually incurred for each bankruptcy; or
- reasonable and customary attorney's fees incurred when the bankruptcy was not routine.

Mortgagees may not claim additional attorney's fees for defending against court-ordered involuntary principal reductions (or "cramdowns") as part of a bankruptcy, nor may Mortgagees claim fees that have already been included in a Loss Mitigation Option.

(2) Required Documentation

The Mortgagee may claim reimbursement for attorney's fees by entering into Part D of the initial filing of form HUD-27011 the following information:

- Item 305, "Disbursements for HIP, taxes, ground rents and water rates (which were liens prior to mortgage), eviction costs and other disbursements not shown elsewhere,": Enter up to the maximum fee set forth in the <u>HUD Schedule</u> for possessory actions.
- Item 306, "Attorney/Trustee Fees": Enter the amount of attorney or trustee fees actually incurred. The Mortgagee must itemize the elements of the fee if the fees exceed the amount that is <u>HUD approved for the area</u>.
- Item 307, "Foreclosure and/or acquisition, conveyance and other costs": Itemize any other legal costs paid by the Mortgagee, not including disbursements shown in Item 306. Mortgagees must not enter attorney's fees in Item 307.
- Item 310, "Bankruptcy": Enter an amount up to the maximum fee set forth in the HUD Schedule for costs actually incurred for each bankruptcy and reasonable and customary attorney's fees incurred when the bankruptcy was not routine.

(L) Foreclosure and Acquisition Costs

(1) Definition

Foreclosure and Acquisition Costs are those costs associated with the Mortgagee's foreclosure of the Property and acquisition of good marketable title to the Property.

(2) Standard

The Mortgagee may request reimbursement for fees and costs that are:
- necessarily incurred in foreclosure proceedings; and
- reasonable and customary in the area.

For all Mortgages endorsed prior to February 1, 1998, HUD will reimburse the Mortgagee's foreclosure costs at two-thirds of the foreclosure costs.

For all Mortgages endorsed on or after February 1, 1998, HUD will reimburse the Mortgagee's foreclosure costs based on the Tier Ranking System (TRS) ranking of the Mortgagee as of the date the Part B claim is received by HUD as follows:
- for non-Tier 1 Mortgagees, 67 percent of foreclosure costs; and
- for Tier 1 Mortgagees, 75 percent of foreclosure costs.

HUD will not reimburse the Mortgagee for the following fees and costs:
- fees and costs in excess of reasonable and customary fees and costs, which lack documentation supporting the amount claimed;
- fees and costs unnecessary for the protection, acquisition, or conveyance of the Property, such as courier services, document retrieval, express mail, or property inspection by attorneys;
- Mortgagee's overhead items such as postage, telephone, duplication, or collection services;
- compensation paid to an attorney or trustee who is a salaried employee of the Mortgagee; or
- extra costs incurred in foreclosures that result from defects in the mortgage transaction or foreclosure or defects in the title existing at or before the time the Mortgage was filed for record. HUD may reimburse these costs if the Mortgage was sold by the Secretary or was executed in connection with the sale of a Property by the Secretary after August 1, 1969.

(3) Required Documentation

The Mortgagee must reflect total foreclosure costs in Items 306, 307, and 310 of form HUD-27011. HUD will then calculate either the two-thirds or 75 percent allowance, as appropriate, for both expenses and interest.

(M) Bankruptcy

HUD will reimburse fees related to bankruptcy as based on the Mortgagee's tier ranking. HUD will reimburse allowable bankruptcy fees in accordance with HUD guidance pertaining to the <u>reimbursement of foreclosure costs</u>.

If there are multiple bankruptcies for a Mortgage in Default, the Mortgagee may request reimbursement for the fees and costs related to each filing.

(1) Extension for Initiation of Foreclosure

(a) Standard

If the Mortgagee is unable to initiate foreclosure due to the Borrower's filing of bankruptcy and the time limit to initiate foreclosure had not expired prior to the bankruptcy petition being filed, the Mortgagee may reflect the use of the 90-Day extension to initiate foreclosure by entering in form HUD-27011:

- the date of the filing of the bankruptcy petition in Item 40;
- the release date of the bankruptcy stay in Item 21;
- a date 90 Days after the release of the bankruptcy stay, including any applicable extensions, in Item 19; and
- the date the foreclosure action was initiated or reinitiated, if canceled due to the bankruptcy, in Item 11.

(b) Required Documentation

The Mortgagee must retain in the Claim Review File:

- dated copies of the court's release form the bankruptcy stay;
- copies of any demand letters or notices required by applicable state law; and
- any approvals for extensions received by HUD.

(2) Extensions for Foreclosure Completion

If the Mortgagee is unable to timely complete the foreclosure due to the filing of a bankruptcy petition, the Mortgagee must:

- note the cause of the delay in the "Mortgagee's comments" section of Part A; and
- retain supporting documentation in the Claim Review File.

(N) Rental of the Property

(1) Standard

HUD will not reimburse the Mortgagee for costs incurred solely in renting the Property prior to conveyance. If rental produces a net profit, HUD will reduce the amount of the claim by that profit.

(2) Required Documentation

If the Mortgagee rents the Property, the Mortgagee must include on form HUD-27011:

- any Rental Income on Item 115, Part B; and
- rental expenses, as an offset to Rental Income, on Item 116, Part B.

(O)Section 235 Assistance Payments

(1) Unapplied Payments

The Mortgagee must return unearned Section 235 assistance to HUD via the Section 235 billing process. The Mortgagee must apply earned payments to the Borrower's account in full installments to advance the date of account and report Partial Payments in Item 123 of Part B.

(2) Overpaid Assistance

For funds that were advanced to repay overpaid Section 235 assistance to HUD and were not recovered from the Borrower, the Mortgagee must enter the unrecovered advance in Item 123, Column B, Part B.

(P) Deficiency Judgments

(1) Standard

When HUD required the deficiency judgment action or when HUD has approved the Mortgagee's request to pursue the Judgment, the Mortgagee may request full reimbursement of the following fees:

- cost of reasonable and customary attorney fees which relate only to obtaining the deficiency Judgment;
- additional filing or recording fees directly related to the deficiency Judgment; and
- if local law required a judicial foreclosure in order to obtain a deficiency Judgment, those costs directly related to the judicial foreclosure.

(2) Required Documentation

The Mortgagee must note costs related to deficiency Judgments in Item 410 of form HUD-27011.

(Q)Late Fees and Interest Penalties

Unless otherwise stated specifically in this *SF Handbook* or otherwise authorized by HUD, the Mortgagee may not request reimbursement for late fees and/or interest penalties on escrowed items.

iii. FHA Refinance of Borrowers in Negative Equity Positions

(A) Submission of Claim to HUD

For claims for Mortgages under the FHA Refinance of Borrowers in Negative Equity Positions, or FHA Short Refinance program, the Mortgagee may file a conveyance claim and request reimbursement for all allowable Part B expenses.

(B) Submission of Claim to the Department of Treasury

After HUD pays the unpaid principal balance on Part A of the conveyance claim, the Mortgagee must contact the Department of Treasury's Claims Processor at ctsclaimsprocessor@wellsfargo.com to register and submit claims for the Emergency Economic Stabilization Act (EESA) portion of the unpaid principal balance to be paid in part by the Department of Treasury. The Mortgagee may contact the Claims Processor for support at (866) 846-4526.

iv. Submission of Claim Form Parts to HUD for Conveyance Claims

(A) Submission of Part A

(1) To HUD

The Mortgagee must submit Part A to HUD headquarters via EDI, FHAC, or paper claim.

The Mortgagee must submit Part A no later than two business days after the date the deed to HUD is filed for record or mailed to the recording authority. For paper claims submitted via mail, HUD will consider the submission timely if HUD receives these documents within 10 Days from the date listed in Item 6.

(2) To P260

The Mortgagee must upload into P260:
- a copy of Part A;
- a copy of the deed to HUD filed for record;
- documentation of the last tax bills paid to each taxing authority;
- a copy of HUD's letter approving damaged conveyance of the Property under 24 CFR § 203.379(a), if applicable;
- the Mortgagee's certificate that the conditions of 24 CFR § 203.379(b), relating to fire damage, have been met, if applicable; and
- a copy of documentation that will verify that appropriate action was taken to protect and preserve the Property.

The Mortgagee must upload these documents no later than two business days after the date the deed to HUD is filed for record or mailed to the recording authority.

(B) Submission of Parts B, C, D, and E

(1) To HUD

The Mortgagee must submit Part B to HUD headquarters via EDI, FHAC, or paper claim. When submitting via paper claim, the Mortgagee must also submit Parts C, D, and E.

The Mortgagee must submit Part B within the later of:
- 45 Days after the deed was filed for record or mailed to the recording authority; or
- 15 Days after the Title Approval Date in FHAC, if the claim was filed electronically (or 15 Days after the Title Approval Letter Date if the claim was filed manually).

The Mortgagee must retain Parts C, D, and E in the Claim Review File.

(2) To P260

The Mortgagee must upload into P260:
- Parts B, C, D, and E; and
- required supporting documentation of amounts claimed.

The Mortgagee must upload into P260 Parts B, C, D, and E within the later of:
- 45 Days after the deed was filed for record or mailed to the recording authority; or
- 15 Days after the Title Approval Date in FHAC, if the claim was filed electronically (or 15 Days after the Title Approval Letter Date if the claim was filed manually).

b. Claim Type 02 - Assignment or Single Family Loan Sale Program

A Mortgagee participating in HUD's SFLS Program or assigning a Mortgage to HUD under the Indian Land or Hawaiian Home Lands programs may submit a claim under Claim Type 02.

i. Hawaiian Home Land Mortgages (Section 247 Mortgages) Claims

The Mortgagee may assign to HUD Mortgages in Default that are insured under Section 247 of the National Housing Act and file claims for mortgage insurance benefits.

(A) Computation of Interest

HUD will pay mortgage note interest accrued and unpaid at the time of assignment. HUD will pay debenture interest on the net claim amount, excluding mortgage note interest, from the date of assignment to the date of claim payment.

If the Mortgagee fails to meet HUD's time requirement to submit the claim, HUD will notify the Mortgagee of the date of curtailment to be entered in form HUD-27011.

(B) Computation of Claims

The Mortgagee may claim up to 100 percent of the unpaid principal balance, plus allowable costs and debenture interest.

HUD will reimburse the Mortgagee for reasonable and customary costs associated with the assignment as follows.

(1) Allowable Costs

The Mortgagee may claim reimbursement for:
- fees paid to recorders of deeds or public trustees;
- costs required by law;
- property and preservation costs performed in accordance with HUD guidance before the date of assignment; and
- other fees and costs necessarily incurred and are customary in the area.

(2) Disallowable Costs

The Mortgagee may not claim reimbursement for the following fees and costs:
- fees and costs in excess of reasonable and customary fees and costs and lacking documentation supporting the amount claimed;
- fees and costs unnecessary for the protection, acquisition, or conveyance of the Property, such as courier services, document retrieval, express mail, or property inspection by attorneys;
- Mortgagee's overhead items such as postage, telephone, duplication, or collection services; and
- costs for title policies.

(C) Submission of Claim Form Parts to HUD for Hawaiian Home Land Mortgages

The Mortgagee may only file a claim after:
- the Mortgagee has notified the Department of Hawaiian Home Lands (DHHL) of the Borrower's Default by letter by the 90th Day of Delinquency;
- the Borrower's Default has remained uncured for 180 Days; and
- the Mortgagee has met all regulatory program requirements, including the face-to-face interview and required loss mitigation evaluation.

The Mortgagee must submit the claim via EDI, with Parts A and B submitted simultaneously, or via paper claim, with all Parts included. The Mortgagee must retain copies of all Parts of the form HUD-27011 in the Claim Review File.

(D) Submission of Claim Form Parts as Part of Request for Title Approval for Hawaiian Home Land Mortgages

At the time the Mortgagee files its claim, the Mortgagee must send copies of the form HUD-27011 with its title evidence package to:

Associate Regional Counsel - Hawaii
Office General Counsel
U.S. Department of HUD
611 W. Sixth Street, 13th Floor
Los Angeles, CA 90017

ii. Insured Mortgages on Indian Land (Section 248 Mortgages) Claims

With HUD approval, the Mortgagee may assign to HUD Mortgages that are in Default and are insured under Section 248 of the National Housing Act and file claims for mortgage insurance benefits.

(A) Computation of Interest

HUD will pay mortgage note interest accrued and unpaid at the time of assignment. HUD will pay debenture interest on the net claim amount, excluding mortgage note interest, from the date of assignment to the date of claim payment, unless interest is curtailed.

(B) Computation of Claim

The Mortgagee may claim up to 100 percent of the unpaid principal balance, plus allowable costs and debenture interest.

HUD will reimburse the Mortgagee for reasonable and customary costs associated with the assignment as follows.

(1) Allowable Costs

The Mortgagee may claim reimbursement for:
* fees paid to recorders of deeds or public trustees;
* costs required by law;
* property and preservation costs performed in accordance with HUD guidance before the date of assignment; and
* other fees and costs necessarily incurred and are customary in the area.

(2) Disallowable Costs

The Mortgagee may not claim reimbursement for the following:
* fees and costs in excess of reasonable and customary fees and costs and lacking documentation supporting the amount claimed;

- fees and costs unnecessary for the protection, acquisition, or conveyance of the Property, such as courier services, document retrieval, express mail, or property inspection by attorneys;
- Mortgagee's overhead items such as postage, telephone, duplication, or collection services; and
- costs for title policies.

(C) Submission of Claim Form Parts for Section 248 Mortgages

(1) Submission of Claim Form Parts to HUD

The Mortgagee must submit via EDI to HUD Parts A and B simultaneously. For paper claim submissions, the Mortgagee must submit Parts A, B, C, D, and E. The Mortgagee must retain copies of all Parts of the form HUD-27011 in the Claim Review File.

(2) Submission of Claim Form Parts as Part of Request for Title Approval

At the time the Mortgagee files its claim, the Mortgagee must send to HUD's Loan Servicing Contractor:
- copies of Parts A and B;
- a copy of the original Mortgage;
- a copy of the original Note with endorsement;
- a copy of assignment to HUD;
- copies of all intervening assignments;
- the Mortgagee's original title policy evidencing the Mortgage's first lien position;
- a copy of Part D;
- a copy of the Title Submission Certificate;
- the original of all hazard insurance policies and a copy of the notice to the insurance carrier requesting that HUD be named beneficiary in the Mortgagee clause;
- documentation of the last tax bill paid;
- all payment records and, if capitalization method is used, a worksheet showing allocation of payments per mortgage terms;
- a copy of the buydown agreement, if any, and all documents which relate to the payment amount or application of the payments;
- a copy of HUD's letter approving assignment of a damaged Property under 24 CFR § 203.379(a), if applicable;
- the Mortgagee's certificate that the conditions of 24 CFR § 203.379(a)(2), relating to fire damage, have been met, if applicable;
- documentation showing that the requirements of 24 CFR § 203.604 have been met;
- a statement relating to title defects if 24 CFR § 203.390 applies; and

- for Section 235 Mortgages, the following documentation, if not otherwise provided to HUD:
  - o the last two recertifications of family income and composition;
  - o employment verifications;
  - o a Notice of Suspension, Termination and Reinstatement of Assistance Payments Contract, if applicable; and
  - o if the case is subject to Section 235 recapture of assistance payments, the total dollar amount of assistance applied to the account through the date of assignment.

iii. Single Family Loan Sales Claims

The SFLS Program is a program through which participating Mortgagees may file assignment claims for insurance benefits.

SFLS claims are only authorized in connection with the execution of a PSA between HUD and the Mortgagee for an identified Distressed Asset Stabilization Program (DASP) sale, which is the sale through which HUD will dispose of the asset after payment of the claim. The SFLS claim is governed by the specific terms of the PSA for the specific DASP sale identified in the PSA.

(A) Claim Submission Process

The Mortgagee must follow the initial claim submission and claim submission report procedures set forth in the PSA. Upon the Mortgagee's compliance with these procedures, HUD will enter an SFLS Claim Identification Date in the claims processing system.

On the business day after the award of the pools of Mortgages, HUD will enter a list of awarded Mortgages (Award Report) in the claims processing system.

For Mortgages with an SFLS Claim Identification Date and that are included in the Award Report, the Mortgagee may submit assignment claims until the Claims Cut-off Date noted on Schedule I of the PSA. The Mortgagee may only submit assignment claims for eligible mortgages as defined in the PSA.

For Mortgages that are not awarded in the sale, the Mortgagee may submit insurance claims under CWCOT procedures and as further described in the PSA.

(B) Submission of Claim Form Parts to HUD for SFLS

(1) To HUD

The Mortgagee must submit Part A and Part B to HUD headquarters via EDI.

Handbook 4000.1
Effective Date: 09/30/2016 | Last Revised: 07/10/2019
*Refer to the online version of SF Handbook 4000.1 for specific sections' effective dates

855

(2) To P260

The Mortgagee must upload into P260:
- a copy of Parts A, B, C, D, and E;
- documentation of the last tax bills paid to each taxing authority; and
- any supporting documentation required by the PSA.

c. Claim Type 05 - Supplemental Claims/Remittances

The Mortgagee may submit a supplemental claim under Claim Type 05.

i. Definition

A Supplemental Claim is a claim readjusting the initial claim payment due to delayed disbursements or claim calculation or payment errors.

ii. Standard

The Mortgagee may submit one supplemental claim within six months of final settlement for conveyance claims or full settlement for all other claim types in the following circumstances:
- when a vendor delays submitting an invoice to the Mortgagee for an allowable expense;
- for amounts paid after the date the original claim was filed if the obligations were incurred before the deed or assignment to HUD was filed for record or was paid on HUD's written instruction;
- requests for reconsideration of disallowed costs; or
- additional attorney fees not paid on the original claim.

The Mortgagee may submit subsequent supplemental claims in the following circumstances:
- overpayments due to HUD;
- hazard insurance refund adjustments;
- deficiency Judgments;
- additional unpaid principal balance, with debenture interest, not paid on the original claim; or
- where the Mortgagee has received approval from the National Servicing Center (NSC) to file a subsequent supplemental.

The Mortgagee may not submit supplemental claims prior to receipt of the original Part B payment except when Part A was overpaid.

iii. Overpayments and Funds due HUD

(A) Definition

An Overpayment is HUD's payment of a claim in an inaccurate amount that results in money owed by the Mortgagee to HUD.

(B) Claim Involves Overpayment

If the claim involves an overpayment, the Mortgagee must:
- remit amounts due; and
- retain in the Claim Review File a supplemental claim Part A explaining how the overpayment occurred in the "Mortgagee's comments" section.

(C) Claim Involves a Computation of Interest

If the amount overpaid or received involved a computation of interest, the Mortgagee must:
- remit amounts due to HUD, including in the reimbursement:
  - o interest calculated by the Mortgagee and included in Part B; and
  - o interest calculated by HUD for the period from the date of claim to the date of payment; and
- retain in the Claim Review File a supplemental claim Part A explaining how the overpayment occurred in the "Mortgagee's comments" section.

(D) Remittance of Amounts Due

The Mortgagee must remit amounts due via pay.gov using the Claim Remittance functions in FHAC.

iv. Hazard Insurance Refund Adjustment

(A) Standard

The Mortgagee may submit a supplemental claim for a hazard insurance refund adjustment when it has met all of the following conditions:
- hazard insurance costs were included in the initial submission of form HUD-27011, Part B; and
- the Mortgagee has documented in its Claim Review File its efforts in diligently following up with the hazard insurance carrier to confirm any necessary adjustment.

When the Mortgagee becomes aware of a hazard insurance refund within six months of final settlement, the Mortgagee must file its supplemental claim within six months of the final settlement; otherwise, the Mortgagee may submit its supplemental claim within one year from the date of final settlement.

(B) Claim Form Preparation

When completing and submitting the supplemental claim, the Mortgagee must:
- include a copy of the carrier's notification with its submission; and
- clearly indicate in the "Mortgagee's comments" section that the supplemental claim is being filed to recover an adjustment to the hazard insurance premium refund.

v. Deficiency Judgments

The Mortgagee may submit one supplemental claim for the additional costs related to the pursuit of the deficiency Judgment when all such known costs were included in the initial submission of Part B of form HUD-27011, or, to the extent possible, are claimed within six months from the date of final settlement of the initial Part B.

vi. Attorney Fees

The Mortgagee may submit a supplemental claim for attorney fees if it believes that it is entitled to an amount more than was actually reimbursed in the initial claim payment. The supplemental claim must include:
- a supplemental claim form HUD-27011, with an explanation of the need for the increased fee in "Mortgagee's comments;"
- a copy of all Parts submitted in the original claim filing;
- a copy of the final Advice of Payment letter; and
- copies of the attorney chronology and any documentation necessary to support the additional claimed amount.

The Mortgagee must retain in the Claim Review File adequate documentation supporting all attorney fees. Should HUD determine in a post-claim review that the claim for attorney fees is greater than allowed amounts or is unsupported by documentation, HUD will bill the Mortgagee for overpayment as:
- an amount statistically calculated for all claims within the review period; or
- the actual amount of the overpayment, if the review was not based on a statistical sample.

vii. Claims for Additional Funds

The Mortgagee may submit one supplemental claim for additional funds within six months of the date of final settlement for conveyance claims or full settlement for all other claim types. The Mortgagee may only file a supplemental claim before receipt of the original Part B payment when Part A was overpaid.

(A) Supplemental Claims for Correction of Dates in Part A

When the claim for additional funds is based on a corrected date on the Part A claim, the Mortgagee must include:

- the form HUD-27011 reflecting the corrected date(s);
- the reason for the supplemental claim in the "Mortgagee's comments" section;
- the certification on the accuracy and validity of all other dates in the "Mortgagee's comments" section; and
- all supporting documentation.

(1) Certification

When the claim for additional funds is based on a corrected date on the Part A claim, the Mortgagee must provide with this supplemental claim a certification as to the accuracy and validity of all other dates on the Part A claim which affect time requirements and the payment of interest on the claim. This certification must include:

- a statement that all such dates have been rechecked against the claim filing instructions in this *SF Handbook*; and
- a statement describing the document referenced by the Mortgagee for each of these dates.

(2) Required Supporting Documentation

The Mortgagee must provide the following supporting documentation for corrected claims:

- Item 8, "Due date last complete installment paid": Include Mortgage Payment history record.
- Item 9, "Date of possession and acquisition of marketable title": Include legal documentation such as sheriff's deed recorded DIL, proof of eviction date, inspection report, and a chronology of events from the date in Item 11 to the date in Item 9.
- Item 10, "Date deed or assignment filed for record or date of closing or appraisal": Include recorded deed or assignment; Closing Disclosure or similar legal document; appraisal report and/or invoice reflecting correct date of the appraisal.
- Item 11, "Date foreclosure proceedings (a) Instituted or (b) Date of deed in lieu": Include documentation of first legal action taken to institute foreclosure, such as the complaint, or publication of notice of sale, or the recorded DIL.
- Item 17, "Unpaid loan balance as of date in block 8": Include copies of the mortgage Note and payment history record.
- Item 19, "Expiration date of extension to foreclose/assign": Include the printout from Extensions and Variances Automated Requests System (EVARS) of HUD's approval (form HUD-50012, *Mortgagee's Request for Extensions of Time*) of the extension.
- Item 20, "Date of notice/extension to convey": Include the printout of the MCM's approval (form HUD-50012) from P260.

- Item 21, "Date of release of bankruptcy, if applicable": Include a copy of the bankruptcy release notice or release of stay.
- Item 31, "Mortgagee reported curtailment date": Include applicable documentation to support curtailment correction.
- "Disbursements for Protection and Preservation": Include the form HUD-27011 Part C filed with the original claim submission, with supporting documentation for all P&P expenses.
- Disbursements (taxes, HIP, possessory action costs), foreclosure costs, attorney fees, bankruptcy costs, all other disbursements: Include documentation showing payment made, including paid receipts or invoices . If cost incurred after the date the deed or assignment was filed for recording, include a printout of the MCM's approval from P260 to pay costs.
- Taxes paid after date of deed to HUD: If taxes were paid after the date the deed or assignment was filed for recording, include a printout of the MCM's approval from P260 for payment before filing a supplemental claim.

(B) Claims for Additional Funds when Subject to Administrative Offsets

The Mortgagee must not claim additional funds when HUD is offsetting amounts.

(C) Claims for Funds Related to Partial Claims

If the Mortgagee claimed less than the actual Partial Claim note amount, the Mortgagee must absorb the cost of the miscalculation and must not:
- claim the additional funds from HUD; or
- add the deficient note amount to the Borrower's mortgage balance.

HUD will not accept corrected Partial Claims.

viii. Submission of Supplemental Claim Form Parts to HUD

(A) To HUD

The Mortgagee must send to HUD:
- the original Part A and Part B of the supplemental claim;
- copies of Parts C, D, and E of the supplemental claim, if applicable;
- supporting documents; and
- copies of all Parts of the original claim.

For supplemental claims relating to SFLS claims, the Mortgagee must send the claim to:

U.S. Department of Housing and Urban Development
Asset Sales Office
451 7th Street, SW Room 3136
Washington, DC 20410
Attn: SFLS [Year]-[Sale Number] Supplemental Claims

For all other supplemental claims, the Mortgagee must send the claims to the
following addresses:

Overnight Mail:

Department of Housing and Urban Development
FHA Single Family Claims Branch
ATTN: SUPPLEMENTAL CLAIMS
451 7th Street, SW, Room 6246
Washington, DC 20410-3000

Regular Mail:

Department of Housing and Urban Development
Office of Financial Services
Single Family Claims Branch
ATTN: SUPPLEMENTAL CLAIMS
P.O. Box 23297
Washington, DC 20026-3297

(B) To P260

The Mortgagee must upload to P260:
- copies of Parts A and B of the supplemental claim; and
- the original Parts C, D, and E, of the supplemental claim, if applicable.

(C) Time Frame for Submission of Supplemental Claims

For supplemental claims involving overpayments identified by the Mortgagee,
including its own QC reviews, the Mortgagee may submit a remittance of
overpayments and funds received by the Mortgagee at any time.

For supplemental claims involving recouping additional unpaid principal balance not
reimbursed on the original Part A claim, the Mortgagee may submit a claim at any
time.

For all other supplemental claims, the Mortgagee must submit supplemental claims
no later than six months after the date of final payment, except where noted below.

(1) Time Frame for Submission of Hazard Insurance Refund Adjustment

The Mortgagee may submit a supplemental claim for a hazard insurance refund adjustment under any of the following conditions:

- within six months from the date of final settlement of the original Part B claim; or
- if the Mortgagee received the insurance carrier's notification more than six months from the date of final payment, the Mortgagee must submit the supplemental claim within 24 Days from the date of the insurance carrier's notification and must document in its Claim Review File its efforts in diligently following up with the hazard insurance carrier to confirm any necessary adjustment. HUD will not accept the supplemental claim for a hazard insurance refund adjustment more than one year from the date of final settlement.

(2) Time Frame for Submission of Deficiency Judgments Costs

When HUD has required the Mortgagee to pursue a deficiency Judgment, the Mortgagee must submit one supplemental claim for the additional costs related to the deficiency Judgment within the latter of:

- one year from the date of final settlement of the initial Part B; or
- three months after the deficiency Judgment.

(3) Extension to Time Frame for Submission

If more than one year is needed to request reimbursement for related Housing Insurance Premium (HIP) adjustments or deficiency Judgments, the Mortgagee must request an extension from the MCM. When using an extension based on deficiency Judgments or HIP adjustments, the Mortgagee may not include in its supplemental claim other types of costs they may have failed to include in the earlier claim.

The Mortgagee must include with its supplemental claim a printout of the MCM's approval (form HUD-50012) via P260.

(4) HUD Requests for Corrections or Additional Information

Supplemental claims previously submitted and returned to the Mortgagee for a correction and/or for further information must be received by HUD as soon as possible but no later than 45 Days from the date of HUD's letter and/or request.

ix. Variance Requests for Additional Supplemental Claim Submissions

The Mortgagee generally may only submit one supplemental claim. When circumstances outside of the Mortgagee's control require the submission of additional supplemental claims, the Mortgagee must submit a request to the Single Family Claims Branch before filing a supplemental claim.

x.   Appeals of Supplemental Claim Disposition

The Mortgagee may submit an appeal of a denied supplemental claim within 60 Days from the date the supplemental claim was denied to:

Department of Housing and Urban Development
Attn: Chief, Single Family Claims Branch
451 7th Street, SW, Room 6248
Washington, DC 20410

The Mortgagee must submit the request in writing and attach a copy of the supplemental claim with the supporting documents.

d. Claim Type 06 - Claims Without Conveyance of Title

The Mortgagee may file a CWCOT under Claim Type 06.

i.   CWCOT Processing Fee Exemption for Small Servicers

(A) Standard

For Paper Claims only, HUD will reimburse the manual claim processing fee for Mortgagees who:
- meet the definition of a small servicer under 12 CFR § 1026.41(e)(4)(ii);
- do not have EDI capability; and
- elect to bid the Commissioner's Adjusted Fair Market Value (CAFMV) at the foreclosure sale under CWCOT guidelines.

(B) Required Documentation

The Mortgagee meeting the small servicer exemption standards above must add the manual processing fee of $200 in Item 305 of Part D of form HUD-27011.

The Mortgagee must maintain documentation verifying that it meets the definition of a small servicer.

ii. Computation of Interest

(A) Debenture Interest

Provided that the Mortgagee has met all time requirements, HUD will pay debenture interest on the unpaid principal balance from the date of Default to either:
- the date the Mortgagee or third-party bidder obtains title; or
- the date the Borrower redeems the Property.

HUD will then pay debenture interest on the difference between the unpaid principal balance and the greater of either the CAFMV, redemption amount, or the third-party bid, to the date of final payment of the claim.

(B) Calculating Interest for an Expenditure using Daily Interest Rate Factors

HUD will pay debenture interest on expenses from the date of expenditure to the date of final payment of the claim, as calculated using the method in Calculating Interest for an Expenditure using Daily Interest Rate Factors.

(C) Calculating Interest for Default after SFB-Unemployment or SFB

When the Mortgagee files a claim for insurance benefits after a Default under an SFB-Unemployment Agreement or SFB, HUD will pay mortgage note interest as calculated under the procedures in Calculating Interest for Default after SFB-Unemployment or Special Forbearance.

(D) Curtailment of Interest

The Mortgagee must self-curtail interest on Single Family claims for the following failures to meet HUD requirements as of the date on which the required action should have been taken:
- failure to timely initiate foreclosure;
- failure to give HUD notice of foreclosure;
- failure to meet Reasonable Diligence Time Frames; and
- failure to file the claim within 30 Days of:
  - the date the Mortgagee acquired good marketable title;
  - the date a third party acquired good marketable title;
  - the date the Borrower or other party redeemed the Property;
  - the date the redemption period expires; or
  - such other date as required by the FHA Commissioner.

If more than one time requirement is missed and there are no applicable extensions, the Mortgagee must calculate the interest for the claim payment to the earliest missed time requirement.

iii. Computation of Claim Amount

(A) Standard

The Mortgagee may claim 100 percent of the unpaid principal balance, plus allowable costs and debenture interest. HUD will deduct from the claim amount the sale bid or redemption price.

(B) Eviction and P&P Costs when Property is Sold to a Third Party

When a third party is the successful bidder at the foreclosure sale, the Mortgagee may not claim reimbursement for costs relating to eviction or Property P&P after the sale. The Mortgagee may request reimbursement for those costs incurred, or for work completed, before the foreclosure sale but not paid until after the sale.

(C) Hazard Insurance Premiums

HUD will not reimburse the Mortgagee for any hazard insurance premiums allocated to the period after acquisition of title by the Mortgagee or a third party.

(D) Deficiency Judgments

When HUD required the deficiency judgment action or when HUD has approved the Mortgagee's request to pursue the Judgment in relation to a CWCOT, the Mortgagee may request full reimbursement of certain fees.

(E) Third-party Auction Service Fees

For successful third-party sales only, HUD will reimburse Mortgagees for independent third-party auction service fees they incur for an amount that does not exceed 5 percent of a Property's net sales price.

iv. Submission of Claim Form Parts to HUD for CWCOT

The Mortgagee must submit Parts A and B simultaneously no later than 30 Days after:
- the date the Mortgagee acquired good marketable title;
- the date a third party acquired good marketable title;
- the date the Borrower or other party redeemed the Property;
- the date the redemption period expires; or
- such other date as required by the FHA Commissioner.

If filing via EDI or FHAC, the Mortgagee must submit Parts A and B no later than two Days after the date the form was prepared.

In all cases, the Mortgagee must also upload into P260:
- all Parts of form HUD-27011;
- the Closing Disclosure or similar legal document for post-foreclosure sales;
- the appraisal;
- appraisal invoices;
- a worksheet reflecting the Mortgagee's application of the CAFMV based on the adjustment provided in the instructions on FHAC; and
- a third-party service fee invoice for auction services; if applicable.

e. Claim Type 07 - Pre-Foreclosure Sales

The Mortgagee may file a claim for a <u>PFS</u> incentive and insurance benefits under Claim Type 07.

i. Computation of Interest

(A) Standard

HUD will pay debenture interest as follows:
- on the unpaid principal balance from the date of Default to the date of the closing of the PFS;
- on the difference between the unpaid principal balance, plus allowable costs and advances, and the net PFS proceeds from the date of the closing of the PFS to the date of claim settlement;
- on allowable costs and advances from the date of expenditure to the date of the closing of the PFS; and
- when a Default under an <u>SFB-Unemployment Agreement</u> or SFB Agreement is involved, from the last date of the mortgage interest calculation to the date of the closing of the PFS.

(B) Calculating Interest for an Expenditure

The Mortgagee must calculate the amount of interest to be claimed for an expenditure as follows:
- multiply the Daily Interest Rate Factor (see Appendix 8.c Daily Interest Rate Factor in the *Claim Filing Technical Guide*) by the amount paid; then
- multiply this result by the number of Days from the date paid (or Default date, if later) for each Item to the date of closing of the PFS, as listed in Item 10.

ii. Computation of Claim Amount

(A) Allowable Costs

HUD will reimburse the Mortgagee for reasonable and customary costs as follows.

(1) Mortgagee Advances for Escrow Funds

The Mortgagee may claim reimbursement for advances of escrow funds as provided for in <u>Escrow Funds</u>.

(2) Property Preservation and Protection Costs

The Mortgagee may claim reimbursement for the cost of inspections and P&P actions performed in accordance with <u>HUD guidance</u> for the current Default, for costs incurred before the Closing Date of the PFS.

(3) Taxes, Assessments, Hazard Insurance, and Other Allowable Items

The Mortgagee may claim reimbursement for disbursements for taxes, assessments, hazard insurance and other allowable items payable which were not satisfied at closing. HUD will only reimburse property-related costs which were incurred before the PFS Closing Date.

(4) Attorney's Fees for Postponed Foreclosure

For a foreclosure that was postponed pending completion of the PFS, the Mortgagee may claim reimbursement for attorney fees commensurate with the work actually performed up to the point of the cessation of the legal action, not exceeding the amount established as reasonable and customary in Appendix 4.0 - HUD Schedule of Standard Attorney Fees (applies to Servicing only).

(5) Satisfaction of Junior Liens

The Mortgagee may claim reimbursement for the amounts paid to satisfy or release junior liens Paid Outside Closing (POC), as long as these amounts are not included in the Closing Disclosure or similar legal document.

(6) Appraisal and Title Search

The Mortgagee may claim reimbursement for reasonable and customary costs of the appraisal and title search, if not included in the Closing Disclosure or similar legal document.

(7) Borrower Consideration

The Mortgagee may claim reimbursement for the amount of the PFS Borrower Consideration as an Acquisition Cost.

(8) PFS Incentive Payment

HUD will pay the Mortgagee a financial incentive for the use of the PFS Option in compliance with all regulatory requirements and procedures relating to the submission of incentive claims in FHAC.

(B) Disallowable Costs

HUD will not reimburse the Mortgagee for the following costs.

(1) Items Already Included on Closing Disclosure

The Mortgagee may not claim reimbursement for costs that have already been included on the Closing Disclosure or similar legal document.

(2) Eviction Costs

The Mortgagee may not claim reimbursement for any costs incurred to evict residents from the mortgaged Property.

(3) Property Preservation and Protection Costs Incurred After Closing

The Mortgagee may not claim reimbursement for Property P&P costs incurred after the date of closing of the PFS.

(4) Hazard Insurance Premiums Paid after Closing

The Mortgagee may not claim reimbursement for hazard insurance premiums for the period after the PFS closing.

(C) Deductions from Claim Amount

HUD will deduct the following items from the total claim amount.

(1) Money Received After Closing

HUD will deduct all amounts received by the Mortgagee on the Mortgage after closing of the PFS.

(2) Rent or Other Income

HUD will deduct from the claim any amount by which Rental Income exceeds rental expenses.

(3) Money Retained by Mortgagee

HUD will deduct from the claim any amounts retained by the Mortgagee for the Borrower's account which have not been applied to reduction of principal.

(4) Sales Proceeds

HUD will deduct from the claim amount all amounts received by the Mortgagee relating to the sale of the Property.

iii. Extensions to the Time Requirement to Initiate Foreclosure

To reflect the use of HUD's automatic extension to the time requirement to initiate foreclosure in order to utilize a PFS, the Mortgagee must enter into form HUD-27011:
- the ending date of the terminated or failed PFS transaction in Item 20 of Part A; and
- in Item 19, a date that is no more than 90 Days after the date listed in Item 20.

iv. Submission of Claim Form Parts to HUD for PFS

The Mortgagee must submit Parts A and B simultaneously to HUD no later than 30 Days after the PFS Closing Date and retain the original Parts in the Claim Review File.

f. Claim Type 31 - Special Forbearance

The Mortgagee may file a claim for an SFB-Unemployment incentive under Claim Type 31. HUD will pay the Mortgagee a financial incentive for the use of an SFB-Unemployment Option in compliance with all regulatory requirements and procedures relating to the submission of incentive claims in FHAC.

HUD must receive a correct and complete claim submission of Parts A and B via FHAC within 60 Days of the execution date of the SFB-Unemployment Agreement or the incentive claim will not be processed.

g. Claim Type 32 - Loan Modification

Prior to March 1, 2017, FHA's Loss Mitigation Home Retention Priority Order (Waterfall) included a standalone Loan Modification option, which featured a Loan Modification incentive. The Mortgagee may file a claim for a Loan Modification incentive under Claim Type 32. HUD will pay the Mortgagee a financial incentive for the use of a Loan Modification in compliance with all regulatory requirements and procedures relating to the submission of incentive claims in FHAC.

The Mortgagee may only file for an incentive fee for the Loss Mitigation Option used to cure the Default.

HUD must receive a correct and complete claim submission of Parts A and B via FHAC within 60 Days of the execution date of the Loan Modification agreement or the incentive claim will not be processed.

h. Claim Type 32 ** - FHA-HAMP Loan Modification

The Mortgagee may file a claim for an FHA-HAMP Loan Modification incentive under Claim Type 32 **. HUD will pay the Mortgagee a financial incentive for the use of an FHA-HAMP Loan Modification in compliance with all regulatory requirements and procedures relating to the submission of incentive claims in FHAC.

The Mortgagee may only file for an incentive fee for the Loss Mitigation Option used to cure the Default. When the FHA-HAMP Partial Claim and FHA-HAMP Loan Modification are used together, the Mortgagee must submit two separate claims for the incentives for these two options.

HUD must receive a correct and complete claim submission of Parts A and B via FHAC within 60 Days of the execution date of the FHA-HAMP Loan Modification or the incentive claim will not be processed.

i. Claim Type 33 ** - FHA-HAMP Partial Claim

The Mortgagee may file a claim for an <u>FHA-HAMP Partial Claim</u> incentive and insurance benefits under Claim Type 33 **. The Mortgagee may include in its claim <u>legal fees and foreclosure costs for partial claims</u> as outlined in the Servicing and Loss Mitigation section of the *SF Handbook*. HUD will pay the Mortgagee a financial incentive for the use of an FHA-HAMP Partial Claim in compliance with all regulatory requirements and procedures relating to the submission of incentive claims in FHAC.

The Mortgagee may only file for an incentive fee for the Loss Mitigation Option used to cure the Default. When the FHA-HAMP Partial Claim and FHA-HAMP Loan Modification are used together, the Mortgagee must submit two separate claims for the incentives for these two options.

HUD must receive a correct and complete claim submission of Parts A and B via FHAC within 60 Days of the execution date of the promissory Note and Mortgage or the incentive will be disallowed.

3. Payment of Claims

a. Processing of Claim Forms

HUD will generate payment to the Mortgagee if:
- the Mortgagee's submission of Parts A and B pass all system edits and control checks; and
- the Mortgagee provides all required documentation or makes all necessary updates to the suspended claim.

HUD may reduce the claim payment if the claim lists unusually high disbursements that are not supported by documentation. HUD may require reimbursement of any amounts that are found to be excessive or not supported by appropriate documentation.

When a Mortgagee files a claim, other than a supplemental claim or Loss Mitigation Incentive claim, after the expiration of a designated time period, HUD will accept these claims, which will be subject to interest curtailment.

i. Initial Payment

(A) Definition

The Initial Claim Payment is the disbursement to the Mortgagee of funds relating to Part A of form HUD-27011.

(B) Standard

HUD will pay the unpaid principal balance plus debenture interest upon receipt and processing of Part A and required attachments.

Before debenture interest is calculated, HUD will reduce the unpaid principal balance by the greater of any damage or insurance recovery reported in Item 27. HUD's Claims system will determine the amount of debenture interest.

ii.   Final and Full Payments

(A) Definition

The Final Claim Payment is the disbursement to the Mortgagee of funds relating to Parts B through E of form HUD-27011 for conveyance claims.

The Full Claim Payment is the disbursement to the Mortgagee of funds relating to Part A and Part B of Form HUD-27011 for claims other than conveyance claims.

(B) Standard

As Final Claim Payment for conveyance claims, HUD will pay the Mortgagee's expenses, allowances, and debenture interest upon receipt and processing of Part B and required attachments.

As Full Claim Payment for claims other than conveyance claims, HUD will pay unpaid principal balance, the Mortgagee's expenses, allowances, and debenture interest upon receipt and processing of Part A and Part B claims and required attachments.

b.   Method of Payment

HUD makes all claim disbursements through the U.S. Treasury Electronic Funds Transfer (EFT) wire transfer application.

c.   Disbursement of Claim

For Claim Type 31 only, HUD will disburse the incentive payment to the Servicer. For all other Claim Types, HUD will not honor requests for claim payments to be disbursed to any Entity other than the holder of the Mortgage.

d.   Negative Claim Amount

If the Net Claim Amount in Part B (Item 137) of the original conveyance claim is a negative amount, HUD will calculate the claim, making the necessary adjustments for the costs of foreclosure, and will bill the Mortgagee for the amount due. For CWCOT and PFS claims, HUD will calculate the claim and issue the Mortgagee a settlement letter.

e.   Advice of Payment and Title Approval

When a claim is processed in the HUD Claims system, HUD will provide the Advice of Payment and Title Approval (where applicable) via FHAC. Mortgagees may locate both the Advice of Payment and Title Approval under the Single Family Insurance Claims Processing menu in the Single Family FHA/Single Family Servicing section of FHAC. Advice of Payment is available by accessing the "Claim Status" function, while Title Approval is available by accessing the "Title Approval Status" function.

When a claim is being processed outside of the HUD Claims system, HUD will provide hard copies of the Advice of Payment and Title Approval (where applicable) letters to the Mortgagee by mail.

Mortgagees should be advised that if claims have been grouped together into one EFT payment, HUD will provide Mortgagees with a separate Advice of Payment for each individual payment in each payment batch via FHAC if claims are filed electronically or via hard copy if claims are filed manually.

4. Withdrawal or Cancellation of Insurance Claims

a. Withdrawal of Application for Insurance Benefits

If the claim has not yet been paid, the Mortgagee may apply in writing to HUD's MCM for consent to withdraw an application of insurance benefits. The Mortgagee must agree to:
- accept Reconveyance of the Property;
- promptly file a Reconveyance for record;
- accept the title evidence it furnished to HUD; and
- reimburse HUD for expenses incurred in holding the Property.

b. Cancellation of Insurance Benefits due to Reconveyance

i. Reconveyance

(A) Definition

A Reconveyance is a conveyance of a Property from HUD back to the Mortgagee due to the Mortgagee's failure to comply with HUD's conveyance requirements or at the Mortgagee's request.

(B) Standard

When HUD reconveys a Property, the Mortgagee must return all insurance funds received from the claim associated with that Property. For Mortgages insured on or after November 19, 1992, the Mortgagee must also reimburse HUD for its holding costs and expenses incurred in the acquisition and Reconveyance of the Property.

(C) Reduction of Insurance Benefits due to Changes in Value

For Mortgages insured on or after November 19, 1992, if there is a reduction in the estimate of value from the time of Reconveyance to the time of reapplication for insurance benefits, HUD will deduct from the claim amount the difference in value.

(D) FHA Short Refinance

For Mortgages under the FHA Short Refinance program, the Mortgagee will be required to repay all claim funds to FHA, including the claim funds paid under EESA, in the event the Property is reconveyed to the Mortgagee.

(E) Costs Relating to Title Defects

(1) Insured On or After November 19, 1992

For Mortgages insured under a Firm Commitment issued on or after November 19, 1992, or under Direct Endorsement processing where the credit worksheet was signed by the Mortgagee's approved underwriter on or after November 19, 1992, HUD may require the Mortgagee to correct title defects within 60 Days after the Mortgagee receives notice from the Secretary or within such further time as the Secretary may approve in writing.

The Mortgagee may retain the insurance benefits already paid, but HUD will not reimburse the Mortgagee for any costs involved in correcting the title.

(2) Insured before November 19, 1992

For Mortgages insured under a Firm Commitment issued before November 19, 1992, or under Direct Endorsement processing where the credit worksheet was signed by the Mortgagee's approved underwriter before November 19, 1992, HUD may require the Mortgagee to correct title defects within such time as the Secretary may approve in writing.

Where HUD allows the Mortgagee time to correct title defects, the Mortgagee may retain the insurance benefits already paid, but HUD will not reimburse the Mortgagee for any costs involved in correcting the title.

(3) Reimbursement to HUD for Holding Costs and Interest

If a title defect is not corrected within HUD's time frame, the Mortgagee must reimburse HUD for holding costs and interest on the paid insurance benefits from the date of the notice to the date the defect is corrected or to the date the Secretary reconveys the Property, within the time frame stated by HUD in its Demand Letter.

(4) Costs Associated with Correcting Title

The Mortgagee is responsible for the costs in correcting title defects and for property expenses pending correction, except where HUD has sold the Property or Mortgage with an adverse interest senior to the Mortgage and causing the title defect.

Handbook 4000.1   873
Effective Date: 09/30/2016 | Last Revised: 07/10/2019
*Refer to the online version of SF Handbook 4000.1 for specific sections' effective dates

(5) Improper Deed to HUD

If the Property was improperly deeded to HUD and the Property has been sold, HUD will remit to the Mortgagee the sales price less expenses of the sale and expenses incurred while the Property was in HUD's inventory.

(F) Property Preservation Costs

(1) Standard

The Mortgagee is responsible for any damages the Property has sustained while in the Mortgagee's possession, if the Property was conveyed without prior notice and approval by HUD.

If a Property is reconveyed because of damage, the Mortgagee must withdraw its claim for insurance benefits and reimburse HUD for property expenditures.

(2) Holding Costs

(a) Definition

Holding Costs are those costs paid by HUD related to taxes, maintenance and operating expenses of the Property, and administrative expenses.

(b) Standard

If HUD finds that the Mortgagee did not comply with its conveyance standards, the Mortgagee must reimburse HUD for holding costs and interest on the paid insurance benefits from the date of the notice to the date the defect is corrected or to the date the Secretary reconveys the Property, as determined by HUD.

(G) Appeals of Reconveyances due to Property Condition

HUD has established a two-stage appeal procedure for disputes between Mortgagees and HUD regarding Reconveyance requests due to property condition.

(1) Appealing to the MCM

If the Mortgagee disagrees with HUD's decision to reconvey, the Mortgagee may appeal the Reconveyance via email in P260 to the MCM within 10 Days from the date the response was due or received from HUD.

(2) Appealing to HUD

If the Mortgagee believes that the MCM's decision is not supported by regulation or circumstances and has exhausted all appeal methods available through the

MCM, the Mortgagee may appeal the decision to reconvey the Property to HUD's Government Technical Representative (GTR).

The Mortgagee must submit the written appeal to the GTR within 10 Days from the date the response was due or received from the MCM.

HUD's decision is final and HUD will not accept further appeals.

ii. Reacquisition by HUD and Resubmission of Claim

(A) Reacquisition

(1) Definition

Reacquisition is the process by which a Mortgagee conveys to HUD a Property that has been previously reconveyed to the Mortgagee.

(2) Standard

After the Mortgagee has corrected the problem causing Reconveyance, the Mortgagee may request reacquisition by HUD of a reconveyed Property and resubmit the claim.

Where a Mortgagee used the CWCOT procedure and the Property was reconveyed, the Mortgagee may choose to retain that Property, instead of requesting reacquisition by HUD.

(B) Reacquisition Package

(1) Standard

The Mortgagee must prepare and submit a reacquisition package to the MCM via email through P260 requesting permission to convey the Property to HUD. The Mortgagee must ensure that this package demonstrates:
- that any title issues have been resolved, if applicable;
- that any required repairs have been completed, if applicable; and
- that the Property is ready to be conveyed to HUD.

The Mortgagee must attach a copy of the Preliminary Notice of Intent to Reconvey in its email to the MCM.

(2) Required Documentation

For Properties reconveyed due to title issues, the Mortgagee must include in its reacquisition package:
- a corrected title package, including a certification of title; andfor mobile housing or Manufactured Housing, an affidavit of affixture.

For Properties reconveyed due to damage, the Mortgagee must include in its reacquisition package:
- current dated color photographs that support repairs; and
- current inspection reports or other documentation evidencing that repairs have been completed and that the Property is in conveyance condition.

(C) Resubmission of Claim

Once the Mortgagee receives MCM approval to convey, the Mortgagee may reapply for insurance benefits. The Mortgagee must send a new original paper form HUD-27011, Parts A and B, with "Re-Conveyance" written at the top, along with any required attachments to HUD at:

U.S. Department of Housing and Urban Development
Single Family Claims Branch
Attention: Chief, Review & Compliance Section
451 7th Street SW, Room 6251
Washington, D.C. 20410

(D) Expenses and Interest after Reconveyance

The Mortgagee must not include on its reacquisition claim any property expenses or debenture interest not included in the initial claim filing. HUD will not reimburse these additional expenses as part of the reacquisition claim.

If necessary, the Mortgagee may submit a supplemental claim for additional property expenses or debenture interest incurred before initial conveyance to HUD. The Mortgagee must submit the supplemental claim based on the time frames set in Time Frame for Submission of Supplemental Claims.

5. Post-Claim Reviews

a. Definition

A Post-Claim Review is a review of the claim file by HUD or its agent to determine the Mortgagee's compliance with HUD's claim guidance and to verify the accuracy and appropriateness of amounts claimed.

b. Standard

HUD or its agent (e.g., FHA Claims Branch, Quality Assurance Division (QAD), Office of Inspector General (OIG), HUD contractors, U.S. Department of Justice (DOJ), etc.) may conduct a post-claim review at any time within three years after the claim is paid. This time frame does not apply to or limit enforcement reviews. If the Mortgagee is notified within the three-year period that its claims will be reviewed by HUD or its agent, all claim files must be maintained until completion and final settlement of the review.

The Mortgagee must be able to show support for all information entered on the application for insurance benefits. When filing a claim, the Mortgagee is responsible for the completeness and accuracy of the claim submission and for any overpayments identified on claims by HUD.

If a question arises regarding the support of an amount reimbursed on an insurance claim, the burden of proof is on the Mortgagee to show that the amount is valid and reasonable.

c. Selection of Claims for Review

HUD may use statistical sampling to select claims for review and, based upon the results of the statistical sampling, may extrapolate the amount of any overpayment over all claims paid during the subject review period to determine the amount due HUD for overpayments.

d. Frequency of Reviews

HUD may review any paid claim file at any time within three years after the claim is paid.

Where state Housing Finance Agencies (HFA) have settled 50 or fewer FHA mortgage insurance claims in a 12-month period, the HFA may elect to defer the review to a biennial (occurring every two years) schedule.

e. Notification to Mortgagee of Claim Review

HUD will notify Mortgagees by letter before beginning its claims review. The Mortgagee must make available to HUD copies of identified claim files, in the format (electronic or hard copy) requested, within 24 hours of a request or such other time as permitted by HUD. Refer to HUD Requests for Information and Missing Claim Files for additional guidance.

Denial of access to a file may be grounds for enforcement action.

f. HUD's Initial Report

HUD will review the result of the claims review prior to the issuance of a report.

After completion of the reviews, HUD will issue the initial report identifying:
- any discrepancies resulting from inaccuracies, omissions, missed time requirements or unsupported claim information;
- the Mortgagee's potential liability (potential amount owed); and
- whether or not the Mortgagee is in compliance with HUD's claim filing guidelines.

g. Mortgagee Response Procedures to HUD's Initial Report

The Mortgagee may provide any additional documentation that could affect the review results within 45 Days from the date of the initial report. If no additional documentation is provided within 45 Days, HUD will consider the report final and the potential liability identified will become the amount owed.

h. Findings Based on Mortgagee Response

HUD will review additional information provided by the Mortgagee within the response timeline and, if applicable, will make adjustments to the potential amount owed. HUD will issue a follow-up report stating the revised Finding, if any, and any new Findings.

i. Mortgagee Response Procedures to HUD's Follow-Up Report

Within 21 Days from the date of the follow-up report, the Mortgagee may provide additional documentation that could affect the review results. If no additional documentation is provided within 21 Days, HUD will consider the report final and the potential liability identified will become the amount owed.

If further documentation is submitted to refute the Findings in the follow-up report, HUD will review the documentation and issue a final report stating:
- the revised Findings (if any);
- any new Findings; and
- that the review is being referred to the Albany Financial Operations Center (FOC) for enforced debt collection, if applicable.

j. Referral for Collections

HUD will send the post-claim review to the Albany FOC for collection of the outstanding amount. HUD will pursue any outstanding amounts via Treasury Offset if the amount remains outstanding.

k. Referral for Enforcement Review

HUD may, at its discretion, refer cases to the appropriate office(s) for enforcement review based on the post-claim review.

6. Debt Collection and Administrative Offset

HUD may use the debt collection and administrative offset process to collect money owed by the Mortgagee due to an improper claim amount.

a. Demand Letter

To establish the debt, HUD will send a Demand Letter to the Mortgagee. Within 30 Days of the date of the Demand Letter, the Mortgagee must:
- remit overpaid amounts; or
- take other such action, including submitting a rebuttal, as provided in the Demand Letter. After receiving a Demand Letter, the Mortgagee may request a review of HUD records related to the debt in accordance with 24 CFR Part 17 and/or as otherwise instructed in the Demand Letter.

b. Notice of Intent to Collect Administrative Offset

i.   Issuance of Notice of Intent to Collect by Administrative Offset

HUD will issue a Notice of Intent to Collect by Administrative Offset to the Mortgagee, should the Mortgagee fail to respond to the Demand Letter or should HUD determine that the Mortgagee's rebuttal fails to demonstrate that the Mortgagee is not responsible for the debt.

ii. Required Mortgagee Action

The Mortgagee must remit funds within 30 Days from the date of the Notice of Intent to Collect by Administrative Offset.

iii. Request for HUD Review

After receiving a Notice of Intent to Collect by Administrative Offset, the Mortgagee may request a review of the case in accordance with 24 CFR Part 17 and/or as otherwise instructed in the Notice.

iv. Departmental Review

Appeals will be reviewed in accordance with 24 CFR Part 17.

c. Initiation of Offset Action

HUD will initiate the offset action if HUD does not receive the funds from the Mortgagee within 30 Days from the date of the Notice of Intent to Collect by Administrative Offset and the Mortgagee has not submitted a request for a HUD review of the determination of indebtedness.

B. TITLE II DISPOSITION

This section provides the standards and procedures applicable to the disposition of Real Estate Owned (REO) Single Family Properties acquired by HUD as a result of foreclosure of FHA-insured Mortgages or special acquisitions. All parties participating in HUD disposition programs must fully comply with all of the following standards and procedures. Terms and acronyms used in this *FHA Single Family Housing Policy Handbook* (*SF Handbook*) have the meanings defined in the Glossary and Acronyms sections and in the specific section of the *SF Handbook* in which the definitions are located.

1. Management and Marketing Program

HUD's Management and Marketing (M&M) program is HUD's contracting network used to manage and market Single Family Properties owned by or in the custody of HUD.

a. HUD Contractors

i. Mortgagee Compliance Manager

Mortgagee Compliance Managers (MCM) are HUD's M&M contractors responsible for ensuring compliance with HUD's conveyance standards related to title, occupancy, and property condition.

ii. Field Service Manager

Field Service Managers (FSM) are HUD's M&M contractors responsible for providing property maintenance and preservation services for Properties owned by or in the custody of HUD.

iii. Asset Manager

Asset Managers (AM) are HUD's M&M contractors responsible for the marketing and sale of Properties owned by or in the custody of HUD.

b. Nondiscrimination Policy

All parties engaged in contracting, occupancy, rental, and sales activities relating to HUD-owned Properties must conduct these activities without regard to race, color, creed, religion, sex, national origin, age, familial status, disability, marital status, actual or perceived sexual orientation, or gender identity.

c. P260 Portal

i. Definition

P260 is HUD's web-based portal for submitting requests and documentation relating to Property Preservation and Protection (P&P), conveyance, and disposition activities.

ii. Standard

HUD-approved Mortgagees and M&M contractors must use P260 or its successor system to report and upload documentation for activities related to the Property.

HUD expects FHA Roster Appraisers, HUD-Registered Real Estate Brokers, and Closing Agents to use P260 to fulfill their documentation submission requirements.

2. REO Property Disposition

a. Property and Sales Condition

i. As-Is Condition

(A) Definition

As-Is Condition refers to the condition of a Property without repairs, representations, or warranties.

(B) Standard

HUD markets Properties under the following categories, based on the as-is condition of the Property at the time of listing as determined by one or more evaluation tools, such as an appraisal, Brokers Price Opinion, or Automated Valuation Model:
- insurable;
- insurable with repair escrow; or
- uninsurable.

ii. Vacant Lots

(A) Definition

A Vacant Lot is a Property without improvements or Structures.

(B) Standard

HUD may raze Structures or offer the vacant lot for sale where Properties are so damaged that repair by HUD or the buyer is not feasible and where one of the following conditions exist:
- the Property has already been unsuccessfully offered for sale in its as-is condition;
- a local ordinance or agreement prohibits as-is sales of such Properties; or
- the Structure must immediately be razed by HUD to remove a serious public hazard.

Where there is no immediate need to raze the Property or where it would be otherwise inappropriate to sell the Property as-is, HUD may sell the Property with the requirement that the buyer raze the Structure after sales closing.

iii. Held Off Market

(A) Definition

Held Off Market is the status of a HUD REO Property that is unavailable for sale.

(B) Standard

HUD may designate a Property as held off market when a property, title, occupancy, or other condition delays or prohibits HUD's ability to market or sell the Property.

Should the adverse condition be resolved, HUD may then list the Property for sale.

b. List Price

i. Definition

List Price is the "asking price" of a Property based on Market Value.

ii. Standard

HUD will offer a Property for sale at the list price based on Market Value, reflecting the highest and best use in the current market, competitive with Properties being offered by other sellers.

The AM will monitor assigned transactions to ensure that Properties are valued and sold in a manner in accordance with market conditions.

For vacant lots, HUD will offer the lots at the estimated Market Value of the lot based on comparable vacant lot prices, considering highest and best use.

c. Marketing Tools

i. Standard

In marketing HUD REO Properties, listing brokers are expected to use those contemporary industry marketing tools used in marketing non-REO Properties in that area, which may include, but are not limited to:
- utilizing yard signage and online advertising;
- encouraging pre-qualification or pre-approval of potential buyers;
- holding open houses or holding webinars, seminars, or workshops on HUD property sales; and
- requesting limited repair of Properties, with approval by HUD.

Listing brokers must ensure that all written advertising includes the Equal Housing Opportunity logo, statement, or slogan.

HUD, at its discretion, may offer bonuses or other sales incentives to real estate brokers.

ii. HUD Home Store

(A) Definition

HUD Home Store is the listing site for HUD REO Single Family Properties.

(B) Standard

HUD will post its inventory of HUD REO Properties for sale on HUD Home Store.

iii. Local Real Estate Agent Associations and Listing Sites

HUD expects listing brokers to work with their local National Association of Realtors (NAR) boards and similar organizations and use a local Multiple Listing Service (MLS) and other industry standard listing sites to market HUD REO Properties.

iv. Online Marketing Tools

Listing brokers are expected to use such contemporary online marketing tools as the following:
- full application of internet tools to present houses in multimedia formats with MLS, with extensive photographs, video, and documentation;
- search engine optimization;
- Quick Response (QR) codes or other technology to assist buyers in accessing property information; and
- marketing blogs or other tailored social media.

v. Hard-to-Sell Properties

(A) Definition

A Hard-to-Sell Property is a HUD REO Property located in a specific market area characterized by such sales conditions as large numbers of non-HUD vacant Properties, declining neighborhoods, or severely depressed local economy.

(B) Standard

The AM is responsible for designating hard-to-sell Properties under HUD guidance.

HUD offers a minimum sales commission for Properties designated as hard-to-sell on HUD Home Store and, at its discretion, may offer bonuses or other sales incentives to real estate brokers.

HUD will prescribe the time frame and conditions under which bonuses or other sales incentives will be offered.

vi. Revitalization Areas

(A) Definition

Revitalization Areas are designated geographic areas in which HUD identifies Properties eligible for disposition through discount sales programs.

(B) Standard

HUD will designate <u>Revitalization Areas</u> based on the following criteria:
- very low income areas;
- high concentration of HUD REO Properties; and
- low homeownership rate.

State, local, or tribal governments or HUD-approved Nonprofits may request that HUD designate a geographic area as a Revitalization Area by sending a written request to the Director of the Jurisdictional Homeownership Center (HOC) for the area.

d. Prospective Buyers

i. Owner-Occupant Buyers

(A) Definition

An Owner-Occupant Buyer is a buyer who intends to use the Property as their Principal Residence.

(B) Standard

A buyer may purchase HUD REO Properties as an Owner-Occupant Buyer if:
- they certify that they will occupy the Property as their Principal Residence for at least 12 months; and
- they have not purchased a HUD-owned Property within the past 24 months as an owner occupant.

The selling broker must not knowingly submit the offer on behalf of a person or Entity that is not an Owner-Occupant Buyer and must discuss the penalties for false certification with the buyer.

The buyer and selling broker must sign an Exclusive Listing Period Purchase Addendum for Individual Owner-Occupant Buyers certifying to the above conditions.

Buyers using FHA-insured financing must begin their owner-occupancy terms as stated in <u>FHA Requirement for Owner Occupancy</u>. Buyers purchasing under the Good Neighbor Next Door (GNND) Sales Program must begin their owner-occupancy terms as stated in <u>Owner-Occupancy Term</u>.

(C) Required Documentation

The Owner-Occupant Buyer and selling broker must complete and submit with their offer an Exclusive Listing Period Purchase Addendum for Individual Owner-Occupant Buyers.

ii. Investor Buyers

An Investor Buyer is a buyer who will not occupy the HUD REO Property as their Principal Residence.

iii. Good Neighbor Next Door Participants

(A) Definitions

Good Neighbor Next Door (GNND) Participants are law enforcement officers, teachers, firefighters, or emergency medical technicians who are eligible to purchase HUD REO Properties under the <u>GNND Sales Program.</u>

Locality is the community, neighborhood, or jurisdiction of the unit of general local government or Indian tribal government.

A Unit of General Local Government is a county or parish, city, town, township, or other political subdivision of a state.

(B) Standard

GNND participants may purchase designated single-unit HUD REO Properties in Revitalization Areas at a discount of 50 percent off the list price.

The GNND participant must bid the full list price; the AM will reflect any applicable discounts in the sales price.

(C) Eligible Participants

Buyers must meet all of the following requirements in order to purchase through the GNND Sales Program. The AM will ensure that Buyers are eligible to participate in the program.

(1) Full-Time Employment as a Law Enforcement Officer, Teacher, or Firefighter/EMT

At the time the bid is submitted and at the time of closing, the buyer must be employed full-time as one of the following:

- a law enforcement officer:
  - who is employed full-time by a law enforcement agency of the federal government, a state, a unit of general local government, or an Indian tribal government;
  - whose full-time employment, in the normal course of business, directly serves the locality in which the home is located; and
  - who, in carrying out such full-time employment, is sworn to uphold, and make arrests for violations of, federal, state, tribal, county, township, or municipal laws;
- a teacher:
  - who is employed as a full-time teacher by a state-accredited public school or private school that provides direct services to students in grades pre-kindergarten through 12; and
  - whose full-time employment, in the normal course of business, serves students from the locality where the home is located; or
- a firefighter/Emergency Medical Technician (EMT):
  - who is employed full-time as a firefighter or EMT by a fire department or emergency medical services responder unit of the federal government, a state, unit of general local government, or an Indian tribal government serving the locality where the home is located.

The buyer must certify to their good faith intention to continue employment as a law enforcement officer, teacher or firefighter/EMT for at least one year after the date of closing.

(2) Purchasing as Owner-Occupant Buyer

The buyer must agree to own, and live in as their sole residence, the purchased Property for the owner-occupancy term of 36 months and certify that occupancy annually.

(3) Execution of Second Mortgage and Note

The buyer must agree to execute a second Mortgage and Note on the house for the difference between the list price and the discounted selling price.

(4) Restrictions Related to Previous GNND Sales Program Purchases

The buyer nor their spouse must not:

- have owned any residential Real Property during the year before they submitted a bid on the Property to be purchased through the GNND Sales Program; and
- have purchased another house under the GNND Sales Program.

(D) Eligible Properties

GNND participants may purchase designated single-unit HUD REO Properties under the GNND Sales Program that are located:
- in a HUD-designated Revitalization Area; and
- in the community where the GNND participant works (applicable to teacher and firefighter/EMT buyers only).

iv. Governmental Entities and HUD-Approved Nonprofits

(A) Definitions

A Governmental Entity refers to any federal, state, or local government agency or instrumentality. To be considered an Instrumentality of Government (IOG), the Entity must be established by a governmental body or with governmental approval or under special law to serve a particular public purpose or designated by law (statute or court opinion). HUD deems Section 115 Entities to be IOGs for the purpose of providing secondary financing.

HUD-approved Nonprofit organizations approved to participate in FHA nonprofit programs are eligible to purchase HUD REO Properties.

(B) Purchasing as Owner-Occupant Buyers

(1) Standard

Governmental Entities and HUD-approved Nonprofits are included in the definition of Owner-Occupant Buyers and may purchase Properties during the same periods in which Owner-Occupant Buyers may purchase. HUD-approved Nonprofits are responsible for compliance with their Affordable Housing Program Plan (AHPP).

(a) Purchases during Direct Sale Periods

When purchasing HUD-owned Properties at a 10 percent or greater discount as part of a direct sale, Governmental Entities and HUD-approved Nonprofits must complete and submit with their offer a Land Use Restriction Addendum (LURA).

(b) Purchases during Competitive Sales Periods

(i) Exclusive Listing Period

Governmental Entities and HUD-approved Nonprofits may purchase Properties during the exclusive listing period as long as they:
- certify that they will own the Property for at least 12 months;
- have not purchased a HUD-owned Property during the exclusive listing period within the past 24 months; and
- complete and submit an Exclusive Listing Period Purchase Addendum for Governmental Entities and HUD-Approved Nonprofits with their offer.

(ii) Extended Listing Period

Governmental Entities and HUD-approved Nonprofits may purchase Properties during the extended listing period and are not required to complete an Exclusive Listing Period Purchase Addendum for purchases made without discount.

(2) Required Documentation

Where applicable, the Governmental Entity or HUD-approved Nonprofit must complete and submit with their offer a LURA or Exclusive Listing Period Purchase Addendum for Governmental Entities and HUD-Approved Nonprofits.

(C) Use of Selling Brokers

HUD will not pay selling broker commission for Properties purchased by Governmental Entities and HUD-approved Nonprofits.

Where guidance in this section directs the selling broker to perform a specific action, a designated agent of the Governmental Entity or HUD-approved Nonprofit may perform this action.

(D) Discounts on Direct Sales

For direct sales, Governmental Entities and HUD-approved Nonprofits may purchase HUD REO Properties at the following discounts on the list price:
- 30 percent off the list price for uninsured Properties located within a Revitalization Area;
- 10 percent off the list price for insured or uninsured Properties located outside of a Revitalization Area;
- 10 percent off the list price for insured Properties located within a Revitalization Area; and

Handbook 4000.1   888

Effective Date: 09/30/2016 | Last Revised: 07/10/2019
*Refer to the online version of SF Handbook 4000.1 for specific sections' effective dates

- 15 percent off the list price for insured or uninsured Properties located outside of a Revitalization Area and insured Properties located in a Revitalization Area when:
  - o the AM has accepted five or more bids from the Governmental Entity or HUD-approved Nonprofit within a 15 business day period; and
  - o the sales are closed in a single transaction.

(E) Restrictions on Resale

Governmental Entities and HUD-approved Nonprofits must comply with the restrictions on resale as stated in an executed LURA or Exclusive Listing Period Purchase Addendum.

To request exceptions to the restrictions on resale, the Governmental Entity or HUD-approved Nonprofit may submit a request in writing to the Director of the Jurisdictional HOC for the area in which the Property is located.

v. HUD Employees

(A) Standard

HUD employees and members of HUD employees' households are eligible to purchase HUD REO Properties as Owner-Occupant Buyers if:
- they do not currently own a house and can demonstrate and certify that they will occupy the Property as their Principal Residence for at least two years;
- they have not purchased a HUD-owned Property within the past 24 months as an owner occupant; and
- they are not prohibited buyers.

Eligible HUD employees and members of their households must obtain supervisor and Office of Single Family Asset Management (OSFAM) approval before bidding on a HUD-owned Single Family house.

(1) Form HUD-50001

The HUD employee must complete form HUD-50001, *HUD Employee/Relative Home Purchase Certification*, by:
- describing their job and/or relationship to the proposed buyer;
- certifying that they have no involvement with the management and oversight of the M&M contractors' activities; and
- obtaining their immediate supervisor's signature.

(2) Approval by the Office of Single Family Asset Management

The HUD employee must email the signed form HUD-50001 to the Director of OSFAM for approval. OSFAM will notify the employee if they are approved to purchase HUD REO Properties.

(3) Period of Eligibility to Bid

The approved HUD employee or member of the HUD employee's household is eligible to bid on HUD REO Properties for up to 12 months from the date of the approval.

(4) Recertification

The approved HUD employee or member of the HUD employee's household must re-certify by completing form HUD-50001 and obtaining the required approvals in the event of any job change.

(B) Required Documentation

The HUD employee must complete and submit with their offer an Exclusive Listing Period Period Purchase Addendum for Individual Owner-Occupant Buyers. The HUD employee must include on the Addendum their Social Security Number (SSN) and date of birth.

vi. Prohibited Buyers

The following are prohibited from purchasing HUD REO Properties.

(A) HUD REO Staff

The following HUD employees and their household members are prohibited from purchasing HUD REO Properties:
- all HUD management personnel who are part of the management chain that has authority over the Single Family REO disposition process;
- all headquarters OSFAM employees;
- all HUD employees that have direct or indirect responsibilities for policy development, procurement, and disposition of Single Family REO Properties; and
- all HOCs, field and regional offices' employees that have direct or indirect oversight responsibilities of M&M contractors.

(B) Participants in HUD REO Marketing and Management

Certain participants in HUD M&M activities and their immediate Family Members may be prohibited by contract from purchasing HUD REO Properties. HUD M&M contractor staff should contact the Government Technical Representative (GTR) for information on eligibility to purchase HUD REO Properties.

(C) Members of Congress

Members or delegates of the United States Congress are prohibited from purchasing or benefiting from a purchase of a HUD REO Property.

(D)Former Borrowers who Defaulted on FHA-Insured Mortgages

Former Non-Occupant Borrowers of FHA-insured Mortgages, whose Default resulted in HUD's payment of a mortgage insurance benefits claim to a Mortgagee, are prohibited from repurchasing the same Property that secured the FHA-insured Mortgage.

e. Lead-Based Paint

REO Property disposition activities are conducted in accordance with 24 CFR 35 subpart F, HUD-Owned Single Family Property.

i. Availability of Inspection Information

For all HUD REO Properties built before 1978 or for which the year of construction is unknown, buyers will have access to available lead-based paint information in the Property Condition Report (PCR), including all available copies of:
- lead-based paint inspection reports;
- risk assessment reports; and
- other records and reports pertaining to lead-based paint and/or lead-based paint hazards.

The buyer may request paper copies of this information from the local AM.

ii. Providing Lead Based Paint Information

The selling broker is responsible for ensuring that the following are provided to the buyer for review:
- form HUD-9545-Y, *Lead-Based Paint Disclosure Addendum to Sales Contract – Seller has pertinent records*, or form HUD-9545-Z, *Lead-Based Paint Disclosure Addendum to Sales Contract – Seller has NO pertinent records*, as applicable;
- all available lead-based paint records and reports; and
- the U.S. Environmental Protection Agency (EPA)-approved pamphlet entitled "Protect Your Family from Lead in Your Home."

iii. Other Lead-Based Paint Information Obtained After Receipt of a Sale Offer

If HUD obtains additional lead-based paint records, reports and/or information after receiving a sale offer, HUD will deliver to the selling broker:
- the additional lead-based paint records, reports and/or information on the subject Property that became available and were not posted on HUD's website for retrieval prior to bid submission; and
- a supplemental form HUD-9545-Y, *Lead-Based Paint Disclosure Addendum to Sales Contract – Seller has pertinent records*, acknowledging receipt of any additional lead-based paint or lead-based paint hazard-related documents.

f. Sales Timeline

i. Tenant Right of First Refusal

(A) Definition

The Tenant Right of First Refusal is a tenant's ability to purchase a HUD REO Property on a non-competitive basis before it is listed for sale.

(B) Standard

HUD's AM will contact eligible tenants regarding their opportunity to purchase occupied Properties at list price under the tenant right of first refusal.

ii. Asset Control Area Program

(A) Definition

The Asset Control Area (ACA) Program is a direct sale program in which eligible local, county, or state governments or HUD-approved Nonprofit organizations may enter into a contract with HUD to purchase vacant HUD REO Properties in designated areas.

(B) Standard

HUD will sell to Entities participating in the ACA Program all or a specified number of vacant HUD REO Properties acquired in designated areas as specified in the ACA agreement.

iii. National First Look Program

(A) Definition

The National First Look Program is a direct sale program in which participating Neighborhood Stabilization Program (NSP) grantees have the exclusive opportunity to purchase HUD REO Properties located in NSP areas.

(B) Standard

HUD will make available to participating NSP grantees information on HUD REO Properties for sale within NSP-designated areas. Eligible NSP buyers may purchase these HUD REO Properties at a discount of 10 percent for insurable Properties or 15 percent for uninsurable Properties off the list price, less the cost of any applicable listing and sales commission.

(1) Eligible Neighborhood Stabilization Program Grantees

The following NSP grantees are eligible to purchase HUD REO Properties at a discount:

- direct recipients of NSP funds; or
- sub-recipients (or sub-awardees) of direct NSP grantees; and
- consortium members under NSP2.

(2) First Look Purchase Period

The NSP grantee must submit an offer for a HUD REO Property within two business days after the date of the property appraisal.

Each First Look Property will remain available for purchase under the First Look Sales Method until an eligible NSP grantee buyer submits an offer to purchase the Property, or through the expiration of the two-day purchase period, whichever comes first.

(3) Confirmation of Location of Property

The NSP grantee buyer is responsible for confirming that the Property is within the boundaries of the NSP designated area. Where the boundaries of any two or more NSP areas overlap and where multiple eligible NSP grantee buyers submit offers to purchase a HUD REO Property in that overlapping area, the right to purchase the Property is granted to the eligible NSP grantee buyer that first submits an offer to purchase that Property.

(4) Use of Neighborhood Stabilization Program Funds

The NSP grantee buyer must use NSP funds, at least in part, in order to purchase a HUD REO Property under the NSP grantee buyer time frame and discount.

iv. Lottery Period

(A) Definition

The Lottery Period is a direct sale period in which Governmental Entities, HUD-approved Nonprofits, and GNND participants may submit bids for designated HUD REO Properties.

(B) Standard

Governmental Entities, HUD-approved Nonprofits, and GNND participants may submit bids equal to the list price during the seven-Day lottery period.

At the end of the lottery period, HUD will select a winning bidder at random. The AM will reflect applicable discounts in the sales contract.

(1) Good Neighbor Next Door

During the lottery period, GNND participants may submit bids for designated HUD REO Properties.

When separate bids are submitted by spouses who are both GNND participants, HUD may approve a bid from only one spouse.

(2) Lottery for Governmental Entities and HUD-Approved Nonprofits

During the lottery period, Governmental Entities and HUD-approved Nonprofits may submit bids at list price for uninsured Properties located within their approved purchase areas.

v. Exclusive Listing Period

(A) Definition

The Exclusive Listing Period is a competitive listing period in which only eligible Governmental Entities, HUD-approved Nonprofits, and Owner-Occupant Buyers may submit bids on HUD REO Properties.

(B) Standard

Governmental Entities, HUD-approved Nonprofits, and Owner-Occupant Buyers may submit bids during the exclusive listing period. HUD will choose the winning bid, which produces the greatest net return to HUD and meets HUD's terms of offering of the Property.

(1) Length of Exclusive Listing Period

For Properties marketed as "insured" or "insured with escrow," the exclusive listing period is 15 Days.

For Properties marketed as "uninsured," the exclusive listing period is five Days.

(2) Review of Bids during Exclusive Listing Period

(a) Bid Opening for "Insured" and "Insured with Escrow" HUD REO Properties

(i) Bids Received from Days 1 through 10

For Properties marketed as "insured" or "insured with escrow," the AM will open all bids received from the 1st through the 10th Day of the exclusive listing period on the next business day after the 10th Day of the exclusive listing period. The AM opening the bids will treat all bids as having been received simultaneously.

(ii) Bids Received from Days 11 through 15

If none of the bids received by the 10th Day are accepted, the AM will open and review bids received during the 11th Day up to the 15th Day daily on the next business day. If a bid is not accepted during the 15-Day exclusive listing period, the AM will extend the listing to all buyers by listing the Property in the extended listing period.

(b) Bid Opening for "Uninsured" HUD REO Properties

For Properties that are marketed as "uninsured," AMs will open and review all bids received from the 1st through the 5th Day on the next business day after the 5th Day of the exclusive listing period. The AM will treat all bids as having been received simultaneously.

If a bid is not accepted in the five-Day exclusive listing period for Properties listed as "uninsured," the AM will extend the listing to all buyers by listing the Property in the extended listing period.

(c) Bid Opening on Weekends and Federal Holidays

HUD considers bids received on Fridays, Saturdays, and Sundays in the same bid period as being received simultaneously during that period. The AM will open those bids on:

- the following Monday; or
- the next business day, if Monday is a federal holiday.

HUD considers bids received on a federal holiday in the same bid period as being received on the previous Day. The AM will open those bids on the next business day.

vi. Extended Listing Period

(A) Definition

The Extended Listing Period is a competitive listing period during which all buyers may submit bids on HUD REO Properties.

(B) Standard

If a Property remains unsold for 15 Days, HUD will extend the listing to all buyers by listing the Property in the extended listing period.

All buyers, including Investors, may submit bids on HUD REO Properties during the extended listing period.

(C) Review of Bids during Extended Listing Period

The AM will open bids at the end of each business day, subject to the policies in Bid Opening on Weekends and Federal Holidays.

vii. Bulk Sales

(A) Definition

A Bulk Sale is a direct sale of five or more HUD REO Properties to eligible buyers.

(B) Standard

HUD may seek to dispose of Properties through bulk sales. HUD will advertise and sell these Properties on an all-cash, as-is basis, without warranty and without FHA-insured mortgage financing.

To be eligible for bulk sale discounts, the Governmental Entity or HUD-approved Nonprofit purchasing in bulk must close on all property sale transactions no later than 60 Days from the date the contract is ratified.

Bulk Sale to Eligible Governmental Entities and HUD-Approved Nonprofits

If a Property is marketed and remains unsold for 60 Days, HUD may elect to sell the Property to eligible Governmental Entities and HUD-approved Nonprofits as part of a bulk sale as follows:
- Properties with an appraised value greater than $100,000 will be priced at a 10 percent discount from the appraised value;
- Properties with an appraised value less than or equal to $100,000 will be priced at a 50 percent discount;
- Properties with an appraised value less than $20,000, and considered "demolition properties" will be priced at $100;
- participants purchasing 50 or more Properties will receive an additional 5 percent discount; and
- under certain conditions, local governments may purchase Properties that have been listed for 180 Days or more for $1, plus closing costs.

viii. Dollar Homes – Government Sales

(A) Definition

The Dollar Homes – Government Sales Program is a direct sales program through which eligible Governmental Entities may purchase certain HUD REO Properties for $1 each, plus closing costs.

(B) Standard

If a Property remains unsold after 180 Days, HUD will remove the Property from the market and offer it exclusively to local governments for 10 Days before returning it to the extended listing period, if no $1 bids are accepted.

Local governments may purchase for $1 each, plus closing costs, certain Properties meeting the following criteria:
- the Property is not under a contract for sale;
- the Property has been offered to the public and marketed for sale for at least 180 Days;
- the Property is within the jurisdiction of the local government;
- the Property is uninsured; and
- the current as-is Market Value of the Property is $25,000 or less.

(C) Commissions and Costs

(1) Commissions

Listing brokers will not receive a commission for a Property sold under the Dollar Homes – Government Sales Program.

HUD will not pay a selling agent commission for Properties sold under the Dollar Homes – Government Sales Program; buyers may submit a bid directly without the service of a selling broker.

(2) Local Government Liens

In those instances where a local government has placed liens against the Properties and fines have been assessed, the local government must remove these liens at no cost to HUD in an effort to facilitate the sale.

(D) Dollar Homes Closing Costs

Buyers will be required to pay closing costs involved with each Dollar Homes - Government Sales Program property sale transaction.

(E) Partnering with HUD-Approved Nonprofits

(1) Standard

Local Governmental Entities may partner with local nonprofits to purchase Properties under the Dollar Homes – Government Sales Program for local housing and community development initiatives.

Governmental Entities may only purchase eligible HUD Properties within their jurisdiction and must:

- identify the intended disposition strategy or strategies and clear public purpose goals and objectives consistent with supporting local housing or community development initiatives, including rehabilitation and resale to first time homebuyers or Low- to Moderate-Income buyers, that it will pursue with Properties purchased through this program;
- affirm that all profits from resale of these Dollar Homes will go to support local housing or community development initiatives; and
- identify what specific local housing or community development programs or uses these profits will support.

(2) Annual Reporting to HOC

Governmental Entities must provide information pertaining to the purchase and subsequent resale of Properties purchased under the Dollar Homes – Government Sales Program in its annual report to HUD's HOC Program Support Division Director via HUD's Nonprofit Data Management System (NPDMS).

The report must include information on:
- the ultimate Owner-Occupant Buyer;
- the amount of profit realized on the final sale; and
- the specific local housing/community development programs or uses these profits were used to support.

(3) Compliance with Program Requirements

Failure of a Governmental Entity to comply with any of the Dollar Homes – Government Sales Program requirements will result in disqualification from participation in the program.

(4) No Direct Purchase by Nonprofits

Nonprofit organizations are not permitted to directly purchase Properties under this sales program on their own behalf. HUD will accept a sales contract from nonprofits only if a Governmental Entity identifies in its intended disposition strategy that the nonprofit will act as its agent to purchase these Properties.

(5) Demolition Consideration

(a) Request to HUD

A local government may recommend to the AM the demolition of any Property that is currently available for purchase by that Entity meeting the Dollar Homes – Government Sales standard. HUD will consider the following criteria in its decision:

- whether HUD's last listed price, plus the cost of rehabilitating the Property to meet HUD's Minimum Property Standards (MPS) is more than 130 percent of the after-rehabilitation value;
- whether the cost of demolition exceeds the cost of rehabilitating the Property to meet MPS; and
- whether the Property is listed on or eligible for the National Register of Historic Places or located in a historic district. If it is, a Section 106 consultation with the State Historic Preservation Officer and other interested parties is required before HUD approves the Property for demolition.

(b) Cost of Demolition

If HUD approves the Property for demolition, HUD will pay for the demolition and clearing of the debris.

(c) Sale after Demolition

Following demolition, HUD will list the land for sale to the general public for 10 Days at its Fair Market Value (FMV).

If no acceptable offers are received from the general public, HUD will offer the land to local governments for $1 for 10 Days.

If the land is not purchased by local governments, HUD will relist the Property to all classes of bidders until the Property is sold.

ix. HUD Rescission of Listing

HUD, at its discretion, may remove a listing or cancel a sales contract and may return all or a portion of a buyer's earnest money deposit if:
- HUD has not acquired the Property;
- HUD is unable or unwilling to remove valid objections to the title prior to closing; or
- HUD determines that the buyer is not an acceptable Borrower.

g. Bid Submission

i. Use of HUD Home Store

Selling brokers, HUD-approved Nonprofits, and Governmental Entities must submit bids for HUD REO Properties electronically through HUD Home Store.

In order to submit bids through HUD Home Store, selling brokers, HUD-approved Nonprofits, and Governmental Entities must:

- have applied for and been issued a Name and Address Identification Number (NAID); and
- be registered on HUD Home Store or successor site.

ii. GNND Bid and Eligibility Documentation

The GNND participant must submit with its bid:
- form HUD 9549, *Good Neighbor Next Door Sales Program Personal Information Questionnaire*;
- form HUD 9549-E, *Employer Verification of Participant Employment*; and
- one of the following pre-qualification questionnaires:
  - form HUD 9549-A, *Good Neighbor Next Door Sales Program - Law Enforcement Officer*;
  - form HUD 9549-B, *Good Neighbor Next Door Sales Program - Teacher*; or
  - form HUD 9549-C, *Good Neighbor Next Door Sales Program - Firefighter/Emergency Medical Technician*.

iii. Back-up Bids

(A) Definition

A Back-up Bid is an acceptable bid for a HUD REO Property, held by HUD, should the winning bid fail to close.

(B) Standard

At the time of bidding, the selling broker may elect to have their bid held as a back-up bid. Should the winning bidder's sale fail to close, HUD may offer the Property to back-up bidders before relisting the Property.

HUD will allow at least one back-up bidder and, in the case of GNND, two back-up bidders.

h. Bid Acceptance During Competitive Sales Periods

i. Standard

For Properties sold in competitive sales, HUD will accept the bid that produces the greatest net return to HUD and meets all the terms and conditions pertaining to HUD's offering, with priority given to Owner-Occupant Buyers for Properties being offered with insured Mortgages.

For Properties marketed as uninsurable, HUD will give priority to Governmental Entities and HUD-approved Nonprofits before Owner-Occupant Buyers.

The net return is calculated by subtracting from the bid price the dollar amounts for financing and closing costs, as stated on Line 5 of form HUD-9548, *Sales Contract*, and real estate sales commissions to be paid by HUD.

(A) Multiple Bids

Selling brokers may submit an unlimited number of bids on a Property, provided that each bid is from a different buyer. If a buyer submits multiple bids on the same Property, HUD will only consider the bid producing the highest net return to HUD.

If a prospective Owner-Occupant Buyer submits a bid on more than one Property, the bid that produces the greatest net return to HUD will be accepted and all other bids from that buyer will be eliminated from consideration. However, if the prospective Owner-Occupant Buyer has submitted the only acceptable bid on another Property, then that bid must be accepted and all other bids from that buyer on any other Properties will be eliminated from consideration.

(B) Identical Net Offer

Where two or more bids result in identical net offers, HUD will give preference to the Owner-Occupant Buyer.

If the identical bids were submitted by two or more Owner-Occupant Buyers, or by two or more Investor Buyers, HUD will choose the winning bid by lottery.

ii. Counteroffers

If all bids received are unacceptable, HUD may, at its discretion, offer counteroffers to one or more bidders via P260, and those bidders may resubmit bids during a specified period of time.

If HUD elects to counteroffer, HUD will accept the highest acceptable net bid received within the specified time period.

i. Selection of Winning Bid

i. Notification by HUD of Winning Bid

HUD will alert the buyer or selling broker if they are the winning bidder.

ii. Submission of Sales Documents

Once HUD has notified the buyer or selling broker that they are the winning bidder, the buyer or selling broker must send the following to the AM within two business days:
- a fully completed form HUD-9548, signed by the buyer and selling broker;
- a pre-qualification letter, certification of cash funds, or other proof of funds; and
- all required addenda, if applicable, including:

- o   an Exclusive Listing Period Purchase Addendum for Individual Owner-Occupant Buyers or an Exclusive Listing Period Purchase Addendum for Governmental Entities and HUD-Approved Nonprofits;
- o   a forfeiture of earnest money deposit addendum;
- o   a Buyer Select Closing Agent Addendum;
- o   closing instructions and certification;
- o   form HUD-9548-B, *Discount Sales Addendum*;
- o   all copies of form HUD-9545-Y, *Lead-Based Paint Disclosure Addendum to Sales Contract – Seller has pertinent records*, and/or form HUD-9545-Z, *Lead-Based Paint Disclosure Addendum to Sales Contract – Seller has NO pertinent records*, providing the original Addendum and any Supplemental Addenda;
- o   form HUD-92564-CN, *For Your Protection: Get a Home Inspection*;
- o   Good Neighbor Next Door addenda;
- o   a flood zone property addendum; and
- o   any disclosures required by state or local law.

The selling broker must complete line 3 of form HUD-9548 to identify the Closing Agent as the party who will be holding the earnest money deposit, unless otherwise instructed by the AM.

iii. Earnest Money Deposit

(A) Definition

The Earnest Money Deposit is a buyer's deposit towards the purchase of real estate to demonstrate that they are serious about wanting to complete the purchase.

(B) Standard

The buyer and selling broker must sign the earnest money forfeiture agreement. The selling broker must submit the earnest money deposit with the completed form HUD-9548, for all sales other than ACA sales, to the AM within two business days of being notified that their buyer is the winning bidder, unless otherwise instructed by the AM, and the AM will forward the deposit to the Closing Agent.

(C) Form of Earnest Money Deposit

The earnest money deposit must be in the form of a cashier's check, certified check, or money order with no termination date or cancellation provision, payable to the Closing Agent or to another Entity as designated by HUD.

Earnest Money Deposit Amounts

The earnest money deposit amount is as follows:
- for Properties with a sales price of $50,000 or less, the earnest money deposit is $500;

- for Properties with a sales price greater than $50,000, the earnest money deposit is between $500 and $2,000, as determined by HUD;
- for vacant lots, the earnest money deposit is 50 percent of the list price; and
- for Properties to be purchased under the GNND Sales Program, the earnest money deposit is 1 percent of the list price, but no less than $500 and no more than $2,000.

The buyer or selling broker may contact the AM for the earnest money deposit amount for a specific Property.

(D) Disposition of Earnest Money Deposits when the Transaction Fails to Close

Should the sales transaction fail to close as scheduled, HUD may consider the earnest money deposit forfeited or may return all or a portion of the earnest money deposit.

(1) Investor Buyer

Forfeiture of Entire Earnest Money Deposit

Subject to state law, the Investor Buyer forfeits 100 percent of the earnest money deposit, unless HUD cancels the sales contract due to HUD's inability to close the transaction for any reason.

(2) Owner-Occupant Buyers

(a) Return of Entire Earnest Money Deposit

Subject to state law, HUD will return 100 percent of an Owner-Occupant Buyer's earnest money deposit in the following circumstances:
- there has been a death in the immediate family (contract holder, spouse, or children living in the same household);
- there has been a recent serious illness in the immediate family that has resulted in significant medical expenses or substantial loss of income, thus adversely affecting the buyer's financial ability to close the sale;
- there has been a loss of job by one of the primary wage earners, or substantial loss of income through no fault of the buyer;
- on an insured sale, HUD determines that the buyer is not an acceptable Borrower;
- on an uninsured sale, the buyer was pre-approved for FHA-insured mortgage financing in an appropriate amount by a recognized Mortgagee but, despite good faith efforts, was ultimately unable to secure mortgage financing;
- within 30 Days of the contract ratification date, the buyer has provided to the AM written documentation from a lender supporting the buyer's inability to secure financing;

- HUD cancels the contract due to the documented presence and/or condition of lead-based paint and/or lead-based paint hazards;
- pursuant to the terms of the VA Amendatory Clause for purchasers using VA financing; or
- other circumstances evidencing equally good cause, as determined by HUD.

In order to receive any part of the earnest money deposit, the Owner-Occupant Buyer must submit documentation to the AM within allowed time limits evidencing the circumstances related to the transaction's failure to close.

(b) Forfeiture of Entire Earnest Money Deposit

Subject to state law, the buyer forfeits 100 percent of the earnest money deposit in the following circumstances:

- the buyer does not submit documentation supporting their reason for the return of any part of the earnest money deposit within 30 Days, or such other time allowed by the AM in writing, following contract cancellation; or
- the buyer's submitted documentation fails to support an acceptable cause for the buyer's failure to close.

(3) Vacant Lots

Subject to state law, buyers of vacant lots will be considered Investor Buyers for the purpose of earnest money deposit disposition.

(E) Failure to Abide by HUD's Earnest Money Policy

Listing brokers who fail to comply with HUD's instructions for the collection and forwarding of the earnest money deposit to the AM (or other party as instructed by the AM) may be subject to such action including:

- Limited Denial of Participation (LDP);
- notification of the state real estate commission or regulatory body;
- referral to the appropriate office(s) for enforcement review; and/or
- suspension or termination of the Broker's NAID.

iv. Failure to Submit Sales Documents

Should the winning bidder fail to submit a ratified sales contract and accompanying documentation and deposits within allowed time limits, the AM may offer the Property to back-up bidders before relisting the Property.

v. Electronic Signatures

The use of electronic signatures is voluntary. HUD will permit the use of electronic signatures conducted in accordance with the Policy on Use of Electronic Signatures on the HUD REO form HUD-9548 and related addenda requiring signatures, unless otherwise prohibited by law.

j. Inspection Contingency

i. Standard

After HUD ratifies the sales contract, the buyer has 15 Days to:
- access the Property to conduct any inspections, tests, or risk assessments at their expense; and
- for Properties constructed before 1978, review all available records and reports relating to lead-based paint or lead-based paint hazards in the Property.

If the HUD REO appraisal was completed without the utilities being activated and the buyer is using FHA-insured financing, the Mortgagee or buyer must complete the systems check while the utilities are activated. The Mortgagee or buyer may contact the Field Service Manager (FSM) to request activation of utilities; HUD may charge a fee for this service.

ii. Repairs Necessary to Comply with Mortgage Lender or State, Tribal, or Local Law Requirements

HUD sells REO Properties as-is. When necessary to comply with mortgage lender requirements or state, tribal, or local law, a buyer may submit a request to the AM for repairs. The buyer must include with its request:
- documentation reflecting that such repairs are necessary to comply with lender or state or local requirements; and
- a copy of a home inspection report identifying the property condition at issue.

HUD will review requests on a case-by-case basis and, at its sole discretion, may make the requested repairs. HUD may impose some or all of the cost of repairs on the buyer.

iii. Withdrawal from Sales Contract

Before the expiration of the inspection contingency period, the buyer may terminate their obligation to purchase the house and request a refund of the earnest money deposit by providing to the AM:
- written notice of its withdrawal from the sales contract; and
- a copy of a home inspection report identifying serious problems or conditions with the Property that were not previously disclosed or corrected, or documentation of the presence and/or condition of lead-based paint or lead-based paint hazards.

Handbook 4000.1
Effective Date: 09/30/2016 | Last Revised: 07/10/2019
*Refer to the online version of SF Handbook 4000.1 for specific sections' effective dates

905

k. Closing

i. Closing Agents

(A) Definition

A Closing Agent is the Entity responsible for conducting the closing of a HUD REO property sales transaction, including submitting closing packages, and wiring sales proceeds to the U.S. Treasury.

(B) Standard

The buyer must select a Closing Agent who meets HUD's Closing Agent Requirements.

(1) Antidiscrimination Laws

Closing Agents and their employees, or persons or Entities otherwise authorized to act for the Closing Agent, must:
- comply with Title VIII of the Civil Rights Act of 1968 (Fair Housing Act, Title VIII, or Public Law 90-284), the Equal Credit Opportunity Act (ECOA), and Executive Order 11063;
- not discriminate on the basis of race, color, creed, religion, national origin, sex, age, familial status, disability, marital status, or actual or perceived sexual orientation and gender identity; and
- instruct their staffs in the policies of nondiscrimination and all applicable local, state, and federal fair housing and non-discrimination laws.

(2) No Conflicts of Interest

A Closing Agent must not participate in a closing where the Closing Agent's spouse, children, or business associates have a financial interest in the Property. Financial interest includes having an equity, creditor, mortgage lender, or debtor interest in any corporation, trust, or partnership with a financial interest in the Property.

(C) Required Documentation

The buyer and selling broker must identify the selected Closing Agent as follows:
- identify the Closing Agent on Line 9 of form HUD-9548; and
- submit the Closing Agent designation form with the sales contract package. The form, at a minimum, must include the following:
  - the name of the Closing Agent;
  - the full address of the Closing Agent; and
  - the telephone number, email address, and contact person.

The Closing Agent must sign and certify in the Closing Instructions and Certification that they meet HUD's requirements and will adhere to HUD's Closing Instructions.

(D) Closing Agent Fee

The buyer is primarily responsible for any and all Closing Agent and closing fees, up to the maximum allowed per state law and regulatory requirements.

The buyer may apply amounts listed on Line 5 of form HUD-9548 for payment of closing fees.

ii. Time Frame for Closing

The time frame for closing is specified in Line 9 of form HUD-9548. The Closing Agent must schedule a firm Closing Date within the time frame set by the AM. The AM will identify the time frame for closing in Line 9 of form HUD-9548 as follows:
- for cash sales, within 30 Days of contract ratification;
- for sales involving mortgage financing, within 45 Days of contract ratification; and
- for sales involving a 203(k) product, within 60 Days of contract ratification.

(A) Requests for Extensions

If scheduled Closing Dates cannot be met, the selling broker or buyer may request extensions of the closing time from the AM before the expiration of the sales contract by:
- submitting the request for an extension in writing; and
- if applicable, including an extension fee for the full amount of the requested 15-Day extension, in the form of certified funds payable to HUD.

The AM will grant extensions in 15-Day increments on a case-by-case basis when extenuating circumstances preclude the buyer from closing as scheduled.

(1) Fees for Extensions

The AM may assess a daily fee for initial or repeat sales contract extensions as follows:
- for a sales price of $25,000 or less, the extension fee is $10 per Day;
- for a sales price of $25,001 to $50,000, the extension fee is a minimum of $10 per Day and a maximum of $15 per Day; and
- for a sales price over $50,000, the extension fee is a minimum of $10 per Day with a maximum of $25 per Day.

(2) No Cost Extensions

The AM will grant extensions at no cost to the buyer if the delay is due to HUD, HUD's contractors, or a title defect.

The AM will also grant an initial extension to Owner-Occupant Buyers who demonstrate that:
- the buyer made a proper and timely loan application;
- the buyer is not responsible for the delay in closing; and
- mortgage approval is imminent.

If approved, the AM will grant a 30-Day extension for Section 203(k) transactions or a 15-Day extension for all other transactions.

(3) Application of Extension Fee

If the sale closes before the expiration of the extension, the extension fee will be applied to the amount due from the buyer and the buyer will be credited with any unused portion of the fee, computed on a daily basis.

(B) Notification from HUD on Extension

The AM will notify the selling broker of the approval or denial of the extension request. The selling broker must place a copy of the approval or denial in the property file.

(C) Closing Time Frame Lapsed

When closing does not occur as scheduled and the buyer has not requested and received an extension of time to close, the AM will cancel the sales contract.

iii. Commissions

(A) Standard

For sales to buyers other than Governmental Entities or HUD-approved Nonprofits, HUD will pay commission to listing brokers and selling brokers as follows, based on averages for the area and depending on the level of service provided to HUD and on value and market conditions. The selling broker may contact the listing broker for transaction-specific commission amounts.

(1) Commission Amounts

(a) Minimum Commission

HUD will pay commissions not less than:
- $200 each for the listing broker and selling broker for sales of vacant lots; and
- $500 each for the listing broker and selling broker for all other sales.

(b) Maximum Commission

For sales of vacant lots, HUD will pay commissions totaling not more than 10 percent of the bid price.

For all other sales, HUD will pay commissions totaling not more than 6 percent of the bid price.

(c) Hard-to-Sell Properties

For sales of Properties designated as hard-to-sell, HUD will pay up to a total sales commission of $2,000, to be split between the listing broker and selling broker.

(2) Split of Sales Commission

Listing brokers and selling brokers will split sales commissions. The selling broker's acceptance of a lower commission does not affect the amount the listing broker will receive.

(3) Calculating Commission on Discounted Sales

For discounted sales to buyers other than Governmental Entities or HUD-approved Nonprofits, the listing broker and selling broker may calculate commission based on the bid price before any discounts are deducted.

(B) Required Documentation

The listing broker and selling broker must enter on form HUD-9548 the actual commissions to be paid.

iv. Closing Costs

(A) Costs Automatically Paid by HUD

HUD will pay the following closing costs:
- proration of property taxes and any special assessments such as Homeowners' Association (HOA) fees and utility bills;
- condominium or HOA transfer fee, if applicable;
- the cost to provide condominium documents to the buyer;
- the repair escrow inspection fee of $200, if applicable;
- recording fees and charges for the deed;
- the overnight mailing fee for the final Closing Disclosure or similar legal document, signed by the buyers and the Closing Agent, and sent to the AM contractor; and
- state and local transfer taxes that are reasonable and customary in the jurisdiction where the Property is located.

For closing costs claimed on discount sales to Governmental Entities and HUD-approved Nonprofits, HUD will deduct any closing costs paid from the total discount amount.

(B) Other Financing and Closing Costs for Properties in Competitive Sales

(1) Standard

For Properties sold in competitive sales and not in GNND transactions, HUD will pay the buyer's actual financing and closing costs as requested on Line 5 of form HUD-9548 in an amount up to 3 percent of the Property's gross purchase price, provided that the costs are reasonable and customary in the jurisdiction where the Property is located. The gross purchase price is the bid price before any subtractions requested by the buyer for financing and closing costs, and the broker's sales commission.

No assistance for financing and loan closing costs or for broker's sales commission will be provided to Investor Buyers.

HUD will retain any Line 5 funds not used at closing.

(2) Required Documentation

The buyer must identify on Line 5 of form HUD-9548 their requested financing and closing costs.

v. Closing Process

(A) Closing Agent Assignments

The AM will provide the Closing Agent with the following items:
- fully ratified sales contract and addenda;
- title evidence (when available);
- wire instructions;
- pre-closing and post-closing instructions;
- HOA documents, if applicable;
- all outstanding property bills; and
- any other documentation deemed necessary by the GTR.

The AM will provide these documents within two business days of the AM's ratification of the sales contract, the issuance of the HUD-issued Title Identification (ID) Number, or, for ACA sales, receipt of the fully executed Notice of Acquisition from the ACA participant.

(B) Pre-Closing Package

(1) Definition

The Pre-Closing package is the documentation, including the Settlement, deeds, and supporting documentation, of a HUD REO Property Sale that is submitted before closing to the AM for review.

(2) Standard

The Closing Agent must upload into P260 and send to the AM a pre-closing package no later than five business days before closing.

(a) Closing Disclosure

The Closing Agent must accurately prepare the preliminary Closing Disclosure or similar legal document and provide it to the AM for their review and approval.

(b) Deed

The Closing Agent must prepare a special warranty or grant deed, where applicable, and provide the deed to the AM for their review and execution.

(3) Required Documentation

The pre-closing package must include the following documents:
- the Closing Disclosure or similar legal document and signature affidavits:
  - If the buyer has obtained new FHA financing, the Closing Agent must ensure that the FHA case number is listed on Line 8; or
  - If the buyer has not obtained new FHA financing, the Closing Agent must ensure that the previous FHA case number associated with that Property is listed in the "Seller Name" block of the Closing Disclosure or similar legal document;
- the deed prepared by Closing Agent;
- supporting documentation of any charges to HUD on the Closing Disclosure or similar legal document, such as past due bills for utilities or HOAs;
- recent tax documentation from the county;
- mortgagee documents itemizing all costs to be paid by HUD;
- copies of the extension fee payment, if applicable;
- the seller's affidavit, if applicable;
- Closing Agent contact information; and
- a signed copy of the Closing Instructions.

(C) HUD Review of Pre-Closing Package

The Closing Agent must ensure that sales documents are prepared accurately and promptly remitted to HUD's AM contractor for review.

The AM will review the pre-closing package prepared by the Closing Agent. If approved, the AM will return the Closing Disclosure or similar legal document and overnight the original, signed deed to the Closing Agent before closing.

(D) Notification to HUD of Closing

The Closing Agent must notify the AM on the same Day as the closing of the transaction.

(E) Deposit of Sales Proceeds

No later than one business day after closing, the Closing Agent must deposit the sales proceeds and initiate the request for wire transfer of the full amount of sales proceeds due HUD. The Closing Agent must include the FHA case number on the wire transfer request.

(F) Delivery of Deed for Recording

No later than one business day after closing, the Closing Agent must deliver the deed for recording and must notify the taxing authority and HOA, if applicable, that title has changed to a new owner.

(G) Final Closing Package

(1) Definition

The Final Closing Package is the documentation, including the final Closing Disclosure or similar legal document and other supporting documentation, which is provided to the AM after a HUD REO Property sale closing.

(2) Standard

Within two business days of closing, the Closing Agent must upload into P260 and mail to the AM a Final Closing Package including all of the following:
- all pages of the Closing Instructions and certifications;
- the final Closing Disclosure or similar legal document and all signed certifications;
- evidence the deed was delivered for recordation or a recorded copy;
- a copy of the wire confirmation proceeds transfer to the U.S. Treasury;
- a copy of form SAMS-1103, *Request to Wire Transfer Funds*;
- a copy of all applicable invoices or receipts of Disbursements; and

- a copy of the disbursement log accounting for all incoming and outgoing funds related to the transaction.

(3) GNND Additions to Final Closing Package

No later than five business days after closing, the Closing Agent must also send to the AM the following:

- the original Note;
- a copy of the Mortgage with evidence that it was delivered for recording; and
- a copy of the recorded Mortgage, when available.

(H)Canceled Closings

To cancel the sales contract after ratification by HUD, the buyer or selling broker must contact the AM and complete any required cancellation documentation provided by the AM.

The Closing Agent must send to the AM the signed deed and any extension fees in their possession.

The AM will ensure the return of the signed deed and forfeited extension fees, if any, to HUD.

The AM may offer the Property to back-up bidders before relisting the Property.

C. TITLE I CLAIMS

RESERVED FOR FUTURE USE

This section is reserved for future use, and until such time, FHA-approved Mortgagees, Servicers and any other interested participants must continue to comply with all applicable law and existing Handbooks, Mortgagee Letters, Notices and outstanding guidance applicable to their participation in FHA programs.

D. TITLE I DISPOSITION

RESERVED FOR FUTURE USE

This section is reserved for future use, and until such time, FHA-approved Mortgagees, Servicers and any other interested participants must continue to comply with all applicable law and existing Handbooks, Mortgagee Letters, Notices and outstanding guidance applicable to their participation in FHA programs.

V. QUALITY CONTROL, OVERSIGHT AND COMPLIANCE

The Quality Control, Oversight and Compliance section in this *FHA Single Family Housing Policy Handbook (SF Handbook)* covers quality control requirements, Federal Housing Administration (FHA) monitoring of Mortgagees, and enforcement actions FHA may take if its requirements are violated. This section covers Title I lenders, Title II Mortgagees, and other FHA program participants. The term "Mortgagee" is used throughout for all types of FHA approval (both Title II Mortgagees and Title I lenders) and the term "Mortgage" is used for all products (both Title II Mortgages and Title I loans), unless otherwise specified.

A Mortgagee must fully comply with all of the following requirements in order to participate in the origination, underwriting, closing, endorsement, servicing, purchasing, holding, or selling of FHA-insured Title I or Title II Mortgages.

If there are any exceptions or program-specific requirements that differ from those set forth below, the exceptions or alternative program requirements are explicitly stated or hyperlinked to the appropriate guidance. Terms and acronyms used in this *SF Handbook* have their meanings defined in the Glossary and Acronyms and in the specific section of the *SF Handbook* in which the definitions are located.

A. QUALITY CONTROL OF LENDERS AND MORTGAGEES

1. Quality Control Program Overview

a. Purpose of Quality Control Program

Quality Control (QC) Programs must be designed to:
- ensure compliance with FHA and Mortgagee policy and guidelines related to FHA Loan Administration;
- protect FHA and the Mortgagee from unacceptable risk;
- guard against errors, omissions, negligence, and fraud from those involved in the Mortgagee's Loan Administration;
- determine the root cause of any deficiencies and identify potential internal and external control weaknesses;
- alert Mortgagee management to patterns of deficiencies with respect to mortgage process and personnel;
- ensure timely and appropriate corrective action;
- ensure the existence of required documentation (e.g., credit, loan, and appraisal information) that is the basis of underwriting and servicing decisions;
- ensure Mortgages are secured by properties with values sufficient to support the Mortgage; and
- ensure compliance with fair lending laws, including the Fair Housing Act and the Equal Credit Opportunity Act (ECOA).

b. Definitions

i. Quality Control Program

A Quality Control (QC) Program is the process and written procedures through which the Mortgagee seeks to ensure that FHA operations and Loan Administration are in compliance with all applicable requirements.

ii. Quality Control Plan

A Quality Control (QC) Plan is a written plan that sets forth a Mortgagee's procedures for ensuring quality control. A QC Plan is the written element of a Mortgagee's QC Program.

iii. Loan Administration

Loan Administration refers to all aspects of the FHA mortgage lifecycle, including origination, underwriting, closing, endorsement, and servicing of FHA-insured Mortgages that are governed by FHA policies and procedures.

c. Standard

The Mortgagee must adopt and implement a QC Program that fully complies with the requirements of this *SF Handbook*, and, where applicable, the additional Multifamily QC requirements outlined in the *Multifamily Accelerated Processing (MAP) Guide*, 4430.G. The Mortgagee must maintain and update its QC Program as needed to ensure it is fully compliant with all applicable FHA requirements at all times.

The QC Program must cover the lifecycle of an FHA-insured Mortgage, including origination, underwriting, closing, endorsement, and servicing functions that are conducted by the Mortgagee.

The QC Program must cover all policies and procedures, whether performed by the Mortgagee or outsourced to a contractor, to ensure full compliance with FHA requirements for Loan Administration.

The QC Program must provide the Mortgagee's management with information sufficient to adequately monitor and oversee the Mortgagee's compliance, and measure performance as it relates to the Mortgagee's FHA mortgage activity.

i. Exception for Multifamily Mortgagees

The following QC Program requirements do not apply to Mortgagees with an Originate Multifamily, Service Multifamily, or Service/Originate Multifamily only authority. For Mortgagees with Originate Single Family/Multifamily, Service Single Family/Multifamily, or Service/Originate Single Family/Multifamily authority, these QC Program requirements do not apply to its Multifamily operations.

- V.A.2.b.iii(A) Rejected Mortgage Applications
- V.A.2.b.iv Escrow Funds
- V.A.2.b.vi Timely and Accurate Submission for Insurance
- V.A.2.d.iv(F) Method of Reporting
- V.A.3.a.i Time Frame for Selection and Review
- V.A.3.a.iii Sample Size Standard
- V.A.3.a.iv Sample Composition Standard
- V.A.3.b Loan Sample Risk Assessment
- V.A.3.c Origination and Underwriting Loan File Compliance Review
- V.A.3.d Quality Control Reviews of Specialized Mortgage Programs
- V.A.3.e Servicing Loan File Compliance Review
- V.A.3.f.ii Servicing Reviews
- V.A.4 Data Integrity
- V.B Quality Control of Other Participants
- V.C.2.a Title I Lender Monitoring Reviews
- V.C.2.c Servicer Tier Ranking System II
- V.C.3 Loan Level Monitoring

- V.D Monitoring of Other Participants
- V.E.3 Program Office Actions and Sanctions
- V.E.5.e Specific Program Participants

d. Required Documentation

The Mortgagee must document the existence of its QC Program and evidence of its implementation, including written procedures, QC reports, and corrective action plans.

i. Time Frame for Retention

The Mortgagee must retain all QC review results, including all selection criteria, review documentation, Findings, and actions taken to mitigate Findings, for a period of two years from the initial QC review, or from the last action taken to mitigate Findings, whichever is later.

ii. Production of Documents

The Mortgagee must make all documentation relating to its QC Program available to FHA at any time upon request.

2. Institutional Quality Control Program Requirements

a. Who May Perform Quality Control

The Mortgagee may use employees or contractors to perform QC functions in accordance with the following requirements.

i. Employees

The Mortgagee must ensure that employees who perform QC Program functions are, at all times, independent of all Loan Administration processes and do not directly participate in any of the Loan Administration processes represented in the QC Plan. The Mortgagee must ensure QC employees are not within any chain of reporting or management that is directly connected to Loan Administration staff.

ii. Contractors

The Mortgagee may contract with outside vendors to perform QC functions if:
- the Mortgagee assumes full responsibility for the contractor's conduct of QC reviews in compliance with FHA requirements;
- the Mortgagee and the contractor have a valid contractual agreement in place that specifies the roles and responsibilities of each party; and
- the Mortgagee acknowledges that the existence of such contract for the provision of QC services does not satisfy the Mortgagee's obligation to have a written QC Plan that fully complies with FHA requirements.

The Mortgagee must ensure that contractor employees who perform QC Program functions on behalf of the Mortgagee do not participate in any of the Loan Administration processes represented in the QC Plan.

b. Operational Compliance

The Mortgagee must ensure that its QC Plan provides for the following required reviews.

i. Personnel

(A) Training

(1) Loan Administration and Quality Control Processes

(a) Standard

The Mortgagee must train all staff involved in FHA Loan Administration and QC processes to ensure that staff know all current FHA requirements for the FHA Loan Administration practices for which the Mortgagee is responsible.

(b) Required Documentation

The Mortgagee must maintain a list of all training provided to staff. For each training, the Mortgagee must include a summary of the content covered.

(2) Access to FHA Guidance

(a) Standard

The Mortgagee must provide all Loan Administration and QC staff with access to current FHA guidance including Handbooks, Mortgagee Letters (ML), Frequently Asked Questions (FAQ), and other guidance issued by FHA.

(b) Required Documentation

The Mortgagee must confirm that all Loan Administration and QC staff have access to the internet or to hard copies of current FHA guidance.

(B) Restricted Participation

(1) Standard

The Mortgagee must confirm it verified, through each of the following systems, that the designated employees and/or Affiliates listed below were permitted to participate in FHA programs. If any of the designated employees and/or Affiliates are found to be ineligible, they are restricted from participating in FHA programs.

Handbook 4000.1   919
Effective Date: 09/14/2015 | Last Revised: 07/10/2019
*Refer to the online version of SF Handbook 4000.1 for specific sections' effective dates

Checks to verify employee eligibility must be conducted at least semiannually.

(a) Excluded Parties List

The Mortgagee must verify employee eligibility for all officers, partners, directors, principals, managers, supervisors, loan processors, loan underwriters, loan originators, and all other employees and Affiliates participating in U.S. Department of Housing and Urban Development (HUD) programs for or on behalf of the Mortgagee, using the System for Award Management (SAM) (www.sam.gov) Excluded Parties List.

(b) Limited Denial of Participation

The Mortgagee must verify employee eligibility for all officers, partners, directors, principals, managers, supervisors, loan processors, loan underwriters, loan originators, and all other employees and Affiliates participating in HUD programs for or on behalf of the Mortgagee, using the Limited Denial of Participation (LDP) list.

(c) National Mortgage Licensing System and Registry

The Mortgagee must verify that all employees and Affiliates participating in HUD programs for or on behalf of the Mortgagee are registered with the National Mortgage Licensing System and Registry (NMLS), unless excluded from NMLS requirements by law or regulation.

(2) Required Documentation

Mortgagees must maintain documentation that supports each employee's eligibility.

ii. Affiliate Quality Control Reviews

(A) Standard

The Mortgagee must perform QC reviews of its Affiliates in the same manner and under the same conditions as required for the Mortgagee's own operations. At a minimum, Affiliate monitoring must include a periodic (semiannual at a minimum) re-verification of the Affiliate's compliance with all applicable laws related to licensing, qualification, eligibility, or approval to originate or subservice Mortgages.

(B) Required Documentation

The Mortgagee must document the methodology used to review Affiliates, the results of each review, and any corrective actions taken as a result of review Findings. The procedures used to review and monitor a Mortgagee's Affiliates must be included in the Mortgagee's QC Plan.

iii. Fair Housing and Fair Lending

The Mortgagee must verify that its operations comply with applicable state and federal fair lending laws, including the following:

- Fair Housing Act (42 U.S.C. § 3601 et seq.)
- ECOA (15 U.S.C. § 1691 et seq.)
- Federal Truth in Lending Act (15 U.S.C. § 1601 et seq.)

(A) Rejected Mortgage Applications

(1) Standard

The Mortgagee must review a random statistical sample of rejected applications within 90 Days from the end of the month in which the decision was made. Reviews must be conducted on a monthly basis and ensure that:

- the reasons given for rejection were valid;
- each rejection has the concurrence of an officer, senior staff person, or underwriter with sufficient approval authority, or a committee chaired by an officer, senior staff person, or underwriter with sufficient approval authority;
- the requirements of the ECOA are met and documented in each file; and
- no civil rights violations were committed in the rejection of the application.

Where possible discrimination is noted, the Mortgagee must take immediate corrective action to ensure its operations comply with applicable state and federal fair lending laws.

(2) Required Documentation

The Mortgagee must document the methodology used to review rejected applications, the results of each review, and any corrective actions taken as a result of review Findings. The procedures used to review rejected applications must be included in the Mortgagee's QC Plan.

(B) Fair Housing Poster and Equal Housing Opportunity Logo

(1) Standard

The Mortgagee must verify that a fair housing poster is prominently displayed in the Mortgagee's home office and any branch offices that deal with Borrowers and the general public. The Mortgagee must verify that the equal housing opportunity logo is prominently displayed on all documents, including both hard copy and electronic documents, distributed by the Mortgagee to the public.

(2) Required Documentation

The Mortgagee must confirm that a fair housing poster is prominently displayed in the Mortgagee's offices. The Mortgagee must be able to demonstrate that all documents distributed by the Mortgagee to the public contain the equal housing opportunity logo.

(C) Fair Housing or Discrimination Violations

(1) Standard

Potential fair housing violations or instances of discrimination must be reported to HUD's Office of Fair Housing and Equal Opportunity (FHEO) immediately.

(2) Required Documentation

Fair housing violations and complaints may be reported online using the HUD Form 903 Online Complaint, contacting HUD's local FHEO Regional Office or by calling the Fair Housing Complaint Hotline at 1-800-669-9777.

iv. Escrow Funds

(A) Standard

The Mortgagee must verify that escrow funds received from Borrowers were used only for the purpose for which they were received, and are in compliance with all Consumer Financial Protection Bureau (CFPB) escrow requirements.

(B) Required Documentation

The Mortgagee must retain the results of each review and any corrective actions taken as a result of review Findings.

v. Mortgage Insurance Premiums

(A) Standard

The Mortgagee must verify that FHA Mortgage Insurance Premiums (MIP) were remitted to FHA within the required time period or, if not, that the remittance included late charges and interest penalties. Mortgagees must address any pattern of late submissions and promptly take corrective measures.

(B) Required Documentation

The Mortgagee must retain the results of each review and any corrective actions taken as a result of review Findings.

vi. Timely and Accurate Submission for Insurance

(A) Standard

The Mortgagee must verify that Mortgages are being submitted to FHA for insurance within the required time frames (see Case Binder Submission – Direct Endorsement Non-Lender Insurance).

(B) Required Documentation

The Mortgagee must retain the results of each review and any corrective actions taken as a result of review Findings.

vii. Advertising

(A) Standard

The Mortgagee must review all advertisements generated by the Mortgagee or on its behalf to verify compliance with HUD/FHA advertising requirements (see Advertising). The Mortgagee must take prompt corrective action upon discovering any violation of advertising requirements described in this *SF Handbook*.

(B) Required Documentation

The Mortgagee must retain copies of any Advertising Device the Mortgagee produces, or that is produced on the Mortgagee's behalf, that is related to FHA programs. The Mortgagee must retain samples of the advertising reviewed, the results of each review, and any corrective actions taken as a result of review Findings.

c. Identifying Patterns

i. Standard

The Mortgagee must review its loan performance data to identify any patterns of non-compliance.

ii. Required Documentation

The Mortgagee must document the methodology used to review patterns of non-compliance, the results of each review, and any corrective actions taken as a result of review Findings. The procedures used to review patterns of non-compliance must be included in the Mortgagee's QC Plan.

Mortgagees may use HUD's Neighborhood Watch Early Warning System (Neighborhood Watch) to assist with identifying patterns.

d. Fraud, Misrepresentation, and Other Findings

i. Definitions

(A) Finding

A Finding is a final determination of defect by the Mortgagee.

(B) Material Finding

In the context of mortgage origination and underwriting, a Finding is Material if disclosure of the Finding would have altered the Mortgagee's decision to approve the Mortgage or to endorse or seek endorsement from FHA for insurance of the Mortgage.

In the context of mortgage servicing, a Finding is Material if it has an adverse impact on the property and/or FHA.

(C) Mitigated Finding

In the context of mortgage origination and underwriting, a Finding has been Mitigated if the Mortgagee has adequately addressed the deficiencies underlying the Finding, and such deficiencies have been remedied so that the Mortgagee's decision to approve the Mortgage or to endorse or seek endorsement from FHA for insurance of the Mortgage is acceptable to FHA.

In the context of mortgage servicing, a Finding has been Mitigated if the Mortgagee has adequately addressed the deficiencies underlying the Finding, and such deficiencies have been remedied through mortgage servicing actions taken by the Mortgagee so there is no longer an adverse impact on the Property and/or FHA.

ii. Standard

The Mortgagee must monitor all FHA-insured Mortgages it originates, underwrites, services, or purchases, including those Mortgages originated by sponsored Third-Party Originators (TPO), for potential fraud, material misrepresentations, or other Material Findings.

Suspected instances of fraud, material misrepresentations, and other Material Findings must be investigated and documented by the Mortgagee's QC team, who must determine whether or not fraud or material misrepresentation actually occurred, or whether Material Findings exist.

iii. Internal Reporting to Senior Management

The Mortgagee's written QC Plan must contain a process for QC staff to report Findings identified through the QC process to senior management that complies with the following requirements.

(A) Time Frame for Reporting

Initial review Findings must be reported to the Mortgagee's senior management within 30 Days of completion of the initial Findings report. The Mortgagee's final report must be issued within 60 Days from the date the initial review Findings were reported to senior management.

(B) Corrective Action Plan

Mortgagee senior management must review and respond to each instance of fraud, material misrepresentation, or other Material Finding. The Mortgagee's final report must identify the corrective and curative actions being taken, the timetable for completion, and any planned follow-up activities.

(C) Follow Up

The Mortgagee must discuss all Findings with the responsible party(ies) in order to ensure corrective action and to prevent similar Findings from occurring in the future.

iv. External Reporting to FHA

(A) Fraud and Material Misrepresentation

The Mortgagee must report to FHA all Findings of fraud and material misrepresentation.

(B) Material Findings

The Mortgagee must report to FHA any Material Findings concerning the origination, underwriting, or servicing of a Mortgage that the Mortgagee is unable to mitigate.

(C) Mitigated Findings

Findings that do not involve fraud or material misrepresentation and were already Mitigated by the Mortgagee do not have to be reported to FHA.

(D) Time Frame for Reporting

The Mortgagee must report any Findings of fraud or material misrepresentation to FHA immediately.

The Mortgagee must report all other Material Findings that the Mortgagee is unable to mitigate to FHA no later than 90 Days after the completion of the initial Findings report.

(E) Corrective Action Plan

For all Findings that must be reported, the Mortgagee must identify what actions have been taken to attempt to mitigate each Finding, and report any planned or pending follow-up activities.

(F) Method of Reporting

The Mortgagee must use the Self-Report feature in the Loan Review System to report Findings to FHA. FHA may request supporting documentation, including the endorsement case binder, the QC report, and any other documentation necessary for FHA to fully evaluate the Finding.

(G) Suspected HUD Involvement

If the Mortgagee suspects HUD employees or contractors were involved in fraud or material misrepresentation, the Mortgagee must refer the matter directly to HUD's Office of Inspector General (OIG) through the HUD OIG website, by sending a written referral to the HUD OIG Hotline at 451 7th Street, SW, Room 8254, Washington, DC 20410, or by fax at (202) 708-4829.

v. Required Documentation

The Mortgagee must retain all QC review results, including all selection criteria, review documentation, Findings, and actions taken to mitigate Findings.

3. Loan Level Quality Control Program Requirements

Mortgagees must perform QC reviews of FHA-insured Mortgages the Mortgagee and its Affiliates originate, underwrite, or service.

a. Loan File Selection

i. Time Frame for Selection and Review

(A) Pre-Closing Reviews

Mortgagees must select Mortgages for pre-closing reviews during each month. Mortgages selected for pre-closing review must be reviewed after the Mortgage is approved by an FHA Direct Endorsement (DE) underwriter, and prior to closing.

(B) Post-Closing Reviews

Mortgagees must select Mortgages for post-closing reviews on a monthly basis. The selection must be comprised of loans closed in the prior one-month period. Mortgages selected must be reviewed within 60 Days from the end of the prior one-month period.

(C) Early Payment Default Reviews

Mortgagees must select Early Payment Defaults (EPD) for review on a monthly basis. EPDs selected must be reviewed within 60 Days from the end of the month in which the loan was selected.

(D) Servicing Reviews

Mortgagees must select Mortgages for servicing reviews on a monthly basis. Mortgages selected for servicing reviews must be reviewed within 60 Days from the end of the month in which the loan was selected.

ii. Scope

The Mortgagee's QC Plan must provide for the thorough evaluation of all Loan Administration functions for which the Mortgagee is responsible. The Mortgagee must expand the scope of the QC review as appropriate when fraud or patterns of deficiencies are uncovered.

iii. Sample Size Standard

The Mortgagee's QC Plan must provide for a combination of both pre-closing and post-closing reviews. The Mortgagee's QC Plan must provide for review of an appropriately sized, statistically valid sample that complies with the following.

The Mortgagee must calculate its FHA QC sample size separately for FHA-insured Mortgages it originates/underwrites versus services.

(A) 3,500 or Fewer FHA-Insured Mortgages per Year

Mortgagees that originate/underwrite or service 3,500 or fewer FHA-insured Mortgages per year must review a minimum of 10 percent of the FHA-insured Mortgages the Mortgagee originates/underwrites or services.

(B) More Than 3,500 FHA-Insured Mortgages per Year

Mortgagees that originate/underwrite or service more than 3,500 FHA Mortgages per year must review either 10 percent of the FHA-insured Mortgages the Mortgagee originates/underwrites or services, or a stratified random sample that is of sufficient size to ensure a 95 percent confidence level with a confidence interval not to exceed 2 percent on an annual basis, based on the defect rates for FHA-insured Mortgages recently reviewed by the Mortgagee.

For origination and underwriting reviews, the stratification should be based on mortgage product type and the source of origination. For servicing reviews, the stratification should be based on servicing functions in the following categories: general servicing; default management and loss mitigation; escrow administration; foreclosure administration; and claims.

(C) Percent of Pre- and Post-Closing Reviews

The Mortgagee's required FHA QC sample size must comply with the following balance of pre- and post-closing reviews:

Type of Review	% of FHA QC Sample Size
Pre-Closing Review	10% or less
Post-Closing Review	90% or more

(D) Exception

Mortgagees that close nine or fewer loans during the prior one-month period must select a minimum of one loan each month for pre-closing review.

iv. Sample Composition Standard

The Mortgagee's QC Plan must contain provisions to select FHA-insured Mortgages for review via random, EPDs, and discretionary sample selection methods that meet the following conditions. Only random and discretionary samples may be included in the sample size standard.

(A) Random

The Mortgagee must select FHA-insured Mortgages through the use of statistical sampling such that each of the Mortgagee's FHA-insured Mortgages has an equal chance of being selected. The random sample must be drawn from all of the Mortgagee's FHA-insured Mortgages, regardless of origination source or program type.

(B) Early Payment Defaults

(1) Definition

Early Payment Defaults (EPD) are all Mortgages that become 60 Days delinquent within the first six payments.

(2) Standard

The Mortgagee must review *all* EPDs underwritten by the Mortgagee, regardless of which Mortgagee services the Mortgage. Mortgagees may use Neighborhood Watch to assist with identifying EPDs.

(C) Discretionary

The Mortgagee must focus discretionary samples on programs, participants, or sources that represent a high level of risk, which may include disproportionate loan volume, default rates, new relationships, or concentration in soft market areas.

v. Required Documentation

The Mortgagee must document how the sample size and selections were determined.

b. Loan Sample Risk Assessment

i. Definition

A Loan Sample Risk Assessment is a method of evaluating loans selected for QC on the basis of the severity of the violations found during QC reviews.

ii. Standard

Mortgagees must establish a Loan Sample Risk Assessment methodology. At a minimum, the methodology must include the categories of risk described below.

The Mortgagee must compare one month's QC sample to previous QC samples in order to conduct trend analysis.

iii. Risk Categories

(A) Low Risk

No issues or minor variances were identified with the origination, underwriting, or servicing of the Mortgage.

(B) Moderate Risk

The records contained unresolved questions or missing documentation. Issues were identified pertaining to processing, documentation, or decisions made during Loan Administration, but none were material. Failure to resolve these issues created a moderate risk to the Mortgagee and to FHA.

(C) Material Risk

The issues identified during the review contained Material Findings which represent an unacceptable level of risk.

iv. Required Documentation

The Mortgagee must document the methodology used to establish the loan sample risk assessment system and conduct trend analysis.

c. Origination and Underwriting Loan File Compliance Review

i. Minimum Requirements

At a minimum, Mortgagees must include the following areas in their QC review to ensure they meet the requirements outlined in the Origination Through Post-Closing/Endorsement section of this *SF Handbook*:

Requirement	Pre-Closing Review	Post-Closing Review
Appraisal	✓	✓
Mortgage application, eligibility, and underwriting documents	✓	✓
Disclosures and legal compliance	✓	✓
Mortgage origination documents	✓	✓
Handling of mortgage documents	✓	✓
Borrower occupancy		✓
Credit reports	✓	✓
Outstanding debt obligations	✓	✓
Verifications of employment and deposit	✓	✓
Self-employed Borrowers	✓	✓
Borrower's source of funds	✓	✓
Underwriting accuracy and completeness, including compensating factors	✓	✓
Property Flipping restrictions	✓	✓
Prohibited restrictive covenants	✓	✓
Qualified Mortgage (QM)	✓	✓
Loan Estimate	✓	✓
Discrepancies in the loan file	✓	✓
Condition clearance	✓	✓
Closing procedures and documents		✓
Closing Disclosure or other similar legal document		✓

Requirement	Pre-Closing Review	Post-Closing Review
Pre-endorsement review		✓
Timely submission for insurance		✓

ii. Document Review and Re-verification

A Mortgagee's QC Plan for origination and underwriting must provide for the review and re-verification of the following information on all FHA-insured Mortgages selected for pre-closing and post-closing review, unless otherwise specified below.

(A) Credit Report

(1) Standard

For all post-closing reviews, the Mortgagee must obtain a new credit report in the same form as the original credit report used to approve the Mortgage, including a Residential Mortgage Credit Report (RMCR), a Tri-Merged Credit Report (TRMCR), or, when appropriate, a business credit report for each Borrower whose FHA-insured Mortgage is selected for review. The new credit report must comply with the credit report standards described in the Credit Report(s) section of this *SF Handbook*. The Mortgagee must compare the new credit report obtained with the original credit report used to approve the Mortgage, and determine whether any discrepancies exist between the reports that may adversely affect the Borrower's eligibility to qualify for an FHA-insured Mortgage.

If discrepancies exist between the credit reports that may adversely affect the Borrower's eligibility to qualify for an FHA-insured Mortgage, then the Mortgagee must obtain a second, full RMCR.

(2) Exceptions

A new credit report does not have to be obtained for pre-closing reviews, or for non-credit qualifying Streamline Refinances.

(3) Required Documentation

The Mortgagee must retain a copy of the new credit report(s).

(B) Income, Employment, Asset, and Housing Expense Information

(1) Re-verification

(a) Standard

For all post-closing reviews, the Mortgagee must analyze the validity and sufficiency of all documents contained in the loan file. The Mortgagee must re-verify, in writing or electronically if available, the following:

- employment;
- income;
- assets;
- gift funds;
- source of funds; and
- Mortgage Payments or rental payments.

If a written or electronic re-verification request is not returned to the Mortgagee, the Mortgagee must attempt a telephone re-verification. Re-verification is not required for pre-closing reviews.

(b) Required Documentation

The Mortgagee must retain evidence of the written, electronic, or telephone verification, and document the due diligence.

(2) Discrepancies

(a) Standard

The Mortgagee must evaluate all discrepancies to ensure that the original documents (except blanket verification releases) were completed before being signed, were as represented, were not handled by Interested Parties, and that all corrections were proper and initialed. All conflicting information in the original documentation must be resolved with the underwriter. Discrepancies in documentation discovered during pre-closing reviews must be resolved prior to closing.

(b) Required Documentation

The Mortgagee must document any discrepancies and retain copies of information used to resolve such discrepancies.

(C) Appraisals

(1) Standard

(a) Property Appraisal Reviews

The Mortgagee must conduct a review of the property appraisal for all FHA-insured Mortgages chosen for a QC review.

At a minimum, Mortgagees must include the following areas in their QC review of the property appraisal:
- the appraisal data;
- the validity of the comparables;
- the value conclusion (as required by FHA guidance);
- any changes made by the underwriter; and
- the overall quality of the appraisal.

(b) Field Reviews

The Mortgagee must perform targeted field reviews on 10 percent of the FHA-insured Mortgages selected for the monthly post-closing QC sample, as well as on all EPDs. The Mortgagee must select Mortgages for field reviews based on the factors used for discretionary targeting, as well as the following characteristics:
- property complaints received from Borrowers;
- discrepancies found during QC reviews;
- large adjustments or variances to value;
- comparable sales more than six months old;
- excessive distances from comparables to the subject Property;
- repetitive sales activity for the subject Property;
- investor-sold Properties;
- identity-of-interest conflicts between Borrower and seller;
- seller identity differs from owner of record;
- HUD Real Estate Owned (REO) sales financed with an FHA-insured Mortgage;
- vacant Properties; and
- soft markets.

Field reviews must be performed by Appraisers listed on FHA's Roster of Appraisers.

(2) Exceptions

Property appraisal and field reviews do not have to be performed for Streamline Refinances, or for HUD REO sales chosen for QC review where the Mortgagee was not required to order a new appraisal for a property financed with an FHA-insured Mortgage.

Field reviews do not have to be performed for pre-closing reviews.

(3) Required Documentation

The Mortgagee must retain all QC review results, including all selection criteria, review documentation, Findings, and actions taken to mitigate Findings.

d. Quality Control Reviews of Specialized Mortgage Programs

i. Standard

QC reviews of specialized mortgage programs (e.g., 203(k), Home Equity Conversion Mortgages (HECM), Energy Efficient Mortgages (EEM), etc.) must monitor compliance with FHA requirements specific to those programs.

ii. Required Documentation

The Mortgagee must retain all QC review results, including all selection criteria, review documentation, Findings, and actions taken to mitigate Findings.

e. Servicing Loan File Compliance Review

i. Minimum Requirements

Mortgagees must review all aspects of their servicing operations, including a review of subserviced Mortgages and activities as they relate to FHA-insured Mortgages, to guarantee that all FHA servicing and loss mitigation requirements are being met. At a minimum, Mortgagees must include the following elements in their QC review to ensure they meet the requirements outlined in the Servicing and Loss Mitigation and Claims and Disposition sections of this *SF Handbook*:
- servicing records
- document retention and legibility
- non-discrimination policies
- Borrower requests, complaints, and escalated cases
- fees
- transfer of servicing notification and records
- documentation of purchased or acquired Mortgages
- mortgage record changes
- escrow account functions
- force-placed insurance
- prepayments
- MIP
- early default intervention

- loss mitigation
- collection activities
- reporting to credit repositories
- home retention option priority order (waterfall)
- home disposition options
- claims for insurance benefits
- Claims Without Conveyance of Title (CWCOT)
- foreclosure proceedings
- property preservation and conveyance
- deficiency judgments
- Single Family Default Monitoring System (SFDMS) reporting
- Adjustable Rate Mortgages (ARM)
- assumptions
- Presidentially-Declared Major Disaster Areas (PDMDA)
- Hawaiian Home Land Mortgages (Section 247 Mortgages)
- Section 184 Indian housing loans
- Section 222 Mortgages
- Good Neighbor Next Door
- Servicemembers Civil Relief Act (SCRA)
- Section 235 Mortgages
- Section 203(k) Mortgages
- servicing of HECM

f. Ineligible Participants

i. Origination and Underwriting Reviews

(A) Standard

The Mortgagee must verify that none of the participants in the mortgage transactions reviewed were debarred, suspended, under an LDP for the FHA program and jurisdiction, or otherwise ineligible to participate in an FHA transaction. This includes participants in an assumption transaction.

Participants in a mortgage transaction may include, but are not limited to, the:
- seller (excluding the seller of a Principal Residence)
- listing and selling real estate agent
- loan originator
- loan processor
- underwriter
- Appraiser
- 203(k) Consultant
- Closing Agent
- title company

The Mortgagee must verify participant eligibility using the SAM (www.sam.gov) Excluded Parties List, the LDP list, and NMLS, as applicable.

(B) Required Documentation

The Mortgagee must maintain documentation that supports each participant's eligibility.

ii. Servicing Reviews

(A) Standard

The Mortgagee must verify that none of the participants in the servicing transactions reviewed were debarred, suspended, under an LDP for the FHA program and jurisdiction, or otherwise ineligible to participate in an FHA transaction. This includes participants in a loss mitigation transaction.

Participants in a servicing transaction may include, but are not limited to:
- Borrowers applying for an FHA-HAMP Loss Mitigation Option
- underwriters
- real estate brokers
- Closing Agent
- title company
- employees of the Mortgagee, or Affiliates participating in HUD programs for or on behalf of the Mortgagee, who have influence or control over the evaluation, approval, or outcome of the servicing loss mitigation, or claims transaction.

The Mortgagee must verify participant eligibility using the SAM (www.sam.gov) Excluded Parties List and the LDP list, as applicable.

(B) Required Documentation

The Mortgagee must maintain copies of each participant's eligibility verification print-outs.

4. Data Integrity

a. Standard

The Mortgagee's QC program must include a review of the completeness and accuracy of the information obtained for each Mortgage for all aspects of the Loan Administration process for which a QC sample is selected. The Mortgagee must report all Findings internally to senior management, and to FHA where appropriate.

i. Origination and Underwriting Information

For origination and underwriting, the review must validate all data elements submitted through the Automated Underwriting System (AUS), Technology Open To Approved Lenders (TOTAL) Mortgage Scorecard, and FHA Connection (FHAC), and validate that documentation exists in the loan file to support all data used to underwrite the Mortgage.

ii. Endorsement and Insurance Information

For endorsement, the review must validate all data elements submitted through FHAC, and validate that documentation exists in the loan file to support all data used to endorse and insure the Mortgage.

iii. Servicing Information

For servicing, the review must validate mortgage information submitted through FHAC, SFDMS, or Home Equity Reverse Mortgage Information Technology (HERMIT), as applicable.

b. Required Documentation

The Mortgagee must retain the results of each review and any corrective actions taken as a result of review Findings.

B. QUALITY CONTROL OF OTHER PARTICIPANTS

1. Direct Endorsement Underwriter

The Direct Endorsement (DE) underwriter is not required to perform any individual Quality Control (QC) reviews. The DE underwriter must review any finding made in the Mortgagee's QC reviews performed in accordance with the Loan Level Quality Control Program Requirements concerning loans underwritten by the DE underwriter.

2. Nonprofits and Governmental Entities

a. Quality Control Plan Overview

i. Definition

A Quality Control (QC) Plan outlines the processes and procedures used by the nonprofit to monitor its compliance with FHA nonprofit program guidelines.

A Finding refers to a final determination of defect by the nonprofit agency.

ii. Standard

The nonprofit must develop and implement a QC Plan that explains its internal and external audit and monitoring procedures and must fully comply with the requirements in the <u>Doing Business with FHA – Nonprofits</u> section of this *SF Handbook*. The QC Plan must include the nonprofit's reports, any reports of fraud, corrective action plans, and review procedures.

The nonprofit must maintain and update its QC Plan as needed to ensure it remains fully compliant with all applicable FHA requirements.

iii. Required Documentation

The nonprofit must retain all QC review results, including all selection criteria, review documentation, Findings, and corrective actions taken to mitigate or resolve Findings. This documentation must be maintained for a minimum of three years. The nonprofit must make all documentation relating to its QC Plan available to FHA at any time upon request.

b. Quality Control Plan Findings and Corrective Action

i.   Records of Quality Control Findings

The nonprofit must maintain records of QC Findings and actions taken, periodic reports, and review procedures. Reports must identify areas of deficiency, including the agency's policies and procedures, errors and omissions, and unacceptable patterns or trends. All violations of law or regulation, any known false statement, or fraud or program abuse must be reported to FHA, the Office of Inspector General (OIG), and the appropriate federal, state or local law enforcement agency.

ii. Corrective Action

The nonprofit must maintain a copy of the corrective actions taken when Findings are discovered. Findings that result in changes to managerial staff or expose any deviance to previously approved processes must be brought to the attention of FHA upon discovery.

c. Fraud, Misrepresentation, and Other Findings

i.   Standard

The nonprofit must take prompt, effective, and corrective measures to investigate and document suspected instances of fraud, misrepresentation, and other related Findings.

ii. Internal Reporting to Senior Management

The nonprofit's QC Plan must contain a process for its QC staff to promptly report and document Findings delivered to senior management. Nonprofit staff must report Findings to senior management no more than 15 business days from the date of discovery.

iii. External Reporting to FHA

The nonprofit's senior management must contact the Program Support Division at the Jurisdictional Homeownership Center (HOC) to submit QC Findings. HUD will review the Findings and determine the appropriate course of action.

3. Real Estate Brokers

HUD's Asset Manager (AM) and Homeownership Center (HOC) staff are responsible for quality control and monitoring procedures for HUD-Registered Real Estate Brokers.

4. Closing Agents

HUD's AM and HOC staff are responsible for quality control and monitoring procedures for Closing Agents.

5. Additional Other Participants

RESERVED FOR FUTURE USE

This section is reserved for future use, and until such time, FHA-approved Mortgagees and Other Participants must continue to comply with all applicable law and existing Handbooks, Mortgagee Letters, Notices and outstanding guidance applicable to their participation in FHA programs.

C. MORTGAGEE MONITORING

1. Cooperation with HUD Investigations and Reviews

Mortgagees must fully cooperate with any investigation(s) or review(s) undertaken by HUD. Mortgagees must make all Corporate Officers and employees available for interviews and provide information and documents requested by HUD in the format and time frame requested.

2. Institutional Mortgagee Monitoring

a. Title I Lender Monitoring Reviews

RESERVED FOR FUTURE USE

This section is reserved for future use, and until such time, FHA-approved Mortgagees and Title I Lenders must continue to comply with all applicable law and existing Handbooks, Mortgagee Letters, Notices and outstanding guidance applicable to their participation in FHA programs.

b. Title II Mortgagee Monitoring Reviews

i. Notice

FHA provides Mortgagees with notice prior to FHA monitoring reviews. Such notice may be transmitted via email to the Mortgagee's administrative contact, which is described in the Doing Business with FHA section of this *SF Handbook*. The Mortgagee may access the Loan Review System for detailed information about such monitoring review.

ii. Production of Loan Files and Records

Mortgagees must have the files requested by FHA available for review. The Mortgagee must provide all records related to the loans selected for review, including any and all files, whether hard copy or stored, in the Mortgagee's systems that include data or information on the specific loans identified.

iii. Scope

FHA will, in its sole discretion, determine the scope of any monitoring review. FHA may conduct limited reviews of a Mortgagee's origination, underwriting, and servicing of FHA-insured Single Family Mortgages, or more comprehensive reviews that include not just the Mortgagee's files, records, and practices, but also the Mortgagee's overall operations and policies with respect to Mortgagee relationships, quality control and risk management, escrow administration, wholesale Mortgages, and certain FHA product lines.

iv. Findings

At the conclusion of a monitoring review, FHA will document any identified Findings in the Loan Review System and will specify the remedies and response that are required from the Mortgagee. For reviews of mortgages conducted as part of a monitoring review, results will be documented in accordance with the Title II Loan Reviews/Findings section of this *SF Handbook*.

c. Servicer Tier Ranking System II

i. Definition

The Tier Ranking System (TRS) II is a methodology for measuring a Mortgagee's performance in complying with HUD's Loss Mitigation Program.

ii. Standard

TRS II evaluates Mortgagees' overall performance in Delinquent mortgage servicing, based on the following elements:
- foreclosure prevention;
- Re-Defaults;
- SFDMS reporting; and
- loss mitigation engagement.

See TRS II – Scorecard Calculation Methodology – Servicer Narrative for complete instructions.

iii. Who Will be Scored

(A) Eligibility

HUD will score Mortgagees meeting the following criteria under TRS II:
- approved to service Single Family Mortgages;
- Mortgagee approval status is active; and
- the Mortgagee is the Mortgagee of record for a seriously Delinquent portfolio of five Mortgages or more, as reflected in Neighborhood Watch for the last month in the scoring quarter.

(B) Opt-Out Option

A Mortgagee may opt out of being rated if:
- the Mortgagee meets the eligibility criteria above; and
- the Mortgagee has a seriously Delinquent portfolio of between 5 and 25 Mortgages, as reflected in Neighborhood Watch for the last month of the scoring quarter.

(1) Use of Scores

HUD will continue to issue TRS II Scorecards to all eligible Mortgagees; HUD will use scores for Mortgagees who have exercised the opt-out option for informational purposes and HUD reviews and metrics only.

(2) Publication

HUD will not make available on a public website the scores of Mortgagees who have opted out of scoring.

(3) Loss Mitigation Financial Incentives

Mortgagees who have opted out of scoring will not be eligible for increased loss mitigation financial incentives for the following calendar year.

(C) Process for Opting Out

To request to opt out of scoring, the Mortgagee must submit a request to NSC via email to sfdatarequests@hud.gov, no later than October 31 of each calendar year for which the Mortgagee requests to opt out of scoring. The Mortgagee must include in the request:
- "TRS II Opt-Out" in the subject line of their email; and
- their Mortgagee five-digit ID number.

Once NSC verifies the Mortgagee's status, the Mortgagee will receive a confirmation email that the Mortgagee has opted out of scoring for the fiscal year.

iv. TRS II Elements

There are four elements that comprise TRS II:
- Foreclosure Prevention: evaluates a Mortgagee's foreclosure initiation actions, time frames, and intervention practices;
- Re-Defaults: evaluates the loss mitigation performance after a permanent Home Retention Loss Mitigation Option is utilized by the Mortgagee;
- SFDMS Reporting: determines a Mortgagee's compliance with Default reporting regulations; and
- Loss Mitigation Engagement: measures a Mortgagee's loss mitigation attempts and utilization of permanent Loss Mitigation Options.

Mortgagees may calculate their own TRS II scores by following the instructions provided in the TRS II – Scorecard Calculation Methodology – Servicer Narrative.

v. Extra Credit

The Mortgagee may receive extra credit added to their final fiscal year end score by attending, participating in, and/or completing delinquent servicing training pursuant to the attendance and completion requirements in the TRS II – Scorecard Calculation Methodology – Servicer Narrative.

vi. Scores, Grades and Tiers

HUD evaluates each scoring element separately, based on activity for each month in the quarter, and then averages the elements for a quarterly score.

HUD will provide Mortgagees with a TRS II Scorecard each quarter, along with a corresponding letter grade and tier ranking. HUD will average quarterly scores to produce a final annual fiscal year score and grade.

Final Fiscal Score	Assigned Grade	Corresponding Tier
90.00% - 100.00+%	A	1
80.00% - 89.99%	B	2
70.00% - 79.99%	C	3
60.00% - 69.99%	D	3
59.99% or Less	F	4

vii. Notification of TRS II Scores

Mortgagees will receive quarterly TRS II Scorecards consisting of the Mortgagee's scores, grades, and Tier via email after the conclusion of each fiscal year quarter.

HUD will only send hard copy letters containing scores, grades, and Tiers if the NSC cannot reach the Mortgagee electronically. See the TRS II – Scorecard Calculation Methodology – Servicer Narrative for information on how to request electronic distribution.

viii. Public Availability of Scores and Grades

All scored Mortgagees, except those which have chosen to opt out, may have their names and scores published on HUD's Tier Ranking System website at the close of each calendar year, after all appeals have been evaluated and after Mortgagees that have submitted appeals have been notified of the results.

ix. Appeals

(A) Basis of Appeal

The only basis for an appeal by the Mortgagee receiving an "F"/Tier 4 is disagreement with the data used by HUD to calculate the Mortgagee's grade. If HUD determines that the Mortgagee's "F"/Tier 4 grade rating was based on incorrect or incomplete data, HUD will recalculate the Mortgagee's performance and will provide a corrected score.

(B) Time Frame

Mortgagees receiving a grade of "F"/Tier 4 may appeal their final score no later than 30 Days after the issue date of the final fiscal year grade.

(C) Process

The Mortgagee must submit the appeal to HUD's Deputy Assistant Secretary for Single Family Housing or their designee and request an informal HUD conference.

x. Increased Incentives

HUD will use TRS II to determine those Mortgagees earning "A"/Tier 1 scores and may therefore qualify for increased loss mitigation financial incentives for the following calendar year.

3. Loan Level Monitoring

a. Title I Loan Reviews

> **RESERVED FOR FUTURE USE**
>
> This section is reserved for future use, and until such time, FHA-approved Mortgagees and Title I Lenders must continue to comply with all applicable law and existing Handbooks, Mortgagee Letters, Notices and outstanding guidance applicable to their participation in FHA programs.

b. Title II Loan Reviews

i. Notice

FHA will notify Mortgagees with Lender Insurance (LI) authority daily via email of its intent to review the Mortgagee's LI case binders. Mortgagees that do not have LI authority can view loans selected for review in the Loan Review System or on the Insurance Application screen in FHAC.

ii. Production of Case Binders

The Mortgagee must provide the requested case binder(s) within 10 business days of FHA's transmittal of a request.

Failure of a Mortgagee with LI authority to submit requested case binders may result in suspension of the Mortgagee's LI authority.

iii. Scope

Title II loan reviews consist of, but are not limited to, the Mortgagee's compliance with FHA guidelines and an assessment of whether the Mortgage represents an unacceptable level of risk to FHA.

iv. Findings

FHA will document the results of each review in the Loan Review System and will use its Single Family Housing Loan Quality Assessment Methodology (Defect Taxonomy) to identify and capture detailed information about any Findings related to compliance with FHA underwriting requirements. FHA will specify the remedies and response that are required from the Mortgagee. The Mortgagee must respond to any Material Findings using the functions provided in the Loan Review System.

D. MONITORING OF OTHER PARTICIPANTS

1. Appraisers

FHA may perform periodic reviews of the work performed by FHA Roster Appraisers to ensure compliance with FHA requirements. FHA Roster Appraisers must provide any additional information requested by FHA to assist in properly evaluating the work performed.

2. 203(k) Consultants

FHA may perform periodic reviews of the work performed by 203(k) Consultants to ensure compliance with FHA requirements. 203(k) Consultants must provide any additional information requested by monitors to assist them in properly evaluating the work performed.

3. Nonprofits and Governmental Entities

a. Monitoring of Governmental Entities and HUD-approved Nonprofits

FHA monitors Governmental Entities and HUD-approved Nonprofits that participate in FHA's nonprofit programs as part of its ongoing QC activities to ensure compliance with FHA requirements. The HOC conducts remote and on-site reviews for monitoring purposes.

i. Notice

FHA will notify Governmental Entities and HUD-approved Nonprofits of its intent to conduct a review of their Affordable Housing Program Plans (AHPP) 30 Days prior to any review.

ii. Scope

FHA will, at its sole discretion, determine the scope of any monitoring review. These reviews may include, without limitation, a review of projects under development, the agency's internal control procedures, and adherence to the goals of the approved program.

iii. Production of Files and Records

Nonprofits must have the files requested by FHA available for review. The HOC may request documentation regarding the nonprofit's progress in implementing its AHPP(s).

The HOC will make review requests in writing, providing the nonprofit with 30 Days to respond and accommodate such requests.

iv. Findings

Following the monitoring review, FHA will discuss Findings with the Governmental Entity or HUD-approved Nonprofit. FHA will provide notification of identified Findings, if any, and specify the remedies and response that is required.

b. Monitoring of HUD Homes Participants

FHA's review and monitoring activity will include a review of the AHPP and verification that HUD Homes purchased at a discount of 10 percent or greater are sold to persons at or below the applicable median income. FHA will review and monitor the program participant's Individual Property File and Net Development Costs (NDC). The NDCs are used to review program compliance and profit margins.

FHA will also monitor to ensure that savings under the HUD Homes program are passed on to Low- to Moderate-Income Borrowers.

The HOC may request access to properties under development or otherwise a part of the nonprofit agency's AHPP.

Additional Documentation Required for Review

The Governmental Entity or HUD-approved Nonprofit must have the Individual Property File and the following additional documentation available for FHA staff completing a review:
- bank statements and monthly reconciliations for the last two years;
- proof of payment documentation for the last two years;
- a current financial statement and evidence of funding sources;
- rental payment history and evidence of funding sources;
- general ledger entries for the last two years;
- contractor licenses and qualifications records;
- a Marketing Plan and evidence of marketing efforts;
- an AHPP; and
- a QC Plan and monitoring reports.

c. Monitoring FHA Mortgagor Participants

FHA reviews the nonprofit's mortgage performance under the program. FHA will monitor foreclosure rates, Default and evidence of fraud.

d. Monitoring of Secondary Financing Program Participants

FHA will review second lien performance. HUD-approved Nonprofit Mortgagees must identify second liens and their performance.

Additional Documentation Required for Review

Upon request, the Governmental Entity or nonprofit must provide copies of fully executed Closing Disclosures or similar legal documents, and recorded secondary financing documents.

4. Real Estate Brokers

HUD-Registered Real Estate Brokers will be monitored by the AM, who will report any deficiency or noncompliance issues to HUD for further investigation and/or action that may result in deactivation of the HUD-Registered Real Estate Broker's Name and Address Identification Number (NAID).

5. Closing Agents

Closing Agents will be monitored by the AM, who will report any deficiency or noncompliance issues to HUD for further investigation and/or action that may result in deactivation of the Closing Agent's Title ID number.

6. Additional Other Participants

RESERVED FOR FUTURE USE

This section is reserved for future use, and until such time, FHA-approved Mortgagees and Other Participants must continue to comply with all applicable law and existing Handbooks, Mortgagee Letters, Notices and outstanding guidance applicable to their participation in FHA programs.

E. ENFORCEMENT

The following provides general information about the processes and procedures normally employed by FHA in its enforcement activities. The following is provided for informational purposes only and does not represent a waiver of any authority of FHA, HUD, or the federal government to carry out enforcement activities to the full extent of its authorities in connection with FHA's Single Family programs.

Handbook 4000.1
Effective Date: 09/14/2015 | Last Revised: 07/10/2019
*Refer to the online version of SF Handbook 4000.1 for specific sections' effective dates

947

1. Referrals for Non-Compliance

FHA may refer any finding for administrative or other enforcement action in its discretion. Referrals may be made to any appropriate body, including:

- HUD's Mortgagee Review Board (MRB);
- HUD's Office of Fair Housing and Equal Opportunity (FHEO) (fair lending issues);
- HUD's Departmental Enforcement Center (DEC) (suspension or debarment actions);
- HUD's OIG (suspected fraud or illegal activities);
- the Consumer Financial Protection Bureau (CFPB);
- the Department of Justice; and/or
- state licensing agencies (e.g., Secretary of State, Real Estate Commissioner, Appraisal Review Board, Department of Banking, Bar Association, etc.).

2. Employee Improprieties Attributed to the Mortgagee

Criminal, fraudulent, or other seriously improper conduct by an officer, director, shareholder, partner, employee, or other individual associated with a Mortgagee may be attributed to the Mortgagee with which the individual is connected when the improper conduct occurred in connection to the individual's performance of duties for or on behalf of the Mortgagee, or with the Mortgagee's knowledge, approval, or acquiescence. Such impropriety may result in appropriate administrative sanctions against the Mortgagee.

3. Program Office Actions and Sanctions

FHA's Office of Single Family Housing is authorized to take the following enforcement actions against Mortgagees that do not comply with FHA requirements.

a. Actions and Sanctions Against Mortgagees

i. Probation of Title II Direct Endorsement Authority

FHA may place a Mortgagee on DE probation for a specified period of time for the purpose of evaluating the Mortgagee's compliance with the requirements of the DE Program. The scope of the probation depends upon the seriousness of the problems and deficiencies exhibited by the Mortgagee. For additional information on this authority, see 24 CFR § 203.3(d)(1). This action is separate and apart from probation imposed by the MRB.

(A) Scope

(1) Training

The Mortgagee's underwriter, or other technical staff, may be required to attend training sessions, as appropriate.

(2) Title II Loan Reviews

FHA may increase the percentage of the Mortgagee's cases subject to Title II loan reviews.

(3) Mortgagee Audit and Monitoring Review

FHA may require the Mortgagee to perform a review or audit of its underwriting processes, or to hire an independent third party to assess the Mortgagee's operational controls and systems, and report the results to FHA. FHA may also conduct an on-site monitoring review of the Mortgagee.

(4) Quality Control Plan

FHA may require the Mortgagee to make changes to its QC Plan.

(5) Test Case Phase Review Status

FHA may place a Mortgagee back in Test Case Phase review status and subject the Mortgagee's cases to technical underwriting reviews and Firm Commitment processing prior to endorsement (see Supplemental Mortgagee Authorities).

(a) Time Frame

Test Case Phase review status continues until the Mortgagee corrects its underwriting deficiencies or until the Mortgagee's DE approval is withdrawn.

(b) Cause

A return to Test Case Phase review status may result from, but is not limited to, the following circumstances:
- final Title II loan review results that demonstrate a Mortgagee's failure to follow FHA requirements;
- a pattern of fraud identified by FHA, of which the Mortgagee was aware, or should have been aware; or
- the results of on-site or other reviews of the Mortgagee.

(6) Additional Elements

FHA may impose additional elements of probation reasonably related to the Mortgagee's underlying violations that allow FHA to monitor the Mortgagee and assist FHA with bringing the Mortgagee into compliance with FHA regulations.

(B) Notice

FHA will send a written notice of probation to the Mortgagee. The probation notice will list the violations that precipitated the probation and explain the elements being applied to the Mortgagee's probation.

(C) Effective Date

Probation is effective immediately upon the receipt of the notice of probation by the Mortgagee.

ii. Withdrawal of Title II Direct Endorsement Authority

FHA may withdraw the DE authority of any Mortgagee that demonstrates a pattern or practice of failing to comply with FHA underwriting guidelines or program requirements. This action is separate and apart from the termination action described in the Credit Watch Termination section.

(A) Scope

FHA may terminate a Mortgagee's approval to participate in the DE Program in a particular jurisdiction or on a nationwide basis.

(B) Notice and Appeal

FHA will provide the Mortgagee with written notice of the proposed withdrawal that identifies the grounds for the action and advises the Mortgagee of its right to an informal conference.

(1) Informal Conference

FHA will expeditiously arrange for a conference where the Mortgagee may present information and argument in opposition to the proposed withdrawal. The Mortgagee may be represented by counsel.

(2) Determination

After consideration of the material presented, FHA will issue a decision in writing stating whether the proposed termination is rescinded, modified, or affirmed.

(3) Appeal and Final Agency Action

The Mortgagee may appeal the decision to the Deputy Assistant Secretary (DAS) for Single Family Housing or his or her designee. A decision by the DAS for Single Family Housing or his or her designee constitutes final agency action.

iii. Credit Watch Termination of Title II Mortgagees

HUD may terminate a Mortgagee's authority to originate or underwrite FHA-insured Single Family Mortgages in any geographic area where the Mortgagee has an excessive rate of early defaults and claims in accordance with the Credit Watch Termination regulations at 24 CFR § 202.3(c)(2). Credit Watch Termination is separate and apart from any action that may be taken by the MRB.

(A) Frequency and Scope

FHA reviews the default and claim rate of FHA-insured Single Family Mortgages on a quarterly basis. FHA compares the rate of each participating Mortgagee with the rates of other Mortgagees in the same geographic area. The review is limited to Mortgages with an amortization date within the preceding 24 months.

(B) Cause

FHA may terminate the origination or underwriting authority of any Mortgagee whose default and claim rate exceeds both the national default and claim rate and 200 percent of the default and claim rate within the geographic area served by a HUD field office.

(C) Notice and Appeal

FHA will issue a Proposed Credit Watch Termination Notice to the Mortgagee prior to terminating the Mortgagee's approval. The Mortgagee may appeal the proposed termination by submitting a written request for an informal conference with the DAS for Single Family Housing or its designee within 30 Days of receipt of the Notice.

(1) Informal Conference

The Mortgagee or its representative may make an oral and/or written presentation to oppose the proposed termination. FHA will only consider presentations that specifically address relevant mitigating factors and present facts and circumstances to explain the Mortgagee's poor performance.

(2) Mitigating Factors

FHA will consider relevant mitigating factors in deciding whether to terminate a Mortgagee's origination and/or underwriting authority.

(3) Determination

After the informal conference, FHA will make a determination whether to sustain or withdraw the termination. FHA will notify the Mortgagee of its decision in writing via a Final Notice of Determination. If sustained, the termination will not take effect until the Mortgagee receives the Final Notice.

(4) Waiver of Appeal

If a Mortgagee does not request an informal conference within 30 Days of receiving the Proposed Credit Watch Termination Notice, the Mortgagee has waived its appeal and its authority will be terminated 60 Days from the date of the Proposed Credit Watch Termination Notice without further notice from HUD.

(D) Effect of Termination

A Mortgagee whose authority has been terminated under Credit Watch is prohibited from originating or underwriting FHA-insured Single Family Mortgages within the area of the HUD field office(s) listed in the Notice. The Mortgagee's general FHA approval and supplemental authorities (see Supplemental Mortgagee Authorities) remain unaffected.

(1) Case Status

(a) Definition

An Approved Mortgage is a Mortgage underwritten and approved by a DE underwriter, or covered by a Firm Commitment issued by HUD.

(b) Standard

During the period of credit watch termination, FHA will not endorse any Mortgage originated by the Mortgagee, unless prior to the date of termination a Firm Commitment has been issued by HUD relating to any such Mortgage or a Direct Endorsement (DE) underwriter approved the Mortgage.

Mortgages that closed or were approved before the termination became effective may be endorsed. Cases at earlier stages of processing cannot be submitted for insurance by the terminated Mortgagee. However, the cases may be transferred for completion of processing and underwriting to another Mortgagee authorized to underwrite FHA-insured Mortgages in that area.

(2) Public Notice

HUD will publish a list of Mortgagees who have had their authority terminated in the Federal Register and on HUD's website with a general explanation of the cause and effect of the termination.

(E) Reinstatement

(1) Waiting Period

A terminated Mortgagee may request to have its authority reinstated no earlier than six months after the effective date of the termination.

(2) Independent Review

The Mortgagee must obtain an independent review of the terminated area's operation and mortgage origination or underwriting, specifically including the FHA-insured Mortgages cited in the termination notice. The analysis must identify the underlying cause for the Mortgagee's high default and claim rate. The review must be conducted and issued by an independent Certified Public Accountant (CPA) qualified to perform audits under Government Auditing Standards as set forth by the General Accounting Office.

(3) Corrective Action Plan

The Mortgagee must submit a corrective action plan to address each of the issues identified in the CPA's report, along with evidence that the plan has been implemented. FHA reserves the right to impose additional requirements for reinstatement.

(4) Application for Reinstatement

The application for reinstatement must be submitted through the Lender Electronic Assessment Portal (LEAP). The application must be accompanied by the CPA's report and the corrective action plan.

iv. Suspension or Termination of Title II Lender Insurance Authority

(A) Definition

The Lender Insurance (LI) Compare Ratio is the percentage of Mortgages underwritten by the Mortgagee that are in claim or default status compared with the percentage of Mortgages in claim or default status for all Mortgagees operating in the same state(s) over the preceding two-year period.

(B) Scope

FHA monitors Mortgagees participating in the LI program whose LI Compare Ratios exceed 150 percent.

(C) Cause

FHA may immediately terminate or temporarily suspend a Mortgagee's LI authority for any cause set forth in 24 CFR § 203.4(d).

(D) Notice and Appeal

FHA will provide written notice to any Mortgagee whose LI authority has been suspended or terminated. Mortgagees may appeal the suspension or termination by requesting an informal conference with the DAS for Single Family Housing or its designee.

(1) Informal Conference

The suspension or termination letter will provide the address to where the request for an informal conference may be sent, and the time frame for the informal conference. The informal conference must be requested in writing within 30 Days of the notice of suspension or termination.

(2) Determination

The DAS or the designee will issue a decision in writing after the informal conference to either affirm the suspension or termination, or reinstate the Mortgagee's LI authority. This decision represents a final agency action pursuant to section 256(d) of the National Housing Act (12 U.S.C. § 1715z-21(d)) and is not subject to further appeal or judicial review.

(3) Waiver of Appeal

If a Mortgagee does not request an informal conference within 30 Days of receiving the suspension or termination letter, the Mortgagee has waived its right to appeal.

(E) Effective Date

The suspension or termination of the Mortgagee's LI authority is effective immediately upon the receipt of the notice by the Mortgagee.

(F) Effect of Suspension or Termination

A Mortgagee must submit every case binder to HUD for a pre-endorsement review and endorsement consideration.

A Mortgagee's DE authority is not affected by the suspension or termination of its LI authority. Mortgagees who have had their LI authority suspended or terminated may continue to underwrite and close FHA Mortgages without prior review by HUD.

(G) Reinstatement

(1) Waiting Period

A Mortgagee whose LI authority has been terminated is prohibited from applying for reinstatement of its LI authority for six months from the date of termination.

(2) Claim and Default Rate

At the time of the application for reinstatement, the Mortgagee must have unconditional DE authority and a two-year claim and default rate that does not exceed 150 percent of the aggregate claim and default rate for the states in which it underwrote Mortgages.

(3) Application for Reinstatement

Applications for reinstatement of LI authority must be submitted to FHA through LEAP. The application must include:

- a copy of the *Acknowledgment of Terms and Conditions for LI* page from FHAC signed by an authorized official registered with HUD;
- a corrective action plan identifying the changes in internal policies and procedures that address the issues that resulted in the termination of LI authority; and
- documentation evidencing that the Mortgagee has implemented the corrective action plan.

b. Loan Level Actions and Sanctions

FHA has the authority to pursue loan level actions and sanctions reasonably related to a Mortgagee's underlying violations.

4. Mortgagee Review Board Actions and Sanctions

The MRB is authorized to impose civil money penalties and take administrative action against any FHA-approved Mortgagee that does not comply with HUD and FHA statutory, regulatory, and any Handbook requirements, the Real Estate Settlement Procedures Act (RESPA), or the non-discrimination requirements of the ECOA, the Fair Housing Act, or Executive Order 11063 on Equal Opportunity in Housing.

a. Actions and Sanctions

The following actions and sanctions may be imposed by the MRB:

- a letter of reprimand;
- probation;
- suspension;
- withdrawal of FHA approval; and
- civil money penalties.

The MRB may also enter into settlement agreements with non-complying Mortgagees.

The following are general descriptions of the types of actions and sanctions that may be taken by the MRB and are for informational purposes only. The specific requirements for and procedures applicable to these actions are set forth in sections 202(c) and 536 of the National

Housing Act (12 U.S.C. §§ 1708(c) and 1735f-14), and Parts 25 and 30 of Title 24 of the Code of Federal Regulations (24 CFR Parts 25 and 30).

i. Letter of Reprimand

The MRB may issue a letter of reprimand to inform a Mortgagee of its violation of FHA requirements. A letter of reprimand is effective upon receipt of the letter by the Mortgagee.

(A) Case Status

A letter of reprimand has no impact on the Mortgagee's authority to originate, underwrite, or service FHA-insured Mortgages.

(B) Duration

There is no time duration associated with a letter of reprimand.

(C) Appeal

The Mortgagee has no right to appeal a letter of reprimand within HUD.

ii. Probation

The MRB may place a Mortgagee on probation for violation of FHA requirements. The MRB will specify the scope, terms, and conditions of the probation, which are designed to allow FHA to monitor the Mortgagee and assist FHA with bringing the Mortgagee into compliance with FHA regulations.

(A) Case Status

Unless specified in the terms of the probation, a Mortgagee on probation retains its origination, underwriting, and servicing authorities, as applicable.

(B) Duration

The MRB may place a Mortgagee on probation for a period of up to six months.

(C) Appeal

The Mortgagee has the right to appeal a probation action in accordance with the provisions of 24 CFR Parts 25 and 26.

iii. Suspension

Suspension is a temporary measure that is applied to a Mortgagee when there is adequate evidence that the interests of HUD or the public would not be served by continuing to allow the Mortgagee to participate in FHA programs, pending the completion of any investigation, other review, or legal or administrative proceedings the Mortgagee is involved in.

(A) Effective Date

If the MRB determines there is adequate evidence that immediate action is required to protect the financial interests of HUD or the public, the MRB is authorized to suspend a Mortgagee's FHA approval immediately upon issuance of the notice of suspension and without prior issuance of a Notice of Violation (NOV) as set forth in 24 CFR § 25.7(d).

Any other suspension is effective upon the Mortgagee's receipt of the notice of suspension as set forth in 24 CFR § 25.5(d).

(B) Case Status

During the period of suspension, HUD will not endorse any Mortgage originated by the suspended Mortgagee unless it was an Approved Mortgage prior to the date of suspension.

The Mortgagee must transfer all other applications in process to another FHA-approved Mortgagee for completion of processing, submission, and endorsement.

(C) Duration

Suspension is generally imposed for a period of six months to one year, but may be extended for an additional six months in accordance with the provisions of 24 CFR Part 25.

(D) Appeal

The Mortgagee has the right to appeal a suspension in accordance with the provisions of 24 CFR Parts 25 and 26.

iv. Withdrawal of FHA Approval

Only the MRB may withdraw a Mortgagee's FHA approval. Withdrawal of FHA approval applies to all offices of the Mortgagee.

(A) Effective Date

If the MRB determines there is adequate evidence that immediate action is required to protect the financial interests of HUD or the public, the MRB is authorized to withdraw a Mortgagee's FHA approval immediately; in this case, the withdrawal is effective upon the Mortgagee's receipt of the notice of withdrawal.

Any other withdrawal is effective upon either:

- the expiration of the 30-Day appeal period, if the Mortgagee does not request a hearing; or
- the receipt of the Administrative Law Judge's final decision, if the Mortgagee does request a hearing within the 30-Day appeal period.

(B) Case Status

HUD will not endorse any Mortgage originated by the withdrawn Mortgagee unless it was an Approved Mortgage prior to the date of withdrawal.

The withdrawn Mortgagee must transfer its servicing portfolio to another FHA-approved Mortgagee (see Transfers of Servicing and Sales of Mortgages).

Withdrawn FHA approval means that the Mortgagee may not originate, underwrite, service, or purchase any FHA-insured Mortgages.

(C) Duration

The MRB's withdrawal of a Mortgagee's FHA approval will be for a reasonable, specified period of time, but not less than one year. The MRB may permanently withdraw a Mortgagee's FHA approval if it finds the Mortgagee's violations to be egregious or willful.

A withdrawn Mortgagee's approval is not reinstated at the end of the period of withdrawal. The Mortgagee may reapply for FHA approval after the period of withdrawal has expired.

(D) Appeal

The Mortgagee has the right to appeal a withdrawal of its FHA approval by the MRB in accordance with the provisions of 24 CFR Parts 25 and 26.

v. Civil Money Penalties

The MRB may impose civil money penalties against any FHA-approved Mortgagee who knowingly and materially violates FHA requirements as set forth in 24 CFR § 30.35.

(A) Complaint

If the MRB elects to seek civil money penalties against a Mortgagee, HUD will file a complaint to initiate legal action. A civil money penalty may be imposed against a Mortgagee in addition to any other administrative action taken by the MRB.

(B) Maximum Civil Money Penalties

The MRB is authorized to impose a civil money penalty, in accordance with the provisions of 24 CFR Part 30, against a party that knowingly and materially violates

FHA program regulations or requirements. A civil money penalty may be imposed with respect to each insured Mortgage or other separate occurrence of a violation up to the maximum permitted under Part 30.

(C) Mitigating and Aggravating Factors

In determining the amount of a civil money penalty, the MRB will consider the following factors:
- the gravity of the offense;
- the Mortgagee's history of prior offenses;
- the Mortgagee's ability to pay the penalty;
- the injury to the public;
- the benefits received by the violator;
- the extent of potential benefit to other persons;
- deterrence of future violations; and
- the degree of the violator's culpability.

vi. Settlement Agreements

The MRB is authorized to enter into settlement agreements with non-complying Mortgagees at any time in order to resolve grounds for an administrative sanction or civil money penalty, as set forth in 12 U.S.C. § 1708(c)(3)(E) and 24 CFR § 25.5(a). Failure by the Mortgagee to comply with the terms of a settlement agreement may result in a suspension or withdrawal of the Mortgagee's FHA approval.

b. Procedures

The following is a brief summary of the procedures of the MRB under 24 CFR Parts 25, 26, and 30.

i. Notice of Violation

The MRB will send the Mortgagee an NOV detailing the Mortgagee's alleged violations.

(A) Mortgage Response

The Mortgagee may provide the MRB with a written response within 30 Days of receiving the NOV. The MRB will consider the Mortgagee's response, as well as other relevant material, when deciding which administrative action to take, if any, and whether to seek civil money penalties against the Mortgagee.

If the Mortgagee fails to respond to the NOV within 30 Days, the MRB will make a final determination based upon the information available to it.

(B) Preservation of Documents

Upon receipt of the NOV, the Mortgagee is required to preserve and maintain all documents and data, including electronically stored data, within the Mortgagee's possession or control that may relate to the violations alleged in the NOV.

ii. Notice of Administrative Action

If the MRB decides to take administrative action against the Mortgagee, the MRB will issue a Notice of Administrative Action to the Mortgagee describing the nature and duration of the action and setting forth the basis for the action being taken.

iii. Appeal

(A) Request for Hearing

Mortgagees may appeal a probation, suspension or withdrawal action by the MRB by submitting a written request for a hearing within 30 Days of receipt of the Notice of Administrative Action. The Mortgagee's request for a hearing must specifically respond to the violations set forth in the Notice of Administrative Action.

(B) Hearing Process and Procedures

Hearings are conducted before an impartial Administrative Law Judge in accordance with the procedures set forth in 24 CFR Part 26, Subpart B.

(C) Waiver of Appeal

If a Mortgagee fails to request a hearing within the 30-Day period, the MRB action becomes final.

iv. Public Notice

(A) Federal Register

Pursuant to the National Housing Act (12 U.S.C. § 1708(c)(5)), HUD publishes a description of and the cause for each administrative action against an FHA-approved Mortgagee in the Federal Register. The Federal Register notices include details on all MRB actions, including letters of reprimand, probations, suspensions, withdrawals of FHA approval, settlement agreements, and civil money penalties.

(B) Agency Notifications

If the MRB suspends or withdraws the approval of a Mortgagee, FHA is required to notify certain state, federal, and other interested agencies that interact with the Mortgagee, including:

- Conference of State Bank Supervisors/NMLS

- CFPB
- Fannie Mae
- Federal Deposit Insurance Corporation (FDIC)
- Federal Reserve
- Freddie Mac
- Ginnie Mae
- National Credit Union Administration (NCUA)
- Office of the Comptroller of the Currency
- U.S. Department of Agriculture Rural Development Housing Authority
- U.S. Department of Veterans Affairs

5. Actions and Sanctions Against Individuals and Other Program Participants

HUD may also impose civil money penalties and take administrative action against individuals and other program participants for violations of FHA mortgage insurance program requirements.

a. Limited Denial of Participation

i. Definition

A Limited Denial of Participation (LDP) is an action that excludes a party from further participation in a specified HUD program area based on the participant's failure to comply with HUD program standards. LDPs are issued under the authority of 2 CFR § 2424.1100.

ii. Cause

An LDP may be issued against an individual or other program participant based upon adequate evidence of any of the causes listed in 2 CFR § 2424.1110.

iii. Effective Date

An LDP is effective immediately upon issuance of the notice by the authorizing official.

iv. Duration

The LDP sanction may be imposed for a period not to exceed 12 months.

v. Processing and Appeals

An individual or other program participant may appeal the LDP by requesting an informal conference with the authorizing official or a hearing before the Departmental Hearing Officer within 30 Days of receipt of the notice of LDP.

LDP processing and appeal procedures are set forth in 2 CFR §§ 2424.1100 through 2424.1165.

vi. Public Notice

A list of individuals and other program participants who have received LDPs is available publicly on the HUD website, as well as through FHAC.

b. Suspension

Violations of statutes or serious or repeated violations of FHA requirements may lead to the suspension of an individual or other FHA program participant.

i. Definition

Suspension is a government-wide action that temporarily renders an individual ineligible to participate in most federal government programs pending the completion of an investigation or legal proceedings.

ii. Cause

FHA may suspend an individual for the reasons listed in 2 CFR § 180.700, including:
- the existence of an indictment for, or other adequate evidence to suspect, an offense listed under 2 CFR § 180.800(a); or
- the existence of adequate evidence to suspect any other cause for debarment listed under 2 CFR § 180.800(b) through (d); and
- a determination made by the suspending official that immediate action is necessary to protect the public interest.

iii. Effective Date

A suspension is effective when the suspending official signs the decision to suspend.

iv. Duration

If legal or debarment proceedings are initiated at the time of, or during a suspension, the suspension may continue until the conclusion of those proceedings. If proceedings are not initiated, a suspension may not exceed 12 months. The suspending official may extend the 12-month limit for an additional six months under limited circumstances described in 2 CFR § 180.760. In no event may a suspension exceed 18 months without initiating legal or debarment proceedings.

v. Processing and Appeals

An individual may appeal a proposed suspension by providing the suspending official with information in opposition to the suspension within 30 Days of receipt of the notice of suspension. Information may be provided orally or in writing; important information provided orally must also be submitted in writing for the official record.

Suspension processing and appeal procedures are set forth in 2 CFR §§ 180.700 through 180.760.

c. Debarment

Violations of statutes or serious or repeated violations of FHA requirements may lead to the debarment of an individual or other FHA program participant.

i. Definition

Debarment is a final determination by an authorizing official that the individual has engaged in prohibited conduct and is not presently responsible. Debarment excludes an individual from participating in most federal government programs for a specified period of time.

ii. Cause

FHA may debar an individual for the reasons listed in 2 CFR § 180.800, including, but not limited to:

- criminal conviction or civil judgment for commission of fraud in connection with obtaining, attempting to obtain, or performing a public or private agreement or transaction;
- criminal conviction or civil judgment for commission of embezzlement, theft, forgery, bribery, falsification or destruction of records, making false statements, tax evasion, receiving stolen property, making false claims, or obstruction of justice;
- criminal conviction or civil judgment for violation of federal or state antitrust statutes;
- criminal conviction or civil judgment for the commission of any other offense indicating a lack of business integrity or business honesty that seriously and directly affects the individual's present responsibilities;
- violation of the terms of a public agreement or transaction so serious as to affect the integrity of an agency program;
- knowingly doing business with an ineligible person;
- failure to pay a single substantial debt, or a number of outstanding debts, owed to any federal agency or instrumentality, provided the debt is uncontested, or, if contested, provided all legal and administrative remedies have been exhausted; or
- any other serious or compelling cause that affects the present responsibility of the individual.

iii. Effective Date

A debarment is not effective until the individual has received a notice of proposed debarment and has had an opportunity to contest the proposed debarment. After the debarring official issues a decision, the debarment is effective immediately.

iv. Duration

The period of debarment is based on the seriousness of the cause(s) upon which the debarment is based. Generally, the period of debarment should not exceed three years. However, if circumstances warrant, the debarring official may impose a longer period of debarment.

v. Processing and Appeals

An individual may appeal a proposed debarment by providing the debarring official with information in opposition to the debarment within 30 Days of receipt of the notice of debarment. Information may be provided orally or in writing; important information provided orally must also be submitted in writing for the official record.

Debarment processing and appeal procedures are set forth in 2 CFR §§ 180.800 through 180.885.

d. Civil Money Penalties

The Assistant Secretary for Housing - Federal Housing Commissioner or its designee is authorized to pursue civil money penalties against any principal, officer, or employee of a Mortgagee, or other participants in a Mortgage insured by FHA, including, but not limited to:

- sellers
- Borrowers
- Closing Agents
- title companies
- real estate agents
- mortgage brokers
- Appraisers
- sponsored TPOs
- dealers
- consultants
- contractors
- subcontractors
- inspectors

The Assistant Secretary for Housing - Federal Housing Commissioner or its designee is authorized to pursue civil money penalties against program participants who knowingly and materially violate FHA requirements as set forth in 24 CFR § 30.36.

e. Specific Program Participants

The following are actions and sanctions available for use in connection with the specific program participant listed.

i. Appraisers

(A) Notice of Deficiency

(1) Standard

A Notice of Deficiency (NOD) refers to a formal notification from FHA to an Appraiser when a review identifies an error or lack of compliance. An NOD is not a sanction and is not considered severe enough to require remedial education or removal.

An NOD is noted on the Appraiser's record and multiple NODs may result in further action by FHA.

(2) Cause

An Appraiser may receive an NOD if an FHA review has determined gaps in due diligence and professionalism or errors or noncompliance.

(3) Notice

FHA will provide the Appraiser with written notice outlining deficiencies found in a specific appraisal.

(4) Appeal

An NOD is not a sanction and no appeal is available.

(B) Remedial Education

(1) Standard

FHA may require an Appraiser to take remedial education on appraisal-related topics for failure to comply with the requirements outlined in this *SF Handbook*.

The Appraiser must complete remedial education within 60 Days of the date of notification and provide proof of successful completion. Failure to comply with a remedial education action may result in escalation of the action to an administrative sanction, including removal from the FHA Appraiser Roster.

(2) Cause

Cause for remedial education includes, but is not limited to, identification of more serious deficiencies in the appraisal report that indicate lack of competence, including incomplete data collection or support for analysis and conclusions.

(3) Notice

FHA will provide the Appraiser with written notice of the required remedial education that identifies the ground for the requirement.

(4) Appeal

Remedial education is not a sanction and no appeal is available.

(C) Removal

(1) Standard

FHA may remove an Appraiser from the FHA Appraiser Roster for failure to comply with the requirements outlined in this *SF Handbook*. The Appraiser may be required to take remedial education in addition to the removal.

FHA will notify the state licensing or certification agency in writing when an Appraiser has received a final notice of removal from the FHA Appraiser Roster. HUD is required by law to refer Appraisers to these boards if HUD considers the actions to be of such magnitude or frequency as to warrant such referral.

(2) Causes

Causes for removal include, but are not limited to, any of the following:
- significant deficiencies in appraisals, including non-compliance with Civil Rights requirements regarding appraisals;
- losing standing as a state-certified Appraiser due to disciplinary action in any state in which the Appraiser is certified;
- prosecution for committing, attempting to commit, or conspiring to commit fraud, misrepresentation, or any other offense that may reflect on the Appraiser's character or integrity;
- failure to perform appraisal functions in accordance with instructions and standards issued by HUD;
- failure to comply with any agreement made between the Appraiser and HUD or with any certification made by the Appraiser;
- issuance of a final debarment, suspension, or limited denial of participation;
- failure to maintain eligibility requirements for placement on the Appraiser Roster as set forth under this subpart or any other instructions or standards issued by HUD; or
- failure to comply with HUD-imposed education requirements.

(3) Notice

An Appraiser that is debarred, suspended, subject to a limited denial of participation or has lost standing as a state-certified Appraiser due to disciplinary action or expiration of a state certification, will be automatically removed from the FHA Appraiser Roster and notified of the removal.

In all other cases, the Appraiser will be given written notice of the proposed removal, and the notice will include the reasons for the proposed removal and the duration of the proposed removal.

(4) Appeal

The Appraiser will have 20 Days from the date of the notice of removal to submit a written response appealing the proposed removal and to request a conference. A request for a conference must be in writing and must be submitted along with a written response.

Within 30 Days of FHA's receipt of the Appraiser's written response, or if the Appraiser has requested a conference, within 30 Days after the completion of the conference, an FHA official, designated by the Secretary, will review the appeal and will send a final decision either affirming, modifying, or canceling the removal from the Appraiser Roster. FHA may extend this time upon giving notice. The FHA official designated by the Secretary to review the appeal will not be someone involved in FHA's initial removal decision nor will it be someone who reports to a person involved in that initial decision.

If the Appraiser does not submit a written response, the removal will be effective 20 Days after the date of FHA's initial removal notice. If the Appraiser submits a written response, and the removal decision is affirmed or modified, the removal or modification will be effective on the date of FHA's notice affirming or modifying the initial removal decision.

(5) Duration

Removal from the FHA Appraiser Roster may be for a period of up to 12 months.

If removal is the result of expiration or a disciplinary action by the licensing state, removal from the FHA Appraiser Roster will remain in effect until the appraisal credentials are reinstated by the issuing state.

ii. 203(k) Consultants

Removal

(A) Standard

FHA may remove a Consultant from the Roster for any cause that HUD determines to be detrimental to HUD or its programs.

(B) Cause

Cause for removal includes:

- poor performance on a HUD QC review;
- failure to comply with applicable regulations or other written instructions or standards issued by HUD;
- failure to comply with applicable civil rights requirements;
- misrepresentation or fraudulent statements;
- failure to retain standing as a state-licensed architect or state-licensed engineer (unless the Consultant can demonstrate the required three years of experience as a home inspector or remodeling contractor);
- failure to retain standing as a state-licensed home inspector, if the Consultant is located in a state that requires such licensing; or
- failure to respond within a reasonable time to HUD inquiries or requests for documentation.

A 203(k) Consultant who is debarred or suspended, subject to a Limited Denial of Participation (LDP), or otherwise ineligible to participate in an FHA transaction will be removed from the Roster.

(C) Notice

HUD will give the Consultant written notice of the proposed removal with reasons for the proposed removal and instructions for appeal or reinstatement.

iii. Nonprofits and Governmental Entities

(A) HUD Homes – Excess Profits

FHA limits the costs that are eligible to be included in the NDC calculation and prohibits the nonprofit organization or Governmental Entity from reselling the repaired or improved properties at prices in excess of 110 percent of the allowed NDCs.

If the Governmental Entity's or HUD-approved Nonprofit's resale price of the HUD Home exceeds 110 percent of the NDCs, or if non-allowable items that are included in the NDCs result in an excessive sales price, the HUD-approved Governmental Entity or Nonprofit must use the excess profit to pay down the existing Mortgage associated with that particular resale.

(B) Removal from Roster

(1) Standard

FHA may remove a nonprofit from the list of HUD-approved nonprofit agencies for any cause that HUD determines to be detrimental to FHA or any of its programs.

Nonprofit agencies removed from the approved list must reapply to HUD in accordance with instructions contained in Nonprofit and Governmental Entities, Application and Approval Process.

(2) Cause

Cause for removal includes, but is not limited to, any of the following:
- failure to comply with applicable Single Family regulations in this *SF Handbook* or other written instructions or standards issued by HUD;
- failure to comply with applicable civil rights requirements;
- holding a significant number of FHA-insured Mortgages that are in Default, foreclosure, or claim status (in determining the number considered "significant," HUD may compare the number of insured Mortgages held by the nonprofit organization against the similar holdings of other nonprofit organizations);
- debarment, suspension, being subject to a Limited Denial of Participation (LDP) or otherwise sanctioned by HUD;
- failure to further all objectives described in the Affordable Housing Program Plan (AHPP);
- misrepresentation or fraudulent statements; or
- failure to respond to FHA inquiries, including recertification requests or other requests for further documentation, within 30 Days.

(3) Notice and Appeal

A nonprofit organization that is debarred or suspended, or subject to an LDP, will be automatically removed from the HUD Nonprofit Roster.

In all other cases, the following procedures for removal apply:
- HUD will give the nonprofit organization written notice of the proposed removal. The notice will include the reasons for the proposed removal and the duration of the proposed removal.
- The nonprofit organization will have 20 Days from the date of the notice (or longer, if provided in the notice) to submit a written response appealing the proposed removal and request a conference. A request for a conference must be in writing and must be submitted along with the written response.
- A HUD official will review the appeal and provide an informal conference if requested. The HUD official will send a response affirming, modifying, or canceling the removal. The HUD official will not have been involved in HUD's initial removal decision. HUD will respond with a decision within 30 Days of receiving the response, or, if the nonprofit organization has requested a conference, within 30 Days after the completion of the conference. HUD may extend the 30-Day period by providing written notice to the nonprofit organization.

Handbook 4000.1
Effective Date: 09/14/2015 | Last Revised: 07/10/2019
*Refer to the online version of SF Handbook 4000.1 for specific sections' effective dates

969

- If the nonprofit organization does not submit a timely written response, the removal will be effective 20 Days after the date of HUD's initial removal notice (or after a longer period provided in the notice). If a written response is submitted, and the initial removal decision is affirmed or modified, the removal will be effective on the date of HUD's notice affirming or modifying the initial removal decision.

iv. Real Estate Brokers

(A) Removal for Good Cause

HUD may rescind real estate brokers' HUD registration and prohibit those brokers from participating in the sale of HUD REO Properties for good cause. Good cause includes, but is not limited to:

- conviction under 18 U.S.C. 371 or 1010 of a broker or by an agent supervised by that broker and acting within the scope of their duties; and
- any of the following actions by a broker or an agent supervised by that broker and acting within the scope of their duties:
  o falsifying mortgage documents or aiding or abetting others in the use of false or misleading information including, but not limited to, forged or fraudulent gift letters and owner-occupant certifications;
  o acting in concert with an Appraiser to arrive at an artificial appraised value;
  o engaging in fraudulent activities that have led to Default and payment of an insurance claim;
  o failing to comply with earnest money collection, management, and disbursement procedures;
  o failing to maintain a current state license;
  o violating the Real Estate Settlement Procedures Act (RESPA);
  o failing to comply with civil rights requirements, including the Fair Housing Act and ECOA, in any real estate related transaction;
  o involvement in, or knowledge of, any fraudulent activity by any person involved in the HUD REO sales transaction; and
  o any other actions or omissions that evidence a lack of business integrity or non-compliance with the laws, regulations, and rules applicable to housing, lending, or real estate sales.

Good cause, as identified above, includes apparent criminal activity. If and when apparent criminal activity is identified, it must be immediately reported to HUD's Office of Inspector General (OIG).

(B) Notice to Real Estate Broker

Once HUD makes an initial Finding that there is good cause to remove a real estate broker, HUD will provide the real estate broker with written notice of the proposed

suspension or termination of the NAID and deactivation of the broker's access to HUD's systems used for HUD REO sales. The notice will:
- state the reasons that HUD is taking the action;
- identify the violations or deficiencies involved;
- provide a citation to the relevant regulation, statute, or policy; and
- state the effective date and duration of the suspension or termination.

(C) Effective Date of Removal

The real estate broker's suspension, termination, and/or deactivation is effective 30 Days from the date of HUD's written notice, unless the broker submits a written response or requests a conference.

(D) Real Estate Broker Response and Conference

Within 20 Days after the date of the notice or within such time provided in the notice, the real estate broker may submit a written response to HUD opposing the proposed removal and may request a conference.

The real estate broker must submit a request for a conference in writing and must submit this request with the written response.

HUD will delay suspension, termination, and/or deactivation until it makes a final determination on the real estate broker's response and conference. HUD will notify the real estate broker in writing of its decision; the written decision by HUD shall constitute final agency action.

(E) Effect of Removal Proceedings on Bids

HUD will honor all bids submitted and commissions earned by the real estate broker before removal, unless HUD determines that the bids or commissions were made under fraudulent circumstances.

v. Closing Agents

HUD reserves the right to sanction or remove any Closing Agent that does not abide by HUD's closing instructions and requirements.

vi. Additional Other Participants

RESERVED FOR FUTURE USE

This section is reserved for future use, and until such time, FHA-approved Mortgagees and Other Program Participants must continue to comply with all applicable law and existing Handbooks, Mortgagee Letters, Notices and outstanding guidance applicable to their participation in FHA programs.

APPENDIX 1.0 – MORTGAGE INSURANCE PREMIUMS

Upfront Mortgage Insurance Premium (UFMIP)
All Mortgages: 175 Basis Points (bps) (1.75%) of the Base Loan Amount.
Exceptions: <ul><li>Streamline Refinance and Simple Refinance Mortgages used to refinance a previous FHA-endorsed Mortgage on or before May 31, 2009</li><li>Hawaiian Home Lands (Section 247)</li><li>Indian Lands (Section 248)</li></ul>
Indian Lands (Section 248) do not require a UFMIP.

Annual Mortgage Insurance Premium (MIP)			
Applies to all Mortgages except: <ul><li>Streamline Refinance and Simple Refinance Mortgages used to refinance a previous FHA endorsed Mortgage on or before May 31, 2009</li><li>Hawaiian Home Lands (Section 247)</li></ul>			
Hawaiian Home Lands (Section 247) do not require Annual MIP.			
Mortgage Term of More Than 15 Years			
Base Loan Amount	**LTV**	**MIP (bps)**	**Duration**
Less than or equal to $625,500	≤ 90.00%	80	11 years
	> 90.00% but ≤ 95.00%	80	Mortgage term
	> 95.00%	85	Mortgage term
Greater than $625,500	≤ 90.00%	100	11 years
	> 90.00% but ≤ 95.00%	100	Mortgage term
	> 95.00%	105	Mortgage term
Mortgage Term of Less than or Equal to 15 Years			
Base Loan Amount	**LTV**	**MIP (bps)**	**Duration**
Less than or equal to $625,500	≤ 90.00%	45	11 years
	> 90.00%	70	Mortgage term
Greater than $625,500	≤ 78.00%	45	11 years
	> 78.00% but ≤ 90.00%	70	11 years
	> 90.00%	95	Mortgage term

Handbook 4000.1
Effective Date: 09/14/2015 | Last Revised: 07/10/2019
*Refer to the online version of SF Handbook 4000.1 for specific sections' effective dates

972

Streamline Refinance, Simple Refinance:

For refinance of previous Mortgage endorsed on or before May 31, 2009 UFMIP: 1 (bps) (.01%) All Mortgages			
All Mortgage Terms			
Base Loan Amount	**LTV**	**Annual MIP (bps)**	**Duration**
All	≤ 90.00%	55	11 years
	> 90.00%	55	Mortgage term
For Mortgages where FHA does not require an appraisal, the value from the previous Mortgage is used to calculate the LTV.			

Hawaiian Home Lands Section 247

Hawaiian Home Lands Upfront MIP (UFMIP)				
	Loan Term in Years			
	≤18	>18 and ≤22	>22 and ≤25	>25
MIP Financed	2.400%	3.000%	3.600%	3.800%
MIP not Financed	2.344%	2.913%	3.475%	3.661%
Annual MIP is not assessed on Section 247 Mortgages.				

Handbook 4000.1   973
Effective Date: 09/14/2015 | Last Revised: 07/10/2019
*Refer to the online version of SF Handbook 4000.1 for specific sections' effective dates

APPENDIX 2.0 – ANALYZING IRS FORMS [TEXT WAS DELETED IN THIS SECTION.]

IRS Form 1040 Heading	Description
Wages, Salaries and Tips	An amount shown under this heading may indicate that the individual: • is a salaried employee of a corporation; or • has other sources of income. This section may also indicate that the spouse is employed, in which case the spouse's income must be subtracted from the Borrower's gross income.
Business Income and Loss (from Schedule C)	Sole proprietorship income calculated on Schedule C is business income. Depreciation, depletion, amortization, and casualty losses may be added back to the gross income.
Business Use of Home	Mortgage interest, Mortgage Insurance Premiums (MIP), real estate taxes, and property insurance deducted for business use of a house may be added back to the gross income.
Rents, Royalties, Partnerships (from Schedule E)	Any income received from rental properties or royalties may be used as income, after adding back any depreciation shown on Schedule E.
Capital Gain and Losses (from Schedule D)	Capital gains or losses generally occur only one time, and should not be considered when determining Effective Income. However, if the individual has a constant turnover of assets resulting in gains or losses, the capital gain or loss must be considered when determining the income. Three years' tax returns are required to evaluate an earnings trend. If the trend: • results in a gain, it may be added as Effective Income; or • consistently shows a loss, it must be deducted from the total income.
Interest and Dividend Income (from Schedule B)	This taxable/tax-exempt income may be added back to the adjusted gross income only if it: • has been received for the past two years; and • is expected to continue. If the interest-bearing asset will be liquidated as a source of the cash investment, the Mortgagee must appropriately adjust the amount.

Handbook 4000.1
Effective Date: 09/14/2015 | Last Revised: 07/10/2019
*Refer to the online version of SF Handbook 4000.1 for specific sections' effective dates

974

IRS Form 1040 Heading	Description
Farm Income or Loss (from Schedule F)	Any depreciation shown on Schedule F may be added back to the gross income.
IRA Distributions, Pensions, Annuities, and Social Security Benefits	The non-taxable portion of these items may be added back to the adjusted gross income, if the income is expected to continue for the first three years of the Mortgage.
Adjustments to Income	Adjustments to income may be added back to the adjusted gross income if they are: • IRA and Keogh retirement deductions; or • penalties on early withdrawal of savings health insurance deductions, and Alimony payments.

Analyzing IRS Form 1120, *U.S. Corporation Income Tax Return*

A Corporation refers to a state-chartered business owned by its stockholders.

To determine the Borrower's income, the adjusted business income must be multiplied by the Borrower's percentage of ownership in the business.

Corporate compensation to the officers, in proportion to the percentage of ownership, is shown on the corporate tax return (IRS Form 1120), and individual tax returns. If the Borrower's percentage of ownership does not appear on the tax returns, the Mortgagee must obtain the information from the corporations' accountant, along with evidence that the Borrower has the right to any compensation.

The table below describes the items found on IRS Form 1120 for which an adjustment must be made in order to determine adjusted business income.

Adjustment Item	Description of Adjustment
Depreciation and Depletion	Add the corporation's depreciation and depletion back to the after-tax income.
Fiscal Year vs. Calendar Year	If the corporation operates on a fiscal year that is different from the calendar year, an adjustment must be made to relate corporate income to the individual tax return.
Cash Withdrawals	The Borrower's withdrawal of cash from the corporation may have a severe negative impact on the corporation's ability to continue operating.

Analyzing IRS Form 1120S, *U.S. Income Tax Return for an S Corporation*

An "S" Corporation refers to a small start-up business, with gains and losses passed to stockholders in proportion to each stockholder's percentage of business ownership.

Income for owners of "S" corporations comes from W-2 wages, and is taxed at the individual rate. The IRS Form 1120S, Compensation of Officers line item is transferred to the Borrower's individual IRS Form 1040.

Depreciation and depletion may be added back to income in proportion to the Borrower's percentage of ownership in the corporation.

The Borrower's income must be reduced proportionately by the total obligations payable by the corporation in less than one year.

Analyzing IRS Form 1065, *U.S. Return of Partnership Income*

A Partnership refers to when two or more individuals form a business, and share in profits, losses, and responsibility for running the company. Each partner pays taxes on their proportionate share of the partnership's net income.

Both general and limited partnerships report income on IRS Form 1065, and the partners' share of income is carried over to Schedule E of IRS Form 1040.

Both depreciation and depletion may be added back to the income in proportion to the Borrower's share of the income.

The Borrower's income must be reduced proportionately by the total obligation payable by the partnership in less than one year.

APPENDIX 3.0 – POST-ENDORSEMENT FEES AND CHARGES BY HOC (APPLIES TO SERVICING ONLY)

Philadelphia HOC

Type of Service	CT	DE	DC	ME	MD	MA	MI	NH	NJ	NY
Substitution of Hazard Insurance Policy	$10	$10	$10	$10	$10	$10	$10	$10	$10	$10
Returned Check*	$25	$15	$15	$25	$15	$25	$20	$25	$20	$20
Modification of performing Mortgage	$50	$50	$50	$50	$50	$50	$50	$50	$50	$50
Modification of the mortgaged Property	$100	$110	$110	$100	$110	$100	$150	$100	$100	$100
Incorporating a Borrower's name change into the Servicer's loan system	No Charge	No Charge	No Charge	No Charge	No Charge	No Charge	No Charge	No Charge	No Charge	No Charge
Re-analyzing escrow accounts and providing new coupon books	No Charge	No Charge	No Charge	No Charge	No Charge	No Charge	No Charge	No Charge	No Charge	No Charge
Copy of Mortgage Note	$10	$10	$10	$10	$10	$10	$10	$10	$10	$10
Copy of Closing Disclosure**	$10	$10	$10	$10	$10	$10	$10	$10	$10	$10
Copy of Amortization Schedule**	$15	$15	$15	$15	$15	$15	$15	$15	$15	$15
Replacement Coupon Books	$5	$5	$5	$5	$5	$5	$5	$5	$5	$5
Verification of Mortgage	$20	$20	$20	$20	$20	$20	$20	$20	$20	$20
Copy of Year-End Statement	$5	$5	$5	$5	$5	$5	$5	$5	$5	$5
Transmittal of Payoff Statement via Facsimile	$5	$5	$5	$5	$5	$5	$5	$5	$5	$5
Additional Payoff Statements***	$10	$10	$10	$10	$10	$10	$10	$10	$10	$10

* Unless prohibited by the Borrower's bank, the Mortgagee must present the check for payment twice before it can be deemed "uncollectible" when returned unpaid.
**other than the statement or schedule provided at closing
*** after two payoff statements have been provided free of charge for the calendar year

Handbook 4000.1
Effective Date: 03/14/2016 | Last Revised: 07/10/2019
*Refer to the online version of SF Handbook 4000.1 for specific sections' effective dates

977

Type of Service	OH	PA	RI	VT	VA	WV
Substitution of Hazard Insurance Policy	$10	$10	$10	$10	$10	$10
Returned Check*	$20	$15	$25	$25	$15	$15
Modification of performing Mortgage	$50	$50	$50	$50	$50	$50
Modification of the mortgaged Property	$100	$110	$100	$100	$110	$110
Incorporating a Borrower's name change into the Servicer's loan system	No Charge	No Charge	No Charge	No Charge	No Charge	No Charge
Re-analyzing escrow accounts and providing new coupon books	No Charge	No Charge	No Charge	No Charge	No Charge	No Charge
Copy of Mortgage Note	$10	$10	$10	$10	$10	$10
Copy of Closing Disclosure**	$10	$10	$10	$10	$10	$10
Copy of Amortization Schedule**	$15	$15	$15	$15	$15	$15
Replacement Coupon Books	$5	$5	$5	$5	$5	$5
Verification of Mortgage	$20	$20	$20	$20	$20	$20
Copy of Year-End Statement	$5	$5	$5	$5	$5	$5
Transmittal of Payoff Statement via Facsimile	$5	$5	$5	$5	$5	$5
Additional Payoff Statements***	$10	$10	$10	$10	$10	$10

* Unless prohibited by the Borrower's bank, the Mortgagee must present the check for payment twice before it can be deemed "uncollectible" when returned unpaid.

**other than the statement or schedule provided at closing

*** after two payoff statements have been provided free of charge for the calendar year

Atlanta HOC

Type of Service	AL	FL	GA	KY	IL	IN	MS	NC	PR	SC
Substitution of Hazard Insurance Policy	$10	$15	$10	$10	$10	$10	$7.50	$7.50	$10	$15
Returned Check*	$10	$20	$15	$15	$20	$25	$15	$15	$10	$20
Modification of performing Mortgage	$50	$50	$50	$50	$50	$50	$50	$50	$50	$50
Modification of the mortgaged Property	$100	$100	$125	$100	$100	$100	$100	$150	$100	$100
Incorporating a Borrower's name change into the Servicer's loan system	No Charge	No Charge	No Charge	No Charge	No Charge	No Charge	No Charge	No Charge	No Charge	No Charge
Re-analyzing escrow accounts and providing new coupon books	No Charge	No Charge	No Charge	No Charge	No Charge	No Charge	No Charge	No Charge	No Charge	No Charge
Copy of Mortgage Note	$10	$10	$10	$10	$10	$10	$10	$10	$10	$10
Copy of Closing Disclosure**	$10	$10	$10	$10	$10	$10	$10	$10	$10	$10
Copy of Amortization Schedule**	$15	$15	$15	$15	$15	$15	$15	$15	$15	$15
Replacement Coupon Books	$5	$5	$5	$5	$5	$5	$5	$5	$5	$5
Verification of Mortgage	$20	$20	$20	$20	$20	$20	$20	$20	$20	$20
Copy of Year-End Statement	$5	$5	$5	$5	$5	$5	$5	$5	$5	$5
Transmittal of Payoff Statement via Facsimile	$5	$5	$5	$5	$5	$5	$5	$5	$5	$5
Additional Payoff Statements***	$10	$10	$10	$10	$10	$10	$10	$10	$10	$10

* Unless prohibited by the Borrower's bank, the Mortgagee must present the check for payment twice before it can be deemed "uncollectible" when returned unpaid.
**other than the statement or schedule provided at closing
*** after two payoff statements have been provided free of charge for the calendar year

Handbook 4000.1
Effective Date: 03/14/2016 | Last Revised: 07/10/2019
*Refer to the online version of SF Handbook 4000.1 for specific sections' effective dates

979

Type of Service	TN	VI
Substitution of Hazard Insurance Policy	$7.50	$10
Returned Check*	$20	$10
Modification of performing Mortgage	$50	$50
Modification of the mortgaged Property	$150	$100
Incorporating a Borrower's name change into the Servicer's loan system	No Charge	No Charge
Re-analyzing escrow accounts and providing new coupon books	No Charge	No Charge
Copy of Mortgage Note	$10	$10
Copy of Closing Disclosure**	$10	$10
Copy of Amortization Schedule**	$15	$15
Replacement Coupon Books	$5	$5
Verification of Mortgage	$20	$20
Copy of Year-End Statement	$5	$5
Transmittal of Payoff Statement via Facsimile	$5	$5
Additional Payoff Statements***	$10	$10

* Unless prohibited by the Borrower's bank, the Mortgagee must present the check for payment twice before it can be deemed "uncollectible" when returned unpaid.
**other than the statement or schedule provided at closing
*** after two payoff statements have been provided free of charge for the calendar year

Denver HOC

Type of Service	AR	CO	IA	KS	LA	MO	MN	MT	NE	NM
Substitution of Hazard Insurance Policy	$10	$10.50	$10	$10	$10	$10	$10	$10.50	$10	$10
Returned Check*	$25	$15	$15	$15	$25	$15	$20	$15	$15	$15
Modification of performing Mortgage	$50	$50	$50	$50	$50	$50	$50	$50	$50	$50
Modification of the mortgaged Property	$110	$100	$100	$100	$110	$100	$100	$100	$100	$110
Incorporating a Borrower's name change into the Servicer's loan system	No Charge	No Charge	No Charge	No Charge	No Charge	No Charge	No Charge	No Charge	No Charge	No Charge
Re-analyzing escrow accounts and providing new coupon books	No Charge	No Charge	No Charge	No Charge	No Charge	No Charge	No Charge	No Charge	No Charge	No Charge
Copy of Mortgage Note	$10	$10	$10	$10	$10	$10	$10	$10	$10	$10
Copy of Closing Disclosure**	$10	$10	$10	$10	$10	$10	$10	$10	$10	$10
Copy of Amortization Schedule**	$15	$15	$15	$15	$15	$15	$15	$15	$15	$15
Replacement Coupon Books	$5	$5	$5	$5	$5	$5	$5	$5	$5	$5
Verification of Mortgage	$20	$20	$20	$20	$20	$20	$20	$20	$20	$20
Copy of Year-End Statement	$5	$5	$5	$5	$5	$5	$5	$5	$5	$5
Transmittal of Payoff Statement via Facsimile	$5	$5	$5	$5	$5	$5	$5	$5	$5	$5
Additional Payoff Statements***	$10	$10	$10	$10	$10	$10	$10	$10	$10	$10

* Unless prohibited by the Borrower's bank, the Mortgagee must present the check for payment twice before it can be deemed "uncollectible" when returned unpaid.
**other than the statement or schedule provided at closing
*** after two payoff statements have been provided free of charge for the calendar year

Type of Service	ND	OK	SD	TX	WI	WY	UT
Substitution of Hazard Insurance Policy	$10.50	$10	$10.50	$10	$10	$10.50	$10.50
Returned Check*	$15	$25	$15	$25	$20	$15	$15
Modification of performing Mortgage	$50	$50	$50	$50	$50	$50	$50
Modification of the mortgaged Property	$100	$110	$100	$110	$100	$100	$100
Incorporating a Borrower's name change into the Servicer's loan system	No Charge	No Charge	No Charge	No Charge	No Charge	No Charge	No Charge
Re-analyzing escrow accounts and providing new coupon books	No Charge	No Charge	No Charge	No Charge	No Charge	No Charge	No Charge
Copy of Mortgage Note	$10	$10	$10	$10	$10	$10	$10
Copy of Closing Disclosure**	$10	$10	$10	$10	$10	$10	$10
Copy of Amortization Schedule**	$15	$15	$15	$15	$15	$15	$15
Replacement Coupon Books	$5	$5	$5	$5	$5	$5	$5
Verification of Mortgage	$20	$20	$20	$20	$20	$20	$20
Copy of Year-End Statement	$5	$5	$5	$5	$5	$5	$5
Transmittal of Payoff Statement via Facsimile	$5	$5	$5	$5	$5	$5	$5
Additional Payoff Statements***	$10	$10	$10	$10	$10	$10	$10

* Unless prohibited by the Borrower's bank, the Mortgagee must present the check for payment twice before it can be deemed "uncollectible" when returned unpaid.
**other than the statement or schedule provided at closing
*** after two payoff statements have been provided free of charge for the calendar year

Handbook 4000.1

982

Effective Date: 03/14/2016 | Last Revised: 07/10/2019
*Refer to the online version of SF Handbook 4000.1 for specific sections' effective dates

Santa Ana HOC

Type of Service	AK	AZ	CA	HI	ID	NV	OR	WA	Pacific Islands
Substitution of Hazard Insurance Policy	$15	$10	$10	$10	$15	$10	$15	$15	$10
Returned Check*	$15	$15	$15	$15	$20	$15	$15	$15	$15
Modification of performing Mortgage	$50	$50	$50	$50	$50	$50	$50	$50	$50
Modification of the mortgaged Property	$125	$100	$100	$100	$125	$100	$125	$125	$100
Incorporating a Borrower's name change into the Servicer's loan system	No Charge	No Charge	No Charge	No Charge	No Charge	No Charge	No Charge	No Charge	No Charge
Re-analyzing escrow accounts and providing new coupon books	No Charge	No Charge	No Charge	No Charge	No Charge	No Charge	No Charge	No Charge	No Charge
Copy of Mortgage Note	$10	$10	$10	$10	$10	$10	$10	$10	$10
Copy of Closing Disclosure**	$10	$10	$10	$10	$10	$10	$10	$10	$10
Copy of Amortization Schedule**	$15	$15	$15	$15	$15	$15	$15	$15	$15
Replacement Coupon Books	$5	$5	$5	$5	$5	$5	$5	$5	$5
Verification of Mortgage	$20	$20	$20	$20	$20	$20	$20	$20	$20
Copy of Year-End Statement	$5	$5	$5	$5	$5	$5	$5	$5	$5
Transmittal of Payoff Statement via Facsimile	$5	$5	$5	$5	$5	$5	$5	$5	$5
Additional Payoff Statements***	$10	$10	$10	$10	$10	$10	$10	$10	$10

* Unless prohibited by the Borrower's bank, the Mortgagee must present the check for payment twice before it can be deemed "uncollectible" when returned unpaid.
**other than the statement or schedule provided at closing
*** after two payoff statements have been provided free of charge for the calendar year

Handbook 4000.1
Effective Date: 03/14/2016 | Last Revised: 07/10/2019
*Refer to the online version of SF Handbook 4000.1 for specific sections' effective dates

983

APPENDIX 4.0 – HUD SCHEDULE OF STANDARD ATTORNEY FEES (APPLIES TO SERVICING ONLY)

State	Non-judicial Foreclosure	Judicial Foreclosure	Bankruptcy Clearance[13]	Possessory Action	Deed-in-Lieu
AK	$1,625		Varies	$500	$400
AL	$1,325[1]		Varies	$500	$400
AR	$1,475		Varies	$500	$400
AZ	$1,350		Varies	$400	$400
CA	$1,425[2]		Varies	$550	$400
CO	$1,650		Varies	$450	$400
CT		$2,450[3,4]	Varies	$400	$400
DC	$1,200[1]	$2,250	Varies	$400	$400
DE		$1,900	Varies	$450	$400
FL		$2,800[11]	Varies	$400	$400
GA	$1,325		Varies	$450	$400
GU	$1,625		Varies	$350	$400
HI		$2,950[7]	Varies	$525	$400
IA	$1,275	$1,850	Varies	$350	$400
ID	$1,250		Varies	$400	$400
IL		$2,300	Varies	$400	$400
IN		$2,050	Varies	$450	$400
KS		$1,800	Varies	$400	$400
KY		$2,250	Varies	$400	$400
LA		$1,900	Varies	$500	$400
MA	$2,550	$2,550[3]	Varies	$625	$400
MD	$2,500[5]		Varies	$500	$400
ME		$2,300	Varies	$525	$400
MI	$1,425		Varies	$425	$400
MN	$1,450	$1,800	Varies	$400	$400
MO	$1,375		Varies	$450	$400
MS	$1,300[1]		Varies	$400	$400
MT	$1,250		Varies	$400	$400
NC	$1,575		Varies	$400	$400
ND		$1,800	Varies	$350	$400
NE	$1,250	$1,950	Varies	$350	$400
NH	$1,450		Varies	$425	$400
NJ		$2,975	Varies	$500	$400
NM		$2,050	Varies	$400	$400
NV	$1,525		Varies	$650	$400
NY	$1,225[9]	$2,900[3,9]	Varies	$725	$400
OH		$2,250	Varies	$600	$400
OK		$2,000	Varies	$350	$400
OR	$1,425	$2,600	Varies	$400	$400
PA		$2,350	Varies	$450	$400

State	Non-judicial Foreclosure	Judicial Foreclosure	Bankruptcy Clearance[13]	Possessory Action	Deed-in-Lieu
PR		$2,050[3,10]	Varies	$300	$400
RI	$1,725		Varies	$525	$400
SC		$2,200	Varies	$450	$400
SD		$1,800	Varies	$400	$400
TN	$1,300		Varies	$375	$400
TX	$1,325	$1,800	Varies	$400	$400
UT	$1,325		Varies	$400	$400
VA	$1,350		Varies	$600	$400
VI		$1,800	Varies	$300	$400
VT	$1,600	$2,250	Varies	$375	$400
WA	$1,500		Varies	$450	$400
WI		$2,050	Varies	$400	$400
WV	$1,250[1,5]		Varies	$400	$400
WY	$1,250		Varies	$500	$400

Footnotes:

1. This fee covers the combined attorney's and notary's fees.
2. This fee applies to completed foreclosures. If the Mortgage is reinstated, the maximum fee is the amount allowed under applicable law, not to exceed $725 for reinstatements after recording the Notice of Default but before mailing the Notice of Sale, or $1,075 for reinstatements after mailing the Notice of Sale but before the trustee's sale.
3. An additional $200 will be permitted when the property is sold to a third party and the attorney must perform additional work to complete the transfer of title to the successful bidder.
4. This fee applies to strict foreclosures. If the court orders a foreclosure by sale (or a foreclosure by market sale on or after January 1, 2015), the fee will be $2,700.
5. This fee includes the attorney's fee, the notary's fee and the trustee's commission (or statutory fee).
6. [Reserved]
7. A fee of $3,950 will be permitted for judicial foreclosures in locations other than Honolulu County.
8. [Reserved]
9. In New York, the non-judicial foreclosure process is to be used only in connection with cooperative share loans. This fee includes all steps in the foreclosure process, including the transfer of the stock and the lease for an occupied cooperative unit. The allowable fee for judicial foreclosures in New York, where judgment is obtained as a result of an uncontested trial, is established at $3,650. For judicial foreclosures in the City of New York and on Long Island (Nassau and Suffolk Counties), the allowable fee is $3,500 (or $4,250 if judgment is obtained via uncontested trial).
10. In addition to the allowable foreclosure fee, HUD will pay a notary fee up to the greater of $250 or one percent (1%) of the bid amount on the Mortgage being foreclosed.
11. The allowable fee for foreclosures in Florida, where judgment is obtained as a result of an uncontested trial, is established at $3,550.
12. When a Mortgagee requests reimbursement from HUD for a fee amount based on specified conditions contained in a footnote above, the Mortgagee's reimbursement request must contain a description or sufficient supporting documentation to allow HUD to properly evaluate the request.
13. This fee assumes that all required procedural steps have been completed. The maximum attorney fee varies based on the chapter under which the bankruptcy action is filed.

   For Chapter 7 bankruptcies, the maximum allowable fee is $1,175.
   - Motion for Relief is $750
   - Proof of Claim Preparation (if required) is $300
   - Reaffirmation Agreement is $125

For Chapter 11 bankruptcies, the maximum allowable fee is $1,600.
- Proof of Claim Preparation and Plan Review is $750
- Motion for Relief is $850

For Chapter 12 bankruptcies, the maximum allowable fee is $2,100.
- Proof of Claim Preparation and Plan Review is $750
- Objection to Plan is $500
- Motion for Relief is $850

For Chapter 13 bankruptcies, the maximum allowable fee is $2,850.
- Proof of Claim Preparation and Plan Review is $650
- Objection to Plan is $500
- Motion for Relief is $850
- Payment Change Notification (if needed) is $50
- Notice of Fees, Expenses, and Charges is $100
- Post-Stipulation Default / Stay Termination is $50 / $200
- Response to Final Cure Payment Notice is $50 (agreed) / $500 (objection)

APPENDIX 5.0 - FIRST LEGAL ACTIONS TO INITIATE FORECLOSURE AND REASONABLE DILIGENCE TIME FRAMES (APPLIES TO SERVICING ONLY)

State Code	State	Typical Type of HUD Security Instrument	Normal Method of Foreclosure	First Legal Action to Initiate Foreclosure	Reasonable Diligence Time Frame (in months)
01	Alabama	Mortgage	Non-Judicial	Publication	6
11	Alaska	Deed of Trust	Non-Judicial	Recording of Notice of Default	10
02	Arizona	Deed of Trust	Non-Judicial	Recording of Notice of Sale	6
03	Arkansas	Deed of Trust	Non-Judicial	Recording of Notice of Sale	11
04	California	Deed of Trust	Non-Judicial	Recording of Notice of Default	12
05	Colorado	Deed of Trust	Non-Judicial	Filing of Foreclosure Documents with Public Trustee	12
06	Connecticut	Mortgage	Judicial	Delivering Complaint to Sheriff	21
07	Delaware	Mortgage	Judicial	Complaint	26
08	District of Columbia[1]	Deed of Trust	Non-Judicial	Notice of Default Mayor	7
		Deed of Trust	Judicial	Complaint	7
09	Florida	Mortgage	Judicial	Complaint	25
10	Georgia	Security Deed	Non-Judicial	Publication	6
83	Guam	Mortgage	Non-Judicial	Posting and Publishing of Notice of Sale	11
14	Hawaii	Mortgage	Judicial	Complaint	30
		Mortgage	Non-Judicial	Publication of Notice of Intent to Foreclose	6
12	Idaho	Deed of Trust	Non-Judicial	Recording of Notice of Default	13
13	Illinois	Mortgage	Judicial	Complaint	17
15	Indiana	Mortgage	Judicial	Complaint	13
16	Iowa	Mortgage	Judicial	Petition	17
		Deed of Trust	Non-Judicial	Filing of Notice or Voluntary Foreclosure Agreement with Recorder	9
18	Kansas	Mortgage	Judicial	Complaint	10

*Refer to the online version of SF Handbook 4000.1 for specific sections' effective dates

State Code	State	Typical Type of HUD Security Instrument	Normal Method of Foreclosure	First Legal Action to Initiate Foreclosure	Reasonable Diligence Time Frame (in months)
20	Kentucky	Mortgage	Judicial	Complaint	14
22	Louisiana	Mortgage	Judicial	Petition for Executory Process	12
23	Maine	Mortgage	Judicial	Complaint	27
24	Maryland	Mortgage	Judicial	Complaint	18
		Deed of Trust	Non-Judicial	Filing an Order to Docket	18
25	Massachusetts	Mortgage	Non-Judicial	Filing of Complaint[2]	9
26	Michigan	Mortgage	Non-Judicial	Publication	9
27	Minnesota	Mortgage Deed	Non-Judicial	Publication	10
28	Mississippi	Deed of Trust	Non-Judicial	Publication	9
29	Missouri	Deed of Trust	Non-Judicial	Publication	5
31	Montana	Trust Indenture	Non-Judicial	Recording of Notice of Sale	9
32	Nebraska	Mortgage	Judicial	Petition	8
		Deed of Trust	Non-Judicial	Publication of Notice of Sale	8
33	Nevada	Deed of Trust	Non-Judicial	Recording of Notice of Default	24
34	New Hampshire	Mortgage	Non-Judicial	Publication	11
35	New Jersey	Mortgage	Judicial	Complaint	19
36	New Mexico	Mortgage	Judicial	Complaint	25
37	New York City	Mortgage	Judicial	Complaint	27
	New York	Mortgage	Judicial	Complaint	21
38	North Carolina	Deed of Trust	Non-Judicial	Notice of Hearing	9
40	North Dakota	Mortgage	Judicial	Complaint	15
41	Ohio	Mortgage Deed	Judicial	Complaint	13
42	Oklahoma	Mortgage	Judicial	Petition	14
43	Oregon	Deed of Trust	Non-Judicial	Recording of Notice of Default	30
44	Pennsylvania	Mortgage	Judicial	Complaint	21
50	Puerto Rico	Mortgage	Judicial	Complaint	21
45	Rhode Island	Mortgage	Non-Judicial	Publication	22

Effective Date: 03/14/2016 | Last Revised: 07/10/2019
*Refer to the online version of SF Handbook 4000.1 for specific sections' effective dates

State Code	State	Typical Type of HUD Security Instrument	Normal Method of Foreclosure	First Legal Action to Initiate Foreclosure	Reasonable Diligence Time Frame (in months)
46	South Carolina	Mortgage	Judicial	Complaint	14
47	South Dakota	Mortgage	Judicial	Complaint	14
		Deed of Trust	Non-Judicial	Publication of Notice of Sale	9
48	Tennessee	Deed of Trust	Non-Judicial	Publication	6
49	Texas	Deed of Trust	Non-Judicial	Posting and Filing of the Notice of Sale	8
52	Utah	Mortgage	Judicial	Complaint	12
		Deed of Trust	Non-Judicial	Recording of Notice of Default	12
53	Vermont	Mortgage	Judicial	Complaint	24
54	Virginia	Deed of Trust	Non-Judicial	Publication	7
82	Virgin Islands	Mortgage	Judicial	Complaint	15
56	Washington	Deed of Trust	Non-Judicial	Recording of Notice of Trustee's Sale	18
57	West Virginia	Deed of Trust	Non-Judicial	Publication	7
58	Wisconsin	Mortgage	Judicial	Complaint	12
59	Wyoming	Mortgage	Non-Judicial	Publication	7

Footnotes:
1. Loans secured by a Deed of Trust are normally foreclosed using non-judicial procedures provided in D.C. Code § 42-815. Mortgagees may elect to foreclose using judicial procedures established pursuant D.C. Code § 42-816 instead when it is determined to be warranted for a particular Mortgage.
2. The Mortgagee must first obtain a Judgment from the Land Court verifying that the Borrowers are not entitled to relief under the Servicemembers Civil Relief Act (SCRA).

APPENDIX 6.0 - PROPERTY PRESERVATION ALLOWANCES AND SCHEDULES (APPLIES TO SERVICING ONLY)

A. MAXIMUM PROPERTY PRESERVATION ALLOWANCES

CLAIM SUBMISSION AND DOCUMENTATION COSTS	
Maximum Property Preservation Allowance	$5,000
Photographs	Maximum $30 per property
Local Requirements (Vacant Property Registration)	Actual cost to register and comply with all VPR ordinance requirements (provide supporting documentation)
INSPECTIONS	
Initial Inspection	$20/$15 per each additional unit
Occupancy Inspections	$20/$15 per each additional unit
Vacant Inspections (Ongoing) • Initial Vacant Property Inspection (One time) • Ongoing Inspections	$35/$15 per each additional unit $20/$15 per each additional unit
SECURING THE PROPERTY	
Emergency Contact Information Posting	
Emergency Contact Posting including Address Posting	$10 one time reimbursement
Lockbox, including duplicate HUD coded keys	$40 one time reimbursement
Locksets	
Lockset replacement – Front or Main Entranceway	$60 per door/door set
Lockset replacement – other than above	$20 each
Re-keying	$10 per keyhole
Padlock/Hasp Installation	$40 each
Doors	
Replace Exterior Door – Pre-Hung Steel	$800 each
Replace Overhead Door	$800 single bay door $1,000 double bay door
Repair Overhead Door	$100 maximum per property
Glazing/Windows	
Re-Glazing	$1.50 per United Inch (U.I.) (Length (in.) of one side + Width (in.) of one side = Total U.I.)
Window Lock Replacement	$5 each; maximum $50 per property
Door slider lock, anti-lift blocks, security bars	$25 each
Boarding/Securing of doors and windows	
Boarding/Securing Materials	$.90 per U.I.

Swimming Pools, Spas, and Hot Tubs	
Swimming Pool Securing – In-ground	Maximum $1,250 for all work, including cover installation
Swimming Pool Securing – Above ground	Maximum $500 for all work, including cover installation
Spa and Hot-tub Securing	Maximum $50 for all work, including cover installation
Swimming Pool Draining	Maximum $300 per property
Above Ground Swimming Pool Removal	Maximum $500 per property
Swimming Pool Maintenance	Maximum $100 monthly
Winterization	
Dry Winterization	Maximum $100 each unit
Wet/Steam Winterization	Maximum $150
Wet/Steam Winterization – additional unit	Maximum $90
Radiant Winterization	Maximum $250
Radiant Winterization – additional unit	Maximum $125
Reduced Pressure Zone (RPZ) Valves	Maximum $150, where required by state or local law
Swimming Pools and Spas	Maximum $200 per property per 12-month period
Re-winterization	$50 each occurrence
Utilities, Power Supply, Water Supply, Gas Supply	
Electricity, Gas, Oil, Propane, Water and Sewer	Actual cost – one time shut off/transfer fee as assessed by local utility entities
Water well closing and disconnection	$80 for all work required – one time shut-off per property
Initial water line pressure testing	$20
Wire Capping	$1 each; maximum $25 per property
Water, Sewer, or Gas Capping	$15 each; maximum $90 per property
Smoke Detectors – when required by AHJ	$15 each
CO2 Monitor – when required by AHJ	$25 each
Roof Assembly Repair	
Temporary Roof Repair/Tarping	Maximum $600 per property
Permanent Roof Repair/Patching	Maximum $1,000 per property
Chimney Capping	Maximum $100 each
Foundation Drainage Systems and Basements	
Basement Water Pumping	Maximum $500 per property
Gutter Cleaning and Repair	$1 per linear foot (LF); Maximum $100 per property
Gutter Replacement (missing sections only)	$4.70 per LF; Maximum $400 per property
Molds, Fungus, Discoloration and Related Moisture Damage and Organic Growth	
Dehumidifier Purchase and Installation	Maximum $250 each
Absorbent Moisture Desiccants	$20 each; maximum $100 per 12 month period

Mold Treatment including Medium Removal, mold inhibitor chemicals, mold inhibiting paints	$300 Maximum per property
Sump Pumps	
Sump Pump Replacement/Installation	Maximum $300 per property
Sump Pump Repair	Maximum $50
Debris Removal, Cleaning, and Minor Repair	
Debris Removal, Interior and Exterior	Maximum $1,250
Debris Removal, Interior and Exterior – additional waste	$50 per cubic yard (CY)
Broom Swept Cleaning	$50
Refrigerator and Freezer Cleaning	$50
Toilet Cleaning	$50
Clothes Dryer Vent Cover Installation	$ 20 each
Pest Extermination (professional services with documented need)	Maximum $300 (provide payment evidence)
Pest Extermination (Over-the-counter products)	$30 each; maximum $90 per 12 month period
Dead Animal Removal	$50 per occurrence
Vehicle/Boat Removal	Maximum $210 per vehicle
Fencing Repair	$300 for all work required
Handrails	$10 per lineal foot (LF) Maximum $200 per property
Carpet Removal including removal of tack strips	$.20 per square foot (SF) Maximum $400 per property
Demolition of Dilapidated/Unsafe Outbuildings and Sheds	$1.00 per square foot; Maximum $400 per property
Professional reports (Hazardous material identification and testing) - Reimbursement for positive results only	Maximum $1,100 per property
Police and Fire Reports	$20 each
Personal Property Storage	
Storage and disposition	Maximum $300 per property
MAINTENANCE	
Yard Maintenance	
Initial Desert Landscaping Maintenance	Maximum $300
Re-Cut Desert Landscaping Maintenance	Maximum $200 per 12 month period
Grass Cuts	Refer Attachment B
Tree Trimming	Maximum $250 per 12 month period
Shrub Trimming	Maximum $200 per 12 month period
Snow Removal	
Snow/Ice Removal	Maximum $75 per occurrence
Utilities	
Utility Costs	Actual costs as invoiced by power and utility entities

Handbook 4000.1
Effective Date: 03/14/2016 | Last Revised: 07/10/2019
*Refer to the online version of SF Handbook 4000.1 for specific sections' effective dates

993

B. WINTERIZATION SCHEDULE

Required Winterization Period	State or Territory
All Year	Alaska
September 1 through April 30	Colorado; Connecticut; Idaho; Illinois; Indiana Iowa; Maine; Massachusetts; Michigan; Minnesota; Montana; Nebraska; New Hampshire; New Jersey; New York; North Dakota; Ohio; Oregon; Pennsylvania; Rhode Island; South Dakota; Vermont; Washington; Wisconsin; Wyoming
October 1 through March 31	Alabama; Arizona; Arkansas; California; Delaware; Florida; Georgia; Kansas; Kentucky; Louisiana; Maryland; Mississippi; Missouri; Nevada; New Mexico; North Carolina; Oklahoma; South Carolina; Tennessee; Texas; Utah; Virginia; West Virginia; Washington, DC
Winterization not required	Hawaii; Guam; Northern Mariana Islands; American Samoa; Puerto Rico; U.S. Virgin Islands

C. GRASS CUT SCHEDULE

State or Territory	Initial Cut (1 - 10,000 sf)	Initial Cut (10,001 sf - 20,000 sf)	Re-cuts (1 - 10,000 sf)	Re-cuts (10,001 sf - 20,000 sf)
NOTE: Add $25 for each additional 10,000 sf for properties greater than 20,000 sf				
ALL YEAR: ONCE PER MONTH				
Arizona	$75	$95	$70	$90
Nevada	$90	$110	$85	$105
New Mexico	$85	$105	$80	$100
ALL YEAR: TWICE PER MONTH				
California	$100	$120	$95	$115
Florida	$85	$105	$80	$100
Hawaii	$110	$130	$105	$125
Guam, MP, AS	$110	$130	$105	$125
Puerto Rico	$110	$130	$105	$125
U.S. Virgin Islands	$85	$105	$80	$100
APRIL 1 TO OCTOBER 31: ONCE PER MONTH				
Colorado	$85	$105	$80	$100
Utah	$85	$105	$80	$100
Wyoming	$85	$105	$80	$100
APRIL 1 TO OCTOBER 31: TWICE PER MONTH				
Arkansas	$70	$90	$65	$85
Connecticut	$100	$120	$95	$115

State or Territory	Initial Cut (1 - 10,000 sf)	Initial Cut (10,001 sf - 20,000 sf)	Re-cuts (1 - 10,000 sf)	Re-cuts (10,001 sf - 20,000 sf)
Delaware	$95	$125	$90	$120
Idaho	$100	$120	$95	$115
Illinois	$85	$105	$80	$100
Indiana	$85	$105	$80	$100
Iowa	$85	$105	$80	$100
Kansas	$85	$105	$80	$100
Kentucky	$85	$105	$80	$100
Maine	$100	$120	$95	$115
Maryland	$100	$120	$95	$115
Massachusetts	$100	$120	$95	$115
Michigan	$85	$105	$80	$100
Minnesota	$85	$105	$80	$100
Missouri	$85	$105	$80	$100
Montana	$85	$105	$80	$100
Nebraska	$85	$105	$80	$100
New Hampshire	$100	$120	$95	$115
New Jersey	$100	$120	$95	$115
New York	$100	$120	$95	$115
North Carolina	$85	$105	$80	$100
North Dakota	$85	$105	$80	$100
Ohio	$85	$105	$80	$100
Oklahoma	$85	$105	$80	$100
Oregon	$100	$120	$95	$115
Pennsylvania	$95	$115	$90	$110
Rhode Island	$100	$120	$95	$115
South Dakota	$85	$105	$80	$100
Tennessee	$85	$105	$80	$100
Vermont	$100	$120	$95	$115
Virginia	$95	$115	$90	$110
Washington	$100	$120	$95	$115
West Virginia	$95	$115	$90	$110
Wisconsin	$85	$105	$80	$100
Washington DC	$95	$115	$90	$110
MARCH 1 TO NOVEMBER 30: TWICE PER MONTH				
Alabama	$70	$90	$65	$85
Georgia	$85	$105	$80	$100
Louisiana	$85	$105	$80	$100
Mississippi	$85	$105	$80	$100
South Carolina	$85	$105	$80	$100
Texas	$85	$105	$80	$100
JUNE 1 TO SEPTEMBER 30: TWICE PER MONTH				
Alaska	$100	$120	$95	$115

Effective Date: 03/14/2016 | Last Revised: 07/10/2019
*Refer to the online version of SF Handbook 4000.1 for specific sections' effective dates

INDEX

Handbook 4000.1
Effective Date: 03/14/2016 | Last Revised: 07/10/2019
*Refer to the online version of SF Handbook 4000.1 for specific sections' effective dates

997

Handbook 4000.1
Effective Date: 03/14/2016 | Last Revised: 07/10/2019
*Refer to the online version of SF Handbook 4000.1 for specific sections' effective dates

998

Handbook 4000.1
Effective Date: 03/14/2016 | Last Revised: 07/10/2019
*Refer to the online version of SF Handbook 4000.1 for specific sections' effective dates

999

Handbook 4000.1
Effective Date: 03/14/2016 | Last Revised: 07/10/2019
*Refer to the online version of SF Handbook 4000.1 for specific sections' effective dates

1002

Handbook 4000.1   1003
Effective Date: 03/14/2016 | Last Revised: 07/10/2019
*Refer to the online version of SF Handbook 4000.1 for specific sections' effective dates

Handbook 4000.1
Effective Date: 03/14/2016 | Last Revised: 07/10/2019
*Refer to the online version of SF Handbook 4000.1 for specific sections' effective dates

1004